A COMPANION TO THE AMERICAN SOUTH

Edited by

John B. Boles

Blackwell
Publishing

BLACKWELL PUBLISHING
350 Main Street, Malden, MA 02148-5020, USA
108 Cowley Road, Oxford OX4 1JF, UK
550 Swanston Street, Carlton, Victoria 3053, Australia

First published 2002
First published in paperback 2004 by Blackwell Publishing Ltd

Library of Congress Cataloging-in-Publication Data

A companion to the American South / edited by John B. Boles.
    p. cm. — (Blackwell companions to American history; #3)
  Includes bibliographical references and index.
  ISBN 978-1-405-12130-9
  1. Southern States—Historiography. 2. Southern States—History. I. Boles, John B.
II. Series

  F208.2.C66 2002
  975—dc21

                                                        2001018473

A catalogue record for this title is available from the British Library.

Set in 10 / 12 pt Galliard
by Kolam Information Services Pvt Ltd, Pondicherry, India

For further information on Blackwell Publishing, visit our website:
http://www.blackwellpublishing.com

Blackwell Companions to American History

This series provides essential and authoritative overviews of the scholarship that has shaped our present understanding of the American past. Edited by eminent historians, each volume tackles one of the major periods or themes of American history, with individual topics authored by key scholars who have spent considerable time in research on the questions and controversies that have sparked debate in their field of interest. The volumes are accessible for the non-specialist, while also engaging scholars seeking a reference to the historiography or future concerns.

Contents

Contributors

James Beeby is an assistant professor at West Virginia Wesleyan College.

John B. Boles is the William P. Hobby Professor of History at Rice University and Managing Editor of the *Journal of Southern History.*

Amy Turner Bushnell is an Invited Research Scholar at the John Carter Brown Library and Adjunct Associate Professor of History at Brown University.

Daniel W. Crofts is a professor of history at the University of New Jersey.

Mary A. DeCredico is a professor of history at the United States Naval Academy.

Daniel S. Dupre is an associate professor of history at the University of North Carolina at Charlotte.

Charles W. Eagles is a professor of history at the University of Mississippi.

Laura F. Edwards is an associate professor of history at Duke University.

Michael W. Fitzgerald is an associate professor of history at St Olaf College.

Wayne Flynt is the University Professor of History at Auburn University.

David R. Goldfield is the Bailey Professor of History at the University of North Carolina at Charlotte.

Ira D. Gruber is the Harris Masterson, Jr., Professor of History at Rice University.

Paul Harvey is an associate professor of history at the University of Colorado at Colorado Springs.

Paul E. Hoffman is a professor of history at Louisiana State University.

Samuel C. Hyde, Jr. is an associate professor of history at Southeastern Louisiana University.

John C. Inscoe is a professor of history at the University of Georgia and Secretary-Treasurer of the Southern Historical Association.

Cynthia A. Kierner is a professor of history at the University of North Carolina at Charlotte.

Daniel Letwin is an associate professor of history at Penn State University.

Sally G. McMillen is a professor of history at Davidson College.

David Moltke-Hansen is President of the Historical Society of Pennsylvania.

Donald G. Nieman is a professor of history at Bowling Green State University.

George C. Rable occupies the Charles E. Summersell Chair of History at the University of Alabama.

Joseph P. Reidy is a professor of history at Howard University.

Stephanie J. Shaw is an associate professor of history at Ohio State University.

Mark M. Smith is an associate professor of history at the University of South Carolina.

Randy J. Sparks is an associate professor of history at Tulane University.

Mart A. Stewart is an associate professor of history at Western Washington University.

Elizabeth Hayes Turner is an associate professor of history at the University of Texas.

Pamela Tyler is an associate professor of history at North Carolina State University.

Samuel L. Webb is an associate professor of history at the University of Alabama at Birmingham.

Betty Wood is a professor of history at Cambridge University.

Preface

The history of the American South continues to fascinate scholars and general readers alike, both in the United States and abroad. The region's long travail with slavery, and then the Civil War, Reconstruction, sharecropping, and segregation, are simply the most obvious features of its history that seem to set the South apart from the rest of the United States. American scholars study the region because of its own distinct history and for how, through contrast, it illuminates the history of the nation as a whole. For scholars around the world, however, the South's historical experience of "military defeat, occupation, and Reconstruction," while it may distinguish the region from the American North, paradoxically makes it seem a more universal history, having much in common with their own nation's historical experience (Woodward 1993: 190). The result is that southern history is studied across the breadth of the United States and throughout the English-speaking world and beyond.

The field is also one of very intense cultivation, with new methodologies and approaches, new questions, and fresh viewpoints enlivening seemingly familiar topics and opening up new topics as well. Even scholars specializing in the history of the South often find that they cannot keep abreast of the torrent of scholarship, and new students and those investigating the southern aspect of some topic they have previously studied in a different geographical setting sometimes hardly know where to begin. This volume is intended for those trying to keep up with the field or simply wanting to find an entry point. Twenty-nine chapters (and of course the pie could have been cut in many other ways or sliced more narrowly or broadly) attempt to divide the region's history into manageable slices that represent how the scholarship has developed. Authors who were intimately familiar with their fields were asked to identify the major themes, interpretative schools, historiographical debates, and basic books of each topic. The authors were asked to imagine readers either new to the topic or wanting to update their understanding, then tell them about the essential scholarship, with some attention to older, classic books but emphasizing more recent scholarship of the last two decades or so. It is my hope that this volume will be an intellectual Baedeker to those setting out to study the history of the American South, a companion they will resort to frequently as they proceed on their course of reading and discovery.

The individual essays have focused on the specific topics, but there are general books and reference guides relevant to the entire field of southern history that do not appear in the separate chapters. Two older guides to the literature of southern history still repay use (Link and Patrick 1965; Boles and Nolen 1987), as do the most recent editions of two college-level textbooks (Cooper and Terrill 1996; Boles 2003). We seem to live in an age of encyclopediazation, and four recent collaborative titles should be considered essential references both for their brief capsule accounts of innumerable topics and also for their brief bibliographies (Roller and Twyman 1979; Hill 1984; Miller and Smith 1988; and Wilson and Ferris 1989). No one should miss the southern and South-related articles and bibliographies in a recent guide to United States history in general (Parish 1997). One of the most important developments in American historical scholarship over the past half century has been the multivolume publications of carefully edited versions of the letters and papers of major (mostly political) figures such as George Washington, Thomas Jefferson, Henry Clay, John C. Calhoun, Jefferson Davis, and Booker T. Washington. All of these volumes contain material far broader than politics, and students of many aspects of the South's history should be alert to the riches found therein. Many scholarly periodicals contain valuable articles on practically every imaginable aspect of southern history; the best guide to this scholarly outpouring is the annual "Southern History in Periodicals: A Selected Bibliography," published in each May issue of the *Journal of Southern History*. That journal also contains reviews each year of approximately 250 books related to the field, along with fourteen to sixteen articles. The Southern Historical Association, which supports the journal, also sponsors a large academic conference each fall at which more than a hundred papers and panels are presented, and every three years the Southern Association for Women Historians sponsors a summertime conference with papers and panel discussions.

Southern history is thriving as a field of study, and there are many venues for reading it, hearing it, and publishing it. The editor and authors of this volume hope that the present book will be accepted as an introduction and an invitation to the history of the American South.

I wish to express my appreciation to the various authors whose individual chapters constitute this book, my extraordinary staff at the editorial offices of the *Journal of Southern History*, and two graduate students, Charles A. Israel at Rice University and Matthew Tyler Penney, then at Baylor University, who checked the bibliographical citations.

BIBLIOGRAPHY

Boles, John B. 2003: *The South Through Time*, 3rd edn, 2 vols. Upper Saddle River, NJ: Prentice-Hall.

Boles, John B. and Nolen, Evelyn Thomas 1987: *Interpreting Southern History: Historiographical Essays in Honor of Sanford W. Higginbotham*. Baton Rouge: Louisiana State University Press.

Cooper, William J., Jr. and Terrill, Thomas E. 1996: *The American South: A History*. New York: McGraw-Hill.

Hill, Samuel S. 1984: *Encyclopedia of Religion in the South*. Macon, GA: Mercer University Press.

Link, Arthur S. and Patrick, Rembert W. 1965: *Writing Southern History: Essays in Historiography in Honor of Fletcher M. Green*. Baton Rouge: Louisiana State University Press.

Miller, Randall M. and Smith, John David 1988: *Dictionary of Afro-American Slavery*. New York and Westport, CT: Greenwood Press.

Parish, Peter J. 1997: *Reader's Guide to American History.* London and Chicago: Fitzroy Dearborn Publishers.

Roller, David C. and Twyman, Robert W. 1979: *The Encyclopedia of Southern History.* Baton Rouge: Louisiana State University Press.

Wilson, Charles Reagan and Ferris, William 1989: *Encyclopedia of Southern Culture.* Chapel Hill: University of North Carolina Press.

Woodward, C. Vann 1993: *The Burden of Southern History,* 3rd edn. Baton Rouge: Louisiana State University Press.

PART I

The Colonial South

CHAPTER ONE

The First Southerners: Indians of the Early South

AMY TURNER BUSHNELL

HISTORIANS whose early modern America falls between the Chesapeake and Massachusetts have been wont to characterize American Indians as hunters, essentially different from the English who came to settle the land and improve it, farmers replacing forest dwellers in a kind of species shifting. But historical knowns change. A larger early modern America has room for Europeans who range and Indians who inhabit, and nowhere is this clearer than in the early South. Earth, water, and sky permitting, the Indians of the South were town oriented and agricultural. Proud heirs of the Mississippian tradition, they did not fade away into the forest at the European approach. Instead, powerful chiefdoms and confederacies emerged to control the eastern woodlands south of the Ohio and Potomac Rivers and east of the Great Plains. As late as 1760, the South outside of Virginia and the Carolinas held twice as many Indians as it did blacks and whites combined (Wood 1989: 90).

Too often, this long period of Indian strength is dismissed as prefatory. The South that emerged in the 1820s presents so strong a unity of interests, expressed in the spread of commercial agriculture and black slavery, that as a historical period it has come to stand without qualification, leaving the preceding three centuries to take such names as the Early South, Colonial South, Colonial Southeast, or, in one book title, "The Forgotten Centuries" of "the American South" (Hudson and Tesser 1994). This is a South without a synthesis, for other than Timothy Silver's study of South Atlantic forests (1990) and James Axtell's Fleming Lectures on the Indians' New South (1997), no early modern historian has yet stepped outside a Spanish, English, or French specialty to consider it as a whole. Moreover, until recently most studies of southern Indians focused on the dramatic early nineteenth century, for the emerging southern identity carried a sense of entitlement to nonwhite lands as well as nonwhite labor; the Louisiana Purchase of 1803 made the relocation of eastern Indians feasible; and the Removal Act of 1830 gave notice that the federal government would not protect Indian persons or properties from the jealousy of the states. Southern history begins with an act of ethnic cleansing.

Once the Indians of the eastern woodlands had lost their power to threaten and been declared surplus, their history became a magnet for myths. Non-Indian Americans constructed a pre-Colombian past of sustainable environments, primitive harmony, and mysterious mound-builders, a colonial past of pristine forests and moccasined deerhunters retreating before the advance of fences and farmers, and an early national past of warriors and purifying violence. In some quarters the feeling persists that Indian history is a special genre, closed to outsiders and exempt from rules of evidence.

In 1954 ethnologists and historians open to nondocumentary sources launched a society and journal of ethnohistory, which came to mean the history of Indian–white relations over the course of conquest, conceived as a linear process marked by the erosion of aboriginal cultures. While the historical profession as a whole accepted the new interdisciplinary social history, early American historians did not integrate Indians, as they did Africans and women, into the main narrative. Ethnohistorians of the colonial period spoke mainly to each other, and their field began to look old-fashioned before they had finished wrestling with their sources.

Historians now speak of "a new Indian history." No longer following what Daniel H. Usner Jr. calls "anthropology's ethnographic preoccupation with single tribal groups, reconstructing precontact societies and then tracing predictably deleterious effects of European colonialism and American expansion upon them" (Usner 1998: 16, 56–72), the new Indian history is more conscious of relationships among Indian nations and of intercultural spaces, conceptualizing them in phrases like Richard White's "middle ground" (1991), James Merrell's "New World" for Indians (1989), and Usner's own "frontier exchange economy" (1992). Combining the sense of Indian agency found in biography and tribal history, the larger landscape of institutional and policy history, and the theories and models of social science, it puts Native Americans center stage in a drama reaching back to when the South was theirs.

The new Indian history was borne into the mainstream of colonial and early national studies by the tides of history at large. Postmodernism made historians better readers of texts, more aware of silences and the unintended sense. A turn away from victor history opened the door to polycolonial histories of early modern America, subaltern histories of the later imperial experience, and contact studies for the European–native encounter worldwide. Advances in historical archeology, semiotics, hieroglyph interpretation, epidemiology, and environmental studies increased the general awareness of protohistory, the interval between first contact and settlement, where artifact meets document. The new Indian history has not gone unnoticed. Gregory Evans Dowd (1992: xii–xiii) was among the first to recognize its importance, and Daniel Usner (1998: 1–13) and Theda Perdue (1998b) recently summarized the new literature and positioned it in the historiography.

Historians have long appreciated the significance of Iroquois diplomacy and warfare in the Northeast and of statesmen like the Mohawk Joseph Brant. As neutrals, the Iroquois were masters of the balance of power, maintaining hegemony over other Indians and deflecting the flow of colonial settlement. The southern story differs from the northern on several points. The South had multiple militarized confederacies and three rival European empires – the Spanish having planted themselves in 1565, the English in 1607, and the French in 1698 – and keeping the peace was like walking a balance beam. By the eighteenth century, many native leaders were of mixed descent; the most adroit negotiator may have been the Creek Alexander McGillivray, son of a Scottish trader and a woman of the Wind Clan. Finally, the South entered the national period with the problem of Indian sovereignty unsolved, leaving the states to deal with Indian sanctuaries for fugitive slaves, powerful trading companies speculating in the exchange of debts for land, and citizens made heady by the rapid expansion of plantation agriculture, who regarded all Indians as conquered and their lands as spoils of war.

Historians of early America appreciate the importance of the European matrix and the classical civilizations of the Mediterranean but give little thought to the ancient peoples of America's Old World. For seventy years textbooks have asserted that the first humans to set foot in America were North Asian nomadic hunter-gatherers who made the crossing from Siberia to Alaska on the Bering Sea land bridge during the Pleistocene epoch some 13,500 years ago, hunting woolly mammoths and other big game with their distinctively fluted "Clovis" spear-points, found in assemblages that archeologists call Paleo-Indian. A revolution against Clovis culture primacy and the Beringian bottleneck is now in progress. One representative theory argues that a separate group of Stone Age explorers, the Solutreans of northern Iberia and southern France, arrived by way of the North Atlantic more than 18,000 years ago, depositing their projectile points from the American desert to Chile. Its opponents counter that the northern British Isles were too glaciated to serve as Solutrean stepping stones (Straus 2000).

Ten thousand years ago, the ice age ended and sea levels began to rise, drowning numerous Paleo-Indian sites beneath the Gulf of Mexico. Whether from climate change or overhunting, the larger, cold-adapted animals disappeared and with them the practice of following the herds. Archeologists of the Southeast tell us that people of the Archaic tradition (8000–700 BC) hunted and foraged from a central base, usually close to wetland sources of fish, clams, and oysters. Late Archaic people made elaborate tools and ornaments of shell, bone, and stone, carved wood, worked fiber into fabric, cordage, and baskets, fired ceramics, and, a thousand years before their descendants adopted Mexican crop husbandry, domesticated numerous plants we now consider sidewalk weeds. Massive earthworks appeared in the Poverty Point culture of Louisiana and Mississippi. The people of the Woodland tradition (700 BC–AD 1000) that followed the Archaic were characterized by larger, more permanent settlements; increasing long-distance trade, a function of greater regional variation; more elaborate mortuary practices; the use of bow and arrow for hunting and war; and increasing reliance on crops such as little barley, knotweed, the pigweeds, sunflower, squash, and bottle gourd.

Archeologists divide the late prehistoric Southeast into five environmental zones. In the Appalachian Highlands, mountain people combined female farming with male hunting and valued their seclusion. The broad alluvial valleys and game-filled forests of the Piedmont Plateau, including the Ozarks, supported sizeable populations. The Mississippi Alluvial Valley had the richest lands and highest population densities. The Coastal Plain, dominated by pine forests, contained three ecological subzones: the alluvial valleys of slow, silt-bearing rivers, the fertile lands between faster-flowing rivers, and the coasts, marginal for agriculture but excellent for seasonal hunting, fishing, and gathering. The fifth and final zone, subtropical South Florida, supported dense populations on marine and estuarine resources alone.

In all of these zones, chiefdoms arose, as the egalitarian eastern woodland communities evolved between AD 800 and 900 into societies of rank supported by economic surpluses. In many inland regions, such as the Mississippian polities, a concomitant of the new political system was a growing dependence on cleared-field agriculture with maize of the cold-resistant eastern flint species developed in the

Mesoamerican highlands as the principal crop. Whether the shift to intensive agriculture is what caused settlements to increase in size or was itself a response to settlement nucleation, the new foods paradoxically supported larger populations in poorer health. According to bioarcheologist Clark Spencer Larsen, the transition to agriculture on the Georgia coast shows up skeletally in decreased body size and stature and increased nonspecific infections, dental caries, and enamel hypoplasia, with females under greater environmental stress than males (Larsen 1987).

The Mississippian tradition (AD 1000–1600) that accompanied the rise of chiefdoms in the Mississippi Valley and the Southeast was characterized by the construction of great ceremonial centers, places having in common the flat-topped platform mounds, militaristic propaganda, and artistic motifs of the Southeastern Ceremonial Cult. Cahokia, largest of the ceremonial centers, flourished in a floodplain called American Bottoms near the confluence of the Mississippi and Missouri Rivers in present Illinois; by the twelfth century it had a population of up to 20,000. How much the Mississippian tradition owed to Mesoamerican influence and how much was indigenous remains a matter of debate.

In the early thirteenth century, Mississippian centers began to show signs of ecological stress, including drought, soil exhaustion, and the depletion of timber and game, and chronic warfare, revealed in defensive fortifications. Population gradually declined until, by the late fourteenth century, places like Cahokia were deserted, their inhabitants dispersed into farming villages. The drought-plagued Anasazi culture centers of the Southwest were abandoned at about the same time. In an important theoretical book with the unlikely title of *Lumbee Indian Histories: Race, Ethnicity, and Indian Identity in the Southern United States*, anthropologist Gerald M. Sider proposes that southeastern stratified societies were "durationally fragile" because they lacked two of the characteristics of early states: centralized management of storage and distribution, and the social or physical barriers to keep people from moving away from state demands (Sider 1993: 218–20). The result was a pattern of cycling in which population flowed between centers and villages as if organically. The question is not why Cahokia declined, but why it appeared in the first place. Maize does not require a floodplain or regimented tilling; a lone farmer can plant it in a forest clearing. The first southerners, like the Mayas, did not really need their cities.

The main language families in the Indian South were Siouan, Algonquian, Iroquoian, Caddoan, the Gulf Languages, and Timucuan. Siouan speakers, who were among the region's earliest inhabitants, included the Osages and Quapaws, later known as Arkansas, of the Central Mississippi river basin, the Biloxis on the Gulf, several small groups in the Carolina lowcountry, and most of the inhabitants of the Carolina and Virginia piedmont from the Catawba River to the Rappahannock. Algonquian speakers, living in Virginia and the Ohio Valley, included the Pamunkeys, nucleus of the Powhatan confederacy, and the restless Shawnees. Iroquoian languages were spoken by the Cherokees of the Appalachian Highlands, the Tuscaroras of North Carolina, and the Westos, who arrived in Carolina not long before the English. Caddoan speakers, loosely grouped into the Hasinai, Kadohadacho, and Natchitoches confederacies, lived in the trans-Mississippi South in present Louisiana, Arkansas, East Texas, and Oklahoma, separated from the Great Plains by the forbidding "*llano estacado.*" The so-called Gulf Languages included Atakapa, Chitimacha,

Natchez, and Tunica, all spoken in what is now Louisiana, and Muskhogean, a wide-ranging family of languages spoken respectively by the Apalaches of North Florida, the Oristas and Cusabos of South Carolina, the Choctaws of Mississippi and Louisiana, the Chickasaws to their north, possibly the Guales and Yamasees of Georgia, and the Muskogees, Alabamas, and Hitichitis (including the Apalachicolas) of Alabama, Georgia, and Tennessee. Even the trade jargon Mobilian, with its eclectic phonology and lexicon, had a Muskhogean grammar. Exceptions to the Muskhogean norm in the Southeast were three South Florida languages closely related to Tunica and spoken respectively by the Calusas, the east-coast Ais and Jeagas, and the inland Mayacas and Jororos, and the Timucuan language of Georgia and North Florida, an isolate with Amazonian origins. That southern Indians frequently spoke more than one language is revealed by their readiness to federate across language barriers. Thus the Creek confederacy was composed not only of people who spoke Muskogee and other Muskhogean languages, but also of Algonquian Shawnees and the probably Siouan Yuchis. In the Catawba confederacy trader James Adair heard more than twenty dialects.

The once crisp contrast between landbound American Indians and sea-roving Europeans no longer holds, as evidence mounts of Polynesian-like canoes and Phoenician-like trade and colonization in the basins of the Gulf of Mexico and the Caribbean Sea and on both sides of the Gulf Stream. Resemblances between the pre-Columbian art and architecture of the Yucatan and of South Florida suggest that Maya cultural influence reached the Southeast by sea. The Taínos and Caribs knew about Florida and the Yucatan; the Calusas on the west coast of South Florida knew about the Maya; and the Maya knew the currents and roamed the seaways in great, flatbottomed canoes with steering oars.

The first Spaniards to visit the South came to kidnap Indians for the slave markets of the Greater Antilles, where the almost complete annihilation of the Arawaks had created an acute demand for labor. Venture capital flowed into the slave trade, and men of substance like Hispaniola judge Lucas Vázquez de Ayllón looked for loop holes to legalize it, claiming that the Indians were guilty of sodomy and cannibalism, or that they were slaves already. Appointments to govern remote islands and provinces, such as Juan Ponce de León's license to discover "Bimini" and Nuño de Guzmán's assignment to Pánuco, were tacit hunting licenses. The distinction between voyages of discovery and of slavecatching blurred, and Indians died by the thousands in collection pens and the holds of ships. By 1520 slavers had picked the Bahamas clean of Lucayans and were ready to turn their attention to the mainland that Ponce de León had seen in 1513. We have abundant information about the voyages, landings, and possession-taking ceremonies through which Europeans added the southeastern littoral to their maps. But the Indians who initially greeted them, disposed to trade, developed a dislike of the people-stealers that could only be expressed by killing castaways and stray missionaries from Padre Island to the Chesapeake.

Álvar Núñez Cabeza de Vaca, most unusual of explorers, embarked for "Amichel" (western Florida, Alabama, Mississippi, Louisiana, and Texas) with Pánfilo de Narváez in 1528, was raft-wrecked on the Texas coast, and eight years later, as if from the dead, walked into a camp of Spanish slavers on the frontiers of New Spain. The narrative he wrote of his and his companions' adventures combined ethnographic information with a plan for peaceful conversion persuasive enough to give pause to Charles V and lead to experiments in counter-conquest. Rolena Adorno and Patrick Charles Pautz's (1999) three-volume critical edition and translation, *Álvar Núñez Cabeza de Vaca: His Account, His Life, and the Expedition of Pánfilo de Narváez*, sets a new standard for the editing of sixteenth-century sources and enlarges our knowledge of southern Indian history by opening a window onto the upper Texas coast, a region of wandering nations that Europeans would not revisit for 150 years.

Rumors of riches beyond the horizon triggered two *entradas* into the wilds of North America, Francisco Vázquez de Coronado riding north from New Spain into the Plains and Hernando de Soto landing in South Florida and heading toward the Appalachian mountains at the pace of his herd of pigs. In the sources of the de Soto expedition (1539–43), *conquistadores* appear at their worst, taking a hard-eyed look at the looting possibilities of a non-Christian world and outraging peoples who received them with the courtesies due a paramount chief and his retinue. Three participants, Rodrigo de Ranjel, Luis Hernández de Biedma, and the anonymous Fidalgo de Elvas, wrote brief accounts of the *entrada*, and a generation later a Peruvian mestizo, Garcilaso de la Vega, produced a semi-fictional history that borrowed from Elvas and, on the principle of Indian uniformitarianism, from Inca ethnography. The four de Soto narratives are available in English translations, but as Patricia Galloway reminds us (Galloway 1997: 11–44), none has yet been published in a critical edition.

In 1986, three years before the 450th anniversary of the de Soto expedition, ten southern governors appointed a regional trail commission to mark a route for National Park Service highway markers. Anthropologist Charles Hudson, prominent in early southern Indian studies, stepped forward, supported by a team of archeologists. Comparing the findings of archeology to a composite itinerary compiled from the three eyewitness sources, Garcilaso, and the reports of two expeditions led by Juan Pardo that covered much of the same ground twenty-five years later, the team quilted prehistory to history, site by site. The route they proposed and circulated for comment, however, drew fire from all sides. Chambers of Commerce were incensed, scholars dissented, and with Columbus quincentenary protesters making old-style celebrations of rapine impolitic, private foundations and state and federal agencies withdrew their support. Hudson published the team's findings anyhow, first in 1994, then in detail in *Knights of Spain, Warriors of the Sun: Hernando de Soto and the South's Ancient Chiefdoms* (Hudson 1997). Spiritedly defending their methodology, he dismissed questions about intertextuality, pseudohistorical genres, and the implicit boosterism of dot-to-dot itineraries as nitpicking, emphasizing the yield of de Soto route research for the prehistory and protohistory of southern Indians. Archeologists have, for example, found the sites of the sixteenth-century chiefdom of Coosa and tracked the descendants of the Coosas into the Creek confederacy.

Scholars continue to debate the impact of the de Soto invasion on the southeastern chiefdoms. The consensus is that Europeans did not trigger the decline of the Mississippian tradition, which had passed its apogee, but that the new diseases that they and their animals introduced probably reduced the aboriginal population to between a twentieth and a twenty-fifth of its size at contact. That all-important size scholars have developed elaborate methods to estimate, calculating the carrying capacity of various environments, noting the mortality rates of documented virgin soil epidemics and applying them to post-epidemic censuses, developing formulae for the ratios between population size and premodern counts of warriors or hearths or Lenten communicants – plucking "numbers from nowhere," in the phrase of David P. Henige (1998). Twentieth-century estimates range from Alfred Kroeber's 1939 low of 8.4 million for the hemisphere, with 0.9 million north of the Rio Grande and 150,000 in the Southeast, to Henry Dobyns's 1966 estimate of 90 to 112.6 million for the hemisphere, with 9.8 to 12.3 million in the North. William Denevan's 1976 estimate of a hemispheric population of 57.3 million, with 4.4 million in the North, and Gerald Sider's 1993 estimate of over 2 million in the Southeast (Thornton 1987: 15–41; Weber 1992: 27–9, 372–3; Sider 1993: 213–14) fall between the two extremes. Whatever their numbers, most American Indians north of Mexico lived in the eastern woodlands and favored regions of agricultural abundance, where soils were fertile, rains sufficient, and the growing season ranged from 180 to 240 days, with a minimum of 120 days frost-free.

Depopulation, accelerating the decline of the Mississippian tradition, forced structural change upon the southeastern chiefdoms. Archeologists have traced these changes in various regions, with Marvin T. Smith (1987) considering the whole. Adoption, incorporation, migration, and confederation, survival strategies for polities in danger of dwindling into unimportance, were old practices capable of creating new collectivities. Patricia Galloway (1995) describes how the Choctaw reinvented themselves after the decline of Mississippian societies in Moundville, Alabama, and Pearl River, Mississippi. As protohistory gave way to history, native polities beyond the pale of European settlement continued to secede, combine, and recombine in fresh confederations, not out of pan-Indian solidarity, but in order to better their chances in a threatening new world.

Europeans came to the South to stay in 1565, when Pedro Menéndez de Avilés, a captain general under contract to Philip II, destroyed a French fort, garrisoned seven harbors along the Gulf Stream, and founded three settlements, including St Augustine. Spanish Florida lay farther north than the present state, the king's writ did not extend into the southern half of the peninsula, and the first capital of "the provinces of Florida" was in present South Carolina. Although eventually the flag of Spain would fly over the continent from Florida to California, in the sixteenth century the two colonies on the northern frontier, Florida and New Mexico, did not communicate.

The natives who met Menéndez presented a spectrum of cultures. The Oristas, Cusabos, Guales, and eastern Timucuans of central Florida and the coast above St Augustine were part-time agriculturalists who left their fields in wintertime to hunt and gather; the Ais and Jeagas of the lower Atlantic coast, like the Mayacas and Jororos along the St Johns River, were nonagricultural and seasonally nomadic; the Apalache and western Timucua of the upper Gulf coast were sedentary and agricultural; the Calusas of the lower Gulf coast, sedentary and nonagricultural. Despite their variety, most of the Florida Indians lived at least seasonally in towns, most towns belonged to chiefdoms, and many chiefdoms recognized a paramount chief.

The 1560s and 1570s were a time of transition in the Spanish empire, when the High Conquest, with its brutal *conquistadores* and slavetraders, was rejected in favor of Pacification, a conquest by contract, Crown-controlled and covenant-based. On the wild frontiers, the Crown resorted to a policy of pacification by gifts and a presidial system of fortified outposts and ports. In those places where the Indians accepted Christianity, the *presidios* were reinforced by mission provinces. Where the Indians rejected Christianity, the frontier did not advance. Indians on the edges of empire who could not be pacified by sword, gospel, or gift were apt to be seasonal nomads, unwilling to live "beneath the bell" in Mediterranean-style farming villages, indifferent to the sacraments, governing themselves by consensus, and impossible to quarantine from contact with Spain's rivals, the French, the English, and the Dutch (Bushnell 1990; Bushnell 2001).

The Jesuits who came at Menéndez's invitation found Florida unable to sustain a mission program. Eight of them set off in 1570 for "Ajacán" in the Chesapeake Bay, with don Luis de Velasco, a young convert from the area, to make the introductions. The party landed at the James River a few miles east of the later site of Jamestown. Don Luis deserted them, and the mission was wiped out before it was five months old. Franciscans replaced the Jesuits in Florida in 1573, when the colony's finances had taken better form. Their *modus operandi* was to raise a cross on the town plaza, preach, and invite the chiefs to St Augustine to receive the king's gifts. There, the lords of the land kissed the governor's hand, negotiated alliances of trade and mutual defense, and registered a request for teaching friars – acts that in Spanish eyes turned them and their vassals into subjects and neophytes. Those who assented to the covenant became part of the self-governing "Republic of Indians," sharing the land with the "Republic of Spaniards" in exchange for protection and gifts (Bushnell 1989). Churches and convents arose in the main towns, giving the chiefs access to exotic goods and spiritual power. From these places, the friars serviced strings of *visitas* that matured into *doctrinas* when they received a resident friar and a 1,000–peso baptismal gift of *sacra*: vestments, linens, images, sacred vessels, parish registers, large bells, and an altarstone. Spanish soldiers turning settler looked to the provinces for wives: in 1600, half of the women in St Augustine were Indians.

During the period of nearer pacifications (1580s–1620s), the Spanish followed the waterways to create a line of missions, starting with the Timucuans of the St Johns River and ending with the Guales of the Georgia coast. These conquests by the gospel were short-lived; within a generation, every group had rebelled and been reconquered by the sword. The Guale Rebellion of 1597 ended in a famine induced by scorched-earth tactics; half of the 16,000 converts in eastern Timucua and Guale died of the plague between 1613 and 1617; and other epidemics followed, until war and disease had virtually emptied the eastern *doctrinas*. The impulse for the farther pacifications (1630s–1670) came from within the colony, as *floridanos* scented opportunities for agriculture, ranching, and trade in the Gulf. The western watershed was subdued with a gunboat, and soon the friars were planting missions in western Timucua and Apalache. With this, the colony seemed to reach its natural limits. Subsequent efforts to convert the Hitchiti-speaking Apalachicolas failed, as did missions to the Calusas, Mayacas, and Jororos.

A military outpost in a maritime periphery, St Augustine provisioned itself with Indian agriculture, secured its perimeter with an Indian buffer zone, and policed the long coastline with Indian surveillance. Garrison detachments were stationed in the provincial capitals. From San Luis de Apalache, settlers, chiefs, and Franciscans conducted a lively trade with Havana merchants in agricultural and ranch products and, by midcentury, deerskins from Apalachicola. Pack animals being scarce and the waters around the peninsula pirate-infested, Spanish authorities employed Indian burdeners, vying for their services and accusing one another of misusing them. Two revolts and an epidemic interrupted this modest economic progress. The Apalache Rebellion of 1647 was a civil war between Christian and non-Christian chiefs. Yellow fever reached Florida in 1650, felling Spaniards and Indians alike. That, and the Timucuan Rebellion of 1656, triggered by the mobilization of Indian militia after the English invasion of Jamaica, left central Florida so depopulated that the governor resettled the remnants of the Timucuans to service the transpeninsular road to Apalache.

At their height in the mid-seventeenth century, the wattle-and-daub missions of Florida numbered as many as forty *doctrinas* with up to 26,000 Christians. To maintain the "divine cult" in all these places, the friars trained the sons and nephews of chiefs in the duties of sacristans, musicians, interpreters, catechists, and overseers and raised orphan boys to serve as gardeners, cooks, and grooms. Like the soldiers, the friars received their support from two sources: the *situado*, an annual subvention from the Mexico City treasury's defense account, and the *sabana* system, the native method of public finance. Each planting season the commoners of a town planted one *sabana* of maize for each leader and one for the community. After joining forces with Spaniards, they planted other *sabanas* for the service of the convent and the service of the king. In times of scarcity the governor pressed them to sell part of their communal surplus to the *presidio* on credit, in what amounted to a forced loan. The colony became increasingly dependent upon the various transfers of labor and produce from the hinterland, sanctioned and brokered by the chiefs. The Florida governor rewarded the rulers of the Republic of Indians with ceremonial staves of office, entertained them at his table, and made them gifts: European clothing and weapons for themselves and cloth, blankets, beads, and tools to satisfy their followers. The expense of "regaling" the Indians was the one open-ended fund in the *situado*.

Unaware of this seventeenth-century frontier in Spanish North America, much less of the sixteenth-century Chichimeca one, Jeremy Adelman and Stephen Aron claim, in a forum essay on borderlands and borders, that Spain, having a "lack of experience handling non-tributary aboriginal peoples," was forced in the 1790s to abandon "the principle of paternalistic pacification" and "belatedly, in response to threats from colonial rivals,... turn to the diplomacy of gift-alliances and commercial exchange" (Adelman and Aron 1999: 829–35). In consenting to solemnize agreements by the exchange of gifts, however, traders and officials in the colonial South – Spanish, and in due time English and French – were accommodating to Indian diplomatic protocols. The importance of these agreements to the course of European empire can be gauged by the large sums Spain, France, and Great Britain authorized their governors to expend annually on Indian allies and trading partners.

Anticipating by two hundred years the adobe missions of California, the Florida missions were little known outside the circle of southeastern historians and historical archeologists until the mid-1980s, when scholars began to put southern Indians within the Spanish sphere of influence before a larger audience. David Hurst Thomas (1990) and David J. Weber (1992) gave the Southeast parity with the Southwest in the Spanish Borderlands; Kathleen A. Deagan (1985) treated Florida as part of the Greater Caribbean; and Amy Turner Bushnell (1994) presented it as a maritime periphery comparable to Chile or the Philippines. After years in the historical backwaters, the provinces of Florida entered the mainstream as an adjunct of historical archeology – the state of Florida having farmed out its non-English past to cultural resource management – and the results have been uneven. The two most productive archival scholars, John H. Hann (1988, 1991, 1996) and John E. Worth (1995, 1998), avoid historical interpretation, while Jerald T. Milanich, foremost interpreter of the archeological literature, wields it with abandon, stating: "Missions *were* colonialism. The missionary process was essential to the goal of colonialism: creating profits by manipulating the land and its people" (Milanich 1999: xiii) – although it is no secret that Spanish Florida was a deficit operation, subsidized out of defense funds.

Southern Indians had their first experience with English-speaking colonists in the mid-1580s, when Sir Walter Raleigh sponsored a reconnaissance of Virginia and northern North Carolina, leading to a settlement at Roanoke on the Outer Banks. War between England and Spain prevented the timely relief of the colony and delayed further colonizing ventures until 1606, when the Virginia Company was chartered. In the thirty-seven years since the Jesuit mission to the Chesapeake, the Pamunkey chief Powhatan had extended his rule over some thirty southern Algonquian chiefdoms and a good half of tidewater Virginia in the paramount chiefdom of Tsenacommacah, better known as the Powhatan confederacy. Moderately Mississippian, on the fringes of the Southeast but with ties to the Algonquian North, Tsenacommacah was less southern than part of the larger culture of the eastern woodlands and less a confederation than an empire of conquest (Rountree 1989: 15, 140–52; 1993). Frederic W. Gleach (1997: 106–22) suggests that Powhatan and his brother, the war chief Opechancanough, sought to bring Jamestown itself into Tsenacommacah, adopting the newcomers in the person of Captain John Smith. But the English were unassimilable. Many of them veterans of the Irish and Spanish wars, they reduced Powhatan power in three Anglo-Indian wars (1609–14, 1622–32, and 1644–6) and seized the confederacy's forests and farmlands in order to grow Indian tobacco. The survivors, congregated in "dependencies," were quiet; when Nathaniel Bacon raided Pamunkey encampments in 1676, he broke a peace of thirty years. After Bacon's Rebellion, the king's commissioners tried to rebuild the Powhatan confederacy for their own purposes, reuniting the chiefdoms under the Pamunkey queen, but the Chickahominys and Rappahannocks refused to be her tributaries, preferring to deal with the English directly. By 1700 the number of free Indians in coastal Virginia had declined to under 2,000. The Virginia of the eighteenth century was effectively post-Indian, which is why historians of that place and period have little to say about them.

Sufficient written records exist to answer the important question of how many people – Indian, African, and European – actually did live in the colonial South. In an important statistical study, Peter Wood (1989) has come up with estimates for all three groups at fifteen-year intervals between 1685 and 1790 for ten subregions, each one the home of Indians important to southern history. According to his calculations, the South contained 199,400 Indians in 1685. Seven out of eight of them, or 176,500, lived in one of seven non-English subregions: 16,000 in Florida; 15,000 in Georgia and Alabama south of the Appalachian mountains, where the Creek confederacy was taking shape; 32,000 in southern Appalachia, home of the Cherokees; 35,000 in Mississippi, mainly Choctaws and Chickasaws; 42,000 in Lower Louisiana, with the largest nations, the Natchez and the Quapaw, located in the Central River area between the mouths of the Red River and the Arkansas; 28,000 in

East Texas, home of the Caddos; and 8,500 below the Ohio River in the "Shawnee interior" of West Virginia, Kentucky, and Tennessee. The remaining 22,900 Indians lived east of the Appalachians in one of the three subregions that at the time had English settlers: 10,000 in North Carolina, 10,000 in South Carolina, and a bare 2,900 in Virginia. In 1685 Indians outnumbered non-Indians four to one in the South, which had a non-Indian population of 50,200 (46,900 white and 3,300 black), four-fifths of whom lived in coastal Virginia. With that one subregion removed, the South was 95 percent Indian.

Gerald Sider divides southern Indian societies of the colonial period into two groups: (1) the confederations of towns, each town a chiefdom with a society of rank, and (2) the small, relatively egalitarian communities. As in pre-Columbian times, population flowed in and out of the confederations, which paradoxically gained strength from the social dislocations produced by epidemic disease and endemic warfare. What confederated the towns were ties of language, religion, clan membership, marriage, mechanisms to override origins and create fictive kin, a jural community for resolving inter-town disputes, shared attachments to "mother towns," inter-town games to channel competition into mock combat, a common trade network, and common enemies, although the towns might disagree on how to meet them. During the colonial period, while the smaller confederations of Catawbas, Tuscaroras, Natchez, and Yamasees struggled to maintain their autonomy, the Cherokee, Choctaw, Creek, and Chickasaw confederacies became what he calls "great trading, warring, slaving, and slaveholding regional empires," useful to the colonies as sources of deerskins and Indian slaves, military allies, and bounty hunters for the recovery of fugitive slaves and indentured servants. Colonial governments insisted on treating the confederations as nations, pressuring the towns to form a single political entity by holding them responsible for each other's behavior (Sider 1993: 231–2).

The smaller, relatively egalitarian hamlets and settlements survived by attaching themselves as clients to one of the colonies. Sider classifies them as either settlement or tributary, based on their location vis-à-vis the pale, or frontier, defined as the line of white settlement. Settlement Indians lived inside the pale, integrated into the colonial political economy; tributary Indians lived outside the pale, serving as buffers and mercenaries (ibid: 226–7). The self-governing "republics of Indians" represent a third, Spanish type in which the pale is religious rather than racial, a line between Christians and non-Christians, with the latter drawn into the colony's sphere of influence by agreements of trade and invitations to join the Pax Hispana (Bushnell 1989).

Beyond the borders of colonial provinces and dependencies, whites and Indians met each other mostly for reasons of exchange, an activity that drew white traders into the interior and that mercantilist-minded governments in England, France, and Spain distrusted as likely to lead to ungovernable territorial expansion. Trade between Virginia and the people of the piedmont, for example, was against the law from 1631 to 1659. But there was always a way to get around a regulation. In 1644, a time of falling tobacco prices, the colonial government established several fall-line forts and leased them to private individuals, and soon James River traders began to travel beyond the falls with packhorses, returning with deerskins and the occasional Indian slave. Hunters taking their own skins to market found Indian middlemen astride the trading paths. That in the mid-1640s Spanish Florida opened a similar deerskin trade out of Apalache province, employing burdeners, suggests that the time was right for southern Indians to participate in an Atlantic market. Gregory A. Waselkov (1989) and Amy Bushnell (1994: 126–32, 169) describe this little-known trade.

Due north of Apalache, the headwaters of three southeastern river systems ran parallel between the north–south ranges of the Appalachians. From west to east, they were the Coosa and Tallapoosa, which joined in the Alabama, the Chattahoochee and Flint, which became the Apalachicola, and the Oconee and Ocmulgee (known in its upper reaches as Ochese Creek), which met to form the Altamaha, flowing into the Atlantic Ocean. On the banks of these rivers were towns with the autonomy of Greek city-states: Coweta, Cussita (or Kasihta), Abeika (or Coosa), Tallapoose (or Okfuskee), Apalachicola, Alabama (or Alibamon), and more. English-speaking traders named them Creeks. J. Leitch Wright Jr. (1986) argues that there was a deep division in the confederacy between Muskogees and non-Muskogees, the *estenkos*. Differences between the two moieties, he suggests, were responsible for most of the conflicts among the Creeks.

Spanish Florida had ceased to enslave southern Indians in the 1570s and was under strict orders not to sell them firearms. The latter policy was often breached – two Virginians visiting the Overhill Cherokees in 1673 reported sixty Spanish flintlock muskets in their possession, and in the 1680s a Dutch captain out of New York entered the St Augustine harbor with suspicious regularity – but Florida lacked the wherewithal to be a major weapons dealer. When the firearms revolution reached the South, Spain lost its trading partners and with them its sphere of influence. People with firearms were not only safer, they could deliver deerskins in volume; they could, furthermore, raid their neighbors with impunity and sell their captives to the English and the French, whose consciences were silent on the subject of Indian slavery. Southern Indians had their own forms of slavery, which left some leeway for adoption or repatriation. Theda Perdue (1979), finding no economic reason for aboriginal bondage, posits a cultural one: a slave, lacking the legal rights and protections afforded by a kinship group, had no claim to humanity; he was an anomaly, and in the Cherokee world deviants confirmed the norm. When southern Indians were drawn into the Atlantic market, however, slaves became commodities. Confederacies that participated in the slave trade, like the Cherokees and Creeks, had a choice of markets. They could take their captives to Virginia, which in 1683 made it legal to enslave any Indian brought into the colony; to South Carolina, which offered bounties for captives as early as 1674; or to Louisiana, where in 1707 a Chitimacha woman or child brought 200 livres. The leitmotifs of Leitch Wright's *The Only Land They Knew: The Tragic Story of the American Indians in the Old South* (1981) are the human cost of the southern Indian slave trade and the submerged Indian heritage of African-Americans.

Shock waves from the Iroquoian wars reached the South in 1659, when the Westos (Chichimecos to the Spanish), an Iroquoian people armed with muskets from Virginia who lived by plunder and slavetaking, emerged from the woods to attack the coastal missions of Guale. They would remain a danger until the English armed their enemies and destroyed them at a remove in the Westo War (1680). In 1683 a group of migratory Shawnees set in motion by Iroquois raids on the Ohio Valley in the 1660s and 1670s settled on the Savannah River and began to raid the Spanish provinces, armed and encouraged by a group of Scots who had recently, to the dismay of Carolina merchants, positioned themselves at the Altamaha River to intercept slaves and deerskins. When a Spanish–Indian expedition of reprisal wiped out the Scottish settlement, Charles Town did not retaliate.

With the Westos and Scots removed, traders from Charles Town burst into the interior. Finding trade to the north monopolized by Virginia – as many as fifty or sixty Virginia traders made the annual trip to the piedmont and the Appalachian Highlands, home of the Cherokees – they pushed westward to the Mississippi and southward into the Spanish sphere of influence. The towns along the Chattahoochee welcomed envoy Dr Henry Woodward in 1685 and helped him to build a stockade. The governor of Florida tried to counter the Anglo advance with hastily founded missions, a trading post, and the torching of empty towns, but the lure of English trade goods was too powerful. Some of the pro-English towns moved east to settle on Ochese Creek, 150 miles from Charles Town. English traders called them Creeks, then extended the name to all of the towns on the trading path westward, the people along the Chattahoochee, Flint, and Ocmulgee Rivers becoming Lower Creeks, and the ones on the Coosa, Tallapoosa, and Alabama Rivers farther "up" the trading path, Upper Creeks.

With their new firearms, warriors from the towns on the trading path launched raids on the missions of Florida, then hurried their captives north to the receivers of stolen persons, who shipped an undetermined number of them to other mainland colonies and the West Indies. Facing unequal odds, the greater part of the Christian Indians deserted their *doctrinas*. First to secede were the Guales, whose towns on the sea islands were also dangerously exposed to pirates. Although their declining numbers were temporarily masked by a countercurrent of Yamasees, by 1696 all that remained of Guale province were three towns of refugees on Amelia Island.

To open Queen Anne's War (1702–13) a combined force of Creeks and Carolinians under the leadership of Governor James Moore overran Amelia Island and destroyed St Augustine, without taking the castillo. The object of their next winter's campaign was the destruction of Apalache province, from which Moore returned to Charles Town with 4,000 women and children and up to 300 men. Some of the Apalaches fled to Pensacola and Mobile, where they continued to practice Catholicism. Some, led in exodus by the chief don Patricio de Hinachuba, migrated first to Timucua, then to St Augustine, hoping to find safety under the guns of the fort (Bushnell 1979). Others left for parts unknown, saying they would not stay to die with Spaniards.

Continuing the southeastern version of the proxy war, the Creeks raided the Indian villages in the outskirts of St Augustine, Mobile, and Pensacola, attacked the Choctaws, who were French allies, and laid siege to what was left of Timucua province. In 1708 the Spanish governor reported that since the beginning of the war, the enemy had carried off between ten and twelve thousand persons. With the mission buffer gone, the Creek conquest pushed into South Florida, driving once elusive peoples into the arms of Spaniards to ask for asylum in languages so strange that the friars despaired of indoctrinating them. Some of the Creeks, tempted by the abandoned cattle and grasslands of Apalache and central Florida, remained, exercising a right of conquest that the British would assent to in 1763. The name these settlers went by, "Seminole," came from the Spanish word *cimarrón*, for something that has reverted to the wild. They must have felt like outlaws, for although the Creeks appreciated the strings of packhorses that came loaded with trade goods and left with peltry, most of them objected to cow keeping and, especially, to cattle drives.

For many southern Indians, the years of warfare, flight, and loss marked a new beginning, as uprooted peoples settled near one another in informal alliance. As in the psychological process of "creative disintegration," in which a dysfunctional personality breaks down and is replaced by a functional one, new societies emerged from the ruins of the old. In the Carolina piedmont, shielded to the north by the Dismal Swamp, refugees from societies shattered by epidemics, slave raids, and war gathered near the Catawba River. By 1677, when Susquehannocks driven out of Maryland joined the Five Nations to make war on the Occaneechees and other Siouan speakers to the south, the Catawba had constructed a nation powerful enough to match them warrior for warrior. James Merrell (1989) uses the Catawba experience – assimilating traders and trade goods but not missionaries, leasing their land to settlers, fighting on the American side in the Revolution, redefining their government as a republic, and becoming part of the local exchange network – to reveal how Indian peoples transformed themselves in response to a series of challenges.

For 150 years after routing the army of de Soto, the Indians who lived along the Mississippi River went about their business unobserved by Europeans, secluded by the inability of Gulf pilots to thread the maze of channels that concealed the river mouth. The exploration of the Mississippi, when it finally occurred, was part of a geopolitical plan by New France to extend the fur trade beyond the Great Lakes and secure a warm-water port. In 1682 René-Robert Cavalier, Sieur de La Salle, journeyed downstream to the Mississippi mouth, claimed the drainage basin for France, and returned upstream, pausing to establish a trading post among the Illinois. Two years later he was back, this time straight from France with ships and colonists, overshooting his destination to land at Matagorda Bay in present-day Texas. As a base, the colony was a failure, but Spain's response, sending eleven expeditions out to find it, generated excitement and focused attention on the Gulf. Five of the expeditions came by land from Coahuila, crossing the territory of the non-agricultural Coahuiltecans into the pine-forested "kingdom of the Tejas," as the Spanish called the Caddos. European rivalry in the Caddo world, as in Florida, took the form of a contest between strategic evangelism and mercantile capitalism. David La Vere (1998) lifts the lid of European rivalry to expose the bitter warfare between the Caddos and their competitors in the hide and horse trades – Quapaw, Osage, Apache, and Choctaw.

As the 300th anniversary of La Salle's first expedition came around, scholars sifted the record for material on all Gulf Indians. Patricia Galloway (1982) edited a collection describing the Choctaw, Chickasaw, and Natchez peoples on the eve of colonization. When Europeans converged on the Lower Mississippi Valley – the French from Canada, the Spanish from New Spain and Florida, and the English from Carolina – they found its peoples familiar with European trade goods and ready for an expanded deerskin market. The first European outposts were fortified warehouses. By 1690 the English had a post among the Alabamas at the forks of the Coosa and Tallapoosa Rivers. In 1698 the Spanish founded Pensacola. The French, led by Pierre Le Moyne, Sieur d'Iberville, founded Biloxi in 1699 and Mobile in 1702. The Indians tolerated French soldiers and settlers and sold them food; the French, undersupplied and outnumbered, used their leverage to keep the Indians at war and undertook an occasional punitive campaign, such as the one in 1707, which left the majority of the Chitimachas enslaved and the rest hiding in the Atchafalaya swamp.

In the early 1700s the family compact between France and Bourbon Spain brought a change of tactics in the Gulf. When in 1714 a party from Louisiana appeared at a *presidio* on the Rio Grande, prepared to trade, the government of New Spain took action. Between 1716 and 1718 the viceroy found the funds and manpower for seven Franciscan missions and a *presidio* in East Texas, extending to within fifteen miles of the French post of Natchitoches, and other settlements followed. The *presidio* and surrounding missions of San Antonio, founded in 1718, the same year as New Orleans, was the only settlement that Spain continued to maintain after Louisiana became Spanish and the border a moot point. Indian responses to the Texas missions and *presidios* varied. The Caddos became middlemen in a growing trade in cattle, hides, and bison robes across the Texas–Louisiana border (La Vere 1998), but the greatest beneficiaries were probably the eastern bands of Apaches, who used the missions as sanctuaries during the Comanches' seasonal sweeps across Apache hunting grounds to raid the frontiers of New Spain.

The Yamasee War (1715–17), an uprising of Carolina Indians backed by Upper Creeks against the traders of Charles Town, altered Indian–white relations throughout the South. The Yamasees fled to St Augustine; the Siouan peoples of the Carolina coast took refuge in the piedmont; and the Upper Creeks withdrew their trade from the English and took it to the French, who enlarged their system of trading forts, beginning with Fort Toulouse near the forks of the Alabama in 1717. In 1720 Louisiana allied itself with the Choctaws, countering Carolina's influence with the Chickasaws, and the Chickasaws and Choctaws fought war upon war to keep their respective allies in Indian slaves, until a faction of Choctaws rebelled against the arrangement in the Choctaw Revolt (1746). The Lower Creeks, who continued their English trade, absorbed numerous Taensa, Natchez, Chickasaw, and Shawnee refugees from foreign wars. The Creeks did not allow themselves to be split into pro-English and pro-French factions; like the Iroquois, they pursued a policy of neutrality toward their colonial trading partners and their partners' client communities.

The most centralized chiefdom in Louisiana, that of the Natchez, was a relic of the mound-building Mississippian tradition. The Natchez caste system, which made room for French and African fugitives, shows how a Mississippian community absorbed outsiders, and the rituals following the death of a chief, or Great Sun, which to the horror of French observers included large numbers of human sacrifices, offer an insight into the southeastern ceremonial cult. As late as 1715 the Natchez were numerous enough to raise 4,000 warriors. When they refused to let one of their towns be taken for tobacco planting, cultural conflict escalated into the Natchez War (1729–31). The victorious French rounded up the remnants of the nation, women and children as well as warriors, and sold them to planters in Guadalupe and Martinique.

Richard White's (1991) engaging study of French and Indian accommodation has encouraged colonial historians to look for other intercultural spaces. J. Russell Snapp finds that the Indians of the South Carolina lowcountry were too numerically insignificant in the 1670s for the English to bother making peace with them. Only after the Yamasee War did the colonists, in self-defense, take steps to reduce the level of Indian exploitation, and even then, "a new generation of traders operated on the middle ground much more effectively than government" (Snapp 1996: 8–20). In the later councils between South Carolina and the Cherokees, M. Thomas Hatley (1993) finds evidence of mediation and the promise of mutuality. But familiarity can be inimical to friendship, and intercultural alliances may work only until the partners realize how truly different they are. Gregory Dowd's (1998) analysis of the collapse of the Cherokee–British alliance is a case in point. The reason why the Cherokees, who had fought beside Britons against the Tuscaroras and come to their rescue in the Yamasee War, turned against them during the Seven Years' War is that they learned that Britons despised mercenaries and expected them to manifest the subordination of inferiors. The origins of the Cherokee War (1759–61) lay not in cross-cultural misunderstandings of the role of gifts or the law of international homicide, but in the Cherokee realization that they and the British were misallied.

Louisiana, like Florida, was an imperial outpost in which overseas commerce, commercial agriculture, and settlement did not realize their potential. Instead, as Daniel Usner (1992) shows, the colony developed a flexible and intercultural economy that the plantation economy of the nineteenth century would supersede but never quite replace. The topic takes him across ethnic boundaries and behind the screen of officers' reports to show the economic ties that connected Indians, slaves, soldiers, *habitants*, and *engagés*. The southern Indians who figure in his monograph were not the great confederations, but the humble and diverse *petites nations* who lived on the margins of colonial society by hunting, fishing, and herding, itinerant peddling, foodstuff marketing, and odd jobs. By the mid-1720s there were twenty different groups in this category, with ten villages around Mobile and Biloxi alone. Although some of these Indians were Catholics, and the government provided them with priests at their request, the colony did little to support conversion in the client communities. In the French empire as in the Spanish, the day was past when missions were an end in themselves.

For many years, the Indians of the trans-Mississippi South were protected from white colonization by their region's poor soils and difficult rivers – logjams prevented navigation on the Red River for 100 miles above Natchitoches. The contributors to *Cultural Encounters in the Early South: Indians and Europeans in Arkansas* (Whayne 1995) describe how the French established the Arkansas Post as a stopover between Louisiana and Illinois, an entrepôt of the fur trade, and a gesture of support for the Quapaw in their wars with the Osage and Chickasaw confederacies. After the Seven Years' War the Spanish took over the Post, continuing the annual gifts. All they asked in return was that the Quapaw recognize the king's authority, arrest fugitives and illicit traders, and when they visited the Post, refrain from drinking and leave their weapons at the gate. Arkansas was a commercial hunting frontier, where whites as well as Indians lived by selling bear oil, tallow, salted buffalo meat, and skins to New Orleans.

The Indian slave trade declined after 1730s, but the deerskin trade continued strong, linking southern Indians to the Atlantic economy through the long eighteenth century. Kathryn E. Holland Braund (1993) deconstructs that trade, examining regulation, consumerism and debt, trading alliances, and production, from the male hunting of the white-tailed deer to the female processing of deerskins into supple leather. As Braund's book shows, historians of southern Indians have learned to use gender as an analytic tool. Works that clearly fall into the category of women's history, such as Theda Perdue's *Cherokee Women: Gender and Culture Change, 1700–1835* (1998a), are not the only ones to take it seriously. Late nineteenth-century attempts by missionaries and Indian agents to "civilize" southern Indians by altering their gender roles, forcing the men to do women's work in the fields and the women to be financially dependent, were culturally disruptive, but so was the eighteenth-century deerskin trade, in which scholars detect the economic roots of gender conflict. According to Thomas Hatley (1989) working conditions for Cherokee women worsened over the eighteenth century. Their labor on deer leather subsidized a commerce dominated by males, and as the men's hunts grew longer, women were left to do men's work, such as cutting and hauling firewood. Claudio Saunt (1999) shows by contrast that the labor of Creek women gave them rights to the product and a degree of economic independence. When in the 1760s a shift in the market in favor of raw deerskins turned the trade into an activity for young, unmarried men, who wasted their proceeds on rum, Creek women lost an important source of income. The simple addition of gender to the equation opens the door to fresh questions and research.

After the Seven Years' War, Great Britain disappointed colonial expectations by coming to terms with the Indians of the eastern woodlands, negotiating treaties, appointing superintendents of Indian affairs – Sir William Johnson in the North, John Stuart in the South – and establishing by proclamation an Indian Boundary designed to keep the peace by protecting Indian territories from the expanding colonies. Russell Snapp (1996) analyzes the failure of this enlightened frontier policy, emphasizing the clash between British officials and British–American frontiersmen.

The motor behind colonization of the backcountry was demographic. In 1775, on the eve of the American Revolution, the population of southern Indians had, by Peter Wood's (1989: 90) calculations, reached a nadir of 55,600, compared to a non-Indian population of 916,900. Only one Indian in forty-three lived in one of the three traditionally English subregions, in which the original inhabitants had become demographically inconsiderable: 300 Indians to 465,900 non-Indians in Virginia, 500 Indians to 209,100 non-Indians in North Carolina, 500 Indians to 178,900 non-Indians in South Carolina. In the non-English subregions, the proportions varied. In the Creek subregion there were 14,000 Indians to 33,000 non-Indians; in the subregion of the Choctaws and Chickasaws, 16,300 to 100; in the Cherokee subregion, 8,500 to 2,200. The Shawnee interior was still a hunting ground, with only 2,000 Indians and 300 non-Indian residents. East Texas contained 8,300 Indians to 2,100 non-Indians. The ratio in Lower Louisiana was 3,700 to 21,500. Florida was no longer a population vacuum, with 1,500 Indians, mostly Seminole Creeks, and 4,800 non-Indians. During the American Revolution the population of these last two subregions would fluctuate with their flags, as Loyalists and their slaves first poured across the borders into French Louisiana and the British Floridas, East and West, then – when Spain recaptured West Florida, France ceded Louisiana to Spain, and Great Britain retroceded East Florida – left for havens where they could complain in English.

In the short period that the Floridas were British, a Scottish merchant house established itself in East Florida and opened stores to serve the Choctaws, Chickasaws, and Upper Creeks. William S. Coker and Thomas D. Watson (1986) reconstruct the deerskin trade as a British firm experienced it. When the British left Florida

in 1784, the firm continued with a Spanish license and until 1821 essentially monopolized the Indian trade east of the Mississippi, from the Bahamas to western
Tennessee. Pragmatically switching its loyalty to the United States in 1812 in order
to collect over $200,000 in accounts receivable from the Choctaw, Chickasaw,
Cherokee, Creek, and Seminole nations, the firm secured land cessions in excess of
12 million acres.

The pressures behind land cessions of this size were demographic, political, economic, and cultural. By 1790, the date of Peter Wood's last set of population figures
for the South (Wood 1989: 90), Indian southerners had managed to arrest their long
demographic decline and stabilize their numbers at 55,900. This would not necessarily have kept other Americans from thinking that they were dying out, for in the
fifteen years before 1790, the non-Indian population increased by 77.8 percent to
1,630,100, causing the Indian share of total population to fall from 6.1 to 3.4
percent. Some natural philosophers believed that Native Americans came from a
weaker stock than Euro-Americans and would in time become extinct. Settlers raised
on stories of wilderness cruelty thought of them as blackhearted savages who with-
held the good land that white men needed for farming in order to indulge their idle
habit of hunting. State governments objected to the Indian nations' intra-territorial,
quasi-sovereign status. The federal government wanted the Indians either to forsake
their communal identities and turn into faux white people or take themselves west.
With diplomacy no longer cost-effective, the United States ceased the formal gifts
that eased alliances.

Once valued as producers of deerskins and consumers of trade goods, southern
Indians saw their economic situation change as a declining demand for deerskins
intersected with a rising demand for cotton lands. The credit on which the deerskin
trade operated became the lever with which to pry deerhunters from their hunting
grounds. Deliberately, the merchant companies allowed Indian debts to mount. In
return for satisfying them, the federal government between 1802 and 1805 obtained
large tracts of land in a series of treaties with the Creeks, Choctaws, and Chickasaws.
These cessions were part of an ongoing process of expansion, as Americans yielded to
the urge to colonize. The contested area between the Mississippi River and West
Florida that Spain ceded to the United States in 1795 became the Mississippi
territory, joined by the territories of Orleans and Louisiana when the United States
divided the Louisiana Purchase in 1804.

An old rule of thumb holds that when a large war ends, small wars break out,
employing restless military men and using up matériel. The Creek War of 1813–14
came hard on the heels of the war of 1812. It began as a conflict between the tribal
council and the Red Sticks, a faction under the influence of the Shawnee leader
Tecumseh that angered southern slaveowners by welcoming runaway slaves. Andrew
Jackson intervened on the council side, moving militia and federal troops into Upper
Creek territory. In the Treaty of Fort Jackson he penalized the Creek nation for its
civil war by seizing half of the present state of Alabama, organized into the Alabama
territory in 1817. The defeated Red Sticks left to join the Seminoles, and Jackson's
pursuit of them across an international border was an affront that Spain could only
protest, its armies being busy with the Spanish American Wars for Independence. The
United States bought East Florida, the last sanctuary, in 1819 and organized it into a
territory three years later.

The first southerners had survived the decline of the Mississippian chiefdoms, contact with European explorers, drastic drops in population, the births and growing pains of new polities, contact with colonists and traders, increased militarization, debt, and land cessions leading to factionalism and civil wars. Although a handful of southern Indians resisted removal, they knew that the price of defiance would, sooner or later, be war. The Indians had lost the land, and as they headed west, the land lost them.

BIBLIOGRAPHY

Adelman, Jeremy and Aron, Stephen 1999: From Borderlands to Borders: Empires, Nation-States, and the Peoples in Between in North American History. *American Historical Review*, 104, 814–41.

Adorno, Rolena and Pautz, Patrick Charles 1999: *Álvar Núñez Cabeza de Vaca: His Account, His Life, and the Expedition of Pánfilo de Narváez*, 3 vols. Lincoln: University of Nebraska Press.

Axtell, James 1997: *The Indians' New South: Cultural Change in the Colonial Southeast*. Baton Rouge: Louisiana State University Press.

Braund, Kathryn E. Holland 1993: *Deerskins and Duffels: Creek Indian Trade with Anglo-America, 1685–1815*. Lincoln: University of Nebraska Press.

Bushnell, Amy Turner 1979: Patricio de Hinachuba: Defender of the Word of God, the Crown of the King, and the Little Children of Ivitachuco. *American Indian Culture and Research Journal* 3: 1–21.

Bushnell, Amy Turner 1989: Ruling "the Republic of Indians" in Seventeenth-Century Florida. In Peter H. Wood, Gregory A. Waselkov, and M. Thomas Hatley (eds.), *Powhatan's Mantle: Indians in the Colonial Southeast*. Lincoln: University of Nebraska Press, 134–50.

Bushnell, Amy Turner 1990: The Sacramental Imperative: Catholic Ritual and Indian Sedentism in the Provinces of Florida. In David Hurst Thomas (ed.), *Columbian Consequences*, 3 vols. Washington, DC: Smithsonian Institution Press, 2: 475–90.

Bushnell, Amy Turner 1994: *Situado and Sabana: Spain's Support System for the Presidio and Mission Provinces of Florida*. Anthropological Papers of the American Museum of Natural History, no. 74.

Bushell, Amy Turner 2001: Spain's Conquest by Contract: Pacification and the Mission System in Eastern North America. In Michael V. Kennedy and William G. Shade (eds.), *The World Turned Upside Down: The State of Eighteenth-Century Studies at the Beginning of the Twenty-First Century*. Bethlehem: Lenign University Press, 239–320.

Coker, William S. and Watson, Thomas D. 1986: *Indian Traders of the Southeastern Spanish Borderlands: Panton, Leslie & Company and John Forbes & Company, 1783–1847*. Pensacola: University of West Florida Press.

Deagan, Kathleen A. 1985: Spanish–Indian Interaction in Sixteenth-Century Florida and Hispaniola. In William W. Fitzhugh (ed.), *Cultures in Contact: The Impact of European Contacts on Native American Cultural Institutions, AD 1000–1800*. Washington, DC: Smithsonian Institution, 281–318.

Dowd, Gregory Evans 1992: *A Spirited Resistance: The North American Indian Struggle for Unity, 1745–1815*. Baltimore: Johns Hopkins University Press.

Dowd, Gregory Evans 1998: "Insidious Friends": Gift Giving and the Cherokee–British Alliance in the Seven Years' War. In Andrew R. L. Cayton and Fredrika J. Teute (eds.), *Contact Points: American Frontiers from the Mohawk Valley to the Mississippi, 1750–1830*. Chapel Hill: University of North Carolina Press, 114–50.

Galloway, Patricia (ed.) 1982: *LaSalle and His Legacy: Frenchmen and Indians in the Lower Mississippi Valley*. Jackson: University of Mississippi Press.

Galloway, Patricia 1995: *Choctaw Genesis, 1500–1700*. Lincoln: University of Nebraska Press.

Galloway, Patricia (ed.) 1997: *The Hernando de Soto Expedition: History, Historiography, and "Discovery" in the Southeast*. Lincoln: University of Nebraska Press.

Gleach, Frederic W. 1997: *Powhatan's World and Colonial Virginia: A Conflict of Cultures*. Lincoln: University of Nebraska Press.

Hann, John H. 1988: *Apalachee: The Land Between the Rivers*. Gainesville: University of Florida Press.

Hann, John H. (ed. and trans.) 1991: *Missions to the Calusa*. Gainesville: University of Florida Press.

Hann, John H. 1996: *A History of the Timucua Indians and Missions*. Gainesville: University of Florida Press.

Hatley, M. Thomas 1989: The Three Lives of Keowee: Loss and Recovery in Eighteenth-Century Cherokee Villages. In Peter H. Wood, Gregory A. Waselkov, and M. Thomas Hatley (eds.), *Powhatan's Mantle: Indians in the Colonial Southeast*. Lincoln: University of Nebraska Press, 223–48.

Hatley, M. Thomas 1993: *The Dividing Paths: Cherokees and South Carolinians through the Era of Revolution*. New York: Oxford University Press.

Henige, David P. 1998: *Numbers from Nowhere: The American Indian Contact Population Debate*. Norman: University of Oklahoma Press.

Hudson, Charles 1997: *Knights of Spain, Warriors of the Sun: Hernando de Soto and the South's Ancient Chiefdoms*. Athens: University of Georgia Press.

Hudson, Charles and Tesser, Carmen Chaves (eds.) 1994: *The Forgotten Centuries: Indians and Europeans in the American South, 1521–1704*. Athens: University of Georgia Press.

Larsen, Clark Spencer 1987: Biological Interpretation and the Context for Contact. In Clark Spencer Larsen (ed.), *The Archaeology of Mission Santa Catalina de Guale: 2. Biocultural Interpretations of a Population in Transition*. Anthropological Papers of the American Museum of Natural History, no. 68: 11–25.

La Vere, David 1998: *The Caddo Chiefdoms: Caddo Economics and Politics, 700–1835*. Lincoln: University of Nebraska Press.

Merrell, James H. 1989: *The Indians' New World: Catawbas and Their Neighbors from European Contact through the Era of Removal*. Chapel Hill: University of North Carolina Press.

Milanich, Jerald T. 1999: *Laboring in the Fields of the Lord: Spanish Missions and Southeastern Indians*. Washington, DC: Smithsonian Institution Press.

Perdue, Theda 1979: *Slavery and the Evolution of Cherokee Society, 1540–1866*. Knoxville: University of Tennessee Press.

Perdue, Theda 1998a: *Cherokee Women: Gender and Culture Change, 1700–1835*. Lincoln: University of Nebraska Press.

Perdue, Theda 1998b: Indians in Southern History. In Frederick E. Hoxie and Peter Iverson (eds.), *Indians in American History: An Introduction*, 2nd edn. Wheeling, IL: Harlan Davidson, 121–39.

Rountree, Helen C. 1989: *The Powhatan Indians of Virginia: Their Traditional Culture*. Norman: University of Oklahoma Press.

Rountree, Helen C. (ed.) 1993: *Powhatan Foreign Relations, 1500–1722*. Charlottesville: University of Virginia Press.

Saunt, Claudio 1999: *A New Order of Things: Property, Power, and the Transformation of the Creek Indians, 1733–1816*. Cambridge: Cambridge University Press.

Sider, Gerald M. 1993: *Lumbee Indian Histories: Race, Ethnicity, and Indian Identity in the Southern United States*. Cambridge: Cambridge University Press.

Silver, Timothy 1990: *A New Face on the Countryside: Indians, Colonists, and Slaves in South Atlantic Forests, 1500–1800*. Cambridge: Cambridge University Press.

Smith, Marvin T. 1987: *Archaeology of Aboriginal Culture Change in the Interior Southeast: Depopulation during the Early Historic Period.* Gainesville: University of Florida Press.

Snapp, J. Russell 1996: *John Stuart and the Struggle for Empire on the Southern Frontier.* Baton Rouge: Louisiana State University Press.

Straus, L. G. 2000: Solutrean Settlement of North America? A Review of Reality. *American Antiquity* 65: 219–26.

Thomas, David Hurst (ed.) 1990: *Columbian Consequences.* Washington, DC: Smithsonian Institution Press.

Thornton, Russell 1987: *American Indian Holocaust and Survival: A Population History Since 1492.* Norman: University of Oklahoma Press.

Usner, Daniel H., Jr. 1992: *Indians, Settlers, and Slaves in a Frontier Exchange Economy: The Lower Mississippi Valley Before 1783.* Chapel Hill: University of North Carolina Press.

Usner, Daniel H., Jr. 1998: *American Indians in the Lower Mississippi Valley: Social and Economic Histories.* Lincoln: University of Nebraska Press.

Waselkov, Gregory A. (1989) Seventeenth-Century Trade in the Colonial Southeast. *Southeastern Archaeology* 8, 117–60.

Weber, David J. 1992: *The Spanish Frontier in North America.* New Haven, CT: Yale University Press.

Whayne, Jeannie (comp.) 1995: *Cultural Encounters in the Early South: Indians and Europeans in Arkansas.* Fayetteville: University of Arkansas Press.

White, Richard 1991: *The Middle Ground: Indians, Empires, and Republics in the Great Lakes Region, 1650–1815.* Cambridge: Cambridge University Press.

Wood, Peter H. 1989: The Changing Population of the Colonial South: An Overview by Race and Region, 1685–1790. In Peter H. Wood, Gregory A. Waselkov, and M. Thomas Hatley (eds.), *Powhatan's Mantle: Indians in the Colonial Southeast.* Lincoln: University of Nebraska Press, 35–103.

Worth, John E. 1995: *The Struggle for the Georgia Coast: An Eighteenth-Century Spanish Retrospective on Guale and Mocama.* Anthropological Papers of the American Museum of Natural History, no. 75.

Worth, John E. 1998: *Timucuan Chiefdoms of Spanish Florida,* 2 vols. Gainesville: University of Florida Press.

Wright, J. Leitch, Jr. 1981: *The Only Land They Knew: The Tragic Story of the American Indians in the Old South.* New York: Free Press.

Wright, J. Leitch, Jr. 1986: *Creeks and Seminoles: Destruction and Regeneration of the Muscogulge People.* Lincoln: University of Nebraska Press.

CHAPTER TWO

Spanish and French Exploration and Colonization

PAUL E. HOFFMAN

HISTORIANS have traditionally presented the Spanish and French explorations and colonizations of the American South as minor parts of the larger narrative of the European "discovery" of the world and as part of the story of national rivalries among the Spaniards, French, and English for colonial possessions. Parkman (1879, 1885), La Roncière (1899–1932), Lowery (1901–5), Folmer (1953), Wright (1971), Quinn (1974), and a host of other historians are examples of this tendency to privilege narrative, national identity, and, in the case of the European writers, their national documentary sources. In addition, they and other writers have often paid scant attention to the social and economic sides of the events they discuss. Native Americans, blacks, and especially women are absent from these narratives, a fact understandable for explorations in which the latter two were not always present, but less so for colonization, in which all three groups interacted with the European male actors who have traditionally held center stage.

Historians of the United States, as distinguished from those interested in the Spanish and French empires in the Americas, if they consider the histories of Spanish Florida (La Florida hereafter to avoid confusion with peninsular Florida, which is but a fragment of the original Spanish claim) and French and Spanish Louisiana (La Louisiane hereafter to denote the entire territory, roughly equal to the Louisiana Purchase territory, but including the Gulf of Mexico coast as far east as Perdido Bay and as far west as the Trinity River in Texas) at all, generally treat French and Spanish explorations and settlements as a brief, curious prologue to the "real story" of United States history that begins at Jamestown in 1607 and is the story of the expansion of anglophone civilization across the face of the continent. In contrast, the historical interactions of the New England colonies with French Canada, and consequently sometimes some of Canada's internal history, do find a place in histories of the United States. The equally significant if less long-lived interactions of Carolina and Georgia and Spanish Florida and of La Louisiane with the British colonies and the early United States pass largely unnoticed, except perhaps in state histories of Carolina, Georgia, and the states formed from the Louisiana Purchase.

Historians of the Spanish empire, except for the famous Borderlands school that flourished in the 1920s, likewise have seldom taken much interest in these peripheral colonies, perhaps because, unlike the Southwest, no significant Spanish-speaking population survived into the national period.

This thralldom to nineteenth-century conceptions of nation and male, Euro-centric, teleological narrative is rightly under challenge in this nation of peoples called the United States. And even were it not, it is scarcely credible that the colonial histories of Carolina and Georgia, and the story of sectional conflict, to mention only the most obvious topics, could be told without paying attention to the histories of La Florida and La Louisiane. On a different plane, the histories of a number of social groups, especially blacks, in the US and Latin America are usefully compared to those of the same people in La Florida and La Louisiane. Some excellent work along these lines has appeared in recent years, as will be noted. The challenge for historians of the South (and of the US and the Spanish and French empires), then, is to appropriately fit the histories of Spanish and French exploration and settlement into their metanarratives. The works reviewed here, to varying degrees, attempt to do that or can be used to that end.

There is no single volume that covers the topics considered here, but David Weber (1992) comes close. A narrative survey of the entire "borderlands" from first explorations to colonization and then annexation into the United States and even to the uses of the Hispanic heritage of the annexed areas, this work summarizes the scholarship to its date of publication. While taking a Spanish point of view, Weber is careful to consider Native Americans and Africans and what they contributed to the story, especially during the formative sixteenth and seventeenth centuries. Too, Weber is aware of how his story fits into the story of US expansion and of the Latin American context of much of what he discusses. Less is said about the French colonial experience, but a reader new to Spanish and French exploration and colonization might well begin with Weber's fine book.

Exploration

The exploration of the South proceeded mostly from the Atlantic coast but also, as Robert Weddle (1985) has reminded us, from the Gulf of Mexico (see below). The basic narratives of both sets of explorations have been in print since the eighteenth century. Woodbury Lowery (1901–5) and some other scholars early in the twentieth century added details and corrections to that older narrative from selected Spanish documentation. David B. Quinn, Susan Hillier, and Alison Quinn (1978) made much of this source material available in translation. They added to the older corpus with their own archival discoveries in England and Spain. They largely left it to their readers to explore the possible interconnections among the voyages and colonization efforts.

The maps that explorers and settlers helped to create are found in William P. Cumming and Louis De Vorsey Jr. (1998). This book handsomely reproduces many of the maps from the earliest years to the late eighteenth century and describes most of the rest. Each of the 491 maps in the list is described as to content, when and why produced, where referenced and reproduced, and the locations of originals and copies. De Vorsey's essay on Native American maps and contributions to cartography, mostly in the Carolinas and Virginia, complements Galloway's discussions (1998; below). Cumming has a bias towards maps of the Carolinas and Georgia, especially in the illustrations.

Robert S. Weddle (1985), the first volume in his trilogy of the history of the exploration and settlement of the shores of the Gulf of Mexico, boldly challenges the standard narrative's emphasis on the Atlantic explorations and the nationalist narratives' minimizing of events not directly tied to the national territory. Weddle argues that the Gulf approach to North America was far more important than Atlantic coast-oriented historians of European exploration and settlement had assumed. Believing that, he produced the best, most detailed narrative of the voyages of discovery that touched not only what became the United States but also Mexico. Those voyages were, he ably shows, interrelated and inseparable as parts of the larger story of exploration and colonization. Juan Ponce de León, Alonso Alvarez de Pineda, Álvar Núñez Cabeza de Vaca, Hernando de Soto, Tristan de Luna, and Angel de Villafañe among sixteenth-century explorers who touched what became US shores, and the more shadowy figures of English, French, and Dutch mariners who plied the Gulf in the seventeenth century, here receive their due. Several of these early explorers are also discussed in Hudson and Tesser (1994). More may yet be learned about the late seventeenth-century voyagers, but until then Weddle is the best source for their stories.

Weddle rightly calls attention to the generation (1539–61) during which Spain's approach to North America *was* via the Gulf Coast. De Soto reoriented the Spanish approach to La Florida by using Cuba as a staging base. Luna used Mexico for his base and tried to colonize at Pensacola and on the Alabama River (1559–61). Luna's failure and Spanish concerns about possible French or Scots colonization of the Point of Santa Elena (Tybee Island, GA) after 1559 ended this approach to North America. After 1561, Spanish exploration and colonization was once again along the Atlantic face of the continent, as it had been in the 1510s and 1520s.

Paul E. Hoffman (1990) is a revision of the traditional idea that La Florida's sixteenth-century history is not important for the narrative of US history, understood as the story of English colonization. Taking European imperial rivalries and a Caribbean (and Atlantic coast) context as givens, Hoffman asked why those rivalries of the 1560s to 1580s focused on particular places on the southeast coast, a question not asked by the older narrative tradition. He found an answer in two misconceptions or legends about the geography of North America that arose in the 1520s. The book argues that all sixteenth-century exploration and attempted settlement in the Southeast after 1521, even if not on the Atlantic coast, including the English settlement of the 1580s, was directly influenced by one or both of these legends.

The first legend, the new Andalucia, is based on the *Licenciado* Lucas Vázquez de Ayllón's claim that a "new land" discovered under his authority in 1521 was at the latitude of Andalucia in Spain and thus, according to Ptolemaic principles, capable of producing wine and olive oil. In addition, Francisco El Chicorano, an Indian kidnapped in 1521, was understood to say that the land yielded freshwater pearls and, inland, "terrestrial gems." This was an early version of the myth of American abundance.

The other legend, "a way to the Orient," originated in the French-sponsored voyage of Giovanni da Verrazzano along the Atlantic coast in 1524 and the cartographic tradition that arose from it. Wroth (1970) showed that this geographical misconception mixed the fact of the sounds behind the Outer Banks and a wish that the Pacific Ocean come close to the Atlantic Ocean at some point in North America (thereby facilitating the voyage to Asia) to give North America an isthmus at about 35 degrees North. Over time, the isthmus widened and moved north on the maps as the vaguely known Great Lakes replaced the North Carolina sounds as the eastern arm of the Pacific Ocean. The fullest expression of this complexity and later geographic knowledge of the St Lawrence and Colorado Rivers is John Dee's map, "Humfray Gylbert knight his charte" of ca. 1582–3, which summarized all the variations of the Verrazzano tradition (Cumming and De Vorsey 1998: plate 8).

Recent scholarship on de Soto has been prolific because of the 450th anniversary of his expedition of 1539–43 and because he encountered late Mississippian chiefdoms that are important to archeologists and ethnohistorians trying to understand how Native Americans got from the mound-building chiefdoms of the twelfth to fourteenth centuries CE to the tribal confederations that eighteenth-century explorers found. Charles Hudson (1997) reconstructs the expedition's route on the basis of the best current knowledge and provides a brief guide to the arguments of his critics. Hudson's book should be read in conjunction with Patricia Galloway (1997), which is a collection of essays that raise questions about Hudson's sources and methods and suggest additional contexts not covered in his book. No satisfactory answers are suggested to the questions raised, for example, about the intertextuality of the sources and what diseases might have traveled with the army's pigs. Rather the way is pointed to studies yet to be done. The vexing question of the location of Mabila (was it at the junction of the Cahawba and Alabama Rivers or further down the Alabama River?) also awaits resolution, most likely by archeological discovery. Hoffman (2000) reviews other books produced for the occasion.

A number of issues connected with sixteenth-century exploration remain under researched. The financing of most of the early expeditions is poorly understood, although we do know something of how Verrazzano, Ayllón, de Soto, and Tristan de Luna paid their bills. We have a prosopographical study of the de Soto survivors (Avellaneda Navas and Chappell 1990), but not of the other French and Spanish expeditions. We know only a little, and much of that circumstantial, about French national policy that governed exploring and colonial activity during the sixteenth century. The old idea that Admiral Gaspard de Coligny sponsored Jean Ribault in hopes that he would find a Huguenot refuge seems to be but part of a larger policy. And there is much we still do not know about the geographical distribution of Native Americans during the early sixteenth century and how that played into what Europeans attempted to do both along the coasts and inland and was in turn affected by the European presence.

Spanish exploration during the early seventeenth century was limited to a few minor Spanish reconnaissances of the interior of Georgia (Worth 1994) until they learned of La Salle's Texas colony. The Spaniards mounted major searches for it that gave them new understandings of East Texas and a truer outline of the northern Gulf of Mexico coast. Weddle (1991) is the best treatment of these developments. The book distills his earlier work on La Salle and the Spanish search for La Salle and then discusses the Spanish and French colonies of Pensacola and La Louisiane (briefly) and subsequent explorations along the Gulf coast, again including Mexico. The fruits of this activity, in which the French took an especially active part, were a series of maps that showed an increasingly accurate and sophisticated understanding of the entire Gulf of Mexico littoral. These maps form the subject of a final chapter.

Because of his focus on the exploration of the Gulf of Mexico, Weddle does not develop the story of growing French knowledge of the interior South – modern

Georgia, Alabama, Mississippi, Louisiana, and Tennessee – after 1699. That story is told in a superb, heavily illustrated chapter based on mostly French cartographic evidence in Patricia Galloway (1995).

Like de Soto, La Salle has been the subject of many works and recent public interest since the discovery and excavation of his ship, *Le Belle*. Peter Wood (1989) has changed our understanding of La Salle and challenged traditional biographies such as Parkman's (1879). Wood shows that La Salle made an error in figuring his latitude while at the head of the Mississippi's bird-foot delta in 1682. With that erroneous calculation of 27 degrees North (29 degrees is the correct figure), La Salle and his patrons at the French court proceeded to take the cartography of their time, probably some knowledge of the de Soto expedition, and a variety of political and economic motives and fashioned a map that showed the Mississippi swinging west in a great arc that came out on the coast of Texas, somewhat to the west of the traditional cartographic location of the mouth of the Río del Espiritu Santo (Sabine River), the largest river flowing into the Gulf on Spanish maps. Thus La Salle was neither mad nor Parkman's "hero" struggling against great odds. Had he not been murdered, he might well have reached the Caddo peoples of western Louisiana and then the Red River and been able to correct his mistake, as his patrons at court quickly did once they had the account of his murderers' long trek. Consequently, when Pierre Le Moyne, Sieur de Iberville, set out for the Mississippi in 1698, he did so with an accurate estimate of where he would find it. Weddle's third volume (1995) carries the story of Gulf explorations and mappings to the end of the colonial era. Surveys of Florida's coasts receive passing mention, with most attention focused on the west coast.

In sum, the exploration of the South by the Spaniards and French is better understood in its narrative details than was the case half a century ago. Progress has been made as well in understanding the larger stories of which it is a part, stories that encompass Native Americans and their histories and also the histories of the English southern colonies. More can be done on almost all of these topics, especially for the seventeenth century.

Colonization: La Florida (East Florida)

Scholarly understanding of Spanish and French colonization also has undergone renovation during the last quarter century. Hoffman (1990) is the best account of the Ayllón colony of 1526. Tristan de Luna y Arellana's colony at Pensacola and Nanipacana (on the Alabama River, location uncertain) of 1559–61 awaits a complete modern treatment, but Galloway's (1995) study of the Choctaw has brought current archeological knowledge to bear on the problem of the location of Nanipacana and provides a good short account of events. Hoffman (1990) also provides the fullest account to date of Lucas Vázquez de Ayllón the Younger's activities of 1562–5, when he apparently planned to colonize the Chesapeake Bay as a follow-up to its exploration by Angel de Villafañe (1561) and the arrival in Spain with Villafañe of Paquequineo, a Powhatan Indian later known as Don Luis de Velasco. Ayllón the Younger never made it to the Chesapeake Bay, but Paquequineo did eventually return to his homeland with the Jesuit mission of 1570–1. Archeological research has recently located Jean Ribault's Charlesfort (1562–3) under one of the Spanish forts on Parris

Island, SC (site of Spanish Santa Elena). René de Laudonnière's Fort Caroline colony (1564–5) has received extensive documentary and narrative coverage, but we still do not know all of the details of its purposes and fitting out; the same can be said of Charlesfort.

The most important recent book on the early years of the permanent Spanish colonization of La Florida is Eugene Lyon (1976). Lyon examined the "enterprise of Florida" as a business venture whose financial aspects are perhaps uniquely well documented, from the Crown's expenditures and gifts to him to what Pedro Menéndez de Avilés claimed (in lawsuits) he had spent or caused associates to spend. Lyon also looked at the social connections among the Asturians who were the Adelantado's key supporters and the ruling elite of the new colony. The result is a richly textured socioeconomic history of a colonization effort set within a more detailed narrative of events than can be found in any previous work (e.g. Lowery 1901–5). A projected second volume will carry the story to and beyond D. Pedro's death in 1574, although a more limited documentary base may well yield less information on the social and economic sides of the colony's history. Lyon (1984) sketches aspects of such a second volume and calls attention to one of the lesser known aspects of the Spanish presence in the South: the town of Santa Elena on Parris Island, SC. Karen Paar also is preparing a history of Santa Elena.

The rest of the history of the Spanish settlement, at St Augustine to 1700, is still only partially known. Weber (1992) provides an overview. Dunkle (1958) and Corbett (1976) provide somewhat contrasting views of the town's demographic history. Hoffman (n.d.) is preparing a book on the history of Florida's frontiers that will cover the story from the 1520s to 1860.

What is known about the seventeenth-century history of St Augustine is found in Amy Bushnell's books. Using a largely topical approach, Bushnell (1981) explored the social and economic hold that the royal treasury officials gained on the economy of La Florida. She shows that, like the Menéndez *comuño* that controlled La Florida in the 1560s and from which some of these men were descended, this group of officeholders used their positions for personal gain, although they had to contend with various restrictive royal orders, with governors out for the same ends, and with other newcomers, who had to be assimilated into the intermarried elite (or ejected!). Too, the colony faced repeated minor and one or two major crises (e.g. Robert Searle's raid of 1659). By the time of James Moore's raids in 1702 and 1704, the elite had established a ranching economy that used areas left vacant by the demographic decline of the Native Americans, although their hold on public office and its benefits was weaker. Bushnell's (1994) book on the missions and their economies supplies additional new and important detail about the seventeenth-century economy and events in St Augustine, as well as among the missions, its primary focus. In both books, Bushnell's analysis is hampered by the fact that most of the treasury accounts and all notarial records for the seventeenth century are missing.

John E. Worth (1998) adds an additional dimension to our understanding of the seventeenth century. Worth's structuralist analysis of the Spanish mission system and the use of previously neglected primary sources allow him to discern not only the mobilization of labor to produce food for St Augustine (a topic Bushnell discusses as well), but also the existence of an Indian militia, for example, and the revolutionary nature of the changes that the Spaniards imposed on the Indians after the rebellion of

1657. This synchronic interpretative framework, for all of the insights it generates, downplays the dynamic effects of sharp population declines in the 1620s–40s and later.

For the early eighteenth century we have only John J. TePaske's *The Governorship of Spanish Florida, 1700–1763* (1964) and Weber's (1992) summary of the recent scholarship. TePaske's topical chapters sketch out the internal administrative and economic history of St Augustine, which was all that remained of the Spanish presence in La Florida after Moore's raids on the missions in 1702 and 1704. He also has materials on English attacks on the colony from the Spanish point of view, a useful counter to the more familiar English accounts. Still, these six decades in La Florida's history offer many opportunities for research.

Much the same situation exists for British East Florida. Charles L. Mowat (1943) is still the best treatment of that period. It is a narrative that focuses on the political struggles of the first governor and the crises of the American Revolution and the transfer to Spain in 1783–4. Wright (1975) provides a detailed look at events in both East and West Florida (especially the latter) during the American Revolution. Here again recent article literature is beginning to deepen our knowledge of aspects of this history, especially the social aspects, but much more needs to be done on the details of economic development, or lack thereof.

The second Spanish period in East Florida, 1784–1821, also is not well studied. Most of the older historical writing focused on governors, William Augustus Bowles, and episodes that relate to the history of the US such as the Anglo-American invasion of 1795 and the "Patriot's War" of 1812–13. That minor border episodes should be the subject of several books illustrates how much the nationalist and romantic traditions have shaped the writing of history about East Florida in this period while larger topics are neglected. Weber (1992) is a useful summary.

A somewhat comprehensive study is Pablo Tornero Tinajero (1979), which examines the demographic and economic history of the colony to show how La Florida became a dependency of the United States well before it was acquired as a result of Spain's weakness and Andrew Jackson's attacks. This slender Spanish dissertation has not been translated and has little narrative of other aspects of the colony's history. It also does not make use of the voluminous East Florida Papers held in the Library of Congress, the Spanish administrative archive that the United States seized at the time of the transfer of East Florida in 1821. Consequently the picture is not as full as it might have been. Still, the book suggests what a more deeply researched treatment of the topic might show.

What Tornero Tinajero's work lacks, Jane Landers (1999) partially supplies via incidental discussions of most of the major military and economic events of the period. Landers begins with considerations of Spanish policies toward both slave and free Africans and the pre-1783 history of African slavery in La Florida, but most of her book is concerned with the post-1783 period. Landers calls special attention to the free persons of African ancestry and their roles as militiamen as well as economic and social agents. Like Hanger (1997), she uses examples to show that their status under Spanish rule was quite different from the status of blacks in the United States. Anglo-American immigrants into northeast Florida found this status and the Spanish policy of granting refuge to fleeing slaves (to 1790) upsetting, as did Americans in Georgia and South Carolina who feared for the security of their slaveocracy. The existence of black communities associated with Seminole villages also incited Americans, giving them another reason to repeatedly invade Florida. Free persons understood this American hostility and played a major role in defending the colony during the invasions, further inciting American anger. The free persons of African ancestry who did not leave with the Spaniards eventually regretted their choice, as Americans imposed the two-caste system of race relations. This is clearly the most important book we have on the internal history of La Florida during the second Spanish period.

The history of West Florida as a British and Spanish colony, like that of East Florida in the eighteenth century, needs additional study. Weber (1992) gives an overview. A somewhat longer one is William S. Coker's (1999) essay that incorporates recent archival and archeological evidence and shows just how much is still not known. Cecil Johnson (1943) remains the standard history of that colony. Wright (1975) provides narrative coverage of the war of 1779–83. Robert R. Rea and Robin F. A. Fabel have added a number of excellent articles to the literature, expanding and correcting Johnson's accounts. The reader is referred to standard bibliographies such as Fabel (1989) and *America: History and Life* for details.

The second Spanish period in West Florida, 1779–1821, awaits a detailed general history. Weber (1992) and Coker (1999) provide overviews. William S. Coker and Thomas D. Watson (1986) describe not only the histories of Panton, Leslie and Company and John Forbes and Company and their trade with the Creek and Choctaw, but also the ever shifting policies of Spain and the United States with respect to the Southeastern Indian nations, especially the Creek. The work, however, provides little information on the colony's European and African residents and their economy. Constructing such a history is more difficult because many of the Spanish administrative records have been lost.

Settlement: La Louisiane

The French colony of La Louisiane was founded in 1699 by Pierre Le Moyne, Sieur de Iberville (1661–1706), with royal support, to serve France's imperial designs for North America. The French had three aims. They wanted to make good their claim to the Mississippi River watershed and its fur trade that arose from La Salle's exploration of 1682. They wanted to provide themselves with a naval base on the Gulf of Mexico from which to attack Spanish shipping and Mexico in wartime and to use as a port for smuggling in peacetime. And they hoped that control of the Mississippi and extension of their fur-trading operations into the South would allow them to confine the English colonies to the seaboard. In pursuit of these aims, Iberville and his successors settled French headquarters first at old Biloxi (modern Ocean Springs, MS) before moving them to Mobile (1702) and eventually New Orleans (1718). A Spanish colony founded at Pensacola in late 1698 denied them use of that superb bay.

The accession to the Spanish throne of Philip V, Louis XIV's grandson, began an off-and-on alliance with Spain but did not change the strategic purposes of the colony. By 1719 that initial alliance had turned to enmity in Europe and on the Gulf Coast. Restored in the 1730s, the alliance (the Family Compact) waned in the 1750s, only to be revived again in 1762 when Spain saw France going down to defeat before the British. Spain's ill-timed and ill-prepared entry into the Seven Years' War followed, with the consequent loss of all of the South east of the Mississippi River in the treaties of 1763. La Louisiane, thus reduced to roughly the area of the later Louisiana Purchase, was given to a reluctant Spain as France pulled out of North America. The two powers again cooperated against the British in 1779–83, and Spain permitted La Louisiane to trade with France and the French West Indies thereafter. Only in 1790 did Revolutionary France turn on Spain, demanding La Louisiane and temporarily ending the common pursuit of containing the British empire. With the 1790s too came increased American pressure to cede to the US the former British territorial holdings and river privileges. Pinckney's Treaty (1795) and then the cession of La Louisiane to France and the subsequent sale to the United States followed (1803).

As with the Floridas, so with La Louisiane, there is no single-volume general history of La Louisiane's colonial era that provides both depth and breadth and considers the colony's development and peopling during both periods and in international context. Hoffman (1992) is a stab in that direction, but it is in Spanish, mostly about the Spanish period, and now available only on CD-ROM as part of a larger collection. An alternative is Weber (1992). Also useful are Dunbar Rowland's *Mississippi Provincial Archives* volumes (Rowland 1911; Rowland, Sanders, and Galloway 1927–84), which cover the French and English presence not only within the bounds of modern Mississippi but more broadly in La Louisiane and West Florida. Volumes 1 (Conrad 1995), 2 (Din 1996), and 10 (Brasseaux 1996) of the University of Southwestern Louisiana's Center for Louisiana Studies' *Louisiana Purchase Bicentennial Series* are collections of important articles and some book chapters. The first two volumes include sections on ethnic groups, religion, economics, administration, and events surrounding the beginnings and endings of each period. These essays do not form a complete history of their respective periods, but they are a good beginning. Volume 10 has two sections that elaborate on immigration, especially of Africans and Acadians.

A word is warranted about the several nineteenth-century histories that are still reprinted. They are so uneven and biased by the French Creole vision of events (especially for the Spanish period) as to be unreliable. Too, they go into great detail about a few episodes while under-analyzing larger developments.

Not unlike Spanish Florida in the 1560s, La Louisiane was viewed by its founding family (the Le Moynes of Canada) and its associates as almost private property, a view that lasted until the 1740s. The first thirty years of the colony are best captured in the work of Marcel Giraud (1953–87) and Charles E. O'Neill (S.J.) (1966). Giraud's five volumes, of which three have been translated and published (Giraud 1974, 1991, 1993), provide the most detailed narrative of the first thirty years of La Louisiane that we are likely to get for some time. The focus is on the economic, administrative, and Indian policies and events and the personalities that shaped the colony. The wealth of information is at times staggering, in part because the author has a tendency (evident in volumes 2–4) to provide précis of the documents rather than use them in the service of a thesis. O'Neill's work examines the struggle between the Capuchin and Jesuit orders for control of the new mission field of the lower Mississippi Valley and the larger issues of church and state relations within the tiny colony, to 1732. O'Neill incidentally considers many other aspects of Louisiana's history besides the issues of who would control missions and parish chapels.

The hold of the "Bienvillists" on the colony's economy and government only began to lessen when Iberville's younger brother, Jean Baptiste Le Moyne, Sieur de Bienville, the longtime commandant of the garrison and then governor, was finally removed from office (1739). The Marquis de Vauderil, later to be the governor of Canada who surrendered it to the British in 1760, replaced him.

Unlike Spanish Florida, La Louisiane rather quickly left its garrison phase behind and developed an economy based on slave labor and a staple export crop, indigo. The architects of this transformation were the Company of the Indies (1717–31) and then royal policy. John G. Clark (1970) provides the best account of these developments and the most detailed general history of the 1731–68 period available. Contrary to what the title suggests, the work considers all parts of La Louisiane but focuses on the *Isle de Orleans*, the colony's economic center. See also Usner (1992) and Hall (1992), below.

The balance of the French period and the first decade of the Spanish period, except for the final years and transition to Spanish rule, are hardly covered either by monographs or articles (except for Clark, 1970). The rebellion of 1768 has claimed the most scholarly attention but little new has been added to the narrative. We still do not have an in-depth study of discussions about La Louisiane in Madrid during the five years before the Rebellion.

Spain's war to gain control of all of La Louisiane (1779–83) was reexamined during the bicentennial of those events in a number of short volumes and lesser studies. Wright (1975) has largely replaced Caughey (1934) as an account of Bernardo de Gálvez's campaigns against British West Florida. Light T. Cummins (1991) offers a different perspective on Spain's policy toward both its British adversary and the United States (with which it was *not* allied). Cummins shows that Spain developed as efficient an information-gathering network centered on Havana and New Orleans as the communications technologies of the time allowed and kept particular watch on Americans' ambitions to gain the old Southwest (the Mississippi and the Gulf Coast in particular), using agents accredited to the Continental Congress.

The subsequent story of the Spanish–US struggle to control the Mississippi Valley is best told by Arthur P. Whitaker (1927, 1934). Both works need revision with more attention to the Spanish side of the struggle and to how certain Americans, and Spaniards, used the various Spanish intrigues to further their own purposes. Too, we need to know more about Spanish policy, which often seems to have run along different lines created by officials in Madrid, New Orleans, and Philadelphia.

The most important recent scholarship on La Louisiane's colonial period has focused on various ethnic groups. Daniel Usner's *Indians, Settlers, and Slaves in a Frontier Exchange Economy* (1992) is in two parts. The first is a succinct history of the development of settlements and how Indian groups responded to the changing trade opportunities that colonial developments presented. Emphasis falls on events to 1730 and again in the 1763–83 period, although there are particularly good accounts of the Indian wars of 1729–47. The second part is a topical examination of aspects of the colonial exchange economy that involved Indian interactions with the other members of the colonial population and their economies. He finds that early in the colonial era there was a high degree of mutual interdependence, and even mutual respect, often expressed in the activities of households of individuals from all three groups (Indians, Europeans, and Africans). This gave way to more rigid hierarchies of power and race wherever commercial agriculture took hold or its influence was felt. The work ends with 1783.

Gwendelin Midlow Hall (1992) and a CD-ROM of supporting databases (Hall 2000) also looks at the sweep of the colonial period in terms of the development of one segment of the population. Her work, like recent studies of the Acadian (Brasseaux 1987) and Isleño (Canary Islander) (Din 1988) immigrations, is strongest for the Spanish period (1765–1803) when the records are extensive. Her argument is that the French West Indies Company imported its slaves from the Senegambian region of West Africa (1719–30), thereby producing a preference that was reinforced when wholesale slave imports resumed during the period (1763–79) when the British had access to the Mississippi under the terms of the Treaty of Paris (1763). This preference was reinforced again under Spanish rule. The result was an Afro-American culture in South Louisiana that is uniquely influenced by the Senegambian origins of the majority of its ancestors. The book has been criticized for lumping many different West African peoples, and somewhat different cultures, under the general Senegambian label and for reliance on data from Pointe Coupee parish, made famous by the alleged slave conspiracy of 1795. Whatever the merits of that criticism, this book together with Hanger (1997) has brought the black experience in the colony to the fore. Gilbert C. Din (1999) offers a different understanding of Spanish slave practices than Hall's, which he finds mistaken in many particulars.

Kimblery S. Hanger's *Bounded Lives, Bounded Places* (1997) is the latest addition to this socioethnic history. This is a rich-in-example study of how free persons of color attained their freedom and, increasingly, bought relatives into freedom, engaged in various occupations, and gradually forged a group identity and social hierarchy by marriage, god-parentage, service in the militia, and participation in religious and public rituals and social events such as dances. The emergence of this group identity and hierarchy, like the growth of the *libre* group itself, accelerated in the last years of the Spanish period as prosperity provided the foundations for freedom, wealth, and status-producing activities and as whites increasingly discriminated against them because of their race. However, the sense of identity was, like so much else in the lives of these people, ambiguous, reflective of their middle position between slaves and whites. Subthemes of the work are that *libres* were ambitious, hardworking persons who took as much advantage of the changing circumstances of the late colonial era as the larger society and the law would allow and that women were numerically and otherwise key members of the community who here receive major attention. There is no comparable study of any other social group, even though the ecclesiastical and notarial records from which Hanger constructed much of her study are readily accessible in New Orleans and rich in detail.

Summation

In sum, the works of Hall (1992), Usner (1992), Hanger (1997), and Landers (1999) have broken the hold of the traditional administrative and military narratives on the later colonial history of La Louisiane and La Florida and have challenged many of the generalizations about slaves and free persons of color that historians of the United States developed from their own studies. Hanger and Landers also situate their subjects within the context of the Spanish empire and its race and gender norms.

These books are important examples of the newer social history that flourished in the 1980s and 1990s and of the richness of perspective that research guided by transnational historical knowledge can produce.

But as this review has suggested, there are many aspects of the histories of these colonies – including their old-fashioned administrative and military histories – that are as yet poorly understood. The same may be said of aspects of their economic histories. The challenge is to examine such traditional topics with a full awareness of the rich social history that they influence and to avoid privileging the national and narrative approaches to such an extent that that rich context is lost. A second challenge is to more fully and carefully draw the connections between the exploration and settlement of La Florida and La Louisiane and the history of the United States into which they were annexed in the early nineteenth century. Progress has been made, but much more can be done to understand the interrelationships of events on both sides of the "line" that the nationalist perspective has drawn. Persons on the frontiers, and even in Philadelphia and New Orleans in the late eighteenth century, were less impressed by that "line" than we have become. And finally, more needs to be done to recover the Gulf–Caribbean connections that crossed the political frontiers of the eighteenth century and made individual lives rich and challenging to our more parochial perspectives.

BIBLIOGRAPHY

Avellaneda Navas, José Ignacio and Chappell, Bruce S. 1990: *Los Sobrevivientes de la Florida: The Survivors of the De Soto Expedition*. Gainesville: P. K. Yonge Library of Florida History.

Brasseaux, Carl A. 1987: *The Founding of New Acadia: The Beginnings of Acadian Life in Louisiana, 1765–1803*. Baton Rouge: Louisiana State University Press.

Brasseaux, Carl A. 1996: *A Refuge for All Ages: Immigration in Louisiana History.* Lafayette, LA: Center for Louisiana Studies, University of Southwestern Louisiana.

Bushnell, Amy Turner 1981: *The King's Coffer: Proprietors of the Spanish Florida Treasury, 1565–1702*. Gainesville: University Presses of Florida.

Bushnell, Amy Turner 1994: *Situado and Sabana: Spain's Support System for the Presidio and Mission Provinces of Florida*. New York: American Museum of Natural History.

Caughey, John Walton 1934: *Bernardo de Gálvez in Louisiana, 1776–1783*. Berkeley: University of California Press.

Clark, John G. 1970: *New Orleans, 1718–1812: An Economic History.* Baton Rouge: Louisiana State University Press.

Coker, William S. 1999: Pensacola, 1686–1821. In Judith A. Bense (ed.), *Archaeology of Colonial Pensacola*. Gainesville: University Press of Florida, 5–60.

Coker, William S. and Watson, Thomas D. 1986: *Indian Traders of the Southeastern Spanish Borderlands: Panton, Leslie & Company and John Forbes & Company, 1783–1847*. Gainesville: University Presses of Florida; University of West Florida Press.

Conrad, Glenn R. (ed.) 1995: *The French Experience in Louisiana*. Lafayette, LA: Center for Louisiana Studies, University of Southwestern Louisiana.

Corbett, Theodore G. 1976: Population Structure in Hispanic St. Augustine, 1629–1763. *Florida Historical Quarterly*, 54, 263–84.

Cumming, William P. and De Vorsey, Louis, Jr. 1998: *The Southeast in Early Maps*, 3rd edn. Chapel Hill: University of North Carolina Press.

Cummins, Light Townsend 1991: *Spanish Observers and the American Revolution, 1775–1783*. Baton Rouge: Louisiana State University Press.

Din, Gilbert C. 1988: *The Canary Islanders of Louisiana.* Baton Rouge: Louisiana State University Press.

Din, Gilbert C. (ed.) 1996: *The Spanish Presence in Louisiana, 1763–1803.* Lafayette, LA: Center for Louisiana Studies, University of Southwestern Louisiana.

Din, Gilbert C. 1999: *Spaniards, Planters, and Slaves: The Spanish Regulation of Slavery in Louisiana, 1763–1803.* College Station: Texas A & M University Press.

Dunkle, John R. 1958: Population Change as an Element in the Historical Geography of St. Augustine. *Florida Historical Quarterly,* 37, 3–32.

Fabel, Robin F. A. 1989: British Florida, 1763–1784. In Paul S. George (ed.), *A Guide to the History of Florida.* Westport, CT: Greenwood Press, 37–48.

Folmer, Henry 1953: *Franco-Spanish Rivalry in North America, 1524–1763.* Glendale, CA: A. H. Clark.

Galloway, Patricia 1995: *Choctaw Genesis, 1500–1700.* Lincoln: University of Nebraska Press.

Galloway, Patricia (ed.) 1997: *The Hernando De Soto Expedition: History, Historiography, and "Discovery" in the Southeast.* Lincoln: University of Nebraska Press.

Giraud, Marcel 1953–87: *Histoire de la Louisiane française,* 5 vols. Paris: Presses Universitaires de France.

Giraud, Marcel 1974: *A History of French Louisiana*: Vol. 1: *The Reign of Louis XIV, 1698–1715.* Trans. Joseph C. Lambert. Baton Rouge: Louisiana State University Press.

Giraud, Marcel 1991: *A History of French Louisiana*: Vol. 5: *The Company of the Indies, 1723–1731.* Trans. Brian Pearce. Baton Rouge: Louisiana State University Press.

Giraud, Marcel 1993: *A History of French Louisiana*: Vol. 2: *Years of Transition, 1715–1717.* Trans. Brian Pearce. Baton Rouge: Louisiana State University Press.

Hall, Gwendolyn Midlo 1992: *Africans in Colonial Louisiana: The Development of Afro-Creole Culture in the Eighteenth Century.* Baton Rouge: Louisiana State University Press.

Hall, Gwendolyn Midlo 2000: *Databases for the Study of Afro-Louisiana History and Genealogy, 1699–1860.* Baton Rouge: Louisiana State University Press (CD-ROM).

Hanger, Kimberly S. 1997: *Bounded Lives, Bounded Places: Free Black Society in Colonial New Orleans, 1769–1803.* Durham, NC: Duke University Press.

Hoffman, Paul E. 1990: *A New Andalucia and a Way to the Orient: The American Southeast During the Sixteenth Century.* Baton Rouge: Louisiana State University Press.

Hoffman, Paul E. 1992: *Luisiana.* Madrid: Editorial MAPFRE. In *Colecciones MAPFRE 1492* (CD-ROM). Madrid: Fundación MAPFRE América.

Hoffman, Paul E. 2000: Hernando De Soto, A Review Essay. *Louisiana History,* 41.

Hoffman, Paul E. n.d. *A History of Florida's Frontiers.* Bloomington: Indiana University Press. Forthcoming.

Hudson, Charles 1997: *Knights of Spain, Warriors of the Sun: Hernando de Soto and the South's Ancient Chiefdoms.* Athens: University of Georgia Press.

Hudson, Charles and Tesser, Carmen Chaves (eds.) 1994: *The Forgotten Centuries: Indians and Europeans in the American South, 1521–1704.* Athens: University of Georgia Press.

Johnson, Cecil 1943: *British West Florida, 1763–1783.* New Haven, CT: Yale University Press.

Landers, Jane 1999: *Black Society in Spanish Florida.* Urbana: University of Illinois Press.

La Roncière, Charles Germain Marie Bourel de 1899–1932: *Histoire de la marine française,* 6 vols. Paris: Plan-Nourrit et Cie.

Lowery, Woodbury 1901–5: *Spanish Settlements Within the Present Limits of the United States,* 2 vols. New York: G. P. Putnam's Sons.

Lyon, Eugene 1976: *The Enterprise of Florida: Pedro Menéndez de Avilés and the Spanish Conquest of 1565–1568.* Gainesville: University Presses of Florida.

Lyon, Eugene 1984: *Santa Elena: A Brief History of the Colony, 1566–1587.* Columbia: Institute of Archaeology and Anthropology, University of South Carolina.

Mowat, Charles Loch 1943: *East Florida as a British Province, 1763–1784*. Berkeley: University of California Press.

O'Neill, Charles Edwards 1966: *Church and State in French Colonial Louisiana: Policy and Politics to 1732*. New Haven, CT: Yale University Press.

Parkman, Francis 1879: *La Salle and the Discovery of the Great West*. Boston: Little, Brown.

Parkman, Francis 1885: *Pioneers of France in the New World*. Boston: Little, Brown.

Quinn, David B. 1974: *England and the Discovery of America, 1481–1620, from the Bristol Voyages of the Fifteenth Century to the Pilgrim Settlement at Plymouth: The Exploration, Exploitation, and Trial-and-Error Colonization of North America by the English*. New York: Knopf.

Quinn, David B., Hillier, Susan, and Quinn, Alison M. (eds.) 1978: *New American World: A Documentary History of North America to 1612*, 5 vols. New York: Arno Press.

Rowland, Dunbar (ed.) 1911: *Mississippi Provincial Archives: English Dominion*. Jackson: Mississippi Department of Archives and History; Nashville, TN: Press of Brandon Printing.

Rowland, Dunbar, Sanders, A. G., and Galloway, Patricia Kay (eds. and trans.) 1927–84: *Mississippi Provincial Archives: French Dominion*, 5 vols. Jackson: Mississippi Department of Archives and History (vols. 1–3) and Baton Rouge: Louisiana State University Press (vols. 4 and 5).

TePaske, John Jay 1964: *The Governorship of Spanish Florida, 1700–1763*. Durham, NC: Duke University Press.

Tornero Tinajero, Pablo 1979: *Relaciones de dependencia entre Florida y Estados Unidos (1783–1820)*. Madrid: Ministerio de Asuntos Exteriores.

Usner, Daniel 1992: *Indians, Settlers, and Slaves in a Frontier Exchange Economy: The Lower Mississippi Valley before 1783*. Chapel Hill: University of North Carolina Press.

Weber, David 1992: *The Spanish Frontier in North America*. New Haven, CT: Yale University Press.

Weddle, Robert S. 1985: *Spanish Sea: The Gulf of Mexico in North American Discovery, 1500–1685*. College Station: Texas A & M University Press.

Weddle, Robert S. 1991: *The French Thorn: Rival Explorers in the Spanish Sea, 1682–1762*. College Station: Texas A & M University Press.

Weddle, Robert S. 1995: *Changing Tides: Twilight and Dawn in the Spanish Sea, 1763–1803*. College Station: Texas A & M University Press.

Whitaker, Arthur Preston 1927: *The Spanish–American Frontier, 1783–1795: The Westward Movement and the Spanish Retreat in the Mississippi Valley*. New York: Houghton Mifflin.

Whitaker, Arthur Preston 1934: *The Mississippi Question, 1795–1803: A Study in Trade, Politics, and Diplomacy*. New York: Appleton-Century.

Wood, Peter H. 1989: La Salle: Discovery of a Lost Explorer. *American Historical Review*, 89, 294–323.

Worth, John E. 1994: Late Spanish Military Expeditions in the Interior Southeast, 1597–1628. In Charles Hudson and Carmen Chaves Tesser (eds.), *The Forgotten Centuries: Indians and Europeans in the American South, 1521–1704*. Athens: University of Georgia Press, 104–22.

Worth, John E. 1998: *The Timucuan Chiefdoms of Spanish Florida*, 2 vols. Gainesville: University Press of Florida.

Wright, J. Leitch 1971: *Anglo-Spanish Rivalry in North America*. Athens: University of Georgia Press.

Wright, J. Leitch 1975: *Florida in the American Revolution*. Gainesville: University Presses of Florida.

Wroth, Lawrence C. 1970: *The Voyages of Giovanni da Verrazzano, 1524–1528*. New Haven, CT: Yale University Press.

CHAPTER THREE

The English Colonial South to 1750

Cynthia A. Kierner

"To write of the South when there was no South is a task not without difficulties," observed Wesley Frank Craven, author of the first volume in the landmark *History of the South* series from Louisiana State University Press (Craven 1949: xiii). The white inhabitants of colonial Maryland, Virginia, North Carolina, South Carolina, and Georgia considered themselves European and, for the most part, English; if they identified with America at all, they saw themselves as belonging to a particular county or province. Reflecting that cultural reality as well as particularity of their sources, historians have rarely studied the southern colonies as a cohesive region. Craven's authoritative *The Southern Colonies in the Seventeenth Century, 1607–1689* (1949) is a notable exception that remains useful, especially as an overview of early political and institutional development.

Readers seeking an introduction to the history of a single colony should consult the appropriate volume in *A History of the American Colonies*, a thirteen-volume series published between 1973 and 1986. The best of these books, such as *Colonial South Carolina: A History* (1983), by Robert M. Weir, and *Colonial Virginia: A History* (1986), by Warren M. Billings, John E. Selby, and Thad W. Tate, synthesize recent scholarship within a chronological narrative of the history of a particular colony. Other volumes are less current in their scholarship but are nonetheless valuable as introductions to the often arcane politics of specific provinces.

The recent emphasis on the social and cultural history of British colonial America has resulted in a movement away from colony-wide studies toward those that focus on specific issues or communities. Britain's five southernmost mainland colonies constituted not a cohesive "South" but rather three distinct subregions during the colonial era. The societies that emerged in each of these subregions were shaped profoundly by the primary economic activities of their white inhabitants: tobacco planting in the Chesapeake colonies of Virginia and Maryland; rice production in the Carolina and Georgia lowcountry; mixed agriculture in the interior or backcountry, an area settled mainly by non-English immigrants after 1750 and thus beyond the scope of this essay. In the tobacco- and rice-producing areas, chaotic and unstable early settlements gradually evolved into relatively orderly and cohesive societies characterized by gentry rule, commercial agriculture, and widespread use of enslaved African labor.

The first-settled Chesapeake dominates the historiography of the southern colonies. The 1970s saw a renaissance in the history of the early Chesapeake, which originated partly in response to a growing body of work on colonial New England that cast the pious, homogeneous, communal Puritan villages as archetypical early

American communities. Since then, scholars have gone a long way toward reconstructing the distinctive demography, social structure, economy, and labor systems of the Chesapeake colonies, especially in the seventeenth century. The literature is richer for Maryland than for Virginia because of the greater availability of records for the smaller colony.

The relative influence of English culture and New World environment on emerging colonial societies is the central issue in the historiography of the early Chesapeake. Scholars debate the extent to which white colonists replicated or repudiated their English cultural baggage, generally viewing the most significant social and cultural changes as resulting from the tobacco economy. Most agree that major political and social transformations occurred in both colonies some time around 1680, but they attribute those developments to a variety of often interrelated factors ranging from fluctuations in tobacco prices to the increasing importation of enslaved African labor.

Edmund S. Morgan's *American Slavery, American Freedom: The Ordeal of Colonial Virginia* (1975) was the first book-length study to address many of what would become the enduring issues in the social history of the colonial Chesapeake. Morgan sought to explain the seemingly symbiotic relationship between white liberty and black slavery, which he deemed the "central paradox of American history" (Morgan 1975: 4). He did so by seeking the origins of slavery, racism, and libertarian ideologies in the Virginia colony. In the process, he presented an important interpretation of Virginia's history that revolves around the issues of demography, class, race relations, and the social consequences of the colony's agricultural economy.

Morgan's portrait of early Virginia is a study in social pathology. The colony, he contends, was populated by selfish and often lazy men who jettisoned the most admirable features of English culture in pursuit of financial gain. Adopting tobacco as their staple crop, white colonists settled on widely dispersed plantations, which impeded the formation of community ties, while the planters' initial preference for white male indentured servants to work the tobacco fields ensured the perpetuation of skewed sex ratios and retarded the development of normal family life. Disease and brutal working conditions made mortality rates alarmingly high in the colony at least until the 1640s, when Morgan believes servants began to outlive their contracts and enjoy some economic opportunity. By the 1660s, however, wealthy planters, most of whom were government officials, had engrossed much of the remaining land, leaving little for lesser men, who resented both the corrupt grandees and the Indians whose presence in the interior prevented them from seeking opportunity farther west.

For Morgan, early Virginia was a volatile society in which poor men, largely bereft of family, community, or church attachments, rebelled against a rapacious and irresponsible elite. Though led by Nathaniel Bacon and other gentry opponents of Governor William Berkeley, Bacon's Rebellion of 1676 attracted a mass following. Like most historians, Morgan sees the rebellion as a watershed, but unlike them he sees racism as the key to its significance. Just as Bacon deployed racism to unify his supporters against the Indians, Morgan argues, later Virginia leaders would use racism to separate white and black workers, both legally and socially. Institutionalized racism, coupled with the subsequent spread of African slavery in the colony, fostered white solidarity across class lines. Virginia's elite assumed the benevolent demeanor of the English gentry in the eighteenth century and white society became more stable and deferential, but Morgan attributes the attainment of social harmony in Virginia primarily to the unifying effects of racism and the shared privileges of white supremacy.

Without disputing the increasing centrality of slavery in the economy of the region, other scholars challenge important aspects of Morgan's portrait of the early Chesapeake. Two collections of essays by leading Chesapeake historians – each of which begins with a superb historiographical overview – reexamine in piecemeal fashion some of the issues Morgan addressed. Published in 1979, *The Chesapeake in the Seventeenth Century*, edited by Thad W. Tate and David L. Ammerman, explores demography, economic development, and the gradual emergence of stable elites in Maryland and Virginia, tentatively revising certain aspects of Morgan's interpretation. The essays in *Colonial Chesapeake Society* (Carr, Morgan, and Russo 1988) go farther, contending that the white residents of the region created viable communities that reflected English values and culture and that many middling and lesser whites prospered as a result of settling in the tobacco colonies.

Contributors to the earlier volume view the seventeenth century as decades of demographic disaster followed by a "pervasive transformation of society, economy, and government" that began both in Maryland and in Virginia some time after 1660 (Tate and Ammerman 1979: 37). Adaptation to difficult circumstances is the major theme of many of these essays: Jamestown's residents, who suffered more from disease than from starvation born of laziness, unwittingly abandoned their microbe-infested peninsula for a healthier environment; colonists countered the devastating effects of high mortality rates by devising strategies to care for their children and preserve family property in the likely event of early parental death. Other essays advance a relatively benign view of white servitude, contending that freed servants enjoyed significant economic and social opportunities, at least in Maryland, through the 1670s, and suggesting that white immigration to the region declined as opportunity diminished, leading planters to fill the void by importing African slaves. Two other essays suggest that the attainment of political stability in both Virginia and Maryland resulted from the rise of entrenched, native-born leaders who identified less with England than with their colony, its elected assembly, and that body's white constituents.

The second collection of essays adheres to the same general interpretation but extends into the eighteenth century, which the editors characterize as a "golden age" of prosperity and social harmony followed by a period of growing instability and popular discontent (Carr, Morgan, and Russo 1988: 10). The authors stress the religious, ethnic, and economic diversity of the Chesapeake colonies and highlight the inhabitants' efforts to adapt their culture to environmental challenges. One essay examines the social experiences of Catholics and Quakers in early Maryland, asserting that neighbors and coreligionists became surrogate kin in demographically unstable immigrant communities. Another uses local records to reconstruct neighborhood networks that fostered social contacts – subject to variations by class, race, and gender – despite dispersed settlement. Studies of economic development in two Maryland counties reveal a growing diversification of agricultural products and a rise in craft activity. Diversification, in turn, encouraged the development of an economy of local exchange, which became a basis for social contact as well as a source of economic stability.

Much of the best recent scholarship on the early history of the Chesapeake suggests that the interplay of English culture and American conditions resulted in the formation of distinctive Anglo-American societies. James P. P. Horn's *Adapting to a New World* (1994) draws on research in Maryland, Virginia, and two English counties to assess the extent to which English values, attitudes, and institutions shaped settlers' adaptation to New World conditions in the seventeenth century. Stressing the imperial perspective, he argues that Maryland and Virginia in the seventeenth century were "far-flung [English] provinces overseas, intimately linked to the parent society by strong and enduring political, cultural, social, and economic ties" (Horn 1994: vii–viii).

Horn examines the varied English origins of those who emigrated and shows how previously unconnected groups of individuals came together to create New World communities. Comparing colonial material culture, religious practice and belief, and family and community life to their English counterparts, he concludes that, despite some significant differences resulting mainly from persistently high mortality rates and unbalanced sex ratios, the Chesapeake was more like England than unlike it during the seventeenth century. Indeed, unlike many scholars who see an "anglicization" of provincial life on the eve of the Revolution, Horn argues that the Chesapeake colonies most resembled England during the seventeenth century, before changes in the labor market would result in a major influx of African slaves whose presence would dramatically alter both the culture and the social structure of the tobacco colonies.

Still, for English immigrants accustomed to producing subsistence crops on small family plots, the choice of labor-intensive tobacco as a staple crop necessitated agricultural innovations. *Robert Cole's World: Agriculture and Society in Early Maryland* (Carr, Menard, and Walsh 1991) scrutinizes the process of farm formation and development through the unusually well-documented estate of Robert Cole, an English-born middling farmer who settled on a 300–acre farm on St Clement's Manor in 1652. Carr, Menard, and Walsh argue that Cole and his seventeenth-century neighbors blended English-style subsistence farming with tobacco cultivation to create a new agriculture that afforded upward mobility to careful husbandmen, who, over the course of an agricultural year, maximized the efficiency of their workers and reinvested much of their earnings in additional land and labor. The authors describe in impressive detail how ordinary people cleared land, tended crops and livestock, made economic decisions, and pursued their livelihoods along Maryland's tobacco coast. In Cole's time, they contend, Maryland was a land of opportunity for farmers and servants alike, and it remained a "good small-man's country" at least until the 1680s (ibid: 15).

In *Tobacco Colony: Life in Early Maryland, 1650–1720* (1983), Gloria L. Main's analysis of probate records indicates that the economic priorities of Marylanders remained unchanged into the eighteenth century. Unlike some other scholars, Main finds little evidence of community life among Marylanders – particularly before the 1680s, when horses became more common in the colony – and she argues that social inequality in Maryland, which had existed since the colony's founding, became more pronounced as a result of late seventeenth-century fluctuations in the tobacco market and the eventual establishment of patrilineal family dynasties. Nevertheless, Main believes that Marylanders who survived despite continually high mortality rates could expect to prosper, and surveys of the conditions of white indentured servants and of the estates left by former servants lead her to conclude that the indenture system worked well for both masters and their bondpeople. Her detailed analysis of housing in the colony, which complements later studies by historical archeologists, reveals relatively little class differentiation and a clear preference for investment over consumption among planters of all social ranks. Main suggests that erstwhile servants and incipient elites lived simply not because they were poor – wealth levels were comparable to those in Old and New England – but as a result of high mortality rates and the scarcity of labor. Houses were insubstantial both because people expected to die before long and because they believed that additional investment in land or workers offered better returns on their own or their servants' labor.

While the impact of tobacco culture on settlement patterns, social structure, and material culture is the chief concern of historians of the early colonial period, many who study the eighteenth century emphasize the larger transatlantic context of the tobacco economy. English demand for colonial tobacco gave rise to a flourishing export economy, but the tobacco trade became increasingly complex and unstable during the eighteenth century. Jacob M. Price examines the growing importance of Scotland and France as export and reexport markets for Chesapeake tobacco and the pervasive role of credit in the tobacco trade in *France and the Chesapeake* (1973) and *Capital and Credit in British Overseas Trade* (1980), respectively. Broader in scope, *The Atlantic Economy and Colonial Maryland's Eastern Shore* (1980) by Paul G. E. Clemens, is the best introduction to both the local and Atlantic dimensions of the Chesapeake economy.

Clemens traces the expansion and eventual decline of tobacco culture in a particular area, showing how the demands of the Atlantic market dictated the economic choices of successive generations of planters on Maryland's eastern shore, where he discerns three phases of the economic development: the adoption of tobacco as a cash crop; the spread of slave labor to maximize production of this agricultural staple; and the subsequent diversification of agricultural output in response to changing trends in the Atlantic market. Planters turned especially to grain both to shield themselves from declining tobacco prices and to take advantage of the growing demand for foodstuffs in New England, the West Indies, and southern Europe. Slave-owning planters grew both tobacco and wheat to maximize the productivity of their labor force by employing them year-round, while farmers in marginal tobacco-producing areas who owned no slaves could grow only wheat, which was less labor intensive than tobacco.

Clemens shows that, like tobacco in the seventeenth century, the growing primacy of wheat shaped subsequent social developments on Maryland's eastern shore. While the area's white inhabitants had marketed their tobacco through English and later Scottish merchants, the grain trade led them to establish commercial contacts with the nearby port of Philadelphia. More important still, while the tobacco economy had discouraged the creation of towns in the Chesapeake, wheat production spurred the development of towns as milling centers and led to the rise of Baltimore as a thriving commercial community.

Did environment or culture, then, predominate in the shaping of the Anglo-American societies of the colonial Chesapeake? Two important syntheses suggest that historians still disagree on this issue and thus on the fundamental nature of Chesapeake colonial society. *A Place in Time* (1984), by Darrett B. Rutman and Anita H. Rutman, focuses on the process of community-building in Middlesex County, Virginia, underscoring the cultural conservatism of white colonists of all social ranks.

By contrast, in *Tobacco and Slaves* (1986), Allan Kulikoff focuses on the issue of class formation and finds the origins of a distinctly southern white culture – and a black one, too – in the social relations largely determined by the Chesapeake's tobacco economy.

A Place in Time (Rutman and Rutman 1984) was the first book-length study of a Chesapeake community to appear in print, and it remains the only study of a Chesapeake county that begins with the earliest years of settlement and continues well into the eighteenth century. The book is a model microhistory, its authors having culled local records to compile data on some 12,000 individuals to trace the formation of social bonds in Middlesex County between 1650 and 1750. The Rutmans argue that the county's white inhabitants consistently organized themselves into neighborhoods and parishes and self-consciously strove to replicate the institutions – family, courts, and church – that provided the bases of English social stability.

In stark opposition to Morgan's interpretation of Bacon's Rebellion and its significance, the Rutmans maintain that support for the rebellion in Middlesex came from across the social spectrum, that racism contributed to neither its causes nor its consequences, and that the episode left no lingering hostilities among the county's inhabitants. Nevertheless, the Rutmans concede that Middlesex changed in the decades after 1680, owing primarily to the spread of slavery. White society became more prosperous but also more stratified; wealthy planters and merchants profited, but small farmers found themselves unable to compete with slave-owners and many eventually left the county. *A Place in Time* ends at mid-century, perhaps looking ahead to an era of instability. Before then, however, the Rutmans portray the white residents of Middlesex as relatively orderly and harmonious, united by formal and informal community networks, and deferring to the authority of a largely benevolent elite.

By contrast, Kulikoff (1986) interprets social relations among white colonists less as expressions of neighborliness or communal identity than as manifestations of class formation and consolidation in an increasingly stratified society. Kulikoff divides the history of the early Chesapeake into three periods, the first two of which basically coincide with the Rutmans' chronology. In the first period, which lasted from the settlement of Jamestown in 1607 until roughly 1680, Kulikoff agrees that the Chesapeake was a society of small planters who suffered horrific demographic conditions but enjoyed modest prospects for economic advancement. During the second period, between 1680 and 1750, Kulikoff credits demographic circumstances – chiefly declining mortality among whites, the curtailment of white immigration to the region, and the resulting large-scale conversion to enslaved African labor – with increasing social inequality and the emergence of an entrenched and self-conscious gentry elite. In the third period, from 1750 through 1800, Kulikoff, unlike most historians, sees more stability than change. During this period, he contends, the tobacco economy collapsed, but the westward migration of small planters, if anything, enhanced the authority of the region's gentry elites.

Drawing on his own research in the records of Prince George's County, Maryland, and on the work of other scholars in other Chesapeake localities, Kulikoff discerns the origins of an allegedly hegemonic antebellum planter class in the colonial era. After 1680, he argues, the biggest planters attained economic dominance by amassing land and slaves; wealth and patronage, in turn, became the basis of an alliance with an emerging yeomanry that ensured the gentry's continued monopoly of political power. Kulikoff suggests that this alliance with the yeomanry enabled the gentry to ignore or antagonize the rest of white society. Far from benign expressions of community identity, family and neighborhood networks that cemented linkages among white colonists also purposefully bolstered the authority of male elites. Decreasing mortality rates encouraged the development of a domestic patriarchy that rendered white women subservient, while expanding kinship networks facilitated the advantageous marriages that strengthened local oligarchies. Like their antebellum counterparts, Kulikoff contends, colonial grandees derived their authority from interlocking class, racial, and gender hierarchies. Domestic patriarchy complemented slavery and class privilege in the creation of stable societies dominated by increasingly self-conscious elites.

Those elites used their wealth to create a class-specific culture that distinguished them from their neighbors and thereby reinforced their putative social authority. The earliest studies of elite culture, such as Louis B. Wright's *First Gentlemen of Virginia* (1940), focused on the intellectual attainments of colonial gentlemen – the books they read, the schools they attended – while social historians later quantified the sudden explosion of genteel material goods among affluent colonists, especially by the second quarter of the eighteenth century. More recently, cultural historians have begun using interdisciplinary methodologies and approaches to discern meaning in the material and ritual worlds of early Americans, often dwelling on the more fully documented perspectives of colonial elites.

The essential work on the cultural history of the southern colonies is Rhys Isaac's *The Transformation of Virginia, 1740–1790* (1982), which traces the evolution of the Old Dominion from a traditional organic society in which the gentry were politically, economically, and culturally dominant, into one that was more competitive, individualistic, and privatistic due to the influence of religious dissent and antiauthoritarian political culture in the prerevolutionary era. The book's first section describes the physical, social, and cultural landscapes of Virginia at mid-century, presenting an array of richly textured tableaux embracing Virginians of all social ranks. Isaac shows that elite and plebeian culture in the colonial period were separate but overlapping. Literacy, classical learning, mansion houses, and access to cosmopolitan culture distinguished the gentry from lesser folk, while the rituals of the courthouse, the muster field, and the Church of England bound people together across class lines into a cohesive organic community. Like a cultural anthropologist, Isaac interprets court-day rituals, electioneering feasts, and the Anglican liturgy as social theater, suggesting that in their heyday these performances simultaneously displayed and reinforced both communal unity and the existing social hierarchy.

Isaac contends that evangelical religious dissent challenged both the Anglican establishment and the social values it promoted and presupposed. The Separate Baptists in particular jeopardized not only the gentry's control of religious institutions – and thus their cultural primacy – but also the organic unity of colonial society. Isaac characterizes the Baptists as a counterculture, the pious vanguard of what would become a sweeping social revolution. Appealing primarily to poor whites and blacks, the success of the early Baptists exposed the insecurity of gentry rule and the limits of popular deference.

Following Isaac's lead, architectural historian Dell Upton examines the material culture of Virginia Anglicanism as an expression of the cultural values of the gentry, who dominated the parish vestries that oversaw the building and furnishing of churches in the eighteenth century. In *Holy Things and Profane* (1986), Upton argues that Virginia parish churches, which combined English and local building styles, sought to reinforce the power of the state and its established church, as well as that of the gentlemen, who, as county justices and vestrymen, embodied the authority of both church and state in their local communities. Upton uses three metaphors – power, hospitality, and dancing – to explore the social meaning of these churches. Power relationships between God and man, king and subjects, gentry and commonfolk, determined the use of space and ornamentation within the churches. Mirroring the secular hospitality of the gentry, the house of God offered shelter and the sustenance of the eucharist to all, displaying the power and benevolence of the host and the grateful dependence of his guests. Finally, like dancing, church attendance was a social ritual that employed a "processional use of space" to demarcate social hierarchies (Upton 1986: 206).

Upton notes that the architectural styles of churches, courts, and plantation houses – where most hospitality and dancing occurred – were remarkably similar in colonial Virginia because gentlemen constructed all three to manifest their social values. Like Isaac, Upton perceives a growing distance between gentry and commonfolk after mid-century, but he attributes that change to the gentry's desire to curtail the social obligations that bound them to their neighbors without relinquishing their social authority. Conversely, evangelical dissenters wished to preserve the bonds of community while eradicating social hierarchy. Upton contends that the gentry's new and more privatistic social ethic found architectural expression in the separate galleries and hanging pews – often accessible only by private stairs and entrances – with which they increasingly equipped their parish churches in the late colonial era.

Studying material culture and social rituals yields insights into the collective world view of early southerners, few of whom produced diaries or other written records that afford glimpses into their interior lives. Only two colonial southerners – William Byrd II and Landon Carter, both white male Virginians – left diaries that went beyond mere tallies of visits, illnesses, and agricultural productivity. Although their authors were hardly typical colonists, the published versions of the Byrd and Carter diaries, along with the journal of the tutor Philip Fithian, are essential sources for the social and cultural history of eighteenth-century Virginia.

Byrd's diary and other writings are the raw materials for Kenneth A. Lockridge's *The Diary, and Life, of William Byrd II of Virginia, 1674–1744* (1987), the most probing biography of a colonial southerner. Lockridge uses literary and psychoanalytical theory to crack the "code" of Byrd's prolific writings and in so doing explore his construction of Anglo-American identity (Lockridge 1987: 1). Byrd's English education and his reading of English etiquette books made him see himself as an English gentleman, but his failures in both imperial politics and London society led him first to despair but eventually to create for himself a more viable social identity. Lockridge argues that Byrd's writing helped him to reinvent himself as a Virginia gentleman, adapting the English gentry ideal to vastly different colonial circumstances. Analyzing Byrd's relations with women, slaves, and poor whites – and his portrayal of those relationships in his diary – Lockridge suggests that gender, race, and class shaped Byrd's understanding of himself. As a white male slave-owning planter, Byrd expected to have mastery over a wide range of dependents. Like many other gentlemen who left far fewer written records, Byrd expressed his mastery by building a mansion, pursuing high political office, and dominating his imagined inferiors, whom he envisioned as the unruly beneficiaries of his wisdom and largesse.

Byrd's misogyny, which pervades his diary, suggests the significance of gender as an analytical category in the study of southern colonial history, but women's history and gender studies had little impact on the field until the 1990s. Although women appeared as wives, widows, and executrixes in demographic studies, and the letters of one exceptional woman – Eliza Lucas Pinckney of South Carolina – have been published, Julia Cherry Spruill's classic *Women's Life and Work in the Southern Colonies* (1938) remains the starting place for understanding the myriad experiences of white southern women during the colonial era. Spruill's impressive but largely descriptive work is now supplemented by Kathleen M. Brown's *Good Wives, Nasty Wenches, and Anxious Patriarchs* (1996), which examines the lives of white and black women in colonial Virginia and explores the intersection of gender and race in the creation of stable social hierarchies.

Brown sees the early seventeenth century as a time of instability, when Virginia's high mortality rates and skewed sex ratios impeded the replication of English gender ideals in the colony. While the scarcity of women may have enhanced their influence, the demand for labor meant that many would work in the tobacco fields with men. By the 1660s, however, as more white men and growing numbers of African slaves of both sexes were available to do field work, white women's work could be circum-scribed more readily within the household. Brown emphasizes the importance of a 1668 law that exempted only the labor of white women from taxation as a key turning point in the erection of racial barriers and the domestication of white women's work. Like Morgan, however, she also sees Bacon's Rebellion as pivotal in the construction of a stable society dominated by a powerful and self-conscious elite.

In some ways a gendered retelling of the story Morgan related in *American Slavery, American Freedom*, Brown's interpretation of Bacon's Rebellion and its aftermath stresses both the systematic degradation of black men and the eradication of white women from meaningful participation in public life. Describing the rebellion as the culmination of a crisis "in which two distinct cultures of masculinity came into open conflict," she argues that Virginia's leaders emerged from it determined to reassert control over their dangerously fractured society (Brown 1996: 140). Part of their agenda, as Morgan suggested, was to separate poor whites from blacks via institution-alized racism, but Brown contends that another dimension of the rebellion's con-sequences involved marginalizing white women's influence, despite or because of their participation in it on both sides. Racism and patriarchal privilege, together, she argues, mitigated class tensions among white male Virginians, who united under the banner of a redefined masculinity the chief characteristic of which was supremacy over both blacks and women. In the decades following 1676, white men celebrated their shared masculinity in an array of new social rituals – militia musters, electioneering, and the like – while they consigned women to domestic dependence. Brown con-cludes that white women's status declined precipitously, even if an increasingly genteel style of living afforded elite women some new social opportunities.

As this review of recent work on the colonial Chesapeake shows, scholars have done impressive research on the social history of the region, especially for the seventeenth century. Scholarship on the region's cultural history – for instance, on the issues of

religious belief, work and leisure, political ideology, conceptualizing imperial connection, and even gender – has been less thorough and often focused primarily on the
eighteenth century. Nevertheless, in both quality and scope, the overall output of
Chesapeake scholars now rivals that of their New England counterparts and far
surpasses that of historians of the other southern colonies.

The recent historiography of the rice-producing colonies of South Carolina and
Georgia – variously known as the lowcountry or Lower South – differs from that of
the Chesapeake in three significant respects. First, there is much less of it, owing both
to a thinness of local records and to the relative lateness of English settlement of the
lowcountry region. Second, and more important, because African slavery dominated
these colonies from the first – as a divisive issue in Georgia under the government of
the antislavery trustees and as a pervasive reality in South Carolina – race and slavery
are central to the most significant studies of their history during the colonial era.
Finally, unlike much of the Chesapeake scholarship that stresses the persistence of
English ways in the tobacco colonies, the recent historiography of South Carolina
and Georgia emphasizes the exotic physical and social environments of these rice-
producing plantation colonies.

Peter H. Wood's *Black Majority* (1974) is the path-breaking study of the lowcountry during the colonial era. Although Wood is primarily interested in the evolution of slavery and African culture in coastal South Carolina, he also has important
things to say about that region's early white inhabitants. Wood emphasizes the
influence of Barbados planters and their slaves on the economic and social development of the colony. Emigrating to coastal Carolina after 1670, the Barbadians used
their cultural baggage and personal contacts to make early South Carolina, in Wood's
words, "the colony of a colony" (ibid: 13).

The prospect of free land and economic opportunity in general brought the
Barbadians to coastal Carolina, while their experience with slavery on a sugar-
producing island led them to employ slave labor from the start in their new settlements. White settlers expected to produce commodities, such as foodstuffs, to export
to the sugar islands, thus capitalizing on their personal contacts there. African labor
and expertise was critical in the production of those commodities – first livestock and
later rice – that emerged as South Carolina's staples. Although whites, blacks, and
Indians often worked together in the colony's earliest decades, Wood explains that
the introduction of rice cultivation accelerated the spread of slavery. Unknown to
whites and Native Americans, rice was a labor-intensive crop with which West Africans
were familiar, and it found ready markets both in the sugar islands and in Europe.
From its first permanent cultivation in 1695, rice shaped the subsequent social
development of the South Carolina colony.

Alone among the mainland colonies, South Carolina had a black majority. Wood
estimates that by 1708, owing to increased slave importations, blacks outnumbered
whites, and that by the 1720s whites accounted for only about one-third of the
province's total population. White population continued to shrink proportionately as
slaves arrived in growing numbers through 1740. White settlement in the rice-
producing lowcountry became even more dispersed than in the tobacco colonies, as
South Carolina planters employed more slaves on larger landholdings, especially after
changes in the British Navigation Acts permitted the exportation of rice to southern
Europe beginning in 1730. Dispersed settlement and minority status generated white

anxiety that, in turn, gave rise to stricter laws controlling black behavior in the 1730s. A major slave revolt, the Stono Rebellion of 1739, led to more white repression and attempts to discourage slave imports, though South Carolina retained its black majority through the end of the colonial era.

In *The Shadow of a Dream* (1989), Peter A. Coclanis builds on Wood's work, expanding his analysis both topically – to include considerations of physical environment and planter ideologies – and chronologically, through the nineteenth century and on into the twentieth. Coclanis notes that elite South Carolinians were the wealthiest residents of British North America during the colonial period but that their fortunes declined both absolutely and relative to those of many other Americans after 1800. He argues that the founding of Carolina and its early prosperity is best understood in the context of the economic expansion of western Europe and the growth of an Atlantic market economy. The economic demise of the lowcountry, in turn, occurred as a result of the region's loss of its export market to competing Asian and American rice producers and its inability to adapt to changing market realities.

Coclanis's first three chapters deal with the colonial period. The first examines the settlement of coastal Carolina from the standpoint of British imperial and mercantilist interests and emphasizes the market orientation of the area's earliest white settlers. The second describes the lowcountry's physical environment, which was good for crops but appallingly bad for people, resulting in high mortality rates throughout the colonial era. The third emphasizes the influence of the market – aided and abetted by the political ideals of classical liberalism and the spread of African slavery – on the evolution of the lowcountry economy as the settlements moved from relatively small-scale production of livestock, grain, and lumber into a large-scale staple-producing plantation economy. Coclanis stresses the interdependence of town and country, a distinguishing feature of the rice economy. Charleston, America's fourth largest city on the eve of revolution and the only significant urban center in the southern colonies, thrived as the rice trade's entrepôt but decayed with the decline in European demand for the Carolina staple.

In a complementary study, Joyce E. Chaplin examines the construction of modernity by whites in the colonies of South Carolina, Georgia, and British East Florida between 1730 and 1815. In *An Anxious Pursuit* (1993), Chaplin argues that these plantation colonies were neither economically nor culturally backward, despite their near-exclusive commitment to slavery and plantation agriculture. At a time when commerce, not industry, was deemed the highest form of economic activity, she maintains, these plantation colonies were valued partners in a thriving transatlantic mercantile economy. Planters, moreover, self-consciously embraced modernity as part of their identity as members of a progressive Atlantic community. The ambivalence with which they did so, however, is a major theme of Chaplin's study.

Chaplin pays particular attention to both agricultural methods and planter ideology, explaining how the white and black inhabitants of the Lower South manipulated their natural environment to produce rice and later cotton and how elite whites thought about the interrelated issues of commerce, technology, and labor. Lower South planters turned to the philosophy of the Scottish Enlightenment, which lauded the benefits of commerce, to articulate and to justify their commitment to economic progress, yet they worried about both the perceived social and cultural costs of over-commercialization and the impediments to full modernization in their slave society.

Planters argued that slavery, in fact, could be a source of social cohesion as well as a source of profit, enabling whites to enjoy commercial prosperity without creating an oppressed working class on the English model. Planters enlisted the efforts of natural and social scientists to counter the widely held assumption that an exotic, semitropical environment such as theirs would necessarily engender laziness and wastefulness – vices that many critics believed slavery also promoted. Embracing an ethic of self-improvement, they asserted the importance of the seasoning process whereby resident colonists might cultivate resistance to disease and climate. Accepting the bourgeois work ethic but adapting it to their purposes, Lower South planters argued that by supervising enslaved people they were themselves working hard and thereby effecting the improvement of their society.

Planters also cultivated rice on North Carolina's southern coast, but tobacco was the main crop in that colony's northeastern counties. Although scholars often consider North Carolina part of the Lower South, its colonial economy combined the staples of its northern and southern neighbors, while many of the province's small and middling farmers engaged in subsistence agriculture, owing in part to the absence of a deep-water port, which inhibited commercial development during the colonial era. Far more diverse and less economically developed than South Carolina or the Chesapeake, colonial North Carolina is difficult to categorize and, perhaps for that reason, its historiography is more descriptive than analytical. Aside from a few important articles devoted to the Regulator uprisings of the 1760s, historians have produced no studies of North Carolina's social or cultural history that are comparable to the best recent work on the other southern colonies.

The best book-length discussion of North Carolina's colonial history is A. Roger Ekirch's *"Poor Carolina:" Society and Politics in Colonial North Carolina, 1729–1776* (1981). Ekirch begins his book with a useful overview of settlement patterns, economic activities, and social structure in North Carolina between roughly 1730 and 1770, but he then goes on to focus primarily on provincial politics under royal government. Ekirch describes the colony as politically unstable and immature, particularly compared to Virginia and South Carolina. He attributes North Carolina's political deficiencies mainly to the absence of a viable ruling elite. Unlike the Virginia and South Carolina gentry who made their fortunes and then set about cultivating the deference of lesser folk, North Carolina's leaders were less prosperous and therefore more inclined to augment their wealth via official corruption. Individual self-interest manifested itself in factional alliances and in the relations between leading North Carolinians and a succession of royal governors. Opportunistic, corrupt, and lacking both the wealth and cultural trappings of a bona fide gentry class, North Carolina's elites captured neither the respect nor the deference of their fellow colonists, who from time to time rebelled against them. Seen in this light, the Regulator movement was the most significant in a series of protests against corrupt and irresponsible government.

Ekirch probably overstates both North Carolina's instability and the harmony of its neighbors, but the comparisons he makes underline the persistent social and economic variations within the region that gradually would coalesce into an increasingly self-conscious South in the postrevolutionary era. What then, if anything, did the southern colonies have in common with each other before 1750? And to what extent were they distinct from Britain's other American colonies?

In *Pursuits of Happiness* (1988), Jack P. Greene contends that all of the southern colonies, along with most of Britain's other American provinces, were established in pursuit of economic opportunity and demonstrated similar patterns of subsequent social development. Greene posits two models of English colonization: the declension model, which best fits the New England experience, and the developmental model, which characterized not only the Chesapeake but also – with some variations – all the other British American colonies. While the declension model describes a linear process of social decay – from communalism to individualism, from unity to fragmentation – the developmental model describes societies evolving from fragility and unsettledness toward greater complexity and order.

Drawing on recent research, Greene describes the Chesapeake as the prototype for the developmental model. Motivated by a desire for economic advancement, English immigrants established precarious and sometimes unruly settlements that gradually became more "settled, cohesive, and coherent" with the attainment of demographic stability and the emergence of family networks, political and religious institutions, more diversified economies, ethnic pluralism, and stable ruling elites (Greene 1988: 81). This process of social elaboration and replication of English social norms and institutions, which began in the Chesapeake around 1660, eventually occurred elsewhere in British colonial America. Greene finds this pattern repeated throughout the southern colonies, particularly in the lowcountry after 1745; he regards northern North Carolina and the nascent backcountry settlements as a later developing subsidiary of the "greater Chesapeake" (ibid: 141). The Chesapeake colonies and the Lower South differed chiefly, Greene asserts, in their mortality rates, the size of their black population, and the wealth of their elites – all of which were greater in the rice-producing regions – and in the timing of their social development.

The fact that all of the colonies south of New England – and even parts of New England itself – fit the pattern of Greene's developmental model should deter historians from finding southern distinctiveness and regional consciousness in the colonial era. Yet in the southern colonies, the English pursuit of opportunity led to the adoption of a particular type of commercial agriculture that was both labor intensive and profitable. Before the Revolution, white colonists throughout British America shared the economic and cultural values that supported slavery, an institution that was not yet peculiar to its southernmost section. At the same time, African slavery was already a defining feature of the society and culture of colonial southerners in a way that it never would be for their northern neighbors. In that distinction lay the origins of the self-conscious sectionalism that would emerge in the postrevolutionary era.

BIBLIOGRAPHY

Bailyn, Bernard 1959: Politics and Social Structure in Virginia. In James Morton Smith (ed.), *Seventeenth-Century America: Essays in Colonial History*, Chapel Hill: University of North Carolina Press, 90–115.

Barbour, Philip L. 1964: *The Three Worlds of Captain John Smith*. Boston: Houghton Mifflin.

Billings, Warren M. (ed.) 1975: *The Old Dominion in the Seventeenth Century: A Documentary History of Virginia, 1606–1689*. Chapel Hill: University of North Carolina Press.

Billings, Warren M., Selby, John E., and Tate, Thad W. 1986: *Colonial Virginia: A History.* White Plains, NY: KTO Press.

Breen, T. H. 1977: Horses and Gentlemen: The Cultural Significance of Gambling among the Gentry of Virginia. *William and Mary Quarterly,* 3rd ser., 34, 239–57.

Breen, T. H. 1985: *Tobacco Culture: The Mentality of the Great Tidewater Planters on the Eve of Revolution.* Princeton, NJ: Princeton University Press.

Bridenbaugh, Carl 1952: *Myths and Realities: Societies of the Colonial South.* Baton Rouge: Louisiana State University Press.

Brown, Kathleen M. 1996: *Good Wives, Nasty Wenches, and Anxious Patriarchs: Gender, Race, and Power in Colonial Virginia.* Chapel Hill: University of North Carolina Press.

Carr, Lois Green and Jordan, David William 1974: *Maryland's Revolution of Government, 1689–1692.* Ithaca, NY: Cornell University Press.

Carr, Lois Green and Walsh, Lorena S. 1977: The Planter's Wife: The Experience of White Women in Seventeenth-Century Maryland. *William and Mary Quarterly,* 34, 542–71.

Carr, Lois Green, Menard, Russell R., and Walsh, Lorena S. 1991: *Robert Cole's World: Agriculture and Society in Early Maryland.* Chapel Hill: University of North Carolina Press.

Carr, Lois Green, Morgan, Philip D., and Russo, Jean B. (eds.) 1988: *Colonial Chesapeake Society.* Chapel Hill: University of North Carolina Press.

Carson, Jane 1965: *Colonial Virginians at Play.* Charlottesville: University Press of Virginia.

Chaplin, Joyce E. 1993: *An Anxious Pursuit: Agricultural Innovation and Modernity in the Lower South, 1730–1815.* Chapel Hill: University of North Carolina Press.

Clemens, Paul G. E. 1980: *The Atlantic Economy and Colonial Maryland's Eastern Shore: From Tobacco to Grain.* Ithaca, NY: Cornell University Press.

Coclanis, Peter A. 1989: *The Shadow of a Dream: Economic Life and Death in the South Carolina Low Country, 1670–1920.* New York: Oxford University Press.

Coleman, Kenneth 1976: *Colonial Georgia: A History.* New York: Scribner.

Craven, Wesley Frank 1949: *The Southern Colonies in the Seventeenth Century, 1607–1689.* Baton Rouge: Louisiana State University Press.

Davis, Richard Beale (ed.) 1963: *William Fitzhugh and his Chesapeake World, 1676–1701: The Fitzhugh Letters and Other Documents.* Chapel Hill: University of North Carolina Press.

Davis, Richard Beale 1978: *Intellectual Life in the Colonial South, 1585–1763,* 3 vols. Knoxville: University of Tennessee Press.

Deetz, James 1993: *Flowerdew Hundred: The Archaeology of a Virginia Plantation, 1619–1864.* Charlottesville: University Press of Virginia.

Earle, Carville V. 1975: *The Evolution of a Tidewater Settlement System: All Hallow's Parish, Maryland, 1650–1783.* Chicago: University of Chicago Press.

Ekirch, A. Roger 1981: *"Poor Carolina:" Politics and Society in Colonial North Carolina, 1729–1776.* Chapel Hill: University of North Carolina Press.

Farish, Hunter D. (ed.) 1943: *Journal and Letters of Philip Vickers Fithian, 1773–1774: A Plantation Tutor of the Old Dominion.* Williamsburg, VA: Colonial Williamsburg.

Greene, Jack P. 1963: *The Quest for Power: The Lower Houses of Assembly in the Southern Royal Colonies, 1689–1776.* Chapel Hill: University of North Carolina Press.

Greene, Jack P. (ed.) 1965: *The Diary of Colonel Landon Carter of Sabine Hall, 1752–1778,* 2 vols. Charlottesville: University Press of Virginia.

Greene, Jack P. 1988: *Pursuits of Happiness: The Social Development of Early Modern British Colonies and the Formation of American Culture.* Chapel Hill: University of North Carolina Press.

Gundersen, Joan Rezner 1986: The Double Bonds of Race and Sex: Black and White Women in a Colonial Virginia Parish. *Journal of Southern History,* 52, 351–72.

Horn, James 1994: *Adapting to a New World: English Society in the Seventeenth-Century Chesapeake.* Chapel Hill: University of North Carolina Press.

Isaac, Rhys 1982: *The Transformation of Virginia, 1740–1790*. Chapel Hill: University of North Carolina Press.

Kierner, Cynthia A. 1998: *Beyond the Household: Women's Place in the Early South, 1700–1835*. Ithaca, NY: Cornell University Press.

Kukla, Jon 1985: Order and Chaos in Early America: Political and Social Stability in Pre-Restoration Virginia. *American Historical Review*, 90, 275–98.

Kulikoff, Allan 1986: *Tobacco and Slaves: The Development of Southern Cultures in the Chesapeake, 1680–1800*. Chapel Hill: University of North Carolina Press.

Land, Aubrey C. 1981: *Colonial Maryland: A History*. Millwood, NY: KTO Press.

Lefler, Hugh T. and Powell, William S. 1973: *Colonial North Carolina: A History*. New York: Scribner.

Lockridge, Kenneth A. 1987: *The Diary, and Life, of William Byrd II of Virginia, 1674–1744*. Chapel Hill: University of North Carolina Press.

McCusker, John J. and Menard, Russell R. 1985: *The Economy of British America, 1607–1789*. Chapel Hill: University of North Carolina Press.

Main, Gloria L. 1983: *Tobacco Colony: Life in Early Maryland, 1650–1720*. Princeton, NJ: Princeton University Press.

Merrell, James H. 1989: *The Indians' New World: Catawbas and Their Neighbors from European Contact through the Era of Removal*. Chapel Hill: University of North Carolina Press.

Merrens, Harry Roy 1964: *Colonial North Carolina in the Eighteenth Century: A Study in Historical Geography*. Chapel Hill: University of North Carolina Press.

Morgan, Edmund S. 1952: *Virginians at Home: Family Life in the Eighteenth Century*. Williamsburg, VA: Colonial Williamsburg.

Morgan, Edmund S. 1975: *American Slavery, American Freedom: The Ordeal of Colonial Virginia*. New York: Norton.

Noël Hume, Ivor 1982: *Martin's Hundred*. New York: Knopf.

Norton, Mary Beth 1996: *Founding Mothers and Fathers: Gendered Power and the Formation of American Society*. New York: Knopf.

Perry, James R. 1990: *The Formation of a Society on Virginia's Eastern Shore, 1615–1655*. Chapel Hill: University of North Carolina Press.

Pinckney, Elise (ed.) 1972: *The Letter Book of Eliza Lucas Pinckney, 1739–1762*. Chapel Hill: University of North Carolina Press.

Price, Jacob M. 1973: *France and the Chesapeake: A History of the French Tobacco Monopoly, 1674–1791, and of Its Relationship to the British and American Tobacco Trades*, 2 vols. Ann Arbor: University of Michigan Press.

Price, Jacob M. 1980: *Capital and Credit in British Overseas Trade: The View from the Chesapeake, 1700–1776*. Cambridge, MA: Harvard University Press.

Quinn, David B. 1985: *Set Fair for Roanoke: Voyages and Colonies, 1584–1606*. Chapel Hill: University of North Carolina Press.

Roeber, A. G. 1981: *Faithful Magistrates and Republican Lawyers: Creators of Virginia Legal Culture, 1680–1810*. Chapel Hill: University of North Carolina Press.

Roeber, A. G. 1993: *Palatines, Liberty, and Property: German Lutherans in Colonial British America*. Baltimore: Johns Hopkins University Press.

Rogers, George C., Jr. 1969: *Charleston in the Age of the Pinckneys*. Norman: University of Oklahoma Press.

Russo, Jean Burrell 1989: *Free Workers in a Plantation Economy: Talbot County, Maryland, 1690–1759*. New York: Garland.

Rutman, Darrett B. and Rutman, Anita H. 1984: *A Place in Time: Middlesex County, Virginia, 1650–1750*. New York: Norton.

Shea, William L. 1983: *The Virginia Militia in the Seventeenth Century*. Baton Rouge: Louisiana State University Press.

Silver, Timothy 1990: *A New Face on the Countryside: Indians, Colonists, and Slaves in South Atlantic Forests, 1500–1800*. New York: Cambridge University Press.

Sirmans, M. Eugene 1966: *Colonial South Carolina: A Political History*. Chapel Hill: University of North Carolina Press.

Smith, Daniel Blake 1980: *Inside the Great House: Planter Family Life in Eighteenth-Century Chesapeake Society*. Ithaca, NY: Cornell University Press.

Sobel, Mechal 1987: *The World They Made Together: Black and White Values in Eighteenth-Century Virginia*. Princeton, NJ: Princeton University Press.

Spindel, Donna J. 1989: *Crime and Society in North Carolina, 1663–1776*. Baton Rouge: Louisiana State University Press.

Spruill, Julia Cherry 1938: *Women's Life and Work in the Southern Colonies*. Chapel Hill: University of North Carolina Press.

Stewart, Mart A. 1996: *"What Nature Suffers to Groe": Life, Labor, and Landscape on the Georgia Coast, 1680–1920*. Athens: University of Georgia Press.

Sydnor, Charles S. 1952: *Gentlemen Freeholders: Political Practices in Washington's Virginia*. Chapel Hill: University of North Carolina Press.

Tate, Thad W. and Ammerman, David L. (eds.) 1979: *The Chesapeake in the Seventeenth Century: Essays on Anglo-American Society*. Chapel Hill: University of North Carolina Press.

Tinling, Marion (ed.) 1977: *The Correspondence of the Three William Byrds of Westover, Virginia, 1684–1776*, 2 vols. Charlottesville: University Press of Virginia.

Upton, Dell 1982: Vernacular Domestic Architecture in Eighteenth-Century Virginia. *Winterthur Portfolio*, 17, 95–119.

Upton, Dell 1986: *Holy Things and Profane: Anglican Parish Churches in Colonial Virginia*. Cambridge, MA: MIT Press.

Ver Steeg, Clarence L. 1975: *Origins of a Southern Mosaic: Studies of Early Carolina and Georgia*. Athens: University of Georgia Press.

Weir, Robert M. 1983: *Colonial South Carolina: A History*. Millwood, NY: KTO Press.

Whittenburg, James P. 1977: Planters, Merchants, and Lawyers: Social Change and the Origins of the North Carolina Regulation. *William and Mary Quarterly*, 3rd ser., 34, 215–38.

Williams, D. Alan 1969: The Small Farmer in Eighteenth-Century Virginia Politics. *Agricultural History*, 43, 91–105.

Wood, Peter H. 1974: *Black Majority: Negroes in Colonial South Carolina from 1670 through the Stono Rebellion*. New York: Norton.

Woodfin, Maude A. and Tinling, Marion (eds.) 1942: *Another Secret Diary of William Byrd of Westover, 1739–1741, with Letters and Literary Exercises, 1696–1726*. Richmond, VA: Dietz Press.

Wright, Louis B. 1940: *The First Gentlemen of Virginia: Intellectual Qualities of the Early Colonial Ruling Class*. San Marino, CA: Huntington Library.

Wright, Louis B. and Tinling, Marion (eds.) 1941: *The Secret Diary of William Byrd of Westover, 1709–1712*. Richmond, VA: Dietz Press.

Yentsch, Anne Elizabeth 1994: *A Chesapeake Family and Their Slaves: A Study in Historical Archaeology*. New York: Cambridge University Press.

CHAPTER FOUR

The Origins of Slavery, 1619–1808

BETTY WOOD

U P until the late 1960s and early 1970s one could have been almost forgiven for believing that the slave societies of the American South sprang into existence in a fully fledged form in 1830 or thereabouts. As far as scholarly interest was concerned, the first century and a half of slavery and race relations in the southern mainland was to all intents and purposes a void. True, there were some notable exceptions to this general rule of neglect. Back in the 1930s, for example, Lewis C. Gray had devoted a goodly portion of the first volume of his *History of Agriculture in the Southern United States to 1860* (1933) to the origins and development of the colonial South's slave-based plantation economies. In the 1940s John Hope Franklin included a discussion of the colonial southern experience in his pioneering work *From Slavery to Freedom*, a book now in its seventh edition. A few years after the publication of Franklin's study, Oscar and Mary Handlin (1950) and Carl Degler (1959) became embroiled in an intense argument as to whether or not the first twenty or so West Africans to arrive in Virginia in 1619 had been immediately enslaved by the English colonists, who were said by John Rolfe to have purchased them from the Dutch.

Although the issues raised by the Handlins and Degler were of fundamental significance, it was to be another ten years before they received any more serious scholarly attention. The main impetus for the flowering of a scholarship that sought to explore more fully the questions they had raised, and to build upon the earlier findings of Gray and Franklin, came from what, initially at any rate, were two entirely separate fields of scholarly inquiry.

During the mid-1950s, thanks mainly to the burgeoning civil rights movement, historians, including a growing number of African-American scholars, launched a campaign that over the next two decades effectively demolished the "Phillips thesis," an interpretation of southern slavery and race relations that had dominated the historiography since the early years of the twentieth century. Yet scholars such as Kenneth Stampp (1956), John Blassingame (1972), and Eugene Genovese (1975), who were in the forefront of the battle to eradicate the baleful influence of U. B. Phillips (1918), seldom strayed very far from the temporal parameters that he had been so instrumental in creating. For these historians, as it had been for Phillips, it was the apogee of the South's slave system, rather than its colonial origins, which was of primary concern. However, despite its continuing fascination with the antebellum South, this vibrant new scholarship would have enormous implications for the subsequent study of earlier periods of southern history. It posed questions, suggested methodologies, and identified previously untapped sources that would be of interest and utility to those scholars who, simultaneously, were beginning to challenge the traditional, rosy image of life in early America advanced by the so-called "Consensus" historians of the 1940s and 1950s.

The social and political turmoil of the 1960s was the backdrop against which a generation of younger scholars, including Gary Nash (1970, 1974) and James Henretta (1973) initiated what amounted to a veritable revolution in the historiography of the colonial period. No longer were the mainland colonies depicted as worlds of boundless opportunity, as worlds in which equality reigned in practice as well as in theory. Colonial historians were now discovering worlds that were characterized by a whole number of inequalities: inequalities of social rank (of class), of gender and, not least of all, of race and ethnicity. Increasingly, those people whom previous scholarship had either ignored or marginalized – under-class colonists, Native Americans, women, and African-Americans – were moved from the outer wings to the very center of the historical stage. True, much of this new scholarship at first focused on New England and the Middle Atlantic colonies, but increasingly more attention came to be paid to the southern mainland.

The first significant fruits of the growing interaction between these two strands of historical inquiry began to appear in the late 1960s and early 1970s. Between 1966 and 1975 four major works were published that effectively initiated the task of surveying the previously unmapped and, as time would show, the immensely complicated terrain of slavery and race relations in the early South. Albeit in rather different ways, the authors of these seminal studies, David Brion Davis, Winthrop D. Jordan, Edmund S. Morgan, and Peter H. Wood, defined research agendas that scholars continue to follow.

As its title suggests, the central focus of Davis's magisterial study, *The Problem of Slavery in Western Culture*, first published in 1966 and reissued with a new introduction in 1999, was a sweeping attempt to explain the origins and subsequent evolution of various slave systems in the Western world, from antiquity to the European colonization of the Americas. His concern in this work, the first of a trilogy that would appear over the course of the next twenty years and carry the story into the nineteenth century, was not so much with the economic dimensions of slavery, or with the lives of the enslaved, as it was with the theoretical arguments devised by European philosophers, politicians, and churchmen in order to justify different versions of this form of bondage. In this interpretation, the slave systems that took root everywhere in British America were part of an intellectual and ideological continuum. There was a very real sense in which southern slavery originated not at some point in the seventeenth century on the shores of Chesapeake Bay but in a long-lived and complex maze of Old World conceptualizations of "slavery" and "freedom."

An essentially similar interpretative framework was employed in a monumental study that appeared in 1968, Jordan's *White Over Black*. Unlike Davis, however, Jordan confined his attention to the British American colonies. His was the first book-length study to consider the question of why it was that, everywhere they settled in the Americas, the English not only opted for systems of bondage that were unknown in the Common Law of England but also for systems that at different times in different places became reserved for people of West African ancestry. Jordan's explanation hinged on cultural, rather than on economic, determinants, and it emphasized the complexity of the evolving relationship between slavery and race, between slavery and racism.

Quite rightly, Jordan argued that the English did not begin their colonizing ventures in the Americas with a view to enslaving anyone if, by that, was meant a bondage that defined the bond servant as a chattel, as a piece of property, rather than as a person who could lay valid claim to at least minimal rights. Rather more controversially, he insisted that sixteenth-century English people had a clear understanding of what enslavement entailed and also subscribed to a cluster of beliefs about West Africa and its inhabitants. Some of those beliefs dated back to medieval times, some of them were derived from classical and biblical sources, and all of them were reinforced during the sixteenth century as the English began to encounter West Africans for the first time. Even before they set out for Virginia, Jordan concluded, the English were already predisposed to see West Africans as potential candidates for enslavement. It took the best part of a century for this potential to be fully realized in Virginia. The process of legal enslavement that culminated in the colony's slave code of 1705 was incremental and reflected the outcome of what Jordan described as a series of "unthinking decisions" rather than the implementation of a clearly worked out blueprint of racial exploitation and oppression.

More recent scholarship, including the work of Breen and Innes (1980), has generally endorsed Jordan's view of an early seventeenth-century Virginia in which race relations were somewhat ambiguous: a Virginia in which skin color alone did not define the individual's legal status. That there were growing signs of racial discrimination in the Virginia of the 1620s and 1630s is indisputable. Yet there is also evidence of European and West African workers collaborating with one another in ways that suggest they attached more significance to their shared lowly social rank than they did to their ethnic differences. There were those in early Virginia who considered themselves to be the cultural superiors of the small number of West Africans in their midst, but this sense of English superiority did not immediately prompt the legal enslavement and dehumanization of the colony's fledgling black population. Over the next half-century, however, racial attitudes hardened. Racism and slavery evolved hand in hand, the one informing the other, to the point where skin color determined, and was equated with, the individual's legal status.

Jordan's richly nuanced analysis of the immensely intricate ways in which English concepts of "white" and "black," of "freedom" and "slavery," were formed and in their turn informed the definition of colonial identities elevated the debate about the origins of slavery in British America to an entirely new level of sophistication. In fact, such was the subtlety and complexity of his thesis that in 1974 a shorter and simplified version of it, intended for students and general readers, was published under the title of *The White Man's Burden: Historical Origins of Racism in the United States*.

Over the years, Jordan has been criticized not so much for what he did say as for what he did not say. In his schemata, the various economic and demographic factors operating on both sides of the Atlantic during the seventeenth century, colonial and metropolitan imperatives that might well have played a significant part in the enslavement of West Africans, rated barely a mention. Jordan also had little time for the argument advanced in 1944 by the Trinidadian historian Eric Williams, in his classic work *Capitalism and Slavery*, that plantation agriculture, and the slave labor and translantic slave trade upon which it depended, was instrumental in the forging of capitalistic societies in the North Atlantic world.

In fact, by the late 1960s there was already a substantial, if controversial body of literature that emphasized the economic imperatives involved in the emergence and subsequent development of the New World's slave systems, including those of the southern mainland. Gray (1933) had highlighted some of those imperatives, and there were British and American scholars who had long been interested in the rise and fall of the British transatlantic slave trade. Some of these scholars had concerned themselves with the precise importance of that trade to the metropolitan economy; others had focused on the relative significance of the economic and moral reasons that prompted the British government to dispense with that trade in 1808. A third area of interest was trying to establish precisely how many West Africans had been shipped to the British American colonies before the closing of the slave trade.

Davis and Jordan had emphasized the intellectual, ideological, and cultural, rather than the economic, roots of early American slavery. In 1975, however, an alternative scenario was scripted by Edmund S. Morgan in his *American Slavery, American Freedom*. As far as he was concerned, one did not have to delve deeply into the world of religious, political, and racial ideologies in order to explain the enslavement of West Africans in seventeenth-century Virginia. For Morgan, both the timing and the character of the transformation of that colony's labor base, from indentured white to involuntary black servitude, was to be sought in the changing configuration of various economic and demographic factors in the seventeenth-century North Atlantic world. The "tobacco revolution" of the 1620s, he argued, generated an insatiable demand for unskilled agricultural workers in Tidewater Virginia, but profit-hungry tobacco planters did not immediately see West Africans as being the solution to their labor problems. The question for Morgan was, why not? These planters had the example of the Iberian powers in South America and the Caribbean to guide them and already had a small number of West Africans at their disposal. Moreover, such were the profits they were making from tobacco production that they could easily have afforded to import more. Why was it that the transformation of Virginia's labor base, and the concomitant legal enslavement of people of West African ancestry, began to get underway in the 1680s and 1690s rather than in the 1620s and 1630s?

For Morgan, the answer lay in the comparative profitability of indentured and involuntary workers at different points in the seventeenth century – in changing patterns of the availability, cost, and assumed productivity of Europeans and West Africans, of servants and slave. In the Morgan scheme of things seventeenth-century Virginia's tobacco producers were nothing if not economically rational beings. When it became more financially advantageous for them to invest in enslaved West African workers, as it did during the latter part of the century, when the supply of inexpensive white indentured servants shrank, then they did so without hesitation or reservation. Racial prejudice and racism, Morgan insisted, had little to do with the choices made by tobacco planters. Questions of profit and loss, and by the 1680s their ruthless determination to protect their interests in the face of heightened competition from less socially eminent whites who sought to emulate, if not to displace, them, explain the timing of the transition to a racially based system of slavery. As that transition was occurring, elite planters employed racism as a political tool in their attempt to secure and to retain the loyalty of those whites in the Tidewater who could not afford or who did not choose to become slave owners. The elite was particularly concerned that under-class whites might conclude that they had a class-based affinity with the rapidly growing number of West Africans being imported into the colony. In this part of his discussion Morgan drew closer to Jordan by emphasizing the ways in which, through the remainder of the colonial period, white Virginian concepts of "freedom" and "bondage," the identities that they were in the process of forging for themselves as political beings, became irrevocably linked to race, to skin color.

As far as the experience of seventeenth-century Virginia was concerned, though, Jordan and Morgan presented starkly different interpretations, neither of which satisfactorily explains the timing and dynamics of the introduction of a racially based system of bondage to the colony. As Betty Wood (1997) has recently suggested, while the economic and demographic factors emphasized by Morgan explain the timing of the transition from indentured white to involuntary black servitude, they do not provide a convincing explanation of why the legal status of "slave" became devised and reserved for people of West African ancestry. It is here that we must incorporate Jordan's discussion of the forging of an English racial awareness, of a sense of self that owed much to sixteenth-century perceptions of the "other." This awareness, the English "identity" that was being shaped in the sixteenth century, would eventually make possible but alone neither dictated nor predetermined the enslavement of West Africans. Moreover, the impression conveyed by Jordan that the English colonists of Virginia inched their way, somewhat uncertainly, towards the definition of a slave status for West Africans must be put in the context of the speed with which their counterparts in Barbados rushed to embrace the institution of slavery. By the mid-1630s the English had devised a slave status for those West Africans already in Barbados; by 1660 the island had an enslaved black majority.

As both Edmund Morgan (1975) and Betty Wood (1997) have argued, the alacrity with which the English in Barbados enslaved West Africans during the middle years of the seventeenth century to meet the enormous labor demands generated by the island's "sugar revolution" goes a long way towards explaining the delay in the transformation of Virginia's labor base. The fact of the matter was that during the 1620s Virginia tobacco planters had a choice of two, rather than three, labor pools to draw from: Native American and European. After the so-called "Massacre" of 1622, planters determined that what they wanted from the former was their land rather than their labor. For the Dutch shippers who dominated the transatlantic slave trade until they were displaced by the English in mid-century, there was little incentive to service Virginia's tobacco economy when much richer pickings were closer to hand in South America and the Caribbean. The English labor market would save tobacco planters. Surplus English labor was both able and willing to satisfy Virginia's demand for workers until the last quarter of the seventeenth century. We can only speculate as to what might have happened had West Africans been made available in significant numbers and low prices to Virginia's tobacco producers during the 1620s and 1630s or had the supply of willing English workers remained sufficient. However, the contemporary example set by English planters in Barbados strongly suggests that had plentiful and inexpensive Africans been available earlier, few "unthinking decisions" would have been made by their counterparts in Tidewater Virginia.

In many ways, of course, the argument about the relative importance of the ideological, cultural, and economic determinants of the seventeenth-century process of enslavement in Virginia can never be finally resolved one way or the other.

However, although it no longer dominates the historiography in the way that it did, it is an argument that continues to fascinate historians of the colonial South. Perhaps now the time is ripe for a reformulation of the argument that takes into account some of the recent research into the social and economic history of early modern England. How, for example, did changing patterns of metropolitan consumption influence the decisions that were taken by colonial planters in respect to their workforces? James Walvin (1997) has recently suggested that a growing British demand for the products of plantation agriculture was of critical importance and, possibly, was just as influential as the cyclical changes in England's labor markets in determining planter decisions regarding their workforces. It may well be that the tide of interpretation is beginning to turn back in Morgan's favor.

Following Edmund Morgan, it is generally accepted that, everywhere in the southern mainland, the planters who orchestrated the introduction of slavery into their colonies were economically rational beings. However, since Gray and Wood's (1976) detailed analysis of indentured white and involuntary black servitude in early Georgia, economic historians have shown little inclination to test the accuracy of the planters' initial assumptions about the comparative profitability of these two types of labor. Similarly, and somewhat surprisingly given the long-lived debate about the profitability of slavery in the antebellum South, relatively little attention has been paid to the profitability of plantation slavery once it had become firmly established in the southern mainland. McCusker and Menard's (1985) excellent discussion notwithstanding, there remains a pressing need for further detailed research on this issue.

There also remains considerable scope for expanding Jordan and Morgan's analyses of the evolving public laws of slavery, laws that did not vary to any great extent between the different southern colonies or from those of the anglophone Caribbean. Despite the pioneering work of Wiecek (1977) and A. Leon Higginbotham Jr. (1978), it is still not clear whether these similarities in both the civil and the criminal laws of slavery were coincidental, which seems utterly implausible, or whether they reflected a quite deliberate process of borrowing from one another on the part of planter-dominated colonial governments. Given the close, and already thoroughly researched, connections between them, this problem needs little further investigation in the case of Barbados and South Carolina, and subsequently that of South Carolina and Georgia. However, we still know comparatively little about the probable interconnections within and between the other southern colonies and the British sugar islands.

Much the same is true when it comes to determining the extent to which these same laws, but particularly the criminal laws of slavery, were shaped and changed by the actual, as well as by the anticipated, behavior of enslaved Africans. Schwarz (1988) produced a compelling and detailed account of the ways in which enslaved people were instrumental in the definition of eighteenth- and nineteenth-century Virginia's criminal laws of slavery. Unfortunately, not as much attention has been paid to this dimension of the criminal laws, and the judicial processes, of the other southern colonies, particularly during the formative years of their slave systems.

Although they produced very different interpretations of the seventeenth-century Virginia experience, there was one crucial respect in which Jordan's (1968) and Morgan's (1975) studies were virtually identical. Both of these scholars attached considerably more importance to the interests, imperatives, actions, and evolving identities of those who were doing the enslaving than they did to those who found themselves in the process of being enslaved. This imbalance, which also characterized the historiography of the antebellum South through the early 1970s, began to be remedied in 1974 with the publication of Peter H. Wood's *Black Majority*. This work also served another function: it alerted its readers to the fact that the colonial southern experience of slavery and race relations amounted to rather more than just that of Tidewater Virginia.

Black Majority was the first, and it remains the definitive, analysis of the origins and early history of lowcountry South Carolina's slave system. Although slavery had been legally sanctioned since the first settlement of Carolina in the 1660s, as in the case of Virginia it was only around the turn of the seventeenth century that West Africans began to be imported into the lowcountry in ever-increasing numbers, including many from Barbados. By the early years of the eighteenth century South Carolina already had a black majority, and would prove to be the only mainland southern colony to hold that dubious honor. This "discovery" of the lowcountry and its black majority was a significant enough contribution. Yet even more important than this in the shaping of subsequent scholarship was the entirely new question posed by Peter Wood and one which he succeeded in answering so very brilliantly: what did it mean in practice to be an enslaved person in the early South, in this case in the Carolina lowcountry?

Simultaneously, and in what proved to be a major sea change in the historiography, Blassingame (1972) and Rawick (1972) were beginning to ask precisely the same question of the antebellum South. At a stroke, Blassingame, Rawick, and Wood displaced slave owners from the center of the stage that they had for so long occupied. Peter Wood's insistence that the literally thousands of West Africans brought against their will to the lowcountry were not mute, passive objects but active players with their own imperatives was indisputably one of the most original and influential contributions ever made to our understanding of the dynamics of slavery and race relations in the early South. Overnight an entire field of scholarly endeavor had been transformed; a new one had been invented.

Like Winthrop Jordan and Edmund Morgan before him, Peter Wood was concerned with what might be described as the public world of slavery that took shape in the Carolina lowcountry between the late 1670s and the late 1730s. But whereas Jordan and Morgan had ascribed the main responsibility for the construction of that world to Europeans, Wood adopted a very different approach. Where he differed from them, and indeed from all previous historians of the early South, was in his emphasis on the various strategies devised by enslaved people as they struggled to survive and to maintain their personal and communal identities in the horrendous circumstances in which they now found themselves. Without ever downplaying the brutality of the lowcountry's slave owners, Wood emphasized black agency. His analysis, which drew to a close at what for him was the defining moment of the abortive Stono Rebellion in 1739, offered entirely new insights into the nature and dynamics of the relationship between owner and slave; it also charted the evolution, character, and significance of the private spaces, the private worlds, that enslaved people fought to carve out for themselves. Their family lives, their religious beliefs and practices, and their domestic economies, as well as their individual and organized acts of defiance, all came under the spotlight for the very first time. It is thanks mainly to *Black Majority*, as well as to the simultaneous contributions of Blassingame, Rawick, Genovese (1975), and Levine (1977) for the antebellum years, that since the mid-1970s considerably more scholarly attention has been paid to the enslaved people of the colonial South than it has been to their owners.

Peter Wood's stunning demonstration of the creative ways in which enslaved people pursued cultural lives that existed independently, or quasi-independently, of their work regimes immediately laid the foundations of a vibrant scholarship that continues to explore and to elaborate on many of the themes first set out in *Black Majority*. Among other things, it drew attention to the indisputable fact that if the racially based slave systems of the early South had been instrumental in the definition of white colonial identities, then precisely the same held true for people of West African ancestry. Back in 1959 Stanley Elkins had argued that West Africans had been traumatized to the point of infantilization – and left practically bereft of their old world culture – by their capture and sale in Africa, their journey to the Americas, and their subsequent experiences of enslavement. In some ways, Wood's *Black Majority* can be seen as part of a continuing critique of Elkins's thesis, a critique that before 1974 had been confined to historians of the antebellum South.

Wood insisted that the West Africans imported into the lowcountry had not been completely traumatized and totally demoralized by their experience of enslavement. They were both able and willing, he argued, to call upon their various pasts in order to explain and cope with present realities and plan for a future that might or might not involve their continuing enslavement.

For Wood's pathbreaking purposes it was both inadequate and erroneous to depict a homogenous West African past. Quite predictably, however, the task of identifying and unraveling the complex skeins of practices and relationships, as well as the more practical knowledge and skills, that in varying degrees survived the Middle Passage, proved immensely difficult. It was far more difficult than what proved to be the relatively simple task of enumerating the West Africans who were bought and sold in Charleston between the 1670s and the 1730s. When it came to identifying exact West African origins, shipping lists and plantation records left something to be desired. The "national" and "ethnic" labels that were attached to West African peoples by European slave traders, colonial merchants, and planters did not necessarily correspond to the actual ethnic identities and affiliations of those concerned. The problem of such labeling continues to vex historians of the transatlantic slave trade as it does those whose main interest is in the changing definition of West African lives and identities after their arrival in the plantation colonies. It is possible, and greatly to be hoped, that at least a part of the problem will be resolved as scholars such as Patrick Manning (1990) and John K. Thornton (1992) continue to probe more deeply into the West African end of the transatlantic slave trade.

Despite the evidential problems posed by European labeling, attempts to pinpoint precise West African backgrounds have been fundamental to the efforts undertaken in recent years to elaborate many of the themes and issues first addressed by Peter Wood in 1974. Daniel Littlefield (1981) delved more deeply than had Wood into the ethnicity of the Carolina lowcountry's enslaved population and a similar effort underscored Allan Kulikoff's (1986) elaboration of the original ethnic mixes that, beginning in the 1670s and 1680s, formed the bedrock upon which the cultures, rather than a single homogenous culture, of the Chesapeake evolved over the course of the next century. It might just be noted here that Kulikoff's analysis drew attention to an aspect of the formation of enslaved peoples' culture that has subsequently attracted comparatively little scholarly interest.

During the 1960s and 1970s, largely in response to the "Phillips thesis" and more immediately to the bleak African-American past depicted by Elkins, students of the antebellum South were understandably eager to emphasize black creativity, black agency, and, not least of all, black solidarity (for example, Blassingame 1972; Genovese 1975; Levine 1977). Yet as Kulikoff discovered in the case of early Virginia, there were important and sometimes violent antagonisms between enslaved people that, if their white contemporaries are to be believed, stemmed from their different West African pasts. Schwarz (1988) too, in his study of the criminal laws of Virginia, revealed an evolving private world of slavery that was by no means free of discord. Enslaved people not only verbally abused one another; sometimes they physically assaulted and even killed one another. Whether this discord was rooted in different West African pasts, in their present world of enslavement, or in a mixture of both, was not always mentioned in the contemporary records.

Since the mid-1970s there has been a scholarly fascination with the definition and redefinition of West African identities in the early South, with the processes associated with acculturation, with the forging of African-American identities. Some scholars, including Ira Berlin (1998), have convincingly demonstrated the changing demographic contexts in which this cultural transformation was rooted. Others, such as Mechal Sobel (1987) and Sylvia Frey and Betty Wood (1998), have emphasized the religious dimensions of that same process. The spatial and temporal parameters favored by scholars vary somewhat. On what might be described as the micro-level, Lorena Walsh (1997) has made a significant contribution with her detailed study of Carter's Grove plantation, an analysis that draws from the archeological record as well as the written records of that estate. Other scholars have focused their attention not on individual plantations but on particular colonies or subregions of the early South. However, there are now some highly illuminating exceptions to this general rule. In two major studies, Michael Gomez (1998) and Ira Berlin (1998) have cast their nets wider and incorporated the entire southern mainland from the seventeenth to the nineteenth century into their analyses. In the process they have elevated the discussion of West African origins and the formation of African-American identities to an entirely new level of sophistication.

Since the mid-1970s the origins and early development of slavery and race relations in each of the southern mainland colonies have received varying degrees of attention. No colony has been completely ignored, although it is worth noting that as far as the Chesapeake is concerned, Maryland has received considerably less attention than Virginia has. There remains a need for a full-length study of the beginnings of slavery in seventeenth-century Maryland, and particularly for an analysis that teases out the significance of the Calverts's Roman Catholicism as well as early Maryland's influential Jesuit presence. John Thornton (1992) and more recently Frey and Wood (1998) have drawn our attention to the prior acquaintance of some of the West Africans who were imported into the southern mainland, but especially Angolans, with a Roman Catholicism that had been presented to them by Portuguese missionaries. As Thornton (1992) and Peter Wood (1974) have argued, this common religion was an important dynamic in the organization of the Stono Rebellion and, by extension, in the shaping of other aspects of the enslaved communities that took root in the lowcountry between the late seventeenth and the mid-eighteenth century. A closer analysis of the West African backgrounds of early Maryland's enslaved population, as well as the religious preferences of their owners, might well reveal a very similar pattern.

Roman Catholicism, at least as far as their European populations were concerned, was not a significant dynamic in shaping either the origins or the initial development of slavery in North Carolina and Georgia, two colonies that have received an increasing amount of scholarly attention over the past few years. In 1984 Betty Wood examined the exceptional case of Georgia, the only British colony anywhere in the Americas in which a sustained attempt was made to prohibit the introduction of slavery. More recently, Kay and Carey (1995) have produced a comprehensive study of slavery and race relations in North Carolina during the last quarter-century of the colonial period. We are still in need of a detailed analysis of the evolution of slavery in that colony during the preceding half-century. Robert Olwell (1998) has taken the South Carolina story begun by Peter Wood (1974) up to the American Revolution, and his decision to concentrate on the post-Stono years eloquently testifies to the fact that, twenty-five years after its appearance, *Black Majority* remains the definitive study of the beginnings and early history of slavery in the Carolina lowcountry.

One of the major changes in the historiography over the past ten years or so, but one that still conceptualizes the beginnings of slavery in the context of the individual colony, has been the somewhat belated recognition by anglophone historians that there were, in fact, slave societies in those parts of the southern mainland that did not declare their independence from Britain in 1776. At the same time that her work added enormously to the ongoing debate about the precise West African origins of enslaved people, Gwendolyn Midlo Hall (1995) was influential in putting the eighteenth-century French colony of Louisiana on the map. More recently, Jane Landers (1999) has done likewise for Spanish Florida.

A few years ago another historian of eighteenth-century Louisiana, Daniel Usner (1992), provided us with a timely reminder of a point made a quarter of a century ago by Gary Nash (1974): the triangular nature of race relations in early America. Although the historiography has always tended to place Native Americans and enslaved West Africans into separate categories, Usner's study illuminates the interactions, the relationships, the sometimes permeable and sometimes more rigid, cultural boundaries that were formed in the Lower Mississippi Valley between Native Americans, enslaved people, and Europeans. It is greatly to be hoped that other scholars will follow Usner's lead and examine the nature and dynamics of similar encounters elsewhere in the early South.

The colonial case studies that have appeared in such numbers since the mid-1970s, including now invaluable analyses of the French and Spanish systems of slavery in Louisiana and Florida, are of enormous value and consequence in their own right. However, they also provide the basis for comparative analyses of the slave systems that emerged in different parts of the southern mainland during the course of the seventeenth and eighteenth centuries. Although many scholars continue to focus their attention on a particular colony, during the past ten years or so there has been an exciting, and highly illuminating, willingness on the part of others to broaden their horizons and undertake comparative studies. What promises to be a highly influential contribution is Philip Morgan's prize winning book, *Slave Counterpoint* (1998), a mammoth study of Virginia and South Carolina that teases out the fundamental differences, as well as some of the essential similarities, between these two slave societies. In his highly innovative and compelling analysis, *Many Thousands Gone*, Ira Berlin (1998) has broadened the comparative framework to incorporate not only Tidewater Virginia and the Carolina lowcountry, but also the northern colonies and Louisiana, from the seventeenth to the early nineteenth century. In each of the regions of the American mainland, Berlin argues, discreet, distinctive, and complex slave societies evolved as enslaved people and their owners continued to negotiate and to renegotiate their relationship.

Ira Berlin is one of the few scholars in recent years who has taken what might be described as the longer-term view of the early South's evolving slave societies. Moreover, his is a perspective that does not compartmentalize slavery and race relations into chronological fragments determined largely by political events and decisions. Yet one event in particular, the American Revolution, had crucial implications for the subsequent history of slavery. Few attempts have been made by scholars interested in adopting a comparative approach to examine the divisions created by the American Revolution, not so much between "North" and "South" as between the southern mainland and the anglophone Caribbean. During the colonial period, and to some extent during the years immediately after the War for American Independence, the southern colonies, but particularly the Lower South, and the sugar islands were components of an integrated world in which ideas and people, as well as goods, circulated with some regularity. Much the same was true of eighteenth-century Louisiana and the French sugar islands. The historiographical reintegration of these mainland and Caribbean worlds is long overdue.

The extent to which the American Revolution was a pivotal period in the history of slavery and race relations in the anglophone South has been closely examined in a number of recent studies. Sylvia Frey (1991) has demonstrated the ways in which wartime disruptions, as well as pragmatic British promises of freedom, raised enslaved peoples' hopes that one of the outcomes of the war might be their own liberation from bondage. The defeat of the British, and in the Lower South particularly their Patriot owners' staunch commitment to the institution of slavery both as an economic regime and as a means of seeking to impose their racial, social, and political control, prompted a reformulation of African-American concepts of freedom. As Frey (1991) and Frey and Wood (1998) have argued, evangelical Protestantism was a central dynamic of this process. During the late eighteenth and early nineteenth century, ever-increasing numbers of enslaved people, everywhere in the southern mainland, embraced the Baptist and Methodist faiths. They interpreted these faiths in ways that both helped them to cope with their continuing enslavement and to anticipate their eventual liberation from bondage. Moreover, the black and biracial churches that sprang up throughout the early national South represented the institutional frameworks within which new communities were formed; communities that were predicated on commonly held religious beliefs and assumptions. The adoption of evangelical Protestantism was one of the most important, if not the most imporant, steps in the transformation of Africans into African-Americans.

With respect to religion, the American Revolution and its aftermath marked a profoundly significant break with the past. However, other aspects of enslaved peoples' lives were not changed dramatically by either wartime disruptions or by the republican ideology of their Patriot owners. For example, this was generally true in terms of the different work regimes favored by owners; it was also generally true of the various activities associated with the enslaved peoples' domestic economies.

Despite the flowering of scholarly activity since the mid-1970s, two aspects of slavery and race relations, everywhere in the colonial and early national South, remain sadly neglected. Regardless of their often innovative and illuminating contributions, all too often the male historians who have dominated the field during the past thirty years have been guilty of conveying the impression that all slave owners were men as were all enslaved people. It is only now that (mainly women) historians are beginning to set the record straight. However, there still remains a significant disparity between the relative amounts of scholarly attention paid to women in the antebellum and the early South. Within the field of early southern history there is a disparity of another sort. Comparatively little detailed attention has been paid to the specific experiences of enslaved women. Whereas historians of the anglophone Caribbean have delved deeply into those experiences, there is no comparable literature for any part of the early southern mainland. True, a handful of articles and essays have appeared that consider some dimensions of enslaved women's lives. Betty Wood (1987, 1995), for example, has examined patterns of female resistance in the Georgia lowcountry as well as the ways in which that region's informal economies were gendered. For her part, Jacqueline Jones (1989) has contributed a pioneering essay that elaborated the ways in which enslaved women's lives were changed, in her view generally for the worse, during the era of the American Revolution. More recently, Frey and Wood (1998) have emphasized the pivotal role of women in shaping the religious lives, the religious transformation, of enslaved people between the early seventeenth century and 1830. However, it remains the case that we still have a great deal more to learn about the lives, experiences, and imperatives of enslaved women everywhere in the early South.

Generally speaking, such scholarship as there is on gender and gender relations in the early southern mainland tends to place free and enslaved women in separate analytical categories. Kathleen Brown (1996) is to be applauded for her recent effort to break down that categorization. Her pioneering study of Virginia addresses the complexity of the relationship between gender, race, and enslavement and, in the process, points to the need for similar analyses of other parts of the South as they too underwent the transition from slaveholding to slave societies. As yet, however, we know comparatively little about those white women in the early South who were either plantation mistresses, the mothers or wives of planters, or slave owners in their own right. Cara Anzilotti (1997) and Betty Wood (2000) have produced short studies of women slave owners in the Carolina and Georgia lowcountry, but otherwise scant regard has been paid to them. By default, this means that, with the notable exception of Brown's (1996) study, we know precious little about relationships that have attracted an enormous amount of interest on the part of historians of the antebellum South: those that were formed between plantation mistresses, or female slave owners, and enslaved women.

Another set of relationships in the early South, those between under-class white and enslaved people, that Edmund Morgan (1975) identified as being so significant in seventeenth-century Virginia's transformation to a slave society, have also not received as much attention as they might in recent scholarship. This is not necessarily to demand a return to, or revival of, the Marxist interpretation favored by Philip Foner (1975). However, the time does seems ripe for a fuller examination of the lives, interests, and imperatives of under-class white women and men and the ways in which they interacted in various contexts, for example in the southern towns, churches, and marketplaces, with enslaved people.

In many, and often in quite fundamental ways, our understanding of the origins of slavery in the different parts of the southern mainland between the early seventeenth and the early nineteenth century has been transformed during the course of the last twenty-five years. Exciting new questions have been posed, revealing new methodologies and approaches have been devised, old sources have been reexamined and new ones brought into play. A quite remarkable amount of progress has been made, and in many areas a significant degree of scholarly consensus has been achieved. However, there are still some aspects of the processes of enslavement, and the mainland South's evolving slave societies, that remain elusive. Much has been accomplished since the late 1960s and 1970s, but the origins of slavery in the early South remain far from being an exhausted field of scholarly investigation.

BIBLIOGRAPHY

Anzilotti, Cara 1997: Autonomy and the Female Planter in Colonial South Carolina. *Journal of Southern History*, 63, 239–68.

Berlin, Ira 1998: *Many Thousands Gone: The First Two Centuries of Slavery in North America.* Cambridge, MA: Belknap Press of Harvard University Press.

Blassingame, John W. 1972: *The Slave Community: Plantation Life in the Antebellum South.* New York: Oxford University Press.

Boles, John B. 1982: *Black Southerners, 1619–1869.* Lexington: University Press of Kentucky.

Breen, T. H. and Innes, Stephen 1980: *"Myne Owne Ground": Race and Freedom on Virginia's Eastern Shore, 1640–1676.* New York: Oxford University Press.

Brown, Kathleen M. 1996: *Good Wives, Nasty Wenches, and Anxious Patriarchs: Gender, Race, and Power in Colonial Virginia.* Chapel Hill: University of North Carolina Press.

Davis, David Brion 1966: *The Problem of Slavery in Western Culture.* Ithaca, NY: Cornell University Press.

Degler, Carl N. 1959: Slavery and the Genesis of American Race Prejudice, *Comparative Studies in Society and History*, 2, 49–66.

Elkins, Stanley M. 1959: *Slavery: A Problem in American Institutional and Intellectual Life.* Chicago: University of Chicago Press.

Foner, Philip S. 1975: *The History of Black Americans*, Vol. 1: *From Africa to the Emergence of the Cotton Kingdom.* Westport, CT: Greenwood Press.

Franklin, John Hope 1994: *From Slavery to Freedom: A History of African-Americans*, 7th edn. New York: Alfred A. Knopf.

Frey, Sylvia R. 1991: *Water From the Rock: Black Resistance in a Revolutionary Age.* Princeton, NJ: Princeton University Press.

Frey, Sylvia R. and Wood, Betty 1998: *Come Shouting to Zion: African American Protestantism in the American South and British Caribbean to 1830.* Chapel Hill: University of North Carolina Press.

Genovese, Eugene D. 1975: *Roll, Jordan, Roll: The World the Slaves Made.* New York: Pantheon Books.

Gomez, Michael A. 1998: *Exchanging Our Country Marks: The Transformation of African Identities in the Colonial and Antebellum South.* Chapel Hill: University of North Carolina Press.

Gray, Lewis C. 1933: *History of Agriculture in the Southern United States to 1860,* 2 vols. Washington, DC: Carnegie Institution.

Gray, Ralph and Wood, Betty 1976: The Transition from Indentured to Involuntary Servitude in Colonial Georgia, *Explorations in Economic History,* 13, 353–70.

Hall, Gwendolyn Midlo 1995: *Africans in Colonial Louisiana: The Development of Afro-Creole Culture in the Eighteenth Century.* Baton Rouge: Louisiana State University Press.

Handlin, Oscar and Handlin, Mary F. 1950: Origins of the Southern Labor System, *William and Mary Quarterly,* 3rd ser., 7, 199–222.

Henretta, James A. 1973: *The Evolution of American Society.* Lexington, MA: Heath.

Higginbotham, A. Leon, Jr. 1978: *In the Matter of Color: The Colonial Period.* New York: Oxford University Press.

Jones, Jacqueline 1989: Race, Sex, and Self-Evident Truths: The Status of Slave Women during the Era of the American Revolution. In Ronald Hoffman and Peter J. Albert (eds.), *Women in the Age of the American Revolution.* Charlottesville: University Press of Virginia, 293–337.

Jordan, Winthrop D. 1968: *White Over Black: American Attitudes Toward the Negro, 1550–1812.* Chapel Hill: University of North Carolina Press.

Jordan, Winthrop D. 1974: *The White Man's Burden: Historical Origins of Racism in the United States.* New York: Oxford University Press.

Kay, Marvin L. Michael and Carey, Lorin Lee 1995: *Slavery in North Carolina, 1748–1775.* Chapel Hill: University of North Carolina Press.

Kulikoff, Allan 1986: *Tobacco and Slaves: The Development of Southern Cultures in the Chesapeake, 1680–1800.* Chapel Hill: University of North Carolina Press.

Landers, Jane 1999: *Black Society in Spanish Florida.* Urbana: University of Illinois Press.

Levine, Lawrence 1977: *Black Culture and Black Consciousness: Afro-American Folk Thought from Slavery to Freedom.* New York: Oxford University Press.

Littlefield, Daniel C. 1981: *Rice and Slaves: Ethnicity and the Slave Trade in Colonial South Carolina.* Baton Rouge: Louisiana State University Press.

McCusker, John J. and Menard, Russell R. 1985: *The Economy of British America, 1607–1789.* Chapel Hill: University of North Carolina Press.

Manning, Patrick 1990: *Slavery and African Life: Occidental, Oriental, and African Slave Trades.* Cambridge: Cambridge University Press.

Morgan, Edmund S. 1975: *American Slavery, American Freedom: The Ordeal of Colonial Virginia.* New York: W. W. Norton.

Morgan, Philip D. 1998: *Slave Counterpoint: Black Culture in the Eighteenth-Century Chesapeake and Lowcountry.* Chapel Hill: University of North Carolina Press.

Nash, Gary B. 1970: *Class and Society in Early America.* Englewood Cliffs, NJ: Prentice-Hall.

Nash, Gary B. 1974: *Red, White, and Black: The People of Early America.* Englewood Cliffs, NJ: Prentice-Hall.

Olwell, Robert 1998: *Masters, Slaves, and Subjects: The Culture of Power in the South Carolina Low County, 1740–1790.* Ithaca, NY: Cornell University Press.

Phillips, Ulrich B. 1918: *American Negro Slavery.* Baton Rouge: Louisiana State University Press.

Rawick, George O. 1972: *From Sundown to Sunup: The Making of the Black Community*. Vol. 1 of *The American Slave: A Composite Autobiography*. Westport, CT: Greenwood Press.

Schwarz, Philip J. 1988: *Twice Condemned: Slaves and the Criminal Laws of Virginia, 1705–1865*. Baton Rouge: Louisiana State University Press.

Sobel, Mechal 1987: *The World They Made Together: Black and White Values in Eighteenth-Century Virginia*. Princeton, NJ: Princeton University Press.

Stampp, Kenneth M. 1955: *The Peculiar Institution: Slavery in the Antebellum South*. New York: Alfred A. Knopf.

Thornton, John K. 1992: *Africa and Africans in the Making of the Atlantic World, 1400–1800*. New York: Cambridge University Press.

Usner, Daniel H. 1992: *Indians, Settlers, and Slaves in a Frontier Exchange Economy: The Lower Mississippi Valley Before 1783*. Chapel Hill: University of North Carolina Press.

Walsh, Lorena S. 1997: *From Calabar to Carter's Grove: The History of a Virginia Slave Community*. Charlottesville: University Press of Virginia.

Walvin, James 1997: *Fruits of Empire: Exotic Produce and British Taste, 1660–1800*. Houndmills, Basingstoke: Macmillan.

Wiecek, William M. 1977: The Statutory Law of Slavery and Race in the Thirteen Mainland Colonies of British America. *William and Mary Quarterly*, 3rd ser., 34, 258–80.

Williams, Eric 1944: *Capitalism and Slavery*. Chapel Hill: University of North Carolina Press.

Wood, Betty 1984: *Slavery in Colonial Georgia, 1730–1775*. Athens: University of Georgia Press.

Wood, Betty 1987: Some Aspects of Female Resistance to Chattel Slavery in Low Country Georgia, 1763–1815. *The Historical Journal*, 30, 603–22.

Wood, Betty 1995: *Women's Work, Men's Work: The Informal Slave Economies of Lowcountry Georgia*. Athens: University of Georgia Press.

Wood, Betty 1997: *The Origins of American Slavery: Freedom and Bondage in the English Colonies*. New York: Hill and Wang.

Wood, Betty 2000: *Gender, Rank, and Race in a Revolutionary Age: The Georgia Lowcountry, 1760–1820*. Athens: University of Georgia Press.

Wood, Peter H. 1974: *Black Majority: Negroes in Colonial South Carolina from 1670 Through the Stono Rebellion*. New York: W. W. Norton.

Young, Alfred F. (ed.) 1976: *The American Revolution: Explorations in the History of American Radicalism*. Dekalb: Northern Illinois University Press.

CHAPTER FIVE

Understanding the South in the Revolutionary Era, 1750–1789

IRA D. GRUBER

THE history of the South in the Revolutionary era has been inextricably bound to the larger history of the American Revolution. The South does have its own rich internal history in the second half of the eighteenth century – a history of a population growing rapidly and shifting away from the seaboard, of an economy tied increasingly to Atlantic markets and slavery, of a society unsettled by aspiring common people and emerging dissenting religious sects, and of a politics fueled by contending interest groups. But that rich internal history has ever been a part of developments outside the South and has blended almost imperceptibly with the American Revolution. The South and southerners had indispensable parts in the political and constitutional struggles that disrupted the British empire, secured independence, shaped the governments of the new United States, and contributed to the reordering of American society. To gain an understanding then of the South in the Revolutionary era requires a reading of books about the Revolution in general and the Revolutionary South in particular. Perhaps even more important, it requires a resolution of conflicting interpretations of the Revolution at large to see how best to explain the South in the Revolutionary era.

For nearly forty years Bernard Bailyn has shaped our overall understanding of the American Revolution. His *Ideological Origins of the American Revolution*, first published in 1965 but refined extensively since then, has proved a remarkably durable explanation of the causes and consequences of the American Revolution. According to Bailyn, the Revolution was primarily "an ideological, constitutional, political struggle," an affair of the mind (Bailyn 1992: x). When after 1763 the British sought to reorganize their empire in North America – to force their colonists to submit to restrictions on currency, trade, and settlement and to pay some of the costs of managing the empire – the colonists saw themselves as victims of a conspiracy against liberty. Having been taught by radical English Whig writers and by their own experience to fear corrupt rulers – to fear men who would use taxes, places, and a standing army to gain power at the expense of the people – the colonists had little trouble deciding that they were being exploited by corrupt British ministers. The colonists interpreted a succession of loosely connected British measures (adopting the Stamp Tax and Townshend Duties, curbing the independence of judges and the jurisdiction of juries, and redeploying the British army from the frontiers to the cities) as parts of a conspiracy against liberty.

In defending themselves against such abuses of power and, eventually, in creating governments for their new states, Americans transformed traditional constitutional and social thinking. When the British argued that the colonists were subject to the Stamp Act because they were virtually represented in Parliament, the colonists replied that they understood representation quite differently, that they expected to be taxed only by representatives of their own choosing. When the colonists challenged the constitutionality of Acts of Parliament and the British replied that Parliament could judge the constitutionality of its own Acts, the colonists began to modify the meaning of a constitution. They argued that only the people could create a constitution and that a written constitution, not Parliament or any other legislature, defined the form of government and the rights of the people. And when the British asserted that Parliament had the ultimate power in the empire – the sovereign power to make laws binding the colonists in all cases whatsoever – the colonists reconsidered sovereignty. They eventually decided that sovereign power lay with the people who through conventions and constitutions parceled power to their governments.

According to Bailyn, these efforts to control power led Americans to reconsider more than the nature of government – to attack slavery, established religion, and aristocratic privilege. Although many southerners were reluctant to face the loss of slaves, the Continental Congress pledged in 1774 to discontinue the slave trade; and four of the new states either abolished slavery or prohibited the importation of slaves. The Revolution also allowed Dissenters to turn resentment of British efforts to strengthen the Anglican church into an attack on all established religion. Dissenters sought relief in the first Congress, won an expression of support in the Virginia Declaration of Rights in June 1776, and at length gained the Virginia Statute for Religious Freedom in 1786. Finally, in trying to control royal governors and their councils, colonists became aware of the advantages of a mixed government, the traditional mixed polity of Britain in which monarch, aristocracy, and commons checked one another. Americans clearly rejected monarchy and aristocracy in their new states, but they sought to prevent excesses of republicanism by preserving the forms of mixed government, by having elected members of the lower house of the legislature choose both the upper house and the executive, and by creating an independent judiciary.

Gordon Wood has added considerable depth and power to Bailyn's radical-Whig interpretation of the American Revolution, particularly to his description of the constitutional and social consequences of the Revolution. In his *Creation of the American Republic* Wood (1969) explored changes in constitutional thinking that emerged while Americans created governments for their new states and for the United States. He confirmed much of what Bailyn had said, but he went beyond Bailyn in analyzing constitution-making in the states, in looking more closely at the changes in American understandings of constitution, representation, mixed polity, conventions, and sovereignty that emerged in the decade after independence. Wood also put more emphasis than Bailyn did on the republican character of the Constitution – on republican justifications of a stronger executive and judiciary and of a stronger national government to thwart legislative abuses of power everywhere.

Wood most comprehensively enriched Bailyn by exploring the social implications of the Revolution. In his wonderfully coherent and readable synthesis, *The Radicalism of the American Revolution*, Wood (1992) argued that measured "by the amount of social change that actually took place," the American Revolution was "one of the greatest revolutions the world has known" (ibid: 5). In little more than a half-century after 1760, Americans transformed a thoroughly monarchical colonial society into the most democratic nation on earth. The citizens of this new nation eliminated monarchy and aristocracy, reconstituted state power, elevated the standing of laborers and labor, revamped American culture and economy, and, most important, made the interests of ordinary people the goals of society and government.

These sweeping changes came largely through a republican revolution, a revolution that accelerated developments already underway in the population and economy. In 1760 Americans accepted a hierarchical society, a society dominated by a king, royal officials, colonial gentlemen, and heads of families. But even then demographic and economic changes were challenging this traditional monarchical order. The extraordinary growth of the population forced individuals to the frontiers where there were simply not enough gentlemen to exercise power and where the family and community began to break down. Similarly, thriving grain exports brought profits, a taste for luxury goods, and an increase in domestic manufacturing – indeed, impersonal market relations that superseded older patronage networks. In the Chesapeake small planters began to sell directly to Scottish factors, thereby gaining the independence to challenge the political power of the great planters. When the colonists subsequently overthrew royal authority and established their own republican governments, they hastened the destruction of the hierarchy that had dominated colonial life. Subjects became citizens. Patriots struck at hereditary distinctions by abolishing primogeniture and entail; they reduced and then eliminated indentured service; they attacked slavery; they sought to make every voter independent; they opened offices to talent; and they so constituted their new governments as to make the people sovereign while protecting minority rights and private property.

When in the 1780s and 1790s anxious conservatives took measures to restore the old hierarchical society, they succeeded mainly in propelling their countrymen from republicanism to liberal democracy. Conservatives tried at first to teach Americans to be virtuous citizens, to subordinate their private interests to the good of the states and nation. Those efforts failing, conservatives sought to regulate selfishness by setting interest against interest in the Constitution of 1787 and by bringing disinterested gentlemen to power in the new national government. Once again they failed. Ordinary Americans, rejecting the idea that anyone could be disinterested, gained control of state and national governments explicitly to serve themselves. To consolidate their hold on power – to offset the political advantages of the rich and wellborn – these ordinary men provided pay for officeholders, extended the vote to nearly all adult white men, and developed permanent political parties to contest elections and reward their followers. They adopted legislation to promote the economic interests of ordinary men – building roads and canals to ease domestic commerce, chartering banks to satisfy the need for currency and credit, and providing general acts of incorporation to favor new industry. So it was, according to Wood, that between the mid-eighteenth century and the early nineteenth century, Americans experienced an "unprecedented democratic revolution" (Wood 1992: 348). They created a "prosperous free society belonging to obscure people," a society bound together by "common people with their common interests in making money and getting ahead" (ibid: 369).

Bailyn's and Wood's understandings of the American Revolution have been sustained by the work of other fine scholars, including Charles Royster, whose *A Revolutionary People at War: The Continental Army and American Character, 1775–1783* (1979) is the most important book about the War for American Independence. According to Royster, leading revolutionaries were determined to win independence without sacrificing their republican ideals – without violating their notions of selfless service to the state or creating the kind of standing army and powerful central government that had threatened them within the British empire and that might still deprive them of their liberties in an independent United States. So it was that Congress tried at first to defeat the British with an army of inspired militiamen serving for no more than a year and supplied by the voluntary contributions of the states. Even after defeats at New York in 1776 forced Congress to create a long-serving professional army with rigorous discipline and training, and even after that army began to prove its worth, revolutionaries wanted to believe that they did not need the army to win independence – that the militia could defeat the British and that ordinary citizens were not obligated to serve in or support the Continental army. Between 1778 and 1780 the army and the American people drifted ever farther apart, the people ignoring the army while pursuing private interests and the army taking pride in its accomplishments in spite of popular neglect. British victories at Charleston and Camden in 1780 and Benedict Arnold's treason temporarily encouraged Americans to reaffirm their commitments to selfless service and independence. Even so, relations between the Continental army and the American people grew worse over the last years of the war, the army wanting a stronger national government to provide soldiers with pay, food, clothes, and pensions; the people, relief from taxes and opportunities to profit from the war. At war's end, when the army sought pay and recognition for what it had done, the people objected, claiming victory for themselves, the virtuous American people. Royster's account makes clear how difficult it was for Americans to win their independence without violating their republican ideals.

Just as Royster built upon and sustained the work of Bailyn and Wood, so too did Jack N. Rakove in his highly reflective *Original Meanings: Politics and Ideas in the Making of the Constitution* (1996). Rakove drew upon Bailyn's and Wood's understandings of Anglo-American politics and of constitution-making in the new United States to illuminate the intentions of the men who wrote and ratified the Constitution. According to Rakove, James Madison and other like-minded men went to Philadelphia in 1787 to free the government of the United States and citizens in the states from the tyranny of state legislatures, of legislatures that were all too responsive to the will of selfish majorities. Madison and his colleagues succeeded in creating a stronger national government and in providing greater protection for the minority of citizens within the states. But the framers of the Constitution, mindful from their own history and political theory of the dangers inherent in governmental power, took care that their new, energetic national government did not destroy liberty – that the Constitution preserved separate spheres for national and state government and that it separated executive, legislative, and judicial powers within the national government. The framers also took care to submit the Constitution to the people for ratification, thereby circumventing the state legislatures and affirming the sovereign power of the people. And when during debates over ratification many complained that the Constitution did not provide adequate security for individual rights, for rights long protected in both the British colonies and the new United States, Madison undertook to secure those rights in the first ten amendments. Although Rakove found it difficult to establish the intentions of the framers, and although the framers themselves could not long agree on what they had intended, their efforts did produce "the one set of consensual political symbols that come closest to universal acceptance" among their countrymen (Rakove 1996: 367).

Unlike Rakove and Royster, who accepted and extended Bailyn's and Wood's understanding of the American Revolution, Joyce Appleby sought to challenge and modify that understanding. Her essays, written in the 1970s and 1980s and republished with a new introduction in *Liberalism and Republicanism in the Historical Imagination* (1992), represent the most sophisticated and comprehensive criticism of Bailyn's and Wood's ideological interpretation of the Revolution. According to Appleby, radical Whig ideas could not adequately explain the causes and consequences of the Revolution. Those ideas might well have swayed leading patriots, but they were not so important in shaping the Revolution as the economic and political interests of ordinary men.

Appleby owed her insight to a reading of late seventeenth-century British economic tracts, especially those of John Locke. Locke had tried to persuade the British government to abandon mercantilism, to give up the idea that economic growth was dependent on a state-controlled and favorable balance of trade and to trust individuals striving within a free domestic market to produce prosperity. Although he failed, although the British embraced mercantilism for another seventy-five years, Locke's arguments contributed to the freeing of the individual and the limiting of government power, particularly in the British colonies of North America. By the middle of the eighteenth century many ordinary Americans were growing prosperous in relatively unfettered pursuits of trade, manufacturing, and commercial agriculture, just as Locke had predicted. But these prosperous men, spreading across the colonies and selling their crops in European markets, were on a collision course both with the mercantilist policies of the British government and with the hierarchical order of their own society. When in the 1760s the British government sought to enforce restrictions on their trade, the colonists reacted violently. The colonists might well have been prompted by radical Whig fears of power to resist Acts of Parliament; but, according to Appleby, emerging liberalism – the pursuit of rational self-interest in commerce and politics – was more important than radical Whig ideology in driving the colonists to rebel. By then, liberal impulses had also thoroughly disrupted Wood's interdependent, hierarchical society of mid-eighteenth century America.

And, Appleby argued, liberalism continued to be a more potent force than republicanism in the new United States. Ordinary men rejected the classical republican ideal of selfless community service, gained control of the early state legislatures, and adopted a number of self-serving measures that favored debtors over creditors. Frightened creditors, members of traditional elites who felt their property and authority threatened, struck back. In the Constitution of 1787 they created a national government to check the power of ordinary men, to control selfish majorities whether in the federal government or in the state legislatures. But in the 1790s state legislatures continued to favor ordinary men – building roads, opening waterways,

and providing a postal service for the small farmers and merchants who were producing foodstuffs for emerging markets in Europe and the West Indies. And when
Thomas Jefferson and his Republican Party came to power in 1800, the national
government was ready to assist the small commercial farmer. Far from fearing
commerce, Jefferson sought to favor it by eliminating governmental regulations,
supporting free trade, opening western lands, and promoting a national market
through uniform currency and contracts. According to Appleby, Jefferson embraced
the ordering of society through the free transactions of individuals.

Appleby's emphasis on liberalism in the Revolution, on the effects that the self-
interest of ordinary men had on the disruption of the British empire and on the
reordering of American society and government in the new United States, was not
meant to replace but rather to complement Bailyn's and Wood's republican interpretations. She urged that they and other historians incorporate her liberalism, or
liberal republicanism, in their understanding of the causes and consequences of the
Revolution. To a considerable extent she has succeeded. Wood's *Radicalism of the
American Revolution* shares her insights far more than his or Bailyn's earlier works;
and the best recent books on the South in the Revolutionary era – books on politics,
religion, regionalism, agriculture, and slavery – support Appleby's reading of the
Revolution.

Although Charles S. Sydnor's *Gentlemen Freeholders: Political Practices in Washington's Virginia* (1952) appeared a decade before historians began to debate the relative
importance of ideology and interest in the Revolution, his study remains one of the
most appealing and instructive books about the South in this era; and it does support
those who would later emphasize interest over ideology. To explain how Virginians
managed to identify and develop so many of the leaders of the Revolution – such
diverse and great men as George Washington, Thomas Jefferson, James Madison, and
John Marshall – Sydnor analyzed Virginia politics from roughly the Seven Years' War
to the ratification of the Constitution. He found in that political system a curious
blending of aristocratic and democratic practices that brought extraordinary men to
power in the new United States. Nearly all Virginians of the mid-eighteenth century
expected their public officials to be aristocrats, white men of wealth, position, and
learning. They also expected those officials to be responsive and responsible servants
of the people, leaders who understood the interests of ordinary men. And in the era of
the Revolution, Virginians had a system that produced just the kind of leaders they
had in mind.

Aspiring politicians had first to win appointment to and prove themselves in local
government, in the county courts which were dominated by other aristocrats. They
then had to stand for and win election to the House of Burgesses, to gain the votes of
independent planters and farmers who came to know the candidates well in intensely
public contests of character and skill. Finally, as members of the House of Burgesses,
they had to prove themselves once again – as committeemen, speakers, and parlia-
mentarians – to secure the support of their fellow legislators for appointment to the
highest offices of state and nation. This political system clearly favored men of wealth
and standing, but it also identified and advanced men of talent who knew enough of
democratic elections and responsible government to flourish as leaders in the new
American republic. Although some of Sydnor's conclusions have been refined in the
past half-century, his book remains a wonderfully persuasive combination of telling

images and thoughtful speculations on the intersection of local and national politics in Revolutionary Virginia.

The hierarchical society that nurtured Washington and Jefferson did not survive the Revolution. Rhys Isaac's *The Transformation of Virginia, 1740–1790* (1982) describes the shattering of that society by a half-century of religious and political revolution, by popular forces inspired far more by rational self-interest than by ideology. In 1740 Virginia's society was dominated by a relatively small number of men of wealth, education, and social standing – gentlemen who often cultivated tobacco on large tidewater estates worked by slaves and who had the leisure to exercise power through county courts, parish vestries, militia companies, and the colonial assembly. These were secular, competitive men who lived extravagantly and were treated deferentially by smaller planters as well as by servants and slaves. But in the middle of the eighteenth century changes in the economy coincided with powerful religious and political movements to overturn this ruling elite. Scottish merchants arrived to deprive the great planters of their role as middlemen in the Atlantic tobacco trade and, as a result, of some of their influence over small planters. Anglican clergy and dissenting sects subsequently battled with the gentry and with each other in complicated struggles that diminished the gentry's power in church and society, weakened the Anglican church, and alienated Virginians from the Crown. During the War for American Independence the gentry made political and religious concessions to ordinary men to win their support for the patriot cause. But ordinary men rejected the republican ideal of selfless service to the state and nation. They elected men of their own class, evaded military service, sought profit from the war, and neglected religion. By the 1780s Virginia's hierarchical society was, according to Isaac, in shambles. The Anglican church had been disestablished; the population was shifting to the west in search of better lands; and the tidewater gentry were having to share political and social control with Dissenters and other ordinary Virginians. Isaac's transformation was complete, the work of ordinary men pursuing what Appleby called their rational self-interests.

So too did Jean B. Lee see self-interest fueling the Revolution in tidewater Maryland. In her comprehensive and authoritative *The Price of Nationhood: The American Revolution in Charles County, Maryland*, Lee (1994) has shown that while some in Charles County were stirred by republican ideals to support the Revolution, many more followed their economic interests and dislike of Lord Baltimore in opposing the proprietary and royal governments of Maryland. On the eve of the Revolution, Charles County was a thriving agricultural community of some 16,000 inhabitants on the banks of the Potomac River, a community dominated by wealthy planters who exploited slaves and sold tobacco and grains in the Atlantic market. These leading planters only gradually became leading revolutionaries. If slow to support opposition to the Stamp Tax and Townshend Duties, they did act forcefully in 1770 to keep proprietary officials from imposing inspection fees on tobacco (fees that had not been approved by the Maryland House of Delegates) and from collecting a tax to support the Anglican clergy. By 1774, after having suffered through several years of declining tobacco prices and prosecutions for indebtedness to British firms, they were ready to move toward revolution, ready to support economic sanctions, committees of correspondence, militia forces, and a Continental Congress. In June 1776 "a great number of the inhabitants" of Charles County met to vote for independence, to instruct their delegates to the Maryland Convention to adopt a government suitable for a "free and independent" state (ibid: 129, 130).

Although the subsequent struggle for independence proved very costly for the people of Charles County, most remained committed to the Revolution and to the new United States; most continued to see in an independent state and nation their best hope for a better life. During the war, while suffering a succession of destructive British raids, they provided men and supplies for the Continental army. Sometimes they resorted to conscription and enforced sales to meet quotas, but they rarely commandeered supplies, and in 1781 they turned out warmly to assist French and American forces en route to Yorktown. After the war they never enjoyed the prosperity they expected. Many of the planters were hard pressed to repay long-standing debts and taxes. To meet these obligations they overplanted tobacco, depressing the market and exhausting their fields; and when they still were unable to pay taxes, they ruined local officials who were held personally liable for revenues. Under these circumstances many of the best qualified men resigned from office or refused to serve, forcing the state to restructure the county courts, to diminish the power and importance of those courts in local government. The people of Charles County supported the Constitution of 1787 to "maintain order and foster American economic development" (ibid: 247); and they did enjoy many benefits from the Revolution – an end to legal disabilities for Catholics, a reduction in indentured service, an expansion of the franchise, an increase in elective offices, a reduction in property qualifications for officeholders, an end to the slave trade, and an increase in the number of free blacks. Even so, by the 1790s Charles County had, according to Lee, paid a high price for its part in establishing the new nation. Its buildings and lands were run-down; its society was disintegrating; and its white population was moving away in search of better lands and lives.

Unlike Lee, Isaac, and Sydnor, whose planters rarely invoked ideas to explain their actions in the Revolutionary era, Timothy Breen has found that the great tobacco planters of tidewater Virginia regularly employed the language of radical English Whigs to explain their economic and social troubles in the 1760s and to justify their subsequent support for the American Revolution. In his unusually insightful *Tobacco Culture: The Mentality of the Great Tidewater Planters on the Eve of Revolution*, Breen (1985) has considered why men with large estates, social prominence, and political power embraced a radical political ideology and became revolutionaries. He discovered the answer outside their politics – in their cultivation of tobacco, mounting indebtedness to British merchants, and fears for their personal autonomy. Although bringing in a good crop of tobacco required luck as well as skill and judgment, planters tended to measure their personal worth (their sense of autonomy) against the value of their crop and the amount of credit they could command from the British merchants who handled their tobacco and furnished them with manufactured goods, with such luxuries as carriages, china, carpets, and furniture. To keep up appearances of success and to nourish their sense of autonomy, the great planters were tempted to go ever deeper into debt. They trusted that their British friends would be generous and patient creditors, just as they sought to be with Virginia neighbors and friends. When British merchants were hard-pressed during international financial crises, when they did call upon Virginians to pay their debts, the Virginians felt betrayed and threatened. They suspected the merchants of being greedy and dishonest, and they feared that they would lose what mattered most to them, their sense of personal independence.

In trying to preserve their autonomy, in resisting their creditors and imperial tax collectors, Breen's great planters progressed from individual protests, to cooperative reforms, to collective political and constitutional action. At every stage they employed English radical Whig ideas to explain or justify their actions. When pressed for payment of debts in the early 1760s individual planters reacted with anger and excuses, saying merchants were conspiring to ruin them, to deprive them of their independence. Subsequently, as individuals became aware they were not alone in their indebtedness – as Virginians pressed one another for money so as to pay British merchants – planters proposed a variety of changes in their tobacco culture to preserve their independence: selling their lands, paying debts, and moving west for a fresh start on the frontier; changing from tobacco to wheat or other crops; and giving up their luxurious way of living. None of these proposals for becoming simple republican farmers appealed to men whose social and political standing had long depended on living in the high style of successful tobacco planters. Not until faced with both parliamentary taxation and fresh demands for payment of debts to British merchants did Virginia planters seek a political solution to their problems, did they see themselves resisting politicians and merchants who were conspiring to deprive them of their liberties through luxuries, debts, and taxes. Only then were they willing to give up their tobacco culture – to adhere to nonexportation of tobacco as well as nonimportation of British goods – to gain their independence of merchants and Parliament. In the new United States tobacco planters aspired to be farmers raising wheat and leading frugal republican lives.

Breen has been more successful than any other historian in linking Bailyn's understanding of the causes of the Revolution to events in the southern colonies. But Breen has, wisely, refused to make exaggerated claims for the importance of ideology in his analysis of the coming of the Revolution. His great planters were only a small fraction of the population of the tidewater; they came relatively late to the Revolutionary cause; and their influence over other, lesser planters – to say nothing of the rest of the people of Virginia – remains to be established. Moreover, in explaining the connections between the great planters' cultivation of tobacco and their fears of debt, luxury, and conspiracies against liberty, Breen has illuminated only one of many causes of the Revolution. He clearly has left room for a much more complex explanation of the coming of the Revolution in the South – an explanation that, to judge by the work of other recent historians, would include more of interests than of ideology. Indeed, in looking beyond independence, Breen has put more emphasis on fears of debt than on fears of conspiracy against liberty. The natural heirs of Breen's great tidewater planters of the prewar era were the Jeffersonian Republicans of the 1790s with their pervasive fears of luxury and debt.

Like Breen, Joyce E. Chaplin has studied commercial agriculture in the Revolutionary South. But her interest in planters and crops has been fundamentally different than his. In her complex and persuasive *An Anxious Pursuit: Agricultural Innovation and Modernity in the Lower South, 1730–1815*, Chaplin (1993) has considered the impact of modern notions of progress on "a seemingly backward-looking slave society and plantation economy" (ibid: vii). Her planters were more concerned with theories of economic and social development – the theories of Scottish historians and economists – than with the republican fears for liberty of English radical Whigs. Eager to increase their profits and resentful of criticisms of their unhealthy climate and reliance on slave labor, the planters of South Carolina and Georgia sought to prove that they were industrious and progressive. They drained swamps and cleaned towns; collected seeds and seedlings from other parts of the world; experimented with different techniques for cultivating crops; imported and improved machines for processing grains, dyes, and fibers; wrote scientific articles; and drew on current ideas of human motivation – and humane behavior – to extract more labor from their slaves. They were suitably anxious about progress based on slavery, particularly about the corrupting effects of luxury on the individual and the community. But they modified Scottish theories to suit their peculiar circumstances and assuage their anxieties – to elevate farming over commerce as a measure of social development and to justify slavery as an extension of man's inherent inequality.

Although planters of the Lower South agreed on the rewards and perils of progress, they struggled over the rewards – the profits to be made in commercial agriculture. Before and during the War for American Independence, the lowcountry planters of South Carolina and Georgia used their wealth and political power to protect their interests and survive a series of crises. They sought control over the slaves, seeds, machines, and capital needed to produce crops for overseas markets; they expected the white inhabitants of inland districts to farm without slaves and to protect the lowcountry against foreign encroachments; and when war and revolution disrupted exports, they experimented with indigo and cotton. After independence, they reverted to the commercial production of rice, which made them the wealthiest planters in North America. They used their slaves, capital, and legislative power to improve the tidal irrigation of their fields and increase yields and profits; and they invested in water- or steam-powered mills to shell their rice. But these great lowcountry planters remained dependent on slaves to manage their plantations and in conflict with upcountry planters over political power and opportunities to profit from slave-supported commercial agriculture, especially from cotton. Planters of the Lower South in the Revolutionary era, planters great and small, were always aware of their rational self-interests. In struggling for access to the lands, slaves, and machines that made men rich, they seemed far closer to Appleby's liberalism than to Bailyn's republicanism.

So too did the backcountry planters that Rachel Klein studied in her *Unification of a Slave State: The Rise of the Planter Class in the South Carolina Backcountry, 1760–1808* (1990). Klein's planters, men with enough slaves to have some freedom from farm work, consistently put self-interest before ideology in struggling for control of their region and for parity with the coastal elite in the new state government. To put down bandits, Loyalists, and debtors who successively threatened the stability of western South Carolina from the 1760s to the 1780s, backcountry planters took the law into their own hands, joining with yeoman farmers to suppress criminals and support the American Revolution. They also persuaded colonial and state legislatures to help them by creating courts, calling out the militia, and, in the 1780s, passing a variety of laws to ease the plight of debtors. But it would take backcountry leaders another two decades to gain a proportional share of power in the state government. A clear majority of the white population lived in the backcountry, and planters throughout the state were by the late 1780s committed to a hierarchical society, commercial agriculture, slavery, and unfettered access to land. Even so, backcountry planters would not be able to persuade the lowcountry elite significantly to reapportion the state legislature until 1808. Only then – only after leaders from all regions were more closely bound together by education, interregional marriages, and, with the development of cotton as a staple, a renewed commitment to commercial agriculture and slavery – were South Carolinians able to agree to reapportion the state legislature according to population and taxable property. Self-interest had done more than republican ideals to unify South Carolina.

Similarly, slaves and slavery were more often affected by liberalism than by republicanism in the era of the American Revolution. Although republican ideals improved the lot of some slaves and inspired others, far more slaves suffered from their masters' pursuit of self-interest – from an unrestrained and perverted liberalism. According to Philip D. Morgan's marvelously thorough and judicious *Slave Counterpoint* (1998) slave culture varied significantly from the Upper to the Lower South and from the early to the late eighteenth century. But its distinctive features were shaped to a greater extent by crops, agricultural practices, slave codes, and lingering African habits of living and working than by republican ideas of power and liberty. Compare, with Morgan, the slave cultures of Chesapeake and lowcountry – of perhaps 80 percent of all slaves in eighteenth-century British North America – to see how and why those cultures differed, what they had in common, and how they changed during the age of the American Revolution.

Slave culture in the Chesapeake was shaped primarily by the staples, tobacco and wheat. Because these staples could be produced on a small scale and in conjunction with other crops and livestock, and because these staples were never as profitable as lowcountry rice, Chesapeake plantations remained smaller than those in the lowcountry; and slaves in the Chesapeake were more likely to live and work in small, integrated communities of blacks and whites. Chesapeake slaves were also more likely to be less skilled and to have less control over their work and lives than their lowcountry counterparts; indeed Chesapeake slaves frequently had to seek husbands and wives away from their home plantations, to live in single-parent households, and to rely heavily on extended kin networks in rearing children. But for all the disadvantages of living on smaller plantations, Chesapeake slaves were usually better treated; had better houses, clothes, and food; and were larger and healthier than slaves of South Carolina and Georgia (the Virginia slave population was the first in the New World to begin, around 1720, to grow naturally). By the late eighteenth century, Chesapeake planters thought of themselves as generous masters and expected their slaves to be grateful and happy – in part, perhaps, because many slaves had refused to join the British during the Revolutionary War.

As in the Chesapeake, slave culture in the lowcountry of South Carolina and Georgia was greatly influenced by the primary staple, rice. Because rice was best cultivated on a large scale and was more profitable than tobacco, plantations were larger and slave communities more stable in the lowcountry than in the Chesapeake. Work on rice plantations was hard. Even after the introduction of flooding to control weeds and the application of horse and water power to milling, rice was more difficult to produce than tobacco; and the slaves of South Carolina and Georgia had poorer housing, clothes, and food than their counterparts in the Chesapeake. No wonder that many slaves died during their first year in South Carolina, that many others were small and unhealthy, and that the slave population was able to grow naturally for only two decades during the whole of the eighteenth century. Even so, lowcountry slaves had an unusual amount of control over their lives. They worked apart from their masters, often under the supervision of other slaves and with opportunities to gain skills and to complete daily tasks so as to have time to manufacture goods and raise food for sale on their own account. They were also better able than slaves of the Chesapeake to organize themselves into stable families and to preserve African words, customs, and beliefs. Many lowcountry slaves returned to their home plantations after the Revolution.

Notwithstanding regional differences, there were some uniform developments in slave culture in the eighteenth-century British South – developments that depended more on growing affluence than on changing ideas. As plantations became larger, the population of slaves increased steadily and drew apart from whites. American-born slaves gradually came to dominate the slave community, speaking English, organizing themselves into families, adopting Christianity, and cooperating with each other both to oppose and to assist their masters. Their material lives also improved gradually through the eighteenth century – not just the quality of their food, clothes, and housing but also the conditions of their work. Slaves benefited from the shift from tobacco to wheat in the Chesapeake (wheat being easier to cultivate) and from improvements in the production of rice in the lowcountry. Although female slaves were increasingly employed as field hands, male slaves had more opportunities to become drivers or foremen and to acquire skills to work as carpenters, cabinet makers, cobblers, masons, smiths, tailors, silversmiths, and domestic servants. The Revolutionary War brought freedom for many slaves (the number and proportion of free blacks increasing in the last decades of the eighteenth century) and a republican emphasis on better treatment for all dependents. But after the war, masters recovered some slaves, reasserted their rights over others, and relocated an ever larger number to the newer states in the west.

As Morgan, Sydnor, Isaac, Lee, Chaplin, Klein, and even Breen suggest, Bernard Bailyn's ideological–constitutional interpretation of the American Revolution cannot alone sustain a comprehensive understanding of the South in the Revolutionary era. Bailyn's emphasis on fears of power encroaching on liberty must be combined with Appleby's pursuits of rational self-interest (much as Wood has begun to do in his *Radicalism*) to gain a full appreciation of the South in the Revolution. Self-interest best explains the actions of southerners who for much of this era were preoccupied with profits from land, slaves, and staples and who sought political power to protect and promote their interests. For such men fears of conspiracies against liberty were a secondary consideration until the 1770s when British coercive measures drove them to become inspired republicans – to support independence, voluntary military service, and a radical restructuring of their governments. But even before the Revolutionary War was over, their self-sacrifice gave way to self-interest. Southerners once again sought political power to enrich themselves, and they got that power both in the states and in the new nation. They opened western lands, built roads and cleared rivers, encouraged free trade, and gained uniform currency and contracts. Southerners had, largely in pursuit of their self-interests, created governments and a society that would serve and protect them – that would allow them to exploit the lands, slaves, and crops that made some men rich.

Such a synthesis would go far toward satisfying the most obvious need in the historiography of the South in the Revolutionary era, the need for a comprehensive history. Since the last such history was written more than forty years ago, scholars have completed scores of valuable and discrete studies of politics, economics, religion, society, and culture; of counties, towns, colonies, states, and regions; and of Indians, Loyalists, and slaves. They have written biographies and edited the papers of principal men. They have not yet studied women as carefully as slaves; or North Carolina and Georgia as thoroughly as Maryland, Virginia, and South Carolina. They certainly have not exhausted the new editions of personal papers for biographies of men like Nathanael Greene and Henry Laurens or for studies of the effects of the Revolutionary War on the southern states. But they have produced more than enough fine monographs and editions to sustain what is needed most, a comprehensive history of the South in the Revolution.

BIBLIOGRAPHY

Anderson, Fred 2000: *Crucible of War: The Seven Years' War and the Fate of Empire in British North America, 1754–1766*. New York: Alfred A. Knopf.

Appleby, Joyce 1992: *Liberalism and Republicanism in the Historical Imagination*. Cambridge, MA: Harvard University Press.

Axtell, James 1997: *The Indians' New South: Cultural Change in the Colonial Southeast*. Baton Rouge: Louisiana State University Press.

Bailyn, Bernard 1986: *Voyagers to the West: A Passage in the Peopling of America on the Eve of the Revolution*. New York: Alfred A. Knopf.

Bailyn, Bernard 1992: *The Ideological Origins of the American Revolution*. Cambridge, MA: Harvard University Press.

Beeman, Richard R. 1984: *The Evolution of the Southern Backcountry: A Case Study of Lunenburg County, Virginia, 1746–1832*. Philadelphia: University of Pennsylvania Press.

Breen, T. H. 1985: *Tobacco Culture: The Mentality of the Great Tidewater Planters on the Eve of Revolution*. Princeton, NJ: Princeton University Press.

Cappon, Lester J. 1976: *Atlas of Early American History: The Revolutionary Era, 1760–1790*. Princeton, NJ: Princeton University Press.

Carp, E. Wayne 1984: *To Starve the Army at Pleasure: Continental Army Administration and American Political Culture, 1775–1783*. Chapel Hill: University of North Carolina Press.

Chaplin, Joyce E. 1993: *An Anxious Pursuit: Agricultural Innovation and Modernity in the Lower South, 1730–1815*. Chapel Hill: Published for the Institute of Early American History and Culture by the University of North Carolina Press.

Ekirch, A. Roger 1981: *"Poor Carolina": Politics and Society in Colonial North Carolina, 1729–1776*. Chapel Hill: University of North Carolina Press.

Frey, Sylvia R. 1991: *Water from the Rock: Black Resistance in a Revolutionary Age*. Princeton, NJ: Princeton University Press.

Greene, Jack P. 1988: *Pursuits of Happiness: The Social Development of Early Modern British Colonies and the Formation of American Culture*. Chapel Hill: University of North Carolina Press.

Hoffman, Ronald, Tate, Thad W., and Albert, Peter J. (eds.) 1985: *An Uncivil War: The Southern Backcountry during the American Revolution*. Charlottesville: University Press of Virginia.

Isaac, Rhys 1982: *The Transformation of Virginia, 1740–1790*. Chapel Hill: Published for the Institute of Early American History and Culture by the University of North Carolina Press.

82   IRA D. GRUBER

Jordan, Winthrop D. 1968: *White Over Black: American Attitudes Toward the Negro, 1550–1812*. Chapel Hill: Published for the Institute of Early American History and Culture by the University of North Carolina Press.

Kay, Marvin L. M. and Cary, Lorin L. 1995: *Slavery in North Carolina, 1748–1775*. Chapel Hill: University of North Carolina Press.

Klein, Rachel N. 1990: *Unification of a Slave State: The Rise of the Planter Class in the South Carolina Backcountry, 1760–1808*. Chapel Hill: Published for the Institute of Early American History and Culture by the University of North Carolina Press.

Kulikoff, Allan 1986: *Tobacco and Slaves: The Development of Southern Cultures in the Chesapeake, 1680–1800*. Chapel Hill: Published for the Institute of Early American History and Culture by the University of North Carolina Press.

Lee, Jean B. 1994: *The Price of Nationhood: The American Revolution in Charles County, Maryland*. New York: Norton.

Lewis, Jan E. 1983: *The Pursuit of Happiness: Family and Values in Jefferson's Virginia*. New York: Cambridge University Press.

Lockridge, Kenneth A. 1992: *On the Sources of Patriarchal Rage: The Commonplace Books of William Byrd and Thomas Jefferson and the Gendering of Power in the Eighteenth Century*. New York: New York University Press.

Morgan, Philip D. 1998: *Slave Counterpoint*. Chapel Hill: Published for the Institute of Early American History and Culture by the University of North Carolina Press.

Onuf, Peter S. (ed.) 1993: *Jeffersonian Legacies*. Charlottesville: University Press of Virginia.

Price, Jacob M. 1980: *Capital and Credit in British Overseas Trade: The View from the Chesapeake, 1700–1776*. Cambridge, MA: Harvard University Press.

Ragsdale, Bruce A. 1996: *A Planters' Republic: The Search for Economic Independence in Revolutionary Virginia*. Madison, WI: Madison House.

Rakove, Jack N. 1996: *Original Meanings: Politics and Ideas in the Making of the Constitution*. New York: Alfred A. Knopf.

Royster, Charles 1979: *A Revolutionary People at War: The Continental Army and American Character, 1775–1783*. Chapel Hill: Published for the Institute of Early American History and Culture by the University of North Carolina Press.

Royster, Charles 1999: *The Fabulous History of the Dismal Swamp Company: A Story of George Washington's Times*. New York: Alfred A. Knopf.

Selby, John E. 1988: *The Revolution in Virginia, 1775–1783*. Charlottesville: University Press of Virginia.

Sloan, Herbert E. 1995: *Principle and Interest: Thomas Jefferson and the Problem of Debt*. New York: Oxford University Press.

Sobel, Mechal 1988: *The World They Made Together: Black and White Values in Eighteenth-Century Virginia*. Princeton, NJ: Princeton University Press.

Sydnor, Charles S. 1952: *Gentlemen Freeholders: Political Practices in Washington's Virginia*. Chapel Hill: Published for the Institute of Early American History and Culture by the University of North Carolina Press. Subsequent editions have been entitled *American Revolutionaries in the Making: Political Practices in Washington's Virginia*.

Titus, James 1991: *The Old Dominion at War: Society, Politics, and Warfare in Late Colonial Virginia*. Columbia: University of South Carolina Press.

Wood, Gordon S. 1969: *The Creation of the American Republic, 1776–1787*. Chapel Hill: Published for the Institute of Early American History and Culture by the University of North Carolina Press.

Wood, Gordon S. 1992: *The Radicalism of the American Revolution*. New York: Alfred A. Knopf.

PART II

The Antebellum South

CHAPTER SIX

The South in the New Nation, 1790–1824

DANIEL S. DUPRE

THE South's role in the early republic was, in one sense, to be a localist thorn in the side of the new nation, a prickly reminder of the sectional divisions that plagued the United States at its birth. The period was roughly bracketed, after all, by the Virginia and Kentucky resolutions of 1798, which cloaked Republican opposition to the Federalist Alien and Sedition Acts in the mantle of states' rights, and the Missouri Controversy of 1819–20, when the South rallied in defense of slavery's expansion and against congressional interference in local affairs. But shift the focus to Thomas Jefferson's Louisiana Purchase in 1803, Andrew Jackson's defeat of the British in 1815 at the Battle of New Orleans, or Henry Clay's articulation of the "American System" in Congress in the 1820s and a different picture emerges, one of the South sharing in, and even leading, the rapid expansion and confident nationalism of early-republic America.

Thomas P. Abernethy reminds us that there could be no deep-rooted sectionalism until there was a nation, and one fact that the events of the early republic make clear is that the process of nation-building did not end with ratification of the Constitution. The dialectical relationship between nationalism and sectionalism points the way toward a more complex portrait of the South's role in the new nation. Rapid geographic expansion, the development of a more complex and integrated economy, and the growth of the federal government all helped to make the imagined nation of the Constitutional Convention solid and real. At the same time, geographic, economic, and political expansion created a variety of tensions that either threatened national unity or challenged nationalist assumptions. Southern citizens and leaders contributed both to the process of national consolidation and to sectionalist reactions to that process. Most historians interested in the South's relationship to the new nation end up exploring, in one way or another, the fault lines generated by national development in all its guises.

Three books that provide readers with overviews of southern and national politics between 1790 and 1824 illustrate the close relationship between nationalism and sectionalism. Thomas Abernethy's *The South in the New Nation, 1789–1819* (1961) minimizes conflict between the North and South and denies slavery's power as a divisive issue. Surprising historians accustomed to viewing the region from the perspective of Jefferson's Virginia, Abernethy instead focuses on the West and tells a story of the promise and perils of geographic expansion. Chapter after chapter details the speculation, political intrigues, diplomacy, and warfare at play in the southern borderlands of the late eighteenth and early nineteenth centuries, concluding with the Great Migration that turned a western frontier into a southern landscape of farms and plantations after the War of 1812. Abernethy pays close attention to the centrifugal forces within the Southwest that threatened to pull the new nation apart. Speculators and settlers eager for fertile and valuable cotton land pushed west beyond the limits of the federal government's reach, encountering the dangerous presence of powerful Indian nations and their European allies on the borders. Speculative adventurers and politicians like William Blount, Aaron Burr, and James Wilkinson plotted separatist schemes in the 1790s and early 1800s, manipulating settlers' fears of Indian attacks, their discontent over uncertain access to the mouth of the Mississippi River, and their alienation from the eastern seaboard and the federal government. The War of 1812, especially Andrew Jackson's victories over first the Creeks and then the British at New Orleans, looms large in Abernethy's account precisely because it silenced those early threats of fragmentation. Control over the Mississippi River, the displacement of European powers on the borders, the cession to the federal government of large tracts of Indian land, and a surge of patriotism all helped to solidify the nation's hold over the Old Southwest.

Charles S. Sydnor in *The Development of Southern Sectionalism, 1819–1848* (1948) takes up the story where Abernethy leaves off, with a confident, nationalistic Republican majority in the South accustomed to dominating federal politics. Not all southerners were optimistic, however. Echoes of the strict constructionist philosophies of the anti-Hamiltonian 1790s emanated from a small group of Old Republicans centered in Virginia through the first decades of the nineteenth century. This minority bloc kept alive the states' rights principles of the Virginia and Kentucky resolutions, but their pessimistic obstructionism and insistence on limited government was out of step with the mood of postwar America. Yet by the early 1820s an increasing number of southerners felt threatened by nationalism and found refuge in an aggressive assertion of both states' rights and sectional economic interests. What accounts for this political transformation? The strains of westward expansion played a role, heightening sectional awareness and competition in the battle over Missouri's admission into the Union as a slave state. But Sydnor stresses other forms of congressional activism in explaining the southern retreat from nationalism, especially the neo-Hamiltonian program of postwar politicians eager to develop a dynamic, integrated American economy through banks, internal improvements, and tariffs. Those policies threatened many southerners committed to export agriculture, while John Marshall's Supreme Court rulings in favor of the nationalists' agenda endangered state sovereignty. The panic of 1819 and the subsequent depression also played a role in shifting southern attitudes by dampening the exuberant confidence of the postwar years and raising the stakes in debates over economic policy. Localism and regional self-interest had always existed, Sydnor argues, but the dramatic increase in the volume of federal economic legislation in the decade after the War of 1812 popularized states' rights in the South by transforming strict constructionism from a constitutional abstraction to a vital political issue. Still, nationalism did not wither away completely in the South during the 1820s, Sydnor cautions; divided opinion on issues like internal improvements demonstrates that the South was far from monolithic in its embrace of states' rights sectionalism.

William Cooper in *Liberty and Slavery: Southern Politics to 1860* (1983) emphasizes sectional tensions between the North and South, bringing slavery to the forefront of his political history. Once the South was linked to a larger political nation, first with the Revolution and then with ratification of the Constitution, its citizens and leaders defended distinct sectional interests in national politics, Cooper argues. Sometimes the politics of slavery sparked overt conflict, as when Quaker antislavery petitions in the early 1790s stirred southern leaders to reject the principle of congressional meddling in the "peculiar institution." But since Congress quickly learned to avoid the divisive issue, slavery caused little political conflict until after the War of 1812 and was not a direct factor in the partisan conflict between Federalists and Republicans. Still, Cooper believes that the so-called First Party System was sectional in nature, that the heart of the Republican Party, both in leadership and ideology, was distinctly southern. And since slavery shaped southern economic interests and white citizens' concepts of liberty, the institution played a vital, if indirect, role in creating a political culture receptive to republicanism. Agrarianism and localist suspicion toward governmental power and outside authority – motivating forces in the creation of the party in the 1790s – became increasingly faint echoes after the election of Jefferson and his Virginia successors. But that changed in the late 1810s and 1820s as a resurgence of sectionalism challenged the nationalist ethos of postwar America. While Sydnor locates that resurgence in the southern reaction to Congress's activist economic policy, Cooper roots it squarely in the Missouri Controversy of 1819–20. Northern opposition to the admission of Missouri as a slave state threatened southern participation in westward expansion and thus challenged southerners' rights as Americans. The Missouri Crisis, by fusing together a strict constructionist ideology that emphasized the limitations of congressional power with a defense of slavery, reinvigorated and popularized states' rights ideals throughout much of the South, sharpening sectional conflict.

The three broad overviews offered by Abernethy, Sydnor, and Cooper raise questions and themes that have captured the attention of most historians of the South's role in the early republic. Many revolve around the complex relationship between nationalism and sectionalism. What role did geographic expansion play in the development of both sectionalist and nationalist ideologies? How did the rapid economic growth between 1790 and the 1820s, and the dramatic booms and depressions of that period, influence southerners' sense of their place within the new nation? To what extent did the South, and the Republican Party, support nationalistic economic legislation and what was the relationship between that legislation and the resurgence of sectionalism in the early 1820s? Was the early states' rights movement of the 1820s the intellectual heir of the Republican opposition of the 1790s and, if so, what were the ideological links between those two periods? Finally, what role did slavery as an economic institution and a political problem play in the tangled unfolding of nationalism and sectionalism?

One important area that needs further exploration is the impact of geographic expansion on southern nationalism and sectionalism. Historians have not neglected the Old Southwest; a number of new works focus on the social and economic development of the region. Others have begun untangling the complex diplomacy and warfare associated with the southern borderlands. But few have thoroughly investigated the relationship between social, diplomatic, military, and political history, or the ways in which the rapid expansion of the southwestern frontier inspired both nationalistic and sectionalistic feelings. One way for readers to understand both the dangers of fragmentation and the opportunities for nationalization that underlay westward expansion is through Robert Remini's *Andrew Jackson and the Course of American Empire, 1767–1821* (1977), the first volume in his biographical series. Remini makes clear the fluidity of frontier Tennessee in the 1790s, where perils and uncertainties could serve as paths to wealth and fame for some. Jackson's political popularity in Tennessee hinged on his military exploits in Indian wars, while financial advancement depended upon his legal skills in prosecuting debtors and his business acumen in speculative ventures. As an ally of William Blount, Jackson was in the thick of efforts to create a new state for the Union *and* various separatist schemes. Remini pays close attention to the competing impulses of nationalism and sectionalism in a region that had closer economic ties to the Mississippi River than the eastern sea-board and that remained isolated from the federal government. Remini also illustrates the central role played by Jackson in harnessing to nationalist purposes the expansion-ist impulses that had threatened fragmentation of the Southwest, first in his victories over the Creeks and the British in the War of 1812, and then in his invasion of Spanish Florida in 1818. Those pivotal events in the solidification of the southern borderlands inspired an optimistic and expansive Jacksonian nationalism that found a home in the South, especially the Southwest, as readily as states' rights sectionalism. Remini's biography reveals much, but both the fragmentary impulses of the early settlement period and the subsequent development of nationalism are topics in need of further exploration.

Students of the early-republic South are fortunate that there are biographies for most of the leading and some of the secondary political figures of that era. While a number of the biographies are quite old and their subjects deserve further analysis, they do offer readers entry into the personalities and political controversies of the day. Even more important, though, are the many volumes of published papers, corres-pondence, and writings of southern leaders like Jackson, Henry Clay, Thomas Jefferson, James Madison, James Monroe, John Marshall, John Taylor, and John C. Calhoun. Those published sources allow students to delve into the political, legal, and ideological history of the early-republic South without travelling to archives and provide direct access to some of the most formative thinkers in American history. By examining, for example, the writings of John Taylor of Caroline and the legal decisions of John Marshall, or the papers of Thomas Jefferson and Henry Clay, one can see clearly the tension of a South that stood at the forefront of both national development and sectional reaction. Some of those biographies and published primary sources can be found in the bibliography.

The greatest number of books on the South in the new nation focus on the rise and fall of the First Party System, from the bitter conflicts of the 1790s to the superficial harmony of the Era of Good Feelings. While the great bulk of those works deal with the Jeffersonian Republicans, readers might want to approach the vast topic by first looking at two groups of southerners who were alienated from the political mainstream of their region. James H. Broussard in *The Southern Federalists, 1800–1816* (1978) traces the Federalist minority through years of decline after Jefferson's election. Despite focusing on a group with very little power, one that was more a collection of like-minded men than a political organization, Broussard's book is a model of comprehensiveness. After tracing the evolution of the southern Federalists through time, Broussard examines their impact in the state legislatures, the creation of a Federalist press and rudimentary party organization, their stance on a variety of issues from banking to slavery, and, finally, the characteristics of Federalist supporters. In the process, Broussard transcends the narrowness of his topic and instead casts his focus across the entire political landscape of the South in the years when the region dominated national politics. One of Broussard's points illustrates the tension between nationalism and localism, the malleability of political ideology, and the weakness of party organization in this period. After the War of 1812, as Republicans adopted "neo-Federalist" economic policies, southern Federalists abandoned their own heritage of nationalism and adopted a "neo-Republican" oppositional stance, especially to the Bank of the United States and protective tariffs. One reason for that shift was the simple fact that the Federalists feared the accumulation of power by a Republican-dominated federal government that might take partisan advantage of expanded patronage networks. But Broussard also argues that southern Federalists often represented districts, primarily in Virginia and North Carolina, with strong localist traditions and voted accordingly.

Those southern Federalists who bucked the nationalist tide following the war found unlikely allies across the partisan divide. A small circle of mostly Virginian Old Republicans carried the banner of a form of localist conservatism, forged in opposition, into the era of Republican majorities to challenge the economic agenda of an activist government bent on national development. In *The Old Republicans: Southern Conservatism in the Age of Jefferson* (1965), Norman K. Risjord analyzes the true believers, men like John Taylor of Caroline and North Carolinian Nathaniel Macon, who embraced the states' rights, strict constructionist mentality of the Virginia and Kentucky Resolutions and refused to let go, even as their fellow Republicans took up the reins of government. While troubled by expressions of disloyalty to their party, the Old Republicans remained committed to the political ideals of limited government and personal liberty and the social ideals of hierarchy and agrarianism. One contribution of this book is Risjord's analysis of the evolution of states' rights ideology. He argues that the combination of economic depression and the Missouri Crisis transformed the ideology and absorbed the Old Republicans into a larger movement. What had, before 1819, been an oppositional philosophy based on constitutional interpretation, became a "self-conscious sectionalism" rooted in economic interests. The pessimistic conservatives of the Old Republican faction were "the missing link," Risjord argues, between the Antifederalists and the states' rights southerners of the Jacksonian era.

Risjord's depiction of the Old Republicans as a group sensitive to abuses of power and the corruptions associated with the growth of a commercial economy and preoccupied with preserving personal liberty fits squarely into a more recent historiographical trend. Broussard and Risjord, by emphasizing the power of ideology over party organization in the early republic, helped pave the way for a new generation of historians interested in the persistence of republican thought in American political discourse. The scholarship is voluminous, but two books offer close examinations of the pessimistic and optimistic strands of republican ideology and make convincing cases for the centrality of the southern experience in the development of that ideology. Both explore the uneasy relationship between republican ideology and a political and social context that was increasingly liberal and capitalistic.

Robert E. Shalhope analyzes the leading ideologue of agrarian republicanism in *John Taylor of Caroline: Pastoral Republican* (1980). In essays and books such as *Arator* and *Constructions Construed and Constitutions Vindicated*, Taylor laid out a cogent defense of agrarian society against the private corruptions of a commercializing society enamored of the artificial wealth of the "paper system" of banks and against the abuses of public power by a government grown too active. Shalhope demonstrates the ways in which Taylor's world view grew out of both his Virginia upbringing and his commitment to republican ideals. Devoted to his plantation world and its promise of harmonious economic relations and productive wealth within a context of stable social hierarchies, Taylor was alarmed by the economic changes of the early nineteenth century, especially as Congress and John Marshall's Supreme Court launched their platform of national development after the War of 1812. Fearing that "paper Speculation and executive partronage" would overwhelm "agriculture and publick economy," Taylor advocated both scientific farming and governmental policies that would support, not destroy, agriculture (Shalhope 1980: 185). The continued good health of agrarian society would ensure the maintenance of popular virtues, while the separation of government from capitalist development would prevent corruptions and abuses of power. Both were necessary for the preservation of republican ideals.

Taylor represented an oppositional strand of republicanism that stood in sharp contrast to liberal capitalism, but other Republicans were more optimistic about economic change. In *The Elusive Republic: Political Economy in Jeffersonian America* (1980), Drew R. McCoy offers a sophisticated analysis of mainstream Jeffersonian ideology that explores the complex relationship between traditional republican ideals and the explosive economic growth of early nineteenth-century America. Social virtues were precariously balanced in an age of rapid change, Republicans believed. A simple economy based solely on subsistence farming could encourage indolence and retard civilizing progress, while a dynamic commercializing economy might lead to corruption and popular addiction to luxury. Seeking a middle path, Jefferson and his allies envisioned an "empire of liberty," an expansive form of republicanism based on the opening of western land and the free trade of agricultural exports and imported manufactured goods. Abundant land and free trade would unleash the energies of the American people, creating a dynamic and growing economy, but would also prevent the social decay of industrialization by keeping commerce "within 'the bounds prescribed by nature'" (McCoy 1980: 158). This commitment to the "empire of liberty" repeatedly led Jeffersonians away from their original philosophy of limited government and contributed directly to the aggressive nationalism of westward expansion, exemplified by the Louisiana Purchase, and the troubled economic relationship with England, which led to Jefferson's embargo and war. Although McCoy's perspective is national in scope, his analysis of Jeffersonian attempts to reconcile agrarianism with economic change by encouraging western settlement and free trade is especially pertinent to the history of the early-republic South.

Students interested in the ideological complexities of Jeffersonian America would benefit from a close investigation of Jefferson himself. Numerous biographies are available, but another place to start would be the collection of essays in *Jeffersonian Legacies* (1993), edited by Peter S. Onuf. Originally presented at a conference celebrating Jefferson's 250th birthday, these essays illustrate the contradictory nature of a man who, as Michael Lienesch notes, later generations claimed as a democratic champion of popular sovereignty and social equality and a conservative who stressed individual liberties and limited government. Two of the essays in this volume connect the contradictions within Jefferson to the broader tensions of an age of explosive economic and geographic growth. Walter LaFeber echoes McCoy in his essay on Jeffersonian foreign policy. Beginning with the contention that the central problem facing the new nation was how to "order and control American expansion and foreign affairs" (Onuf 1993: 371), LaFeber argues that Jefferson's "empire of liberty" precipitated a series of foreign-policy crises that ultimately undermined Jeffersonian ideals. Responses such as the Embargo and the declaration of war against England not only led Jefferson and his successors away from their traditional philosophy of limited government, but also encouraged the rapid development of a financial and industrial infrastructure. Those economic changes posed a serious challenge to agrarianism, LaFeber argues, leaving Jefferson embittered about the transformations of his republic. John Lauritz Larson also examines Jefferson's contradictory legacy by focusing on the possibilities and limitations of nationalism. John C. Calhoun and Henry Clay, leaders of the second generation of Republicans, applauded the rapid westward expansion encouraged by Jefferson's "empire of liberty" but also worried about the possibility of sectional fragmentation. So they embarked on an ambitious legislative program of federally financed internal improvements, seeking, in the words of Calhoun, "to 'bind the republic together with a perfect system of roads and canals'" (Onuf 1993: 341). But they ran headlong into the opposition of Republicans devoted to Jeffersonian orthodoxy who were wary of any attempt to expand the limited powers of the national government or to erode state sovereignty. Calhoun and Clay's efforts, inspired by the optimistic strand of Jeffersonian nationalism, ultimately were frustrated by the legacy of Jeffersonian paranoia about the dangers of governmental power.

If Jefferson was a sometimes reluctant proponent of national expansion, he also played an important role in defining citizenship and the boundaries of inclusion in the nation. Joyce Appleby's essay in *Jeffersonian Legacies* focuses on Jefferson's concept of natural rights, the foundation of his belief in popular sovereignty and inevitability of American liberation from the constraints of tradition. But that emphasis on natural rights, as expansive as it was, also blinded Jefferson to the full possibilities of freedom and citizenship, for he believed that nature, not society, placed women and African-Americans in subordinate positions. The "natural" dependence of those groups upon the support of independent white men prevented their full inclusion in the new nation. While Appleby argues that Jefferson and his society were caught within the limitations of their beliefs, Paul Finkelman portrays a man unwilling "to transcend his economic interests" to extend his libertarian ideals to slaves, both his own and the South's (Onuf 1993: 181). Jefferson might have declared the birth of a nation in 1776, but he was fundamentally a sectional man, Finkelman argues in his essay, preoccupied above all with protecting slavery.

Finkelman's indictment of Jefferson for his failure to act on his misgivings about slavery is a more strident reflection of a common historiographical theme that the early republic represented a lost opportunity. As the northern states began to abolish slavery and Virginia slaveholders with troubled consciences manumitted their slaves and considered emancipation laws in the 1780s and early 1790s, national freedom seemed within reach, a number of historians argue. But racism and the tremendous economic and geographic expansion that gave rise to the cotton kingdom overwhelmed those tentative gropings toward abolition in the upper South, leaving the nation divided soon after its birth. Three historians, Winthrop Jordan, David Brion Davis, and William W. Freehling, use Jefferson as a symbol of the ambivalence of a nation balanced on the edge of freedom and slavery.

In *White Over Black* (1969) Jordan argues that Jefferson's ambivalence about slavery stemmed, not from sectional or economic interests, but from his deep-rooted belief in black inferiority, a subject Jordan explores in detail. By centering the dilemma of slavery around race, Jordan pulls Jefferson from the South and restores him to the nation as "an effective sounding board for his culture" (Jordan 1969: 429). But it was in the South that the limitations of the postrevolutionary antislavery impulse were most deeply felt during the Age of Jefferson. The contagion of disorderly liberty unleashed by the French Revolution encouraged a conservative backlash in the region, especially as refugees from the Saint Domingue slave rebellion flooded into Charleston in the 1790s. At the same time, Eli Whitney's cotton gin and the opening of the Gulf states to settlement boosted slavery's economic fortunes and carried the institution deep into the Southwest, linking enslavement to the national experience of expansion. Foreign events and economic changes eroded support for abolition, but Jordan emphasizes the moral failings of Founding Fathers like Jefferson. Their inability to act upon their ideals crippled the antislavery movement and prevented the unfolding of emancipation "as a glorious triumph" and "capstone of the Revolution" (ibid: 374).

David Brion Davis questions whether there really was any opportunity for emancipation to be lost in the 1790s and offers a much more skeptical look at the ideals of Jefferson and his revolutionary generation in his classic book *The Problem of Slavery in the Age of Revolution, 1770–1823* (1975). While Davis acknowledges Jefferson's private misgivings about slavery, he stresses the man's failure to support abolition publically, arguing that Jefferson's "icy caution" and "immense silence" set a conservative precedent for the next generation (Davis 1975: 176, 179). The revolutionary ideals embraced by Jefferson might have encouraged some doubt about the morality of a slaveholding republic, but those same ideals also set real limits on emancipation. Because republicanism permeated the political culture of postrevolutionary America, "any scheme of emancipation ran the risk of undermining property, of increasing the powers of government, and thus of endangering the very foundation of liberty" (ibid: 259). Davis locates the one true challenge to slavery not in the intellectual ferment of revolutionary Enlightenment, but in the evangelical revival that swept through the South before and after the war. But Baptist and Methodist opposition to slavery weakened around the turn of the century. That brief period of dissent ultimately strengthened slavery, Davis argues, because it demonstrated the South's ability "to resolve a moral challenge by assimilating and transmuting it" (ibid: 211).

Winthrop Jordan and David Brion Davis portray Jefferson as a connecting bridge between an early-republic South when apologists defended slavery as a necessary evil and the Jacksonian South when ardent sectionalists trumpeted slavery as a positive good. While Davis faults Jordan for exaggerating postrevolutionary antislavery sentiment, both agree that the Jefferson who failed to act on his misgivings faded from view in the 1820s, along with whatever vestiges of revolutionary doubt that might have existed, to be replaced by John C. Calhoun.

William W. Freehling argues in *The Road to Disunion* (1990) that it was the power of Jefferson's doubts and not the weakness of his actions that made him the "most dominating Southerner" all the way to the point of secession in 1860. Jefferson embodied the Upper South's indecision about slavery, which Freehling terms a commitment to "Conditional Termination" of the institution. Jefferson "would terminate nothing…if conditions seemed to him wrong" (Freehling 1990: 122). Those conditions for emancipation included colonization of freed blacks and a process gradual enough to prevent social convulsions and to ease the financial burdens of slaveholders. Freehling's depiction of Jefferson as "a reformer trembling at reforms" (ibid: 127), forever skeptical that conditions would ever be right for emancipation, is reminiscent of Winthrop Jordan's portrayal of the man. The real success of *The Road to Disunion* lies in the broader social and political context in which Freehling analyzes Jefferson, especially the impact of national expansion. Eli Whitney's invention of the cotton gin in 1793 and westward settlement created a cotton empire and revitalized slavery in the early nineteenth century, but that economic and geographic growth exacerbated sectional tensions within the South. The Upper South became increasingly white with the sale of slaves to the cotton plantations of the Deep South, especially after Congress banned the African slave trade in 1808. Maryland and Virginia, once home to 60 percent of the South's slaves in 1790, contained only 18 percent by 1860. This diffusion of slavery south and southwestward fueled Jeffersonian dreams of a white republic without slavery, created *naturally*, without the social and political upheaval of emancipation. But diffusion also left southerners committed to slavery wondering if they could count on the support of the Upper South in any political struggle over the "peculiar institution." Outside pressure could mute, but not erase, that sectional tension. When northern politicians sought to impose gradual emancipation upon Missouri in 1819, the South rallied in defense of slavery's expansion. But expansion could serve two different purposes; John C. Calhoun would "expand slavery to perpetuate it," while "Jefferson would diffuse the institution to end it" (Freehling 1990: 156). The persistence of that weak-hearted cautious reform so exemplified by Jefferson, Freehling argues, motivated extremists to search for ways to test the resolve of the Upper South, to find ways to create a united South in defense of slavery.

Historians recently have enriched our understanding of the place of the South in the new nation by diverting attention away from the region as a whole and focusing on particular states and communities. The more narrow bounds of their studies might obscure the broader strokes of tension between the South and the North, but they more fully illuminate the political impact of national development in all its complex details. They help us understand the ways in which geographic expansion, the market revolution, and political ideology and partisanship transformed the early-republic South.

In *Politics on the Periphery: Factions and Parties in Georgia, 1783–1806* (1986) George R. Lamplugh asks two simple questions. Did Georgians react most to national issues or local affairs in their politics, and were those politics organized around factions or parties? His answers to those questions offer a more subtle and complicated portrayal of the emergence of the First Party System, one that transcends the usual focus on the high political competition in Congress between Hamiltonians and Jeffersonians. Lamplugh argues that factions centered around particular leaders and local issues formed in the 1780s and persisted well into the 1790s. National policies did play a role. For example, the Washington administration's treaty with the Creeks in 1790 guaranteeing Indian control of much of the western land claimed by Georgia angered many in the state. While that hostility made many Georgians anti-Federalist in the early 1790s, it did not turn them into Democratic-Republicans; party organization remained weak at the nation's periphery. But the land hunger of speculators and settlers in those years after Whitney's cotton gin opened up the economic possibilities of the Southwest proved a defining issue. It was the Yazoo scandal of 1794–5, the sale of millions of acres of western land, that upset the political balance in Georgia and eventually led to the development of parties in the state. Senator James Jackson adroitly manipulated popular outrage at the state legislature's corrupt bargain with speculators to forge a powerful faction and then helped transform that faction into a party by aligning himself with the Jeffersonian Republicans in the late 1790s. The small numbers of Federalists centered in Savannah and Augusta could not compete with Georgia's dominant Republican Party. But even as he acknowledges the formation of party politics in Georgia, Lamplugh emphasizes their fragility. When Senator Jackson unexpectedly died in 1806, his Republican "machine" split, once again, into competing factions organized around the ambitions of George Troup, William Crawford, and John Clark.

Rachel N. Klein looks at the evolution of political parties in early-republic South Carolina but pays more attention to social change than does Lamplugh. She emphasizes the role of economic development in muting sectional tensions within South Carolina in her book, *Unification of a Slave State: The Rise of the Planter Class in the South Carolina Backcountry, 1760–1808* (Klein 1990). Historians interested in the transformation of the Carolina backcountry from a yeoman region at odds with the plantation lowcountry to a willing ally in a slave-based society have traditionally traced a simple story. Yeomen became planters when Whitney's cotton gin made upland cotton profitable; and the increasing number of slaves working the upcountry fields marked the social unification that made political reform possible, resulting in the constitutional reform of 1808 giving the backcountry a more favorable apportionment in the state legislature. Lacy Ford's (1988) superb analysis of South Carolina's antebellum political culture begins with this transformed upcountry. Klein, however, sets out to trace a more complex story, although she too ultimately acknowledges the importance of cotton's expansion.

Klein is primarily interested in the role played by backcountry elites in the decades before the cotton boom. Upcountry planters balanced concerns of region and class, forging connections to their yeomen neighbors while simultaneously maintaining their economic and social ties to the more aristocratic coastal elite. They played a mediating role in a state fractured along sectional lines, but the apportionment rules that gave the coastal elite disproportionate political power made their position precarious. The backcountry elite championed constitutional reform and equitable representation of their region, solidifying their support among the yeomen, but the elites also were careful not to push too hard lest they alienate the lowcountry planters. That local sectional split contributed to the emerging partisanship of the 1790s as backcountry elites gravitated toward the Republican Party while many of their coastal counterparts remained Federalist. Those Federalists viewed the backcountry, with its preponderance of nonslaveholding yeomen and its Republican political culture, with alarm; and the French Revolution and the subsequent slave uprising in Saint Dominque only intensified those fears. By the early nineteenth century the expansion of cotton cultivation and slavery facilitated political unity within South Carolina, building on the sectional ties initiated by the backcountry elite in the preceding decades. As more and more yeomen purchased slaves in order to plant cotton, coastal fears of an uncertain commitment to slavery in the upcountry faded. That shared commitment to slave-based agriculture, more than anything else, led to the constitutional reform of 1808 that granted the backcountry more representation.

Lamplugh and Klein both explore the ways in which the economic development of land, either through speculation or the cultivation of cash-crops, transformed the political systems of Georgia and South Carolina. In *How the West Was Lost: The Transformation of Kentucky from Daniel Boone to Henry Clay* (1996), Stephen Aron examines the political and social impact of the clash of competing interests struggling over control of land and its rich resources in frontier Kentucky. He traces the transformation of Kentucky from a borderland society of hunters, "a crossroads where Indian and European cultures collided" and also "coincided" (Aron 1996: 3), to a complex, settled society committed to market agriculture and dynamic economic growth. That process of American "conquest, colonization, and consolidation" (ibid: 1) of the frontier is reminiscent of Abernethy's *The South in the New Nation*. But while Abernethy tells a political story of western migration with the federal government playing a major role, Aron focuses almost exclusively on the internal dynamics of social and economic change within Kentucky and, like Klein, emphasizes sectional and class tensions.

The two forces that propelled Kentucky from Daniel Boone's world of hunters to Henry Clay's world of planter-capitalists were the expansion of legislative and judicial legal authority and the avid pursuit of economic opportunity. Both processes were dominated by, and favored, settlers most committed to a more hierarchical and market-oriented society, but change did not happen overnight. Yeoman farmers predominated when Kentucky reached statehood in the 1790s, and many were ambivalent about economic growth. Frustration over the complex tangle of land claims left over from the days when Kentucky was Virginia's frontier fueled popular resentment toward speculators; many settlers harbored antislavery sentiments and hostility toward the planter elite. Still, Kentucky entered the new century with the gentry's rights to land and slaves secure in part because the legal system worked in their favor and because expanded economic opportunities widened the base of support for the emerging market-oriented economic system. Geographic divisions persisted in the early nineteenth century. Henry Clay's Bluegrass region around Lexington was home to a slaveholding gentry committed to a diversified economy of cash-crop agriculture, commerce, and manufacturing, while the Green River region, Kentucky's "best poor man's country" (Aron 1996: 150), remained a bastion of smaller, nonslaveholding farmers. But over the first two decades of the nineteenth century, economic development and the planting of tobacco blurred the lines of distinction between the two regions. Green River legislators stopped resisting the banking system that provided the financial infrastructure for the Bluegrass region and began working "to secure a fair share of its spoils for themselves and their constituents" (ibid: 169). Aron's argument that political consolidation followed the expansion of market agriculture is reminiscent of Klein's depiction of early nineteenth-century South Carolina. But in tracing the story of Kentucky from the conquest of Indian hunters, through the colonization of the frontier by yeoman farmers, to the consolidation of a gentry-dominated, slave-based, market-oriented society, Aron emphasizes the worlds that were lost when a portion of the West became the South.

The inexorable march westward of the market revolution took several decades in Kentucky, but in parts of the Old Southwest wilderness became plantations in several years. Daniel S. Dupre's *Transforming the Cotton Frontier: Madison County, Alabama, 1800–1840* (1997) examines one such frontier and explores the political and social impact of economic upheaval during the settlement period. Small farmers and planters with their slaves flocked to Madison County on the Tennessee River in North Alabama in the years just before and after the War of 1812. The prime cotton land of the region encouraged widespread speculation and fueled ordinary farmers' dreams of wealth, especially during the postwar economic boom. Many fell deeply into debt as they bought high-priced government land on credit, confident that high cotton prices would carry them through. Instead, the panic of 1819 struck and its impact was great. The tremendous debt burdening settlers throughout the western frontier, but especially in the South, forced the federal government to reform its land-sale policies. The panic also transformed the political landscape of Madison County, polarizing the community around the different priorities of debtor relief and economic revitalization. The *Huntsville Democrat*, voice of the county's farmers and planters, lashed out against the "royalists" of the community, the merchants and bankers whose speculative activities had brought economic disaster down upon the heads of the ordinary citizens. Merchants and bankers decried those attacks and called for community consensus around a platform of economic recovery through internal improvements and expanded credit. The conjunction of westward expansion and economic crisis shaped popular attitudes toward a whole host of political issues, from banking to government-financed internal improvements. Dupre argues that the ideological foundations of the Jacksonian party system began to coalesce in the contentious decade of the 1820s as citizens debated the causes of and solutions to the panic of 1819.

Recent studies of southern states and communities in the early republic have shifted the historiographical focus from the sectional strains caused by the geographic, economic, and political development of the new nation to tensions internal to the South. The implications of that shift are clear. Abernethy's descriptions of the separatist schemes that accompanied westward settlement and Sydnor's argument that the resurgence in states' rights localism was a reaction to the federal government's activist economic agenda are examples of attempts to sketch out the broad contours of the relationship between nationalism and sectionalism. But historians like Lamplugh, Klein, Aron, and Dupre are less interested in the place of the South within the new nation than in the impact national consolidation had on particular communities and people within the South. All place the transformation of various backcountries at the heart of their arguments because it is there that one can see the pressures of national development in all its guises. Two pictures emerge from these state and local studies. The first is of the backcountry as contested ground where squatters clashed with speculators, planters suspected the loyalties of nonslaveholders, and yeomen resented the pretensions of the elite. Southerners who confronted the development of the backcountry fought over legislative representation and apportionment and debated large questions of political economy and, in the process, helped to shape the ideologies and organizations of the First and Second Party Systems. But if backcountries were contested ground, they also were territories that were transformed. The second picture to emerge from these books is of the inexorable expansion of the market revolution in its southern form. Slavery and cash-crop agriculture, especially cotton, marched west with settlers, and that economic transformation played a major role in the consolidation of the new nation.

African-American slaves and Native Americans suffered most from the expansion of a market economy across the South because the cotton kingdom was built on Indian land and slave labor. Their history does not have a prominent place in the story of the South's role in the new nation. Political historians generally have not looked at southern history through the eyes of slaves and Indians; both groups were barred from citizenship and thus were not political actors in the conventional sense. And the antebellum period, not the early-republic years, have drawn the most attention from historians interested in exploring slavery at its fullest stage of development or examining the struggle over Indian removal. But two historians, William G. McLoughlin and Douglas R. Egerton, have written books that treat Indians and slaves as political actors. They suggest that a close look at those most dispossessed by national development will reveal the limits of citizenship in the early republic and the contested nature of national identity itself.

In *Cherokee Renascence in the New Republic* (1986) McLoughlin delves into the close relationship between shifting American attitudes toward the Indians and the cultural and political transformation of the Cherokee nation between 1783 and 1833. Although he pays attention to the workings of government policy and its impact on Cherokee politics, McLoughlin is more interested in changing concepts of nationalism among both Americans and Indians. The operative Indian policy from George Washington to John Quincy Adams was "civilization," an effort to Americanize Indians through education, Christianity, and the promotion of farming in lieu of hunting. McLoughlin argues that the "civilization" policy was rooted in Enlightenment beliefs in the universality of human existence and in a postrevolutionary optimism that Indians could be integrated into the American nation. But after 1815 pressures began to build for Indian removal instead of absorption. While acknowledging that the land hunger of southern settlers contributed to that pressure, McLoughlin emphasizes the importance of shifting cultural concepts of national identity. Americans were beginning to embrace a romantic nationalism that was more "particularistic," and racial categories took on more significance among a people trying to discover "who they were by deciding who they were not" (McLoughlin 1986: xvii). Cherokee "civilization" and integration seemed less plausible or desirable, McLoughlin argues, when "republican ideology ceased to be universal and became exclusionary" (ibid: xvii).

While American concepts of nationalism were shifting in the years following the War of 1812, the Cherokee were becoming a nation for the first time. Although the Cherokee had fought against American independence, many embraced the "civilization" policy and some entertained the hope of integration and citizenship. But by the 1820s they had abandoned those hopes and begun to develop a national identity that "rested upon a cultural heritage imbedded in history, language, culture, and a distinct and identifiable 'homeland' " (ibid). The Cherokee became adept at using their understanding of American politics to create governmental institutions and a constitution to resist removal and preserve their own ethnic nationalism. Ironically, those efforts forced the Cherokee to turn to the federal government for support against the southern leaders who used states' rights to promote Indian removal. The Cherokee understood that their fate hung in the balance between a national commitment to the federal treaty power and states' desires to control the territory within their borders. The election of Andrew Jackson in 1828 tilted that balance in favor of the southern states, sealing the fate of the Cherokee nation.

Like the Cherokee, African-American slaves were both part of, and separate from, the larger society. In *Gabriel's Rebellion: The Virginia Slave Conspiracies of 1800 and 1802* (1993) and *He Shall Go Out Free: The Lives of Denmark Vesey* (1999), Douglas Egerton offers biographies of two men who plotted the most ambitious and complex slave rebellions in American history. Both Gabriel, a skilled blacksmith who often travelled from the countryside to work in Richmond and sometimes shared his master's surname of Prosser, and Denmark Vesey, a former slave who had purchased his freedom and lived in Charleston, were exposed to a wider world of political discourse, and both were conscious of divisions within white society. Gabriel was caught up in the sharp partisan debate that preceded the election of 1800, while Vesey was heartened to read newspaper accounts of northern opposition to the spread of slavery westward during the Missouri Controversy of 1819–20. Each also faced similar difficulties bridging the gap between urban and country slaves in their recruitment efforts. But Gabriel and Vesey lived in different worlds. When Gabriel travelled to Richmond, he entered a "back-alley culture" of white and black artisans who worked together and socialized in neighborhood grog shops, a culture where class appeared to supersede race (Egerton 1993: 30). Gabriel and his fellow artisans were steeped in a more radical, artisanal variation of Democratic-Republicanism, which identified Richmond's Federalist merchants as the enemy, not just for their political beliefs, but because their control of capital and raw materials weakened the economic power of the laboring classes. Vesey, on the other hand, lived in a far more segregated culture, one that taught him that resistance to oppression sprang from a people, not a class. He had long been fascinated by the Saint Domingue revolution of the 1790s, but even more influential were his leadership experiences in the African Methodist Episcopal Church.

The different social worlds of Gabriel and Vesey shaped the goals of their rebellions, revealing the contested nature of American nationalism. Gabriel thought that his rebel army could take Richmond in 1800 and negotiate, not just for their freedom, but for political and economic equality. Caught up in the radical rhetoric of Democratic-Republicanism, he entertained hopes that white artisans would join his strike against the Federalist merchants, that together they would transform the political order. Like the Cherokee, Gabriel could embrace dreams of integration into a perfected American society because of his experiences in Richmond's "back-alley culture." But Egerton also makes clear that the slave rebels, by conspiring to fight for citizenship, were true revolutionaries. When one of Gabriel's compatriots invoked the name of General Washington at his trial and stated that "I have adventured my life in endeavouring to obtain the liberty of my countrymen, and am a willing sacrifice in their cause" (ibid: 102), he challenged the very heart of American nationalism. Denmark Vesey lived in a more deeply entrenched slave society and was steeped in the traditions of the black church and thus was far more skeptical of integration than Gabriel. He knew that American nationalism precluded African-American citizenship and that freedom for enslaved blacks could only be achieved through escape. Vesey's plan to attack Charleston in 1822 was not an attempt to transform American society but instead was to be the first step in an exodus from the land of slavery to freedom in Haiti.

Historians of the early-republic South have long been interested in the close relationship between national development and sectionalism. For example, they have shown how the resurgence of states' rights politics and strict constructionism in the years after the War of 1812 grew out of reactions to the nationalistic economic policies of Congress and demonstrated that westward expansion evoked threats of national fragmentation or encouraged a prickly defense of southern interests in the case of Missouri. Those older staples of political history deserve deeper analyses that might, for instance, consider the ideological connections between voters and political leaders, or explore the wider contexts of economic change and a shifting political culture. The work of recent historians suggests, however, that we should broaden our concept of sectionalism when considering the impact of nation-building in the early republic. The rapid settlement of an expanding southern borderlands, the dynamic economic transformations of the market revolution, and the emerging partisanship and struggle over the growing power of the national government all shaped, and in turn were shaped by, divisions within the South. One cannot understand the political history of the South in the new nation without focusing on the complexities of region, class, and race in southern society and their relationship with national development.

BIBLIOGRAPHY

Abernethy, Thomas P. 1961: *The South in the New Nation, 1789–1819*. Baton Rouge: Louisiana State University Press.

Adams, Charles Francis (ed.) 1970: *Memoirs of John Quincy Adams, Comprising Portions of His Diary From 1795 to 1848*, 12 vols. New York: AMS Press.

Adams, John 1959: *The Adams–Jefferson Letters: The Complete Correspondence between Thomas Jefferson and Abigail and John Adams*, 2 vols. Edited by Lester J. Cappon. Chapel Hill: University of North Carolina Press.

Appleby, Joyce 1993: Introduction: Jefferson and His Complex Legacy. In Peter S. Onuf (ed.), *Jeffersonian Legacies*. Charlottesville: University Press of Virginia.

Aron, Stephen Anthony 1996: *How the West Was Lost: The Transformation of Kentucky from Daniel Boone to Henry Clay*. Baltimore: Johns Hopkins University Press.

Banning, Lance 1978: *The Jeffersonian Persuasion: Evolution of a Party Ideology*. Ithaca, NY: Cornell University Press.

Beeman, Richard R. 1984: *The Evolution of the Southern Backcountry: A Case Study of Lunenburg County, Virginia, 1746–1832*. Philadelphia: University of Pennsylvania Press.

Broussard, James H. 1978: *The Southern Federalists, 1800–1816*. Baton Rouge: Louisiana State University Press.

Buel, Richard, Jr. 1972: *Securing the Revolution: Ideology in American Politics, 1789–1815*. Ithaca, NY: Cornell University Press.

Calhoun, John C. 1959: *The Papers of John C. Calhoun*, 24 vols. Edited by Robert Lee Meriwether, William Edwin Hemphill, and Clyde Norman Wilson. Columbia: University of South Carolina Press.

Clark, Thomas D. and Guice, John D. W. 1989: *Frontiers in Conflict: The Old Southwest, 1795–1830*. Albuquerque: University of New Mexico Press.

Clay, Henry 1959: *The Papers of Henry Clay*, 8 vols. Edited by James F. Hopkins. Lexington: University of Kentucky Press.

Cooper, William J., Jr. 1983: *Liberty and Slavery: Southern Politics to 1860*. New York: Alfred A. Knopf.

Cox, Joseph W. 1972: *Champion of Southern Federalism: Robert Goodloe Harper of South Carolina*. Port Washington, NY: Kennikat Press.

Cunningham, Noble E., Jr. 1957: *The Jeffersonian Republicans: The Formation of Party Organization, 1789–1801*. Chapel Hill: University of North Carolina Press.

Cunningham, Noble E., Jr. 1978: *Circular Letters of Congressmen to Their Constituents, 1789–1829*, 3 vols. Chapel Hill: University of North Carolina Press.

Cunningham, Noble E., Jr. 1996: *The Presidency of James Monroe*. Lawrence: University of Kansas Press.

Dangerfield, George 1952: *The Era of Good Feelings*. New York: Harcourt, Brace & World.

Davis, David Brion 1975: *The Problem of Slavery in the Age of Revolution, 1770–1823*. Ithaca, NY: Cornell University Press.

Dupre, Daniel S. 1997: *Transforming the Cotton Frontier: Madison County, Alabama, 1800–1840*. Baton Rouge: Louisiana State University Press.

Egerton, Douglas R. 1993: *Gabriel's Rebellion: The Virginia Slave Conspiracies of 1800 and 1802*. Chapel Hill: University of North Carolina Press.

Egerton, Douglas R. 1999: *He Shall Go Out Free: The Lives of Denmark Vesey*. Madison: Madison House.

Elkins, Stanley and McKitrick, Eric L. 1993: *The Age of Federalism*. New York: Oxford University Press.

Ellis, Joseph J. 1997: *American Sphinx: The Character of Thomas Jefferson*. New York: Alfred A. Knopf.

Ellis, Richard 1971: *The Jeffersonian Crisis: Courts and Politics in the Young Republic*. New York: Oxford University Press.

Finkelman, Paul 1993: Jefferson and Slavery: "Treason Against the Hopes of the World." In Peter S. Onuf (ed.), *Jeffersonian Legacies*. Charlottesville: University Press of Virginia.

Finkelman, Paul 1996: *Slavery and the Founders: Race and Liberty in the Age of Jefferson*. Armonk: M. E. Sharpe.

Ford, Lacy K., Jr. 1988: *Origins of Southern Radicalism: The South Carolina Upcountry, 1800–1860*. New York: Oxford University Press.

Freehling, William W. 1990: *The Road to Disunion: vol. 1, Secessionists at Bay, 1776–1854*. New York: Oxford University Press.

Frey, Sylvia R. 1991: *Water from the Rock: Black Resistance in a Revolutionary Age*. Princeton, NJ: Princeton University Press.

Green, Michael D. 1982: *The Politics of Indian Removal: Creek Government and Society in Crisis*. Lincoln: University of Nebraska Press.

Heyrman, Christine Leigh 1997: *Southern Cross: The Beginnings of the Bible Belt*. New York: Alfred A. Knopf.

Hobson, Charles F. 1996: *The Great Chief Justice: John Marshall and the Rule of Law*. Lawrence: University Press of Kansas.

Hoffman, Ronald and Albert, Peter J. (eds.) 1996: *Launching the "Extended Republic": The Federalist Era*. Charlottesville: University Press of Virginia.

Jefferson, Thomas 1950: *Papers*, 27 vols. Edited by Julian P. Boyd, et al. Princeton, NJ: Princeton University Press.

Jefferson, Thomas 1964: *Notes on the State of Virginia*. Edited by Thomas Perkins Abernethy. New York: Harper & Row.

Jordan, Daniel P. 1983: *Political Leadership in Jefferson's Virginia*. Charlottesville: University Press of Virginia.

Jordan, Winthrop D. 1969: *White Over Black: American Attitudes Toward the Negro, 1550–1812*. Baltimore: Penguin Books.

Klein, Rachel N. 1990: *Unification of a Slave State: The Rise of the Planter Class in the South Carolina Backcountry, 1760–1808*. Chapel Hill: University of North Carolina Press.

Knupfer, Peter B. 1991: *The Union As It Is: Constitutional Unionism and Sectional Compromise, 1787–1861*. Chapel Hill: University of North Carolina Press.

Lafeber, Walter 1993: Jefferson and an American Foreign Policy. In Peter S. Onuf (ed.), *Jeffersonian Legacies*. Charlottesville: University Press of Virginia.

Lamplugh, George R. 1986: *Politics on the Periphery: Factions and Parties in Georgia, 1783–1806*. Newark; London: University of Delaware Press; Associated University Presses.

Larson, John Lauritz 1993: Jefferson's Union and the Problem of Internal Improvements. In Peter S. Onuf (ed.), *Jeffersonian Legacies*. Charlottesville: University Press of Virginia.

Lewis, James E., Jr. 1998: *The American Union and the Problem of Neighborhood: The United States and the Collapse of the Spanish Empire, 1783–1829*. Chapel Hill: University of North Carolina Press.

Lewis, Jan 1983: *The Pursuit of Happiness: Family and Values in Jefferson's Virginia*. Cambridge and New York: Cambridge University Press.

Lienesch, Michael 1993: Thomas Jefferson and the American Democratic Experience: The Origins of the Partisan Press, Popular Parties, and Public Opinion. In Peter S. Onuf (ed.), *Jeffersonian Legacies*. Charlottesville: University Press of Virginia.

McColley, Robert 1964: *Slavery and Jeffersonian Virginia*. Urbana: University of Illinois Press. 2nd edn, 1973.

McCoy, Drew R. 1980: *The Elusive Republic: Political Economy in Jeffersonian America*. New York: W. W. Norton.

McCoy, Drew R. 1989: *The Last of the Fathers: James Madison and the Republican Legacy*. Cambridge: Cambridge University Press.

McLoughlin, William G. 1986: *Cherokee Renascence in the New Republic*. Princeton, NJ: Princeton University Press.

Madison, James 1962: *Papers*, 17 vols. Edited by William T. Hutchinson, William M. E. Rachal, and Robert Allen Rutland. Chicago: University of Chicago Press.

Marshall, John 1974: *The Papers of John Marshall*, 8 vols. Edited by Herbert A. Johnson, Charles T. Cullen, and Charles F. Hobson. Chapel Hill: University of North Carolina Press.

Mathews, Donald G. 1977: *Religion in the Old South*. Chicago: University of Chicago Press.

Matthews, Richard K. 1984: *The Radical Politics of Thomas Jefferson: A Revisionist View*. Lawrence: University Press of Kansas.

Melton, Buckner F., Jr. 1998: *The First Impeachment: The Constitution's Framers and the Case of Senator William Blount*. Macon: Mercer University Press.

Miller, F. Thornton 1994: *Juries and Judges Versus the Law: Virginia's Provincial Legal Perspective, 1783–1828*. Charlottesville: University Press of Virginia.

Miller, John Chester 1977: *The Wolf by the Ears: Thomas Jefferson and Slavery*. New York: Free Press.

Onuf, Peter S. (ed.) 1993: *Jeffersonian Legacies.* Charlottesville: University Press of Virginia.

Owsley, Frank Lawrence, Jr. and Smith, Gene A. 1997: *Filibusters and Expansionists: Jeffersonian Manifest Destiny, 1800–1821.* Tuscaloosa: University of Alabama Press.

Pearson, Edward A. (ed.) 1999: *Designs against Charleston: The Trial Record of the Denmark Vesey Slave Conspiracy of 1822.* Chapel Hill: University of North Carolina Press.

Peterson, Merrill D. 1970: *Thomas Jefferson and the New Nation: A Biography.* New York: Oxford University Press.

Peterson, Merrill D. 1987: *The Great Triumvirate: Webster, Clay, and Calhoun.* New York: Oxford University Press.

Remini, Robert V. 1977: *Andrew Jackson and the Course of American Empire, 1767–1821.* New York: Harper & Row.

Risjord, Norman K. 1965: *The Old Republicans: Southern Conservatism in the Age of Jefferson.* New York: Columbia University Press.

Robinson, Donald L. 1971: *Slavery in the Structure of American Politics, 1765–1820.* New York: Harcourt Brace Jovanovich.

Rose, Lisle A. 1968: *Prologue to Democracy: The Federalists in the South, 1789–1800.* Lexington: University of Kentucky Press.

Shalhope, Robert E. 1980: *John Taylor of Caroline: Pastoral Republican.* Columbia: University of South Carolina Press.

Sharp, James Roger 1993: *American Politics in the Early Republic: The New Nation in Crisis.* New Haven, CT: Yale University Press.

Sidbury, James 1997: *Ploughshares into Swords: Race, Rebellion, and Identity in Gabriel's Virginia, 1730–1810.* New York: Cambridge University Press.

Sydnor, Charles S. 1948: *The Development of Southern Sectionalism, 1819–1848.* Baton Rouge: Louisiana State University Press.

Taylor, John 1992: *Tyranny Unmasked.* Edited by Frederick Thornton Miller. Indianapolis: Liberty Fund.

Travers, Len 1997: *Celebrating the Fourth: Independence Day and the Rites of Nationalism in the Early Republic.* Amherst: University of Massachusetts Press.

CHAPTER SEVEN

The Plantation Economy

MARK M. SMITH

ANTEBELLUM southern society was defined in no small part by the shaping and working of large tracts of land whose soil was tilled and staples tended by enslaved African-American laborers. This was, in short, a society dependent on what historians have variously referred to as the plantation system, the southern slave economy or, more commonly, the plantation economy.

From the end of the Revolution until the outbreak of the Civil War in 1861, the plantation economy, spurred by the invention and subsequent refinement of the cotton gin in the 1790s, powered its way westward. Thanks to burgeoning demand for cotton by New England and British textile manufacturers, short-staple cotton quickly overshadowed other crops by the 1820s. Indigo "was a thing of the past; hemp was of negligible importance; tobacco was losing in the east what it gained in the west; rice and sea-island cotton were stationary," and although sugar production "was growing in local intensity" in Louisiana especially, "upland cotton was 'king' of a rapidly expanding realm" (Phillips 1918: 205). Slaveholders' demand for labor increased apace. The number of southern slaves jumped from under one million in 1790 to roughly four million by 1860. By the middle decades of the antebellum period, the Old South had matured into a slave society whose plantation economy affected virtually every social and economic relation within the South.

Given the centrality of the plantation economy and the precision one has come to expect of historians who deal with matters economic, it is surprising that defining this institution, even in a mildly rigorous way, has at times proven problematic. Although there is agreement that plantations tended to organize labor by the gang system and cultivate profitable staples (principally cotton) for export, there is only a brittle consensus on other, fundamental matters. For example, both historians and contemporaries sometimes disagreed on what constituted a plantation and a planter. While some historians consider ownership of twenty or twenty-five bondpeople as the cutoff for planter status, planters themselves often defined plantership in terms that were location specific (Ransom and Sutch 1977: 332, n. 52; Smith 1998: 15–16). In Mississippi's Natchez District, where holdings tended to be large, possession of thirty or more slaves conferred planter status (Wayne 1990: 848; Fogel and Engerman 1974: 200). Even Ulrich B. Phillips, a historian who tended toward precision and detail, spoke vaguely of "Types of Large Plantations" (Phillips 1918: 228).

Disputes have not ended here. As the economic historian William N. Parker remarked in 1970, "Surrounding all studies of the American antebellum South, the subject of slavery lies like a great fetid swamp from which historians emerge like alligators to snap at one another" (Parker 1970: 1). One question in particular has been central to these snappings: was the plantation economy a profitable one? Freighted though it is with moral judgments about the efficiency of a historical enormity, this pivotal question has been the driving force behind the examination of the plantation economy for the past century. Embedded in this broad and admittedly clumsy question is a distinction that historians of the plantation economy tend to make and answer either implicitly or explicitly: was the plantation economy profitable for the individual planter (the micro-profitability of the business) and/or profitable for the southern economy as a whole (the macro-profitability as a system)? (Woodman 1963, 1972).

These questions are not new. They were debated with heated enthusiasm in the antebellum period and have lost none of their spark since (Phillips 1918: 344–58; Woodman 1963). The economic history of the plantation South, then, has one of the oldest pedigrees in historical writing on the Old South. Moreover, in a profession that sometimes prides itself on the rapid turnover of historical interpretations, some of the earliest work written on the subject has resounded for a relatively long time and, as such, it is important to examine some of it in detail.

Inasmuch as it helped shape debate up until the 1970s, Ulrich B. Phillips's *American Negro Slavery: A Survey of the Supply, Employment and Control of Negro Labor as Determined by the Plantation Regime*, first published in 1918 and since reprinted, has become something of a classic. Although Phillips was interested primarily in the micro-economics of plantation slavery, he also had a few things to say about the profitability of plantation slavery as a system. Phillips characterized the plantation business as economically inefficient. He maintained that masters' preoccupation with paternalism, their desire to promote social harmony among what masters liked to consider "their people," and slaves' putative inability to labor assiduously produced plantations that were only moderately profitable to individual masters. More damaging still was slavery's impact on the southern economy generally. As he put it: "A further influence of the plantation system was to hamper the growth of towns. . . . As for manufactures, the chronic demand of the planters for means with which to enlarge their scales of operations absorbed most of the capital that might otherwise have been available for factory promotion. A few cotton mills were built in the Piedmont where water power was abundant, and a few small ironworks and other industries; but the supremacy of agriculture was nowhere challenged" (Phillips 1918: 339–40). In other words, slavery's tendency to undermine the status of labor, its deterrence of white immigrant workers, its check on diversification into manufacturing and industrial pursuits, its dependence on northern capital, and the outpouring of capital from the South in the form of loans and planters' reliance on northern manufactured goods hurt the southern economy. Planters were to blame, primarily. Their obsession with the status of slave owning led to inflated prices for less than productive workers and their heavy focus on cotton-exhausted land. Because it was detrimental to individual planters and to the South generally, the plantation economy, suggested Phillips, was doomed to remain inefficient and counterproductive.

Phillips's contempt for black people was matched only by his respect for empirical research for, however racist *American Negro Slavery* may be, it is a meticulously researched volume. Although Phillips referred occasionally to census data, he was very careful not to use "the asseverations of politicians, pamphleteers, and aged survivors" because he thought them "unsafe even in supplement" (ibid: viii). On the whole, the work is characterized by its extensive use of qualitative evidence, its blending of social and economic history, and its broad treatment of the South as a whole.

Lewis C. Gray's monumental two-volume study, *History of Agriculture in the Southern United States to 1860*, published in 1933, came to some very different conclusions about the micro- and macro-profitability of the Old South's plantation economy. Gray began his work in 1908, and it is characterized by an abundance of detail and solid use of census data. Although he appeared to share some of Phillips's highly questionable assumptions about the nature of African-American labor, his more liberal view allowed him to see plantation slave labor as potentially and, at times, actually profitable. Gray agreed with Phillips that the southern plantation was a force for civilizing "ignorant savages" but, unlike Phillips, thought that the "training" provided by the plantation was effective. Phillips, he maintained, had "failed to allow for the progress made by [slaves] during the late ante bellum period" (Gray 1933, I: 467).

Gray challenged not only Phillips but also the work of classical economists who, Gray argued, incorrectly "assume[d] that all the laziness and incapacity exhibited by the Negro are ascribable to his status as a slave" (ibid: 462). True, conceded Gray, slavery inhibited economic diversification and the acquisition of skills by laborers, "but such qualities are not necessarily a severe handicap for an extractive economy." Consequently, Gray argued, "Frequently slave labor was very profitable" (ibid: 463). Gray came to this conclusion about the micro-efficiency of slavery because he believed that slaveholders' concentration on "a one-crop system," such as cotton, allowed them to routinize plantation production. Moreover, he suggested that within plantation agriculture no time was lost because crops required "year-round employment of labor" and that the problem of labor supervision was minimized by single-staple production which permitted the "employment of a large amount of labor on a small amount of land" (ibid).

Gray's evidence was impressive. His comparative analysis of farm wages paid to free laborers and hired slaves showed that "the superiority of white laborers was not sufficiently great to lead to a very notable difference in the valuation of the services of the two classes of labor" (ibid: 468). Indeed, argued Gray, slave labor was more competitive than free because the "appropriable surplus" of the former, by virtue of the fact that "the minimum level of competition in the case of slave labor was bare subsistence," was always greater than that of the latter (ibid: 474).

Gray was more ambivalent about the macro-economic effects of slavery. He did not believe that by the eve of the Civil War the South was about to be "strangled for lack of room to expand" (ibid: 476). Slave ownership had certainly become concentrated in fewer hands by 1860, but productive soil still existed; and Gray countered Phillips's point concerning the reduction in cotton prices and the over-capitalization of slaves with the argument that such a dual tendency was "only a temporary phenomenon" (ibid: 529–30, 476). But Gray did concede that slavery, and the political interests of the planter class who championed agriculture, placed limits on the region's ability to diversify. The South's failure to attract skilled immigrants, a scarcity of investment capital, and the almost total commitment to plantation agriculture as a way of life "afforded an effective check to the evolution of diversified industry" in the region (Gray 1933, II: 934). Although the South's investment in manufacturing increased by 76 percent between 1840 and 1850, it was "falling behind the rest of the country in relative amount of all manufacturing" (ibid: 935). By 1850 the South's manufacturing capital was only 17.6 percent of the total for the entire country. From this, Gray argued that: "Although slavery was profitable from an individual point of view and for certain uses conferred a competitive superiority as compared with free labor, its ultimate influence upon the economic well-being of the South was pernicious" (ibid: 940).

The South's macro-economic problems were due in part to slavery but also typical of any "predominantly agricultural country" (ibid). The sparseness of the population meant that roads, schools, and other basic infrastructure were lacking in the region. This, combined with "the absence of local centers of population and of local markets" and the virtually wholesale capitalization of southern labor, hurt the older plantations of the eastern seaboard particularly. In sum, slavery "retarded the development of the compensating conditions – immigration and industrial diversification – which in the North alleviated the 'growing pains' of agricultural expansion. Hence we have the near-paradox of an economic institution competitively effective under certain conditions, but essentially regressive in its influence on the socio-economic evolution of the section where it prevailed" (ibid: 942).

In many respects both Phillips and Gray, whatever their different emphases, shaped much of the debate about the nature of the plantation economy until the mid-1970s. With the notable exception of Kenneth M. Stampp's brief but insightful argument that "the high valuation of Negro labor during the 1850s was the best and most direct evidence of the continued profitability of slavery" and that slavery did not retard southern industrialization, most subsequent monographs argued that slavery's effect on the southern economy was negative (Stampp 1956: 414). Richard C. Wade's influential 1964 study of antebellum southern urbanization, for example, supported both Phillips and Gray in their contention that slavery was deleterious to the macro-economic growth of the region because, as Wade argued, the peculiar institution was fundamentally incompatible with urbanization. Wade showed that the relative cost of maintaining the peculiar institution (and policing slaves) in southern cities began to exceed the cost of plantation slavery by the 1850s. This, combined with heightened fears among whites of servile insurrection, served to retard the growth of southern urban centers.

Similarly, three years before Wade's study, Douglass C. North published *The Economic Growth of the United States 1790–1860*, which lent further support to the arguments advanced by Phillips and Gray concerning the plantation economy's generally negative effects on the region's economic development. Plantation slave labor and the "economic and social consequences of investment in this form of capital [slavery]," affected urbanization, income distribution, and economic profitability (North 1966: 122). North suggested that the heavy emphasis on cotton cultivation by planters was damaging to the region as a whole. True, apart from a huge slump in the mid-1840s, the price of cotton was never low enough to encourage planters to reallocate their labor and capital into some other endeavors. Indeed, part of the problem was that even with "the enormous growth in demand of the English cotton textile industry," the South's supply of cotton, primarily through rapid expansion westward between 1815 and 1839, outstripped demand (ibid: 124). But this, in turn, limited the profitability of cotton cultivation for certain planters, particularly those in the Old Southeast. Although the price of slaves increased over the antebellum period and southwestern plantations flourished, the heavy focus on cotton cultivation, especially on southwestern plantations in Texas, caused severe problems for the economy as a whole. Because slaves were capitalized labor, they did not earn income for themselves and, consequently, did not consume goods and services. This had the effect of limiting urban and industrial growth within the region. More importantly, the South's plantation economy was a dependent one basically because its focus on staple production discouraged planters from growing foodstuffs. As such, North argued, the South was forced to import much of its food from the Northwest. Whatever profits were made from plantation agriculture, then, were either reinvested in slaves or squandered on the purchasing of foodstuffs from outside the region, which resulted in a drain of capital from the South. More recent research has largely refuted North's argument and has shown that the South did not, for the most part, run large food deficits. In those few, usually urban, areas that did experience periodic deficits, shortfalls were met by imports of food from surplus-producing areas within the South itself (Fishlow 1964; Gallman 1970; Lindstrom 1970).

Phillips's argument that the plantation economy was unhealthy for both individual planters and the southern economy as a whole received support from unexpected quarters in the 1960s. Eugene D. Genovese's 1965 Marxist interpretation, *The Political Economy of Slavery: Studies in the Economy and Society of the Slave South*, relied on many of the same sources mined by Phillips and Gray and also treated the South as a whole. Genovese started from the premise that the Civil War was waged between two socially and economically distinct sections: a democratic, capitalist, efficient, northern economy and a southern social and economic order riddled with irrationalities. He noted that because masters owned labor for life, they found it difficult to allocate labor efficiently and flexibly in response to changes in demand. He also endorsed the point made by Gray and North that slavery necessarily limited the South's overall purchasing power. Wageless slaves could not purchase goods and services and so, unlike northern laborers, did not stimulate economic growth in the region's market economy. Planters only made things worse, maintained Genovese (echoing Phillips), because their commitment to slavery as a social system – their close identification with slave ownership as a reflection of their self-worth, status, and power – only encouraged them to buy more hands. Their consumption of slaves warped the process of economic reinvestment and this, combined with their heavy importation of northern and European manufactured goods, choked all but the most modest tendencies toward economic diversification in the Old South. Slavery and by extension the plantation economy, because it was controlled by a class of paternal, quasi-aristocratic masters who invested in slaves more out of identity and less out of profit, constituted a premodern force of impressive proportions. By championing this system, planters stunted the economic development of the Old South because they channeled capital away from industrial and urban pursuits. Plantations were not as productive or as efficient as they should have been for individual planters, Genovese maintained, following Wade's lead, not least because slaveholders feared the emergence of a skilled class of urban slave laborers who might resist their enslavement. In Genovese's formulation, then, plantation slavery proved unprofitable to individual planters and was damaging to the South's economic development generally.

While Genovese's *Political Economy of Slavery* was not the last to make this argument in the 1960s – Harold D. Woodman, for example, added support, again from a Marxist perspective, in 1968 by exploring the subservient role of cotton factors in the slaveholders' economy – Genovese's book represented the culmination of a traditional school of thought and methodology. Although Genovese shared none of Phillips's racist assumptions about the nature of blacks or black labor (Genovese's explanations for the plantation economy's inefficiencies were structural and social, not racial), and although both writers represented very different ideological and political extremes, they nonetheless shared a passion for economic history written in a particular style. As Genovese remarked in 1968, Phillips rightly showed that "slavery cannot properly be understood in economic terms alone," and Genovese applauded Phillips's sensitivity to the interplay of social and economic forces (Genovese 1968: viii). For the most part, those who examined the nature of the plantation economy between 1918 through to the late 1960s did so by placing economic questions in larger social contexts. Their sources were qualitative as well as quantitative, and their questions (if not their answers) were basically the same: was the plantation economy viable, profitable, and efficient for planter and/or region?

In the early 1970s historians asked essentially the same questions but used new methodologies and, perhaps as a consequence, came up with different answers. The New Economic History, "the self-conscious application of economic analysis and econometric techniques to historical subjects" as one historian defined it, marked a distinct departure in the way economic historians and, increasingly, economists with an interest in historical problems, evaluated the plantation economy (Wright 1978: xii–xiii). The econometric analysis of the plantation economy reached fruition in 1974 with the publication of Robert William Fogel and Stanley L. Engerman's *Time on the Cross: The Economics of American Negro Slavery.* To be sure, there had been some earlier work of an econometric nature. Alfred Conrad and John Meyer, for example, published an important essay in 1958 that argued that, based on a computation of average input costs (land and slaves, particularly) and outputs (natural increases among slaves and staple crops), the rates of return for the entire South were as healthy as northern investments. Also, Douglass North's argument had been subject to considerable scrutiny by, among others, Albert Fishlow (1964), Robert Gallman (1970), and Diane Lindstrom (1970) whose application of evidence in a slightly different, more econometric framework than North's more traditional variety of economic history suggested that census data showed that the South did not run large food deficits and that planters were not single-minded specializers. But Fogel and Engerman went much further in their wholesale application of econometric analysis to the plantation economy.

Time on the Cross offered ten "principal corrections of the traditional characterization of the slave economy" (Fogel and Engerman 1974, I: 4). The most important of these revisions were, first, that the "purchase of a slave was a generally highly profitable investment" for individual planters and yielded rates of return equal to those in manufacturing; second, that slavery as a system was healthy by the eve of the Civil War; third, that plantation agriculture was not inefficient when compared with free agriculture (large economies of scale, for example, made "southern slave agriculture 35 percent more efficient" than the northern family farm); fourth, the average slave hand was not inept or indolent but, rather, "harder-working and more efficient than his white counterpart;" and, fifth, that slavery was not necessarily antagonistic to industrial or urban growth (ibid: 4–5). The authors' marshaling of quantitative data drawn from census schedules, planters' business papers, and a variety of other documents, combined with their sensible and often explicit comparative analysis, not only made a good case for the absolute profitability of individual plantations but for the relative health of the southern slave economy generally. Most slaveholders, they showed, could expect returns of about 10 percent on their investments, which was competitive with the return of the most successful New England textile manufacturers, 1844–53, and higher than the return from investment in southern railroads, 1850–60 (ibid: 70).

At the macro-economic level, Fogel and Engerman tried to show that slavery did not retard southern economic growth by examining per capita income levels for the region. The "extraordinarily high income of the Northeast" notwithstanding, the authors argued that the per capita income of the North central states was "14 percent lower than the per capita income in the South" (ibid: 249). Moreover, compared to other countries, the per capita income of the South made it "the fourth richest nation of the world in 1860" (ibid: 249). Slavery and the plantation economy, then, did nothing to impede the economic development of the region. Fogel and Engerman's study was a methodological and interpretive break with what they called the "traditional interpretation" of slavery and the plantation economy (ibid: 3). For the first time, here was an interpretation that stressed the health of the plantation economy for individual planters and the South as a whole.

Time on the Cross met with mixed reviews. For some historians, it was a needed endorsement of the African-American work ethic and a validation of the econometric method. For many others, though, the findings of the study were disturbing (Fogel and Engerman had warned readers as much in their Prologue) and flawed methodologically and interpretatively. Within two years of *Time on the Cross*'s publication, two book-length studies and several important articles challenged some of the specific evidence and assumptions of the work and complained that the wholesale application of the econometric approach tended to uncouple the social from the economic, thus flattening the contours of a complex world in which social values and cultural imperatives were lost under an avalanche of quantitative data (Gutman 1975; David et al. 1976; Haskell 1974).

Among the most telling critiques of *Time on the Cross* (and there were several) was that offered by the economic historian, Gavin Wright. First in essays, then in his landmark 1978 study, *The Political Economy of the Cotton South: Households, Markets, and Wealth in the Nineteenth Century*, Wright challenged Fogel and Engerman and, in the process, advanced and refined our understanding of the nature of the Old South's plantation economy (Wright 1975, 1976). Wright frankly and generously acknowledged his indebtedness to the work of Fogel and Engerman but also his disagreement with it. Furthermore, while he noted the fruits of the econometric analysis of slavery, he self-consciously fashioned his study as an exercise in economic history and not simply as a study of "economics applied to old data" (Wright 1978: xiii). *The Political Economy of the Cotton South*, Wright explained, "addresses the old standbys of Southern history," among them "the profitability of slavery before the Civil War [and] the effects of slavery on regional progress" (ibid: 1).

Wright agreed that antebellum slavery was in fact profitable but refused to accept Fogel and Engerman's emphasis on the efficiency of slave labor as the explanation for that profitability. Instead, argued Wright, the plantation economy was profitable simply because the burgeoning world demand for cotton and the South's virtual monopoly of its supply ensured huge returns on investments for planters. Wright argued that slavery not only contributed to a high degree of inequality measured by the distribution of wealth, but that slavery stunted economic diversification by tying planters to agriculture and reducing entrepreneurial activity. He also showed that southern per capita incomes were, contrary to Fogel and Engerman, "somewhat below antebellum northern levels, an inequality traceable to the weakness of manufacturing growth in the Southeast" (ibid: 126). Combined, these structural characteristics of the plantation economy made the region hostage to changes in world demand for cotton. When this demand was high, as it was between 1820 and 1850, the plantation economy was healthy. But when demand stagnated, as it did in the late nineteenth century, slavery and the plantation economy would have imploded. The slave-based plantation economy "of the late antebellum period could not have persisted," Wright concluded (ibid: 127).

Wright's critique of *Time on the Cross* was a healthy reminder that interpretations of the plantation economy could argue for elements of profitability *and* economic backwardness without surrendering conceptual integrity. This kind of nuanced analysis was furthered in 1981 with the publication of a detailed study devoted to explaining why the South's plantation economy failed to stimulate the development of an industrial sector. In *A Deplorable Scarcity: The Failure of Industrialization in the Slave Economy*, Fred Bateman and Thomas Weiss found (not unlike Fogel and Engerman's point concerning comparative per capita income levels) that, compared with the "Northeast, the South appears to have been laggard in manufacturing development, but relative to the rest of the nation its industrial accomplishments were not uniquely modest" (Bateman and Weiss 1981: 157). Based principally on a rigorous statistical analysis of seventeen variables listed in the manufacturing censuses for 1850 and 1860, *A Deplorable Scarcity* demonstrated that plantation slavery was profitable and viable. But, as the study showed, "profitability" was a slippery concept. Slavery was profitable for individual masters and, in fact, beneficial to the overall southern economy. Nevertheless, Bateman and Weiss concluded that "the South could have done better than it did" (ibid: 158). Returns from investment in southern industry were higher than those available from cotton farming and, therefore, according to "market dictates, industrial expansion should have occurred" in the Old South (ibid: 159).

The authors offered two explanations for such a failure, explanations that lent partial support to earlier arguments about the incompatibility of slavery and industrial–urban development. Social factors were at work, argued Bateman and Weiss, in deterring investment in industrial pursuits. Planters were averse to the high risks that investment in industry demanded. They were also afraid, as Genovese and Wade had argued, that industrialization would give rise to a dangerous class of urban factory slaves; and Bateman and Weiss additionally contended that potential "industrial maverick[s]" were deterred from investing in factories for fear of being "ostracized by the agricultural society" (ibid: 162). But slaveholders' economic reasoning was at work too. As long as profits from cotton production were good, planters shied away from risking resources in industrial ventures. Slaveholders should have been more adventurous, suggested Bateman and Weiss, but, given their world view, their caginess was understandable if wrongheaded.

By the early 1980s, then, scholarship on the antebellum South's plantation economy had undergone significant changes but also reflected important continuities since U. B. Phillips's 1918 work. Investigatively and interpretatively, there had been several major advances since Phillips's day, with *Time on the Cross* acting as a turning point. Thanks largely to refinements in computing, statistical analysis, and data correlation, the investigative tools available to economic historians were more sophisticated than ever before. And yet some economic historians were trying to avoid what they perceived as the excesses of econometrics. Interpretatively, as Wright and Bateman and Weiss demonstrated, the understanding of the workings and impact of the plantation economy by the early 1980s was one that stressed the "somewhere between" nature of the Old South's economy (Bateman and Weiss 1981: 163). The economy could be profitable in some respects though not necessarily in others. This was a return to Gray's older, more nuanced way of thinking about the nature of the Old South's economy and society that had been muffled by the diametric and dichotomous tone of the debate of the 1960s and mid-1970s.

Perhaps as a result of this "settling" and the dulling of the rhetorical edge in the historiographical debate, analyses of the plantation economy, of the profitability and inefficiency of slavery, became scarcer after the early 1980s. Drawing on debates begun in the early 1970s, scholars focused increasingly on the social and cultural history of the slave community and, in effect, divorced the study of slave society from the study of the plantation economy. A relatively recent interest in the workings of the slaves' economy (one supplemental to the plantation economy in which slaves acted as market agents, albeit on a modest scale) notwithstanding, there have been few works produced since the late 1980s devoted solely and explicitly to the South's plantation economy. Scholars' interest in cultural history and theory has, it seems, increased at the expense of questions concerning the profitability of slavery and the workings of the plantation economy.

Although this is not to suggest that historians abandoned the study of the plantation economy during the 1980s and 1990s, there was a discernible if subtle bifurcation in the way that studies of the plantation economy were conceived, conceptualized, and written. On the one hand, work was still produced asking essentially the same questions about the profitability of the plantation economy. Alternatively, the late 1980s also saw the emergence of new studies of the plantation economy that focused on regions within the South and, in effect, reflected a growing sensitivity to the situational variables of place and time.

Work dealing with the plantation economy in a traditional way did not disappear altogether, of course. At the end of the 1980s, some historians still debated the old questions in familiar ways. Robert William Fogel's 1989 *Without Consent or Contract: The Rise and Fall of American Slavery* and the volumes accompanying the study (which included some important essays) basically restated, with perhaps a touch less fervor and rather more evidence, the essential findings of *Time on the Cross*. To be sure, Fogel offered new research on the diet and heights of slaves and the efficiencies of the gang system. He also conceded that econometricians had yet to resolve important questions concerning the efficiency of child slave labor and the operations of the slave trade. That much said, Fogel's study, part of which contained an argument concerning not the economics of slavery but rather the politics of antislavery, reiterated the point that the plantation economy was profitable and healthy as both system and business. The more innovative work was found not so much in the volume by Fogel but scattered in the accompanying volumes. Most of these essays, such as John F. Olson's, which maintained that although slaves worked fewer hours per year than free laborers, those working in the gang system worked more intensively per hour, tended to advance as well as confirm some of the points made in *Time on the Cross* (Olson 1992).

In the same year that *Without Consent or Contract* appeared, Roger L. Ransom's *Conflict and Compromise: The Political Economy of Slavery, Emancipation, and the American Civil War* was published. Although not about the southern plantation economy *per se*, the book included a chapter on "The Economics of Slavery" that contained some interesting and new arguments on the old chestnut of plantation profitability. Ransom's work was sympathetic to the claim that slave-based plantation agriculture was "profitable" and "productive" for both planters and the southern economy generally, and he noted, as had some others, that higher productivity on fertile western soils helped sustain the value of slaves in the older regions (Ransom 1989: 45–6; Foust and Swan 1970). But Ransom did refine Fogel and Engerman's argument about the high per capita income levels of the antebellum South and its implications for southern economic growth. He agreed that Fogel and Engerman's per capita income estimates accurately reflected the income of cotton producers, 1790–1860; and he conceded that if slaves had been owned by a majority of white southerners, then the figures would indeed point to a general economic prosperity for the region as a whole. Ransom noted, however, that only about one-third of southern households owned any bondpeople. Because this minority received all of the income produced by their slaves, the per capita income estimates used by Fogel and Engerman warped a true picture in which nonslaveholders were less prosperous but more numerous than slaveholders. There were, then, two Souths according to Ransom, and Fogel and Engerman's figures represented only one of them.

At the same time as Ransom and Fogel published their work, though, other economic historians and, indeed, nonhistorians, were beginning to look at the plantation economy within specific subregions of the South. This much is clear from the work of Richard H. Kilbourne (a lawyer), Wilma Dunaway (a sociologist), and the economic historian Peter A. Coclanis. Coclanis focused on a specific area of the South (the South Carolina lowcountry) and for a much longer duration than just the antebellum period (his study covered the years 1670–1920) in an effort to explicate the complex workings of a particular region economically, socially, and culturally. Refusing to disassociate questions economic from matters sociological, cultural, and literary, Coclanis argued that the market for rice shaped myriad aspects of the South Carolina lowcountry. By the time of the Civil War, argued Coclanis, the lowcountry had locked itself into the production of a staple that, while profitable for some individual planters, nevertheless hampered the region's ability to diversify its economy. Consequently, when rice cultivation collapsed at the turn of the nineteenth century, so too did the South Carolina lowcountry. Coclanis's focus on a specific region and crop and his ability and willingness to place economic developments within other contexts represented a shift in terms of focusing on a specific subregion of the Old South's plantation economy, but also a return to a form of economic history that was as sensitive to the social as it was to the economic.

Because Coclanis's study was one of the first book-length works dedicated to the detailed examination of the operations of the plantation economy from a subregional perspective, it marked a gradual movement away from examining the plantation economy of the entire South. Regional specificity has since become the hallmark of much work on the plantation economy. In short, by the mid-1990s, observers of the plantation economy were beginning to ask slightly different questions of the past, questions framed around more specific geographic areas and, sometimes, along longer axes of time.

Consider Richard H. Kilbourne's 1995 study, *Debt, Investment, Slaves: Credit Relations in East Feliciana Parish, Louisiana, 1825–1885*. Like Coclanis, Kilbourne focused his attention on one particular region of one particular state. Kilbourne also asked new questions and came up with new answers. This was "the first systematic study of the role of slave property on credit contracts" (Wright 1995: xi). It mattered little that Kilbourne's study centered exclusively on Louisiana's East Feliciana Parish because his findings for this region had to do with market fundamentals concerning credit and slaves that probably differed little in other regions of the South. Kilbourne found that slave property was a powerful form of wealth not least because the liquidity of slave assets formed the basis of a considerable extension of collateralized credit. Land, by comparison, was far less useful as a basis for credit because it was both immobile and illiquid. That slave assets and the plantation economy of which these assets were an inextricable part constituted a more sophisticated form of agriculture than their free counterparts in northern states, Kilbourne implied, was clear if unhappy testimony to the efficiency and profitable nature of the South's slave-based plantation economy.

Based as it was not so much on census data, which he found unreliable, but, rather, on a survey of thousands of parish mortgage records and transactions, 1825–68, Kilbourne's study was refreshing and new both empirically and conceptually. While there had been some work on formal banking in the Old South (Schweikart 1987), much of the actual financing of plantation agriculture was outside such regular channels and, as such, Kilbourne's work was highly innovative. Although a good deal of Kilbourne's study was devoted to examining the collapse of the credit market as a result of the Civil War, the sections on the antebellum years showed that the slave South was not crippled by debt. Nor was the plantation economy heavily dependent on northern credit. Instead, slaves formed the single most important sources of planters' collateral and, as such, were used to produce a unique credit market that was both flexible and effective in financing the plantation economy. Moreover, slave assets "represented a huge store of highly liquid wealth that ensured the financial stability and viability of plantation operations even after a succession of bad harvests, years of low prices, or both" (Kilbourne 1995: 5). Here, then, was an efficient, rational aspect of the plantation economy that had remained overlooked by most economic historians of the slave South and detectable primarily because Kilbourne approached the subject from a local perspective using local sources.

Insofar as it interrogated the economy of a defined and limited geographic area, Wilma Dunaway's 1996 *The First American Frontier*, subtitled "Transition to Capitalism in Southern Appalachia, 1700–1860," continued the trend toward book-length, regional studies of the plantation economy. This detailed study applied world-systems analysis to Southern Appalachia in an effort to revise the conventional wisdom concerning the backwardness of the region. Dunaway's emphasis, like Cocla-nis's, was on the *longue durée*, but her application of the world-systems paradigm, a model first advanced by Immanuel Wallerstein explaining regional capitalist develop-ment within a much larger context, marked her work as distinctive. Dunaway's methodology enabled her to offer some useful and thoughtful insights. By embracing an inclusive definition of capitalism – a definition that allowed for "forces internal to the rural communities that were shaping agents for the transition to capitalism" (Dunaway 1996: 9) – she offered the argument that because the settlers who ventured to Appalachia after the Revolutionary War had already "been incorporated into the modern, capitalist system before the region was repopulated ... it is historically and theoretically inappropriate to categorize the region's inhabitants as precapitalist." "Settler Appalachia," in essence, "was *born capitalist*" (ibid: 16).

Dunaway showed that "subsistence farming was *not* characteristic of antebellum Southern Appalachia" (ibid: 125). Only about one-tenth of the region's farm owners were subsistence producers. The remainder produced and sold crops and home manufactures for the market or were wage earners of one kind or another. About half of the region's surplus-producing farm owners were nonslaveholders, and the vast majority were small-to-middling slaveholders. Although Southern Appalachia's plantations were few and only 8 percent or so used the labor of more than ten slaves on farms of more than 500 acres, they nevertheless produced nearly one-fifth of the regional output of grains and livestock and thereby generated a highly dispropor-tionate share of the region's agricultural production. This alone suggested that even the region's smallest plantations were efficient and productive. This production, much of which was for the market, was, in Dunaway's view, a "quest for profits" (ibid: 137).

In terms of the region's contribution to the southern economy overall, "Southern Appalachia's farm owners *exceeded* national averages in per capita production of wheat, corn and hogs" (ibid: 131). They were roughly equivalent to national averages in the per capita production of cattle and tobacco and only slightly below the national averages in per capita production of cotton. Moreover, for all crops except cotton, the region's farm owners cultivated at a higher level than that of the average southern farm.

Neither did Southern Appalachia's admittedly unusual plantation and agricultural economy deter industrial enterprises. Extractive industries were the most common, but there was a good deal of manufacturing too that was tied closely to agriculture (particularly in the leather and tobacco industries) and helped stimulate urban devel-opment. Dunaway, though, did detect the conservative influence of Genovese's planter class in Southern Appalachia which, she maintained, served to stifle the extent of the region's industrial development. Planters' class interests – particularly their commitment to plantation slavery and their fear of the emergence of a southern proletariat – led to the undercapitalization of the region's manufacturing plants and the overconcentration of fixed capital in slaves. Appalachian slavery, then, locked capital into slaves. Not unlike Bateman and Weiss's larger findings for the South as a whole, Dunaway concluded: "The astonishing reality is that Southern Appalachia might have paralleled the American Northeast in its development trajectory if local

elites had invested their capital in diversified manufacturing rather than slaves"
(Dunaway 1996: 311).

On balance, work on the plantation economy published since 1918 suggests that
slavery was profitable as a business but probably damaging for the southern economy
as a whole. Although the studies by Phillips and Genovese point to the utter
inefficiencies of slavery at all levels and work by Fogel and Engerman argues for the
absolute profitability of the plantation economy, most studies suggest that the
efficiency of the plantation economy was contingent. Further analyses of subregions
within the South will help refine this formulation further, although, if the work of
Coclanis and Dunaway is indicative, such studies will probably confirm rather than
refute this basic conclusion. Careful reading of recent studies also suggests that the
methodological and conceptual echoes of U. B. Phillips and other early historians of
the plantation economy can still be identified. For a while, some econometric history
threatened to divorce the plantation economy from its social context and was in
danger of reifying the institution. Phillips's concern with viewing economic history in
social context has been resurrected by recent historians, most notably by Coclanis but
also by Dunaway. Moreover, very recent work suggests that this trend will continue so
that, for example, questions of the plantation South's economic performance will
increasingly be answered in the context of legal and social history (Wahl 1998; Smith
1997).

It would also be sensible, though, if cultural and social historians reciprocated and
engaged more fully with the work of economic historians and students of the plantation economy. That some studies of, for example, slave culture have divorced questions of culture from economics is perhaps a reflection of a reorientation in southern
historical writing toward the cultural and social. Heavily statistical work that purports
to represent objective facts is sometimes viewed with suspicion by historians of
cultural history and embraced only gingerly. This slighting of economic history is
unfortunate not least because relatively recent work on such topics as the slaves'
economy could probably benefit from situating some of its findings in larger, economic contexts as, indeed, some helpful and recent work on slaves' independent
economic activities suggests (Campbell 1993; Morris 1998). After all, it should be
remembered that the existence of the slaves' economy was first noted and alluded to
by historians of the plantation economy (Phillips 1918: 410–14; Fogel and Engerman 1974, I: 151–2). In other words, by looking at the margins of the plantation
economy, particularly at the local level, we may better understand how slaves in
particular contributed not only to their own economic security but also how their
independent social, cultural, and economic activity helped shape the performance of
the plantation economy as both business and system.

BIBLIOGRAPHY

Bateman, Fred and Weiss, Thomas 1981: *A Deplorable Scarcity: The Failure of Industrializa-
tion in the Slave Economy.* Chapel Hill: University of North Carolina Press.
Campbell, John 1993: As "A Kind of Freeman"?: Slaves' Market-Related Activities in the
South Carolina Up Country, 1800–1860. In Ira Berlin and Philip D. Morgan (eds.),
Cultivation and Culture: Labor and the Shaping of Slave Life in the Americas. Charlottesville:
University of Virginia Press, 243–74.

116 MARK M. SMITH

Coclanis, Peter A. 1989: *The Shadow of a Dream: Economic Life and Death in the South Carolina Low Country, 1670–1920.* New York: Oxford University Press.

Conrad, Alfred H. and Meyer, John R. 1958: The Economics of Slavery in the Ante-Bellum South. *Journal of Political Economy,* 66, 95–130.

David, Paul A., Gutman, Herbert G., Sutch, Richard, Temin, Peter and Wright, Gavin 1976: *Reckoning with Slavery: A Critical Study in the Quantitative History of American Negro Slavery.* New York: Oxford University Press.

Dunaway, Wilma A. 1996: *The First American Frontier: Transition to Capitalism in Southern Appalachia, 1700–1860.* Chapel Hill: University of North Carolina Press.

Fishlow, Albert 1964: Antebellum Interregional Trade Reconsidered. *American Economic Review. Papers and Proceedings of the Seventy-Sixth Annual Meeting of the American Economic Association,* 54, 352–64.

Fogel, Robert William 1989: *Without Consent or Contract: The Rise and Fall of American Slavery.* New York: W. W. Norton.

Fogel, Robert William and Engerman, Stanley L. 1974: *Time on the Cross: The Economics of American Negro Slavery,* 2 vols. Boston: Little, Brown.

Foust, James D. and Swan, Dale E. 1970: Productivity and Profitability of Antebellum Slave Labor: A Micro-Approach. In William N. Parker (ed.), *The Structure of the Cotton Economy of the Antebellum South.* Washington, DC: Agricultural History Society, 39–62.

Gallman, Robert E. 1970: Self-Sufficiency in the Cotton Economy of the Antebellum South. In William N. Parker (ed.), *The Structure of the Cotton Economy of the Antebellum South.* Washington, DC: Agricultural History Society, 5–23.

Genovese, Eugene D. 1965: *The Political Economy of Slavery: Studies in the Economy and Society of the Slave South.* New York: Pantheon.

Genovese, Eugene D. 1968: Introduction: Ulrich Bonnell Phillips as an Economic Historian. In Ulrich Bonnell Phillips, *The Slave Economy of the Old South: Selected Essays in Economic and Social History.* Baton Rouge: Louisiana State University Press, vii–xiv.

Gray, Lewis C. 1933: *History of Agriculture in the Southern United States to 1860,* 2 vols. Washington, DC: Carnegie Institution.

Gutman, Herbert G. 1975: *Slavery and the Numbers Game: A Critique of Time on the Cross.* Urbana: University of Illinois Press.

Haskell, Thomas L. 1974: Were Slaves More Efficient? Some Doubts about "Time on the Cross." *New York Review of Books,* 21, September 19, 38–42.

Kilbourne, Richard Holcombe, Jr. 1995: *Debt, Investment, Slaves: Credit Relations in East Feliciana Parish, Louisiana, 1825–1885.* Tuscaloosa: University of Alabama Press.

Lindstrom, Diane 1970: Southern Dependence upon Interregional Grain Supplies: A Review of the Trade Flows, 1840–1860. In William N. Parker (ed.), *The Structure of the Cotton Economy of the Antebellum South.* Washington, DC: Agricultural History Society, 101–13.

Morris, Christopher 1998: The Articulation of Two Worlds: The Master–Slave Relationship Reconsidered. *Journal of American History,* 85, 982–1,007.

North, Douglass C. 1966: *The Economic Growth of the United States, 1790–1860.* Englewood Cliffs, NJ: Prentice-Hall.

Olson, John F. 1992: Clock Time versus Real Time: A Comparison of the Lengths of the northern and southern Agricultural Work Years. In Robert William Fogel and Stanley L. Engerman (eds.), *Without Consent or Contract: The Rise and Fall of American Slavery; Markets and Production: Technical Papers.* Vol. 1. New York: W. W. Norton, 216–40.

Parker, William N. 1970: Introduction. In William N. Parker (ed.), *The Structure of the Cotton Economy of the Antebellum South.* Washington, DC: Agricultural History Society, 1–4.

Phillips, Ulrich Bonnell 1918: *American Negro Slavery: A Survey of the Supply, Employment and Control of Negro Labor as Determined by the Plantation Regime.* New York: Appleton.

Ransom, Roger L. 1989: *Conflict and Compromise: The Political Economy of Slavery, Emancipation, and the American Civil War.* New York: Cambridge University Press.

Ransom, Roger L. and Sutch, Richard 1977: *One Kind of Freedom: The Economic Consequences of Emancipation.* Cambridge: Cambridge University Press.

Schweikart, Larry 1987: *Banking in the American South, from the Age of Jackson to Reconstruction.* Baton Rouge: Louisiana University Press.

Smith, Mark M. 1997: *Mastered by the Clock: Time, Slavery, and Freedom in the American South.* Chapel Hill: University of North Carolina Press.

Smith, Mark M. 1998: *Debating Slavery: Economy and Society in the Antebellum American South.* Cambridge: Cambridge University Press.

Stampp, Kenneth M. 1956: *The Peculiar Institution: Slavery in the Ante-Bellum South.* New York: Alfred A. Knopf.

Wade, Richard C. 1964: *Slavery in the Cities: The South, 1820–1860.* New York: Oxford University Press.

Wahl, Jenny Bourne 1998: *The Bondsman's Burden: An Economic Analysis of the Common Law of Southern Slavery.* New York: Cambridge University Press.

Wayne, Michael 1990: An Old South Morality Play: Reconsidering the Social Underpinnings of Proslavery Ideology. *Journal of American History,* 77, 838–63.

Woodman, Harold D. 1963: The Profitability of Slavery: A Historical Perennial. *Journal of Southern History,* 29, 303–25.

Woodman, Harold D. 1968: *King Cotton and His Retainers: Financing and Marketing the Cotton Crop of the South, 1800–1925.* Lexington: University of Kentucky Press.

Woodman, Harold D. 1972: Economic History and Economic Theory: The New Economic History in America. *Journal of Interdisciplinary History,* 3, 323–50.

Wright, Gavin 1975: Slavery and the Cotton Boom. *Explorations in Economic History,* 12, 439–51.

Wright, Gavin 1976: Prosperity, Progress, and American Slavery. In Paul A. David, Herbert G. Gutman, Richard Sutch, Peter Temin, and Gavin Wright (eds.), *Reckoning with Slavery: A Critical Study in the Quantitative History of American Negro Slavery.* New York: Oxford University Press, 302–36.

Wright, Gavin 1978: *The Political Economy of the Cotton South: Households, Markets, and Wealth in the Nineteenth Century.* New York: W. W. Norton.

Wright, Gavin 1995: Foreword. In Richard Holcombe Kilbourne Jr., *Debt, Investment, Slaves: Credit Relations in East Feliciana Parish, Louisiana, 1825–1885.* Tuscaloosa: University of Alabama Press, 1995, i–ii.

CHAPTER EIGHT

The Maturation of Slave Society and Culture

STEPHANIE J. SHAW

THE first half of the nineteenth century witnessed important changes in the institution of slavery. The number of slaves in the South increased more than five fold, and accompanying this numerical increase was westward migration as more territory came under American control through purchase (the Louisiana Territory), treaties (involving Indian removal), and war (with Mexico). The majority of southern whites never owned slaves, but during the nineteenth century before the Civil War slaveholding became even more concentrated, with the percentage of small slave-holders declining and the percentage of large holders increasing. The increased concentration of slaveholding even in the midst of migration, which involved more slave communities than individuals, enhanced the development and maintenance of slave culture and to some extent the stabilization of slave society. This essay explores the study of these phenomena. It is a scholarship that, early on, focused primarily on the institution of slavery and its characteristics, moving later to the interior lives of slaves themselves, then moving back to the larger picture with increasing attention given to master–slave relationships.

When Ulrich Bonnell Phillips published *American Negro Slavery* in 1918, it was the first major scholarly work published on the topic since James Ford Rhodes's antislavery polemic in 1893 (Rhodes 1893). Phillips saw his own work as objective, but even his preface betrayed his biases. Suggesting a historically harmonious social relationship between black and white southerners, Phillips wrote from a Georgia army base that the white soldiers, though living in separate (segregated) barracks, "seek out their accustomed [black] friends and compare home news and exper-iences". He drew a straight line between slaves of the antebellum South and the early twentieth-century black soldiers at Camp Gordon by characterizing both in terms of their "easy-going, amiable, serio-comic obedience," their "personal attach-ments to white men," and their "sturdy light-heartedness" and "love of laughter and of rhythm". The pride of the black noncommissioned officers compared to that of the old plantation foremen, and, predictably, their white commanding officers resembled the old plantation masters who mixed "tact with firmness," exercised "patience of instruction," and evinced "crisp though cordial reciprocation of sentiment" (Phillips 1959: viii). Phillips's characterization of both groups of men was overly simplistic and stereotypic, and his work suggested to subsequent historians another major pitfall to avoid – static characterizations, even within a generation.

Still, Phillips's book was a masterwork. Although eventually and appropriately criticized for its racism, it continues to influence scholarship, and, indeed, in its structure at least, bears a striking resemblance to the most sophisticated recent work published on the subject (see Berlin 1998). Phillips began his exploration in Africa, Europe, and the West Indies. He examined "the tobacco colonies," "the rice coast," and "the northern colonies" separately. He saw the importance of staple crops to regional, national, and international developments after the Revolutionary Era. And he paid close attention to the annual routines of cotton, sugar, and tobacco production in the different regions of the plantation South.

But Phillips accepted, absolutely, the word of the planters (and partially informed travelers) as proof of the nature of the system. Based on their records, slaves were well cared for when they were ill, rewarded when they achieved, and, in general, happy with their lot in life. The slave system was a benevolent one in which masters "raised" their slaves much like they claimed to raise their children – providing them with all the necessities of life without spoiling them; chastising them whenever necessary, but never too harshly; encouraging them to work hard, but never overtaxing them. Phillips recognized the importance of discipline in this labor system and the necessary give-and-take in order to achieve it, which the most successful planters observed. But slaves had to be disciplined to the plantation regime not because people normally have to become conditioned to any particular regime, but, according to Phillips, because of the innate characteristics – intellectual shortcomings – of Negroes. Ultimately, Phillips characterized plantations as "the best schools yet invented for the mass training of that sort of inert and backward people which the bulk of the American negroes represented" (Phillips 1959: 343). Thus, according to Phillips, slavery was paternalistic and benevolent, and slaves were the beneficiaries: southern slavery was good (at least better than slavery had historically been), slaves were content, and they were better off than had they been free.

The plantation-school thesis held sway until the World War II era, during which time Herbert Aptheker's *American Negro Slave Revolts* appeared. Aptheker paid closer attention to the extensive evidence of public and private fear of slave rebellion among whites and the elaborate formal and informal mechanisms established by them to control slaves. This served as proof that few people believed slaves were content. Aptheker found patterns in slave rebellion, related to goings-on in the larger political economy. But the small number of rebellions he uncovered (about 250), given the number of years slavery legally existed, suggested to some that if slaves were not satisfied with their lot, perhaps neither were they altogether discontented. Given that Aptheker defined rebellion narrowly, excluding many acts that otherwise might have been counted, his book had implications that reached much farther than was obvious. His work compelled subsequent scholars to think more about resistance, identity, consciousness, and nationalism.

Because Phillips's study (and others before and after him) characterized black and white people almost as if they were of different species, it is not difficult to understand Kenneth Stampp's beginning *The Peculiar Institution* (1956) with the assertion that black men were no more or less than white men in dark skin. Others later criticized the assertion, but Stampp deserves much credit for giving a tremendous push to the revisionist scholarly project of studying slavery. Antebellum slavery, according to Stampp, was not the benevolent and paternalistic institution that Phillips described, or an inheritance that whites had to make the best of, which Phillips had also posited, but a deliberate choice of slaveholders based on profit motives. The struggle to maintain control was ongoing, as Aptheker had suggested, and to the extent that whites won for a time was less a tribute to their alleged noble cause of bringing civilization to a needy and accepting backward race than to slaveholders' ability to establish and maintain a certain level of tyranny.

By the time Stampp's book was published, the momentous *Brown* decision and the successful conclusion of the Montgomery, Alabama, bus boycott had just highlighted both the historical failure of black Americans to achieve freedom to that time and their organized efforts to reverse the injustice. These and subsequent events greatly influenced the way post-World War II scholars would look at the history of slavery and the lives of slaves, in general. Stampp, as did other revisionists, began his work by acknowledging that "American Negroes still await the full fruition of their emancipation" (Stampp 1956: vii). The struggle for freedom, best characterized for slaves in a much later work (Harding 1981), was an important theme of *The Peculiar Institution*. Although the next major work in this historiography also conceded the humanity of slaves, it utilized different methods to demonstrate it, with different implications.

Stanley Elkins's *Slavery* (1959) was neither an attempt to refute Phillips's conclusion about the childlike personality of the slaves nor to corroborate Aptheker's opposing conclusion, which some saw as equally extreme. Instead, using the tools of the social psychologist, and continuing a comparative approach begun by Frank Tannenbaum, Elkins studied personality formation as it pertained to slaves and sought to account for it. The so-called Sambo, most profoundly introduced by Phillips, was Elkins's case study. This personality type was "docile but irresponsible, loyal but lazy, humble but chronically given to lying and stealing;...full of infantile silliness and his talk inflated with childish exaggeration. His relationship with his master was one of utter dependence and childlike attachment: it was indeed this childlike quality that was the very key to his being" (Elkins 1980: 82).

Elkins took the position that "closed institutions" had the ability to infantilize individuals. Basing his argument on role theory, Elkins argued that a series of "shocks" – capture, march to the slave ships, middle passage, and seasoning in the West Indies – effectively made the Africans into slaves, destroying all aspects of their cultural pasts and forcing them to draw new standards from their masters. North American slavery allowed for this effect because, as in Nazi concentration camps and unlike in South America, the northern system was a closed one that had no major social, cultural, or legal institutions working effectively to maintain the humanity of slaves and the possibility of their eventual emancipation. Consequently, in order to survive, slaves assumed the social role provided to them by their masters, the father figure, who expected "obedience, fidelity, humility, docility, cheerfulness and so on" (ibid: 130). Slaves became childlike, looking to their master for every cue, identifying with him/her totally. Thus, according to Elkins, Sambo was a personality type that, under these conditions, was easily explained.

Though generationally and conceptually representing different schools of thought, these four works form cornerstones for the historiography of antebellum slavery. They established perspectives and suggested issues that historians have continued to debate and to build upon. Scholars subsequently sought to determine the extent to which paternalism ever existed and the impact of it on people who were enslaved. Wide-ranging questions about slave personality also arose, for although Elkins was writing about personality rather than slaves, and his study was theoretical rather than empirical, if the plantation South was indeed a closed society, a total institution, there would have been no way for slave identity, consciousness, or culture, distinguishable from their owners' or the white South in general, to exist. These studies left questions unanswered about "time and space," as Ira Berlin later put it (Berlin 1980). And none of these four paid enough attention to women and children or the social divisions that generally existed among slaves. This small group of works spawned these and other questions, laying the bases for the multidimensional and increasingly complex literature that followed. This literature came to focus on slaves themselves, then on relations between slaves and slaveholders.

The issue that received the most attention earliest was slave resistance. U. B. Phillips had remarked upon runaways, truancy, and even rebellions among slaves. But he never provided a sustained discussion of resistance as a sociopolitical phenomenon. The idea of resistance in any systematic way was simply inconsistent with his characterization of the plantation South as paternalistic. But Raymond A. Bauer and Alice H. Bauer (1942) posited that absenteeism and general misbehavior (malingering, theft, carelessness, and the like) were indeed acts of resistance rather than evidence of weak character or immaturity, as Phillips characterized them. What Aptheker called "individual acts," the Bauers had labeled day-to-day acts of resistance, and they insisted on our considering the cumulative impact of these covert acts and, consequently, our calling them acts of resistance rather than evidence of inferiority. George M. Fredrickson and Christopher Lasch (1967) took issue with the Bauers, positing that real resistance reflected political (collective) consciousness, that anything short of attempting to overthrow the system did not reflect such consciousness, and, therefore, that these day-to-day (primarily individual) acts were merely reactionary.

Very recent literature draws our attention back to slave resistance. John Hope Franklin and Loren Schweninger (1999) published the first book-length study of runaways during the antebellum period. And William Dusinberre's *Them Dark Days* (1996) is the first study since the Bauers' to provide a clear conceptual framework for addressing subversion, in general, as systemic. Dusinberre goes much farther than Stampp in describing white domination of the slave South in terroristic terms; and to describe the actions of slaves he uses the expression *dissidence* rather than *resistance*, the latter of which in its nineteenth-century usage involved overt, physical opposition. In the rice swamps that Dusinberre studied, the system of control was so overwhelming, the chances for success so limited, and the punishment upon failure so severe, that slaves, themselves, drew the line between dissidence and resistance. Still, dissidence, nonviolent but very often collective, was endemic. Dusinberre's conclusion not only suggested the absence of infantilization, but it also ran counter to the most provocative discussion of resistance published since Elkins's *Slavery.*

Without ascribing to paternalism all the warm and fuzzy characteristics that Phillips gave it, though still moving away from the general conclusions offered by Stampp, the Bauers, and especially Aptheker, Eugene D. Genovese in *Roll, Jordan, Roll* explored paternalism as ideology, with profound implications for slave resistance. Genovese described the paternalism of the Old South as embodying a reciprocal relationship between masters and slaves based on mutual obligations. In exchange for their involuntary labor, slaves expected and received protection, sustenance, and supervision. What slave owners understood as their duties, slaves interpreted as their rights, regularly demanding and receiving them. But slaves' successes in redressing grievances merely "improved" circumstances enough to mitigate against their working to overthrow the system. For Genovese, the conditions under which slaves lived (out-gunned and within a growing back country and a strengthening planter regime), and their own culture, which he describes as accommodationist and anti-millinealist, precluded any revolutionary action. And Genovese, like Fredrickson and Lasch, saw insurrection as "the only genuine resistance since it alone directly challenged the power of the regime" (Genovese 1974: 598). And so day-to-day resistance was another form of accommodation – an indication that the norms slaves defined for themselves under paternalism had been violated, and they sought simply to have them reestablished. For Genovese, this type of resistance "weakened [slaves'] self-respect and their ability to forge a collective discipline appropriate to the long-term demands of their national liberation" (ibid: 609).

It is almost ironic that discussions of (white) paternalism and total institutions would lead to discussions of (black) nationalism. But that is one of the directions this scholarship took. Even before Elkins's series-of-shocks theory, scholars had posited that the survival of African heritage and culture among slaves was unlikely because of the diverse origins of the hundreds of thousands of slaves brought to North America (Frazier 1939). Melville Herskovits, an anthropologist, refuted that conclusion by 1941 in *The Myth of the Negro Past*, and Aptheker's *American Negro Slave Revolts* clearly suggested the existence of a certain level of community self-identification or consciousness. Even Genovese, who characterized slave society as prepolitical and accommodationist, conceded that slaves manifested collective consciousness. But more recent localized historical studies offer more convincing evidence. Several show that whites in different regions preferred (or ended up with) Africans from particular areas and, therefore, that these individuals often began life in America with some common understandings and potential for collective consciousness (see Little-field 1981; Wood 1974; Creel 1988; Hall 1992). Sterling Stuckey provided a different basis for the same conclusion and a direct case for nationalism in his chapter entitled "Slavery and the Circle of Culture" (Stuckey 1987: 3–97).

Stuckey's chapter demonstrated the increasing sophistication of the literature in which resistance, nationalism, and culture were more and more difficult to separate. He argued that "African ethnicity, an obstacle to African nationalism in the twentieth century, was . . . the principal avenue to black unity in antebellum America" (ibid: 5; see also the discussion of Atlantic creoles in Berlin 1998). In his essay, rather than the common heritage of people from the same area serving to unite slaves in their new environment, or the shock of enslavement serving to wipe out the African past, the "common horror" provided a basis for uniting diverse people and, more important, the diverse groups possessed common cultural traditions that provided a basis for social cohesion and a nationalistic identity. Stuckey's title refers to the centrality of the circle in various West African ceremonies. It was a form taken during rituals performed at, and leading to, marriages, births, deaths, funerals, and other observances. It was central to socializing and sermonizing. But the circle was also a metaphor for the process by which African traditions and values were transported, transmitted, and transformed among diverse African and African-American peoples. And, finally, the circle was a description of the culture itself – a culture in which the young are linked to the old, and both to the ancestors; the living to the dead; the sacred to the secular; each member of the community to every other member; the past to the present, the present to the future; and, finally, Africa to America. According to Stuckey, this common cultural idiom provided a basis for unity in America, even under slavery.

The 1960s development of massive civil disobedience on behalf of civil rights undoubtedly influenced the search for slave identity and the general quest to learn more about slavery than Stampp revealed in his 1956 study, which portrayed slaves primarily as victims, and Elkins's study that validated the existence of Sambo. John W. Blassingame's *The Slave Community* and George P. Rawick's *From Sundown to Sunup*, both published in 1972, were among the first detailed examinations of slavery to reveal more clearly the perspective of slaves. Using ex-slave autobiographies, Blassingame gave some attention to cultural survivals – evident in music, religion, folk tales, funerary practices, and language. He did not believe that African traditions survived intact over the generations, but he argued for the creation of a distinct culture based on an African heritage that was adapted to the American environment and influenced by European (and Euro-American) traditions. Some aspects of African culture were strong enough to survive (e.g. music and folk tales), and others (e.g. work and folk tales) had enough similarities to European culture to be adaptable rather than destroyed. Blassingame's work also stood apart from Stampp's, which accepted the humanity of slaves and thereby helped to revise popular portraits to that time but still demonstrated little about slave life that represented a culture distinct from that of white southerners. For Blassingame, slaves were not merely black human beings but people who had a history prior to their becoming enslaved. That history continued to influence their lives throughout their enslavement.

Blassingame also spoke directly to questions about personality. He believed that the Sambo stereotype said more about planters, who needed to justify the institution, than about slaves; that the plantation South was not a "total institution"; and that however useful psychological theory might be, applying it to stereotypes was a useless project. For Blassingame, the pervasive examples of overt and covert resistance provided the most obvious evidence of the failure of the "shocks" Elkins described to wipe out individual personality. But more important, Blassingame differentiated between *primary* and *secondary* environments, the former of which was the slave community. According to Blassingame, it was the ethics and values of *this* community that shaped personality. The slave family in particular, though regularly assaulted by a variety of means and, consequently, rarely unbroken, was the heart of this community and the source of individual and collective esteem and survival. In the secondary environment, which masters and overseers controlled, slaves merely assumed social roles – particular responses to particular circumstances. Slaves outnumbered white supervisors too dramatically to be constantly surveiled, a requirement of a total institution. Consequently, they were rarely totally dependent on whites. For Blassingame, interpersonal theory was much more relevant than role theory for studying slave personality; the relevant "significant others" for slaves were members of the slave community rather than the members of the master class; and ultimately, "the same range of personality types existed in the quarters as in the mansion" (Blassingame 1972: 213). Although others have commented further on slave personality – William Dusinberre follows Orlando Patterson's suggestion that we consider group, rather than individual, psychological theory, and in doing so himself Dusinberre proposes characterizations of determined slaves, truculent slaves, cunning slaves, upright conformists, demoralized opportunists, and proud slaves – Blassingame's characterizations of Nat, Jack, and Sambo provided some direct stimulation for the subsequent, more complex presentations.

Rawick (1972), as his title suggests, also recognized the substantial self-control that slaves manifested, and he provided additional detail on the day-to-day lives of slaves. But the historiographical significance of *From Sundown to Sunup* is also the utilization of Work Projects Administration (WPA) interviews. Rawick demonstrated the richness of the WPA reports for studying this understudied group, and through them he also showed that rather than having been "deculturalized" in the process of enslavement, African heritage provided the foundation for the creation of a black American community in which there occurred a process of "enculturation" of "successive generations" (ibid: 9). This process occurred largely outside the purview of the master, *from sundown to sunup*, and, as Blassingame concluded, it prevented the slaves becoming total victims. Rawick rejected Elkins's representation of the plantation South as a totalitarian society, and he also rejected Kenneth Stampp's postulation that slaves were merely white men with dark skin because it suggested that white behavior was "normal" behavior, and that slaves, being denied the opportunity to live as whites lived, existed "in a kind of cultural chaos" (ibid: 78). Instead, WPA records showed that slaves' religious practices, cultural symbols, and family relationships were "part of a distinct, viable black culture, adapted to slavery and deprivation" (ibid: 79).

Studies that focus on particular aspects of culture reveal this vitality more thoroughly. For example, Sterling Stuckey's (1967) "Through the Prism of Folklore" posited not only that enslavement failed to destroy the personality of slaves, but that a study of folklore revealed the evidence of a "black ethos" – a fundamental set of beliefs and values that could be attributed to and might even have been peculiar to slaves. It was, however, Lawrence W. Levine's (1977) *Black Culture and Black Consciousness* that provided the detail for this position and more fully illustrated the power of culture to allow individuals to transcend their conditions and maintain their humanity. The songs and stories he studied reflected an African worldview in America. But Levine was discussing more than African survivals, which he showed clearly in the structure, rhythm, and purpose of songs, and the character, content, and meaning of stories. And he saw more than evidence of enculturation, passing on traditions from one generation to another. Levine discussed culture as a dynamic and infinite process of constant re-creation in which the structure, performance, and process of transferal put the "individual in continual dialog with his community" (ibid: 33). Levine discerned a defining feature of Stuckey's "black ethos" and Blassingame's "ethos": it was communalistic. Certain traditions not only demonstrated the survival of Africanism and the existence of culture, but these social and cultural phenomena occurred in the context of a community that they helped to create in form and function through their own form and function as well as their content.

Margaret Washington Creel's (1988) *"A Peculiar People"* continues the study of cultural origins and transformations. But while with folk tales in particular it was sometimes easier to demonstrate Africanness in their delivery rather than their origins, Creel, focusing on religion, was able to show precisely which African and Euro-American traditions came together to form African-American ones. Focusing on South Carolina's Gullahs, Creel traced the attempts of Anglicans, Methodists, and Baptists to convert Africans and African-Americans to Christianity. Baptists had the most success, Creel believes, because of similarities between their processes and those of the secret societies in the particular areas of Africa from which most of South Carolina's Gullahs came. The process of initiation into the societies involved isolation in the bush (seekin', in the Methodist and, later, Baptist tradition); lessons from the elders in responsibilities, roles, conduct, and history; and learning to maintain one's individuality while subsuming it in the context of a community. The end of the process was marked by emergence from the wilderness dirty and ragged, suggesting a struggle with demons (the devil), being bathed (baptized), renamed, and welcomed into the community (becoming a member of the praise house and gaining the ability to participate in the ring shouts). Creel's work illustrates perfectly what Blassingame implies and Levine notes explicitly in saying, "Black slaves could absorb so many Euro-American beliefs not because their own African culture had been reduced to a negligible force but because these beliefs fit so easily beside and often in place of their traditional outlooks and convictions" (Levine 1977: 60).

Creel's work sometimes paralleled its predecessor, Albert J. Raboteau's (1978) pathbreaking book, *Slave Religion*. But in other ways, she offered some notable contrasts. Both works examined spirituality in its African context and similarities between African traditions and tenets of Christianity. Both Raboteau and Creel realized the significance of revivalism to the conversion of slaves and the constant tension between slave owners' efforts to provide religious instruction and their need to control it lest it liberate the minds if not the bodies of their human chattel. But Raboteau, studying the entire South, believed slave religion was more hidden, drew more parallels beween Catholicism and African religions, and saw slaves' acceptance of the Baptist denomination as reflecting not only the emphasis Baptists placed on the conversion experience but the prevalence also of black Baptist preachers.

Creel and others revealed the tremendous value in providing a detailed study of a single aspect of the institution of slavery. Richard Wade's *Slavery in the Cities* suggested the same. Most of what had appeared about slaves to that time (1964) focused on plantations. Thus Wade's work was unique. In the commercial, transportation, manufacturing, and trade centers he studied, women sometimes dramatically outnumbered men, and slaves comprised from 20 percent to the majority of the population. There was a higher incidence of slaveholding in cities as compared to the countryside, excluding Richmond, where corporations owned large numbers of slaves. But there were many fewer slaves per household, and the urban population was never as stable as the rural population. Because of some of these conditions, Wade concluded, the bonds between urban slave and master tended to be looser than those of their rural counterparts. But there were other reasons as well. As many urban slaves were hired, there occurred the first break in the system of control that traditionally existed between master and slave. Municipal efforts to control hiring by selling badges to owners placed another person between master and slave, and slaves frequenting urban institutions (e.g. churches, grog shops, markets) and residing off the premises furthered this process of loosening the bonds. Every intervention of local police and courts eroded more of the owner's control; and Wade concludes that the drop in the percentage of urban slaves by 1860 was not for want of work, but a result of the difficulty of controlling slaves when they were not working. Although urban slavery did not manifest the hegemonic controls that others described for rural settings, that lack of control caused owners to start selling young black males to the country, making it difficult to emancipate slaves, and increasing the rules of segregation. Claudia Dale Goldin's (1976) quantitative study of urban slavery has since shown that urban slaves were sold because of their value and the availability of cheaper free black and immigrant labor in the cities. Yet both of these volumes attest to the differences between urban and rural slavery.

Deborah Gray White's *Ar'n't I a Woman?* makes the point of perspective again. Slavery was as different for women when compared to men as it was for those in cities as compared to rural dwellers. For example, slave women were stereotyped by antebellum whites as much as men were, but women were not Sambos and Nats but Jezebels and Mammies. Jezebel was an image in the white mind resulting partly from the nature of slavery itself – a system that sold women's bodies, kept them poorly clothed, and punished them sadistically. Women who used their bodies as a ticket out of the harsh and inhumane conditions helped to reinforce the image and in some instances to make it real. But Jezebel's image, real or imagined, allowed antislavery advocates to raise questions about the lust, abuse, and lack of self-control among many southern white men and the complicit silence of white women. The creation of Mammy, therefore, became a logical response. Mammy was the epitome of unconditional (maternal rather than sexual) love for all those in her care. She was real to the extent that black women bore substantial responsibility for the care of the house, the preparation of food, and the rearing of white children on plantations. But three-fourths of white children lived in families that did not own slaves. Thus, White sees Mammy's origin in patriarchy. She was "the personification of the ideal slave and the ideal woman" (White 1985: 58).

There was, however, more to women's world than these images. White people perceived women differently from men, as less dangerous. While women worked in fields alongside men, they also bore the primary responsibility for caring for children. And women's capacity to reproduce subjected them to different maladies compared to men, but because of the value of that capacity, they had different ways of avoiding or reducing their work – resisting. When resistance involved leaving, they rarely attempted to leave permanently (as men more often did) because of their children, but when they tried to run away, they took their children with them.

White's work contributes to the developing historiography in two additional ways. Her discussion of the female network shows that upon adolescence, when boys and girls began to function in different worlds, a female world developed for girls that supported and sustained them throughout their lives. It was, to be sure, a world of work – in fields and big houses, in nurseries and weaving houses – but it was a world that also fostered sex-segregated socializing, thus enhancing the development of a *female* culture and identity. And second, slave women's roles as mothers seemingly allowed them to escape being reduced to Sambo (Elkins 1980). Frazier (1939) had characterized women as matriarchs. And in the process of restoring manhood to male slaves, others either ignored women as women altogether or saw them, ironically, as Victorians, generally supportive of their men and even demure (Blassingame 1972; Fogel and Engerman 1974; Genovese 1974). White concludes that slave women were not dominant in their families, but they did possess some authority. And in the end, men and women contributed differently but equally to the survival of the family, which was neither matriarchal nor patriarchal but egalitarian.

Scholarship from the 1960s through the 1980s made clear the benefits of focusing slavery studies on slaves. Enslavement was certainly the context, but slaves' humanity was equally influential. Slaves' lives were not defined totally by master–slave relationships; there was also an influential slave community. And finally, slave communities existed in different places and encompassed different kinds of people at different times. These differences conditioned and helped to explain their experiences. Charles Joyner's *Down by the Riverside*, building on this substantial body of work, reflected these and other considerations.

Using quantitative techniques of demographers, social historians, and economists, *Down by the Riverside* reconstructs the slave community of All Saints Parish in the Georgetown District of the South Carolina lowcountry. It adds the methods and sources of folklorists, anthropologists, and linguists to those of the historian to analyze the lives of the slaves. Joyner is easily able, by this time, to get beyond the old debates on whether and the extent to which African culture survived and, like Levine and Creel, to focus on its transformation. But even here, Joyner goes further in his conceptualization. His analysis of how the gap was bridged between African cultural traditions and the new environment in which they existed comes to focus *explicitly* on creolization and, ultimately, on decreolization. Joyner assumes the presence of a "grammar of culture" based on African aesthetics (something Stuckey, Blassingame, and Levine characterized as an "ethos"). This African-born grammar, as any grammar would, served as a foundation. Yet here, it was not only for language but for life, slave life, and the creolization of cultures, black and white.

The black-to-white ratio in this South Carolina community was nine to one, the highest in all of North America. And between 1730 and the legal closing of the African slave trade, these Africans came overwhelmingly from Angola, Senegambia, and the Windward and Gold coasts. With few whites and almost no free blacks present in this South Carolina plantation district, the transference, maintenance, and transformation of African traditions was not difficult. The process was evident in work, where, for example, slaves transformed the highly individualized tasks assigned to them into collective processes. Creolization was evident in food preparation, resulting in what became known as "soul food". How slaves dressed revealed it more than what they wore. The interior space of cabins was more relevant than their exterior appearance. And syncretized religious practices ("I totes mah powder en sulpher en carries mah stick in mah han en puts mah truss in Gawd") further illustrate the phenomenon exquisitely (Joyner 1984: 153).

The Gullah language, a traditional topic of creolization, allowed members of different African language communities to communicate with each other. This pidgin was becoming a creole language with native speakers by the early eighteenth century. But increased contact with whites, and the transformation of Gullah from a spoken to a written language, resulted in its becoming more English-based – decreolized. House servants had a significant impact on both creolization and decreolization. But here they are not the conservative human force, mediating master–slave relations in ways that diminished the autonomy of the slaves and accommodated them to slavery, as Eugene Genovese described. Rather, in this case, house servants are intermediaries in the creolization of black *and* white culture – taking "elements of black culture into the culinary, religious, and folkloristic patterns of the Big House" and bringing "elements of white culture to the [slave] street". Joyner notes, "it was through the house servant that black southerners derived much of their European heritage, and white southerners derived much of their African heritage" (Joyner 1984: 86).

Studies on slave labor have evolved similarly, from discussions of productivity and efficiency – work results, to the inclusion of culture – to a focus on workers. U. B. Phillips found slave labor inefficient, its productivity lower than that of immigrant labor, and the cost of slave labor higher. After exploring a wide variety of economic theories and diverse evidence left by planters, he concluded that slavery for planters "was less a business than a life". Phillips insisted that it "kept money scarce, population sparse and land values accordingly low" (Phillips 1959: 401), resulting in the underdevelopment of men and resources. The only consequential result was that slavery provided the mechanism for organizing and controlling the labor force. For Eugene Genovese, the issue was not the slothful nature of slaves that Phillips described, but the preindustrial character of planters and the South and a rural economy tied to the natural routines of agriculture, that explained the lack of productivity and efficiency. This peasant orientation led slaves to reject the clock orientations of factory systems and, based on seasons and nature, to work hard but not with regularity. Genovese describes the rejection as "a defense against an enforced system of economic exploitation and an autonomous assertion of values generally associated with preindustrial peoples" – a form of resistance (Genovese 1974: 286). But Mark M. Smith provides an alternative to Genovese's conclusions about clock time, and Smith links his conclusions tenuously to West African trade economies, which had demanded significantly more than "a task-oriented, natural time sensibility" (Smith 1997: 131). By Smith's account, the plantation South was definitely clock-time oriented, and slaves, while maintaining some aspect of their natural (circular) time orientations, adapted to clock (linear) time demands. Wake-up bells, call-to-work bells, and other announcements of time socialized slaves to time *obedience* if not time *discipline*. And the penalty for failure to accept it, possibly a whipping, was a compelling inducement.

Robert William Fogel and Stanley L. Engerman in *Time on the Cross* (1974) spoke to Phillips's conclusions in a different way. By their account, over 25 percent of slaves were nonmenial laborers. By examining all that slaves produced, not just agricultural crops, and therefore broadening the scope of "productivity," and by eliminating children from the workforce total, Fogel and Engerman concluded that cotton production (which became central to the southern economy during the antebellum period and a critical component of the westward migraton) used only about 34 percent of slave labor time. This fact had profound implications for questions about efficiency.

Fogel and Engerman said it was not true that slavery was profitable only under a complex set of conditions, including the availability of land, the cost of free labor, the agricultural labor regime, and the price of slaves, which Phillips had concluded, nor was slavery profitable merely because slaves were cheaper than free labor, which Stampp concluded. Fogel and Engerman dismissed claims that breeding provided the profit margin for some. And they rejected Phillips's conclusion that paternalism caused owners to sacrifice profits and Genovese's assertions that these were "pre-capitalist" planters with paternalistic commitments (Fogel and Engerman 1974: 64). Rather, planters were shrewd businessmen, selling slaves at the age and of the sex that was most profitable, and buying them not for the sake of owning them or as a status symbol but because slave laborers made money for their owners.

Fogel and Engerman concluded that slaves returned a 10 percent profit, comparable to other investments. Their *explanation* for the related productivity was stunning. They maintained that slaveholders successfully used a system of rewards and, to a lesser degree, punishments that "imbue[d] slaves with a 'Protestant' work ethic and . . . transform[ed] that ethic from a state of mind into a high level of production" (ibid: 47). Slaves (willingly) worked so well, according to Fogel and Engerman, that large plantations were 35 percent more efficient than any other type of American agriculture. And, "Far from being 'ordinary peasants' unused to 'preindustrial rhythms of work,' black plantation agriculturalists labored under a regimen that was more like a modern assembly line than was true of the routine in many of the factories of the antebellum era" (ibid: 208).

Fogel and Engerman's sophisticated economic theories and complex mathematical formulae suggested the end of the story. But in addition to Herbert Gutman's and others' close scrutiny and critique of their work (Gutman 1975; David et al. 1976), more recent scholarship reiterates the need for reconsideration. William Dusinberre's *Them Dark Days* argues compellingly that slave dissidence could make slave labor inefficient, even if white domination and brutality made slaves profitable. He reminds us of the importance of keeping the two issues separate. And Charles Dew's *Bond of Iron* provides a striking example of the same. William Weaver's Buffalo Forge (and Bath Iron Works and Etna Foundry) slaves earned tremendous profits for him (and his various co-owners) as early as the 1820s. But when Buffalo Forge produced about "200 tons of iron bar per year," other mills were yielding *thousands* of tons (Dew 1994: 333).

Bond of Iron's approach to the study of slave labor is different, in general. Because Dew provides as much focus on the slaves as on their work, his book marks a turning point in the study of slave labor, one that helps to illustrate further slaves' larger lifestyles and their relationships with the whites who owned them. William Weaver, at different times co-owner or sole owner of Buffalo Forge, Etna Furnaces, and Bath Iron Works in the western Virginia iron-producing valley, eventually operated his holdings *entirely* with slave labor. He purchased *none* whose prior work, apprentice-ship, or calculated potential did not guarantee the level of skill he needed. His near total dependence on slaves from the beginning is illustrated by his shutting Buffalo Forge down only six weeks after it opened because his workforce, at that time primarily hired slaves, left to rejoin their families for the Christmas holiday.

Weaver did not rely on the whip to motivate his slaves, as Dusinberre's South Carolina planters did without compunction or mercy. For resistance (or dissidence) in this context could easily result in the destruction (by fire) of the whole plant. He used a system of positive incentives – cash and goods paid for overwork. The overwork system discussed here is not as vague as it is in *The Peculiar Institution*. Nor was it exclusively a masters' means of achieving a desired effect among slaves, which *Time on the Cross* suggests. Buffalo Forge slaves increased their overwork and, therefore, their earnings, upon getting married, having a child, or the approach of a holiday. They used their earnings to purchase Christmas presents, birthday presents, special baptismal and wedding outfits and gifts, to supplement the family diet, to better clothe family members, and to furnish their houses. Participation not only enhanced the material conditions of their lives, but also their value to their owners and, thereby, their ability to determine the fate of family members. Masters might have designed the system to control the behavior of slaves, but Buffalo Forge slaves participated according to their own interests. When they chose not to participate, they were neither whipped nor sold; the work was simply left undone.

Dusinberre's study augments two other important works. The detail in the records he examined allowed for a more systematic study of the internal economy of slaves than Roderick McDonald could pursue for Louisiana slaves in *The Economy and Material Culture of Slaves* (1993). And as a study of *industrial* slaves, Dusinberre's study, by its focus, helps to bridge the tremendous gap still open since Robert Starobin's more general book, *Industrial Slavery in the Old South* (1970), the first major work to draw our attention away from strict plantation economics. But Starobin's work was of that generation of scholarship focusing on profitability and efficiency rather than slave society and culture. In his study of that 5 percent of slaves working in industrial settings, the influence of Phillips is evident. And although Starobin's revisionist conclusions on profit, efficiency, capitalization, flexibility, resistance, etc., seem rather simplistic in light of Dew's study nearly thirty years later, Starobin was first to answer these questions for industrial slaves and to counter, systematically, Phillips's long-standing conclusions about slave laborers.

Dew's *Bond of Iron*, as already suggested, was as much a social as an economic study. And his discussion of work is hardly separable from his discussion of family. William Weaver's first purchase of slaves (in 1815) was a family that included Tooler, a skilled ironworker, his wife Mary, a cook, and their four children. By the end of 1840 Weaver's key ironworkers came exclusively from the families he owned, including and descending from the first three forgemen he purchased. Thus Dew's study, because of Weaver's business practices, is necessarily a study of slave families. But the focused study of black families was thirty years old by this time, having received its most substantial push from Daniel Patrick Moynihan's 1965 study, *The Negro Family*, which, building on such earlier work as Frazier's, portrayed the black family as pathologically matriarchal with devastating antisocial consequences. The root of this problem, Moynihan argued, lay in the destructive forces of slavery. And so between Moynihan's and Dew's publications, the latter of which revealed none of this dysfunction, scholars had to grapple with questions related to family function, stability, structure, and the family's reflection of and contribution to culture.

Some of the earlier discussed works paid attention to slave families. The family in John Blassingame's *The Slave Community* was "primarily responsible for the slave's ability to survive on the plantation without becoming totally dependent on and submissive to his master" (Blassingame 1972: 79). Still, the family was fractured as an institution because about 33 percent of slave unions were destroyed by slave owners; most, says Blassingame, before their sixth anniversary. Although Blassingame argued that the black family contributed much to the stability and survival of slaves, his numbers infer a context, if not the conclusions, of Frazier and Moynihan. Fogel and Engerman posited that the slave family was so central to the maintenance of discipline, order, and productivity that slave owners encouraged its stability. The families were patriarchal, with fairly strict divisions of labor, and they were nuclear not simply because of slave owners' interest, but because "African family forms . . . did not satisfy the needs of blacks who lived and worked under conditions and in a society much different from those which their ancestors experienced" (Fogel and Engerman 1974: 142). Herbert Gutman would take the discussion of adaptability to a new level in what was arguably the most important book on the black family published to that time.

Gutman's *The Black Family in Slavery and Freedom, 1780–1925* was also a quantitative study, but Gutman was especially interested in what the numbers suggested about behaviors and values. He conjectured that if slavery destroyed the black family, which Frazier and Moynihan indicated was the genesis of and the explanation for post-migration, twentieth-century fractured families, then such characteristics should have been equally evident in the years just before and after the Civil War. But Gutman found strong, stable family traditions, patriarchal families, even, which he attributed to the belief system of the slaves and the adaptive culture they possessed (rather than the economic and political interests of owners). Moreover, these strong families were not limited to elite slaves, whom others argued patterned their families after those of whites (Frazier 1939). Rather, the head of typical slave families was a male common laborer or field hand (the majority was overwhelming), and they were participants in longtime unions. These conclusions held in the Upper and Lower South, in urban and rural areas, in places where sex ratios were even and uneven, in areas with varying black population density and ownership patterns (size and age of holdings). Gutman's study of the family was a major contribution to the study of slave culture not merely because the family is a major cultural institution, but also because the family is the conduit for much cultural phenomena. Reaching back to the late-eighteenth century, Gutman revealed the process of this institutional family's maturation and its reflection of slave culture.

Gutman's study provided proof of the stability of slave families, cautioning those who might draw or had already drawn conclusions about slaves based on the study of a short span of time. Married slaves in Louisiana and Mississippi on the eve of emancipation, for example, included a large percentage (35 percent among those over 40 years of age) who had suffered a marriage broken by force. But the marriages they were in at the time of emancipation were committed relationships. Gutman showed that such values or traditions originated in the slaves' cumulative experience and was a cultural tradition itself. Their culture was adaptive and therefore undoubtedly influenced by their circumstances, but it was not mimetic of white culture. Young slaves observed and learned these behaviors from other slaves.

Numerous examples illustrate this point. While the prevalence of nuclear families suggested imitating planter families, naming practices among slaves suggested otherwise. Slave owners recognized the descent of the enslaved child from its mother, but slave naming practices more often linked the child (sons especially) to their fathers. Unlike white families, slave children were regularly named for deceased siblings and distant kin. And the exogamy of slaves contrasted sharply to slave owners' endogamy. These practices indicated cultural traditions distinct from those of the slave-owning class and contrary to Elkins's lack of "alternative social bases" theory (Gutman 1977: 260). Slaves were bicultural: they practiced their own, as well as mainstream, traditions at the same time. They regularly conferred kinship meaning and functions to nonkin relations. While they participated in marriage ceremonies, committed unions did not depend on these rituals for legitimacy. Premarital sex and pregnancy were not uncommon, but fidelity was an expectation after marriage. And long, monogamous marriages were typical. To be sure, slave reproduction gave slave owners a source of discipline over slaves; they could threaten to sell slave children. But the traditions embedded in slave families, traditions of long marriages, strong families, and durable kinship and community ties, pre-existed the establishment of plantation economies and revealed that slave culture depended not on their treatment – what was done to slaves – but rather on an internal system of values and traditions reflecting and influencing behavior.

Ann Patton Malone's *Sweet Chariot* (1992) continued this process of combining long-range quantitative and qualitative methods to learn even more about slave families. Through her further delineation of household/family *types*, and her considering them carefully in different time-based contexts, she offered more insights as to the process of slave family stabilization *and* the factors that influenced that process. Malone established a model based on records documenting family/household relationships for more than ten thousand Louisiana slaves. Almost three-fourths of these individuals lived in simple families (nuclear families with husband and wife or parent and child). Within this group, 49 percent were standard nuclear families (parents with children); 14.5 percent single females with children; 1.8 percent single men with children; and 8.1 percent married couples alone. What Malone established most profoundly is that although enslaved individuals lived overwhelmingly with other relatives, slaves had *less than half* a "chance of being part of a family consisting of children and both parents" (Malone 1992: 18). The conclusion is more important than it might seem. After the Moynihan conclusions about the destruction of the family under slavery, the literature swung in the opposite direction. Several historians stopped short of arguing that the two-parent family was the norm under slavery, perhaps because their studies lacked the quantitative basis for showing such. But after Herbert Gutman showed that most of the children in his study grew up with both of their parents, his conclusion was easily read as if the standard nuclear structure was the norm among slave families. Malone showed that it was not. Malone's work corrected another older apparent truism concerning the setting in which slave families were likely to experience the most stability. A fairly common belief was that the work routine in sugar regions was devastating to the maintenance of slave families. Malone found that slaves in sugar parishes were more likely to live in simple and standard nuclear families than those in the cotton parishes and that there was a higher percentage of women heading households in the cotton parishes compared to the sugar parishes. And while earlier conclusions indicate that sugar regions depended on the labor of young single men, Malone also found that the river cotton parishes contained the highest percentage of solitaires.

The greatest threats to slave family stability were national economic downturns, the establishment of new plantations, and the death of an owner and the subsequent dispersal of his assets. But these threats had different impacts. The greatest threat to families was estate division. The dissolution of marriages and the separation of children from parents, however, was more often the result of death. Local and regional sales more often separated older children from parents than husbands from wives or younger children from mothers. But in spite of all the factors that wreaked havoc with the stability of these families, the community could and did, with time, recover, and eventually manifest "model" conditions – healthy sex ratios, diverse household structures, adequate numbers of men and women in their most productive ages, and the presence of children and elders. As Malone put it, the slave family was obviously mutable, but it was also constant.

Malone revealed that *the slave family* was a much more complex institution than any other study had revealed; William Dusinberre's *Them Dark Days* further complicates the picture. Dusinberre studied the plantations owned by Charles Manigault, Robert Allston, and Pierce Butler in the South Carolina lowcountry. And he returns to a topic of one of the initial discussions that helped to stimulate and animate scholarship on slavery: paternalism. Dusinberre insists, at the outset, that slaveholders were operatives in "a system of domination and of social alienation which could be combined with any number of different economic systems" (Dusinberre 1996: 27). "Callousness, not paternalist benevolence" defined slaveowners' relationship with their slaves (ibid: 48).

Plantation mortality rates and slave treatment in general suggest additional factors to consider before drawing conclusions about slave family stability. Some 32 percent of the marriages at Gowrie lasted for over 16 years. And 37 percent of those broken among slaves in their twenties were the result of a death. Eleven percent of the second marriages (following deaths and deportations) were long-lasting unions. But only one-third of the children at Gowrie grew up in stable, two-parent families. In fact, the most common nuclear group at Gowrie (a Manigault plantation) was slave parents and *no* children. And that is only a partial picture. Between 1833 and 1864, *90 percent* of the children born at Gowrie died before reaching the age of 16. That number did not include still births and miscarriages. Dusinberre conceded that Gowrie was not typical. St Simons, Pierce Butler's cotton plantation, lost one-third of its children before the age of six between 1819 and 1834. His rice plantation, Butler Island, lost half by the age of six, 61 percent by the age of 16. Compared to the figure for southern slave children in general – 46 percent – these were all deadly regimes for slave families, however stable the families might appear.

The Manigaults, Allstons, and Pierce Butler were paternalist ideologues, but when business mattered, they were not always paternalistic, which would have required them to fulfill certain expectations as a moral duty on behalf of their slaves. Dusinberre believes that they adhered more to racial ideology than to paternalist ideology. And he resists using the term "paternalism" precisely because it implies noncapitalist motives. Because capitalist motives dictated these men's actions, Dusinberre proposes the use of different language with more precise meanings to help explain conditions in the antebellum South. He posits that *paternalist ideology* relates exclusively to beliefs; *paternalism* should be used to address the motives behind slaveholders' behavior; and Dusinberre defines *slavery* as "the system of punishments, allowances, and privileges" that the plantation South embodied. By these definitions, a planter could be a capitalist and a paternalist (Dusinberre 1996: 201). But Manigault, especially, was not. Few of the privileges he granted were benevolent. He even considered food, clothing, and housing to be privileges that could be, and frequently were, withdrawn as punishment. The slave owners Dusinberre studied had *no* fear of revolts regardless of their being so overwhelmingly outnumbered, for their system of control was that forceful. Indeed, Dusinberre brings us, almost squarely, back to

Kenneth Stampp's depiction of the terror under which slaves lived. But slaves' personalities were not destroyed as Elkins suggested people under circumstances like these might experience. Instead, slaves matched constant domination with persistent dissidence. Thus, while Dusinberre's discussion of paternalism brings this discussion full circle, his conclusions do not leave us where we started.

With or without the political upheavals of the 1960s and 1970s, the plantation-school theory of slavery might easily have been uprooted. For the process of change in the historiography followed a logical course. Early studies of *slavery* left enough questions unanswered about *slaves* that they logically became the focus of subsequent studies. General studies of slaves led to more detailed examinations of slave culture, and they were followed by studies of particular cultural phenomena – religion, family, or resistance, for example. They uncovered evidence of the existence of culture, then explored its content and meaning. They looked first for the survival of Africanisms and later for their transformation to African-Americanisms. They focused on slaves in their own communities, then demonstrated the utility of looking at blacks and whites together.

The study of antebellum slave society and culture has, indeed, come a long way, but there is yet much work to be done. Discussions of slave health, for example, covered much ground and then stalled. Fogel and Engerman's 1974 conclusions suggesting that slaves ate well (sometimes exceeding 1960s daily nutritional recommendations) were easily revised by Leslie Howard Owens's (1976) narrative, *This Species of Property*, which also factored housing and clothing, not just nutrition, into a broader discussion of health. But Owens also linked nutritional deficiencies to disease and behavior, yielding new ideas about work habits and personality. Kenneth F. Kiple and Virginia Himmelsteib King's *Another Dimension to the Black Diaspora* (1981) more firmly established links between slave diet and health and placed their findings in the context of the southern social, and the general medical, environment. They, along with Todd Savitt (1978) in his more comprehensive *Medicine and Slavery*, factored genetics into the diet of slaves and in predisposing Africans/African-Americans to contracting some and resisting other diseases. As some of the earliest scholars posited but could not explain, race mattered in the health of slaves. Given the childhood mortality rates recently revealed in *Them Dark Days*, we should pay even more attention to health-related issues – what threatened and protected it, and the roles of slaves and slave owners in both. Because of the elementary level of antebellum medical knowledge, and the distance historians have already come in discussing slave health in the context of traditional medical science, future studies on the health of slaves will probably need to focus more closely on the slave community and homeopathic medicine, which numerous older studies address but not in great detail.

There are also still major gaps in the study of slave labor. Charles Dew's *Bond of Iron* stops short of using phrases common to studies of twentieth-century wage laborers like *workers' control of production* and *work culture*, but given all that his narrative reveals, he could have used them. We know much about how hard slaves worked, about what and how much they produced. And studies of slavery have moved from an emphasis on the organization and economy of work to including aspects of the culture of workers. But much of the evidence of slave work culture remains illusive. In an environment of scarce skilled laborers, experience gave Buffalo Forge ironworkers a tremendous amount of control over their work process and their lives outside of work even if it did not give them real power. We also know that the establishment of rice cultures depended as much on slave knowledge and skill as their labor. Future studies must treat the work culture of slaves in the detail that studies of slave culture manifest. Dew's ironworkers and William Van Deburg's slave drivers are a start. But historians must continue this pursuit and move beyond skilled, elite workers.

Social and occupational stratification within the slave community, and the relationship between the two, deserve much more attention, as well. Aptheker, Raboteau, and Starobin pointed out that rebellion leaders were often religious leaders and artisans. But Genovese doubts the ability or even the inclination of the *leaders* to leverage their status in radical ways on behalf of this group. He concludes that they were "suspended between two politics," and ultimately the "integrationist tendency" of the elites won over the field slaves' "protonationalist tendency" (Genovese 1974: 365, 438). Moreover, comparing skilled workers in *Bond of Iron* to those in *Them Dark Days*, it seems that whether or not these skilled occupations were privileged positions *or* intergenerational (an aspect of privilege) warrants reconsideration. The *privileged* domestic slaves on the Manigault holdings were never guaranteed their positions. But Buffalo Forge's ironworkers were generally irreplaceable. Short of running away, none of their acts of recalcitrance resulted in their being moved to some other work. (Would-be runaways – only one woman was ever successful – were immediately sold.) Studies of stratification, social and occupational, are critically needed if we are to understand fully the dynamics of the slave community and of master–slave relations. Which slaves comprised the *privileged* group is now questionable. Perhaps how we have used the term *elite* is as well.

Social groups in general remain somewhat neglected. We have seen detailed arguments for matriarchal, patriarchal, and egalitarian families (marriages); we have but one detailed study of women and none of men as men. Most existing studies acknowledge the revered position of the elderly in slave communities, but no books focus on them as a social group. And considering the importance of the family to survival and to the transmission of culture, children, whose centrality to the family and this process is paramount, have been the focus of only one book, Wilma King's *Stolen Childhood* (1995).

Compared to other areas in southern history, the study of slave society and culture is still relatively young – the bulk of this work debuted since the 1970s. And so gaps in our knowledge are understandable. In addition to filling some of those already noted, we must also pay closer attention to relations between and among slaves. Such attention could yield as much new information as recent studies on master–slave relations have allowed. Future work should continue to move away from the heavily studied geographical areas where extensive records and "black majorities" allowed and demanded sustained attention. Scholars *are* moving back to much-needed state-level studies. Very recent publications addressing slavery focus on Arkansas and Florida; an earlier study concerns Texas. These states deserve more attention, along with Mississippi and Alabama, the latter of which has not attracted detailed study for more than a generation. Even old slave states like Virginia are lacking study for the antebellum period. And, finally, none of the major works on slaves have paid much attention to those on small holdings. Between the 1820s and 1860 plantation economies became firmly entrenched, most slaves were held in such settings, and planters wielded political power beyond their numbers and their residences, to the exent that they controlled Congress as well as state governments. But the overwhelming majority of slaveholders were not planters. The general experiences of slaves in that setting is still not very well known.

Altogether, historians must continue to look closely at many of the old topics and issues with new eyes. The inestimable value of such study has already been proven. We must, however, also pursue *new* issues with vision enhanced by all the work that has come before. By this process we will learn more fully what it meant to be a slave in the antebellum South.

BIBLIOGRAPHY

Aptheker, Herbert 1943: *American Negro Slave Revolts*. New York: Columbia University Press. 6th edn: New York: International Publishers, 1993.

Bauer, Raymond A. and Bauer, Alice H. 1942: Day to Day Resistance to Slavery. *Journal of Negro History* (27) 4, 388–419. Reprinted Indianapolis: College Division, Bobbs-Merril.

Berlin, Ira 1980: Time, Space, and the Evolution of Afro-American Society on Mainland British North America. *American Historical Review*, 85, 44–78.

Berlin, Ira 1998. *Many Thousands Gone: The First Two Centuries of Slavery in North America*. Cambridge, MA: Harvard University Press.

Blassingame, John W. 1972: *The Slave Community: Plantation Life in the Antebellum South*. New York: Oxford University Press.

Boles, John B. 1982: *Black Southerners, 1619–1869*. Lexington: University Press of Kentucky.

Creel, Margaret Washington 1988: *"A Peculiar People": Slave Religion and Community Culture Among the Gullahs*. New York: New York University Press.

David, Paul A., Gutman, Herbert G., Sutch, Richard, Temin, Peter, and Wright, Gavin 1976: *Reckoning with Slavery: A Critical Study in the Quantitative History of American Negro Slavery*. New York: Oxford University Press.

Dew, Charles B. 1994: *Bond of Iron: Master and Slave at Buffalo Forge*. New York: W. W. Norton.

Dusinberre, William 1996: *Them Dark Days: Slavery in the American Rice Swamps*. New York: Oxford University Press.

Elkins, Stanley M. 1980: *Slavery: A Problem in American Institutional and Intellectual Life*. 3rd edn, revd: Chicago: University of Chicago Press, 1959.

Fogel, Robert William and Engerman, Stanley L. 1974: *Time on the Cross: The Economics of American Negro Slavery*. Boston: Little, Brown.

Franklin, John Hope and Schweninger, Loren 1999: *Runaway Slaves: Rebels on the Plantation*. New York: Oxford University Press.

Frazier, E. Franklin 1939: *The Negro Family in the United States*. Chicago: University of Chicago Press.

Fredrickson, George M. and Lasch, Christopher 1967: Resistance to Slavery. *Civil War History*, 4, 293–314.

Genovese, Eugene D. 1974: *Roll, Jordan, Roll: The World the Slaves Made*. New York: Pantheon Books.

Goldin, Claudia Dale 1976: *Urban Slavery in the American South, 1820–1860: A Quantitative History*. Chicago: University of Chicago Press.

Gutman, Herbert G. 1975: *Slavery and the Numbers Game: A Critique of Time on the Cross*. Urbana: University of Illinois Press.

Gutman, Herbert G. 1977: *The Black Family in Slavery and Freedom, 1750–1925.* New York: Pantheon Books.

Hall, Gwendolyn Midlo 1992: *Africans in Colonial Louisiana: The Development of Afro-Creole Culture in the Eighteenth Century.* Baton Rouge: Louisiana State University Press.

Harding, Vincent 1981: *There is a River: The Black Struggle for Freedom in America.* New York: Harcourt Brace Jovanovich.

Herskovits, Melville J. 1941: *The Myth of the Negro Past.* New York: Harper and Brothers.

Joyner, Charles W. 1984: *Down by the Riverside: A South Carolina Slave Community.* Urbana: University of Illinois Press.

King, Wilma 1995: *Stolen Childhood: Slave Youth in Nineteenth-Century America.* Bloomington: Indiana University Press.

Kiple, Kenneth F. and King, Virginia Himmelsteib 1981: *Another Dimension to the Black Diaspora: Diet, Disease, and Racism.* Cambridge: Cambridge University Press.

Levine, Lawrence W. 1977: *Black Culture and Black Consciousness: Afro-American Folk Thought from Slavery to Freedom.* New York: Oxford University Press.

Littlefield, Daniel C. 1981: *Rice and Slaves: Ethnicity and the Slave Trade in Colonial South Carolina.* Urbana: University of Illinois Press.

McDonald, Roderick A. 1993: *The Economy and Material Culture of Slaves: Goods and Chattels on the Sugar Plantations of Jamaica and Louisiana.* Baton Rouge: Louisiana State University Press.

Malone, Ann Patton 1992: *Sweet Chariot: Slave Family and Household Structure in Nineteenth-Century Louisiana.* Chapel Hill: University of North Carolina Press.

Owens, Leslie Howard 1976: *This Species of Property: Slave Life and Culture in the Old South.* New York: Oxford University Press.

Parish, Peter J. 1989: *Slavery: History and Historians.* New York: Harper and Row.

Patterson, Orlando 1982: *Slavery and Social Death: A Comparative Study.* Cambridge, MA: Harvard University Press.

Phillips, Ulrich Bonnell 1959: *American Negro Slavery: A Survey of the Supply, Employment and Control of Negro Labor as Determined by the Plantation Regime.* Gloucester, MA: Peter Smith.

Raboteau, Albert J. 1978: *Slave Religion: The "Invisible Institution" in the Antebellum South.* Oxford: Oxford University Press.

Rawick, George P. 1972: *From Sundown to Sunup: The Making of the Black Community.* Westport, CT: Greenwood Publishers.

Rhodes, James Ford 1893: *History of the United States from the Compromise of 1850 to the Final Restoration of Home Rule at the South in 1877.* New York: MacMillan.

Savitt, Todd L. 1978: *Medicine and Slavery: The Diseases and Health Care of Blacks in Antebellum Virginia.* Urbana: University of Illinois Press.

Smith, Mark M. 1997: *Mastered by the Clock: Time, Slavery and Freedom in the American South.* Chapel Hill: University of North Carolina Press.

Stampp, Kenneth M. 1956: *The Peculiar Institution: Slavery in the Ante-Bellum South.* New York: Alfred A. Knopf.

Starobin, Robert S. 1970: *Industrial Slavery in the Old South.* New York: Oxford University Press.

Stuckey, Sterling 1967: Through the Prism of Folklore: The Black Ethos in Slavery. *Massachusetts Review*, 9, 417–37.

Stuckey, Sterling 1987: *Slave Culture: Nationalist Theory and the Foundations of Black America.* New York: Oxford University Press.

Tannenbaum, Frank 1946: *Slave and Citizen: The Negro in the Americas.* New York: Alfred A. Knopf.

Van Deburg, William L. 1979: *The Slave Drivers: Black Agricultural Labor Supervisors in the Antebellum South.* New York: Oxford University Press.

White, Deborah Gray 1985: *Ar'n't I a Woman? Female Slaves in the Plantation South.* New York: W. W. Norton.

Wood, Peter H. 1974: *Black Majority: Negroes in Colonial South Carolina from 1670 through the Stono Rebellion.* New York: Alfred A. Knopf.

Young, Jeffrey 1999: *Domesticating Slavery: The Master Class in Georgia and South Carolina, 1670–1837.* Chapel Hill: University of North Carolina Press.

CHAPTER NINE

Plain Folk Yeomanry in the Antebellum South

SAMUEL C. HYDE, JR.

FEW features of the antebellum South fail to stimulate passions among both casual observers and serious scholars alike. Slavery, secession, war, and the plantation elite continue to command the greatest interest. Yet there are aspects of the Old South that receive marginal attention at best, and accordingly they highlight the sustained presence of a misunderstood, or perhaps overlooked, South.

The role and relevance of the common white people remains among the most misinterpreted aspects of antebellum southern society. Alternately regarded with utter contempt or considered virtually irrelevant, non-elite southerners have frequently enjoyed little more than the peripheral interest of scholars just as they often serve as the whipping boys of popular culture. The neglect of the non-elite remains abundantly manifest in the ambiguous nature of their identity as well as in the very appellations assigned them. Scholars have as yet failed to reach a consensus regarding the precise identity of the vast group of middling southerners variously known as plain folk, common whites, yeomen, and/or a variety of seemingly related terms. Sometimes they are identified in terms of wealth, and on other occasions by ethnic or attitudinal factors. Some see them as nonslaveholders, while others identify them as those owning up to nine slaves. Often they are described as exclusively farmers, while some historians include some merchants and townspeople among their ranks. Critics often disparage the absence of a standardized terminology or even agreement regarding the exact identity of the yeomen, but they seldom offer any definitive guidance.

Despite their previous failure to deem the yeomen worthy of the intensive scrutiny afforded planters or the slaves, historians have in recent years increasingly acknowledged the fundamental significance of the yeomen to southern society. Still they remain the least-studied subset of the southern population. In the late nineteenth and early twentieth centuries, many students of the South interpreted the seeming absence of abundant primary documentation – letters, diaries, and the like – highlighting the lives of the yeomen as indicative of their limited role in regional development. Other scholars acknowledged the presence and even influence of the common folk but provided little insight into their relevance because they too believed the yeomen left few if any records. Such a situation has left us in the ironic position of knowing more about the bondsmen than many of their masters and has necessitated reconsideration of sources of evidence relevant to the lives of the yeomen.

One of the earliest descriptions of antebellum southern yeomen emerged from the writings of Frederick Law Olmsted. A native of Connecticut, Olmsted embraced the

New England affection for quaint country inns and efficient service, qualities that remained at best limited in the antebellum South. In 1852 Olmsted agreed to travel through the South as a special correspondent for the New York *Daily Times* and prepare reports on "the influence of slavery, as a mode of employing labor, and on the development of general resources in the South." Olmsted personally opposed slavery, but, unlike some radical abolitionists of his time, he favored a peaceful resolution to the controversy. Rather than concentrating on the condition of the slaves or the dynamics of the great plantations, Olmsted instead emphasized in his newspaper reports what he regarded as the degradation of whites that accompanied slavery. In his view slavery everywhere determined ways of living, political inclinations, customs, manners, and law to the point that it enslaved the white man almost as much as the black. It is Olmsted's interest in the societal implications slavery mandated for the collective South that makes his work useful to interpreters of the yeomen (Olmsted 1953: xv).

Olmsted submitted his observations to the *Daily Times* where they appeared in a sequence of articles. The series compilation first appeared in 1861, designed primarily to influence English public opinion during the Civil War. His determination to minimize discussion of the planters became obvious; his most startling revelations involved the work ethic and living conditions of the common people. Instead of portraying rustic lives filled with leisurely charm, Olmsted reported only poverty and despair. He described the outward appearance of their living conditions as wretched, noting that their cabins were "mere hovels, such as none but a poor farmer would house his cattle in at the North." Olmsted reported a virtual monolithic existence among the yeomen, arguing that from Virginia to the southwest the average southerner was destitute of the things even day laborers possessed in the North. While he acknowledged that they did not want for what he termed "coarse food," he maintained that the number of common southerners who lived as well as the working class in the North was very small. His observations led him to conclude that the yeomen "work little and work badly, earn little, sell little, buy little, and have very little of the common comforts and consolations of civilized life. The destitution is not material only; it is intellectual and moral" (ibid: 11–12).

Undoubtedly, there were some southerners who conformed to the image Olmsted described. His observations, however, clearly reflected his New England upbringing and his preconceived expectations. In one of the sharpest departures from conventional notions of the yeomen he asserted that "they are not generous or hospitable; and to be plain, I must say that their talk is not the talk of even courageous men elsewhere. They boast and lack self-restraint, yet, when not excited, are habitually reserved and guarded in expressions of opinion very much like cowardly men elsewhere" (ibid: 12).

Olmsted reported conditions certain to confirm the assumptions of many in the North of the 1850s, but his observations nonetheless remain a rare and valuable account of antebellum southern society. Yet his description of the common folk suffered from his ignorance of their actual circumstances as well as his distaste for their attitudes and mannerisms. Had he not possessed preconceived notions of poverty and degradation, he might have observed substantial wealth amid the cumulative product of the fields and livestock maintained by most yeomen. He took the absence of sturdy New England-type barns as an indication of southern laziness, not recognizing that the warmer climate in much of the South obviated the need for such barns. A more balanced assessment of wealth may have enabled him to understand that the white southern social structure did not consist of only great planters, lesser planters, and poor whites. It remains unclear if Olmsted ever grasped the social position and relevance of the yeomen.

Finally, Omsted employed terms such as "hospitality" and "courage" in a manner inconsistent with standard usage in the South. It seems puzzling that Olmsted could describe scores of families who would open their door, share their food, and, as best they could, accommodate his every need for little or no compensation, as unhospitable. Yet flawed as his accounts of the South are, they remain central to understanding the contemporary prevailing impression of common southerners.

A radically different interpretation of the yeomen, and one that in many ways was constructed to dispute the claims of Olmsted and other like-minded observers, emerged in the writings of Daniel Hundley. Unlike Olmsted, Hundley was a native southerner who relied on lifelong experiences to shape his account. He included both criticism and praise in his discussion of southern society, which he divided into numerous classifications ranging from "cotton snobs" to "poor white trash." His precise representation of the social structure challenged the assumption maintained by Olmsted and others that only two classes of white southerners existed: poor whites and cavaliers. In particular, Hundley's analysis permitted the emergence of a more detailed assessment of the yeomen whom he regarded as the country-dwelling portion of the middle class (Hundley 1979: 77–83).

Simply put, Hundley emphasized the positive elements of the same characteristics of life in the South that Olmsted condemned. He explained the preparation and praised the quality of Olmsted's "coarse food," such as corn pone and hoe cake, and argued that southern yeomen remained as intelligent and generally better versed in politics than middle-class farmers of the North. Although he acknowledged that most yeomen possessed little material wealth, he described their existence as comfortable, noting that the ability to earn an honest livelihood by the sweat of their own brows served as their greatest inheritance. In Hundley's view, effusive hospitality served as one of the most identifiable characteristics of the yeomen, one of the many traits shared between common and elite southerners.

Most important, Hundley argued that the yeomen, by strength of numbers and conviction, enjoyed impressive political power. Political harmony existed in the South because the common people and the elite viewed politics identically amid a political system that allowed for meaningful participation of all white males. Far from a mindless rabble assenting to the demands of the planters, Hundley insisted that the yeomen, along with the urban middle class, made the greatest contribution to southern society, acting as equals with the planters in the direction of their lives.

Hundley's work appeared on the eve of the Civil War, and his sweeping generalizations clearly reflected a desire to refute the assumptions held by many outsiders; but it did provide a more meaningful analysis of the relevance of the yeomen. Regrettably, defeat in war and a troublesome Reconstruction period nullified sympathetic portrayals of the South in the minds of many nonsoutherners. As Olmsted's interpretation accordingly achieved renewed prominence, Hundley's faded.

The widely disparate contemporary depictions of the antebellum yeomanry presented in the work of Olmsted and Hundley defined popular impressions of the southern common folk prior to the Civil War. Not surprisingly, the era of the Civil War and Reconstruction marked a transition in scholarship just as it served as a watershed in American development. Little serious analysis of southern social classes occurred in the late nineteenth and early twentieth centuries. Most scholars concentrated instead on praising the exploits of the Grand Army of the Republic or debating the might-have-beens associated with the Lost Cause. The resurgent nationalism that accompanied the Allied effort during World War I encouraged new analysis of the course of American development, with a special emphasis on the peculiarities of the antebellum South. The greatest interest by far centered on the planters and their slaves.

The intense emphasis on the plantation system not surprisingly served to shape impressions of the yeomen. Although the leading scholars of the period did not ignore the common folk altogether, they typically depicted them as, at best, of only limited significance to southern development. William E. Dodd's *The Cotton Kingdom: A Chronicle of the Old South* (1919) emerged as one of the first such studies suggesting the near irrelevance of the yeomen. Dodd described the common people as victims of planter exploitation, "willing hangers-on of a system which, if they but knew it, could give them no promise of better things." Despite outlining the victim status of common whites, he remained inconsistent in his discussion of their significance to southern society. He acknowledged that the common folk did have value, insisting that their political participation secured for them the interest and affection of the planters. He also described them as "the inarticulate masses" who remained "tributary in their small way to the great planter aristocracy." Dodd seemed to suggest that the plain folk's relevance related exclusively to their value in the eyes of the planters (Dodd 1919: 30–2).

In Dodd's analysis, little of distinction separated the poor whites and yeomen excepting that the yeomen appeared somewhat cleaner and aspired to become planters. He argued that the great majority of southerners belonged to these "poorer classes," some of whom owned a few slaves but whose net income typically amounted to less than two hundred dollars per year. They lived on the poorer lands of the cotton belt, which sustained a hard and monotonous life with few opportunities for improvement. Many yeomen were distant cousins of the elite; all suffered exploitation amid a system that in Dodd's view facilitated the transferal of southern wealth to the ultimate beneficiaries of the cotton economy in the North.

Dodd's treatment of the yeomen reflected the limits of historical research that characterized the early twentieth century. The virtual absence of non-elite southerners in traditional sources of evidence – primarily written records – dramatically decreased appreciation of their relevance. Arguably the most influential southern historian of his time, Ulrich B. Phillips, noted "the letters they wrote were few, and their significant, explicit items fewer still" (Phillips 1929: 340).

Like Dodd, Phillips cautioned against ignoring the presence of the yeomen, although he too downplayed their significance. In a variety of seminal studies of antebellum southern society, Phillips demonstrated that he shared with Dodd a belief in the absolute social, political, and economic dominance of the planter class. He argued, nonetheless, that the plain folk numbered in the millions and that the sweeping statements often employed to characterize them were typically "as false as they are facile." According to Phillips, most of the yeomen maintained a modest existence that afforded relative comfort provided the family avoided illness or enerva-tion. If the breadwinner became in any way debilitated, the family could remain impoverished for generations. Phillips described a yeoman class that sustained itself in varying degrees of comfort but otherwise contributed little to antebellum society. Like their counterparts in the North, they remained "provincial in speech and out-look, jealous of authority, resentful of superior pretenses, matter of fact in daily life, self-respecting and substantial." Yet unlike common farmers in the North, they had little impact on the course of social and political development (ibid: 346, 353).

The image of southern society evident in the works of Dodd and Phillips continued to shape impressions of the yeomen through the course of the early twentieth century. Although few, if any, challenges to the Dodd–Phillips notion of the yeomen emerged, during the depths of the Great Depression there arrived a study of major significance that furthered the prevailing opinion. In 1933 Lewis C. Gray released his massive two-volume *History of Agriculture in the Southern United States to 1860*, a work that continues today as an influential tool for many historians. Although Gray's study is prized for its intensive examination of southern agricultural practices, it also provides insightful analysis of antebellum society.

Gray divided antebellum white southerners into ten groups, ranging from the wealthiest planter elite to the desperately poor. Some of his divisions related to the environment, such as distinctions between residents of highland or lowland areas. Other categories centered on skills and trades, such as contrasts between commercial farmers and free white agricultural laborers, so that in the final analysis, he identified approximately six classes of southerners.

Gray sought to be as specific as possible regarding the diversity that existed within white society. In his most basic division, he separated southerners into plantation and nonplantation classes. The plantation class included varying divisions among the slaveholding elite, while the nonplantation group consisted of everyone else. Even though Gray assigned one specific group the appellation "yeoman," his description of the various classifications of non-elite southerners indicates that several possessed qualities typically associated with the yeomen.

According to Gray, the bottom rung of southern society consisted of the poor whites who served as meaningless outcasts. In his analysis the propertyless, aimless, shiftless, and utterly lazy members of white society described by Olmsted belonged to this group. Seemingly related to, but in Gray's view distinctly separate from the poor whites, were the highlanders: poor hill dwellers who lacked a compelling motive but whose poverty did not make them social outcasts. The highlanders maintained a similar existence to the lowland farmers, or yeomen, but differed in that they owned no slaves. Likewise, the yeomen remained distinctive from planters primarily due to their reliance on general farming rather than the production of staple crops.

Despite the centrality of agriculture to his work, Gray provided precise analysis of the southern social structure, identifying subtle characteristics other than wealth and agricultural practices that separated the yeomanry from other classes of southerners. In particular he stressed differences in personal characteristics and social life. Like other nonplantation classes, the yeomen largely originated from immigrants who came to America as indentured servants, particularly the southward-moving groups of German and Scotch–Irish farmers. The yeomen, or in Gray's words "commercial farmers," constructed large frame and brick houses with substantial barns for livestock surrounded by fruit orchards that made their dwellings separate and distinct from those of poorer whites (Gray 1958, I: 489).

Gray acknowledged that a wide variance of means and ability existed within the yeoman class, a circumstance he attributed to their distance from initial coastal settlements and how quickly they progressed beyond the pioneer stage. According to Gray, the yeomen collectively enjoyed more material comforts than any other antebellum southern group except the large planters. Their quality of life surpassed even that of middle-class planters, who, unlike the yeomen, concentrated on a one-crop system rather than a diversified economy but who otherwise closely resembled the yeomen. The benefits of producing large varieties of grains, fresh milk, butter, eggs, and livestock distinguished yeomen from middle-class planters.

Slaveholding, though producing a powerful common bond, likewise provided important distinctions that both separated the yeomen from middle-class planters and contributed to a superior quality of life. Gray described large, or upper-class, planters owning fifty or more slaves and middle-class planters who maintained between ten and fifty. He noted that many yeomen resembled smaller planters in that they were frequently slaveholders, but he demonstrated that they rarely kept more than a slave or two. Gray argued further that most yeomen slaveholders enjoyed friendly, almost intimate, relations with their slaves in contrast to the hard demands of life on many single-crop middle-class plantations.

As a class, Gray described the yeomen as independent and self-respecting, hospitable and democratic, and intelligent though lacking extensive education. Although they often drank to excess, they remained intensely religious as evidenced by their camp meetings. Gray's conclusions concerning the yeomen echoed many of the themes presented earlier by Daniel Hundley, yet he differed in an important respect. Much like Dodd, Phillips, and even Olmsted, Gray believed in the absolute dominance of the plantation class. Slavery, of course, served as the identifiable basis of their power. Gray compared circumstances in the South to conditions that transformed the Roman Empire, arguing that free farmers eventually proved incapable of competing with slave labor and were driven from the best lands. According to Gray, small farmers "were compelled either to become great planters – and many did not possess sufficient ability and command over capital to accomplish this – or to reestablish a regime of rude self-sufficing economy in a region less favorable for commercial agriculture" (Gray 1958, I: 444).

The image of the yeomen that emerged from the writings of Dodd, Phillips, and Gray profoundly shaped perceptions of southern society for the first half of the twentieth century. Although their portrayal remained distinct from the pathetic class of individuals described by Olmsted, the most enduring stereotype furthered by the Dodd–Phillips–Gray perspective centered on the near irrelevance of the yeomanry. Popular impressions of the antebellum South typically concentrated on planters, slaves, and poor white trash. Plantation society and the slave system commanded the interest of millions worldwide as evidenced by the dramatic success of such books, and films, as Margaret Mitchell's *Gone With the Wind*, while the attention given poor whites confirmed the belief that the mass of southerners remained ignorant dupes of the ruling elite. Through the first decades of the twentieth century little or no interest developed in the seemingly less dramatic lifestyle of the yeomen. Even depictions of the twentieth-century southern poor whites like Erskine Caldwell's

Tobacco Road – made into a Broadway play and a movie – presented them as lazy and both physically and morally deformed.

The popular as well as scholarly neglect of the yeomen did not relate exclusively to their presumed insignificance. Traditional research methods seemed to indicate that the common people left few records to document their existence. But by the middle of the 1940s newly emerging research procedures demanded reconsideration of the yeomen and their influence as scholars mined previously untapped sources of evidence. At the forefront of a more aggressive analysis of common southerners emerged a historian whose work would have a profound impact on future scholarship.

Frank L. Owsley personified a new departure in southern history in the aftermath of World War II. Far from one who could be easily dissuaded in his purpose, Owsley had an established reputation for challenging prevailing stereotypes of the South. Early in his career he joined with a group of southern literary figures in 1930 to produce *I'll Take My Stand: The South and the Agrarian Tradition*, a response to the contemptuous portrayals of the South evident in works such as H. L. Mencken's "Sahara of the Bozart." Consciously intent on neither glorifying antebellum society nor vilifying the South, Owsley, himself a native southerner, concentrated instead on determining the true relevance of the yeomen whom he defined as "the small slaveholding farmers; the nonslaveholders who owned the land which they cultivated; the numerous herdsmen on the frontier, pine barrens, and mountains; and those tenant farmers whose agricultural production, as recorded in the census, indicated thrift, energy, and self respect" (Owsley 1949: 8).

Where others decried the absence of records documenting the lifestyles of common people, Owsley found an abundance of evidence to revise existing interpretations. Supported in his research by his wife, Harriet Chappell Owsley, and numerous students, the so-called Owsley school poured over manuscript census returns, county court minutes, church records, tax records, mortgage books, travel accounts, and the like to uncover an antebellum society that contrasted sharply in many ways with existing beliefs. The appearance of Owsley's primary work *Plain Folk of the Old South* in 1949 not surprisingly provoked both immediate consternation and praise.

Many of Owsley's conclusions challenged notions that had guided historical scholarship for generations. Owsley's plain folk proved vital to antebellum society, serving as an essential determinant of southern economic and political development. He argued that small farmers inhabited every arable region of the South, sharing the best agricultural lands with the planter elite. Owsley's research indicated that in the lower South "from 80 to 85 percent of the agricultural population owned their own land." Perhaps most surprising, Owsley suggested that the opportunity to obtain land remained greater in the South than in the North and that those who did settle on the more rugged lands did so as a result of farming opportunities and not from pressure created by the slave system. In sharp contrast to Olmsted, Dodd, and others, Owsley insisted that nearly all yeomen ascended the economic ladder during the course of their lives (Owsley 1949: 16).

Owsley's analysis of the southern plain folk forced a reconsideration of antebellum social and economic development. Yet an equally important component of his research centered on the insight he provided into the mind of the yeomen. Owsley disputed the contentions of some historians of his era, such as Roger Shugg (1939), who argued that bitter class divisions separated white society. According to the Shugg version of events, the plain folk remained deeply resentful of the elite, whom they regarded as oppressors.

Owsley instead argued that a fundamental difference in values, related primarily to ambition, separated the plain folk and the elite. Although most yeomen did not aspire to great wealth, the knowledge that the opportunity remained open to them stifled the development of bitter class consciousness. Owsley noted that the plain folk generally admired the elite and looked with approval on their success; often in fact they were related by kin to members of the elite. The abundance of cheap land, the high prices they typically received for their agricultural products, and the steady expansion of democracy also served to mitigate frustration and resentment toward the wealthy. Moreover, the regular association rich and poor enjoyed at religious gatherings, schools, and court sessions – as well as family ties and the general folkish bearing of the elite – convinced Owsley that plain-folk discontent remained minimal at most.

The egalitarian perspective maintained by the Owsley school proved almost revolutionary, challenging even the time-tested notion of planter political dominance. Owsley questioned the very mechanisms of planter power, noting that the elite commanded few devices capable of denying an independent people their rights. He argued that intimidation would not have worked against so many well-armed men; neither would economic coercion, since most yeomen owned their own land and means of production and were accordingly dependent on no one. Owsley dismissed the power of bribery and corruption in the electoral process, arguing that such behavior remained virtually nonexistent in a region characterized by honor-bound relationships.

Although he rejected the notion of planter dominance, Owsley acknowledged that the elite exercised powers of influence over the common people. Many of the plain folk respected the character and judgment of community leaders whom they typically knew personally. Owsley described political barbeques and other efforts practiced by the elite to secure the votes of the common people and concluded that the planters' only real mechanism of influence over the plain folk was persuasion.

Owsley's interpretation of the South highlighting the centrality of the plain folk, cooperative and cordial relations between all classes of white southerners, and a reduced emphasis on the slave system, obviously proved controversial. His methodology, however, encouraged a more aggressive analysis of southern culture that allowed for substantive consideration of the yeomen. Owsley conducted groundbreaking research employing manuscript census returns to demonstrate that previously unconsidered sources of wealth and abundance remained widespread among the plain folk. He nonetheless presented his views more as essays than as carefully reasoned works of analysis solidly grounded in his extensive census research. His essays also presented what must be termed a romantic version of yeomen life, perhaps partially in reaction to the popularity of Erskine Caldwell-like portrayals of the common folk of the South. Although numerous historians joined in the debate stimulated by Owsley's ongoing research, the controversy concerning the plain folk and their place in history quickly receded. More than twenty years passed before substantive new contributions to our understanding of the yeomen emerged. As new studies finally began to appear, the enduring legacy of the Dodd–Phillips–Gray perspective as well as the impact of Owsley's contribution proved readily apparent.

In 1974 Dickson D. Bruce Jr., a professor of comparative culture at the University of California, Irvine, released a study that exemplified an emerging synthesis of the traditional and Owsley schools of thought. Bruce concentrated on camp-meeting religion, a phenomenon that attracted considerable attention from Owsley. He borrowed significantly from *Plain Folk of the Old South*, acknowledging that he incorporated Owsley's "plain folk" in his title as the most fitting appellation for the people he described. His exclusive emphasis on the role of the Baptist and Methodist faiths, as well as his concentration on the social aspects and seeming anti-intellectualism of the camp meetings, stands in contrast to the perspective of other scholars such as John Boles (1972), whose expanded focus not only included Presbyterians among the denominations involved, but suggested that the revivals were far more complex than Bruce's more narrowly defined interests indicated.

Bruce's analysis centered on the society from which the movement emerged, the folksy spiritualism evident in the revivals, and the people, primarily the yeomen, who participated in such events. Consistent with earlier studies, he agreed that the plain folk included the largest number of antebellum southerners. The majority of that vast group, in his view, were not particularly religious prior to the emergence of the camp meetings. They accordingly served as the object of greatest interest to early Baptist and Methodist evangelists, both of whom recruited most of their leaders from yeomen ranks. The centrality of the plain folk to both the Baptists and Methodists eventually affected the theology of each, so that over time the two faiths emerged as the spiritual reflection of the yeomanry. Bruce described a near symbiotic relationship between spiritually driven yeomen and the two denominations. Just as the values of the yeomen affected the faith, so the religion came to shape the lives of the plain folk.

Like Owsley, Bruce highlighted the value of nontraditional sources in our effort to understand the yeomen. Otherwise, his study demonstrated the remarkable power of tradition. Instead of embracing Owsley's expanded formula for determining wealth in the antebellum South, Bruce returned to the notion that staple crops and slaves served as the only analytically significant aspects of the agricultural economy. He referred to the plain folk as simple subsistence farmers who "were never important to the staple crop economy of the ante-bellum period." He noted that the yeomen never produced more than 7 percent of the cotton crop in Mississippi or 5 percent of Virginia's tobacco crop. Nowhere did they occupy the most productive land. Borrowing directly from Olmsted, Bruce asserted that the economic marginality of the plain folk was accompanied by political impotence, arguing that the planter elite exercised hegemony over the antebellum South. Perhaps most curious, he echoed the perspective presented by William Dodd more than a half century earlier, suggesting that the plain folk often exhibited bitter resentment toward the elite. Only the hope of improving their status and sharing in the power and prestige enjoyed by the elite contained the rebellious impulses of the yeomen (Bruce 1974: 4–5, 18–19).

Some may conclude that Bruce's perspective merely adhered to pre-Owsley notions of the antebellum South. A more accurate assessment would acknowledge that his work, as well as that of others appearing in the same period, was responsive to Owsley. Beginning in the early 1970s, a number of projects emerged that essentially revised Owsley's revisionism. The value of many of the most significant contributions centered on aggressive statistical analysis.

In a series of studies completed both independently as well as in association with fellow historian Richard Lowe, Randolph Campbell conducted intensive statistical surveys of Texas with a special emphasis on Harrison County. The work of Campbell and Lowe clearly reflected the influence of Owsley as they consistently acknowledged the majority status of the yeomen and assaulted the notion of plain-folk poverty. In 1983 Campbell published *A Southern Community in Crisis: Harrison County, Texas, 1850–1880,* in which he employed statistical data to outline the region's late antebellum social structure. Following the lead of economic historian Gavin Wright, he employed the Lorenz Curve and Gini Index to measure degrees of agricultural wealth among the various classes of southerners. He concluded that by 1860 the value of yeomen home manufactures surpassed that of any other class. More important, the plain folk of Harrison County demonstrated impressive food-production abilities. Even those who were not well off by yeomen standards produced abundant corn, sweet potatoes, and other vegetables as well as impressive amounts of milk, butter, and other fruits of livestock production.

Their statistical analysis allowed Campbell and Lowe to conclude that in the late antebellum period the yeomen served as an expanding class that enjoyed relative comfort and economic security. The increasing number of yeomen landowners did not, however, translate to economic parity between slaveholders and nonslaveholders, nor did it imply political democracy. Campbell noted that although the numbers of landowning farmers increased, it remained difficult for the yeomen to rise higher on the economic scale, and "they were notably less wealthy than the groups above them on the social ladder." He argued further that in the late antebellum period the wealth of the yeomen declined in every category in comparison to their planter neighbors. Although Campbell admitted that his research primarily emphasized economics, he argued that the evidence also suggested planter dominance of the political process (Campbell 1983: 39).

The work of Campbell, Lowe, and others also proved useful for demonstrating the value of micro-studies of the South. Whereas the yeomen often remained the forgotten people of larger studies, they typically emerged as a central component of specific case studies, suggesting that the historical neglect of them related more to research methods rather than to an absence of relevance. The 1980s and 1990s witnessed increasing emphasis on the value of micro-studies, many of which proved crucial to promoting current notions regarding the plain folk. In 1985 Orville V. Burton published an exhaustive micro-study of Edgefield County, South Carolina, that highlighted the relevance of such studies for advancing our understanding of the antebellum yeomen. Burton demonstrated consistency between his own work and that of Owsley, Campbell, and Lowe, by arguing that the majority of Edgefield's population "resembled the self-sufficient yeomen that Frank Owsley called the plain folk of the South" (Burton 1985: 57).

Burton returned to a common theme of the Owsley school that discouraged viewing the various segments of the Old South as separate and distinct. Instead, he encouraged students of the South to acknowledge that all parts of antebellum society bore a relation to the whole. According to Owsley, "it is then that the plain folk appear not as supernumeraries but as a vital element of the social and economic structure of the Old South" (Owsley 1949: 134).

Burton argued that the line separating poor whites and yeomen was never very distinct. Where Campbell and Lowe found abundance among the yeomen, Burton noted that many plain folk remained one economic step away from poverty. The condition of people frequently remained subject to the eyes of the beholder. In Burton's view, "the dividing line between destitution and respectable poverty was drawn by different people in Edgefield at different levels." To accommodate his reasoning, he divided Edgefield society into the poor, the respectable, and the prosperous, the yeomen most often occupying the middle category (Burton 1985: 51).

The obvious divisions in wealth did not affect community obligations in Edgefield, where poor and affluent whites lived side by side relying on one another for support and services. Burton's study did not include the intensive agricultural statistics that supported the work of Campbell and Lowe, but he did acknowledge the centrality of the cotton economy to all aspects of Edgefield society, a condition that advanced interaction between classes. Yeomen rarely maintained their own cotton gins or agents; instead they remained dependent on their planter neighbors to process and market their crop. Burton noted that basic problems of living – such as poor roads, bad weather, and insects – also crossed class lines, furthering the notion of community.

Wealth did contribute to differences in lifestyles. Few among the yeomen commanded the financial resources necessary to engage in the finer things of life that the elite took for granted, such as enjoying imported food and wine or a night at the opera in Charleston. Strong drink often served as the basis of entertainment for many yeomen, while others embraced the strictures incumbent upon evangelical Christians. Burton confirmed the findings of Bruce and others noting that the yeomen tended to avoid the elite-dominated Episcopalians in favor of the more accommodating Baptists and Methodists.

Although Burton emphasized the charitable and cooperative ties that bound whites, he also identified conflict as a social determinant. He argued that the yeomen, like their elite neighbors, frequently settled personal quarrels violently. Honorable resolution of conflict served as another tie that united Edgefield society, but conflict also furthered group identity among the various classes of whites. Burton demonstrated that Edgefield yeomen often harbored deep resentment against medical doctors, lawyers, and other professional classes. Much like the ancient Chinese who typically regarded merchants as the bottom feeders of society, the yeomen resented those "who made their livings other than by the sweat of their brows" (Burton 1985: 75).

Burton's comprehensive treatment of Edgefield society advanced appreciation of the social standing of the yeomen. Perhaps even more significant, it strengthened the notion that the plain folk had a group identity. Historical awareness of the presence of an "us versus them" attitude among social classes in the antebellum South can be traced all the way back to Olmsted and Hundley. Most observers concentrated on economic or political condition as the most obvious determinant of group association. By the middle of the 1980s a new perspective emerged that assigned ethnic background, rather than economic or political condition, as the foremost distinguishing attribute of the yeomen.

In 1988 Grady McWhiney published his culminating work highlighting the southern folk, *Cracker Culture: Celtic Ways in the Old South*. McWhiney, often working in conjunction with Forrest McDonald, had for some years promoted the notion that a herding culture predominated among common southerners. In *Cracker Culture* McWhiney remained consistent with Owsley, arguing that southerners were a genuine folk long before the shared calamity of the Civil War. He also acknowledged a constancy of life in the South that characterized the entire antebellum period. Yet his study represented something of a departure from previous scholarship in that he emphasized the common national origin of the bulk of the people as the source of southern unity. McWhiney argued that the term "Cracker" signified not economic condition but instead defined a culture that persisted across time and geography. Therefore, with the exception of a few planters and professional people, all white southerners were a part of Cracker culture.

In McWhiney's view, southern culture very nearly resembled that sustained by the Celtic tribes who had inhabited the northern and northwest regions of the British Isles and remained distinct from the English. The Celtic connection separated southerners from persons of English descent who predominated in the northern states. Although a scattering of the ethnic variety that characterizes America remained evident in the South, southerners of all classes, McWhiney argued, overwhelmingly traced their ancestry to an Irish or Scotch–Irish origin.

McWhiney's cultural interpretation assigned a near-monolithic sameness to southerners regardless of wealth or standing. In his words, "all poor whites were Crackers even though not all Crackers were poor whites." In so doing he challenged long-standing notions of the South that acknowledged sharp distinctions between the culture of the elite and that of the plain folk. Even Owsley treated the two groups as separate and distinctive. McWhiney claimed to be speaking about southerners generally. On closer inspection, however, it seems clear that his conclusions were more applicable to the lifestyle of the backcountry yeomen than the great planters (McWhiney 1988: xvi).

McWhiney's controversial approach attracted considerable attention from both supporters and antagonists; rarely did it go unnoticed, and even more rarely was it fully accepted. On a note of particular relevance for this essay, he raised the issue of terminology by denying that any southerners could be yeomen. Embracing a rigid nineteenth-century English interpretation of the term "yeomen," one roughly defined as a "settled or staid" freeholder, McWhiney concluded that even common southerners "were too lazy, too unstable, too migratory, and too committed to sensual pleasures to be yeomen." While such an interpretation augments McWhiney's cultural approach, it remains inconsistent with the image of the sturdy, self-reliant farmer described by the Owsley school that McWhiney clearly admired (McWhiney 1988: 264). In fact, much about McWhiney's depiction of Crackers was decidedly unflattering.

McWhiney's emphasis on a common identity for southerners signaled that notions of well-defined class and cultural divisions in the antebellum South were coming into question. *Cracker Culture* also further obscured the identity of the yeomen as an identifiable group and raised new questions concerning terminology. These same issues have remained central to the emerging scholarship of the 1990s.

In 1992 Bill Cecil-Fronsman, a native New Yorker and converted student of the South, added an interesting new perspective to the debate. His *Common Whites: Class and Culture in Antebellum North Carolina* directly addressed the issue of homogeneity among southerners and provided a new twist in the discussion of terms appropriate for describing the yeomen. Like McWhiney, Cecil-Fronsman stressed a commonality among the white people of the South, though he argued that it existed only among the non-elite. He rejected use of the term "yeomen" as well as "plain folk" to describe the common people, specifically because each implied prosperous independent farmers "whose conditions contrasted sharply with the squalid poverty implied by the term poor white." According to Cecil-Fronsman, no matter how different in character the poorest white trash and most prosperous yeoman may have been, they maintained so much in common that a single term should describe them; hence common whites (Cecil-Fronsman 1992: 1).

Although his study also concentrated on culture, it did not conform to the ethnic perspective central to *Cracker Culture*. Instead, Cecil-Fronsman treated culture as class identity distinct and separate from that of the elite. He disputed the Owsley image of plain folk living in harmony with the planters, but he also challenged the planter hegemony argument championed by Eugene Genovese in his *The Political Economy of Slavery* (1965) and other works. According to Genovese's theory of hegemony, the yeomen failed to challenge the absolute power of the elite because the planters convinced them that the planters' own interests were synonymous with those of society at large, including the yeomen. The antebellum South accordingly functioned as it did in the belief that a fair social order prevailed.

Cecil-Fronsman described a different image of the South. Echoing the arguments of both Dodd and Genovese, he acknowledged planter hegemony and the corresponding exploitation of the common people. He insisted that antebellum North Carolina remained a society in which common whites and planters routinely clashed. Far from a class living in harmony with an accommodating elite, as the Owsley school described, or an exploited people essentially ignorant of their own condition, as depicted by Genovese and others, Cecil-Fronsman instead described a group aware of their circumstances and willing to challenge their betters to secure change. In short, common white culture operating within the boundaries of planter hegemony served as the focus of Cecil-Fronsman's study.

The work of Cecil-Fronsman, McWhiney, and others demonstrates an interesting trend emerging in research centered on the yeomen. It should be remembered that most early historical accounts divided antebellum southern society into planters, slaves, and poor whites. Subsequent research generally conformed to that pattern until the Owsley school demonstrated much greater diversity in southern society and, most importantly, highlighted the majority status of a thriving middle class. By the late 1980s some historians proved willing again to blur distinctions between social groups largely based on a cultural pretext. Hence we find McWhiney's Crackers and Cecil-Fronsman's common whites including people obviously inconsistent with the standard notion of antebellum yeomen.

The once-forgotten people of the South have emerged as the ambiguous southerners, a status that at least suggests increasing historical scrutiny. The escalating interest has by no means produced a consensus regarding precise terminology, nor has it resolved the ambiguity surrounding the specific identity of the plain folk. Efforts to answer such questions have complexified the study of the southern yeomanry, but the variety of terms and interpretations appearing demonstrates the continuing near absence of standardization.

Recent influential studies indicate an apparent desire for a consistent definition and at the same time dramatize the absence of consensus. In their respective studies of the Georgia and South Carolina upcountry, historians Steven Hahn and Lacy Ford employed the term "yeomen," while J. William Harris utilized "plain folk" in the title of his work on the Augusta, Georgia environs. Hahn and Ford did each provide a more precise definition of yeomen, generally describing them as those small farmers owning 200 acres or less and no more than five slaves.

Studies highlighting poor whites in the antebellum South have added to the confusion. In his study of tenants and laborers in central North Carolina and northeast Mississippi, Charles Bolton (1994) cautioned that although nearly half the white population in his focus area owned no land, poor whites should not be confused with the yeomen. Bolton argued that although both groups typically contained those who remained materially impoverished, the term "poor" was assigned only to those of low social standing due to certain negative stereotypes such as laziness. By contrast, in a comprehensive study of southern poor whites Wayne Flynt insisted that "it is impossible to separate poor white from middle-class yeomen, so similar were their common interests" (Flynt 1979: 12). Other historians have suggested alternative considerations that may assist in identifying the common folk.

In her study of antebellum society in the South Carolina lowcountry, Stephanie McCurry (1995) sought to provide some guidance. McCurry's suggestions were not unprecedented, but they did directly address the problems involving terminology and the yeomanry's specific identity. Her analysis conformed to traditional interpretations identifying planters as those with 20 or more slaves, great planters with more than 100 slaves, and small planters as those with more than 9 and less than 20. She described the yeomen as "self-working farmers" who differed from planters by the character of their labor. Unlike the planters whose role on the plantation remained managerial, in the yeomen household the family composed the primary labor supply. In McCurry's view, the key to identifying the yeomen was not slaveholding in itself but whether the specific family merely managed labor or worked alongside their bondsmen. Farmers who owned as many as nine slaves but worked the fields with them should, according to her analysis, be considered yeomen.

McCurry argued that the yeomen remained clearly distinguishable from poor whites due to their ownership of real property, specifically fewer than 150 acres of improved land and less than ten slaves. The fine line dividing the yeomen and small planters related almost exclusively to whether they worked among their slaves or not.

McCurry's quantitative analysis furthered efforts to assign specific numerical identifiers to the yeomen class. Her conclusions regarding land and slaveholding remained reasonably consistent with other quantitative studies that appeared in the 1980s and 1990s. Yet her study devoted little space to the relevance of culture, placing her at odds with the conclusions of McWhiney, Cecil-Fronsman, and others who emphasized lifestyle over possessions as the fundamental determinant for identifying antebellum classes.

Southern historians have increasingly demonstrated a willingness to acknowledge and investigate the fundamental relevance of the antebellum yeomen. Regrettably, the plain folk have yet to enjoy the intensive analysis that characterizes the recent historiography of slavery and the planter elite. Current research demonstrates that the study of the antebellum yeomanry has become increasingly more complex, moving from descriptions of housing and food to sophisticated analysis of class consciousness. Problems of terminology and the need to establish a specific identity for the yeomen remain. Scholars continue to confuse readers with a myriad of labels assumed to carry a virtual synonymous meaning with yeomen but whose descriptions frequently transcend expectations of them. A commonly accepted definition of the plain folk or yeomanry would greatly facilitate comparative studies.

The terminology problem relates directly to that of the yeomanry's identity. Some of the most useful research in coming years regarding the common people of the antebellum South may serve to provide an acceptable basis to categorize the yeomanry economically and politically. Other necessary studies should emphasize social and cultural characteristics that may make it possible to determine whether the yeomen were exclusively rural or also urban dwellers, farmers as well as shopkeepers and craftsmen, of one primary ethnic identity or many, and whether they were rulers as well as the ruled. Each of these issues has been addressed, but few have been resolved to the satisfaction of the historical community.

The absence of standards regarding the antebellum yeomanry suggests the opportunity prevailing in the field. One need look no further than a typical bibliography highlighting yeomen studies to acknowledge the limits of related research. Scholars will remain challenged by the absence of abundant primary evidence (letters, diaries, memoirs) detailing the lives of the common people. Serious researchers, nonetheless, continue to demonstrate the existence of a plethora of less obvious evidence to support studies of the yeomen. In the coming years students of the southern yeomanry willing to embrace and overcome the challenges confronting the field will undoubtedly find a bright future as a reward for their efforts.

BIBLIOGRAPHY

Ash, Stephen V. 1991: Poor Whites in the Occupied South, 1861–1865. *Journal of Southern History*, 57, 39–62.

Boles, John B. 1972: *The Great Revival, 1787–1805: The Origins of the Southern Evangelical Mind*. Lexington: University Press of Kentucky.

Bolton, Charles C. 1994: *Poor Whites of the Antebellum South: Tenants and Laborers in Central North Carolina and Northeast Mississippi*. Durham, NC: Duke University Press.

Bond, Bradley G. 1997: Herders, Farmers, and Markets on the Inner Frontier: The Mississippi Piney Woods, 1850–1860. In Samuel C. Hyde, Jr. (ed.), *Plain Folk of the South Revisited*. Baton Rouge: Louisiana State University Press, 73–99.

Bruce, Dickson D., Jr. 1974: *And They All Sang Hallelujah: Plain Folk Camp-Meeting Religion, 1800–1845*. Knoxville: University of Tennessee Press.

Burton, Orville Vernon 1985: *In My Father's House Are Many Mansions: Family and Community in Edgefield, South Carolina*. Chapel Hill and London: University of North Carolina Press.

Caldwell, Erskine 1940: *Tobacco Road*. New York: Duell, Sloan, and Pearce.

Campbell, Randolph B. 1974: Planters and Plain Folk: Harrison County, Texas, as a Test Case, 1850–1860. *Journal of Southern History*, 40, 369–98.

Campbell, Randolph B. 1983: *A Southern Community in Crisis: Harrison County, Texas, 1850–1880*. Austin: Texas State Historical Association.

Campbell, Randolph B. and Lowe, Richard G. 1977: *Wealth and Power in Antebellum Texas*. College Station: Texas A & M University Press.

Cecil-Fronsman, Bill 1992: *Common Whites: Class and Culture in Antebellum North Carolina.* Lexington: University Press of Kentucky.

Clark, Blanche Henry 1942: *The Tennessee Yeomen, 1840–1860.* Nashville: Vanderbilt University Press.

Dodd, William E. 1919: *The Cotton Kingdom: A Chronicle of the Old South.* New Haven, CT: Yale University Press.

Flynt, J. Wayne 1979: *Dixie's Forgotten People: The South's Poor Whites.* Bloomington: Indiana University Press.

Ford, Lacy K., Jr. 1988: *Origins of Southern Radicalism: The South Carolina Upcountry, 1800–1860.* New York: Oxford University Press.

Ford, Lacy K., Jr. 1997: Popular Ideology of the Old South's Plain Folk: The Limits of Egalitarianism in a Slaveholding Society. In Samuel C. Hyde, Jr. (ed.), *Plain Folk of the South Revisited.* Baton Rouge: Louisiana State University Press, 205–27.

Genovese, Eugene D. 1965: *The Political Economy of Slavery: Studies in the Economy and Society of the Slave South.* New York: Pantheon Books.

Gray, Lewis Cecil 1958: *History of Agriculture in the Southern United States to 1860.* Gloucester, MA: Peter Smith.

Hahn, Steven 1982: The Yeomanry of the Nonplantation South: Upper Piedmont Georgia, 1850–1860. In Orville Vernon Burton and Robert C. McMath, Jr. (eds.), *Class, Conflict, and Consensus: Antebellum Southern Community Studies.* Westport, CT: Greenwood Press, 29–56.

Hahn, Steven 1983: *The Roots of Southern Populism: Yeoman Farmers and the Transformation of the Georgia Upcountry, 1850–1890.* New York: Oxford University Press.

Harris, J. William 1985: *Plain Folk and Gentry in a Slave Society: White Liberty and Black Slavery in Augusta's Hinterlands.* Middletown, CT: Wesleyan University Press.

Hobson, Fred 1978: *Serpent in Eden: H. L. Mencken and the South.* Baton Rouge: Louisiana State University Press.

Hundley, Daniel R. 1979: *Social Relations In Our Southern States.* Baton Rouge: Louisiana State University Press.

Hyde, Samuel C., Jr. 1996: *Pistols and Politics: The Dilemma of Democracy in Louisiana's Florida Parishes, 1810–1899.* Baton Rouge: Louisiana State University Press.

Hyde, Samuel C., Jr.(ed.), 1997: *Plain Folk of the South Revisited.* Baton Rouge: Louisiana State University Press.

Linden, Fabian 1946: Economic Democracy in the Slave South: An Appraisal of Some Recent Views. *Journal of Negro History,* 31, 140–89.

Lowe, Richard G. and Campbell, Randolph B. 1987: *Planters and Plain Folk: Agriculture in Antebellum Texas.* Dallas: Southern Methodist University Press.

McCurry, Stephanie 1995: *Masters of Small Worlds: Yeoman Households, Gender Relations, and the Political Culture of the Antebellum South Carolina Low Country.* New York: Oxford University Press.

McDonald, Forrest, and McWhiney, Grady 1975: The Antebellum Southern Herdsman: A Reinterpretation. *Journal of Southern History,* 41, 147–66.

McMillen, Sally G. 1992: *Southern Women: Black and White in the Old South.* Arlington Heights, IL: Harlan Davidson.

McWhiney, Grady 1988: *Cracker Culture: Celtic Ways in the Old South.* Tuscaloosa: University of Alabama Press.

Mitchell, Margaret 1936: *Gone With the Wind.* New York: MacMillan.

Olmsted, Frederick Law 1904: *A Journey in the Seaboard Slave States.* New York: G. P. Putnam's Sons.

Olmsted, Frederick Law 1953: *The Cotton Kingdom.* Edited by Arthur M. Schlesinger Sr. New York: Alfred Knopf.

Olmsted, Frederick Law 1970: *A Journey in the Backcountry.* New York: Shocken.

Owsley, Frank Lawrence 1930: The Irrepressible Conflict. In *I'll Take My Stand: The South and the Agrarian Tradition.* New York: Harper and Brothers, 61–91.

Owsley, Frank L. 1949: *Plain Folk of the Old South.* Baton Rouge: Louisiana State University Press.

Phillips, Ulrich Bonnell 1929: *Life and Labor in the Old South.* Boston: Little, Brown.

Shugg, Roger W. 1939: *Origins of the Class Struggle in Louisiana: A Social History of White Farmers and Laborers During Slavery and After, 1840–1875.* Baton Rouge: Louisiana State University Press.

Sparks, Randy J. 1994: *On Jordan's Stormy Banks: Evangelicalism in Mississippi, 1773–1876.* Athens: University of Georgia Press.

Weaver, Herbert 1945: *Mississippi Farmers, 1850–1860.* Nashville: Vanderbilt University Press.

Wright, Gavin 1970: Economic Democracy and the Concentration of Agricultural Wealth in the Cotton South, 1850–1860. *Agricultural History,* 44, 63–93.

CHAPTER TEN

Religion in the Pre-Civil War South

RANDY J. SPARKS

IN 1987 John B. Boles announced the discovery of southern religious history, and the outpouring of scholarship over the past decade indicates that the field has reached a remarkable stage of maturity (Boles 1987). This essay will explore the most significant works published on the history of southern religion, focusing on those monographs that have appeared during the last decade or since the cutoff date for the titles in Boles's article. He observed that the field of southern religious history had come into existence only in the 1960s; before that time, historians of religion had focused their attention on New England Puritans, and only lay historians interested in the histories of their own churches and denominations had paid much attention to religion in the South. Historians of southern religion might be excused, then, for making the South their only field of labor. In general, southern historians work within their own historiographical confines and rarely venture out to place their work in a larger frame of reference. To some extent, the entire field of southern history is built upon the idea of southern exceptionalism: the idea that there is a distinctive region called the South with a distinctive history worthy of examination on its own terms. It has become increasingly clear over the past decade that the history of southern religion refuses to remain within these boundaries. The South's dominant religious movements did not originate there, but in Europe. European religions were undoubtedly transformed in the South by the complex interaction with African religious traditions, but even that process was not limited to the South.

If historians of southern religion are to move beyond traditional paradigms and shatter the old concepts of southern exceptionalism, they should begin with a reconsideration of religion in the colonial period. For too long, historians have assumed that southern history began with English settlement at Jamestown, a view that essentially excluded the Spanish and French settlers in the Deep South, who were either ignored or dismissed. The emergence of the field of Atlantic history, which might be dated to the late 1980s, marks a major paradigm shift in American historiography with important implications for the study of religion. Atlantic historians see the ocean not as a barrier but as a bridge that linked Europe, Africa, and the Americas in a complex web of interactions. Underlying most of the scholarship is an assumption that the colonial Atlantic World developed through a process of adaptation whereby social and cultural institutions were transferred across the Atlantic. Religion was crucial to this process in a variety of ways. At the most abstract level the Protestant Reformation profoundly affected European societies and fueled the national rivalries that helped define the Atlantic World, and the social upheavals set off by the Reformation played a major role in shaping the Americas. In the words of historical geographer D. W. Meinig, one of Atlantic history's most influential founders, "Among the countless evidences of social disruption emanating from the Reformation none was more portentous for America than the thousands of refugees: individuals, families, whole groups gravitating from a thousand localities into this... region. ... The prominence of persons carrying these new religious identities... becomes a major feature" (Meinig 1986: 50). Many of these religious refugees made their way to the South, though we are only beginning to understand their histories (Butler 1983; Hagy 1993; Jones 1984; Sensbach 1998; Thorp 1989).

This formulation of the Atlantic World, and the importance of religious institutions and refugees within it, offers exciting possibilities for the integration of southern religious history into a larger, more comprehensive theoretical framework. Many of the scholars who have proposed frameworks for understanding the evolution of the Atlantic World agree that the American colonies can be divided into distinct cultural regions that shaped subsequent development (Bailyn, Meinig, Berlin, and Greene). In most of these formulations (e.g. Bailyn 1986b; Meinig 1986; Greene 1988) the South claims two cultural hearths: one in the Chesapeake region and another in the Carolinas, while Berlin adds a third in the Deep South. The Atlantic model and the concept of cultural hearths offer compelling concepts for understanding the development of southern colonial religion, and the reconceptualization of southern religious history to include Spanish and French colonies offers exciting potential for future research. Though the study of religion among the Spanish and French has not been fully integrated into southern religious history, important work has been done in these areas as a part of the dynamic borderlands school of historical inquiry. For students of southern religion, David J. Weber's *The Spanish Frontier in North America* (1992) is an indispensable introduction to the Spanish missionary efforts in the South.

Religion figured prominently in European colonization of the Americas from the very beginning and became part of the rivalry between Protestant and Catholic powers. Spain's vast North American territory offered a rich opportunity for Catholic missionaries, who were among the first Spaniards in the Southeast. Franciscan friars began their work in Florida in 1573 and were soon scattered throughout the lower South in present-day Florida, Georgia, South Carolina, and Alabama. By the 1720s the Spanish had also built ten missions in Texas concentrated in East Texas near their French enemies. These priests, seldom exceeding fifty in the lower South, nevertheless had a dramatic impact on the lives of Indians in the regions they served. Conceptually, Weber sees frontiers as "zones of interaction between two different cultures – as places where the cultures of the invader and of the invaded contend with one another and with their physical environment to produce a dynamic that is unique to time and place" (Weber 1992: 11). Clearly, religion was an important part of that cultural frontier. Unlike the English, who largely excluded natives from their societies, the Spanish sought to include them. Their extensive missionary efforts differed markedly from English efforts to convert the Indians and provide a fruitful comparison of European colonization efforts in the South. Weber has less to say about the religious lives of the Spanish settlers themselves, though some information about religious life in St Augustine has recently appeared (Bushnell 1994; Landers 1999; Thomas 1989).

There is no comparable recent study of the French colony of Louisiana and the missionary efforts there. Indeed, New Orleans is a promising site for research on colonial religion, though southern historians' long concentration on the English colonies and the difficulties associated with using seventeenth- and eighteenth-century Spanish and French records have discouraged scholars. While there is no monograph on the topic, younger historians are producing exciting research on this ethnically diverse city that promises to greatly enhance our understanding of the Deep South (see the essays by Kimberly S. Hanger, Virginia Meacham Gould, and Gwendolyn Midlo Hall in Clinton and Gillespie 1997: 205–61; Clark 1997). Employing a model borrowed from cultural geography, Weber suggests that the first group to establish a viable society "are of crucial significance for the later social and cultural geography of the area, no matter how tiny the initial band of settlers may have been" (Weber 1992: 334). Only further comparative research can test that hypothesis for the earliest history of American religion, but a consideration of the Spanish and French presence in the South suggests how the field of religious history might be changed by placing it in the larger context of Atlantic history.

One study of American religion has successfully employed an Atlantic model: Jon Butler's *Awash in a Sea of Faith: Christianizing the American People* (1990). Though not limited to the South, Butler's stunning reconception of American religious history offers the most convincing picture to date of the colonial South's religious history and how that history relates to larger American and Atlantic trends; in fact, he contends that "a transatlantic focus is a *sine qua non*" for understanding the history of American religion. The close connections between colonial America and Europe, the conscious attempt on the part of Americans to follow European models, and the "overwhelmingly derivative nature" of American society demand such a focus (Butler 1990: 5). His story opens, necessarily, with an exploration of the European spiritual background.

In Butler's view, early modern Europe was characterized by state churches supported through taxes, through laws prohibiting heresy and blasphemy, and by other means. The men and women in church service made up the largest bloc of non-agricultural workers in Europe, and churches defined the landscape. Still, Christianization was incomplete and irregular throughout the continent. Belief in the occult was deeply embedded in all ranks and classes, and though occultism fell in repute among the educated elite after 1680, it remained strong among the common folk. Protestant and Catholic leaders across Europe launched major proselytizing campaigns after 1700, though there is little evidence that they produced substantial results apart from encouraging reform and sectarian movements including German Pietism and English Methodism.

Such was the ambivalent religious legacy that the Old World extended to the New. Virginia's early leaders were deeply religious, and many had Puritan leanings. In keeping with the tradition of a state church, Virginia's rulers built a chapel, enforced religious conformity on pain of death, and required church attendance. The colony's settlers, composed mostly of young single men and indentured servants, proved to be an unruly and irreligious lot, church construction failed to keep pace with population growth, and interest waned from 1630 to 1680. Maryland fared even worse; Lord Baltimore's dream of a Catholic haven never materialized, though only Catholic worship was practiced in the early years. A handful of Anglican ministers worked in the colony before 1690, and Quakers made some inroads, but Christianity was largely absent from practice and from the landscape. It hardly seems possible, but the

Carolinas were even more destitute. The only church in Charleston before 1695 was the French Huguenot church, and the first Anglican minister enjoyed getting drunk and baptizing bears. North Carolina had no settled clergyman of any denomination nor any church buildings before 1700, and only a handful of Quakers held regular worship services. It should come as no surprise that magic, astrology, and occultism flourished under such conditions, and Butler's examination of this topic throughout the colonies invites closer scrutiny.

Butler highlights the importance of the eighteenth century in shaping the future contours of religious life. He joins other historians of religion, including Patricia Bonomi, who see the eighteenth century not as a period of religious declension as portrayed in Puritan historiography but rather as a period of dramatic growth (Bonomi 1986: 6–9). Here, again, the scholarship on religion intersects with that of Bailyn, Breen, Greene, and other Atlanticists who see the eighteenth century as the period during which the English colonies became more complex and achieved the social coherence that enabled them to more successfully emulate the English cultural model. For Butler, the changes of the "eighteenth-century transformation" (Butler 1990: 98) included the establishment of the Church of England throughout the southern colonies, the renewal and reorganization of religious authority, and the arrival of clergy and commissaries from England. Colonial governments and vestries imposed taxes, "sacralized" (ibid: 108) the landscape by building new churches, and forged a close alliance between the church and local elites. A similar process occurred among southern Dissenters including Presbyterians, Baptists, and Quakers, all of whom moved toward greater denominational regulation and authority. Butler's characterization of this period creates a number of avenues for exploration. Have religious historians been swayed by the evangelical view of colonial Anglicanism and underestimated its vigor, particularly for the eighteenth century? What popular forms of Anglican religious worship and lay services existed? What role did Dissenters play in the larger process of social articulation underway during the period?

By far the most ambitious and influential look at a dissenting sect in the colonial period is Rhys Isaac's Pulitzer Prize-winning classic *The Transformation of Virginia*. First published in 1982 and reissued in 1999 with a new preface by the author, Isaac's brilliant evocation of life in Virginia from 1740 to 1790 has left an indelible mark on the study of southern religion. Isaac's study has shaped the debate over the origins of evangelicalism and its stance toward the South's larger culture. He paints a compelling portrait of colonial Virginia at the height of its achievement, at the moment of its greatest maturity and refinement. His study opens with a rich portrayal of the lives of the gentry, their elegant and well-proportioned great houses, and their churches and court houses, which served as stages for the rituals of power that shaped and ordered their lives. Their behavior at court and the polls, at militia meetings and taverns, at horse races and cockfights, all displayed the hierarchical social order they labored to create and maintain. Through the churches, particularly through their control of the vestries, the gentry found divine favor for the ordered community they created. Churches provided settings for rituals that reflected the gentry's status; seating, for example, was based on rank. More importantly, through the vestries gentlemen not only allocated the preachers' salaries but also imposed taxes to support the churches, to repair, refurbish, and build them. Vestries also allocated poor relief, and the gentry thereby found yet another avenue to exert their power over their inferiors.

As impressive as the gentry's edifices and rituals of power were, they had no sooner established their dominance than challengers to it appeared. The clergy, anxious to strengthen their own positions as they attempted to strengthen the Anglican church, became more assertive and clashed with the gentry over control of the vestries. More importantly, the religious community itself was beginning to come undone. Beginning in the 1740s the gentry faced a "popular upsurge" (Isaac 1982: 161) from religious Dissenters, first from the Presbyterians and then followed by the much more aggressive Baptists and Methodists in the 1760s and 1770s. Drawn primarily from the lower orders, the evangelicals attacked almost every aspect of the refined culture the gentry had created, and the elite stage settings for ritual displays of social dominance became cultural battlegrounds. Ruffles and silks became emblems of sinful vanity and indulgence; drunkenness, dancing, and gambling evidence of worldliness and dissipation. The evangelicals defined themselves as a "counterculture," and in their closely knit communities they embraced an egalitarian fellowship. They called one another brother and sister, recognized no superiority except that of the spirit, and some even questioned slavery as they welcomed slaves into their fellowship. Emboldened by the transforming effects of the New Birth, evangelicals entered a new religious community with values dramatically at odds with that of the elite.

The coming of the Revolution greatly complicated the situation, and Isaac proposes a subtle analysis of the overlap between the religious and political revolutions underway in the 1770s. As elite Virginians began to question their ties to the mother country and to join English country-party critics of moral decay and luxurious vices, they found common ground with evangelicals and even adopted the stirring rhetorical devices of the evangelical preachers. The success of the Revolution called into question the old religious establishment, and the gentry and evangelicals joined forces to dismantle it. Religion became an individual matter, and the old order, with its structured, hierarchical community, was diminished. The stark division between the austere evangelicals and the proud gentry continued, however. Indeed, Isaac identifies a "fundamental incompatibility" between the two that resulted in a "polarized world" and "an enduring legacy of conflicting value systems" (ibid: 321–2).

For all its power, its elegance, and its enduring influence, Isaac's work is not without flaws, though the problems it presents continue to define the debate. One of the strengths of Isaac's "reimagined landscape" (ibid: xxvi) is his ability to recreate the evangelical world view, but that view may also color his portrayal of the Anglican church. No comparable examples of Anglican piety fill his pages, no suggestion that its adherents may have had their own equally fervent, if less emotionally demonstrative faith. While he provides ample evidence that evangelicals irritated the gentry who responded by harassing them, that may not constitute evidence that the gentry perceived them as a genuine threat. Isaac does not address the fact that the evangelicals were more often harassed by small farmers and plain folk who had good reason to resent evangelical intrusions into their families and communities. While evangelicals may have occasionally stumbled onto the stages the gentry usually controlled, Isaac acknowledges that the religious folk did not seek to control the political or economic systems. Isaac admits that "it was clearly a mark of the strength of the gentry's hegemony and of the rigidities of the social hierarchy that had slavery at its base that the evangelical revolt should have been so restricted in scope" (ibid: 173).

Herein lies Isaac's chief oversight – Virginia could never be truly transformed so long as it was a slave society. The degradation and enslavement of Africans and African-Americans served as the ultimate basis of Virginia's society, and the "polarization" of white Virginia society would be quickly healed on that basis. The depth and sincerity of the evangelical challenge to slavery continues to be one of the hotly debated issues among historians of the antebellum period – those who seek to carry Isaac's story of evangelical revolt forward into the nineteenth century where its limits were most clearly tested.

In a recent study of colonial and revolutionary South Carolina, Robert Olwell has dissected the role of the Anglican church in the process of cultural articulation underway in the eighteenth century. His study covers the same time period as Isaac's, but his picture of South Carolina society is vastly different from Isaac's Virginia. Olwell examines "the institutions, rituals, and languages within which masters, slaves, and metropolis contested and negotiated" by focusing on "four different pillars of the social order" (Olwell 1998: 3, 13): the law, the established church, the marketplace, and the political economy of the plantations. English traditions had to be molded to suit a colonial slave society, and both the law and the Anglican church lent themselves to the task of maintaining control over the slaves and upholding the social order.

The Anglican church provides an ideal example of how colonial elites, desperate to imitate metropolitan institutions as closely as possible, were forced to adapt to provincial realities. He provides a creative and insightful look at the southern Anglican church; his focus on ritual is particularly innovative and produces some surprises. For instance, his examination of Anglican missionary records revealed that 97 percent of white church members were baptized as infants, but 53 percent of blacks were baptized as adults (ibid: 119). Adult baptism required a period of instruction, and the records indicate that slaves received such preparation. That training not only led to some slaves learning to read, it also resulted in the establishment of a thriving school for blacks that operated for twenty-five years. Enslaved church members were more likely to be creole, skilled, and fluent in English. Not surprisingly, only a tiny fraction of slaves became Anglican converts.

Masters sought to use conversion as a means to incorporate an elite segment of the slave population into their ritual community and resisted mass conversion. Some slaves clearly sought the advantages conversion offered, such as literacy and higher status, but then interpreted Christianity in their own way and sometimes used it to subvert the slave system. Olwell's inclusion of the Anglican church into his conceptualization of South Carolina's "culture of power" restores the established church to its rightful position in an examination of maturing colonial society. It also raises even more questions about the mechanisms through which elites exercised their power within the churches. More details on the vestry system, on the selection of vestrymen and ministers, and the construction of churches and chapels, for example, would give such a concept additional weight. While Olwell focuses on how masters used religion to incorporate some slaves into their ritual community, he does not explore how the church shaped elite whites' relationship with poor whites, and since his study focuses on masters, the role of women in the Anglican church is ignored completely. But unlike Isaac's portrait of a white society in turmoil, South Carolina's society was one where the bonds of empire and slavery were equally powerful, strong enough to give greater coherence to a wealthy white society confronting a black majority. Eighteenth-century South Carolina was "a mature colonial slave society in an era that was largely devoid of collective and violent challenges to the masters' dominion" (Olwell 1998: 9).

One of the most controversial topics in the study of colonial religion is assessment of the African religious heritage. Here, again, Butler has helped sharpen the debate; in his view, "the single most important religious transformation to occur in the American colonies before 1776" was "an African spiritual holocaust that forever destroyed traditional African religious systems as *systems* in North America and...left slaves remarkably bereft of traditional collective religious practice before 1760" (Butler 1990: 129–30). His three-tiered model suggests that between 1680 and 1760 slaves in British North America were unable to maintain their traditional African religious systems, even though some religious practices survived. Beginning as early as 1730 in Virginia and several decades later in South Carolina, Christian and African religious practices developed within slave communities fostered by stronger families and kinship systems. Finally, continuing through the remainder of the colonial period, a more thoroughly European Christian practice emerged among slaves, a practice that became less European and more African-American after 1800.

Unfortunately, Butler abandons the comparative framework that he employs so successfully in discussing the English colonial background when he turns to the African experience. Certainly, problems abound in reconstructing African religious systems from the seventeenth and eighteenth centuries. Indeed, Butler may very well have been responding to historians such as Mechal Sobel (1987) and Margaret Washington Creel (1988), who traced African-American religious practices back to their African roots. Sobel focused on cultural interactions among "prebourgeois" whites and slaves in eighteenth-century Virginia and found a convergence of Anglo and African religious beliefs. Blacks, she contended, accepted most of the Christian eschatology while white evangelicals embraced the trances and visions of African faith, their sense of a spirit journey, and of a reunion with ancestors after death. Margaret Washington focused on the Gullahs of lowcountry South Carolina and Georgia, who, given their isolation, had the strongest African retentions among any group on the North American mainland. She argued that Gullah religion developed from the convergence of cultures from Upper Guinea and Kongo-Angola. For example, she found that important features of the mandatory secret societies so important on the Windward Coast also functioned in Gullah religion, and that significant elements of Bakongo cosmology survived in the Gullah world view. Both Sobel and Washington have been criticized for their interpretations of African cosmology which rely heavily on evidence about African religion drawn from the nineteenth and twentieth centuries.

Recent scholarship suggests how such problems might be resolved. First, in an important work entitled *Africans and Africans in the Making of the Atlantic World* (1992), John Thornton, a historian of Portuguese Africa, has pointed out that the conversion of Africans to Christianity actually began in Africa and was a continuous process from there to the Americas. Africans who were enslaved in the Americas and returned to Africa or those who otherwise moved around the Atlantic World had an important impact on African culture, a process we are only now beginning to understand. He also warns of the pitfalls in trying to fix African cosmologies and then find their American counterpart. Thornton suggests that "If one approaches the issue of conversion in a different way and stresses the dynamic elements (revelations) rather than the more stable one (cosmologies) the nature of conversion is changed.' Viewed in this way, Africans "converted because they received 'co-revelations,'" that is, revelations in the African tradition that dovetailed with the Christian tradition" (Thornton 1992: 255). That same emphasis on the conversion experience can explain why some Europeans accepted the revelations of African religious diviners.

The most compelling study of the Christianization of Africans and African-Americans is Sylvia R. Frey's and Betty Wood's *Come Shouting to Zion* (1998), and the authors acknowledge Thornton's influence. Frey and Wood offer a masterful synthesis of the emergence of African-American Protestantism in the British Caribbean and the South before 1830. Well aware of the gaps in our understanding of African religions during the period of the slave trade, they offer a fascinating and judicious exploration of African religions in West Africa and an overview of the spread of Christianity and Islam in that region. Africans sold into slavery represented "a variety of cultural forms: traditional religions, Africanized Christianity, and Africanized Islam" (Frey and Wood 1998: 33). Africans could not recreate their traditional religious systems anywhere in the Americas, but "What they were able to do, and often very successfully, was to piece together new systems from the remnants of the old" (ibid: 40). Occasionally, startling glimpses of religious retentions appear, as among the Africans involved in South Carolina's Stono Rebellion in 1739. Evidence suggests that the rebels were Kongolese Christians who identified with their fellow Catholics in Spanish Florida and were encouraged by offers of freedom issued from St Augustine. Even the resurgent Anglicanism of the mid-eighteenth century offered little appeal to enslaved Africans and African-Americans in the South, but the evangelical Protestantism just emerging in that period would bring a profound transformation to slaves' religious culture.

Frey and Wood go much further than Isaac in explaining the attraction of evangelicalism to slaves. In their view, "what more than anything else differentiated evangelical Protestantism from the Anglicanism that fell on such stony ground in the slave quarters, was a powerful integrating ideology and an ethos whose emphasis on spiritual equality had the potential for creating the first distinctive changes in African values in relation to Protestant Christianity" (ibid: 82). A remarkable group of African religious leaders emerged throughout the South during the Great Awakening; their congregations served as the "citadels of African evangelism" (ibid: 117) and produced the first generation of black missionaries after the Revolution.

For Frey and Wood, the major turning point for the Christianization of African-Americans is the period from 1785 to 1830. Before 1785, Christianity affected only an "insignificant minority" of slaves, but after 1785 it began to make rapid inroads in the slave community, so that by 1815 Christianity was the "dominant religious influence among Afro-Atlantic peoples" (ibid: 118). In the South, that process was divided into two phases, a short but intense postrevolutionary phase from 1785 to 1790 that was largely confined to Virginia, and a more widespread phase from 1800 to 1830 fueled by the Great Revival. The authors explore the biracial character of the Great Revival that "decisively shaped black and white religious culture" (ibid: 140). While cultural interaction and exchange was an important feature of biracial worship, the larger trend was toward the creation of a distinctive Afro-cultural identity. Black

Christians created their own moral universe, an "integrating theology" that incorporated blacks and whites and men and women (ibid: 181). In their ritual and practice, black Christians emphasized a more expressive and participatory worship where music and ecstatic behavior expressed different religious expectations.

Independent black churches, often called African churches, were an important feature of the early evangelical movement. Historians have identified these churches in the South, in the North, and in the Caribbean; it is important to recognize them as a feature of Afro-Protestantism throughout the Atlantic World (ibid; Hatch 1989). Historians should also pay closer attention to the connections that linked these churches; for instance, black Methodists in Charleston sought ordination from Bishop Richard Allen of Philadelphia's African Methodist Church in 1815; George Liele organized the First African Baptist Church in Savannah, Georgia, and also planted the church in Jamaica in 1784; another Baptist from Georgia, Brother Amos, established a church in the Bahamas in 1788.

Philip Morgan in *Slave Counterpoint*, his monumental comparative study of slave life in colonial Virginia and South Carolina, also explored slaves' religious culture. Like Frey and Wood, he pointedly dismissed Butler's idea that Africans lost their religious culture through a spiritual holocaust, but cautions that "Assumptions about the timelessness or uniformity of West African religion must be strenuously rejected" (Morgan 1998: 610). Still, he argued that West African cultures shared a two-tiered belief system that focused on lesser gods who were primarily concerned with local events, with the microcosm of everyday life. Ideas about a supreme being were more complex; some cultures believed in one creator god, some in two, and some in none at all. African religion was creative, pluralistic, and innovative. Morgan believes that the importance of lesser gods in controlling everyday events is exaggerated in slave societies in the Americas, a development that accounts for the inflated role of lesser gods in their cosmology. That emphasis on the powers of lesser gods is reflected in the importance of magic and conjure in slave culture. Less attuned than Frey and Wood to the spread of Christianity in precolonial Africa, he does acknowledge the role of Islam in encouraging syncretism among some slaves. Even when slaves converted to Christianity, which they did in relatively small numbers in the colonial period, "They engaged in a process of selective appropriation or structured improvisation in which values and practices were reinterpreted as they were incorporated" (ibid: 658). That reinterpretation was reflected in their funeral rites, their emotionally demonstrative worship, their visionary experiences, and the spiritual power of their preachers. As useful and important as Morgan's discussion of colonial slave religion is, it opens up further questions for exploration. He makes a few distinctions between religious life in Virginia and the lowcountry, but if these regions functioned as distinctive cultural hearths, one might expect the differences in slaves' religious culture to be more pronounced. Much research remains to be done, particularly in the colonial church records in South Carolina, North Carolina, and Georgia.

Historians of both black and white religion see the American Revolution as a major turning point. Indeed, Nathan O. Hatch, who has done more than any other historian of religion to shape the current understanding of the postrevolutionary period, has called the war "the most crucial event in American history" (Hatch 1989: 5). The Revolution resulted in the disestablishment of the Anglican church throughout the South, and while some states experimented with other forms of support, the final result was the complete separation of church and state. The religious field was thrown open, and religious populists were quick to take advantage of the new realities. The Revolution called old ideas about authority, organization, and leadership into question. Religious revivalists linked conversion to new democratic concepts, and common people of both races took part in shaping the new religious landscape. Hatch focuses on three important themes. First, popular religious movements redefined leadership and drew their preachers from among the common folk. Second, they empowered ordinary people whose language, music, and folk beliefs found acceptance and validation. Third, populist religious movements made Christianity a liberating force. Hatch's sweeping reassessment of the Second Great Awakening is national in scope, and like Butler's work, provides a useful antedote to southern exceptionalism by integrating the history of southern religion into the larger story. His interpretation of African-American religion and the evangelical position on slavery is especially relevant. In his view, white Methodists and Baptists in the South were genuinely committed to converting slaves and to antislavery. He wrote: "However shallow and short-lived this evangelical attack on slavery appears in light of events after 1800, it must be seen for what it was in its time and place: a radical challenge to the doctrines of paternalism and absolute slave obedience that Anglican evangelizers had so actively formulated" (ibid: 103).

The degree to which southern evangelicalism can be considered revolutionary and the extent of its antislavery sentiment are issues that dominate scholarship on antebellum religion. That scholarship has been shaped by the view that evangelicalism began as a revolutionary movement among the plain folk who consciously set themselves in opposition to the dominant culture of the gentry. In their egalitarian services and in their personal lives, these converts challenged the hierarchical structure of their society and welcomed slaves into the churches on terms approaching equality. As these small sects grew to become major denominations during the early decades of the nineteenth century, they were forced to compromise on issues of slavery and patriarchy to accommodate the realities of southern life. Articulated by Isaac and many historians of antebellum southern religion (e.g. Boles 1972; Farmer 1985; Mathews 1977; Sparks 1994), this paradigm continues to shape much of the debate among scholars of the period.

The most creative reassessment of these questions comes from Christine Heyrman, whose work covers the period from the 1760s to the 1830s. She recaptures the spirit that propelled the dramatic growth of the tiny, despised evangelical sects of the 1760s to the thriving, respectable denominations of the 1830s. In order to recapture that spirit, which she calls the "language of Canaan," she focused her study on the preachers who led the army of Jesus into holy war. In less capable hands, a focus on the ministerial elite might be little more than a throwback to traditional church histories that were often more hagiography than history. She avoids that trap by using the preachers to examine provocative topics essential to understanding the transformation of southern evangelicalism, particularly the ways in which evangelicals "struck at those hierarchies that lent stability to their daily lives" (Heyrman 1997: 26). Most southerners guarded their emotions with care and subordinated them to the demands of kin and community. Evangelical preachers sometimes played on those pent-up emotions, conjured up vivid pictures of a fiery hell, grappled with the Devil incarnate, relied on dreams and portents, and otherwise threatened to upset individuals, their families, and their communities.

Evangelical leaders quickly realized that such a strategy could backfire. More than a few southern skeptics accused evangelical preachers of practicing "devilish necromancy" (ibid: 64) much like black conjurers and Indian shamans. Evangelicals artfully managed to distance themselves from the dark side without ever completely abandoning the mysteries of the faith. One of the ways evangelical leaders pushed occultism to the sidelines was by segregating worship by race. The early emphasis on the equality of believers brought many African-Americans into evangelical churches, but ministers set their sights on converting whites, and they were willing to pay almost any price to do so.

One of the mysteries of the faith was the dramatic conversion of young people who offered vivid testimony of their visions and revelations. In a society where over half the white population was under the age of sixteen, attracting young people was of paramount importance, and evangelical clergymen cleverly targeted this audience. As the churches grew, more and more young men filled the ministerial ranks. Zealous and enthusiastic, they faced a variety of challenges from the faithful who sometimes disputed their decisions in disciplinary cases, disagreed with their interpretation of scripture, and carefully monitored their social lives for any hint of scandal. The most serious challenge, however, came from husbands and fathers who questioned the authority of these neophytes and openly defied their authority.

Evangelical conversion often posed a threat to family stability. Given the centrality of family and household in southern culture, conversion could threaten the entire social structure by pitting family members against one another and by placing loyalty to God above all else. Preachers set a poor example as heads of households because they were often absent, sometimes neglected their farms and families, and preached that obligations to kin took a backseat to duty to God. They further exasperated southern patriarchs by openly interfering in family matters through church discipline, by encouraging evangelical women to marry within the fold, by replacing blood relations with spiritual brothers and sisters, and by their hostility to slavery. In short, "evangelicals challenged the primacy of the family, undercut the privacy of households, and diminished the authority of husbands and parents" (ibid: 141). Evangelical leaders reached out to husbands and fathers by abandoning their hostility to slavery. As preachers pushed their way into the professional class, they earned higher salaries, took better care of their families, and stood shoulder to shoulder with other white fathers, husbands, and masters. Churches abandoned the discipline of white members and celebrated the family as the cornerstone of society.

Largely due to its celebration of the equality of all believers and the opportunities it offered to godly women, evangelicalism attracted large numbers of women from the start. In the early years many female conversions took place over the objections of husbands and fathers, and clergymen encouraged the women's defiance. Though barred from the pulpits in evangelical churches, women prayed, prophesied, exhorted, and otherwise exercised their spiritual gifts. Clergymen and devout women often developed close relationships, but some ministers feared being upstaged by them. Threatened by a growing female majority and confronted by the desires of men to control their own households, preachers took steps to accommodate white men. Beginning about 1800, the clergymen began to rein in these women by limiting their public role in services and by stripping them of the right to vote in churches. They tailored their message on slavery to gain access to slaves scattered on plantations, and restricted black preachers. Increasingly, ministers adopted a muscular, martial Christianity and embraced the code of honor. The infusion of an evangelical ethos throughout southern culture testified to their success.

Heyrman's focus on evangelical clergymen does give rise to certain biases. For instance, it skews her vision away from relationships between lay members and the powerful sense of community that they inspired. She underestimates the importance of female organizations and networks, for example, ignores Sunday schools, and has little to say about the invisible church in the slave community. Her conclusions about church discipline are drawn from only three Baptist churches, hardly a representative sample. The broad outlines of Heyrman's story are familiar, but her unique perspective, combined with the depth of her research and the breadth of her argument, make this one of the most important monographs on southern religion to appear in a decade.

Other historians are more skeptical of the revolutionary nature of early evangelicalism and the degree to which it threatened slavery and patriarchy. Stephanie McCurry, in her study of yeoman households in antebellum South Carolina, has offered the most sustained critique of the what she calls the "declension theory." She agrees that evangelicalism began in lowcountry South Carolina as a movement among yeomen. It was not until a dramatic revival in 1831–3, at the height of the Nullification Crisis, that evangelicals made inroads among the planter elite. Evangelicalism held out the promise of spiritual equality, and slaves certainly read that message in revolutionary ways, but she finds that the message of spiritual equality and "its relation to social equality or status in this world was, even in the early years, deeply contested" (McCurry 1995: 141). In her view, white South Carolina evangelicals never endorsed antislavery. The yeomen who governed these churches were deeply committed both to slavery and patriarchy; they "installed their own considerable prerogatives at the heart of postrevolutionary evangelicalism, lending it a largely conservative and nascent proslavery shape that shored up their own claims to power and authority at home and abroad" (ibid: 147). That commitment gave them common cause with the planter elite, who adopted evangelicalism as a means of garnering moral and ideological support for their own local and regional political culture.

McCurry's work also has important implications for the study of southern women's religious history. She found that women constituted a majority of church members and were attracted to evangelicalism by the lure of spiritual equality, but once in the churches women found themselves governed by men. Men used the churches' disciplinary procedures to enforce the rules of patriarchy, and only men decided who was fit to be admitted or expelled. Men selected preachers, controlled church finances, and held exclusive rights to church offices. McCurry contrasts the experience of southern church women with their northern sisters who found religious authority in their homes and communities that led them to create a vigorous female benevolent empire. In McCurry's view, southern women did not exercise religious authority either in the home or in their communities; southern women found "no clearly gendered domain of moral authority" (ibid: 189). She found, for example, that "the number of female-sponsored or female-directed benevolent institutions or even charitable events numbered very few in the entire antebellum period." From that small number of female societies she inferred that "The distinctiveness of evangelical women's experience in the Low Country, and by extension in the slave South...lies in evangelical women's inability to fashion for themselves, as their northern counterparts managed to do, a common identity as women, a positive definition of women's nature, and a claim to moral authority in home, church, and community" (ibid: 190–1).

No topic in southern religious history is more important or more contested than the role of women. In his landmark study of southern religion published in 1977, Donald Mathews forcefully reminded us that "women made southern Evangelicalism possible" (Mathews 1977: 102). Over twenty years have elapsed since Mathews first made that striking observation, but the full story of how southern women made Protestantism possible has yet to be told. The effort to reconstruct women's contributions to Christianity is an ongoing project fraught with difficulties, none more challenging than a historical legacy that has largely obscured women's involvement. For that reason feminist scholars have insisted that historians must apply a "hermeneutic of suspicion" (Murphy 1998: 16, 134) to a religious history that has omitted or downplayed the essential role of faithful women. Indeed, the scope of women's contributions to southern churches, the role religion played in women's lives, and the emergence of a women's culture closely tied to southern churches and religion are topics that remain either understudied or contested by scholars of southern religion and southern women.

Suzanne Lebsock spoke directly to this problem in her study of the women of Petersburg, Virginia. She found that men often inflated "their own efforts" and minimized "those of the women." In her view, "The most striking feature of the records left by the men of the white churches is their persistent failure to acknowledge women's collective contributions" (Lebsock 1984: 216–17, 224–5, 197). That yawning gap in the historical record has led many women's historians to underestimate the prevalence of women's religious organizations in the South. Historian Jean Friedman found a few scattered examples of women's groups, and those only in urban areas. She focused on the difficulties women faced in organizing and contended that "Women's religious societies did not penetrate much beyond the perimeter of the South" (Friedman 1985: 19–20). Historian Elizabeth Fox-Genovese in her study of elite southern women argued that the South's rural character "excluded southern women from many of the opportunities that were opening up for their northern sisters, notably...to form voluntary associations of various kinds." On a more troubling note, Fox-Genovese dismissed the work of southern church women: "Groups of women might join together to decorate a church for a holiday, or even to put on one of the South's noted 'benevolent fairs.' But these events remained exceptional," she wrote (Fox-Genovese 1988: 70, 80–1). Friedman, Fox-Genovese, and McCurry all have a larger and quite legitimate point to make: southern women did not take the same path their northern sisters took, and southern women's organizations did not follow a "feminist-whig" trajectory that led from benevolence to the women's rights movement. However, one need not downplay women's contributions to southern religion to make that point, as Lebsock reminded us.

Cynthia Lynn Lyerly has brought full circle the historiographical debates surrounding the revolutionary potential of early evangelicalism and the role of women and blacks with the movement in *Methodism and the Southern Mind, 1770–1810* (1998). By focusing on the crucial time period surrounding the American Revolution, her innovative study recaptures the revolutionary nature of early Methodism that Isaac first proposed. She homes in on Methodist doctrine, values, and practices and demonstrates how these inverted power structures and upset relations between sexes, races, and classes. She found, for example, that white southern men reacted violently to Methodist conversions among their wives, children, and slaves for a complex set of reasons that included the spiritual empowerment that conversions brought, the sense of moral superiority that converts felt over nonbelievers, and because Methodists branded male values and behaviors as sinful and robbed men of their moral authority. She explores the attractions that drew women and slaves to Methodism, most importantly the respect, the spiritual equality, and the substantive leadership opportunities that it offered. Only powerful motivators could lure converts to a religion so "ridiculed, feared, and harassed" (Lylerly 1998: 101).

She boldly returns to the declension model and defends the proposition that early Methodists were genuinely committed to antislavery. That commitment faltered as Methodists decided to Christianize an institution they could not abolish, as women and blacks lost their positions of leadership and authority when the Methodists moved from sect to denomination, as southerners became more vocal in their defense of slavery, and as domesticity became a cherished ideal. She suggests that one reason historians have doubted that early evangelicals were genuinely antislavery is that church historians, many of them at work during the antebellum period, attempted to rewrite their past and deny the antislavery position of the founders. Lyerly reminds us that evangelicalism was a powerful force for change, and that, for a time at least, this "peculiar people" threatened to turn the world upside down.

The topic of biracial worship among evangelicals has attracted considerable scholarly attention. John B. Boles focused attention on the topic with an edited volume published in 1988. Biracial worship began during the First Great Awakening and characterized worship among early evangelicals. Though the extent of biracial worship varied across time and place and among denominations, some generalizations can be made. There were three primary types of biracial churches: semi-independent black churches under the supervision of a white church; churches where blacks used the same building as whites, but at different times; and churches where slaves attended the same service as their masters but were segregated from whites. The semi-independent black churches were most common in urban areas and had often begun as autonomous African churches until southern laws forced them to form some sort of relationship with a white church. White attendance and white supervision over these churches was usually slight. The second type, where black congregations met separately, was probably more common and usually began once the black membership grew too large to be accommodated comfortably with whites. The third type, where whites and blacks attended the same services but were seated separately, continued to be common throughout the antebellum period. The pervasiveness of biracial worship raises important questions: what was the relationship between biracial worship and the invisible church in the slave quarters? How did the rituals and practices of these churches change over time, and how are those changes to be interpreted? What were the regional and denominational variables? What significance should historians attach to these religious communities? As Boles wrote, "Without claiming too much or failing to recognize the multitude of ways slaves were not accorded genuine equality in these biracial churches, it is still fair to say that nowhere else in southern society were they treated so nearly as equals" (Boles 1987: 9).

It is useful to note that these biracial churches continued to flourish as white clergymen and churches became more and more committed to the institution of slavery. Many scholars have explored the origins of biblical proslavery, but Larry Tise wrote the most compelling reassessment of that ideology. He proposed a bold thesis that rejected the central arguments of virtually all the previous scholarship. He examined the defense of slavery in America from 1701 to 1840 with startling results. He found, for example, that proslavery was not uniquely southern; in fact, he proposed that the primary tenets of proslavery thought were developed in Great Britain, the West Indies, and New England during the eighteenth century and further elaborated by New England Federalists in the early nineteenth century. His composite picture of 275 proslavery clergymen revealed that southerners came relatively late to the discussion, only after the abolitionist controversies of the 1830s, and even then contributed nothing new to the proslavery ideology. Tise's definition of proslavery is unusually broad – some critics might say overly broad – and includes clergymen "favoring the continuation of the institution of Negro slavery, or opposed to interference with it" (Tise 1987: xv), but his reinterpretation of this important topic has radically changed our understanding of proslavery thought. His work fits within an Atlantic model and opens up exciting possibilities for further comparative research. As for the impact of proslavery on the Civil War, he concluded that "historians will have to look elsewhere than proslavery" (ibid: 362) to understand the origins of that conflict.

Increasingly, historians have turned to religion to help explain the causes of the Civil War and have made a compelling case for a close link between southern proslavery and southern nationalism. Beginning in the 1960s, political historians moved away from their emphasis on class conflict to focus on religious, ethnic, and cultural antagonisms as primary factors in shaping American politics. The most persuasive examination of the links between religion and the rise of southern sectionalism is Mitchell Snay's *Gospel of Disunion* (1993; see also Goen 1985). His work opens where Tise's ends, with abolitionist controversies of the 1830s, and continues through the secession crisis of 1861. He identifies four stages of white southern clerical thought: the first was a defense of slavery, followed by a more radical biblical proslavery, which led to the third stage marked by the division of the leading evangelical denominations along sectional lines, and finally to religious sanction for southern nationalism and secession.

The biblical defense of slavery did not originate with southerners, but in the 1830s they fully embraced the doctrine and promulgated it from their pulpits and through the religious press. Beyond that, they developed a slaveholding ethic to make Christian slaveholders responsible for the physical and spiritual well-being of slaves, which was accompanied by an aggressive mission to the slaves. Through those means, they provided a powerful moral justification for slavery that contributed to the religious schisms of the 1840s. After 1850 southerners grew increasingly defensive, and southern churches threw the entire weight of their denominational structures – their pulpits, presses, schools and colleges – into the creation of their New Israel. As the crisis of the Union deepened, southern clergymen offered their enthusiastic support for disunion and helped inflame popular passions. Using an artful blend of biblical-ism, evangelicalism, and civil religion, they justified seceding from a corrupted and fallen North. In a volume co-edited with John R. McKivigan, Snay has assembled a group of essays to further explore the connection between religion, slavery, and sectionalism in both the North and the South (McKivigan and Snay 1998).

From the study of antebellum politics and the causes of the Civil War, from southern women's history to the history of slavery, from the study of southern culture to the origins of the colonial South, the study of religion is now fully integrated into the historical mainstream. Fueled in large part by the emergence of the new social and cultural history, with their focus on the nature of society, the integrative structures, power dynamics, authority, and ideology that structured social systems, a new generation of scholars has discovered religion as a vital dynamic in southern society. The study of religion can contribute to the breakdown of southern exceptionalism by linking the study of southern history to larger patterns throughout the Americas and the Atlantic World. As southern historians continue their efforts to reconstruct the lives of ordinary people, as they labor to understand the meanings embedded in southern culture, as they continue to grapple with the perennial questions surround-ing race, class, and gender, religion will play an increasingly important role in recreating the lost world of the colonial and antebellum South.

BIBLIOGRAPHY

Bailyn, Bernard 1986a: *The Peopling of British North America: An Introduction*. New York: Alfred A. Knopf.

Bailyn, Bernard with the assistance of Barbara DeWolfe 1986b: *Voyagers to the West: A Passage in the Peopling of America on the Eve of the Revolution*. New York: Alfred A. Knopf.

Berlin, Ira 1998: *Many Thousands Gone: The First Two Centuries of Slavery in North America*. Cambridge, MA and London: Belknap of Harvard University Press.

Blethen, H. Tyler, Wood, Jr., Curtis W., and Weaver, Jack W. (eds.) 1997: *Ulster and North America: Transatlantic Perspectives on the Scotch–Irish*. Tuscaloosa and London: University of Alabama Press.

Boles, John B. 1972: *The Great Revival, 1787–1805: The Origins of the Southern Evangelical Mind*. Lexington: University Press of Kentucky.

Boles, John B. 1987: The Discovery of Southern Religious History. In John B. Boles and Evelyn Thomas Nolen (eds.), *Interpreting Southern History: Historiographical Essays in Honor of Sanford W. Higginbotham*. Baton Rouge: Louisiana State University Press, 510–48.

Boles, John B. (ed.) 1988: *Masters and Slaves in the House of the Lord: Race and Religion in the American South, 1740–1870*. Lexington: University Press of Kentucky.

Bolton, S. Charles 1982: *Southern Anglicanism: The Church of England in Colonial South Carolina*. Westport, CT: Greenwood Press.

Bonomi, Patricia U. 1986: *Under the Cope of Heaven: Religion, Society, and Politics in Colonial America*. New York and Oxford: Oxford University Press.

Bruce, Dickson D., Jr. 1974: *And They All Sang Hallelujah: Plain-Folk Camp-Meeting Reli-gion, 1800–1845*. Knoxville: University of Tennessee Press.

Bushnell, Amy Turner 1994: *Situado and Sabana: Spain's Support System For the Presidio and Mission Provinces of Florida*. [New York] Athens, GA: American Museum of Natural History, distributed by the University of Georgia Press.

Butler, Jon 1983: *The Huguenots in America: A Refugee People in New World Society*. Cam-bridge, MA and London: Harvard University Press.

Butler, Jon 1990: *Awash in a Sea of Faith: Christianizing the American People*. Cambridge, MA: Harvard University Press.

Byrnside, Ron 1997: *Music in Eighteenth-Century Georgia*. Athens, GA and London: University of Georgia Press.

Calhoon, Robert McCluer 1988: *Evangelicals and Conservatives in the Early South, 1740–1861*. Columbia: University of South Carolina Press.

Carwardine, Richard J. 1978: *Transatlantic Revivalism: Popular Evangelicalism in Britain and America, 1790–1865*. Westport, CT: Greenwood Press.

Carwardine, Richard J. 1993: *Evangelicals and Politics in Antebellum America*. New Haven, CT: Yale University Press.

Censer, Jane Turner 1984: *North Carolina Planters and Their Children, 1800–1860*. Baton Rouge: Louisiana State University Press.

Clark, Emily 1997: "By All the Conduct of Their Lives": A Laywomen's Confraternity in New Orleans, 1730–1744. *William and Mary Quarterly*, 54 (4), 769–95.

Clinton, Catherine and Gillespie, Michele (eds.) 1997: *The Devil's Lane: Sex and Race in the Early South*. New York and London: Oxford University Press.

Conkin, Paul K. 1995: *The Uneasy Center: Reformed Christianity in Antebellum America*. Chapel Hill: University of North Carolina Press.

Creel, Margaret Washington 1988: *"A Peculiar People": Slave Religion and Community-Culture Among the Gullahs*. New York: New York University Press.

Eslinger, Ellen 1999: *Citizens of Zion: The Social Origins of Camp Meeting Revivalism*. Knoxville: University of Tennessee Press.

Farmer, James O., Jr. 1985: *The Metaphysical Confederacy: James Henry Thornwell and the Synthesis of Southern Values*. Macon, GA: Mercer University Press.

Finke, Roger and Stark, Rodney 1992: *The Churching of America, 1776–1990: Winners and Losers in Our Religious Economy*. New Brunswick, NJ: Rutgers University Press.

Fox-Genovese, Elizabeth 1988: *Within the Plantation Household: Black and White Women of the Old South*. Chapel Hill and London: University of North Carolina Press.

Frey, Sylvia R. 1991: *Water from the Rock: Black Resistance in a Revolutionary Age*. Princeton, NJ: Princeton University Press.

Frey, Sylvia R. and Wood, Betty 1998: *Come Shouting to Zion: African American Protestantism in the American South and British Caribbean to 1830*. Chapel Hill and London: University of North Carolina Press.

Friedman, Jean E. 1985: *The Enclosed Garden: Women and Community in the Evangelical South, 1830–1900*. Chapel Hill and London: University of North Carolina Press.

Fulop, Timothy E. and Raboteau, Albert J. (eds.) 1997: *African American Religion: Interpretive Essays in History and Culture*. New York and London: Routledge.

Gallay, Alan 1989: *The Formation of a Planter Elite: Jonathan Bryan and the Southern Colonial Frontier*. Athens, GA and London: University of Georgia Press.

Genovese, Eugene D. 1974: *Roll, Jordan, Roll: The World the Slaves Made*. New York: Pantheon Books.

Goen, C. C. 1985: *Broken Churches, Broken Nation: Denominational Schisms and the Coming of the American Civil War*. Macon, GA: Mercer University Press.

Greene, Jack P. 1988: *Pursuits of Happiness: The Social Development of Early Modern British Colonies and the Formation of American Culture*. Chapel Hill and London: University of North Carolina Press.

Hagy, James William 1993: *This Happy Land: The Jews of Colonial and Antebellum Charleston*. Tuscaloosa: University of Alabama Press.

Hanger, Kimberly S. 1997: *Bounded Lives, Bounded Places: Free Black Society in Colonial New Orleans, 1769–1803*. Durham, NC and London: Duke University Press.

Hatch, Nathan O. 1989: *The Democratization of American Christianity.* New Haven, CT: Yale University Press.

Heyrman, Christine Leigh 1997: *Southern Cross: The Beginnings of the Bible Belt.* New York: Alfred A. Knopf.

Hill, Samuel S., Jr. 1980: *The South and the North in American Religion.* Athens: University of Georgia Press.

Hill, Samuel S., Jr. 1984: *Encyclopedia of Religion in the South.* Macon, GA: Mercer University Press.

Holifield, E. Brooks 1978: *The Gentlemen Theologians: American Theology in Southern Culture, 1795–1860.* Durham, NC: Duke University Press.

Hood, Fred J. 1980: *Reformed America: The Middle and Southern States, 1783–1837.* Tuscaloosa: University of Alabama Press.

Horn, James P. P. 1994: *Adapting to a New World: English Society in the Seventeenth-Century Chesapeake.* Chapel Hill: University of North Carolina Press.

Isaac, Rhys 1982: *The Transformation of Virginia, 1740–1790.* Chapel Hill and London: University of North Carolina Press. Reprinted with new introduction, 1999.

Johnson, George Lloyd, Jr. 1997: *The Frontier in the Colonial South: South Carolina Backcountry, 1736–1800.* Westport, CT: Greenwood Press.

Jones, George Fenwick 1984: *The Salzburger Saga: Religious Exiles and Other Germans Along the Savannah.* Athens: University of Georgia Press.

Kolchin, Peter 1987: *Unfree Labor: American Slavery and Russian Serfdom.* Cambridge, MA and London: Belknap Press of Harvard University Press.

Lambert, Frank 1994: *Pedlar in Divinity: George Whitefield and the Transatlantic Revivals, 1737–1770.* Princeton, NJ: Princeton University Press.

Landers, Jane 1999: *Black Society in Spanish Florida.* Urbana: University of Illinois Press.

Lebsock, Suzanne 1984: *The Free Women of Petersburg: Status and Culture in a Southern Town, 1784–1860.* New York and London: Norton.

Levine, Lawrence W. 1977: *Black Culture and Black Consciousness: Afro-American Folk Thought from Slavery to Freedom.* New York: Oxford University Press.

Lewis, Jan 1983: *The Pursuit of Happiness: Family and Values in Jefferson's Virginia.* Cambridge: Cambridge University Press.

Loveland, Anne C. 1980: *Southern Evangelicals and the Social Order, 1800–1860.* Baton Rouge: Louisiana State University Press.

Luker, Ralph 1984: *A Southern Tradition in Theology and Social Criticism, 1830–1930: The Religious Liberalism and Social Conservatism of James Warley Miles, William Porcher Dubose, and Edgar Gardner Murphy.* New York: E. Mellen Press.

Lylerly, Cynthia Lynn 1998: *Methodism and the Southern Mind, 1770–1810.* New York and Oxford: Oxford University Press.

McCurry, Stephanie 1995: *Masters of Small Worlds: Yeoman Households, Gender Relations, and the Political Culture of the Antebellum South Carolina Low Country.* New York and Oxford: Oxford University Press.

McKivigan, John R. and Snay, Mitchell (eds.) 1998: *Religion and the Antebellum Debate Over Slavery.* Athens, GA and London: University of Georgia Press.

Mathews, Donald G. 1965: *Slavery and Methodism: A Chapter in American Morality, 1780–1845.* Princeton, NJ: Princeton University Press.

Mathews, Donald G. 1977: *Religion in the Old South.* Chicago: University of Chicago Press.

Meinig, D. W. 1986: *The Shaping of America: A Geographical Perspective on 500 Years of History: Atlantic America, 1492–1800.* New Haven, CT: Yale University Press.

Miller, Randall M. and Wakelyn, Jon L. (eds.) 1983: *Catholics in the Old South: Essays on Church and Culture.* Macon, GA: Mercer University Press.

Miller, Randall M., Stout, Harry S., and Wilson, Charles Reagan (eds.) 1998: *Religion and the American Civil War.* New York: Oxford University Press.

Morgan, Philip D. 1998: *Slave Counterpoint: Black Culture in the Eighteenth-Century Chesapeake and Lowcountry.* Chapel Hill and London: University of North Carolina Press.

Murphy, Cullen 1998: *The Word According to Eve: Women and the Bible in Ancient Times and Our Own.* Boston: Houghton Mifflin.

Olwell, Robert 1998: *Masters, Slaves, and Subjects: The Culture of Power in the South Carolina Low Country, 1740–1790.* Ithaca, NY: Cornell University Press.

Owen, Christopher 1998: *The Sacred Flame of Love: Methodism and Society in Nineteenth-Century Georgia.* Athens, GA and London: University of Georgia Press.

Parker, Anthony W. 1997: *Scottish Highlanders in Colonial Georgia: The Recruitment, Emigration, and Settlement at Darien, 1735–1748.* Athens, GA and London: University of Georgia Press.

Puglisi, Michael J. (ed.) 1997: *Diversity and Accommodation: Essays on the Cultural Composition of the Virginia Frontier.* Knoxville: University of Tennessee Press.

Raboteau, Albert J. 1978: *Slave Religion: The "Invisible Institution" in the Antebellum South.* New York: Oxford University Press.

Rankin, Richard 1993: *Ambivalent Churchmen and Evangelical Churchwomen: The Religion of the Episcopal Elite in North Carolina.* Columbia: University of South Carolina Press.

Richey, Russell E. 1991: *Early American Methodism.* Bloomington: Indiana University Press.

Schmidt, Leigh Eric 1989: *Holy Fairs: Scottish Communions and American Revivals in the Early Modern Period.* Princeton, NJ: Princeton University Press.

Sensbach, Jon F. 1998: *A Separate Canaan: The Making of an Afro-Moravian World in North Carolina, 1763–1840.* Chapel Hill: University of North Carolina Press.

Snay, Mitchell 1993: *The Gospel of Disunion: Religion and Separatism in the Antebellum South.* New York: Cambridge University Press.

Sobel, Mechal 1979: *Trabelin' On: The Slave Journey to an Afro-Baptist Faith.* Westport, CT: Greenwood Press.

Sobel, Mechal 1987: *The World They Made Together: Black and White Values in Eighteenth-Century Virginia.* Princeton, NJ: Princeton University Press.

Sparks, Randy J. 1994: *On Jordan's Stormy Banks: Evangelicalism in Mississippi, 1773–1876.* Athens, GA and London: University of Georgia Press.

Startup, Kenneth Moore 1997: *The Root of All Evil: The Protestant Clergy and the Economic Mind of the Old South.* Athens, GA and London: University of Georgia Press.

Stuckey, Sterling 1987: *Slave Culture: Nationalist Theory and the Foundations of Black America.* New York: Oxford University Press.

Thomas, David Hurst (ed.) 1989: *Archaeological and Historical Perspectives on the Spanish Borderlands East.* Washington, DC and London: Smithsonian Institution.

Thornton, John 1992: *Africa and Africans in the Making of the Atlantic World, 1400–1680.* Cambridge: Cambridge University Press.

Thorp, Daniel B. 1989: *The Moravian Community in Colonial North Carolina: Pluralism on the Southern Frontier.* Knoxville: University of Tennessee Press.

Tise, Larry E. 1987: *Proslavery: A History of the Defense of Slavery in America, 1701–1840.* Athens: University of Georgia Press.

Upton, Dell 1986: *Holy Things and Profane: Anglican Parish Churches in Colonial Virginia.* Cambridge, MA and New York: MIT Press and the Architectural History Foundation.

Weber, David J. 1992: *The Spanish Frontier in North America.* New Haven, CT: Yale University Press.

Wigger, John H. 1998: *Taking Heaven By Storm: Methodism and the Rise of Popular Christianity in America.* New York and Oxford: Oxford University Press.

Williams, William Henry 1984: *The Garden of American Methodism: The Delmarva Peninsula, 1769–1820*. Wilmington, DE: published for the Peninsula Conference of the United Methodist Church by Scholarly Resources.

Wilson, Charles Reagan (ed.) 1985: *Religion in the South*. Jackson: University Press of Mississippi.

Worth, John E. 1998: *The Timucuan Chiefdoms of Spanish Florida*, 2 vols. Gainesville: University Press of Florida.

Wyatt-Brown, Bertram 1982: *Southern Honor: Ethics and Behavior in the Old South*. New York: Oxford University Press.

CHAPTER ELEVEN

Politics in the Antebellum South

DANIEL W. CROFTS

THIS assessment of modern scholarship on antebellum southern politics divides
into four categories: (1) an introductory segment examining the broad contours
of society and politics in the Old South, looking particularly at the intrinsic tensions
between oligarchy and democracy; (2) a segment on the rise of the two-party system
in the South during the 1830s; (3) a segment on political developments at the state
level during the 1840s and 1850s; (4) a concluding segment on the South's position
in the nation during the period of increased sectional tension in the 1840s and 1850s.

To understand politics in the Old South one must first seek a wider context. In the
early to mid-nineteenth century most people in the world were peasants. Few could
read or write and few enjoyed any political rights or economic independence. Typically living under the thumbs of the rich and powerful, peasants had no choice but to
continue doing what their parents and grandparents had done. Their mental horizons
were local, with identity rooted in attachments to community, family, and clan. In
many parts of the world promoters were attempting to build national consciousness,
but the impact of their work mostly lay in the future. Few peasants considered
themselves citizens of nations.

The United States of America was full of exceptions to the patterns just described.
It was the first "new nation." Americans had an emphatic national identity. They
revered the architects of national independence, the "Founding Fathers." The Euro-
pean-derived male population in the United States either owned land or could
reasonably consider moving to frontier regions where new land was available for
settlement. Most could read and write. White males enjoyed broad legal equality,
and by mid-century all, whether landowning or not, could exercise the franchise. No
white male American considered himself a peasant.

In many ways the Old South shared these national characteristics. White southerners considered themselves patriotic Americans, and the most celebrated Founding
Father of all ("first in war, first in peace, and first in the hearts of his countrymen")
was a southerner. From the Great Lakes to the Gulf of Mexico, rapid population
growth pushed the agricultural frontier westward as pioneer farmers settled ever-
larger sections of the interior. White male southerners gained full political equality,
just as did their counterparts in the North. Nevertheless, the Old South was also very
different. The backbone of its most productive agricultural labor force was an
enslaved and racially stigmatized peasantry. Slaves produced the single-most valuable
American export, cotton, together with large amounts of sugar, rice, and tobacco. As
the system expanded rapidly to fertile land in the Gulf South, slave prices appreciated.
The Old South's investment in slaves came to exceed the combined value of southern

lands and improvements. Embracing slavery both as a social system and a sound investment, slaveholders vigilantly defended their prerogatives. They built a social and economic order less committed to industrial development and more tightly bound by tradition than in the free states.

Most white southerners either stood outside the plantation economy or participated in it only peripherally. Between one-quarter and one-third of white families in the Old South owned neither land nor slaves. An even larger segment (more than half) owned land best suited for family farming. By 1860 only one southern white family in four owned slaves. Yeomen slaveholders, for whom slave labor supplemented white labor, far outnumbered middling slaveholders who owned at least ten slaves, and the latter likewise outnumbered planters, the owners of twenty or more slaves. In short, ordinary whites and white smallholders together constituted close to 90 percent of southern white families (Crofts 1992: 11–19; Bode and Ginter 1986: 125–6, 136–7; Hahn 1983: 26–32, 64–9; Freehling 1990: 41, 573 n. 6).

A hybrid system of politics developed in the Old South, containing elements of both oligarchy and democracy. The privileged minority of planters, middling slaveholders, and professionals used wealth, education, and family connections to exercise disproportionate influence over southern society. Those who commanded the labor of others inevitably had aristocratic outlooks and temperaments. They lived, however, in a nation that prized equality and gave ordinary whites a voting majority. Elite southerners privately chafed at the need to treat common whites as equals, but they recognized the wisdom of doing so. Mary Chesnut penned an account of how her husband, James Chesnut, was "solemnly polite and attentive" to Squire MacDonald, a common white well digger. She wasn't pleased but knew that "Mr. C. would never have forgiven me if I had shown impatience" (Woodward 1981: 193, 205). Through such means, elites managed to dampen class antagonisms and prevent white democracy from encroaching on planter privileges.

However different the circumstances of planters and yeomen, and however contrasting the social and economic life of the plantation districts and the southern uplands, formidable ties linked most white southerners together. W. J. Cash, author of the most widely read book ever written about the history of the South, wrote of the "proto-Dorian" bond through which common whites saw planters not as antagonists but more as old friends and kinsmen, thereby defusing the Old South's political order of any "essential conflict in interest among groups or classes." Resentment at outside criticism further affirmed "the common brotherhood of white men" (Cash 1941: 54, 81). Cash's insights hold up well under modern scrutiny, though Cash himself rarely gets credit from academicians (Wyatt-Brown 1985: 131–54, esp. 152–3; Clayton 1991: 199–201, 220–2). Eugene D. Genovese made much the same point as Cash, imagining the ties that bound a typical "dirt farmer," Josh Venable, to his cousin, Jeff Venable, owner of "the district's finest Big House." Whatever resentment Josh felt toward Jeff was more than counterbalanced by Jeff's continued readiness to play the role of helpful patron (Genovese 1983: 258–9). Steven Hahn and Paul Escott, both keenly sensitive to latent tensions that had the potential to divide planters from yeomen, recognized that the plantation economy functioned so as to allow substantial individual and local autonomy. Hahn noted that small farmers and nonslaveholders prized their independence and typically enjoyed sufficient "economic, social, and cultural space" to forestall complaints about class inequalities

(Hahn 1983: 84–5, 105–14). Escott likewise found that the prewar southern social system afforded yeomen "a large degree of functional independence," shielding them from the realities of "class privilege" (Escott 1985: 81). The relative absence of class conflict in the Old South allowed leadership to pass to those who enjoyed advantages of wealth and education.

Every historian who writes about the Old South must wrestle with the interlocking questions of oligarchy, democracy, regional cohesion, and the extent to which the South differed from the rest of the nation. The preceding several paragraphs attempt to strike a reasonable balance on the characteristics and shortcomings of southern democracy and to identify what might be called the white southern social consensus. Was the Old South therefore a planter-led monolith, culturally distinct from the rest of the nation and predestined to go to war against the nonsouthern majority? As will be developed more fully in the concluding segment, some historians may have exaggerated the polarities.

A nationwide two-party system (the so-called Second Party System) that formed in the 1830s added to the challenges facing southern oligarchs. A shrill minority, conspicuously led by John C. Calhoun, came to believe that the South should steer clear of national parties and unite to defend slavery and other sectional interests, but most southerners enlisted by 1840 as Jacksonians or Whigs, not Calhounites. The catalytic partisan of the era, Andrew Jackson, was a southerner. In his home state of Tennessee and elsewhere in the Old South, intense partisan rivalries flourished and massive voter turnouts became the norm. Charles S. Sydnor's famous quip, that partisan combat in the Old South "had the hollow sound of a stage duel with tin swords," understates the extent to which partisanship complicated the preservation of elite privilege. Partisan politics, in the words of Lacy K. Ford, Jr., both "engaged and divided whites." Any process that mobilized whites into opposing camps had the potential to fuel class resentments (Sydnor 1948: 316; Ford 1989: 70–1).

The Second Party System evolved amid a clash of personalities. Four key south-erners – Jackson, Calhoun, Henry Clay, and James K. Polk – have attracted the attention of modern biographers and have been the focus for extensive modern letterpress editions of published papers. Robert V. Remini has been particularly industrious, with a three-volume biography of Jackson and a hefty volume on his rival, Clay (Remini 1977–84, 1991). Two modern biographies of Calhoun and Charles G. Sellers's uncompleted biography of Polk also are available (Niven 1988; Bartlett 1993; Sellers 1957–66). The published papers for each of the above include a wealth of detail. The Clay project is complete (Hopkins 1959–92); Calhoun and Polk are close to the finish (Meriwether et al. 1959–; Weaver et al. 1969–); the Jackson project is still pre-presidential (Smith et al. 1980–). Other important studies with a biographical orientation include Merrill D. Peterson's *Great Triumvirate* (Clay, Calhoun, and Daniel Webster) and Drew McCoy's linkage between the elderly James Madison and a younger generation of southern Whigs (Peterson 1987; McCoy 1989).

Biography reminds modern readers that arresting personalities and outsized egos did much to kindle partisan rivalry, but more specialized monographs have shaped the interpretative agenda. William J. Cooper's *The South and the Politics of Slavery* contended that slavery was the paramount issue in southern politics from the incep-tion of the two-party system in the 1830s. Cooper showed that politicians in the Old

South routinely questioned the proslavery orthodoxy of partisan rivals, taking particular aim at the other party's "abolitionist" supporters in the free states. He traced the pattern to the uproar over abolitionist petitions that began in 1835 and carried forward into the presidential campaign of 1836, just as the Second Party System was taking shape (Cooper 1978; see also Cooper 1983). More has since been written about the anti-abolition furor of 1835–6, which William W. Freehling dubbed "the Pearl Harbor of the slavery controversy" (Freehling 1990: 308; see also Grimsted 1998; Miller 1996; Wyly-Jones, forthcoming).

Cooper minimized other sources of party rivalry. Several historians, led by Harry L. Watson, contend that partisan differentiation resulted primarily from matters other than slavery. Looking at Cumberland County, North Carolina, Watson provided an assessment that differs markedly from Cooper. Slavery was, Watson acknowledged, a volatile lightning rod with "intense emotional power," but "the white community's underlying solidarity on the subject" made "swapping charges on the slavery issue" an ineffective way "to summon voters to the polls." Instead, Watson found that Whigs and Democrats disagreed about the economic future. The pace of social and economic change divided those who welcomed change from those who feared it. The Democratic Party gave "at least the appearance of involvement and participation to those who doubted the benefits of progress" while actually "diverting most challenges to economic development into noisy but harmless rituals." The Second Party System thus "knitted up the seams in a straining social fabric." Parties polarized the electorate into two groups, but they functioned symbiotically to promote national integration (Watson 1981: 292–6, 324).

Watson judged that the Old South had much in common with the rest of the United States. Both within and without the South, Jacksonian Democrats who were ambivalent about the social and economic changes associated with the "Market Revolution" opposed anti-Jacksonian Whigs, who welcomed economic development. Jackson and his supporters feared that the rise of banks, corporations, and large-scale business enterprise endangered liberty and equality. They suspected that corruption would result if government attempted to promote economic development or enterprise. Whigs, by contrast, contended that everyone benefited when canals and railroads were built, when commerce was extended, and when industry took root. Whigs wanted individual improvement as well as economic development; they were more likely than Democrats to support public education and moral reform. By 1840 the overwhelming majority of white males in the United States had developed a firm attachment to one of the two national parties, the Democrats or the Whigs (Watson 1990: 28–9, 237–48).

Two recent local studies, Crofts's book on Southampton County, Virginia, and Daniel Dupre's on Madison County, Alabama, dovetail well with Watson. The Whig party in Southampton coalesced among small and medium landholders who were receptive to economic and social innovation. The Whig electorate included an egalitarian minority whose cultural outlook diverged sharply from slaveholding traditionalists. Democrats did best in a part of the county where planters discouraged any deviation from the status quo. Southampton is especially well suited for studying party constituencies because records survive showing how individuals voted (Crofts 1992: 137–40, 186–92). Whigs in Madison County tended to favor transportation improvements and moral reform. Democrats, who found identity in the masculine culture of honor, feared that pious busybodies would infringe upon personal liberty. Like Watson, Dupre emphasized the integrative role of partisan competition, which served to deflect conflict away from the community "by absorbing it within a national institutional framework" (Dupre 1997: 7, 137–9).

A series of books, most of which focus on the experience of single states, has given new depth to the study of antebellum southern politics. Several key themes emerge from these studies: the ubiquitous invocation of republican values, coupled with partisan jockeying to identify and squelch threats to liberty and equality; the complex interconnections between local, state, and national politics, with the system ultimately dependent on the loyalty and motivation of ordinary citizens at the local level; and the increasingly dissimilar characteristics of politics in the Upper and Lower South, especially after 1850.

J. Mills Thornton III set out to show what the world of the mid-nineteenth century looked like to the average white Alabamian. From such a perspective, cherished principles of freedom, equality, and autonomy appeared threatened, both by the expansion of market relations within the state and by the looming menace of hostile foes in the free states. Partisan leaders skillfully manipulated "the popular dread of manipulation," conjuring up ever-more sinister threats to popular liberty. Their "eschatological oratory" convinced grassroots activists that society was engulfed in crisis and that only drastic remedies would suit. Thornton concludes by explaining how ordinary white southerners came to see secession as the solution for their problems. Indignant that a hostile northern majority threatened their liberty and equality, white southerners rallied exuberantly to preserve their way of life (Thornton 1978: 141, 160–1, 458).

Thornton's writing contains more than its fair share of hyperbole, and he may be challenged on several particulars. Alabama was not a microcosm of the entire South, and his findings must be used with care in trying to understand the Upper South. Moreover, he fails to make a convincing case that the small farmers from the Jacksonian hill counties of northern Alabama headed the state's secession bandwagon. He would not seriously have impaired his main argument had he said the upcountry acquiesced in secession once it happened, rather than led it. Nevertheless, Thornton has done much to shape subsequent historiography. In at least four different ways, his ideas have proven consequential: (1) in identifying a discourse about threatened liberty and equality in antebellum southern political rhetoric; (2) in suggesting that local-level political leaders transmitted ideologically charged abstractions to credulous voters; (3) in showing the untapped benefits of focusing on a single state; and (4) in obliging historians to think more carefully about what the Lower South and Upper South did and did not have in common.

Thornton's discovery that partisan leaders routinely attempted to identify and combat "antirepublican monsters" has been echoed by Marc W. Kruman, who found that North Carolina's antebellum politicians postured as "the people's surrogate sentinels guarding the fortress of popular liberty," and by Michael F. Holt, who concluded that an obsession "to protect self-government, liberty, and equality for whites" was the key force that "drove Americans to the point of killing each other in 1861" (Kruman 1983: 5; Holt 1978: x; see also Jeffrey 1989: 118–21). Lacy Ford unearthed plenty of politically significant anxiety about endangered liberty in upcountry South Carolina, even without the catalyst of ties to national parties

(Ford 1988). Most recently, Thornton's own student, Jonathan Atkins, has demonstrated how partisan spokesmen in antebellum Tennessee incessantly smeared their opponents for endangering popular liberty (Atkins 1997).

Although less has been done to corroborate Thornton's emphasis on the importance of face-to-face contact between party activists and plain folk, his insights are likely sound. Compared to the North, southern life was more rural, dispersed, and isolated – and more dependent on the spoken rather than the written word. Diarist Daniel Cobb, a Virginian with an above-average share of tangible possessions, knew what he did about politics only because of oral encounters (Crofts 1997: xix, 61). Random distribution cannot explain the remarkably polarized pattern of partisan allegiance in Cobb's native Southampton County, which included two voting districts where over 80 percent of voters routinely cast Whig ballots and three other districts that returned equally decisive Democratic margins. Across the South, voters were more likely than their northern counterparts to reflect the shared outlook of a neighborhood or a community. Most southern counties, and especially most voting districts within each county, had a pronounced partisan identity. Such patterns suggest that ordinary southerners took partisan cues from local elites and party activists, who carried the burden of prodding voters to the polls. These activists had motive (and likely predisposition) to employ ideologically charged stereotypes. Ultimately, Democratic activists provided the cutting edge for secession (Thornton 1978: 158–60; Crofts 1992: 126–31, 155–62, 178–92; Crofts 1989: 47–8; Watson 1981: 310–11).

Thornton established the state as a useful unit of analysis, blazing a trail that has attracted several insightful successors. He rejected the idea that antebellum political history could be understood "as if it had taken place for the most part in Washington" (Thornton 1978: xvi). Instead he explicated the dynamic in a single state, Alabama, and showed how ideologically charged partisans at the local level shaped the contours of statewide politics. In certain ways Thornton built upon the insights of Roy Franklin Nichols, whose masterwork, *The Disruption of American Democracy*, depicted the national Democratic Party as an unstable coalition of state parties (Nichols 1948). Thornton (and Nichols) directly influenced Michael Holt, who has recently published a compendious history of the Whig Party. For Holt, state governments in the nineteenth century "often had far more impact on people's lives" than did the federal government and state elections "were the equivalent of modern public opinion polls." Therefore, "local and state politics were just as crucial as national developments in shaping the political crisis of the 1850s" (Holt 1999: ix, 442; Holt 1978: xi, 4, 14, 104–5, 263). Able state studies by Kruman, Atkins, William G. Shade, Thomas E. Jeffrey, and Anthony Gene Carey, further discussed below, likewise build upon Thornton's example.

Thornton also renewed interest in a key matter that has been assessed more fully in subsequent work: the widening political dissimilarities separating the Lower and Upper Souths, especially in the 1850s. If Alabama's pace of economic change by the 1850s had become a source of instability, why was the sense of crisis far less acute in the Upper South, where the pace of economic and social change was more rapid than in Alabama or other Deep South states? Quite plainly, the Deep South harbored particular demons that were less salient in the Upper South.

What made the Deep South different? Overall it was socially and economically more homogeneous than the Upper South, with a deeper commitment to plantation slavery. Probably as a consequence, two-party politics atrophied in the Deep South. The Whig Party in the Deep South disintegrated between 1850 and 1852, undermined by the free-soil position of northern Whigs. For the rest of the decade, political choices in the Deep South narrowed to factional disagreements within a Democratic Party that provided cover for dangerous malcontents, bitter-enders, and secession extremists. These tendencies endangered intersectional cooperation with northern Democrats. Cooper sees the presence of "fire-eaters" as the key explanatory variable; more fire-eaters, especially at the face-to-face level, generated more political extremism (Cooper 1983: 233–4, 268–81). A chicken-and-egg argument may be involved here. Did fire-eaters transform the Deep South into a secessionist hotbed? Or did the Deep South's underlying social, economic, and ideological characteristics create a fertile field for the fire-eater message?

Efforts to define the distinctive aspects of the Deep South's political culture continue. Anthony Gene Carey's recent study of antebellum Georgia depicts partisanship as a well-defined game, with agreed-upon rules that prevented the players from challenging basic social and economic arrangements. In Carey's view, white men loudly disagreed about means but not about ends. Partisan rhetoric obscured a more fundamental unity that "sharply constricted political debate" (Carey 1997: 7, 18). Kenneth Greenberg downplays even ritual disagreement, suggesting instead that elite southerners thought of themselves as disinterested statesmen, unsullied by selfishness or partisanship. They preferred consensus and harmony, or at least the appearance of such. His research focuses on South Carolina, the one state national political parties failed to penetrate. Greenberg contends that the "political culture of slavery" also eroded partisan competition elsewhere in the Deep South in the 1850s. He recognizes that his interpretation works least well for the eight slave states in the Upper South, where differing cultural norms prevailed (Greenberg 1985: 45–51). Lacy K. Ford's South Carolina was more rambunctious and democratic than Greenberg's, paralleling Thornton's Alabama. Like Thornton, Ford argues that growing economic interconnections between the South Carolina upcountry and the outside world increased popular anxieties, ultimately predisposing yeomen to embrace the secessionist cause (Ford 1988). Neither Thornton nor Ford attempt to explain why the faster pace of economic change in the Upper South failed to produce equivalent political extremism. Christopher Olsen contends that antebellum Mississippi had a "localized political culture" which prevented either political party from capturing a "widespread following." Instead, voters relied on face-to-face cues from trusted friends and neighbors. Interpreting free-soil partisan rhetoric as "personal insult," white males in Mississippi responded angrily. Olsen suggests that the Upper South had a more "viable partisan culture" that inhibited sectional polarization. He does not consider, however, why a comparably localized political culture in the Upper South was less susceptible to extremist politics (Olsen 1996: x, 6, 327; see also Morris 1995: 143–55, 169–79, which shows that in Mississippi's Warren County, which included the city of Vicksburg, localism declined and pro-secession politics failed to attract a majority).

Several discerning modern biographies of prominent Deep South leaders – including Jefferson Davis, Alexander Stephens, James Henry Hammond, and John A. Quitman – deserve attention. The most radical of these men, Quitman, was born and raised in upstate New York but found a congenial new home among Mississippi militants. The future Confederate president, Davis, who attempted to balance between Mississippi's extremist elements and his own national ambitions, served as Secretary of War during the Pierce administration. The modern letterpress edition of the Davis papers contains much of value. Hammond became less radical as he aged; by the 1850s he hoped the South could remain in the Union. Stephens, always a Unionist at heart, was more in his element as a prominent Whig than as the Confederate vice president (Davis 1991; Monroe et al. 1971–; May 1985; Faust 1982; Schott 1988). Edited diaries penned by two otherwise obscure South Carolinians and a Louisianan offer revealing insights into the social mosaic that the politicians confronted (Rosengarten 1986; Racine 1990; Davis 1967).

Compared with the Deep South, the Upper South combined greater industrial development, urban growth, and social diversity with healthier, more integrative political arrangements. Proportionately fewer white families in Virginia, North Carolina, and Tennessee relied on plantation slavery than in the Deep South. Although Virginia still had more total slaves than any other state, its social order varied greatly by region. In many respects two separate states had emerged, even before the war. West of the Blue Ridge, only 15 percent of the population was enslaved, less than in any state that seceded in 1861. Northwestern Virginia beyond the Alleghenies, the fastest growing part of the state, was 95 percent white, comparable to adjacent free states. Regional disparities in Tennessee were nearly as stark as in Virginia, with yeoman-dominated East Tennessee separated from the rest of the state by the Cumberland Plateau. North Carolina was less geographically segmented than Virginia or Tennessee, but significant pockets of its piedmont "Quaker Belt" and mountainous western uplands had no stomach for southern-rights grandstanding. Political structures reflected each of these three states' social and economic diversity. Both parties necessarily competed for the votes of upcountry yeomen and others with little stake in the plantation system. Closely fought two-party politics continued in the Upper South throughout the antebellum era. Whigs and their successors (the American, Opposition, and Constitutional Union parties) obliged Democrats to pull together and to spurn Deep South-style fire-eating (Crofts 1989: 37–65).

Several books reveal a political environment in the Upper South unlike what Thornton encountered in Alabama. Noting that "the politics of the Upper South differed greatly from that of the Lower South," Kruman explains how partisanship in late-antebellum North Carolina continued to provide a mechanism to address and relieve "potentially explosive social conflict." Democrats found it politically inexpedient to identify with Deep South firebrands. Instead, they vied with Whigs to pose as egalitarians and friends of the common man (Kruman 1983: xv, 86–103, 131–3, 191). Jeffrey likewise calls attention to the way that North Carolina Whigs often rejected "the politics of slavery," appealing instead to "the Unionist sensibilities of the North Carolina electorate" (Jeffrey 1989: 297, 305). One may read lengthy sections of the fascinating diary of Basil Armstrong Thomasson of Yadkin County, North Carolina, without finding any mention whatsoever of slavery or the sectional crisis (Escott 1996).

Partisan competition in antebellum Tennessee, like North Carolina, featured very close statewide contests from the late 1830s to the early 1850s, with a narrow Democratic advantage thereafter. According to Atkins, Whigs championed the expansion of "material well-being" while Democrats warned about the misuse of power by "those seeking special privileges." Democrats depicted themselves as pro-Union, concerned for "the liberty of all citizens and not just the interests of slaveholders" (Atkins 1997: 108, 212–13). Most in Tennessee took a dim view of Deep South extremism. One state legislator proposed during the Nullification Crisis that Andrew Jackson rally a force of indignant Tennesseans "to stand on Saluda Mountain and piss enough ... to float the whole nullifying crew of South Carolina into the Atlantic Ocean" (Barnwell 1982: 43). *The Papers of Andrew Johnson* reveal a proud, self-styled plebeian and lone wolf, who disdained elite privilege. In most respects a loyal southerner until 1860, Johnson reached the turning point of his political career when secessionists attempted to hijack the Democratic Party (Graf and Haskins et al. 1967–).

William Shade's prize-winning book, *Democratizing the Old Dominion*, rejects the familiar view that antebellum Virginia remained frozen in a late eighteenth-century time warp. Shade contends instead that the sprawling and diverse state experienced "the same dynamic economic and social development that characterized the country as a whole." Virginia's two party groupings differed. A nucleus of Democratic traditionalists led by US Senators Robert M. T. Hunter and James M. Mason acted as if Virginia were part of the Deep South. But once Virginia governors became popularly elected in 1851, Democrats decided to nominate middle-of-the-roaders with appeal to western nonslaveholders. Virginia's Whig and Whig successor parties remained sectionally moderate, notwithstanding some use of southern rights rhetoric in the 1859 campaign for governor (Shade 1996: 3–6, 19–22, and passim; see also Crofts 1989: 57–9; Crofts 1999). The most trenchant assessment of a late-antebellum Upper South political leader is Craig Simpson's biography of Henry A. Wise, governor of Virginia from 1855 to 1859. Because Wise knew that the South must change and develop, he fought the reactionary traditionalists who loomed large in Virginia's Democratic Party. To gain the upper hand over his intraparty rivals, Wise courted nonslaveholders, suspecting that they might otherwise become recruits for the South's external critics. At heart a conservative, Wise posed as an egalitarian and followed an increasingly erratic course. The tightening noose of North–South estrangement thwarted Wise's presidential ambitions and ultimately ripped apart his home state (Simpson 1985).

Conclusive evidence that the Lower South and Upper South had diverged politically came in the secession crisis. Deep South elites feared both slave discontent and class antagonisms among ordinary whites at a moment when control of the federal government appeared to have fallen into dangerous hands. Extremists within the ascendant Democratic parties of the Deep South fueled a surge of popular indignation and encountered no more than halfhearted resistance. J. William Harris's especially well researched local study makes these points with convincing authority (Harris 1985). (For an iconoclastic dissent, which denies that planters feared "slave insurrection" or "the disloyalty of nonslaveholding whites," and instead explains secession as an angry response to northern insult and a vindication of white southern "manliness and honor," see Olsen 1996: 6, 329.)

The Upper South responded differently. Secessionists gained support in some high-slaveholding and high-Democratic localities, but elsewhere they stirred a furious backlash. The anti-secession coalition that took shape in the Upper South in early 1861 contained in embryo a new political order that was nonplanter if not yet antiplanter. Never before had a political grouping bid for power in the Old South with such a trivial base of support among slaveholders. Forced to choose sides by the outbreak of war in April 1861, many anti-secessionists in the Upper South became loyal Confederates while continuing to resent secessionists for having polarized matters and destroyed the middle ground (Crofts 1989: 153–63, 193–4).

Thornton and most others who wrote before 1990 about southern antebellum politics had little to say about women and gender relations. Elizabeth Varon's salutary monograph shows that some elite women in Virginia, not content to be passive observers, actively sought to influence the electoral process (Varon 1998). If the crucial nexus of partisan politics in the Old South was the face-to-face encounter of party activist and voter, however, women were plainly at a great disadvantage in playing even an indirect political role. A different case for the significance of gender in southern politics has been advanced by Stephanie McCurry, who suggests that South Carolina yeomen were attracted to extreme politics because antislavery agitation threatened both racial and sexual hierarchy (McCurry 1995). She does not consider why white men in the Upper South, equally advantaged by their race and sex, took a less hysterical view of the situation.

The modern understanding of antebellum southern politics has been much influenced by several scholars whose writings cannot fit a narrow definition of political history. Neither Eugene Genovese nor Bertram Wyatt-Brown has ever delved into the realms of elections, partisanship, or governance, but both stand at the forefront of southern studies and deserve consideration here. Perhaps more than anyone else, Genovese established the paradigm of a South that ceased to enjoy any real commonality with the North, a fundamentally separate culture and civilization that had no choice but the strike for independence in 1861. His South was ruled by and for the planter class. These leaders had tangible material reasons for seeking new slave territory, knowing that "the system had to expand or die" (Genovese 1965: 267). The Republican Party's containment policy confronted them with a deadly threat. Wyatt-Brown has reinforced the case for North–South difference by portraying the South as an aristocratic culture of honor, one in which loss of face within the external community did more to shape behavior than did feelings of individual guilt. Each section had mutually exclusive definitions of such key concepts as freedom, liberty, and equality, all of which gained a proslavery slant in the South. Such "moral dichotomies" placed North and South on a collision course. By mid-century each section was becoming ethically and politically more distinctive and estranged (Wyatt-Brown 1985: 1–10; see also Wyatt-Brown 1982).

Genovese and Wyatt-Brown's emphases on North–South polarities converge with the dominant trend of modern historical interpretation. Both Eric Foner and James M. McPherson, whose writings on the wartime era have probably reached a wider general audience than any other modern academic historians, depict a widening gulf of material, moral, and ideological differences dividing the free North from the slave South. For Foner, "the nation was every day growing apart and into two societies whose ultimate interests were diametrically opposed" (Foner 1980: 50). McPherson quotes with approval the comments of a Georgia secessionist who observed that northerners and southerners had become "so entirely separated by climate, by morals, by religion, and by estimates so totally opposite of all that constitutes honor, truth, and manliness, that they cannot longer exist under the same government" (McPherson 1988: 41).

Nevertheless, the dominant paradigm may well overstate North–South differences. David M. Potter, perhaps the shrewdest and most discerning analyst of the political crisis that led to war, never accepted the view that North and South had become culturally polarized. His masterwork, *The Impending Crisis*, depicted southern feelings of estrangement and separatism as products of "anger and fear." In Potter's view, "southern nationalism was born of resentment and not of a sense of separate cultural identity," and "the crisis of 1860 resulted from a transfer of power, far more than from what some writers have called the divergence of two civilizations" (Potter 1976: 29–50, 469, 471–2; see also Potter 1968).

When the Union collapsed and war broke out, most Americans were astonished. Michael Holt notes that most Republicans including Abraham Lincoln expected a peaceful sequel to the 1860 presidential election because they had no plan or intent to attack slavery. They did hope to undercut the political power slaveholders had amassed in the southern-dominated Democratic Party, but only by winning an election, not by starting a revolution. Holt likewise contends, I believe correctly, that a majority of white southerners opposed independence until Lincoln called for troops and undermined the antisecession coalition in the Upper South (Holt 1978: 183–259). Edward Ayers's acclaimed website, "The Valley of the Shadow" (Ayers n.d.), which has taken primary historical data into more homes and classrooms than any book, allows viewers to explore in detail two counties, one in southern Pennsylvania, the other 150 miles south in Virginia. One was in a free state and the other in a slave state, but any reasonable comparison will suggest many points of similarity. The Virginia Valley was only peripherally involved in the plantation economy. In effect Ayers dramatizes how the actions of resolute minorities undercut moderate majorities. Until April 15, 1861, the middle ground was larger than the dominant paradigm allows and it was unthinkable that soldiers from one part of the valley would soon burn and destroy the homes and farms of the other. One risks imposing a dichotomous view of the antebellum world that can only be sustained with hindsight.

Only one contemporary scholar, William W. Freehling, has attempted a full accounting that integrates modern scholarship on the Old South and retraces the political crisis that led to war (Freehling 1990). His first volume of *The Road to Disunion* appeared in 1990; the sequel will cover the pivotal years from mid-1854 to mid-1861. Freehling's work will provide a narrative of the South's role in national politics from the Age of Jackson through to the start of the war. The completed volume already stands alone among books considered in this essay. It is more than a worthy successor to Charles Sydnor's justly acclaimed survey of southern history, 1818–48, published more than half a century ago (Sydnor 1948). In an era of monographic studies, Freehling has dared to try something much bigger. His ultimate focus is political, but his writing is sensitive to the outpouring of new scholarship on slavery, class dynamics, and gender relations in the Old South.

Freehling stands outside the dominant paradigm. He rejects any exclusive focus on North–South polarities. He emphasizes, instead, the relentless negotiating process among many Souths, with the Border and Middle Souths often distancing themselves from the Deep South. Even though white southerners agreed that they had to decide about slavery for themselves without outside interference, they disagreed about whether they wanted to perpetuate slavery forever. Many in the Middle and especially the Border South did not, seeking instead a freesoil or industrial future in which slavery either would play a diminished role or would disappear.

These differing outlooks had political consequences. Leaders of the Deep South (and especially South Carolina) repeatedly clamored for sectional unity. But leaders of the Middle and Border Souths embraced the national two-party system with its integrative ability to transcend sectional divisions. For Freehling more than for any previous scholar, the Border South had an outlook and agenda of its own, the ultimate proof coming when Delaware, Maryland, Kentucky, Missouri, and northwestern Virginia sided with the Union in wartime. Anticipating Michael F. Holt's massive study of the Whig Party, Freehling insists that party differences mattered, that southern Whigs and their successors were more amenable to sectional accommodation, that their failures cannot be ascribed entirely to insurmountable systemic obstacles, that random bad luck played a role (i.e. John Tyler as president), and that a sectional crisis with the potential to explode into unlimited bloodshed was hardly foreordained (Freehling 1990; Holt 1999).

Freehling has something significant to say about nearly every matter addressed in this essay. He recognizes that presidential campaigns in the South lent themselves to proslavery one-upmanship, but he rejects Cooper's thesis that "slavery was *always* the issue." Most of the time (except during the months before presidential elections) it was not, and only during the 1850s did slavery start "overshadowing everything else" (Freehling 1990: 299, 599–600 n. 19). Freehling partially accepts the findings of Thornton and others about politicians both North and South decrying threats to liberty. He suggests, however, that northern egalitarians had a more inviting target ("the haughty Slavepower") and so achieved greater political resonance. The sectional vise tightened when southerners reacted against anti-southern outcries from the North, complaining that northerners had insulted the South and rejected the South's equal moral worth in the Union (Freehling 1990: 461, 612–14 n. 13; see also Wyatt-Brown 1985: 126, 169). As of mid-1854, where Freehling's first volume concludes, it seems almost impossible to believe that a politically marginal group of "reactionary revolutionaries" could ever do what we already know they did do – spur eleven states in a divided South out of the Union and force an epic confrontation. Only southern recklessness – a "Slavepower minority provoking a northern majority" – assured the success of anti-southern politics in the North between 1854 and 1861. And only then could southern extremists rally enough of their countrymen in the Lower and Middle Souths to commit collective suicide (Freehling 1990: 492, 557).

BIBLIOGRAPHY

Atkins, Jonathan M. 1997: *Parties, Politics, and the Sectional Conflict in Tennessee, 1832–1861.* Knoxville: University of Tennessee Press.

Ayers, Edward K., et al. n.d. The Valley of the Shadow. http://jefferson.village.virginia.edu/vshadow2/

Barnwell, John 1982: *Love of Order: South Carolina's First Secession Crisis.* Chapel Hill: University of North Carolina Press.

Bartlett, Irving H. 1993: *John C. Calhoun: A Biography.* New York: Harper Collins Publishers.

Bode, Frederick A. and Ginter, Donald E. 1986: *Farm Tenancy and the Census in Antebellum Georgia*. Athens: University of Georgia Press.

Carey, Anthony Gene 1997: *Parties, Slavery, and the Union in Antebellum Georgia*. Athens: University of Georgia Press.

Cash, W. J. 1941: *The Mind of the South*. New York: Alfred A. Knopf.

Clayton, Bruce 1991: *W. J. Cash: A Life*. Baton Rouge: Louisiana State University Press.

Cooper, William J., Jr. 1978: *The South and the Politics of Slavery, 1828–1856*. Baton Rouge: Louisiana State University Press.

Cooper, William J., Jr. 1983: *Liberty and Slavery: Southern Politics to 1860*. New York: Alfred A. Knopf.

Crofts, Daniel W. 1989: *Reluctant Confederates: Upper South Unionists in the Secession Crisis*. Chapel Hill: University of North Carolina Press.

Crofts, Daniel W. 1992: *Old Southampton: Politics and Society in a Virginia County, 1834–1869*. Charlottesville: University Press of Virginia.

Crofts, Daniel W. (ed.) 1997: *Cobb's Ordeal: The Diaries of a Virginia Farmer, 1842–1872*. Athens: University of Georgia Press.

Crofts, Daniel W. 1999: Late Antebellum Virginia Reconsidered. *Virginia Magazine of History and Biography*, 253–86.

Davis, Edwin Adams 1967: *Plantation Life in the Florida Parishes of Louisiana, 1836–1846*. New York: AMS Press (reprint of 1943 edn).

Davis, William C. 1991: *Jefferson Davis: The Man and His Hour*. New York: Harper Collins Publishers.

Dupre, Daniel S. 1997: *Transforming the Cotton Frontier: Madison County, Alabama, 1800–1840*. Baton Rouge: Louisiana State University Press.

Escott, Paul D. 1985: *Many Excellent People: Power and Privilege in North Carolina, 1850–1900*. Chapel Hill: University of North Carolina Press.

Escott, Paul D. (ed.) 1996: *North Carolina Yeoman: The Diary of Basil Armstrong Thomasson, 1853–1862*. Athens: University of Georgia Press.

Faust, Drew Gilpin 1982: *James Henry Hammond and the Old South: A Design for Mastery*. Baton Rouge: Louisiana State University Press.

Foner, Eric 1980: *Politics and Ideology in the Age of the Civil War*. New York: Oxford University Press.

Ford, Lacy K., Jr. 1988: *Origins of Southern Radicalism: The South Carolina Upcountry, 1800–1860*. New York: Oxford University Press.

Ford, Lacy K., Jr. 1989: "Ties That Bind?" *Reviews in American History*, 64–72.

Freehling, William W. 1990: *The Road to Disunion*, Vol. 1, *Secessionists at Bay, 1776–1854*. New York: Oxford University Press.

Genovese, Eugene D. 1965: *The Political Economy of Slavery: Studies in the Economy and Society of the Slave South*. New York: Pantheon.

Genovese, Eugene D. 1983: Yeoman Farmers in a Slaveholders' Democracy. In Elizabeth Fox-Genovese and Eugene D. Genovese, *Fruits of Merchant Capital: Slavery and Bourgeois Property in the Rise and Expansion of Capitalism*. New York: Oxford University Press, 249–64.

Graf, LeRoy P. and Haskins, Ralph W. et al. (eds.) 1967–: *The Papers of Andrew Johnson*, 15 vols to date. Knoxville: University of Tennessee Press.

Greenberg, Kenneth S. 1985: *Masters and Statesmen: The Political Culture of American Slavery*. Baltimore: Johns Hopkins University Press.

Grimsted, David 1998: *American Mobbing, 1828–1861: Toward Civil War*. New York: Oxford University Press.

Hahn, Steven 1983: *The Roots of Southern Populism: Yeoman Farmers and the Transformation of the Georgia Upcountry, 1850–1890*. New York: Oxford University Press.

Harris, J. William 1985: *Plain Folk and Gentry in a Slave Society: White Liberty and Black Slavery in Augusta's Hinterlands*. Middletown: Wesleyan University Press.

Holt, Michael F. 1978: *The Political Crisis of the 1850s*. New York: Wiley.

Holt, Michael F. 1999: *The Rise and Fall of the American Whig Party: Jacksonian Politics and the Onset of Civil War*. New York: Oxford University Press.

Hopkins, James F., et al. (eds.) 1959–92: *The Papers of Henry Clay*, 10 vols plus supplement. Lexington: University Press of Kentucky.

Jeffrey, Thomas E. 1989: *State Parties and National Politics: North Carolina, 1815–1861*. Athens: University of Georgia Press.

Kruman, Marc W. 1983: *Parties and Politics in North Carolina, 1836–1865*. Baton Rouge: Louisiana State University Press.

McCoy, Drew R. 1989: *The Last of the Fathers: James Madison and the Republican Legacy*. New York: Cambridge University Press.

McCurry, Stephanie 1995: *Masters of Small Worlds: Yeoman Households, Gender Relations, and the Political Culture of the Antebellum South Carolina Low Country*. New York: Oxford University Press.

McPherson, James M. 1988: *Battle Cry of Freedom: The Civil War Era*. New York: Oxford University Press.

May, Robert E. 1985: *John A. Quitman: Old South Crusader*. Baton Rouge: Louisiana State University Press.

Meriwether, Robert L., et al. (eds.) 1959–: *The Papers of John C. Calhoun*, 25 vols to date. Columbia: University of South Carolina Press.

Miller, William Lee 1996: *Arguing About Slavery: The Great Battle in the United States Congress*. New York: Alfred A. Knopf.

Monroe, Haskell M. and McIntosh, James T., et al. (eds.) 1971–: *The Papers of Jefferson Davis*, 10 vols to date. Baton Rouge: Louisiana State University Press.

Morris, Christopher 1995: *Becoming Southern: The Evolution of a Way of Life, Warren County and Vicksburg Mississippi, 1770–1860*. New York: Oxford University Press.

Nichols, Roy Franklin 1948: *The Disruption of American Democracy*. New York: Macmillan.

Niven, John 1988: *John C. Calhoun and the Price of Union: A Biography*. Baton Rouge: Louisiana State University Press.

Olsen, Christopher John 1996: Community, Honor, and Secession in the Deep South: Mississippi's Political Culture, 1840s–1861. Ph.D. Dissertation, University of Florida.

Peterson, Merrill D. 1987: *The Great Triumvirate: Webster, Clay, and Calhoun*. New York: Oxford University Press.

Potter, David M. 1968: The Historian's Use of Nationalism and Vice Versa. In *The South and the Sectional Conflict*. Baton Rouge: Louisiana State University Press, 34–83.

Potter, David M. 1976: *The Impending Crisis, 1848–1861*. Completed and edited by Don E. Fehrenbacher. New York: Harper and Row.

Racine, Philip N. (ed.) 1990: *Piedmont Farmer: The Journals of David Golightly Harris, 1855–1870*. Knoxville: University of Tennessee Press.

Remini, Robert V. 1977–84: *Andrew Jackson*, 3 vols. New York: Harper and Row.

Remini, Robert V. 1991: *Henry Clay: Statesman for the Union*. New York: Norton.

Rosengarten, Theodore 1986: *Tombee: Portrait of a Cotton Planter* (with "The Journal of Thomas B. Chaplin, 1822–1890," edited and annotated with the assistance of Susan W. Walker). New York: William Morrow.

Schott, Thomas E. 1988: *Alexander H. Stephens of Georgia: A Biography*. Baton Rouge: Louisiana State University Press.

Sellers, Charles G. 1957–66: *James K. Polk*, 2 vols to date. Princeton, NJ: Princeton University Press.

190 DANIEL W. CROFTS

Shade, William G. 1996: *Democratizing the Old Dominion: Virginia and the Second Party System, 1824–1861*. Charlottesville: University Press of Virginia.

Simpson, Craig M. 1985: *A Good Southerner: The Life of Henry A. Wise of Virginia*. Chapel Hill: University of North Carolina Press.

Smith, Sam B., et al. (eds.) 1980–: *The Papers of Andrew Jackson*, 5 vols to date. Knoxville: University of Tennessee Press.

Sydnor, Charles S. 1948: *The Development of Southern Sectionalism, 1819–1848*. Baton Rouge: Louisiana State University Press.

Thornton, J. Mills, III 1978: *Politics and Power in a Slave Society: Alabama, 1800–1860*. Baton Rouge: Louisiana State University Press.

Varon, Elizabeth R. 1998: *We Mean to Be Counted: White Women and Politics in Antebellum Virginia*. Chapel Hill: University of North Carolina Press.

Watson, Harry L. 1981: *Jacksonian Politics and Community Conflict: The Emergence of the Second American Party System in Cumberland County, North Carolina*. Baton Rouge: Louisiana State University Press.

Watson, Harry L. 1990: *Liberty and Power: The Politics of Jacksonian America*. New York: Hill and Wang.

Weaver, Herbert, et al. (eds.) 1969–: *The Correspondence of James K. Polk*, 9 vols to date. Nashville: Vanderbilt University Press (vols 1–7). Knoxville: University of Tennessee Press (vols 8–9).

Woodward, C. Vann (ed.) 1981: *Mary Chesnut's Civil War*. New Haven, CT: Yale University Press.

Wyatt-Brown, Bertram 1982: *Southern Honor: Ethics and Behavior in the Old South*. New York: Oxford University Press.

Wyatt-Brown, Bertram 1985: *Yankee Saints and Southern Sinners*. Baton Rouge: Louisiana State University Press.

Wyly-Jones, Susan n.d.: The Antiabolitionist Panic and the Politics of Slavery in the US South, 1835–44. Forthcoming Ph.D. Dissertation, Harvard University.

CHAPTER TWELVE

Women in the Old South

SALLY G. MCMILLEN

THE study of southern women has been an exciting area of scholarship for three decades. For too long, research on American women had focused on those living in the Northeast; southern women, if included, were an afterthought. This is hardly the case today; southern women's history stands on its own. A growing number of historians and graduate students have found this a rewarding field of research. The Southern Association for Women Historians' triennial conference has fostered interest in the subject and resulted in the publication of some excellent papers. Journals occasionally devote an entire issue to southern women.

Scholars engaged in this field face several challenges. The Old South was anything but monolithic; female experiences varied significantly in this biracial, geographically diverse society. It is almost impossible to ignore the impact of race when examining black and white southern women. Historians also must move beyond the myths surrounding women that tend to portray black women as matriarchal or wanton and white females as pious, submissive, and delicate. The reality of women's lives was far different than the images that still persist in the public mind. Historians must avoid presentist thinking and not draw conclusions based on contemporary norms or assume that black and white women embraced similar values.

Historians have pursued different approaches to this subject. Some have compared southern women to northern women, trying to determine how a plantation slave society affected the former and whether their situation was exceptional. Fruitful also are studies that compare the experiences of free black, slave, and white women or compare them to black and white men. Because most antebellum women were tied to household and farm labor, understanding their economic contributions and their activities beyond the domestic sphere is important. Scholars have explored how this patriarchal society and the region's laws and religious and social conventions constrained southern women. Some historians have identified a female culture and tried to understand if and how women accepted their situation or chafed against social and legal restrictions. Others have examined women's activities within the family or considered elite women's role in upholding or undermining slavery. Nearly all offer some perspective on the impact of the Civil War, considering how much freedom, if any, black women gained in 1865 or whether white women emerged from the conflict with greater strength and self-assurance or returned to a more traditional, subordinate role.

Though comprising only a minority of the South's population, white plantation women have attracted the most scholarly attention, undoubtedly because primary sources are both numerous and accessible. Literate, privileged females corresponded frequently or poured their personal thoughts into a diary. Many of their manuscripts reside in library and university archives, making it relatively easy for historians to investigate elite women's lives.

Anne Firor Scott's *The Southern Lady: From Pedestal to Politics, 1830–1930* launched the field in 1970. This classic study, half of it covering the antebellum period, addresses the discrepancy that Scott observed between the professed ideal of elite white women and the reality of their lives. Prescriptive writings placed females atop a proverbial pedestal, but Scott finds that a dominant patriarchy, a rural existence, and demanding family and household responsibilities constricted women's lives.

Scott sees educated women of the landowning class as far more than ornamental creatures; they were hardworking, pious women and mothers, devoted to their family. Numerous pregnancies, constant child rearing, and endless chores aged them prematurely. They tried to live up to the social prescriptions defining their lives. Scott finds elite women expressing discontent over slavery and argues that some acted as quiet abolitionists by ameliorating the worst aspects of slavery or expressing compassion for their slaves. Elite white women's dream of a companionate marriage did not always result in this ideal. Yet women accepted their secondary status in order to uphold a hierarchical slave society and defend the region's social order.

The most contested argument of Scott's analysis is her belief that the Civil War unleashed women's abilities and autonomy, a conclusion challenged by recent scholars. She calls the Civil War a watershed in southern women's history, for during it women stood on their own, managed farms and plantations, and took charge of their family. These wartime experiences, according to Scott, undermined the Old South by challenging patriarchal assumptions and opened doors for women who put their newly acquired skills to good use.

More than a decade later, Catherine Clinton addressed privileged white women in *The Plantation Mistress: Woman's World in the Old South* (1982). Adopting a sweeping approach and examining numerous themes, Clinton challenges the myths and romantic assumptions surrounding elite women. Her book explores female education, kin relationships, attitudes toward slavery and work, marital and sexual roles, health, and daily activities. Clinton makes a strong case for the power of the patriarchy and women's dependency and oppressed situation. Compared to northern women, she feels that southern women were victims of their culture, with little means to fashion a life of their own. She claims that privileged white women, limited by an isolated existence and controlled by a patriarchal ideology, were the "slave[s] of slaves" (Clinton 1982: 16).

Clinton's elite women did not lead charmed lives. They played a critical role in domestic production, performing demanding tasks to ensure plantation self-sufficiency, such as managing household slaves and overseeing domestic industries. Women were responsible for the well-being of both white and slave family members. Unlike northern urban women, few elite southern white women had an opportunity to develop female relationships in such isolated, rural circumstances. Kin and family members constituted their principal support system. Symbolizing virtue, they tried to conform to prescriptive behavior that rewarded them for being pious, maternal, fertile, and chaste. Laws and customs prescribed their lives; the sexual double standard prevailed. In some detail, Clinton sees a "virtual revolution in female education," arguing that privileged southern girls benefited by substantial schooling, much like their northern counterparts, even if education's ultimate purpose was to help them serve their family and fulfill their domestic role.

An interest in sexuality takes Clinton into areas that she and other scholars have explored more extensively in recent years (see Bardaglio 1995; Clinton and Gillespie 1997; Hodes 1997). She finds evidence of widespread miscegenation between white men and black women. Southerners justified and excused these relationships but at the same time condemned those involving white women and black men. She feels that sexual transgressions often prompted white women's cruelty toward female slaves, for they were more likely to take their revenge out on a slave than on their husband. Child bearing, fertility, and infant rearing were central issues in women's lives and Clinton concludes, unlike McMillen (1990), that southern mothers began to depend more on wet nurses and slaves to assist them. Though little changed in women's lives during the period covered here, Clinton challenges many assumptions. Like Scott, she destroys the idea that southern women were weak, pampered, idle, and helpless. The demands on them were unending – as they were on most women at this time.

Jane Turner Censer presents a more cheerful picture of elite women in *North Carolina Planters and Their Children, 1800–1860* (1984). She explores family relationships and plantation households among that state's several dozen wealthiest slaveholding families. Unlike Clinton and Scott, she does not depict women as oppressed or dominated by a strong patriarchy. The sentimentalization and child-centeredness of family life in the eighteenth and early nineteenth centuries is reflected in her view of North Carolina families. Most households are happy, and the marriages are companionate. Censer finds kindly adults using "parental indirection" to influence their children's marital and career choices. Parents could relinquish tight controls over their offspring since most children internalized and accepted parental expectations by marrying in their class and achieving high social status.

Though white families were usually large, Censer finds parents exhibiting equal affection toward every child, showing that numerous children did not dilute parental attention. Nor did high infant mortality diminish parental emotion and sorrow when a baby died. She sees both mothers and fathers demonstrating interest in their children, in contrast to a more gender-demarcated approach to parenting that began to typify genteel urban households in the Northeast. More surprisingly, according to Censer, parents exhibited egalitarianism toward sons and daughters. They made equivalent provision for them in their wills and provided both with a solid education, believing that girls also needed academic training. Though domestic arts were important to a young woman's future, parents did not favor ornamental aspects of female education over academics.

A single chapter covers master–slave relationships. Not surprisingly, the affection exhibited among whites did not cross racial boundaries. Racism, white fears, and ingrained perceptions of African-Americans as property created an unbridgeable racial chasm. Masters might refer to their slaves as "family," but they treated them more harshly than they did their own children. Black servants rarely developed close ties to the white families they served.

In many respects, Censer's families resemble privileged families in the Northeast, countering the concept of southern exceptionalism. Parents encouraged education, achievement, material success, independence, and affectionate relationships.

Southern mothers and fathers wanted to be friends and confidants of their offspring as well as figures of authority when necessary. North Carolina parents, in Censer's view, taught their children the importance of hard work, thrift, and self-discipline. Little familial dissension is depicted in this analysis; privileged families were decent and loving, at least among themselves.

Motherhood in the Old South: Pregnancy, Childbirth, and Infant Rearing, 1800–1860 (1990) by Sally G. McMillen examines child bearing and rearing, an experience common to most southern women. She focuses on literate white mothers and the medical attendants and care involved in birthing and infant health. She sees southern motherhood as both similar and distinctive compared to that of women in the North. Southern women shared experiences with mothers everywhere, turning to other females for support and assistance. Mothers viewed their maternal role as a "sacred occupation" and devoted their lives to their children. Yet she also finds the South unique, for maternal and infant morbidity and mortality were higher there than in the North due to the region's unhealthy climate, the large number of doctors still employing risky procedures, limited medical knowledge, and the presence of so many endemic diseases, especially malaria. Also, while the fertility rate declined nationwide, southern women bore more babies than the norm, contributing to higher maternal mortality. Southerners prized large families, despite the toll exacted on females.

McMillen uses the personal comments of parturient women and mothers to reveal an agonizing but highly intimate and poignant tale. Family responsibilities consumed women's lives, even those in families owning numerous slaves. Pregnancy for most women was a normal, if worrisome, time, and they spent months fearing a life-threatening delivery ahead. For many women, confinement remained an exclusively female event. Many elite women depended on female midwives, their mothers, and women friends to assist in delivering their baby. Yet by the late antebellum period, more southern families engaged male doctors to assist with childbirth, not because physicians had yet proved themselves more skillful but because an educated doctor in attendance delivered a positive message about family status.

Like Censer, McMillen sees most southern women as devoted mothers who worried excessively about their infants and spent days or weeks tending a sick child. The majority of southern mothers – except when they were ill or lacked adequate breast milk – breast-fed their infants rather than relegating wet-nursing to slaves. Though slave women performed some routine duties associated with child rearing, southern women rarely relinquished their maternal duties to other caregivers. Like Censer, McMillen dismisses the idea that bearing many children meant that mothers invested less attention or emotion in each one. Personal writings reveal that females devoted themselves to their family, especially in the South where infant health was so precarious. She shows how wrenching the death of any child was and how most mothers learned to bear their intense sorrow by internalizing it, turning to God, journal writing, or even drugs.

A study exploring the meaning of antebellum southern marriage is Anya Jabour's *Marriage in the Early Republic: Elizabeth and William Wirt and the Companionate Ideal* (1998). This book looks at a single relationship that was long-lived and intimately described in decades of correspondence. The plethora of letters between the Wirts allows Jabour to scrutinize their daily lives and intimate thoughts in detail.

But it also reveals an important characteristic of this relationship: Elizabeth and William spent much of their married life apart. Nevertheless, they struggled to fit their own expectations about marriage into the norms of a companionate ideal, one based on mutual respect and love.

This one marriage suggests a good deal about relationships and marital expectations among the southern elite. Both Wirts approached marriage self-consciously, aware of social norms that outlined an ideal antebellum relationship. Jabour shows the challenges and rewards they faced in trying to forge their relationship and its shifting nature due to their changing physical and emotional circumstances, a growing family, and William's career as an ambitious lawyer and prominent public official. At least in his letters, William professed his desire to be a loving husband, companion, and responsible bread winner. Over time, however, Elizabeth was less able to depend on his fulfilling the role of spouse and father; more responsibilities fell to her. Jabour describes Elizabeth's significant economic contributions to the household, such as gardening and preparing, storing, and even marketing food. These duties declined as child rearing and her husband's career occupied more of her time.

Whether the Wirts' relationship typified antebellum marriage among privileged southerners will require other studies (see Bleser 1991; Stowe 1987). In Jabour's tale, we see the ups and downs of one elite antebellum relationship with lengthy absences, several career changes and attendant household relocations, economic distresses, the challenges of educating children, professional disappointments and accomplishments, illnesses, and the death of children. Jabour concludes that the promise of creating a marriage partnership defined by mutuality and reciprocity proved unachievable for the Wirts and probably for most antebellum couples. Fundamental inequalities between men and women made a companionate relationship difficult to achieve.

An ambitious book emphasizing class concerns and elite white women's public and private roles is Cynthia A. Kierner's *Beyond the Household: Women's Place in the Early South, 1700–1835* (1998). Kierner focuses her attention on Virginia and Carolina women and examines how and why their private and public lives evolved between the colonial period and the early nineteenth century. The first half of her study covers women in the colonial and revolutionary South, where she finds women playing a visible, important public role in establishing and reinforcing elite culture and mores. Usually depicted as domestic, colonial southern women participated in and helped to shape the public sphere and fashion a culture of gentility that reinforced their elite status. The Revolutionary War offered them new political opportunities as they protested, boycotted goods, penned letters and essays, petitioned, wore homespun, or observed patriotic parades.

Major changes followed the war. Many southerners, horrified by the French Revolution, feared their women might become as radicalized as French women. Endless debates ensued over women's appropriate role in the new nation. Spokespersons insisted that women be subservient and focus on home, family, and church. Contemporary observers celebrated marriage, women's nurturing, pious nature, and motherhood; and they vilified the life of single women and bachelors. In the home, virtuous womanhood could flourish; here most experienced their greatest joys and greatest trials. Kierner argues that a decline in public social rituals heightened southern women's isolation. Balls and royal celebrations, where colonial women had played important roles, lost their popularity and were replaced by militia demonstrations and military parades that excluded females except as observers.

Kierner sees several changes in women's lives by the early nineteenth century. Their domestic roles expanded as society's expectations increased for creating happy, well-functioning households. Improvements in slave life (although relative) meant that providing slaves better clothing, food, and health care fell to women. Unlike some historians, Kierner feels that southerners accepted the concept of separate spheres and women's special domestic role. Evangelical Protestantism, which became more appealing to the elite, offered a Christian message that reinforced and popularized the image of southern women as the embodiment of virtue, modesty, and domesticity.

While acknowledging women's importance in the home, Kierner also explores elite women's role in public life. She agrees with other scholars who argue that privileged southern women benefited from a rigorous education, even if its ultimate purpose was to help them become more pleasing companions and better mothers. Women's moral influence gave them the opportunity to engage in benevolent and religious reform, aiding the downtrodden and working through churches or female associations. Unlike northern women, southern women shunned political and egalitarian reforms that might challenge the South, for they understood the need to uphold their society's standards and class interests.

Joan Cashin's *A Family Venture: Men and Women on the Southern Frontier* (1991) places gender at the center of her study of planter families who moved from seaboard states to the southern frontier. Much has been written about the mid-nineteenth-century trek to the far West, but Cashin enriches our understanding of southern migration. Thousands were on the move by the 1820s as diminishing opportunities at home and the attraction of cheap land and potential wealth prompted them to pick up and move.

Cashin shows the importance of gender in this migration. Not surprisingly, women responded differently than did men. Kin, family, and interdependent relationships were central to women's happiness, and most found it wrenching to sever these ties when they had to move. For men, personal ambition and greed overshadowed familial and friendship obligations. While women feared the dangers ahead, men welcomed new challenges and found migration liberating. Few women valued material success over their desire for the comfortable and familiar. Removed from societal and familial constraints, migration gave men the opportunity to test their manhood and engage in what Cashin calls "daredevil masculinity." Women wanted to recreate what they had left behind.

This study shows the importance of understanding southern men to shed light on women, though Cashin's portrait of men is not especially flattering. We see males often making the decision to move and ignoring the toll that migration exacted on their family. Because adults often moved when relatively young, this put strain on women during their child bearing years. Cashin finds marriages to be less affectionate and companionate than those portrayed by Censer and even Jabour. The paternalism she finds whites exhibiting toward slaves on the seaboard was less visible on the frontier, where men treated blacks less humanely. In the absence of community constraints, slave women were more likely to become victims of male sexual abuse.

Overall, Cashin sees migration reinforcing southern women's powerlessness and dependency. The move strengthened, rather than weakened, gender barriers, patriarchal dominance, and stratified roles. The threat of Indians, wild animals, and unforeseen dangers made women more dependent on men. Undertaking the long, arduous journey, settling an untamed wilderness, clearing land, planting new crops, and experiencing months of deprivation made frontier life especially hard on women. Many now had to perform tasks familiar to their ancestors, such as cooking over an open fire and hauling water, reminders of how different their lives were from what they had known back home.

Two studies examine southern women by exploring the black and white experience. A theoretical, boldly argued work is Elizabeth Fox-Genovese's *Within the Plantation Household: Black and White Women of the Old South* (1988). She sees gender, race, and class shaping the lives of elite southern women. Fox-Genovese sets her study within the plantation household, identifying it as the principal unit of production, in contrast to the Northeast where an emerging capitalist economy led to a decline in the household's importance. Though antebellum southerners were drawn into an emerging market economy, she argues that they continued to depend on precapitalistic slave labor. Separate spheres, which began to define gender relationships, among privileged northerners, were less important in southern households where Fox-Genovese finds overlapping relationships and duties. Her southern home is not an exclusive female sphere.

Though incorporating slave and white women in her analysis, Fox-Genovese concentrates more attention on privileged white women and raises more provocative questions about their lives than she does with slave women. She makes a strong case for their unique, contradictory, and shifting lives. Focusing on the years between 1820 and 1861, Fox-Genovese compares elite rural white women to activist women in the Northeast and to female slaves working in white households.

Her slave-owning women were not quiet abolitionists, and in contrast to Clinton, her females were not held captive by patriarchal dictates. In fact, Fox-Genovese insists that women relished their privileged status, one that depended on slave labor and a strong patriarchy. Class interests were at stake. Southern women collaborated in their own domination and supported slavery because male-headed households and slave labor served them well. Slave ownership gave white women status, leisure time, and the opportunity to avoid grubby household chores. Slavery "provided privileges and amenities for its women that they had no intention of surrendering," Fox-Genovese insists (Fox-Genovese 1988: 370).

The overall view of the female slave community here is fairly bleak. African traditions, stable families, and female networks could not protect slave women from the harsh aspects of oppression. If slave women seemed strong and held more power in the family than did black men or white women, it was because slavery stripped black men of traditional forms of power. And while slave women might be less beholden to black male domination, they, like white women, were always controlled by white men. Fox-Genovese urges historians to ask different questions when studying slave women, sensing that they may not have wanted to replicate whites' ideas of the nuclear family and two-parent household or found middle-class ideals appealing.

The relationships between slave women and white women in households, which Fox-Genovese calls "conflict-ridden intimacy," did not foster biracial sisterhood.

Fox-Genovese claims black and white female relationships were rarely affectionate. Mistresses and slaves "shared a world of mutual antagonism and frayed tempers." Though she feels many privileged white women were generous, warm, and decent, their racism was "generally uglier and more meanly expressed than that of the men" (Fox-Genovese 1988: 308, 35, 349). Her privileged white women do not toil as hard as Scott, McMillen, and Clinton claim or devote themselves selflessly to motherhood. Few plantation women here engage in charitable reform, except on an individual basis. Her depiction of female education minimizes the importance of substantial schooling, unlike the findings of Clinton (1982) and Farnham (1994).

Though Fox-Genovese presents elite women's lives as circumscribed by law and tradition and their households often filled with tension, southern women tolerated their lot and did not yearn for a different life. They accepted a hierarchical society and their own subordination, knowing they were more privileged than other southern women. Everything they read, heard in church, and shared in conversation celebrated male dominance and slavery as the natural order. The ideal of the southern lady dictated their behavior. Plantation women stood beside their men and collaborated in supporting the slave South, even if that meant their own subordination.

Brenda E. Stevenson's *Life in Black and White: Family and Community in the Slave South* (1996) examines white, slave, and free black women living in Loudoun County, Virginia, between the Revolutionary and Civil Wars. Stevenson finds a diverse population of both tidewater and upcountry residents, making the area an interesting setting to compare women's lives and study them in depth. She sees race as the determining factor in defining status and shows how profoundly family and community life differed depending on skin color.

This book looks at family life among black and white, slave and free. Stevenson's information on elite white women covers familiar ground, including women's desire to marry well; their difficulties in adjusting to married life; the demanding domestic tasks they undertook; the maternal role; managing household slaves; and the challenges in winning a divorce. The book also describes female cultural rituals such as debuts, courtships, weddings, and honeymoons. Class made a difference in women's adjusting to marriage; yeomen farm wives found it easier than elite women since household chores were part of their upbringing.

Stevenson offers interesting perspectives on slave and free black women. We see a fairly bleak view of slave families, with many defined by inequality and instability. She emphasizes the economic importance of slavery, with market forces and the profit motive influencing slave owners' actions. Whites often forced slaves to work harder in order to increase output, and when market prices declined and owners needed cash, they traded slaves without concern for slave family stability. The internal slave trade had a devastating impact, splitting families apart and often leaving women alone to care for their children. Unlike White (1985), Stevenson finds female slaves with few advantages and with few opportunities to escape or avoid work. Gender, not African antecedents, determined work roles and reflected the dictates of white owners who controlled the slave system. More male slaves than female became skilled artisans, giving men greater opportunities to purchase their freedom, hold positions of authority, or escape.

Like Fox-Genovese, Stevenson finds that slaves did not embrace genteel white visions of monogamous relationships and nuclear families as an ideal. Family patterns varied widely depending on circumstance; many slave children did not grow up in two-parent households. Yet the family was a bulwark against the dehumanization of slavery and thus, Stevenson claims, a vehicle of resistance and source of strength.

We also see the precarious situation of free blacks. Racial discrimination made it difficult for them to own property, hold jobs, or maintain stable households. For free black women, their situation was especially devastating since they were less likely to have special skills and be able to earn money to purchase their own property. Courts often interceded in single-parent families, removing black mothers as custodians of their children.

Two historians have studied antebellum southern women's involvement beyond the household, countering the image that southern women were confined to the domestic sphere. Suzanne Lebsock's *The Free Women of Petersburg: Status and Culture in a Southern Town, 1784–1860* (1984a) is an articulate, well-researched account and the only monograph we have to date on antebellum urban southern women. Lebsock finds a unique female culture in Petersburg, and she shows how free-black and white female behavior, values, and status altered between the American Revolution and the Civil War. She also tackles large historical questions, such as defining black matriarchy and the cult of domesticity and explaining the effect of coverture, female personalism, and women's happiness in the home.

Lebsock argues that Petersburg women's lives improved slightly during the antebellum period, at least compared to their situation in the late colonial period. Some gained more autonomy from particular men by choosing not to marry or remarry. Others found economic independence by writing their own wills, purchasing and dispensing property, working for wages, or establishing a separate estate before marriage. A few wealthy widows and free black women chose to remain single, not wanting to be restricted by laws that applied to married women or be dependent on a man. But she shows how Petersburg women lost ground in the public world by being excluded from political activities and by men who eventually co-opted their charity work.

This book offers the clearest understanding of matriarchy, a term that some scholars have used too freely to define the black family. Lebsock sees it as a relative term, one more reflective of whites' perception of patriarchy and who should hold power rather than evidence of black women's actual position. Females seemed strong relative to their men because whites stripped black men of traditional sources of power. And while black women might maintain equal relationships with black men, they were always beholden to whites. She also explores the meaning of female autonomy, noting that our idea of female independence, which we often associate with paid work and being single, often implied poverty rather than power. Working for wages did not symbolize female assertiveness, nor did southern society condone it. Women worked only if they had to or if the benefits outweighed the inconveniences.

Lebsock finds a distinct female culture in Petersburg, with values that differed from men's. Women might dispense of their property in a highly personal manner, giving it to favorites or to those who needed or deserved it. Like Jabour and Clinton (1982), she finds few marriages conforming to a companionate ideal; in most relationships, men held power. Though Lebsock does not claim that women were abolitionists at heart, she feels they exerted a "subversive influence" over slavery by operating from this personal frame of reference.

The Free Women of Petersburg shows the rewards of studying a single community in order to address large historical issues. Lebsock argues that the cult of true womanhood, which celebrated women as pious, maternal, pure, and domestic, was persuasive because it served so many purposes and often was true – these ideal characteristics often matched female behavior. She also thinks that southern women rarely questioned their demanding lives because society valued their productivity. Domestic work proved satisfying because women understood how critical their role was to family survival. And since few alternatives existed, why would they question it?

This book falls into the camp of those who see southern women sharing norms with women living elsewhere. Like northern women, Petersburg women engaged in charitable work and influenced the moral life of their city. Like Kierner, Lebsock finds women maintaining and running autonomous female organizations. They supported a local orphanage, worked for their churches, participated in ladies' fairs, and taught Sunday school, long before benevolent work attracted men's interest. When men began to engage in charity work in the late 1850s, Lebsock shows how and why they usurped women's benevolent efforts and pushed them aside. She ultimately concludes that the Civil War did little to alter gender relations and southern women's subordinate status.

Also exploring southern women's public lives is Elizabeth R. Varon's *We Mean to Be Counted: White Women and Politics in Antebellum Virginia* (1998). Varon challenges the perception that southern women avoided the political arena and rarely engaged in reform, arguing that a number of privileged Virginia women were actively involved in public life and in local, state, and national politics. Her small sampling of females engaged in benevolent reform verbalized their political sentiments in writing and participated in political events.

Virginia women's political and public interests changed as the nation's and region's interest in various issues shifted. Varon's tidy chronology shows that in the 1820s, southern women supported orphan asylums and the temperance cause. They moved to the controversial American Colonization Society in the 1830s, wrongly assuming that colonization ultimately might dismantle slavery. With the rise of the Whig Party in the 1840s, women began to attend political rallies, sew banners, write opinionated essays, and imbue family members with Whig principles. Party officials encouraged female participation, believing that women's moral influence could have a positive impact on male voters and lend compassion to the rough-and-tumble of political life. By the 1850s secessionist fire-eaters identified women as important crusaders who would foster support for their cause. Though women initially encouraged national harmony, they now defended southern nationalism and slavery against outside critics. A few even penned "anti-Tom" novels to counter Harriet Beecher Stowe's *Uncle Tom's Cabin* (1852), depicting slavery as a benevolent institution compared to the North's free labor system. Southern women became indispensable allies of proslavery defenders; by the 1860s, most fell in line and championed the Confederacy.

The boldest argument here is Varon's assertion that Virginia women became temporary partners with men in forging a political consensus. Her women are more politically involved than those examined by other scholars. In part, this is because her definition of female political involvement, like Kierner's, is broad and encompasses almost anything that brought women into the public arena, as participants or symbols, or encouraged them to speak, act, or write on a public issue. Also, the book focuses on a select group of privileged Virginia women. One must remember that most females were hard at work, too busy or distracted to do anything but care for home and family. Virginia was also an atypical state, being more urban and industrial than others in the South and near the political hubbub of Washington DC. Whether Virginia women's activism holds true for those in other southern states demands more research. Nevertheless, Varon makes an important contribution by dispelling the idea that southern women were politically inactive.

Slave women have attracted the attention of several historians. The first book to acknowledge their important contributions was Deborah Gray White's *Ar'n't I a Woman?: Female Slaves in the Plantation South* (1985). She uses familiar sources to examine the lives of enslaved females, often comparing them to elite southern white women and to male slaves. She identifies two slave systems – one male, one female – and insists that men and women, despite their relatively egalitarian relationships, did not experience slavery in a similar manner. She deflates the well-worn myths of slave women as Mammys and Jezebels, showing how these terms developed and helped whites justify their enslavement and treatment of black women. Like the first chapter in Jacqueline Jones's *Labor of Love, Labor of Sorrow* (1985), White emphasizes women's productive and reproductive contributions and shows how important women were to the plantation economy and to the black community. She places equal value on men's and women's skills and work.

Like Lebsock, White also discusses the meaning of black matriarchy, preferring the term "matrifocal" when describing the black community. Slave women may have been the center of family life but did not hold ultimate power. White's slave women often rely on themselves and other women in the slave quarters rather than on men. Her female slave community is supportive, and her women fairly independent and savvy. Women's reproductive capability might give them status both in the slave community and with the plantation owner who profited by any children she bore. Unlike Stevenson, she feels that bearing children gave them some power by discouraging possible sale or providing an excuse to avoid work. Not all miscegenous relationships were coercion or rape. A consensual sexual liaison was one female option, gaining a slave woman some influence, better living conditions, and, in rare cases, freedom for herself or her children.

Leslie A. Schwalm shows the importance of slave women's labor in the lowcountry in *A Hard Fight for We: Women's Transition from Slavery to Freedom in South Carolina* (1997). Though much of her book covers the Civil War and Reconstruction, she also examines antebellum plantation life in one of the wealthiest areas of the antebellum South. Schwalm argues for slaves' distinctive experiences here. These huge lowcountry slave communities were relatively stable, with hundreds of slaves and skilled laborers. More than other historians, Schwalm argues that slave women's contributions on rice plantations were significant; in fact, she calls women the "backbone" of the plantation labor force here. On some lowcountry plantations, female laborers comprised the majority of workers. They helped clear the land, maintained the elaborate tidal rice plantation system, and cultivated the crop, in addition to caring for their own home, garden, and family. She relates female labor to its West African antecedents where women were primary cultivators of rice. Kin networks rather than a nuclear family model define her black families. Ultimately Schwalm finds slave women taking an active role in defining their freedom after the Civil War.

Compared to extensive scholarship on privileged white and slave women, the study of southern yeomen wives and poor women has suffered, primarily due to a paucity of primary sources. Most poor women were illiterate or had no free time to write. Victoria E. Bynum's *Unruly Women: The Politics of Social and Sexual Control in the Old South* (1992) broke new ground by examining marginalized poor women, at least those who entered the public record. Her descriptive exposition looks at women in only three North Carolina Piedmont counties, but Bynum feels they serve as a microcosm for the South. Bynum looks at females who sought a divorce or protested spousal abuse; those who engaged in deviant or illegal sexual relations; and those who resisted or protested Confederate policies during the Civil War. The court cases she uses involving these women suggest community responses to female deviants and reflect a good deal about the region's mores and standards.

This book is more a study of gendered jurisprudence and male control over powerless women than an examination of poor women's lives. These women were not unruly as much as they were victims of abusive husbands and indifferent county authorities. Bynum shows how subjectively, but often harshly, men dispensed justice, for the region's social structure depended upon the cooperation and subordination of women. Defiant, unladylike behavior might unravel the fabric of southern society. Women who were married and of good background and character were more likely to gain a judge's sympathy than single women with a bad reputation. The state supreme court used a heavy hand when delivering its rulings; often it was more concerned with protecting society than defending women. Courts often failed to protect females against spousal abuse, upholding the sanctity of marriage or believing that such matters should be addressed at home. Southern paternalism had its limits when it came to unruly women.

Bynum falls on the side of southern exceptionalism, finding North Carolina officials exercising more coercive control over white women's sexual behavior than judges in northern states. And though poor women expressed common grievances, a female culture did not develop among them. Nor did unhappiness over their shared bleak situations foster unified action until the Civil War. Patriarchal laws and dictates controlled women's lives, especially those who were poor and single.

An interesting section in this book shows how courts took on the role of guardian in order to control or punish deviant mothers, using the apprenticeship system to dictate the future of poor, fatherless children. Courts also tried to regulate women's reproduction rights and sexuality, more often punishing white females involved in relationships with black men than white men involved with black women. During the Civil War, Bynum argues that unruly women "hastened the collapse of the Confederacy;" they undermined southern society by engaging in more theft, rioting, complaining, and out-of-control behavior (Bynum 1992: 11). They put their needs above those of the Confederacy. Though Bynum sees these women as victims of particular men and of the legal and social order, she also shows that some spunky or angry females acted in an assertive manner, defining their needs, protesting injustice, challenging restrictions, and demanding greater autonomy. It is refreshing to realize that some antebellum women were defiant or rebellious.

Two topics critical to an understanding of southern women that have received little attention to date are education and religion. Christie Anne Farnham's *The Education of the Southern Belle: Higher Education and Student Socialization in the Antebellum*

South (1994) examines southern white women's education. Both Clinton (1982) and Kierner show the importance and rigor of southern women's schooling, but Farnham's study extends the argument. She feels that females had access to a demanding education, one nearly equal to that offered southern men. She also insists that the antebellum South made a greater commitment to women's higher education than did the North, claiming the region was in the "spotlight" of women's education.

Farnham examines the formal and informal curriculum of women's schools and how southern institutions prepared privileged young ladies for their future role in the planter class. After the 1830s individuals, churches, and communities founded a surprising number of schools, in part to educate southern women on home turf. A liberal arts curriculum offered them a southern approach to education, including both rigorous academic courses and lessons in ladylike behavior. The idea was to fashion genteel women to take their place in planter society. Southerners did not see educated women as a threat since southern women understood their proper place, unlike some educated northern women who began demanding more rights. Southern ladies' goal was marriage and family, and they accepted their secondary status.

Farnham describes a variety of schools in the Old South. Many were run and taught by a single proprietor. French-based seminaries expanded educational opportunities, as did female academies, offering what Farnham claims was even a college-level education. The curriculum might include courses in the classics, modern languages, sciences, and mathematics. Yet the southern character of these schools was evident in courses in the fine arts and domestic skills. Farnham also examines cultural and social life in these schools. A female subculture of pageants, rituals, and intimate female friendships was important in educating the southern belle.

This study is by no means the definitive word on southern women's schooling. Farnham's assertion that men and women enjoyed a substantial education and that the South was committed to female colleges before the North deserves verification. Understanding how urban and rural schools differed and the number and background of the pupils who attended are also important. Nevertheless, Farnham's emphasis on the value of female education and its role in perpetuating an elite culture is important. She sees the situation changing after the Civil War when the image of the southern belle received more attention than that of an intellectual woman.

Jean E. Friedman's *The Enclosed Garden: Women and Community in the Evangelical South, 1830–1900* (1985) is the only full-length study of women and religion; surprisingly few books on antebellum women even mention a topic that was so central to females. Despite its subtitle, much of Friedman's book focuses on the antebellum and Civil War periods. She seeks to explain why southern women's reform efforts lagged well behind the North and why the South seemed to inhibit the formation of female autonomy and collective identity. Many historians might conclude that slavery and the patriarchy were barriers, but Friedman delves deeper. Though discounting neither of these forces, she looks at faith and family as causative factors. Friedman, like Clinton, portrays southern white women as victims of their society. The evangelical community and family relationships confined women's lives, she claims, creating a fairly static, limited, and private world in which they functioned. Like Fox-Genovese but unlike Farnham, Friedman feels women's education lagged behind that offered northern women. By contrasting southern women to activist northern women, the former suffer by comparison.

Though the narrative lacks a strong chronological thread and is sometimes difficult to follow, Friedman's ideas and themes challenge historians to test them further. The rural women she examines did not develop support networks or female associations like Lebsock's urban women or their counterparts in the North. Southern society upheld traditional values; its women were tied to family, household, and church. Friedman does not see white women as quiet abolitionists and finds conflict and rivalry more common than sisterhood in biracial relationships. She sees the Civil War strengthening traditional values and women continuing to define their lives through family and church in the postwar years.

No single book examines Native American women during the antebellum period, though two on Cherokee women deserve mention: Theda Perdue's *Cherokee Women: Gender and Culture Change, 1700–1835* (1998) and Sarah Hill's innovative study, *Weaving New Worlds: Southeastern Cherokee Women and Their Basketry* (1997), which uses the metaphor of basket weaving to unfold their past. Both relate a similar story using different approaches. They argue that as the tribe assimilated white ideas and interacted with them, Cherokee women's lives were transformed. Women had possessed a good deal of power before the arrival of Europeans, but their culture began to absorb white concepts of patriarchy, demarcated gender roles, and family structure. This led to a precipitous decline in Cherokee women's participation and position in the community. Hill studies different types of baskets woven by Cherokee women to show how the shapes and materials they used reflected larger issues in tribal history. Before white settlers interacted with the tribe, Cherokee women had access to abundant reeds that grew throughout the southern Appalachians. As whites encroached upon their land and forced the tribe westward, women had to use other materials. They also began to weave different shapes that reflected a lucrative trade with whites.

In recent years, gender has become an important window into understanding the Old South. Kathleen M. Brown's provocative study on colonial history, *Good Wives, Nasty Wenches, and Anxious Patriarchs* (1996), will encourage historians to reconfigure their understanding of the early South, using gender as an important construct of the past (see ibid: 75–104). Similar approaches to the antebellum period place gender at the center of their analysis. *Celia, A Slave* (1991) a provocative study by Melton A. McLaurin, looks at gender and race, examining a troubling case involving a slave woman, Celia, accused of killing her master, John Newsome, in 1855. Newsome, a fairly prosperous Missouri farmer and widower, purchased Celia when she was fourteen. He raped her on the journey home and then established Celia in a cabin and expected her to serve as maid, mistress, and substitute mother for his children. Subsequently she bore him two children. Celia ended the relationship with Newsome by bludgeoning him to death and then burying and burning the evidence.

The fact that Celia was not immediately hanged when discovered but defended by court-appointed white attorneys may seem surprising. Celia's lawyers used a Missouri statute that claimed a woman could kill someone if trying to defend her honor. The court ruled that Celia, a slave and therefore merely property, had no honor to protect, and she was consequently found guilty and hanged. The all-white jury did not feel a slave deserved the same consideration as a white woman.

This chilling tale is less about slave women than about how white society perceived them. McLaurin engages in a good deal of speculation due to limited sources, but he puts Celia's situation and her trial into a larger historical context, examining questions on history, gender, and race. Here, a private act affected the political and forced the South to reexamine itself. This case, even with little evidence, raises important questions that deserve additional study.

Stephanie McCurry looks at plain folk in *Masters of Small Worlds: Yeoman Households, Gender Relations, and the Political Culture of the Antebellum South Carolina Low Country* (1995). The book's importance lies in its use of gender to examine antebellum political discourse and provide a deeper reading of southern history. Focusing on the South Carolina lowcountry, an area assumed to be dominated by huge plantations and wealthy slave owners, McCurry found a majority of whites to be farmers who owned small farms and – at the most – no more than a handful of slaves. Like their elite neighbors, these men treasured their positions as independent property-owners and defended a system that defended their rights. McCurry argues that a gendered ideology depicting such men as masters of their "small worlds" consisting mainly of household dependents (wives and children) helped to fashion and strengthen a patriarchal prerogative that applied to all southern white males, defending their authority over all who were labeled dependents, including slaves.

McCurry finds it important that proslavery defenders used familial, gendered language to express their beliefs. They understood the importance of patriarchal households and the need to draw all white men to their cause. Gendered language in antebellum southern politics helped to support the proslavery argument, connecting the public world of politics and the private world of household relationships. Evangelical clergy also supported this message, legitimizing and empowering it by using biblical dictates to argue men's right to wield authority over their household.

McCurry uses women's history and feminist theory to reinterpret political discourse and help explain why small farmers ideologically supported the planter class. Yeomen and planters "forged a workable alliance," sharing a concept of free men as masters of their household (ibid: 112). Here the seemingly benign domestic exploitation of women became a tenet of southern ideology, legitimizing male authority over women and dependents as a cornerstone of the slavery edifice. McCurry feels it is little wonder that yeomen defended the Confederacy, trying to protect their role as masters of their small worlds.

In *White Women, Black Men: Illicit Sex in the Nineteenth-Century South* (1997) Martha Hodes offers a provocative reading of miscegenous relationships, in this case, those between white women and black men. She seeks to prove some historians' assertions (see Sommerville 1995) that the myth of "black beast rapists" became part of the southern vocabulary only after the Civil War. She discovers that antebellum southern whites expressed "uneasy tolerance" toward these liaisons and that they rarely led to prosecution, violence, or lynching of the black man involved, despite the seriousness of the situation and their challenge to white male honor. Hodes's primary evidence comes from fragments of antebellum court cases and comments that entered the public record, usually when the paternity of the couple's offspring was contested. Most of her examples are poor white women, not because elite women were chaste, but because the power of their class could hide such transgressions and because they were more likely to have access to contraceptive devices.

Her examples show the complexity of these situations. A colonial marriage between a white woman and black slave confused the status of their descendants who subsequently sued for their freedom. In another situation, a pregnant servant woman accused a slave of raping her. The white community was not unduly shocked by this revelation and eventually rallied behind the slave, knowing that the couple had been having an affair long before the woman became pregnant. In another case, a white man brought suit against his much younger wife who had been freely consorting with a black man for years and bore at least two mulatto children, whom she insisted her husband raise and support. The court refused to grant him a divorce because he mistreated her and because ending a marriage had serious consequences.

Here we see the fluidity of the color line in the antebellum South. Even as proslavery defenders developed strong racial theories, the color line was unclear. Mulattoes fell into an intermediate category that clouded their status, especially when some could pass as white. Just as likely, swarthy whites might be presumed to be black. It was not until the end of the nineteenth century that southerners clarified this ambiguity with their "one drop" rule. Hodes shows that in the antebellum period, color often seemed to be in the eye of the beholder.

The Civil War, traditionally seen as a male event, has gained historians' attention in revealing the significant role of Confederate women and how the conflict affected them. George C. Rable first placed southern women front and center in *Civil Wars: Women and the Crisis of Southern Nationalism* (1989). He examines the varied experiences of all social classes of women on the homefront. Nearly all southern women struggled to raise their children, manage the farm, and ensure family survival. Life lost its sense of order as women faced marauding soldiers, fled to safe havens when the enemy approached, and traded with Union soldiers in order to feed their hungry children. Poor women resented laws that gave preferential treatment to the wealthy. Desperate women engaged in bread riots. Those who could write urged their men to desert or insisted that officials send their husbands home. Lonely, fearful, and exhausted, facing shortages of basic goods, uncontrollable inflation, and unproductive farms, Confederate women found the Civil War anything but ennobling. Rable's vision does not show Confederate women as standard bearers for the southern cause. In fact, he suggests that women's growing sense of despair may have hastened the Confederate defeat.

Rable joins other historians who argue that the Civil War did little to change southern women or alter gender relations. Few enjoyed their wartime independence or endless, exhausting work. Most were ill-prepared for the demands of war and longed for their men to come home. He depicts the post-Civil War South as fairly grim economically and, unlike Scott (1970), argues that women willingly returned to their subordinate role in the household. War showed them the value of security. They favored having men in charge over female autonomy.

Drew Gilpin Faust's *Mothers of Invention: Women of the Slaveholding South in the American Civil War* (1996) presents a different vision with its focus on the elite. She sees women's wartime roles as complex and contradictory. Faust examines numerous details, including the books women read, the writing they did, the clothing they wore, their mourning rituals, and the difficulties they faced in undertaking unfamiliar domestic chores and farm management. Though deeply affected by the conflict, females helped to shape the Confederate experience. While many women made an outward commitment to the effort, others were reluctant to accept change or engage in activities that offended their class sensitivities.

Faust claims that the most telling wartime change was the breakdown of slavery. Women in charge of home and plantation lacked the power to enforce slave labor and ensure obedience. As women became more dependent on slaves to run their farms, slaves became more independent and defiant. Women began to perceive themselves as the victims of slavery rather than its beneficiaries. Like Rable, Faust sees women becoming increasingly frustrated by many aspects of the war and urging their men to come home. Confederate women did not emerge with a desire for more independence but began to act with greater self-interest, for their men had let them down. With the emancipation of slaves, women made a silent bargain with men to uphold their privileged position, one based on patriarchal assumptions and white supremacy.

As must be apparent, historians view antebellum southern women through different lenses; generalizations invariably fall short or are riddled with exceptions. To students, these conclusions may seem confusing; to historians, they are challenging. With conflicting opinions on many issues, one may wonder who or what to believe. One must remember that what historians write about and how they interpret the material often depends upon who is doing the writing. Scholars approach their subject with a fair degree of subjectivity, influenced by their own upbringing, values, experiences, and the culture and time in which they live. Their conclusions also depend on what evidence they find and what facts they feel are important. Evidence that catches the eye of one scholar may be overlooked by another.

In the case of southern women, conclusions also vary for good reason. Slave women's experiences depended on numerous factors, including the size of the plantation and the area of the South where they lived, the crops that were grown and the type of labor they performed, their owner's treatment, their health and that of their family, the number of children they bore and raised, and whether they were married or single. Class was a critical factor for white women, as was their marital status, the number of children they had, their living environment, their health, their level of education, their husband's character, as well as their faith.

Despite the richness and variety of books discussed here, the coverage of antebellum southern women remains uneven. Future scholars will need to pay attention to the female experience in Deep South and frontier states; Virginia women and those on the seaboard have received disproportionate attention so far. The diversity of the region affected women, especially in relation to their health, education, and legal constraints, and those differences need more analysis. Comparing rural and urban experiences also deserves additional research. The role of religion and whether and how denominational affiliation influenced women needs more research, since faith played such a central role in women's lives. We need to know more about poor and farm women who comprised the majority of the South's female population; this may require the use of more innovative sources to uncover their lives. Health and the medical resources women had available remain understudied for a region where illness and disease were constant threats to all families. Examining conjugal relationships will give us greater insight into the influence (if any) black and white women had over their husbands and in their households. We also need to know more about the private lives and experiences of southern men and relate those to southern women. The question of southern exceptionalism continues to engage historians who seek to understand whether and how southern women were different from females living elsewhere. Some historians have encouraged a reconfiguration to this approach by anointing southern women, rather than northern, as the paradigm for all antebellum women. Others (Hall 1989) have urged scholars to pursue a multicultural, inclusive history of American women. Whatever the method and approach, additional research will continue to reveal the complexity of women's lives in this fascinating region of the country and engage historians for years to come.

BIBLIOGRAPHY

Alexander, Adele Logan 1991: *Ambiguous Lives: Free Women of Color in Rural Georgia, 1789–1879.* Fayetteville: University of Arkansas Press.

Bardaglio, W. Peter 1995: *Reconstructing the Household: Families, Sex and the Law in the Nineteenth-Century South.* Chapel Hill: University of North Carolina Press.

Bernhard, Virginia, Brandon, Betty, Fox-Genovese, Elizabeth, and Perdue, Theda (eds.) 1992: *Southern Women: Histories and Identities.* Columbia: University of Missouri Press.

Bleser, Carol (ed.) 1991: *In Joy and In Sorrow: Women, Family, and Marriage in the Victorian South, 1830–1900.* New York: Oxford University Press.

Bleser, Carol (ed.) 1996: *Tokens of Affection: The Letters of a Planter's Daughter in the Old South.* Athens: University of Georgia Press.

Brown, Kathleen M. 1996. *Good Wives, Nasty Wenches, and Anxious Patriarchs: Gender, Race, and Power in Colonial Virginia.* Chapel Hill: University of North Carolina Press.

Burr, Virginia Ingraham (ed.) 1990: *The Secret Eye: The Journal of Ella Gertrude Clanton Thomas, 1848–1889.* Chapel Hill: University of North Carolina Press.

Burton, Orville Vernon 1985: *In My Father's House are Many Mansions: Family and Community in Edgefield, South Carolina.* Chapel Hill: University of North Carolina Press.

Bynum, Victoria E. 1992: *Unruly Women: The Politics of Social and Sexual Control in the Old South.* Chapel Hill: University of North Carolina Press.

Campbell, Edward D. C., Jr. and Rice, Kym S. (eds.) 1996: *A Woman's War: Southern Women, Civil War, and the Confederate Legacy.* Richmond: Museum of the Confederacy; Charlottesville: University Press of Virginia.

Campbell, John 1984: Work, Pregnancy, and Infant Mortality among Southern Slaves. *Journal of Interdisciplinary History,* 14, 793–812.

Carr, Lois Green and Walsh, Lorena S. 1977: The Planter's Wife: The Experience of White Women in Seventeenth-Century Maryland. *William and Mary Quarterly,* 34, 542–71.

Cashin, Joan E. 1991: *A Family Venture: Men and Women on the Southern Frontier.* New York: Oxford University Press.

Cashin, Joan E. (ed.) 1996: *Our Common Affairs: Texts from Women in the Old South.* Baltimore: Johns Hopkins University Press.

Censer, Jane Turner 1981: "Smiling Through Her Tears": Ante-Bellum Southern Women and Divorce, *American Journal of Legal History,* 25, 24–47.

Censer, Jane Turner 1984: *North Carolina Planters and Their Children, 1800–1860.* Baton Rouge: Louisiana State University Press.

Clinton, Catherine 1982: *The Plantation Mistress: Woman's World in the Old South.* New York: Pantheon.

Clinton, Catherine (ed.) 1994: *Half Sisters of History: Southern Women and the American Past.* Durham, NC: Duke University Press.

Clinton, Catherine and Gillespie, Michele (eds.) 1997: *The Devil's Lane: Sex and Race in the Early South.* New York: Oxford University Press.

Coryell, Janet L. 1998: *Beyond Image and Convention: Explorations in Southern Women's History.* Columbia: University of Missouri Press.

Farnham, Christie Anne 1994: *The Education of the Southern Belle: Higher Education and Student Socialization in the Antebellum South.* New York and London: New York University Press.

Farnham, Christie Anne (ed.) 1997: *Women of the American South: A Multicultural Reader.* New York: New York University Press.

Faust, Drew Gilpin 1996: *Mothers of Invention: Women of the Slaveholding South in the American Civil War.* Chapel Hill: University of North Carolina Press.

Fox-Genovese, Elizabeth 1988: *Within the Plantation Household: Black and White Women of the Old South.* Chapel Hill: University of North Carolina Press.

Fraser, Jr., Walter J., Saunders, Jr., R. Frank, and Wakelyn, Jon L. (eds.) 1985: *The Web of Southern Social Relations: Women, Family, and Education.* Athens: University of Georgia Press.

Friedman, Jean E. 1985: *The Enclosed Garden: Women and Community in the Evangelical South, 1830–1900.* Chapel Hill: University of North Carolina Press.

Garcia, Celine Fremaux 1987: *Celine Remembering Louisiana, 1850–1871,* ed. Patrick J. Geary. Athens: University of Georgia Press.

Gaspar, David Barry and Hine, Darlene Clark 1996: *More Than Chattel: Black Women and Slavery in the Americas.* Bloomington: Indiana University Press.

Giddings, Paula 1984: *When and Where I Enter: The Impact of Black Women on Race and Sex in America.* New York: William Morrow.

Goodheart, Lawrence B., Hanks, Neil, and Johnson, Elizabeth 1985: "An Act for the Relief of Females...": Divorce and the Changing Legal Status of Women in Tennessee, 1796–1860, *Tennessee Historical Quarterly,* 44, 318–39 and 402–16.

Gould, Virginia Meacham (ed.) 1998: *Chained to the Rock of Adversity: To Be Free, Black, and Female in the Old South.* Athens: University of Georgia Press.

Hagler, D. Harland 1980: The Ideal Woman in the Antebellum South: Lady or Farmwife? *Journal of Southern History,* 46, 405–18.

Hall, Jacquelyn Dowd 1989: Partial Truths: Writing Southern Women's History, *Signs,* 14, 902–11.

Hill, Sarah H. 1997: *Weaving New Worlds: Southeastern Cherokee Women and Their Basketry.* Chapel Hill: University of North Carolina Press.

Hodes, Martha 1997: *White Women, Black Men: Illicit Sex in the Nineteenth-Century South.* New Haven, CT: Yale University Press.

Hughes, Sarah S. 1978: Slaves for Hire: The Allocation of Black Labor in Elizabeth City County, Virginia, 1782 to 1810. *William and Mary Quarterly,* 3rd ser. 35, 260–86.

Jabour, Anya 1998: *Marriage in the Early Republic: Elizabeth and William Wirt and the Companionate Ideal.* Baltimore: Johns Hopkins University Press.

Jacobs, Harriet A. 1987: *Incidents in the Life of a Slave Girl, Written by Herself,* ed. L. Maria Child; new edn. ed. Jean Fagan Yellin. Cambridge, MA: Harvard University Press.

Johnston, Mary Tabb, with Lipscomb, Elizabeth Johnston 1978: *Amelia Gayle Gorgas: A Biography.* Tuscaloosa: University of Alabama Press.

Jones, Jacqueline 1985: *Labor of Love, Labor of Sorrow: Black Women, Work, and the Family from Slavery to the Present.* New York: Basic Books.

Kemble, Frances Anne 1961: *Journal of a Residence on a Georgia Plantation in 1838–1839,* ed. John A. Scott. New York: Alfred A. Knopf.

Kierner, Cynthia A. 1998: *Beyond the Household: Women's Place in the Early South, 1700–1835.* Ithaca, NY: Cornell University Press.

King, Wilma (ed.) 1993: *A Northern Woman in the Plantation South: Letters of Tryphena Blanche Holder Fox, 1856–1876.* Columbia: University of South Carolina Press.

Lebsock, Suzanne 1984a: *The Free Women of Petersburg: Status and Culture in a Southern Town, 1784–1860.* New York: W. W. Norton.

Lebsock, Suzanne 1984b: *"A Share of Honour": Virginia Women, 1600–1945*. Richmond: Virginia Women's Cultural History Project.

Lerner, Gerda 1967: *The Grimke Sisters from South Carolina: Rebels Against Slavery*. Boston: Houghton Mifflin.

Lerner, Gerda (ed.) 1972: *Black Women in White America: A Documentary History*. New York: Pantheon.

Leslie, Kent Anderson 1995: *Woman of Color, Daughter of Privilege: Amanda America Dickson, 1849–1893*. Athens: University of Georgia Press.

Lewis, Jan 1983: *The Pursuit of Happiness: Family and Values in Jefferson's Virginia*. Cambridge: Cambridge University Press.

Lounsbury, Richard C. (ed.) 1997: *Louisa S. McCord: Selected Writings*. Richmond: University Press of Virginia.

McCurry, Stephanie 1995: *Masters of Small Worlds: Yeoman Households, Gender Relations, and the Political Culture of the Antebellum South Carolina Low Country*. New York: Oxford University Press.

McLaurin, Melton 1991: *Celia, A Slave*. Athens: University of Georgia Press.

McMillen, Sally G. 1990: *Motherhood in the Old South: Pregnancy, Childbirth, and Infant Rearing, 1800–1860*. Baton Rouge: Louisiana State University Press.

McMillen, Sally G. 1992: *Southern Women: Black and White in the Old South*. Arlington Heights, IL: Harlan Davidson.

Malone, Ann Patton 1992: *Sweet Chariot: Slave Family and Household Structure in Nineteenth-Century Louisiana*. Chapel Hill: University of North Carolina Press.

Morton, Patricia (ed.) 1996: *Discovering the Women in Slavery: Emancipating Perspectives on the American Past*. Athens: University of Georgia Press.

Moss, Elizabeth 1992: *Domestic Novelists in the Old South: Defenders of Southern Culture*. Baton Rouge: Louisiana State University Press.

Muhlenfeld, Elizabeth 1981: *Mary Boykin Chesnut: A Biography*. Baton Rouge: Louisiana State University Press.

Myers, Robert Manson (ed.) 1972: *The Children of Pride: A True Story of Georgia and the Civil War*. New Haven, CT: Yale University Press.

Norton, Mary Beth 1980: *Liberty's Daughters: The Revolutionary Experience of American Women, 1750–1800*. Boston: Little, Brown.

O'Brien, Michael (ed.) 1993: *An Evening When Alone: Four Journals of Single Women in the South, 1827–67*. Charlottesville: University Press of Virginia.

Pease, Jane H. and Pease, William H. 1999: *A Family of Women: The Carolina Petigrus in Peace and War*. Chapel Hill: University of North Carolina Press.

Perdue, Theda 1998: *Cherokee Women: Gender and Culture Change, 1700–1835*. Lincoln: University of Nebraska Press.

Rable, George C. 1989: *Civil Wars: Women and the Crisis of Southern Nationalism*. Urbana: University of Illinois Press.

Rankin, Richard 1993: *Ambivalent Churchmen and Evangelical Churchwomen: The Religion of the Episcopal Elite in North Carolina, 1800–1860*. Columbia: University of South Carolina Press.

Salmon, Marylynn 1986: *Women and the Law of Property in Early America*. Chapel Hill: University of North Carolina Press.

Schwalm, Leslie A. 1997: *A Hard Fight for We: Women's Transition from Slavery to Freedom in South Carolina*. Urbana: University of Illinois Press.

Scott, Anne Firor 1970: *The Southern Lady: From Pedestal to Politics, 1830–1930*. Chicago: University of Chicago Press.

Scott, Anne Firor 1974: Women's Perspective on the Patriarchy in the 1850s, *Journal of American History*, 61, 52–64.

Smith, Daniel Blake 1980: *Inside the Great House: Planter Family Life in Eighteenth-Century Chesapeake Society.* Ithaca, NY: Cornell University Press.

Smith, Margaret Supplee and Wilson, Emily Herring 1999: *North Carolina Women: Making History.* Chapel Hill: University of North Carolina Press.

Sommerville, Diane Miller 1995: The Rape Myth in the Old South Reconsidered, *Journal of Southern History,* 61, 481–518.

Stevenson, Brenda E. 1996: *Life in Black and White: Family and Community in the Slave South.* New York: Oxford University Press.

Stowe, Steven M. 1987: *Intimacy and Power in the Old South: Ritual in the Lives of the Planters.* Baltimore: Johns Hopkins University Press.

Varon, Elizabeth R. 1998: *We Mean to Be Counted: White Women and Politics in Antebellum Virginia.* Chapel Hill: University of North Carolina Press.

Weiner, Marli F. 1998: *Mistresses and Slaves: Plantation Women in South Carolina, 1830–1880.* Urbana: University of Illinois Press.

Weisenburger, Steven 1998: *Modern Medea: A Family Story of Slavery and Child Murder from the Old South.* New York: Hill and Wang.

White, Deborah Gray 1985: *Ar'n't I a Woman?: Female Slaves in the Plantation South.* New York: W. W. Norton.

Whites, LeeAnn 1995: *The Civil War as a Crisis in Gender: Augusta, Georgia, 1860–1890.* Athens: University of Georgia Press.

Wolfe, Margaret Ripley 1995: *Daughters of Canaan: A Saga of Southern Women.* Lexington: University Press of Kentucky.

Woodward, C. Vann (ed.) 1981: *Mary Chesnut's Civil War.* New Haven, CT: Yale University Press.

CHAPTER THIRTEEN

Intellectual and Cultural History of the Old South

DAVID MOLTKE-HANSEN

IN the 1970s many historians still smiled at the notion of treating the Old South's intellectual history. They found it easy to dismiss the subject as an oxymoron, to accept the judgment that the region's elite had little mental life, however tormented their psychology (Cash 1941; Channing 1970). Scholars scarcely bothered to disentangle the claim that the Old South was intellectually stuck in the eighteenth century (Hubbell 1940) from the claim that it was besotted by romantic visions drawn from Sir Walter Scott (Osterweis 1949). Most accepted, and many still accept, that the commitment to slavery fundamentally shaped and, thereby, deformed what was written or said by most educated southerners, though there were some dissidents who escaped this onus (Rubin 1975, 1989; Degler 1974). Fundamental shifts in perceptions, priorities, and agendas had to occur before the Old South's cultural and intellectual development, life, and character would begin to earn consideration as vital subjects by most southernists. The transformations took place over the last quarter of the twentieth century.

The subjects had not been ignored earlier. Vivid portraits by travelers and residents alike date back to the seventeenth century, and scholarly treatments began to appear in growing numbers late in the nineteenth century. Yet these had little impact on the most influential narratives and interpretations of the region's rise.

Only a few scholars used the strategies of the burgeoning American Studies movement of the 1940s and 1950s to analyze the South's character through literature and folklore (Eaton 1961, 1964b; Osterweis 1949; Taylor 1961). In part this was because southern literary study did not recruit many students or earn much professional standing until the initial American Studies wave had crested (Kreyling 1998). In part, too, it was because the politics and economics of race and desegregation overshadowed other dimensions of the South's past and nature in scholarly debates through the 1970s.

These preoccupations seemed increasingly inadequate, however, in the aftermath of the civil rights movement's successes, the political rise of the Christian Right across the Bible Belt, and the dramatic spread of the influence of country, rock and roll, and other, southern-flavored musics. Clearly more than race and class mattered in the region. Acknowledgment of the point encouraged cultural analyses that fundamentally reshaped understandings of the region's evolution and character.

Scholars developed new cultural perspectives on the Old South in at least three overlapping contexts: political, intellectual, and historiographical. The politics were multifaceted. Communism had fallen in most of the world by the early 1990s, at the same time as historians were reducing their attention to political ideology in intellectual discourse in the Old South. Over the preceding decade-and-a-half or so, conservatives had gained offices, patronage, and intellectual influence in most developed nations, including the United States, and foundations also had revised their research agendas. Partly as a result of these changes, increased funding went to studies of the roles of traditions, the family, religion, and community in shaping Americans' politics, lives, and relationships. At the same time, the rise of multiculturalism and feminism directed funding and attention to studies of groups defined by ethnicity or gender rather than (or in addition to) socioeconomic status and race. The next step – the study of ethnic, women's, and men's cultures – would have accelerating impact on southern studies after the mid-1980s.

Interacting with these environmental influences on the cultural study of the Old South were intellectual developments of the third quarter of the twentieth century that came late to southern studies. Symbolic anthropology equipped people to analyze southerners' collective rituals and behaviors (Breen 1985; Stowe 1987). Ethnology helped southernists conceptualize cultural communities and their study (Isaac 1982; Joyner 1984). Postmodernist critical theory directed scholars to uncover, decode, and contextualize the implicit or covert meanings of southerners' literary and other cultural productions and purchases (Jones and Donaldson 1998). In turn, the perspectives of postcolonialists have begun to help southernists grapple with the cultural dynamics and manifestations of inequalities between ruling and subaltern populations in the region (Mullin 1992; Olwell 1998; Stuckey 1987). In this intellectual climate, southern culture(s) and intellectual life could finally be taken seriously.

Earlier work had debated the emerging political, economic, and ideological unities of southern whites and the extent to which those unities differentiated the South from the North. The new cultural history brought the questions of regional unity and distinctiveness to other dimensions of the southern experience. In the process, the new scholarship made clear that the cultural was not necessarily the same as the political South (Zelinsky 1992). The Confederacy was not coterminous with the territory colonized by southerners over the first half of the nineteenth century. Thanks to migration patterns, that territory spilled across the Ohio River into southern Ohio, Indiana, and Illinois, areas that were north of slavery but nonetheless for some time culturally and socially southern – parts of a contiguous, greater South (Davis 1977; McClelland and Zeckhauser 1982; Etcheson 1996; Fischer and Kelly 1993). Including Abraham Lincoln and the other sons and daughters of Dixie in these areas and in those parts of the Upper South that remained in the Union, perhaps 40 percent or more of the roughly nine million southern whites either lived outside of the Confederacy or were part of the significant minority who did not support their new country in 1861–5 (Crofts 1989; Noe and Wilson 1997; McPherson 1988; Faust 1988).

The plantation South was much smaller even than the Confederacy. Just three of the eleven states in the new republic – South Carolina, Louisiana, and Mississippi – had as much as half of their territory dominated by plantation agriculture. And of these, only the Palmetto state had a legislature dominated by planters – that is, larger slave owners. In Tennessee, Texas, and Florida, as in the border states, slaves, though widespread, made up the majority of the population in less than 10 percent of the territory in 1860.

Clearly, ideological consensus did not unify southerners in 1861 either. Many secessionists were reluctant; a substantial minority of voters simply rejected secession, and those who did vote to secede did not agree on what they were accomplishing. Some saw their departure from the Union as a reenactment of the revolution of 1775–6; others saw it as the birth of a nation out of diverging social, economic, and political interests (Moltke-Hansen 1988; 2000: ch. 3).

Since the mid-1970s these divisions within the Old South have been reframed through cultural analyses. By 1989 it had become reasonable to argue that the South was broadly a sociocultural region developed by migrant streams out of plantation states on the Atlantic and Gulf seaboards but spread far beyond the reach of planters and plantations. This identity was politically, economically, or ideologically intensified for people who saw themselves belonging to a political South, defending the plantation regime, or maintaining the states' rights republican tradition. Without the influence of one or more of these intensifiers, people might think of themselves or be identified by others as southern in some sense, but the label was not enough to inspire them to commit collectively to the Confederacy (Wilson and Ferris 1989: xv; Moltke-Hansen 2000: conclusion).

Over the last quarter of the twentieth century a great deal of work went into understanding the cultural ground of southern identity. Some of the questions addressed were about southerners' cultural origins, melding, and development. Some were about the meanings and functions of people's collective identities, cultural expressions, and consumption patterns. Some were about the relationships among cultural networks, influences, and hierarchies; some about the impact on these relationships of racial, class, and gender as well as political, commercial, and professional networks, influences, and hierarchies. Still others were about the relations of southerners' thoughts and aspirations to American or transatlantic fashions.

The most significant books in these probings have not always been works on the Old South. Southernists have brought to their work broad intellectual agendas shaped by studies of other cultural regions, producers, and consumers (e.g. Anderson 1991). Critics have contended that these influences have not only enabled but also, to some degree, directed the conclusions as well as the conduct of much of the recent work.

Yet, when teaching, debating, or refining understandings of the Old South's intellectual and cultural life, development, and character at the dawn of the twenty-first century, scholars generally have focused on their colleagues' works on the region. The distance traveled in the study of the intellectual and cultural life of the Old South over the last quarter of the twentieth century can be measured by the degree to which the 1989 *Encyclopedia of Southern Culture* remains useful or has become increasingly dated. Coedited by Charles Reagan Wilson, Director of the Center for the Study of Southern Culture at the University of Mississippi, and William Ferris, who left the Center's directorship to become Chairman of the National Endowment for the Humanities, this massive, 1,655–page volume was a surprise, national bestseller. The sales demonstrated the South's growing popularity with lay as well as scholarly audiences. They also marked acceptance of the concept of the South as a cultural region and intellectual domain.

Widely praised for its remarkable range, the volume garnered acclaim as well for its accessibility and its use of more than eight hundred scholars and writers, many of them leading specialists on the subjects about which they wrote. Reviewers appreciated, too, the understanding of culture informing the volume. Quoting T. S. Eliot, the editors defined culture as "all the characteristic activities and interests of a people," so "a *way of life*" (Wilson and Ferris 1989: xvi). This definition naturally led to emphasis on lifeways, experiences, and artistic expressions that at once united southerners and differentiated them from other Americans and other Old World, diaspora populations. Though giving considerable space at various junctures to diverse areas and peoples of the region and devoting one section out of twenty-four to "Women's Life" and another to "Black Life," the volume nevertheless emphasized the dominant, hegemonic, or common features of the region's cultural life and development. The subject was "Southern Culture" in the singular rather than "Southern Cultures" in the plural. Consequently, differences fundamental to the South were incidental to the *Encyclopedia*. The dialectics and distance between tidewater and backcountry or between plantation and frontier or between urban and rural lifeways or between Native and African-Americans or between the South and Latin America were more important than the volume showed.

Despite the earlier work of cultural geographers (Zelinsky 1992), the Old South as multicultural matrix only began to come into its own in the scholarship of the 1990s. True, specialists on Native, European, and African-American contact in the colonial period had been applying similar concepts for at least a decade longer (Silver 1990; Usner 1992), and colonialists had been writing of the "Southern Mosaic" for a generation longer still (Bridenbaugh 1952; Ver Steeg 1975). Preoccupation with the dynamics of white–black relations in the antebellum period, however, had helped insulate scholars of this later era from consideration of other cultural and social complexities. Tellingly, despite the huge volume of work done on Native Americans in the area now known as the American South, the *Encyclopedia of Southern Culture* had no section devoted to the region's aboriginal inhabitants. Indeed, there were only a handful of indexed references to "cultural contributions" of Indians, despite the continued dominance of Native Americans and the frontier over much of the geographic extent of the Old South through the early 1830s.

While these Native Americans may not have had a central role in the South's course to secession, they were a critical part of the region's life and cultural exchanges. Competition for alliances with Native American confederacies helped at once integrate and divide the region politically and diplomatically through the eighteenth century. The *Encyclopedia*, however, emphasized later over earlier chapters in the South's cultural evolution and experience. The Old South was given greater attention than the colonial but not as much as the postbellum. In part, at least, this was because southerners in general only became self-consciously sectional in the second quarter of the nineteenth century. Consequently, in some senses history in the region is much deeper than the history of the region.

Yet, as the *Encyclopedia* demonstrated, scholars have preoccupied themselves increasingly with the cultural antecedents as well as nature of that self-conscious region. Some have emphasized the European and African origins of southerners' attitudes, beliefs, and behaviors. Other scholars have emphasized rather the creation of new societies and cultures in the new world.

The most extreme cases for the European origins of southern distinctiveness have been asserted by Grady McWhiney and Raimondo Luraghi. As Forrest McDonald noted in his introduction to his sometime collaborator's *Cracker Culture: Celtic Ways in the Old South* (1988), McWhiney argued there that

> by virtue of historical accident, the American colonies South and west of Pennsylvania were peopled during the seventeenth and eighteenth centuries mainly by immigrants from...the western and northern uplands of England, Wales, the Scottish Highlands and Borders, the Hebrides, and Ireland...and...the culture these people brought with them and to a large extent retained in the New World accounts in considerable measure for the differences between them and the Yankees of New England, most of whom originated in the lowland southeastern half of the island of Britain. (McWhiney 1988: xxi).

Italian Marxist historian Raimondo Luraghi's very different but equally reductionist argument, in his *Rise and Fall of the Plantation South* (1978), was that southern society and culture owed their fundamental values and orientations to the gentlemanly ideal and the seigneurial traditions inherited from the European Renaissance.

McWhiney virtually ignored the elite in his analysis as well as the cultural influences of African-Americans and other racial and ethnic strands in the southern tapestry. Luraghi ignored the white majority as well as minorities. He followed the Italian Marxist theoretician Antonio Gramsci in arguing that elites culturally dominate and control their societies by imposing their values. In the case of the South, furthermore, the elite also co-opted most opposition, using paternalism to assert social bonds, hierarchy, and reciprocal expectations. Luraghi's Old South, therefore, was radically different from McWhiney's. It was as if the one's aspiring gentlemen and the other's Crackers lived in parallel universes.

Yet, critics have argued, however disparate the origins and strands of colonizing populations, over time many of these diverse groups nevertheless did become more and more entwined. The economy promoted such interaction as the plantation's influence spread with cotton culture and the railroad across the Deep South into Texas. As a result, researchers have insisted, yeomen (whether Celtic or not) could not successfully continue to isolate themselves. When subjected to the pull of the market economy, they almost invariably surrendered self-sufficiency and elements of self-determination (Hahn 1983; Dunaway 1996). Despite this tendency, however, many southerners remained relatively isolated by rough terrain and poor transportation or unrewarding soil and killing climate (Hsiung 1997; Kirby 1995). Even in remote areas, however, many different ethnic groups interacted and intermingled with each other as well as with Native Americans. Such mixing reduced differences but not all at once. Welsh Quakers, Presbyterian Scots–Irish, and Highland Catholics remained different from one another for at least so long as they used their original identities and lived in more-or-less segregated communities. The notion of a common, Celtic folk culture did not, therefore, withstand close scrutiny. Rather, it derived from efforts to construct ethnic genealogies to support nationalist or regionalist cultural revivals and political movements (Kidd 1999).

Despite these criticisms, however, some scholars and many heritage-oriented southerners have continued to insist that the South has an ethnically or class-derived culture or one that is at once ethnically and class based. More scholars have accepted another ethnologically inspired analysis. In *Southern Honor: Ethics and Behavior in the Old South* (1982), Bertram Wyatt-Brown argued that people of diverse origins in the South retained a shared, premodern concept of individual and family honor long after they immigrated and long after it had been largely superceded by newer, corporate social norms and controls in broadening areas of the North. This sense of honor, he continued, influenced behaviors, attitudes, and values in surprising and complex ways across the range of antebellum southerners' activities and relationships. Associated with patriarchalism in the household, individualism in the community, and equality among white men in public arenas, it manifested itself in the mannerliness and violence of men ready to respect others' honor and defend their own. In such a culture the avoidance of shame motivated many even more than the hope for honors, although this too was a powerful stimulant.

The argument appealed because of the ways it connected disparate facets of life, bridged the experiences of planters and backwoodsmen, and allowed for the South's racial and ethnic diversity and the stages of the region's social development while asserting regional commonalities and continuities as well as growing distinctiveness. Studies of male culture in the region, of intergenerational and gender relations, and of class and racial interactions all have drawn on the "honor" thesis (Greenberg 1985, 1996; McCurry 1995; Stowe 1987). Yet that thesis, critics have observed, asserted rather than compared regional differences and anachronistically argued for essential uniformity in the functions and meanings of a cultural concept, honor, across widely different societies, geographic and cultural settings, and time periods.

Some scholars have similarly demurred at the sweeping nature of the argument of folklorist John Michael Vlach. In his seminal *The Afro-American Tradition in Decorative Arts* (1978) Vlach explored African influences on expressive forms from houses to quilts and ironwork. The explicit purpose of the book, and the exhibition on which it was based, was to assert the African aesthetics and origins shaping African-American culture. Africans brought with them to America, Vlach contended, expressive traditions and sensibilities that not only continued to shape how their American descendants thought and worked artistically, but also influenced European Americans in profound and surprising ways. Shotgun houses – homes one room wide and two or more deep – were African in origin, Vlach insisted. So were many pottery, textile, and wrought-iron forms and the improvisational spirit they displayed. So, many have contended, were swept dirt yards and livestock herding on unfenced lands.

Yet, critics observed, the Greek temple form inspiring much European American architecture in the Old South organized space in the same way as did the shotgun house. Many of McWhiney's Celts also had dirt yards and herded livestock on the open range. So did the Spaniards in Florida, Louisiana, and Texas. Moreover, African-Americans descended from very different African populations and cultures. To assert shared African antecedents was, therefore, in some reviewers' eyes, to ignore crucial differences in much the way critics in time accused McWhiney and Wyatt-Brown of doing. On the other hand, most scholars have agreed with Vlach that African-Americans inherited and used African cultural influences, even if the functions of these legacies changed to one degree or another over time. Most have agreed, too, that African-Americans developed and sustained distinctive communities and culture(s) while influencing European Americans in sometimes subtle but nonetheless important respects (Genovese 1974; Stowe 1987).

This emphasis on transatlantic inheritances, whether African or European, has countered the tendency of many southernists to treat their subjects only in a national or regional context. The notion that southerners' roots help explain southern developments has given historical depth to analyses of the South's nature and rise. On the other hand, critics have agreed, southerners' roots alone do not adequately explain the culture(s) created in the region. In the South, as elsewhere in America, root often was grafted on to root and always bore signs of having been transplanted to new soil. Cultures that had little or no contact on the eastern side of the Atlantic developed complex interactions on the western side. Over time, too, southerners' folk inheritances changed portions of their functions and meanings. In part this was because of the radically different environments in which these inheritances were deployed, in part because of historical events and developments that transformed people's opportunities or impinged on people's daily lives, beliefs, and behaviors.

Scholars intent on understanding the consequences of these New World cultural and social interactions for the Old South's evolution have had agendas very different from those colleagues focused on the region's transatlantic roots. Two local studies among a growing number have remained especially influential: Rhys Isaac's *The Transformation of Virginia, 1740–1790* (1982) and Charles Joyner's *Down by the Riverside: A South Carolina Slave Community* (1984).

Australian historian Isaac argued that the society and culture planters dominated in Virginia in 1740 were fundamentally altered by the rise of evangelical religion and the swelling tide of immigration that brought hundreds of thousands of religious Dissenters – particularly Scotch–Irish and Germans – down the Great Wagon Road into the southern backcountry between 1740 and 1790. These new settlers and their fellow evangelicals, many recruited in the first Great Awakening, resisted the plantation regime politically as well as culturally. For them the American Revolution was a chance to shoulder their way into the commonwealth's governance while altering the commonwealth's political ethos. To appeal to this evangelical population, Patrick Henry and others began sounding more like preachers and less like gentlemen. The protopopulist ideology to which Patrick Henry gave voice during the war became an American legacy. In social and cultural as well as political and ideological terms, therefore, the Revolution helped transform the Old Dominion. It went from a plantation colony defined in critical respects by the market demands, fashions, and governing interests of the metropolis and the great planters to a complex society and polity progressively integrating the new state into the equally new American nation and expanding world markets.

Reviewers liked the ways Isaac combined anthropologically informed understanding of community development and structure with political and religious history. They liked as well the emphasis on social transformation and cultural emergence and conflict, so the shift of attention away from folk legacies to historical development and away from continuities to change. Some wondered, however, if Isaac had not overdrawn his case. After all, they observed, through aggressive land speculation planters profited dramatically from the immigrant tide, and a growing number of evangelicals became slave owners. Morcover, while tidewater planters may not have continued their virtual stranglehold on public offices through the antebellum period, they still were at the center of the society and culture their ancestors had formed. In time, they also made political, marital, and financial alliances with the descendants of the backcountry leadership. Many also became evangelicals. Over the long term, there simply was not as much conflict in the Old Dominion as Isaac argued there was. Even the religion that had divided Virginia's elite from a growing percentage of whites came instead in the end to unite whites in a broad evangelical culture (Boles 1972; Heyrman 1997).

Joyner's very different focus was on the culture and community created by Africans and African-Americans on the rice coast of South Carolina. For him the emergence of Gullah (a creole language using mostly English vocabulary together with elements of African grammars and pronunciations) mirrored the creation of a creole culture and community. This slave society melded diverse European and Native American with African and Caribbean influences into a distinctive whole. By definition such a society was different from all those on which it drew. It was a new creation in the New World and manifested itself in the lifeways and expressive habits and productions of the Gullah people and also in the lives and expressions of the Gullahs' European American masters and neighbors.

Though enthusiastic, some reviewers still wondered about the degree of relevance of the Gullah story for African-Americans more generally. Because the rice coast's population was overwhelmingly slave by the mid-eighteenth century, Africans and African-Americans there had more need as well as opportunity to create a full-blown, creole language and culture to unite as well as distinguish them. Rather than typical, the Gullah experience seemed extreme to critics. Elsewhere African-Americans often were more integrated into, not isolated from, dominant, European American culture(s) (Morgan 1998). Yet, as other scholars have noted, even in areas with low African American populations, black influenced white culture, hence demonstrating the power of cultural syncretism as well as the compulsions to assimilate to the dominant culture. Old Timey string music in Appalachia, for instance, developed its subregional character in part after the introduction of the African-derived banjo into upland communities (Conway 1995).

Broader critiques of such analyses of cultural community creation have come from economic, social, and political historians. These critics have contended that community cultures must be analyzed politically, socially, and economically as well as ethnologically if their fissures, functions, and power are to be understood. The corollary contention is that one must read communities in the contexts of broad market, political, and social developments. One must remember, too, that the emergence of a creole culture reflects the subordination or elimination of many aspects of the creole population's antecedents as well as accommodations to an often oppressive and alien cultural hegemony.

The creolization phenomenon is worldwide, occurring wherever diverse, uprooted peoples are forced together over a long period of time in locales where they are the majority and no element of the population predominates linguistically or culturally (Hall 1992; Palmie 1995). The majority of African diaspora as well as many other plantation and colonial populations have been caught up in the process. In a broader sense, the linguistic and cultural syncretism at the heart of creolization has also been central to the American experience. To understand the southern cases fully, therefore, requires comparative as well as global perspectives. One also needs to look beyond the

shared bonds of folkways and language to the subordination, exploitation, or marginalization of many of the people involved.

Some scholars have turned to Marxism for perspective. The first to be influential
was a student of African-Americans' resistance to slavery, Herbert Aptheker (1943).
Not until the 1950s did scholars begin to inform the emerging scholarship by
following Marx himself in analyzing how southerners could be participants in the
broad patterns and trends of western social and cultural development yet create, live
in, and be shaped by what most Marxists thought was a distinctive regime. Another
problem these analysts posed themselves also became central in the historiography.
How, they asked, could the plantation regime impose ideological and cultural dominance over polities, people, and daily lives even though the plantation dominated
land use in only a fraction of the South?

The answers proved complex. According to the evolving argument, the plantation
regime not only helped the elite accumulate great wealth, status, and power over
generations, but also committed the society to forms of economic and social development, co-opting most citizens and framing many aspirations. Moreover, the
regime shaped understanding of social obligations, in the process using the impetus
to male authority and religious devotion to forge a paternalistic ideology with which
planters defined class, gender, and racial relations or, at least, ideals. So, the South
became ideologically as well as economically and socially more and more divergent
from a North that was at once eliminating slavery and industrializing. These differences manifested themselves increasingly in politics, in sermons, in social analyses,
and even in fiction (Snay 1993; Genovese 1985, 1992; Ambrose 1996; Moss 1992;
Tracy 1995); the differences mattered more and more as slavery spread across the
Lower South and as growing numbers of northerners organized to suppress it.

No scholar has more forcefully and influentially argued elements of this case than
Eugene Genovese. He gathered his initial insights into books through the 1960s
(Genovese 1965, 1969). His monumental and pathbreaking *Roll, Jordan, Roll*
(1974) appeared at the dawn of the new cultural history of the Old South and
continued his examination of the ideological, cultural, and human concomitants of
slavery and the plantation system. It focused on the slave community and the ways
African-Americans resisted, adapted to, and shaped the plantation regime, in the
process creating their own culture. While scholars have long awaited his and Elizabeth
Fox-Genovese's equally sweeping and monumental, projected, multi-volume work
on "The Mind of the Master Class," they now do so in a different spirit than
formerly.

In part, anticipation has been colored by the Genoveses' growing reputation as
Catholic and conservative, though how this conversion has affected their interpretive
approach is not as obvious as critics aver (Kreyling 1998: 167ff.). More intellectually
significant is the diminishment of Marxism's value in scholars' thinking over the
last twenty years. Then there are many feminist scholars' disagreement with Fox-
Genovese's insistence, in her *Within the Plantation Household* (1988), that planter
women's commitment to their class undermined and limited their participation in
cross-class and interracial gender solidarity. The disagreements have been evidentiary
but also ideological. In an oppressive, male-centered culture, some critics have insisted,
elite women may normally have appeared to express support for the regime they
served, but their suppressed, true feelings emerged either as fleeting expressions of

rebellion or resistance or as subtexts in more conventional compositions and actions or as telling silences. On her side, Fox-Genovese has insisted that one must not privilege silences with an evidentiary value not given texts, that the preponderance of the evidence must be taken into account, and that there is little reason to doubt women's general acceptance as well as focused criticisms of their culture and class.

Other scholars have disagreed vehemently with the Marxists' conviction that planters behaved or thought differently than other, capitalistic profit seekers either on the western frontier or in eastern urban centers. A number of critics have concluded as well that putative planter paternalism did little to humanize the planter regime or ameliorate slaves' conditions. Yet, despite the now almost ritual observations by reviewers that scholarship either has moved or should move beyond debates over whether the plantation regime was capitalistic or not, work by numerous young scholars still reflects the continuing power of the Genoveses' argument that the Old South developed a distinct planter culture shaped by the economic and social obligations and norms of slavery and the plantation system. Many scholars continue to follow the Genoveses as well in their belief that this culture expressed itself ideologically, using contemporary as well as inherited ideas to shape both a world view and more-or-less systematic responses to the intellectual and religious assaults on slavery.

The belief that the Old South was a distinct cultural and social region has at once made plausible and defined aspects of the separate study of southern art and architecture, literature, and intellectual as well as family and professional life. One of the reasons there were over eight hundred scholars and writers on whom the editors of the *Encyclopedia of Southern Culture* could call is that a growing number of southern artists, authors, and scientists were drawing specialist attention. Moreover, recent broad surveys, bio-bibliographies, and other compendia made much of this swelling volume of research accessible (Bain, Flora, and Rubin 1979; Poesch 1983; Rubin et al. 1985). While generally not highly analytical or theoretically sophisticated or reflective about its assumptions, the work behind these surveys and compendia had helped prepare scholars and members of the public to make the *Encyclopedia* a bestseller.

Jessie Poesch's *The Art of the Old South: Painting, Sculpture, Architecture and the Products of Craftsmen, 1560–1860* (1983) surveyed the fine and decorative arts and architecture of the region from the eve of the Spanish establishment of St Augustine in Florida until the Civil War. Its focus was on regional production for local elites. Its characteristics were careful use of the accumulated scholarship, mastery of detail, and attention to the broad developments and fashions shaping southern artistic production and consumption. Making the work much richer than it otherwise would have been was Poesch's ability to draw both on large, private collections of regional art and growing museum collections of artisanal works likewise made increasingly available through exhibitions and surveys in the years she was finishing her own overview.

Poesch also was able to draw on Wayne Andrews's handsomely illustrated and idiosyncratically focused *Pride of the South: A Social History of Southern Architecture* (1979). The title suggested a growing preoccupation among scholars with the social and symbolic functions of built environments in the elite, white South. The tradition reached back to Marxists such as Arnold Hauser, whose social history of European art was widely used in classrooms through the 1970s. Andrews, however, did not dig as deeply as Kenneth Severens's (1988) later study of antebellum Charleston's civic architecture. Yet Severens's similar focus on prideful forms and examples also slighted the vernacular forms scholars had been examining increasingly to learn both about the operation and influence of folk traditions and about the nature of the lives lived in and meanings given to vernacular structures (Upton and Vlach). While noting such limits, scholars have nevertheless been very grateful for the guidance such pioneering (if partial) treatments have continued to give in fields studied only fragmentarily by earlier generations.

On the other hand, there have been anthologies and histories of southern literature since the late nineteenth century. What Louis D. Rubin and his colleagues accomplished, therefore, was different than what a Poesch or an Andrews achieved. These latter pulled together elements of subjects that had never been surveyed, much less analyzed. Rubin et al. (1985) were explaining what they and their students had learned and concluded since the great survey by Jay B. Hubbell, *The South in American Literature*, published in 1954. Like the *Encyclopedia of Southern Culture* it informed, *The History of Southern Literature* (Rubin et al. 1985) summed up the state of the scholarship at the end of a period of development as well as at the dawn of emerging understandings.

Contextualizing and critiquing these developments was Michael Kreyling's *Inventing Southern Literature* (1998). In Kreyling's view Rubin, together with colleagues at the University of North Carolina at Chapel Hill and Yale, had dramatically enhanced southern literary study as a separate field. The premises of the field, however, had remained conservative, in Kreyling's eyes, despite the political liberalism of some of its exponents. It was not enough that Rubin asked why antebellum southern authors had failed to produce literature comparable in quality in his judgment to works of such contemporaries in the North as Hawthorne and Melville. Neither was it enough that he argued – *pace* Kreyling (1998: ch. 3) – that white southerners' commitment to the slave regime deprived them of the social and intellectual distance they needed to produce good literature (Rubin 1975, 1989). Rubin largely failed to look for the authors among African-Americans and women in the Old South who did have greater degrees of distance. According to Kreyling, this was because he basically accepted the southern literary canon and critical approaches defined by the very conservative southern Agrarians in the 1920s and later.

This canon gave priority to published poetry and fiction by the culturally sophisticated and critically successful, so mostly middle- and upper-class, white men. In part this was because the so-called New Criticism of the Agrarians made preferable works of formal elegance and complex, ambivalent, or ambiguous texts reflecting rich, social, intellectual, and aesthetic tensions. As a result of these preconceptions and biases, the (re)discovery of writings by most women and African-American authors would not redirect antebellum southern literary scholarship until the 1980s. Though telling, this critique does not acknowledge that Rubin's students and colleagues did much of the work to recover women's and African-Americans' texts or that many of the contemporary South's women and African-American writers are products of Rubin's seminars (Andrews et al. 1997). In his ritual slaying of his predecessors, Kreyling all too easily conflated the attitudes and orientations of those who irritated him. Still, elements of his chronology and analysis do help historicize the flowering of southern literary study in the late 1960s and 1970s.

Just as it was not until the 1980s that scholars escaped the constraints of the southern literary canon, it was only in the 1980s that they began to pay serious attention to the essay, memoir, and other forms most composed by antebellum southerners when writing for publication. It was only more recently still that scholars joined colonialist David Shields (1997) in considering the functions of writings circulated in manuscript. The scholar most influential in redirecting the attention of colleagues to the non-fictional writings of the Old South has been Michael O'Brien. Intellectual historians keenly anticipate his "The Intellectual History of the Old South." Yet, through conferences (O'Brien and Moltke-Hansen 1986), essays (O'Brien 1988), and editions (O'Brien 1982, 1993) as well as an intellectual biography of US Attorney General Hugh Swinton Legaré of South Carolina (O'Brien 1985), O'Brien has already done more than anyone to call attention to the range of antebellum southerners' secular, humanistic, intellectual engagements and productions, the influences shaping them, and their circulation and impact. In addressing these abiding concerns of intellectual historians, he at the same time has persistently challenged the preoccupations and analyses that have enabled historians to ignore most of what antebellum southerners thought and wrote. The results have included a much more complex understanding of Romanticism's efflorescence in the South than could be gleaned from prior accounts. Too, O'Brien has pioneered both in recovering antebellum southerners' historical interests and in focusing attention on the thoughts, experiences, and circumstances of educated single women writing in their diaries.

What O'Brien has not yet done is pursue equally the authors and works of scientific and religious thought, fiction, and poetry or the intellectual activities and preoccupations of Native Americans, African-Americans, German and Irish immigrants, apprentices and artisans, or "plain" white folk in the countryside. On the other hand, he already has been slowly recovering the Old South's part in transatlantic and American intellectual history by focusing on the development of intellectual institutions, the diffusion of ideas and shifts in intellectual fashions among cultural elites, and the development and productions of intellectual networks and communities, as well as the work and influence of figures central in the intellectual life of the region. He has done so in ways scholars had scarcely considered before, much less credited. In the process, he has undermined the long-held conviction that southern intellectuals and their audiences went from being open to new ideas in Thomas Jefferson's lifetime to being more and more closed to new intellectual developments by the 1850s (Eaton 1964a).

Over the years O'Brien has been researching the Old South's intellectual history, colleagues (many of whom have joined him in the informal Southern Intellectual History Circle) have transformed aspects of the subject. Biographies of central or revealing figures – Bachman, Hammond, Harby, Hughes, Nott, Petigru, Ramsay, Ruffin, Simms, Thornwell, Tucker – have helped make plausible the study of the mind of the Old South. So have editions of the writings of other key thinkers – for instance, Gildersleeve and McCord – as well as group studies of economic thinkers, the intellectual circle in Drew Faust's pioneering first book, the writers and subjects of the slave narratives, southern nationalists, naturalists, physicians, pastoralists, women writers, legal thinkers, theologians, and defenders of slavery. In turn, studies of the education and culture of elite families and of popular taste have provided a bridge between the Old South's intellectual and cultural histories (Stowe 1987; Lewis 1983; Greenberg 1996; Farnham 1994).

Nevertheless, in critical respects these histories have yet to be written. Scholars know little of the region's antebellum print culture, elementary and secondary education, and social institutions' roles in intellectual commerce and cultural diffusion in the nineteenth century. They have only begun to analyze the networks and intellectual frameworks binding communities of faith, ethnicity, and professions (Snay 1993; Holifield 1978; Bell 1996; Bodenhamer and Ely 1984; Numbers and Savitt 1989). The extent to which the Old South's religious and literary, intellectual and scientific, legal and cultural histories are still separate subjects and discourses continues to frustrate integrated understanding of the experiences, thinking, and feelings of antebellum southerners. Though the Old South is now conceived as a cultural region, what this means is still in debate.

In the first volume of a pioneering comparative study of Boston, Massachusetts, and Charleston, South Carolina, in the Age of Jackson, Jane Pease and William Pease (1985, 1990) argued that, at least in the cases of those cities, one of the central differences was the prevailing attitude toward progress: the northern community again and again invested in and accommodated railroads, factories, and other forms of modernity, while the southern community again and again limited progress's intrusion on and roles in its life. Yet Joyce Chaplin (1993) found South Carolinians anxious investors in agricultural improvements, and Mark Smith (1997) found southern planters increasingly adopting a modern, clock-measured, quasi-industrial model of plantation workforce management by the mid-nineteenth century. So, if the South was a distinct cultural region, its distinction did not obviously or incontrovertibly lie in its relation to broader western values and developments.

Drawing on scholarship that looked at the material and demographic bases of regional culture (Kulikoff 1986), as well as lifeways in the region (Wilson and Ferris 1989), Christopher Morris (1995) has argued that the Old South's distinction lay rather at the intersection of the ways southerners lived, worked, mingled, and used as well as shaped their environment. As he has observed, Confederate President Jefferson Davis's home county of Warren, Mississippi, only became southern gradually and, even having done so, did not leap to embrace secession. First, about the time of the American Revolution, frontiersmen moved in. Following them, in the wake of the decline of the local fur trade, came farmers. The successful among them acquired ever-larger blocks of land, first dealing in timber, naval stores, and foodstuffs, then planting cotton. Plantations became the engine driving the local economy by the 1810s and the introduction of steamboats on the Mississippi and Yazoo Rivers. The area was still rough hewn, but by 1861 Warren County had become one of the increasingly elegant plantation districts of the South, the process having taken three generations. In the course of this development the land, the society, and the culture, as well as the economy, had all acquired recognizably southern attributes.

Morris's analysis has attracted praise for its integration of social and economic with cultural and environmental change. Critics have had trouble, however, generalizing the model. Parts of the region had been southern in Morris's sense for a century or more before Warren County came into existence. Large parts of the region, however, whether considered demographically or geographically, were not yet southern in Morris's sense at the outbreak of the Civil War. Though sophisticated, Morris's model is too simple. Nevertheless, the assumption that people gradually became southern or recreated in newly settled areas aspects of a southern way of life has appeal. It flows naturally from the understanding that the South emerged gradually, though unevenly, out of an evolving mix of people in a distinct sociocultural and physical environment and in particular market and geopolitical circumstances.

Scholars have developed sophisticated understandings of aspects of those market and geopolitical circumstances (Coclanis 1989). Despite the pioneering work of Michael O'Brien, however, scholars know much less about the region's participation in global cultural processes and intellectual exchanges. By 2010 the situation will have changed dramatically. The Genoveses' studies of "The Mind of the Master Class" and O'Brien's volumes on "The Intellectual History of the Old South" will have appeared, been debated and absorbed, and become new milestones. The "History of the Book" project of the American Antiquarian Society will have put the South's print culture and history in national perspective, and scholars will have begun to fill the gaps still yawning in the scholarship.

One can anticipate other developments as well. More work has been done on women writers after 1860 than before; scholars have already begun to redress the balance (Moss 1992; O'Brien 1993). Intellectual historians will do yet more to capture the intellectual lives and interests of free blacks, artisans, apprentices, immigrants, and other groups (Levine 1977; Cornelius 1991; Fleischner 1996; Gillespie 2000; Sobel 1993; Bell 1996). The pioneering efforts of Steven Hahn, Stephanie McCurry, and others to enter the minds of the yeomanry have not yet led to the posing of the full range of questions many intellectual and cultural historians want to ask. Such questions can now be considered much more easily, however, than formerly. In turn, the artificial distinction between people's intellectual discussions in religious and secular settings will diminish but not disappear. More scholars will follow Joyce Chaplin in integrating scientific, technological, and economic with cultural and intellectual issues. Scholars will also move increasingly beyond the isolated treatment of the legal and medical communities and their professional concerns to consider broader societal and cultural issues (McCandless 1996; Hindus 1980).

Intellectuals and their discourses will similarly emerge in new contexts. Scholars will give more sophisticated readings than they often have of the subtexts and contexts as well as the texts in southerners' antebellum literary and intellectual productions. In the process, presumptive or thesis-ridden judgments will give way to informed ones. So, authors such as William Gilmore Simms, arguably the region's preeminent man of letters on the eve of the Civil War, will less often be dismissed by people daunted by the size and conventions of his literary work or his proslavery position (Guilds 1992; Guilds and Collins 1997). Reviewer on average of a book a week over forty years, Simms, along with other cultural mediators, will increasingly serve as a window on the South's changing involvement in the broader worlds of letters and ideas.

Scholars will also follow O'Brien in categorizing, quantifying, and assessing the influence of the books and periodicals southerners read. When mapped, networks of intellectual correspondents and collaborators will help reveal the changing geographic shape and dynamics of southern intellectual life and the differing degrees to which individuals and groups were involved at subregional, regional, national, and international levels in the South's intellectual economy. The same kind of mapping of communication flows will reveal the evolving geography and dynamics of the region's cultural life and commerce. The cultural meaning of relative isolation from the market economy will become even clearer as a result. So will more of the cultural consequences of growing involvement in the market (Hahn 1983; Watson 1990).

The process of the acculturation of immigrants will invite more study as well (Bell 1996). Scholars of the antebellum South will deepen and extend analyses of racial interactions in the market, in church, on the street, in the work place, in households, in public places (Boles 1988; Ownby 1993). Studies of July 4th and other civic occasions will extend to include more of the activities and perceptions of women, immigrants, and African-Americans, and so reveal saliences and tensions in the Old South's evolving civic culture (Travers 1997; Waldstreicher 1997). While often considered a region with an etiolated public sphere, the Old South will provide scholars the opportunity to revise their understanding to include in that sphere the range of those places and occasions where southerners interacted and performed publicly and politically: church, barbecues, clubs, salons, reading rooms, the gardens on the bluff in Natchez, Mississippi (Lebsock 1984; Shields 1997). The interpenetration of the social, the religious, and the political will continue to confound some theoreticians but should exhilarate more flexible thinkers, in part because of the invitation it offers to integrate political and cultural analyses (Faust 1982; Ford 1988; Isaac 1982; Snay 1993; Tise 1987).

In short, the imminent conclusion of the magisterial series by the Genoveses and O'Brien may mark the culmination of some trends in the study of the cultural and intellectual history of the Old South, but will also serve as departure points for researches that will transform this study again. Already the easy dismissal of the Old South's cultural and intellectual life seems jejune, and the simplicities of some bold, pioneering theses seem less and less useful. The consequence is that, although many – perhaps most – brief articles in the *Encyclopedia of Southern Culture* will continue to be useful until new work on more of these thousand-plus subjects appears, the judgments organizing the volume and framing its leading questions and its criteria of inclusion and exclusion are already proving less and less constructive. In a future encyclopedia, the changing demographics of, and the divergent ways of life in, the broad socioculturally defined region should receive more attention. So should intra-regional, interregional, and transnational comparative perspectives. So should the intersections of many of the structuring topics of the current *Encyclopedia*. Intellectual history and aspects of cultural transmission and influence should loom larger, as probably should some forms of popular (in contradistinction to folk) pastimes. The interactions between elite and other population and cultural elements should gain additional attention as well. Hard questions about the impact of subaltern status or marginality on elements of the population should figure also. Such changes would reflect the cumulative impact of the transformations wrought in southern studies, beginning in the mid-1970s, when the New Cultural History came to the Old South.

BIBLIOGRAPHY

Ambrose, Douglas 1996: *Henry Hughes and Proslavery Thought in the Old South*. Baton Rouge: Louisiana State University Press.
Anderson, Benedict 1991: *Imagined Communities: Reflections on the Origin and Spread of Nationalism*, revd edn. London: Verso.

Andrews, Wayne 1979: *Pride of the South: Social History of Southern Architecture*. New York: Athenaeum.

Andrews, William L., et al. (eds.) 1997: *The Literature of the American South: A Norton Anthology*. New York: W. W. Norton.

Aptheker, Herbert 1943: *American Negro Slave Revolts*. New York: Columbia University Press.

Bain, Robert, Flora, Joseph M., and Rubin, Louis D., Jr. (eds.) 1979: *Southern Writers: A Biographical Dictionary*. Baton Rouge: Louisiana State University Press.

Bell, Michael Everette 1996: *"Hurrah fur dies susse, dies sonnige Leben"*: The Anomaly of Charleston, South Carolina's Antebellum German America. Ph.D. dissertation, University of South Carolina.

Bodenhamer, David J. and Ely, James W., Jr. (eds.) 1984: *Ambivalent Legacy: A Legal History of the South*. Jackson: University Press of Mississippi.

Boles, John B. 1972: *The Great Revival, 1787–1805: The Origins of the Southern Evangelical Mind*. Lexington: University Press of Kentucky.

Boles, John B. (ed.) 1988: *Masters and Slaves in the House of the Lord: Race and Religion in the American South, 1740–1870*. Lexington: University Press of Kentucky.

Breen, T. H. 1985: *Tobacco Culture: The Mentality of the Great Tidewater Planters on the Eve of Revolution*. Princeton, NJ: Princeton University Press.

Bridenbaugh, Carl 1952: *Myths and Realities: Societies in the Colonial South*. Baton Rouge: Louisiana State University Press.

Cash, W. J. 1941: *The Mind of the South*. New York: Alfred A. Knopf.

Channing, Steven A. 1970: *A Crisis of Fear: Secession in South Carolina*. New York: W. W. Norton.

Chaplin, Joyce E. 1993: *An Anxious Pursuit: Agricultural Innovation and Modernity in the Lower South, 1730–1815*. Chapel Hill: University of North Carolina Press.

Coclanis, Peter A. 1989: *The Shadow of a Dream: Economic Life and Death in the South Carolina Low Country, 1670–1920*. New York: Oxford University Press.

Conway, Cecilia 1995: *African Banjo Echoes in Appalachia: A Study of Folk Tradition*. Knoxville: University of Tennessee Press.

Cornelius, Janet Duitsman 1991: *"When I Can Read My Title Clear"*: Literacy, Slavery, and Religion in the Antebellum South. Columbia: University of South Carolina Press.

Crofts, Daniel W. 1989: *Reluctant Confederates: Upper South Unionists in the Secession Crisis*. Chapel Hill: University of North Carolina Press.

Davis, James E. 1977: *Frontier America, 1800–1840: A Comparative Demographic Analysis of the Settlement Process*. Glendale, CA: Arthur H. Clark.

Degler, Carl N. 1974: *The Other South: Southern Dissenters in the Nineteenth Century*. New York: Harper and Row.

Dunaway, Wilma A. 1996: *The First American Frontier: Transition to Capitalism in Southern Appalachia, 1700–1860*. Chapel Hill: University of North Carolina Press.

Eaton, Clement 1961: *The Growth of Southern Civilization, 1790–1860*. New York: Harper and Row.

Eaton, Clement 1964a: *Freedom of Thought Struggle in the Old South*. New York: Harper and Row.

Eaton, Clement 1964b: *The Mind of the Old South*. Baton Rouge: Louisiana State University Press.

Etcheson, Nicole 1996: *The Emerging Midwest: Upland Southerners and the Political Culture of the Old Northwest, 1787–1861*. Bloomington: University of Indiana Press.

Farnham, Christie Anne 1994: *The Education of the Southern Belle: Higher Education and Student Socialization in the Antebellum South*. New York: New York University Press.

Faust, Drew Gilpin 1977: *A Sacred Circle: The Dilemma of the Intellectual in the Old South, 1840–1860*. Baltimore: Johns Hopkins University Press.

Faust, Drew Gilpin 1982: *James Henry Hammond and the Old South: A Design for Mastery.* Baton Rouge: Louisiana State University Press.

Faust, Drew Gilpin 1988: *The Creation of Confederate Nationalism: Ideology and Identity in the Civil War South.* Baton Rouge: Louisiana State University Press.

Fischer, David Hackett and Kelly, James C. 1993: *Away, I'm Bound Away: Virginia and the Westward Movement.* Richmond: Virginia Historical Society.

Fleischner, Jennifer 1996: *Mastering Slavery: Memory, Family, and Identity in Women's Slave Narratives.* New York: New York University Press.

Ford, Lacy K. 1988: *Origins of Southern Radicalism: The South Carolina Up-Country, 1800–1860.* New York: Oxford University Press.

Fox-Genovese, Elizabeth 1988: *Within the Plantation Household: Black and White Women of the Old South.* Chapel Hill: University of North Carolina Press.

Genovese, Eugene 1965: *The Political Economy of Slavery.* New York: Pantheon.

Genovese, Eugene 1969: *The World the Slaveholders Made.* New York: Vintage.

Genovese, Eugene 1974: *Roll, Jordan, Roll: The World the Slaves Made.* New York: Pantheon.

Genovese, Eugene 1985: *"Slavery Ordained of God": The Southern Slaveholders' View of Biblical History and Modern Politics.* Gettysburg, PA: Gettysburg College.

Genovese, Eugene 1992: *The Slaveholders' Dilemma: Freedom and Progress in Southern Conservative Thought, 1820–1860.* Columbia: University of South Carolina Press.

Genovese, Eugene 1998: *A Consuming Fire: The Fall of the Confederacy in the Mind of the White Christian South.* Athens: University of Georgia Press.

Gillespie, Michele 2000: *Free Labor in an Unfree World: White Artisans in Slaveholding Georgia, 1789–1860.* Athens: University of Georgia Press.

Greenberg, Kenneth S. 1985: *Masters and Statesmen: The Political Culture of American Slavery.* Baltimore: Johns Hopkins University Press.

Greenberg, Kenneth S. 1996: *Honor and Slavery: Lives, Duels, Noses, Masks, Dressing as a Woman, Gifts, Strangers, Humanitarianism, Death, Slave Rebellions, the Proslavery Argument, Baseball, Hunting, and Gambling in the Old South.* Princeton, NJ: Princeton University Press.

Guilds, John C. 1992: *Simms: A Literary Life.* Fayetteville: University of Arkansas Press.

Guilds, John C. and Collins, Caroline (eds.) 1997: *William Gilmore Simms and the American Frontier.* Athens: University of Georgia Press.

Hahn, Steven 1983: *The Roots of Southern Populism: Yeoman Farmers and the Transformation of the Georgia Up Country, 1850–1890.* New York: Oxford University Press.

Hall, Gwendolyn Midlo 1992: *Africans in Colonial Louisiana: The Development of Afro-Creole Culture in the Eighteenth Century.* Baton Rouge: Louisiana State University Press.

Heyrman, Christine 1997: *Southern Cross: The Beginnings of the Bible Belt.* New York: Alfred A. Knopf.

Hindus, Michael Stephen 1980: *Prison and Plantation: Crime, Justice, and Authority in Massachusetts and South Carolina, 1767–1878.* Chapel Hill: University of North Carolina Press.

Holifield, E. Brooks 1978: *The Gentlemen Theologians: American Theology in Southern Culture, 1775–1860.* Durham, NC: Duke University Press.

Hsiung, David C. 1997: *Two Worlds in the Tennessee Mountains: Exploring the Origins of Appalachian Stereotypes.* Lexington: University Press of Kentucky.

Hubbell, Jay B. 1940: "Literary Nationalism in the Old South," in David K. Jackson (ed.), *American Studies in Honor of William Kenneth Boyd.* Durham, NC: Duke University Press.

Hubbell, Jay B. 1954: *The South in American Literature, 1607–1900.* Durham, NC: Duke University Press.

Isaac, Rhys 1982: *The Transformation of Virginia, 1740–1790.* Chapel Hill: University of North Carolina Press.

Jones, Anne Goodwyn and Donaldson, Susan V. (eds.) 1998: *Haunted Bodies: Gender and Southern Texts.* Charlottesville: University Press of Virginia.

Joyner, Charles 1984: *Down by the Riverside: A South Carolina Slave Community.* Urbana: University of Illinois Press.

Kidd, Colin 1999: *British Identities before Nationalism: Ethnicity and Nationhood in the Atlantic World, 1600–1800.* Cambridge: Cambridge University Press.

Kirby, Jack Temple 1995: *Poquosin: A Study of Rural Landscape and Society.* Chapel Hill: University of North Carolina Press.

Kreyling, Michael 1998: *Inventing Southern Literature.* Jackson: University Press of Mississippi.

Kulikoff, Allan 1986: *Tobacco and Slaves: The Development of Southern Cultures in the Chesapeake, 1680–1800.* Chapel Hill: University of North Carolina Press.

Lebsock, Suzanne 1984: *Free Women of Petersburg: Status and Culture in a Southern Town, 1784–1860.* New York: W. W. Norton.

Levine, Lawrence 1977: *Black Culture and Black Consciousness: Afro-American Folk Thought from Slavery to Freedom.* New York: Oxford University Press.

Lewis, Jan 1983: *The Pursuit of Happiness: Family and Values in Jefferson's Virginia.* Cambridge: Cambridge University Press.

Luraghi, Raimondo 1978: *The Rise and Fall of the Plantation South.* New York: Viewpoints.

McCandless, Peter 1996: *Moonlight, Magnolias, and Madness: Insanity in South Carolina from the Colonial Period to the Progressive Era.* Chapel Hill: University of North Carolina Press.

McClelland, Peter D. and Zeckhauser, Richard J. 1982: *Demographic Dimensions of the New Republic: American Interregional Migration, Vital Statistics and Manumissions, 1800–1860.* Cambridge: Cambridge University Press.

McCurry, Stephanie 1995: *Masters of Small Worlds: Yeoman Households, Gender Relations, and the Political Culture of the Antebellum South Carolina Low Country.* New York: Oxford University Press.

McPherson, James M. 1988: *Battle Cry of Freedom: The Civil War Era.* New York: Oxford University Press.

McWhiney, Grady 1988: *Cracker Culture: Celtic Ways in the Old South.* Tuscaloosa: University of Alabama Press.

Moltke-Hansen, David 1988: Protecting Interests, Maintaining Rights, Emulating Ancestors: US Constitution Bicentennial Reflections on "The Problem of South Carolina," 1787–1860, *South Carolina Historical Magazine,* 89: 160–82.

Moltke-Hansen, David 2000: Southern Genesis: Regional Identity and the Rise of "the Capital of Southern Civilization," 1760–1860. Ph.D. dissertation, University of South Carolina.

Morgan, Philip D. 1998: *Slave Counterpoint: Black Culture in the Eighteenth-Century Chesapeake and Lowcountry.* Chapel Hill: University of North Carolina Press.

Morris, Christopher 1995: *Becoming Southern: The Evolution of a Way of Life, Warren County and Vicksburg, Mississippi, 1770–1860.* New York: Oxford University Press.

Moss, Elizabeth 1992: *Domestic Novelists in the Old South: Defenders of Southern Culture.* Baton Rouge: Louisiana State University Press.

Mullin, Michael 1992: *Africa in America: Slave Acculturation and Resistance in the American South and the British Caribbean, 1736–1831.* Urbana: University of Illinois Press.

Noe, Kenneth W. and Wilson, Shannon H. (eds.) 1997: *The Civil War in Appalachia: Collected Essays.* Knoxville: University of Tennessee Press.

Numbers, Ronald L. and Savitt, Todd L. (eds.) 1989: *Science and Medicine in the Old South.* Baton Rouge: Louisiana State University Press.

O'Brien, Michael (ed.) 1982: *"All Clever Men, Who Make Their Way": Critical Discourse in the Old South.* Fayetteville: University of Arkansas Press.

O'Brien, Michael 1985: *A Character of Hugh Legaré.* Knoxville: University of Tennessee Press.

O'Brien, Michael 1988: *Rethinking the South: Essays in Intellectual History.* Baltimore: Johns Hopkins University Press.

O'Brien, Michael (ed.) 1993: *An Evening when Alone: Four Journals of Single Women in the South, 1827–67.* Charlottesville: University Press of Virginia for the Southern Texts Society.

O'Brien, Michael and David Moltke-Hansen (eds.) 1986: *Intellectual Life in Antebellum Charleston.* Knoxville: University of Tennessee Press.

Olwell, Robert 1998: *Masters, Slaves, and Subjects: The Culture of Power in the South Carolina Low Country, 1740–1790.* Ithaca, NY: Cornell University Press.

Osterweis, Rollin G. 1949: *Romanticism and Nationalism in the Old South.* New Haven, CT: Yale University Press.

Ownby, Ted (ed.) 1993: *Black and White Cultural Interaction in the South.* Jackson: University Press of Mississippi.

Palmie, Stephan (ed.) 1995: *Slave Cultures and the Cultures of Slavery.* Knoxville: University of Tennessee Press.

Pease, Jane H. and Pease, William H. 1990: *Ladies, Women, and Wenches: Choice and Constraint in Antebellum Charleston and Boston.* Chapel Hill: University of North Carolina Press.

Pease, William H. and Pease, Jane H. 1985: *The Web of Progress: Private Values and Public Style in Boston and Charleston, 1828–1843.* New York: Oxford University Press.

Poesch, Jessie 1983: *The Art of the Old South: Painting, Sculpture, Architecture and the Products of Craftsmen, 1560–1860.* New York: Alfred A. Knopf.

Rubin, Louis D., Jr. 1975: *William Elliott Shoots a Bear: Essays on the Southern Literary Imagination.* Baton Rouge: Louisiana State University Press.

Rubin, Louis D., Jr. 1989: *The Edge of the Swamp: A Study in the Literature and Society of the Old South.* Baton Rouge: Louisiana State University Press.

Rubin, Louis D., et al. (eds.) 1985: *The History of Southern Literature.* Baton Rouge: Louisiana State University Press.

Severens, Kenneth 1988: *Charleston: Antebellum Architecture and Civic Destiny.* Knoxville: University of Tennessee Press.

Shields, David S. 1997: *Civil Tongues and Polite Letters in British America.* Chapel Hill: University of North Carolina Press.

Silver, Timothy 1990: *A New Face on the Countryside: Indians, Colonists, and Slaves in South Atlantic Forests, 1500–1800.* Cambridge: Cambridge University Press.

Smith, Mark M. 1997: *Mastered by the Clock: Time, Slavery, and Freedom in the American South.* Chapel Hill: University of North Carolina Press.

Snay, Mitchell 1993: *Gospel of Disunion: Religion and Separatism in the Antebellum South.* New York: Cambridge University Press.

Sobel, Mechal 1993: *The World They Made Together: Black and White Values in Eighteenth-Century Virginia.* Princeton, NJ: Princeton University Press.

Stowe, Steven M. 1987: *Intimacy and Power in the Old South: Ritual in the Lives of the Planters.* Baltimore: Johns Hopkins University Press.

Stuckey, Sterling 1987: *Slave Culture: Nationalist Theory and the Foundations of Black America.* New York: Oxford University Press.

Taylor, William R. 1961: *Cavalier and Yankee: The Old South and the American National Character.* New York: Braziller.

Tise, Larry E. 1987: *Proslavery: A History of the Defense of Slavery in America, 1701–1840.* Athens: University of Georgia Press.

Tracy, Susan J. 1995: *In the Master's Eye: Representations of Women, Blacks, and Poor Whites in Antebellum Southern Literature.* Amherst: University of Massachusetts Press.

Travers, Len 1997: *Celebrating the Fourth: Independence Day and the Rites of Nationalism in the Early Republic.* Amherst: University of Massachusetts Press.

Upton, Dell and Vlach, John Michael (eds.) 1986: *Common Places: Readings in American Vernacular Architecture*. Athens: University of Georgia Press.

Usner, Daniel 1992: *Indians, Settlers and Slaves in a Frontier Exchange Economy: The Lower Mississippi Valley Before 1783*. Chapel Hill: University of North Carolina Press.

Ver Steeg, Clarence L. 1975: *Origins of a Southern Mosaic: Studies of Early Carolina and Georgia*. Athens: University of Georgia Press.

Vlach, John 1978: *The Afro-American Tradition in Decorative Arts*. Cleveland, OH: Cleveland Museum of Art.

Waldstreicher, David 1997: *In the Midst of Perpetual Fetes: The Making of American Nationalism, 1776–1820*. Chapel Hill: University of North Carolina Press.

Watson, Harry L. 1990: *Liberty and Power: The Politics of Jacksonian America*. New York: Hill and Wang.

Wilson, Charles Reagan and Ferris, William (eds.) 1989: *Encyclopedia of Southern Culture*. Chapel Hill: University of North Carolina Press.

Wyatt-Brown, Bertram 1982: *Southern Honor: Ethics and Behavior in the Old South*. New York: Oxford University Press.

Zelinsky, Wilbur 1992: *The Cultural Geography of the United States*. Englewood Cliffs, NJ: Prentice-Hall.

PART III

Civil War and Reconstruction

CHAPTER FOURTEEN

Sectionalism and the Secession Crisis

MARY A. DeCREDICO

DAVID Potter once wrote that hindsight was "the historian's chief asset and his main liability" (Potter 1976: 145). That he was writing about the 1850s was no coincidence, because as he pointed out perceptively, historians studying the years leading up to southern secession and Civil War have all too often treated the turbulent 1830s, 1840s, and 1850s as leading inexorably toward war. For the average Virginian or Mississippian, the late antebellum period was a time of great flux. From controversies over the national bank, the tariff, the Mexican War, and countless political debates, southerners watched and waited while they pursued the day-to-day activities of living. Many hoped a crisis could be averted; others prayed for the confrontation that would precipitate secession and the establishment of a southern nation. When that crisis did come, in Charleston Harbor in April 1861, southerners – some with glee and others with regret – embraced the Confederate standard.

How the people in the eleven states that formed the Confederacy came to that point is a question that has fascinated scholars ever since the final shots were fired in that bloody conflict. As might be expected, the earliest works, written by participants, tended toward apologia. People such as former vice president of the Confederacy Alexander Stephens and President Jefferson Davis devoted countless hours to explaining – and justifying – how events in the late antebellum period forced southerners to sever their connection to the Union. Endeavoring to restore the republic the founders had so painstakingly established, Davis and Stephens went to their deathbeds convinced of the legality, one might even say necessity, of secession.

As the participants in that great conflict passed away, a new generation of professional historians took up the challenge of analyzing and assessing the growth of southern sectionalism and the coming of the Civil War. Not surprisingly, these scholars found myriad reasons for the growth of southern sectionalism and the ultimate secession of the southern states. Often, their interpretations mirrored the times in which they lived. If any generalization can be made about the scholarship, it is that this era has sparked some of the most innovative and controversial literature in southern history.

In many ways, Ulrich Bonnell Phillips occupies a special place in the pantheon of southern historians. Born and raised in Georgia, he counted among his relatives many former Confederates. It was Phillips who first argued "The Central Theme in Southern History"(*American Historical Review*, XXXIV: 1928) was the white determination to control blacks, which for the antebellum period essentially meant slavery. Answering the somewhat rhetorical question of what constituted the South's "essence," Phillips dismissed such popular concepts as states' rights or an adherence to laissez-faire economics. For Phillips, slavery was the defining feature of the region and its people: "Slavery was instituted," wrote Phillips in 1939, "not merely to provide control of labor but also as a system of racial adjustment and social order." As abolitionist attacks mounted, southerners closed ranks to defend their peculiar institution "not only as a vested interest, but with vigor and vehemence as a guarantee of white supremacy" (Phillips 1964).

Phillips's interpretation of the South and how slavery made it a distinct section has been challenged and revised but never totally abandoned. Later scholars who undertook to write broad surveys of the antebellum period were forced to acknowledge Phillips's substantive scholarship.

Three scholars who succeeded Phillips wrote works on the origins and evolution of southern sectionalism that are still considered classics. To be sure, these books are a bit dated, but they still command popular and scholarly attention: Charles S. Sydnor's *The Development of Southern Sectionalism, 1819–1848* (1948), Avery O. Craven's *The Growth of Southern Nationalism, 1848–1861* (1953), and David M. Potter's *The Impending Crisis, 1848–1861* (1976).

Sydnor's volume treated the South on two levels. For Sydnor, the development of sectionalism between the Panic of 1819 and the end of the Mexican War occurred as a result of changes inside and outside the region. Deeply affected by the panic and depression, many southerners became wary of banks because they seemed to amass so much power and appeared to be oblivious to the needs of the public. Similarly, the Missouri Crisis struck the region like a "firebell in the night" and caused great anxiety over the future of slavery in the Missouri territory. Finally, the national government's embrace of tariffs and federal aid to internal improvements smacked of an abandonment of "laissez-faire philosophy" and the development of big government (Sydnor 1948: 134).

Thomas Jefferson's death in 1826 also presaged the end of an era: the culmination of the Virginia Dynasty. The mantle of southern leadership – and the doctrine of states' rights – passed to John C. Calhoun and South Carolina. There it would become "more extreme and radical" than ever envisioned in the Old Dominion (ibid: 177). It would be Calhoun who in 1828 first tested the waters of secession with his *South Carolina Exposition and Protest*. In the ensuing Nullification Crisis, South Carolina stood alone, but increasingly other southern states saw their interests at odds with those of the Northeast. As a result, allegiance to section replaced allegiance to the nation, especially as the reality that the South occupied a minority position within the country became apparent (Sydnor 1948: ix).

Sydnor's volume ends where Craven's begins, with the United States's victory in the Mexican War and the discovery of gold in California. Craven, one of the original revisionists who viewed the Civil War as a "repressible conflict," modified his views in this contribution to Louisiana State University's multivolume History of the South series. Craven argued here that during the period 1848–61 slavery proved to be an intractable issue. Attacks on the peculiar institution, along with northern economic and industrial development, placed the South on the defensive. According to Craven, secession could not have been avoided "unless either the North or the South had been willing to yield its position on an issue that involved the matters of 'right' and 'rights' and the fundamental structure of society" (Craven 1953: 396). Craven underscored how slavery became the *sine qua non*: "Neither the North nor the

South could yield its position because *slavery had come to symbolize values in each of their social–economic structures for which men fight and die but which do not give up or compromise*" (ibid: 397, author's italics).

David Potter, too, saw slavery as a central element that led to secession and war. He assessed the scholarship on the 1850s and discovered that whether historians emphasized cultural differences between North and South, ideological differences between North and South, or economic differences between North and South, slavery remained a constant. Indeed, "slavery had an effect which no other sectional factor exercised in isolating North and South from each other" (Potter 1976: 43). As a result, the sectional divide widened as both sections began reacting, rather than acting, to perceived stereotypes of the other.

As Potter surveyed the course of Manifest Destiny and the problems it created, he urged readers to remember that Americans in both sections during the 1850s "went about their daily lives, preoccupied with their personal affairs, with no sense of impending disaster nor any fixation on the issue of slavery" (ibid: 143). Potter's warning was a needed caveat. It continues to caution students not to view the turbulent decade before the war as a game of dominoes. The average American did not foresee in 1854 that a bill to build a transcontinental railroad would touch off Civil War on the plains of Kansas, prompt violence in the hallowed halls of Congress, or irreparably divide the Democratic Party. Bearing that in mind, the reader gains a new appreciation of what Potter called "the impending crisis."

Potter died prematurely before he could finish his volume. But the final chapter he penned (the manuscript was completed by Don E. Fehrenbacher) demonstrates again his nuanced understanding of the South. Potter saw the region as one with duelling loyalties. Southerners were Americans, but they were also consciously aware that they were southern. As fire-eater rhetoric became more inflammatory, southerners were forced to decide whether they could best preserve their rights within the Union or outside of it. Even if they could not agree on that, they could agree that they had the right to secede if need be (ibid: 484). And so the stage was set.

In many ways the work of Sydnor, Craven, and Potter set the standard for narrative analyses of sectionalism and the secession crisis. But they also stimulated new examinations of the period. For example, their emphasis on the slave issue as the major element leading to the breakup of the Union was taken up by Eugene Genovese, but he gave it a different twist. A Marxist, Genovese maintains that slaveholder hegemony created a precapitalist economy. External threats forced these planters to endorse secession; it was the only alternative left to protect their way of life.

Genovese's *Political Economy of Slavery: Studies in the Economy and Society of the Slave South* (1965) argues, through a series of thoughtful essays, that "slavery gave the South a social system and a civilization with a distinct class structure, political community, economy, ideology, and a set of psychological patterns. . . . [A]s a result, the South increasingly grew away from the rest of the nation" (Genovese 1965: 3). According to Genovese, the South grew throughout the antebellum period, but it never developed. Plantation agriculture extended from the Atlantic to the Trans-Mississippi, and although the region enjoyed unparalleled prosperity, it functioned as a colonial appendage to the rapidly diversifying and industrializing North (ibid: 17). Here is the central paradox: the southern planters who dominated the society functioned in a capitalistic system, but they were precapitalist or even anticapitalist. To be sure, planters exhibited the trappings of capitalism – they invested and reaped profits from their investments – but they plowed those earnings back into land and slaves. Planters only used capitalistic devices to further their agricultural interests (ibid: 19–23).

The ruling planter elite was thus dependent upon expansion. Cotton was a voracious crop, so slaveholders were determined to reap the benefits that Manifest Destiny and, ultimately, war with Mexico, wrought. Concomitantly, slaveholders saw in the expansion and settlement of new territories and states a way to regain their control of the national Congress, an issue that was painfully played out during the debates over Congressman David Wilmot's proposal to restrict slavery in any territories gained from Mexico. Genovese succinctly observes that "The South had to expand, and its leaders knew it" (ibid: 266). Without expansion, slavery and the system of plantation agriculture would be extinguished. He argues forcefully that slavery created the foundation of southern society. Should slavery be eliminated, planters would be confronted with the values of a society that were antithetical to the system they created. "When the slaveholders rose in insurrection," Genovese concludes, "they knew what they were about: in the fullest sense, they were fighting for their lives" (ibid: 270).

Genovese's Marxist interpretation of southern sectionalism and secession attracted other Marxist scholars. All focused on the way the minority planter class seduced the majority yeomanry to join them in secession and the establishment of a southern nation. For Barrington Moore (1966) and more recently, John Ashworth (1995), secession was the South's only alternative because it had developed an economic system that was incompatible with the free-labor and free-market society of the North. Hence, the Civil War that ensued represented the "last revolutionary offensive on the part of . . . [the] urban or bourgeois capitalist democracy" (Moore 1966: 112).

Not until the late 1970s was the Marxist interpretation challenged. The scholars who took up the cudgel agreed that slavery remained a fundamental cause of sectionalism and ultimately secession. But they interpreted slavery in a much broader sense than the Marxists, and in doing so demonstrated how the southern white majority – the yeomen farmers – were induced to endorse secession and embrace war.

Michael Holt's *The Political Crisis of the 1850s* (1978) was the ground-breaking monograph in this area. Interestingly, Holt came upon his interpretation almost accidentally. Setting out to study two-party systems with a behavioral methodology, Holt was increasingly drawn to the role of ideology during the Second Party System (1832–54). He discovered that the idea of republicanism, with its "premises" about the type of government and society that would best safeguard individual liberties (ideas that dated back to 1776), dominated popular thought. "It was that obsession," Holt maintains, "that drove Americans to the point of killing each other in 1861" (Holt 1978: viii).

Holt's study surveys the historiography of the coming of the Civil War. He takes issue with those historians who focus on the growing cleavage between North and South during the 1840s and 1850s. For Holt, the issue is not what made North and South different but "how the nation could contain or control that division for so long and then allow it suddenly to erupt into war" (ibid: 3). The answer to the question of why the nation broke apart in 1860 and 1861 is to be found, as his title suggests, in the political events – and crises – of the 1850s.

Though Holt focuses on the breakdown of the Second Party System, his book is not a traditional political history. Nor does he follow other scholars who studied the Second Party System only in an attempt to understand how and why it failed. Holt's revisionist stance is evident when he argues that party *conflict*, not consensus, kept the republic together. Intense partisan conflict between Democrats and Whigs on a variety of issues served to underscore the major differences between the parties. That competition made voters feel as if their interests were being served. As a result, Americans had a deep faith in "the political process" (ibid: 35).

Holt traces the path of partisan politics through the issues that dominated the late 1840s and early 1850s. Though economic issues loomed large, it was the debate over slavery in the territories that destroyed the national nature of the rival parties. Yet Holt argues the "sectionalization" of the parties was not because of "popular disagreements over black slavery" (ibid: 184). Instead, it was due to the demise of the Whig Party in the South, which produced more consensus than conflict: it was hard for the surviving Democrats to pose as the champion of the South's interests without an opposition party to serve as a foil. In contrast, the emergence of the purely sectional Republican Party, with a platform antithetical to southern interests and its message of containing the "slave power" and restoring republican values, gave northern voters a renewed sense of confidence in the political process.

Republican attacks on the slave power and their pledge to halt the westward expansion of slavery conjured up dire consequences in the minds of white southerners. Here is where the ideological component of Holt's argument weighs in. According to Holt, southerners had long defined "slavery" and "slave" in very complex terms. For white southerners, especially the yeomanry who had less of a tangible investment in the institution, slavery went beyond the notion of chattel servitude. It implied subordinate or second-class status, a loss of liberty and a loss of property. Fire-eaters encouraged white southerners to believe the Republican Party's victory would mean southern whites' liberty would be taken away, leaving them little different from the black slaves who tilled their fields. This was a consequence no freedom-loving southerner could countenance.

Still, Lincoln's election prompted only the seven states of the Deep South to secede. There, the immediatists – those who believed Lincoln's election by itself was cause enough to sever the bonds of Union – were well-organized, highly vocal, and convinced a Republican in the White House portended leadership they could no longer trust to safeguard slavery. The death of Whiggery in the Deep South meant that only one party, the Democrats, remained. Consequently, national, state, and local politicians could assume militantly proslavery stances; there was also, as Holt notes, "no institutionalized check on extremism" that active two-party conflict would provide (Holt 1978: 236).

If the lack of two-party competition encouraged the embrace of radicalism in the Deep South, its presence in the Upper South produced an alternative belief. The Upper South did maintain closer economic ties to the North, and it had a more diversified economy. But those factors, argues Holt, were not decisive. Rather, it was the reality that Virginia, Tennessee, North Carolina, and Arkansas had weathered the party system crisis. Indeed, though the Whigs died nationally, they maintained strong roots on the state and local level in the Upper South. Consequently, party competition remained vibrant and convinced southerners in those states that the political process worked and that some remedy or compromise could be effected through political means (ibid: 252–56).

Sadly for those cooperationists – people who embraced a wait-and-see attitude – crisis preceded compromise. The Confederate bombardment of Fort Sumter and Lincoln's subsequent call for volunteers to "quell" the rebellion convinced Virginia, Tennessee, North Carolina, and Arkansas that the Republican administration was being coercive. By late June 1861 those four crucial states were part of the Confederacy.

William J. Cooper Jr. also sees notions of liberty and slavery crucial to the development of sectionalism and secession. In both *The South and the Politics of Slavery, 1828–1856* (1978) and *Liberty and Slavery: Southern Politics to 1860* (1983), Cooper surveys the political developments that affected the Second Party System. He admits that in both volumes he focused exclusively on "*politically active white Southerners*" (Cooper 1983: vi, author's emphasis) because they were the group who elected the local, state, and national leaders who pressed southern interests to the forefront. Moreover, this was the group that would take up arms and die for their vision of liberty.

Cooper believes the birth of the Second Party System (between 1832 and 1836 with the rise of the Whigs) allowed the debate between southern Whigs and Democrats to create the politics of slavery. According to Cooper, what emerged was a "political world" that contained the "major forces influencing antebellum southern politics: the institution of slavery, parties and politicians, the political structure, and the basic values of white society" (ibid: 195). To be sure, these were not new elements; but with the rise of the militant abolition movement, the ability to pose as the defender of southern interests became *de rigeur*. Indeed, by 1840, southerners' commitment to liberty had become "ferocious" (ibid: 196–7).

It was the territorial issue, and specifically the Wilmot Proviso of 1846, that terrorized southerners anew. Prohibiting the expansion of slavery into the newly won territories gained from Mexico implied that the South "would become the American Ishmael," a second-class region. No honorable southerner could accept that. The Proviso passed the House of Representatives but was defeated in the Senate. That was not enough to allay southern fears. Hence, beginning in 1846, southerners and their political leaders became even more vigilant in defense of their liberty (ibid: 220).

Echoing Holt, Cooper maintains that the yeomen supported the planters and endorsed the vote for secession because they had become convinced white liberty depended on black slavery. Although the Upper South held out longest, largely because it lacked the powerful presence of the fire-eaters, the politics of slavery would ultimately force them to join their Deep South brethren in the Confederate states.

John M. McCardell tackles the issue of slavery and liberty creating a distinct southern identity in *The Idea of a Southern Nation: Southern Nationalists and Southern Nationalism, 1830–1860* (1979). McCardell rejects the notion that northerners and southerners were "two distinct people." As he correctly points out, residents of both sections shared a common language, a common history, common traditions, and common beliefs. Yet southerners saw in the institution of slavery "a whole ideological configuration – a plantation economy, and a pattern of race relations –

which made Southerners believe they constituted a separate nation" (McCardell 1979: 3–4).

It was the Nullification Crisis of 1832 that fostered the emergence of southern nationalism. At that point, "sizeable numbers of Southerners began to perceive that their own set of shared interests were becoming increasingly incompatible with those of the rest of the Union and were, in fact, being threatened" (ibid: 6). The Mexican War, disputes over the territorial issue, and fears about what a Republican administration might mean to southern liberty, convinced southerners that their only alternative to being enslaved to the North was to secede and establish a "better" Union. Interestingly, McCardell concludes that southern defeat in the Civil War "forced Americans to think about their nature and purpose as a nation and hastened the emergence of a modern, integrated, and more genuinely United States." Thus southern nationalism, which precipitated a bloody war, catalyzed American nationalism (ibid: 9, 338).

Holt, Cooper, and McCardell's works paralleled the publication of a number of state studies that examine the role of liberty and slavery in southern politics. One of the more persuasive and provocative monographs they spawned is J. Mills Thornton III's *Politics and Power in a Slave Society: Alabama, 1800–1860* (1978). Thornton's state study endeavors to illuminate how Alabama's "institutional, ideological and political context" was affected by national developments (Thornton 1978: xvii).

Ultimately a hotbed of fire-eater sentiment, Alabama was, according to Thornton, a state "obsessed with the idea of slavery" (ibid: xviii). Imbued with the ideology of the American Revolution, Alabamians fiercely guarded their liberty. Any policy, event, or politician that threatened that liberty was suspect. Thus, as economic development progressed and national issues intruded, Alabamians were caught in a vortex of change. Suddenly, it seemed to many, towns and industrial and commercial enterprises threatened to dominate the landscape. Traditional values appeared obsolete, and new political leaders with new ideas rose to the forefront of the state government. The result of shifting factions and contesting visions was secession (ibid: 442).

The road to secession was not without detours. Alabamians were deeply divided, but those divisions were complex: they did not cut across interstate regions, or landholdings, or social classes. Ultimately, fire-eaters were able to convince all sections of the state that the Republicans were the enemy. The Republican platform of prohibiting slavery in the territories appeared to planters, yeomen, and merchants alike as a threat to white liberty. Exclusion was just a step away from emancipation and a degraded status. The fire-eaters were therefore "able to make their crusade for secession a crusade for the only two things that really mattered in Alabama – liberty and equality" (ibid: 449). The yeomen majority followed because notions of liberty resonated so strongly. Without it, one was a slave.

Mississippi suffered similar symptoms. According to Bradley G. Bond's more recent work, *Political Culture in the Nineteenth Century South: Mississippi, 1830–1900* (1995), social and economic changes fostered fears about what impact those changes would have on liberty. As the state became drawn into battles over expansion and economic development, all Mississippians subordinated other concerns to the maintenance of white supremacy, which was the guarantor of white freedom (Bond 1995: 7–8).

The idea that liberty and slavery dominated the white South during the antebellum era and tipped the balance toward disunion is also the main theme in state studies of South Carolina and Georgia. Steven A. Channing's *Crisis of Fear: Secession in South Carolina* (1974) examines the underlying issues that caused South Carolinians to revolt. For him, the catalyst was fear of a slave insurrection. Having a black majority had always frightened white South Carolinians. They had read about the Stono Revolt in 1739 and Gabriel Prosser's rebellion in Richmond in 1800; they had lived through Denmark Vesey's 1822 conspiracy in Charleston; they had been chilled to learn about Nat Turner's revolt in Southampton County, Virginia, in 1831. But it was the rise of the abolitionist movement and John Brown's attempt to start a slave uprising at Harpers Ferry that galvanized them. As Channing aptly notes, "John Brown had plunged a knife deep into the psyche of Southern whites, and life would never be quite the same again" (Channing 1974: 23).

As national events kept the slavery issue on the front burner, South Carolina divided internally: should the Palmetto State take the lead in the secession movement? Eventually, the fire-eaters in the state gained the upper hand and convinced their less zealous brothers that disunion was "the only guarantee of security for the kind of Southern civilization they idealized" – one where slavery was protected (ibid: 142).

According to Channing, secession was precipitated "by a revolutionary elite which was identified with the traditional ruling class" (ibid: 155). This planter elite succeeded in ensuring that the slaveholders stayed in charge of the slaveholders' revolution. Michael P. Johnson finds similar forces at work in his study of Georgia, *Toward a Patriarchal Republic: The Secession of Georgia* (1977). Johnson sees secession as a divisive issue in Georgia. Governor Joseph Brown was so concerned about how close the tally for immediatists and cooperationists was that he altered the final count to allow for a greater secessionist margin of victory. But secession did not allay the General Assembly's fears for the future. Aware that revolutions have a tendency to get out of hand, legislators rewrote the state constitution to ensure that slavery – and their individual rights – were protected. Georgia's new constitution created the "patriarchal republic," a government of and by slaveholding planters and protected from the whims of the masses (Johnson 1977: 33–4, 46, 119–20).

Extremism and political polarization came to the Deep South first. Thus it is no coincidence that those seven states precipitated the secession crisis. Equally compelling is how and why the Upper South, and in particular the states of Virginia, North Carolina, Tennessee, and Arkansas, hesitated. Scholars have also grappled with this phenomenon: the Upper South's tortured path to secession.

Daniel W. Crofts's *Reluctant Secessionists: Upper South Unionists in the Secession Crisis* (1989) provides a detailed analysis of Virginia, North Carolina, and Tennessee from Lincoln's election in 1860 to the winter of 1861. Echoing Michael Holt, Crofts maintains that one needs to "take into account both slaveholding and previous patterns of party allegiance to understand why the upper and lower South took such different stances during the months after Lincoln's election" (Crofts 1989: xvi).

Croft's monograph portrays a healthy, volatile political culture in the states of Virginia, North Carolina, and Tennessee. Throughout the antebellum period, those three states experienced great party competition. Divisions in each emerged over economic issues and economic change, not ethnicity, slaveholding patterns, or religious differences (ibid: 37–47). All embraced the republican world view and feared the loss of liberty. When Whiggery disappeared in the Deep South, it remained a viable entity in the Upper South.

Lincoln's election did not set off the alarm bells in the Upper South as it did in the Lower South, largely because of this very different political experience. Perhaps as a result of that, three forms of Unionism emerged: the "unconditional" Unionists, who would stay loyal no matter what; the "anticoercionists," who would stay loyal only if the North did not make war on the South; and the "extended ultimatumists," who would stay loyal until every effort had been exhausted (ibid: 104). These Unionists weathered the tense winter months well, but they were dependent on a lenient Republican policy, a policy that slowly eroded during that same time. Still, the firing on Fort Sumter alone did not precipitate the Upper South's secession. Rather, it was Lincoln's call for troops that led to a "striking reversal of public opinion" and the decision to join their sister states in the Confederacy (ibid: 323, 338).

While most recent scholarship has focused on the republican ideology and the party process, one scholar has identified another value worthy of comment. Bertram Wyatt-Brown first explored how southerners equated honor with their way of life in *Southern Honor: Ethics and Behavior in the Old South* (1982). According to Wyatt-Brown, notions of honor created a complex system that determined virtually every facet of southern society. It was only natural that honor and slavery would be inextricably bound together.

Wyatt-Brown elaborated on this theme in his 1985 work, *Yankee Saints and Southern Sinners*. The essay "Honor and Secession" examines how notions of southern honor (as distinct from the northern variety) led directly to secession. Southern honor, according to Wyatt-Brown, is multifaceted. It involves one's view of one's self, one's view of one's self within the community, and, finally, the "acceptance of that self-evaluation" by the larger public which "enables the claimant to know his place in society" (Wyatt-Brown 1985: 186). Lest one think such a definition was limited only to the planter elite, Wyatt-Brown hastens to add that the essence of the honor ethic permeated the yeomanry as well. The "common folk" valued honor "because they had access to the means for its assertions themselves – the possessing of slaves – and because all whites, nonslaveholders as well, held sway over all blacks. Southerners regardless of social position were united in the brotherhood of white-skinned honor" (ibid: 187).

The language of honor permeated southern ideals and southern politics. Politicians spoke to tightly knit communities in terms that touched deeply. They talked of threats to the southern way of life in language that conjured up images of subordinate status. Those leaders used words with pejorative connotations, such as "betray," "treachery," vindicate," and "vengeance," to stress their arguments. As Wyatt-Brown notes, "In societies where honor thrives, death in defense of community and principle is a path to glory and remembrance, whereas servile submission entails disgrace" (ibid: 196–200). That was the picture painted for southerners during the period from the Missouri Crisis in 1819 to the election of Lincoln in 1860.

Wyatt-Brown takes issue with Thornton's and Holt's views of secession: he denies that "white freedom," as opposed to "black slavery, was the source of the calamity." Nor does he dismiss slavery as a central cause of sectionalism and secession. Rather, Wyatt-Brown posits that "Racism, white freedom and equality...were an inseparable part of personal and regional self-definition" (ibid: 203). Because all southern whites viewed honor and slavery in those terms, it was a given they would rally behind the fire-eaters' banner: "The common denominator for both the domestic and the labor institutions was the exigency of honor. Ordinary citizens, not just politicians, felt obliged to close ranks behind the Stars and Bars on the fundamental principle of honor, family, and race supremacy, one and indivisible" (ibid: 212).

The men who convinced the southern people that a point of no return had arrived were the fire-eaters. Thanks to Eric H. Walther we have a better sense of who these men were and what they attempted to effect. *The Fire-Eaters* (1992) argues that fire-eaters and radicals were not necessarily the same thing. Many men were fire-eaters, but not all fire-eaters were southern radicals (Walther 1992: 2). The fire-eaters' activities varied, but they were united in a common goal: the secession of the South. They viewed secession as the only vehicle to save the Republic from being unalterably corrupted. Walther maintains that this vision, rooted more in eighteenth-century political ideology than nineteenth, gathered together planter, yeoman, and merchant. For these men, secession would create a "truly republican society" that would protect slavery and individual liberty (ibid: 298).

As does Wyatt-Brown, Walther sees language as a key to fire-eater success. Each fire-eater (Walther devotes a chapter each to such men as J. D. B. DeBow, Louis T. Wigfall, William Lowndes, Edmund Ruffin, and Robert Barnwell Rhett) focused on a particular theme, but their ideas were the same: "They believed that southerners faced an overwhelming and unconquerable political threat from the North. ... By describing the political struggle of the South as a choice between submission to an alien people or independence, fire-eaters struck a sensitive nerve" (ibid: 300). Those men succeeded in convincing the vast majority of white southerners that their liberty and freedom were only safe in an independent Confederacy (ibid: 301).

As might be gathered from the foregoing analysis, the literature on southern sectionalism and secession is rich and varied. Happily, two historians have endeavored to synthesize the multiplicity of interpretations into narrative works.

William W. Freehling's *The Road to Disunion: Secessionists at Bay, 1776–1854* (1990) is the first volume of a projected two-volume history of the secession crisis. Freehling openly admits in his preface that he embarked upon this project because he was dissatisfied with other accounts. According to him, previous studies of the secession crisis too frequently treated the South as a monolithic entity. Freehling maintains there were many Souths and that, much earlier than other scholars have recognized, these "clashing Souths wove patterns insidious to perpetual Union." Because of this, Freehling believes that sectional conflict antedated the 1850s, the decade most historians point to as wracked by sectional issues, by about fifty years (Freehling 1990: ix).

Freehling is quite interested in the clash between what he terms "despotism" and "democracy" – the conflict between slaveholding and the revolutionary ideals of liberty and equality that coexisted in the antebellum South. Freehling explores this tension in chapters devoted to the master–slave dynamic and its role in the South. For a white to disagree with the system was to commit the cardinal sin of disloyalty. White society's remedy was lynching, though ostracism and exile also served their purpose (ibid: 98–110). As might be expected, the debate over emancipation in Virginia in 1831–2 renewed concerns about the safety and viability of the "peculiar institution."

Because of that, fire-eaters could find fertile ground to spread their gospel, especially in the Upper South. Freehling maintains the rise of the fire-eaters is traceable to "the long, losing campaign to extinguish Monticello's master's vision in more northern sections of the South" (ibid: 121).

Crisis came early to the South, and Freehling deftly tells the tale of the Missouri Crisis and the Nullification Crisis. Out of such conflicts came what Freehling calls the "reorganization of Southern politics." Both Whigs and Democrats ran for office promising to protect and uphold southern interests. Over time, this became a test of party loyalty. These confrontations with the North affected southerners on all levels, but it was the debate over the gag rule that pointed southerners toward secession. It was, to quote Freehling, "the Pearl Harbor of the slavery controversy," the unexpected and unanticipated conflagration that shocked both sections (ibid: 308).

Freehling's treatment of the gag rule controversy provides an interesting and innovative segment to his work. As he correctly points out, few scholars have paid much attention to the South's drive to clamp-off debate on abolitionist petitions that flooded Congress beginning in the mid-1830s. Through careful political planning, southerners succeeded in getting all abolitionist petitions tabled instead of presented for debate. The passage of this "gag resolution" succeeded in censoring, on both the state and now the national level, all incendiary material that attacked slavery. Even more importantly, " 'Tabling' rather than 'receiving' petitions because abolition was 'inexpedient' rather than 'unconstitutional' were code words declaring that abolition could not be stopped without revolutionizing the two-party system." Basically, this allowed southern and northern Democrats to keep the party intact (ibid: 308, 331, 336).

Freehling views the annexation of Texas as the turning point on the road to secession. Coming on the heels of the gag rule controversy, it served to convince the mass of northerners that there was a slave-power conspiracy to control the country. Yet, just as Potter warned over twenty years ago, Freehling, too, cautions his readers that events in the early 1850s did not push the South inexorably toward disunion. Instead, Freehling sees such things as the 1850 Compromise and the debates over Kansas as "little bumps on a trail wandering to heaven knows where" (ibid: 453). Before secession could happen, southerners had to perfect their proslavery ideology and become more united – divisions in the hinterland localities, far from the Washington fray, belied the sense of southern unity (ibid: 564–5).

James M. McPherson's contribution to the literature is the magisterial *Battle Cry of Freedom* (1988), which won the Pulitzer Prize in 1989. McPherson is also interested in the way notions of liberty and freedom and definitions of slavery and liberty registered differently in North and South (McPherson 1988: viii).

McPherson's volume begins with an overview of the nation in 1850. He maintains, as do other scholars, that the institution of slavery had the potential to tear the country apart. "But it was the country's sprawling growth that made the issue so explosive" (ibid: 8). This growth took a variety of forms. It was manifested in an urban explosion, in demographic shifts, in a transportation revolution, and in the development of an industrial and commercial revolution. But even as the country grew and developed, North and South moved farther apart. Instead of focusing on their common history and heritage, northerners and southerners emphasized their differences, the most notable of which was slavery (ibid: 39–40).

The slavery issue flared anew when the United States went to war with Mexico in 1846 and won. The acquisition of thousands of square miles of territory, not to mention the discovery of gold in California, pushed the debate over slavery and freedom in the territories to a new level. President Zachary Taylor along with Senators Henry Clay, John C. Calhoun, and Daniel Webster discussed, debated, and disagreed what procedures should be followed. Clay's Omnibus Bill, designed to placate both sections, served only to create stalemate before it was voted down. Into this vacuum strode Stephen A. Douglas. Breaking the bill into constituent parts, Douglas succeeded in getting the individual pieces of Clay's bill passed. But the result was less a compromise than an armistice: neither North nor South had conceded anything (ibid: 70–7).

Southerners abided by the so-called Compromise of 1850, but through the medium of the Georgia Platform they let it be known that their loyalty was conditional. That condition rested squarely on northern enforcement of the Fugitive Slave Act. For northerners, that was the rub. They found the idea of returning escaped slaves to their southern masters odious and totally incompatible with individual liberty. It is no coincidence that opposition to the Fugitive Slave Law came in the guise of personal liberty laws. Nor should the appearance of Harriet Beecher Stowe's classic *Uncle Tom's Cabin* seem unrelated to that Act. McPherson concedes that it is difficult to gauge the effect Stowe's novel had on the political situation. But there is no doubt that it cut the South to the quick and led the region to adopt what McPherson terms a "defensive–aggressive temper" (McPherson 1988: 89–90).

Part of the reason for the South's defensive stance was the reality that the region was growing rapidly and prospering agriculturally but was not developing industrially; indeed, the South was falling further and further behind the North. Efforts to encourage diversification via the Southern Commercial Convention movement soon segued into a push to expand slavery west and south, into the Plains and down to the Caribbean. It was this push toward expansion that also touched off Civil War in Kansas and led to the rise of the first major sectional party, the Republicans.

Kansas formed the backdrop to the presidential election of 1856. McPherson argues that only issues dealing with "slavery, race and above all Union" had any pull for voters. When the dust settled, Democrat James Buchanan had won the White House. Southerners delighted in having a dough face, a northern Democrat with southern sympathies, at the helm of their party, but they would soon discover that Buchanan's embrace of a slave Kansas would prove, as other "victories" in the 1850s had, "pyrrhic" indeed (McPherson 1988: 158–64).

The major beneficiary of southern "victories," in Kansas and in the 1857 Supreme Court decision *Dred Scott v. Sanford*, was the Republican Party. If southerners feared Republicans were only a front for the abolitionists, they received confirmation of a sort when John Brown attempted to incite a slave rebellion at Harpers Ferry, Virginia. Brown's attempt aborted, but not before he chilled southerners to the bone. As McPherson notes, fear swept the South and produced great confusion as to what would happen in the presidential campaign of 1860 (McPherson 1988: 212 –13).

Abraham Lincoln's election in 1860 stunned the South, but not solely because a "Black Republican" had won. The disturbing feature was the "magnitude of the Republican victory north of the 41st parallel" (ibid: 232). Lincoln's margin hovered near 60 percent. That statistic convinced southerners that they were indeed threatened by a Republican majority in the North.

As might be expected, South Carolina led the South's exodus out of the Union. That venerable old state was followed in rapid succession by the other six states in the Deep South. But then secession slowed. McPherson maintains that all southerners agreed secession was legal; most endorsed the establishment of the Confederacy because they believed it was their only hope to protect slavery and their interests in the western territories. The challenge would be to convince the nonslaveholding majority that they, too, were threatened by a Republican regime. McPherson traces how fire-eaters carefully crafted their message to the white southern majority. The message was not subtle. Secessionist proponents argued virulently that the alternative to secession was abolition, the end of white supremacy and thus the "first step toward racial equality and amalgamation" (ibid: 243). McPherson agrees with other historians who observed that southerners defined white liberty as dependent on black slavery. It would take the assault on Fort Sumter and Lincoln's call for troops to push North Carolina, Tennessee, Virginia, and Arkansas to cast their lot with the Confederacy.

This brief survey of some of the most significant works on the growth of southern sectionalism and the drive toward secession points up some recurring themes. Scholars still see slavery as a fundamental issue that divided North and South, but they have paid increased attention to the way antebellum northerners and southerners interpreted that word. Each region saw in the term "slavery" something distinctly different, but both identified in it the foundation of the early republic. To lose one's liberty implied a degraded, second-class status. In the South, that had added meaning.

Similarly, most works treat the 1840s and 1850s as discrete decades. More than in older works, there is little sense of the inevitability of the conflict. Historians are increasingly aware that average Americans had other concerns during this period; politics did intrude, but they were not the be-all-to-end-all. Still, when the political realm became engulfed in controversy and when radicals in both sections surged to the forefront, northerners and southerners faced the reality that the Founders' experiment was in jeopardy. For southerners, the only alternative was to physically separate and form a "more perfect Union" – one in which slavery and southern rights would be nurtured and protected. As we know, President Lincoln would not allow that to happen.

The years leading to the Civil War will continue to fascinate students and scholars. It marked an era of drama and crisis; it witnessed some of the finest political oratory in American history; and it proved, though not until 1865, that the Union was indivisible.

BIBLIOGRAPHY

Ash, Stephen V. 1988: *Middle Tennessee Society Transformed, 1860–1870: War and Peace in the Upper South*. Baton Rouge: Louisiana State University Press.

Ashworth, John 1995: *Slavery, Capitalism, and Politics in the Antebellum Republic*. Vol. 1: *Commerce and Compromise, 1820–1850*. Cambridge: Cambridge University Press.

Barney, William L. 1974: *The Secessionist Impulse: Alabama and Mississippi in 1860*. Princeton, NJ: Princeton University Press.

Bond, Bradley G. 1995: *Political Culture in the Nineteenth Century South: Mississippi, 1830–1900*. Baton Rouge: Louisiana State University Press.

Buenger, Walter L. 1984: *Secession and the Union in Texas*. Austin: University of Texas Press.

Channing, Steven A. 1974: *Crisis of Fear: Secession in South Carolina*. New York: W. W. Norton.

Cooper, William J., Jr. 1978: *The South and the Politics of Slavery, 1828–1856*. Baton Rouge: Louisiana State University Press.

Cooper, William J., Jr. 1983: *Liberty and Slavery: Southern Politics to 1860*. New York: Alfred A. Knopf.

Craven, Avery O. 1953: *The Growth of Southern Nationalism, 1848–1861*. Baton Rouge: Louisiana State University Press.

Crofts, Daniel W. 1989: *Reluctant Confederates: Upper South Unionists in the Secession Crisis*. Chapel Hill: University of North Carolina Press.

Freehling, William W. 1990: *The Road to Disunion*. Vol. 1: *Secessionists at Bay, 1776–1854*. New York: Oxford University Press.

Genovese, Eugene D. 1965: *The Political Economy of Slavery: Studies in the Economy and Society of the Slave South*. New York: Pantheon Books.

Hahn, Steven 1983: *The Roots of Southern Populism: Yeoman Farmers and the Transformation of the Georgia Upcountry, 1850–1890*. New York: Oxford University Press.

Holt, Michael F. 1978: *The Political Crisis of the 1850s*. New York: John Wiley and Sons.

Johnson, Michael P. 1977: *Toward a Patriarchal Republic: The Secession of Georgia*. Baton Rouge: Louisiana State University Press.

Klein, Maury 1997: *Days of Defiance: Sumter, Secession, and the Coming of the Civil War*. New York: Alfred A. Knopf.

McCardell, John 1979: *The Idea of a Southern Nation: Southern Nationalists and Southern Nationalism, 1830–1860*. New York: W. W. Norton.

McPherson, James M. 1988: *Battle Cry of Freedom: The Civil War Era*. New York: Oxford University Press.

Moore, Barrington, Jr. 1966: *Social Origins of Dictatorship and Democracy: Lord and Peasant in the Making of the Modern World*. Boston: Beacon Press.

Nevins, Allan 1947–71: *Ordeal of the Union*, 8 vols. New York: Charles Scribner's Sons.

Phillips, Ulrich Bonnell 1964: *The Course of the South to Secession*. New York: Hill and Wang.

Potter, David M. 1976: *The Impending Crisis, 1848–1861*. Completed and edited by Don E. Fehrenbacher. New York: Harper Torchbooks.

Sydnor, Charles S. 1948: *The Development of Southern Sectionalism, 1819–1848*. Baton Rouge: Louisiana State University Press.

Thornton, J. Mills, III 1978: *Politics and Power in a Slave Society: Alabama, 1800–1860*. Baton Rouge: Louisiana State University Press.

Walther, Eric H. 1992: *The Fire-Eaters*. Baton Rouge: Louisiana State University Press.

Woods, James M. 1987: *Rebellion and Realignment: Arkansas's Road to Secession*. Fayetteville: University of Arkansas Press.

Wyatt-Brown, Bertram 1982: *Southern Honor: Ethics and Behavior in the Old South*. New York: Oxford University Press.

Wyatt-Brown, Bertram 1985: *Yankee Saints and Southern Sinners*. Baton Rouge: Louisiana State University Press.

CHAPTER FIFTEEN

The Civil War: Military and Political Aspects along with Social, Religious, Gender, and Slave Perspectives

GEORGE C. RABLE

THE historical literature concerning the American South during the Civil War is of both staggering scope and peculiar character. In volume and influence, the more popular works have surpassed the academic tomes, and in several respects neither genre has much shaped the other. The result has not only been differences in the selection of topics, interpretations, and especially style between the books written for larger audiences and those directed toward scholars, but also a persistent and growing fragmentation in the literature. To be sure, historians have long focused on defining the nature of the Confederate experiment and exploring reasons for its failure, and the literature on campaigns and generals continues to grow, but changing interests and fresh ideas have produced far more diffusion than synthesis, as evidenced in several historiographical essays dealing with the more recent literature in the field (McPherson and Cooper 1998).

Given the flood of popular works and the range of academic output, it is perhaps not surprising that the standard survey of the Confederacy, *The Confederate Nation, 1861–1865* (1979), by Emory M. Thomas is now twenty years old and still unrivaled. Beginning with an earlier important collection of essays (Thomas 1971), Thomas set out to reinterpret much of the Confederate experience. Far from being a bastion of cautious conservatism and states' rights, the Confederate States of America underwent a "revolutionary experience" that transformed not only military strategy but especially state administration. Conscription, the suspension of the writ of habeas corpus, and various economic controls all led to the accumulation of power in Richmond regardless of contrary ideological commitments. This nascent centralization also proceeded in the states where governors and legislators dramatically expanded public welfare measures. As government was being transformed, agricultural decline and the pressures of war led to a kind of forced industrialization, complete with expanded administration and urban growth. Even the foundations of slavery were shaken by Confederate policies, and indeed the war caused some fascinating reversals in thinking among politicians and ordinary folk as well. In short, Thomas discovered remarkable fluidity in the Confederacy and much less consistency and rigidity than previous historians had found. By the end of the war, the Confederate experiment had proven to be far more revolutionary than the founders at the Montgomery convention could have envisioned.

Thomas integrated political, military, and diplomatic history into his interpretative analysis but did not create a sweeping narrative. That task was left to a gifted novelist who devoted some twenty years to producing a massive three-volume work. In every page of Shelby Foote's *The Civil War: A Narrative* (1958–74), the author's gift for the well-turned phrase, the beautiful sentence, and finely crafted paragraph carried the reader along almost effortlessly. With admittedly no thesis to advance or vast interpretive scheme, Foote set out simply to tell a story. His narrative favored the Confederate side of the ledger, though more in emphasis and tone because Foote hardly embraced a Lost Cause nostalgia and in fact doubted that southern nation had ever stood much chance of achieving independence. He also set out to restore some geographical balance to popular accounts of the war by devoting many pages to the western theater, including the Trans-Mississippi. With both an eye and ear for the telling anecdote and a remarkable ability to sharply sketch complex characters, Foote created an American epic that for general readers in recent years has largely supplanted the long-beloved volumes of Bruce Catton. Foote's presence in Ken Burns's Civil War television series made him an instant celebrity and solidified his place as the master storyteller of what has often been called an American Iliad.

It is easy for professional historians to criticize Foote for not understanding much about American politics in the Civil War era, for shortchanging their learned studies, and for too often relying on outdated works, but there may also be petty jealousy at work here. The *Journal of American History*, in a remarkable abdication of profes-sional responsibility, did not even deign to review Foote's final volume. What better way to symbolize the gap between the gifted amateurs and professional historians that has both plagued and enlivened the writing of Civil War history.

Like the books of Catton or Allan Nevins, Foote's work represented an older narrative tradition, and one that has been especially rich in the study of military history. In the vast literature on the Army of Northern Virginia, for example, the work of Richmond newspaper editor Douglas Southall Freeman remains preeminent. In his four-volume life of Robert E. Lee (1934–5), but especially in his deeply researched, well-written, and remarkably durable *Lee's Lieutenants* (1942–4), Freeman created monumental works that have cast a long shadow over the entire field. Even today much of the information and even many of the interpretations about the course of the war in the eastern theater can be traced back to this critically important set of books.

No one has examined the published or many of the manuscript sources on the Army of Northern Virginia any more carefully than Freeman. As the subtitle "A Study in Command" announced, Freeman's primary concern was Lee's search for capable subordinates. His explicit assumption was that with better generals Lee could have led his army to victory, and even though there was relatively little about the common soldier in his pages – except for anecdotes that shed light on his analysis of command relationships – Freeman assumed that the rank and file of the Army of Northern Virginia were men who would have won many more victories had not so many corps, division, and brigade commanders been killed or disabled. Freeman handled his large cast of characters with impressive skill, and he has not often been given proper credit for his scrupulous fairness. His attempt to write history as the generals saw it – the much maligned "fog of war" technique – for all its problems, yet had the virtue of seeing the past as indeterminate ground where despite the looming influence of strategic, political, economic, and social factors, human strengths, foibles, and decisions mattered.

Many of the questions and issues raised by Freeman have persisted in Confederate military historiography. More recently, in a conscious attempt to survey southern strategy much like T. Harry Williams had done for the northern side in *Lincoln and His Generals*, Steven Woodworth has offered companion studies of the war's western and eastern theaters. In *Jefferson Davis and His Generals: The Failure of Confederate Command in the West* (1990), Woodworth presented a sympathetic but at the same time critical portrait of a president who, despite enormous ability and commitment, sometimes lapsed into indecision and petulance. Woodworth agreed with other scholars that Davis overlooked the weaknesses of friends and failed to appreciate the virtues of enemies, but he also perceptively noted that the Confederate president performed better during some periods of the war than others. For example, he praised Davis for the planning that culminated in the Shiloh campaign – the Confederacy's best chance for victory in the West. It must have been tempting for Woodworth to boost Davis's standing by turning a notoriously ineffective and unpopular general such as Bragg into a scapegoat, but instead he criticized Davis for not moving against the incompetent and quarrelsome generals in the Army of the Tennessee who undermined Bragg. Indeed, Woodworth attempted to rehabilitate Bragg's historical reputation along with that of Albert Sidney Johnston. In the end, Woodworth argued that a basic insecurity prevented Davis from making bold and timely decisions about a distant theater.

Woodworth's succeeding volume (1995) turned to the war in the East and especially the relationship between Davis and Lee. Here he emphasized Davis's penchant for a defensive strategy to wear down a government far superior in manpower and resources. In contrast, Lee favored the strategic and often the tactical offensive. Yet despite these differences in thinking, the ever tactful Lee never challenged Davis's authority and soon won his unqualified trust. In contrast, neither the flamboyant and ambitious P. G. T. Beauregard nor the secretive and passive Joseph E. Johnston ever worked well with Davis. Yet in one ironic sense neither did Lee. Davis and Lee, Woodworth argued, each offered viable military strategies for their fledgling nation, but the administration followed neither strategy consistently and therefore was bound to fail given the Confederacy's thin margin for error. Despite these problems, however, Woodworth not only praised Lee but also gave the Confederate president unusually high marks for political and military strategy.

Nor was Woodworth alone in rehabilitating Jefferson Davis. In Confederate historiography the study of leaders has loomed large, and during the past two decades new biographies have appeared not only of less important figures but also of the Confederacy's central characters. Even now several scholars are at work on studies of Jefferson Davis, but William C. Davis's *Jefferson Davis: The Man and His Hour* (1991) has set a high standard.

For historian Davis, a basic insecurity lay at the core of the Confederate president's personality, but the tasks of building a nation from the ground up and winning a bloody war against a formidable opponent may have required superhuman abilities. Unfortunately for the Confederacy, Davis was quite ordinary in several respects. His virtues were commonplace and so were his weaknesses: oversensitive to criticism, vacillating, stubborn, excessively loyal to friends, relentlessly unforgiving of enemies.

Yet in several ways Davis's achievements and failures transcended personality flaws. He deserved credit for managing Congress, working with the governors, and creating a civil administration. Despite strategic failure in the West, he prolonged the war beyond what many observers in 1861 might have anticipated.

Biographer Davis of course wrestled with the paradox of a man with vast military knowledge and experience struggling to find a workable strategy and capable generals. He described Davis as an often difficult but not unattractive man, and his biography is at once sharply critical and humanely sympathetic. In several chapters a warmer, more human Davis emerged, a man who could unwind with his family and a few friends, but there also persisted the nagging suspicion that Davis's icy disposition and his often infuriating indecisiveness, combined with a doggedness that could be both impressive and irritating, concealed some unknown problems or unresolved conflicts.

Though a much different personality, Robert E. Lee has presented similar biographical problems, not to mention the fact that Freeman's massive Pulitzer Prize-winning study has deterred other scholars from tackling the subject whole. Emory Thomas admitted as much in the foreword to his recent Lee biography (Thomas 1995), but still managed to carve out a niche in a sizeable literature. For Thomas, Lee's greatness stemmed more from the way he lived than what he accomplished, but even his character contained elements of ambiguity and tragedy. Thomas nicely described how as a young man Lee felt shame for the less than exemplary life of his father Light Horse Harry Lee. Nor did Lee find happiness in a troublesome marriage and large family, and indeed he spent much of his time away from home. A firm believer in self-control, Lee was always dutiful but often frustrated by what he saw as empty or incomplete achievements. Yet Thomas admitted that Lee seldom revealed much of himself in letters or conversation, so to go beyond the traditional portrait of Lee as the model Christian gentleman often required some creative speculation.

Like Woodworth, Thomas argued that Lee believed that a decisive battlefield victory marked the Confederacy's best hope for achieving national independence. Because of his leadership style, Lee could function much more effectively with independent-minded, capable subordinates than with generals who required more direction and supervision. He never lost his taste for the tactical or even the strategic offensive, even when he no longer had enough soldiers to carry out such audacious plans. Thomas's book was hardly a traditional military biography. The author wove Lee's religious convictions and often fatalistic attitudes into the narrative and wrestled with the question of why Lee kept fighting when the cause was presumably lost. In several moving chapters on Lee after the war, Thomas carefully delineated the consistency of Lee's conservative political principles and his paternalistic views on race. Thomas proved to be an empathetic but not uncritical biographer. His coverage of the Confederate period was too brief, and his book does have a certain quirkiness to it, but he gave students of the war the single-volume life of Lee that has so long been needed.

James I. Robertson Jr. accomplished the same feat for Thomas J. "Stonewall" Jackson, but produced a much fatter and fuller biography. A lifelong labor of love, *Stonewall Jackson: The Man, The Soldier, The Legend* (Robertson 1997) is a fitting tribute to author and subject alike. The subtitle suggested the biography's scope, but Robertson also presented Jackson in the full context of his times. More thoroughly than any previous biographer, Robertson probed Jackson's orphan childhood, a period filled with separation and death from which he emerged with an all-consuming sense of duty. Beset by a variety of physical ailments, Jackson showed a remarkable ability to work hard and persevere both as a teacher at the Virginia Military Institute and as a general in Lee's army. Careful attention to medical detail helped Robertson illuminate Jackson's less appealing personality traits, but the extended and sympathetic treatment of Jackson's religious views was even more insightful.

His assessment of Jackson the soldier was fair-minded and detailed, arrived at by weighing conflicting evidence and also weaving in much fresh material from officers, enlisted men, and civilians. Robertson meticulously separated out fact from legend, and his painstaking research uncovered much new information. The story of Jackson's life is of course familiar, and Robertson is no debunker; indeed, this long book should convince most readers that Jackson's skills were critical to prolonging the Confederacy's life beyond its first year of national existence. Robertson went overboard in defending Jackson's lackluster performance during the Seven Days campaign and engaged in a bit of unnecessary bashing of that always tempting target James Longstreet, but his superb book instantly became a remarkable achievement in Confederate biography.

The works of Freeman, Thomas, and Robertson all indirectly illustrate a persistent historiographical problem that has bedeviled scholarship on the war: in reading the literature, it is easy to forget that there was a war outside Virginia. This has hardly been the fault of Thomas Lawrence Connelly, who set out single-handedly to rectify the imbalance. In two substantial volumes on the Army of Tennessee, Connelly (1967, 1971) made the case for the West's importance largely by showing how many bunglers held critical commands in that theater. His focus was intrigue and generals rather than the performance of the soldiers, but even that fairly narrow field left him with abundant material. Like Freeman, he probed command relationships, but Connelly's analysis was much more sharply etched and much less generous. Nor was he an admirer of Jefferson Davis, whose department system of organization had produced delay and disaster.

Connelly's research was prodigious, especially in manuscript collections and National Archives records, his prose supple and appealing. He created the classic standard work but not by avoiding controversy. Long before his later iconoclastic study of Lee (Connelly 1977), Connelly directly confronted the Virginian's (and Virginia's) dominance of Confederate historiography. A key distinction was geography: Army of Tennessee commanders had to defend comparatively large expanses of territory, including the southern nation's agricultural heartland, and that task greatly complicated the usual transportation and logistical problems. Connelly conceded that the Army of Tennessee lost more major battles than it won, yet its fighting men showed remarkable resilience. Connelly was less critical of Braxton Bragg than previous writers, but as several reviewers noted, there were no heroes in these volumes. Instead, Connelly described in loving detail the shifting alliances and petty disputes that dogged the western high command throughout the war and placed them in a larger and properly political context. The government's penchant for transferring troublesome generals to the western theater along with the steady attrition of corps and division commanders produced no end of troubles. So, ironically, Connelly sought to redress an imbalance in the literature by presenting an unattractive portrait of a neglected army.

He later joined with Archer Jones to reexamine the military strategy and politics of the western theater. The much shorter but more analytical *The Politics of Command* (Connelly and Jones 1973) exerted far more influence on subsequent scholarship than the fuller and more readable Army of Tennessee volumes. The authors criticized Lee for lacking both knowledge and interest in the western theater and described the great Confederate chieftain as essentially a parochial Virginian. The so-called western concentration bloc – a complex alliance of Virginia and South Carolina families, anti-Bragg generals, Kentucky stalwarts, and friends of P. G. T. Beauregard – all dreamed of grand offensives in the West.

Connelly and Jones documented a veritable tug-of-war between Lee and the westerners over transferring troops between the two theaters. Thwarted by divisions in their own ranks, poor performance, and Davis's unwieldy department system, western generals had trouble making their case to the administration. Davis's tendency to leave troops where they were, along with his deep distrust of Beauregard and Joseph Johnston, fatally undermined the Confederacy's position in the West, while it allowed Lee to launch costly offensives in the East. Yet, as the authors point out, at least through much of 1863 Davis proved surprisingly responsive to the strategic suggestions of the western concentration bloc. Moreover, there was a curious kind of tension between the sympathetic treatment of these generals in this volume and Connelly's scathing indictments in his work on the Army of Tennessee. Had the Richmond administration paid more attention to the western theater, would the defeats and disasters simply have occurred on a larger scale?

Not surprisingly, the Connelly–Jones thesis has influenced work on Confederate strategy but has generated far more controversy than consensus. In an excellent though brief book, *Two Great Rebel Armies*, Richard McMurry (1989) offered a well-reasoned critique. McMurry agreed that the Army of Tennessee had been relatively neglected by historians. The eastern battlefields had received far more visitors, the Army of Northern Virginia attracted far more attention from Civil War buffs, and even the sources for studying the western armies could not compare to the vast array of materials on the Army of Northern Virginia. Like Connelly, McMurry argued that geography (including problems with communication and organization) played a crucial role, but he added, much like George Pickett after Gettysburg, that a group of capable Yankee generals also contributed to Confederate losses in the West.

But even conceding these points, the Army of Northern Virginia was simply the stronger of the two armies. The superior Virginia militia system, more officers and non-commissioned officers with military experience (including training at various military schools), and better educated troops gave Lee's army built-in advantages. An even more telling comparison involved general officers. Not only did the Army of Northern Virginia have more experienced generals, it also benefited from Lee's steady leadership. In contrast, the Army of Tennessee went through a series of tumultuous command changes involving generals who could never measure up to Lee. In short, the Army of Northern Virginia performed above expectations and, except at the battle of Chickamauga, the Army of Tennessee proved consistently disappointing. Turning Connelly's argument on its head, McMurry concluded that a concentration of forces should have taken place in Virginia rather than in the West.

All this scholarship assumed that the quality of the enlisted men in each army was roughly equal, but no one has yet tackled this most difficult of comparative studies.

Instead, beginning with Bell Irvin Wiley's (1943) classic, *The Life of Johnny Reb: The Common Soldier of the Confederacy*, historians have focused on the experiences of Confederate soldiers in general rather than on close examinations of men in particular armies. At a time when most Civil War historians did not look far beyond the *Official Records* and a few other standard published sources, Wiley introduced his readers to the fascinating diaries and letters (many unpublished) of the common soldiers. Although his work did not immediately change the course of scholarship, he was writing "new military history" before anyone had even thought of coining the term.

Wiley did not ignore the blemishes and shortcomings of Confederate fighting men, but he considered these yeomen in the ranks to be the heart and soul of the southern war effort. He unabashedly admired their endurance and courage in the face of persistent supply shortages and formidable enemy armies. In topical chapters, Wiley presented his heroes in their own words. Here were men complaining about food, writing to their home folks, facing their first battle, shivering in winter quarters, indulging in a few vices, praying to their God, dying of disease, and struggling with loneliness and boredom. More recent works on soldiers in the Army of Tennessee (Daniel 1991) and on men who served in the Army of Northern Virginia during the war's final year (Power 1998) have added more detail and analysis to this general picture.

By carefully examining available muster rolls and making some simple computations, Wiley discovered a surprising number of foreign-born soldiers in Confederate ranks. Although both the young and the old were well represented in the armies, the bulk of the soldiers were between eighteen and twenty-nine years of age. Some were quite well educated, though most of the privates were barely literate at best. Class resentments occasionally flared up, and most soldiers exhibited parochialism and state pride. The typical Confederate private had all the strengths and weaknesses of his yeoman background. A man of sometimes contradictory virtues and vices who was not always well disciplined and whose morale sometimes sagged, he became an excellent soldier where it counted most, on the battlefield. The deep research and appealing style of Wiley's book made it an enduring one and still the best single volume on the Confederate soldier (see also Linderman 1987; McPherson 1997; Mitchell 1988; Robertson 1988).

Although Wiley devoted a few chapters to weapons, fighting, and courage, like the Johnny Rebs he studied he spent far more time in camp than in battle. Many subsequent studies of the common soldier, North and South, have had trouble linking combat with camp life, but by the same token, grand strategy could not achieve much apart from the enlisted men's devotion and bravery. Hence the study of tactics necessarily filled a gap between works focusing on command decisions and studies most concerned with daily routine. In the popular imagination, dramatic Confederate infantry charges at Gettysburg and elsewhere epitomized the southern war effort. In their unfailingly provocative *Attack and Die: Civil War Military Tactics and the Southern Heritage*, Grady McWhiney and Perry Jamieson (1982) argued that Confederates strongly preferred the tactical offensive and paid a heavy price in blood. As a consequence Confederates lost a high percentage of officers, an extraordinary number of generals, and in essence "murdered themselves" (ibid: 24).

Many Confederate officers had led charges with muzzle-loaders during the Mexican War, but the advent of the rifle (and to a lesser degree rifled artillery) made such tactics obsolete. Yet Confederates did not adjust their tactics to the technology and instead suffered casualties that their young nation could ill afford against a much stronger opponent. McWhiney and Jamieson presented useful descriptions of tactical formations and noted how the use of skirmishers and entrenchments evolved during the war. They added depth to the discussion by considering all three branches of the service: infantry, artillery, and cavalry.

The explanation of the supposed southern penchant for the offensive became the most controversial element in the book. The authors argued that the Confederates' Celtic heritage made them more aggressive and reckless; they discussed in some depth perceived differences between the supposedly "Cavalier" South and "Puritan" North. Critics have raised questions about the meaning of the casualty figures, demanded more direct evidence of Celtic influence, and generally rejected the argument for being reductionist. Yet by introducing their cultural argument, McWhiney and Jamieson – perhaps unintentionally – raised larger questions about the very character of Confederate nationalism.

Figuring out why so many white southerners fought and died has presented a major problem for historians, just as sustaining morale severely taxed the political, economic, and ideological resources available to Confederate politicians and generals. For the past twenty years historians have vigorously debated the strengths and weaknesses of Confederate nationalism. In his influential work *After Secession: Jefferson Davis and the Failure of Confederate Nationalism*, Paul Escott (1978) portrayed the Confederate president as a reluctant secessionist who in many ways well represented the ambivalent opinions of many southern whites. Aware of the explosive potential of class divisions, Davis sought to forge national unity along racial lines, while at the same time downplaying slavery as an important element of the Confederate cause. In messages and speeches Davis talked of fighting for traditional liberties and compared the war for southern independence to the American Revolution. Rhetoric, however, could not paper over internal divisions. Indeed, the Richmond administration's centralizing policies offended both planters and plain folk.

Escott's most original contribution was his analysis of disaffection among the nonslaveholders. Thoroughly mining neglected War Department records, he used telling quotations from letters and petitions to show how economic problems and conscription exacerbated class tensions and helped sap morale. The result was a high rate of desertion from southern armies and much suffering on the homefront. Individual states adopted unprecedented relief measures, but the Confederate government never came to grips with the crisis in public welfare. In Escott's view, Governor Joseph E. Brown of Georgia had a much better grasp of ordinary people's needs than Jefferson Davis. By 1863 the president increasingly appealed to fears of Yankee occupation and depredations to sustain public unity, but such negative rhetoric merely signified desperation. Escott carefully documented growing internal political divisions that fostered disaffection and eventually produced a peace movement. During the war's final months some Confederate leaders were even willing to sacrifice slavery for independence. In the end Davis failed to inspire loyalty to the cause, could not work with military and political critics, and, most importantly, never understood the problems of ordinary southerners.

Escott's appraisal of Jefferson Davis was much more subtle than can be suggested by a brief summary, but his basic arguments laid the groundwork for scholars to question the viability of Confederate nationalism. In a major work that combined ambitious synthesis, historiographical discussion, and provocative arguments, Richard E. Beringer, Herman Hattaway, Archer Jones, and William N. Still Jr. (1986) moved away from conventional battlefield explanations for Confederate defeat. Answering the question posed in their title, *Why the South Lost the Civil War*, the authors maintained that white southerners lacked the will to win.

The authors began by rejecting several traditional explanations for Confederate defeat. Despite disadvantages in manpower and industry, the seceding states raised formidable armies and underwent remarkable economic changes. Their real weakness lay in a defective nationalism. Following the lead of an earlier essay by Kenneth M. Stampp (1980), Beringer and his colleagues strongly denied the existence of a distinctive South or a prevailing sense of southern unity; instead guilt over slavery undermined the Confederate cause from the beginning. Building on the earlier work of Hattaway and Jones (1983), Beringer et al. emphasized the indecisive nature of Civil War combat. Both sides fought according to roughly the same military principles and therefore produced a battlefield stalemate for nearly four years. Even Union victories created logistical headaches for armies forced to occupy vast stretches of enemy territory. Nor did states' rights seriously undermine the Confederacy. Like Escott, these authors maintained that governors such as Brown in Georgia and Zebulon Baird Vance in North Carolina won important concessions from the Richmond government and served their people well.

Religion had earlier buttressed Confederate confidence in their cause, but battlefield losses raised questions about whether God was now punishing the southern people for sins ranging from swearing to slavery. Using the psychological theory of cognitive dissonance, the authors argued that uncertainty and guilt led Confederates to doubt their own virtue and criticize their own government.

In the end, the surrender of southern armies came because too many Confederates no longer believed strongly enough in their own cause. Had there been a deeper commitment the soldiers would simply have melted into the countryside and launched a guerrilla struggle that the North could not have won. But religious fatalism, guilt over slavery, and dissonance about the Confederate experiment prematurely ended the struggle for southern independence. After the war many southern whites claimed that they had fought for states' rights rather than for slavery, but they had really lost the war because of their own defective nationalism.

The authors attempted to link military events with their other arguments but with only limited success; their frequent references to military theorists were both enlightening and baffling, and their efforts to portray the Union blockade as ineffective were unpersuasive. Did battlefield losses cause morale to sink, or did a defective sense of purpose undermine Confederate determination? No one could deny that Beringer and his colleagues had presented a long and thought-provoking answer to an old question, but recognition of this achievement did not win widespread acceptance for their unconventional conclusions.

Instead, scholars either rejected their interpretations or set out to examine Confederate nationalism for its own sake rather than as an explanation for southern defeat. In a series of deeply researched and cogently argued lectures, Drew Faust (1988) focused on the intellectual elements of the problem. In her view, any sense of nationalism had to be created. Rejecting distinctions between spurious and genuine nationalism, she set out to explore Confederate nationalism on its own terms, but in doing so ran into some of the same problems faced by earlier scholars. Northerners and southerners shared a common language and history; ethnic differences were hardly clearcut; the Confederacy's founding fathers had closely identified themselves with the American Revolution. Like Escott, Faust recognized the potential import- ance of class divisions among southerners and agreed that the spokesmen for Con- federate nationalism represented the views of a planter elite that nevertheless had to win the support of a much broader constituency.

According to Faust, Christianity became the "most fundamental source of legit- imation for the Confederacy" (Faust 1988: 22). Davis and other Confederate leaders frequently invoked divine assistance for their cause. Yet from the beginning religion also proved a source of weakness. A supposed covenant between God and the south- ern people brought the Almighty's favor but could also provoke his wrath. Reverting to the earlier form of the Jeremiad, southern preachers scrutinized the sins of their fellow southerners while linking evangelical and republican ideologies. In some respects the clergy, part of the intellectual class but committed to spreading the gospel among the common people, embodied the tensions between elitism and democracy that frustrated Confederate nationalists. Their preaching against materi- alism and greed might focus on sins such as extortion but could not resolve the tensions between markets and paternalism.

In dealing with slavery, Faust moved far beyond the guilt thesis. Southern clergy criticized the selfishness of slaveholders while upholding the institution itself. The proslavery argument retained its vitality throughout the war yet was severely strained by pressures from both Union armies and restless slaves. Talk of reform could have both strengthened and undermined slavery, but in the end the war simply produced many of the changes secessionists had hoped to avoid. By attempting to address Confederate nationalism on its own merits, Faust revealed both strengths and weak- nesses while leaving the viability of the Confederate experiment still open to question.

In turn that issue raised a more narrowly political question about what sort of state Confederate leaders were attempting to create. For years, Frank Owsley's (1959) argument that a passion for states' rights had sapped the national government's strength and resources had been the dominant view and one that focused on explain- ing why the Confederacy lost the war. A perceptive comparative study of the two governments revealed some complex and surprising differences between centraliza- tion in the two nations (Bensel 1990). Following Faust's lead, George C. Rable in *The Confederate Republic: A Revolution Against Politics* (1994) analyzed Confederate political culture in its own right. Because of a growing disillusionment with political parties during the antebellum period, the Confederacy's founding fathers intention- ally set out to create a Christian slaveholders' republic without a political party system. Their vision emphasized social harmony, though they had to downplay antidemocratic elements in their conservative ideology. Given the role of veteran politicians at the Montgomery convention that created the Confederate States of America and the exuberant political participation by southern voters before the war, this revolution against politics promised to be difficult if not abortive.

But in trying to curtail such staples of partisanship as executive patronage and pork barrel legislation, the Confederate Constitution became a reforming document. The president of the Confederacy would serve a six-year term and be ineligible for reelection. Everyone from ministers to textbook writers extolled the virtues of a purified republic that would deserve divine favor. Jefferson Davis and other Confederates invoked the spirit of 1776 to defend their classical notions of political culture.

In their dreams for national unity, the Confederacy's founders hoped citizens would rally around Jefferson Davis as a second George Washington. The barely publicized elections in the fall of 1861 promised social and political harmony, but battlefield losses and the inevitable political carping caused serious divisions in the Confederacy. Strong believers in the liberty of states, communities and individuals resisted conscription and the suspension of habeas corpus; but their attacks on political centralization still occurred within an antiparty framework. State elections along with 1863 congressional contests provided opportunities for expressing disagreement and even disaffection, although except in North Carolina did not produce rival political organizations. Skillful politicians such as Brown and Vance created headaches for Davis, who nevertheless received almost everything he asked for from the Congress. Because the opposition to the administration refused to coalesce into a political party, it became both fragmentary and ineffective. Rather than being a liability as several other scholars argued, Rable maintained that the absence of a party system was a source of strength in the Confederacy. Despite a peace movement that gathered momentum after the summer of 1863, the political support for the war effort and for the Davis government remained remarkably strong across the South.

This last point became the centerpiece of Gary W. Gallagher's tightly argued *The Confederate War* (1997). Vigorously responding to the "loss of will" arguments, Gallagher criticized recent scholarship on internal divisions in the Confederacy and drew the deceivingly simple conclusion that the Confederates lost the war on the battlefield. To Gallagher, the most remarkable fact about the experiment in southern nationalism was not its weakness but its strength and staying power. The willingness of soldiers and civilians alike to make incredible sacrifices for their cause belied attempts to explain Confederate defeat by exploring social, economic, or political fissures. Gallagher questioned the extent of yeoman discontent and marshaled statistics and other evidence to demonstrate the relative absence of class conflict. The problem of desertions proved more troublesome to his case, and he also tended to understate problems on the homefront.

Gallagher denied that guilt about slavery undermined Confederate nationalism by pointing out that the advocates of such a position have offered precious little evidence to support it. He duly noted that common suffering and sacrifice and even theological questions about God's purpose fostered renewed commitment more than disaffection, and he offered especially telling evidence of how both soldiers and civilians expressed devotion to the cause quite late in the war. Students of the conflict should never mistake war weariness for loss of will. Gallagher showed an appreciation for the strength of simple patriotism that is too often lost in our own more cynical age. His point that the armies became the focal point for Confederate nationalism provided a helpful answer to an old question.

Gallagher also confronted directly the scholarly second-guessing on Confederate military strategy. The southern people themselves insisted that their armies take the offensive, and Gallagher pointed out that a defensive strategy would have exacted high political costs and considerable casualties. The "offensive defensive" then was the best strategy the Confederacy could have adopted and the one most likely to have brought victory. He thus accorded Lee high marks, as did a monograph focusing on the critical months of 1862 (Harsh 1998). Gallagher likewise dismissed the guerrilla warfare option for running counter to the antebellum military heritage, involving the abandonment of too much territory, making foreign diplomatic recognition less likely, and greatly weakening a slaveholding society. And of course the paradox remained that many yeomen continued to fight for the independence of a republic based on chattel slavery. So the question became explaining Confederate persistence rather than exploring internal weaknesses.

In a fine study of Virginia that offered the kind of detailed research necessary for not only unraveling this difficult question but also probing the nature of Confederate loyalty, William Blair (1998) explored the ways in which both state and national governments addressed the problems faced by soldiers and their families. Blair cleverly finessed the issue by acknowledging the strength of internal dissent and arguing that both national and state governments responded to Virginians' problems and that public discontent did not become disloyalty. Even during the halcyon days right after Lincoln's call for troops, Virginians entered into the fight with their prickly sense of independence intact. They readily supported their state and national governments while freely criticizing their leaders.

Blair's book paid particular attention to Albermarle, Campbell, and Augusta counties – three interior areas chosen on the basis of their diverse agriculture and rich extant primary sources. Blair found evidence of resistance to conscription, food shortages, burdensome taxes, and even desertion, but he completely upset traditional notions – originating with Bell Wiley – of how Confederate morale went into steady decline (Wiley 1956). Indeed, amidst the early privations – and Blair was especially good at analyzing problems with food supplies – hopes remained high each time the Army of northern Virginia won another battle.

Blair recognized that the expansion of government power often came at the behest of Virginia citizens. Numerous petitions to the War Department requested various occupational exemptions from conscription. As the war dragged on and especially after the 1863 elections, political leaders showed much less favoritism toward the planters and worked to equalize the war's burdens. Increasingly, therefore, complaints about impressment, for example, came from more prosperous farmers. Limited resources and federal armies stymied these efforts at rallying the people. Yet images of barbaric Yankees and the reality of plundering soldiers, not to mention memories of shared sacrifice, helped forge a greater ideological loyalty even in defeat.

But of course whether historians argued that Confederate nationalism was defective from the start or that southern citizens had fought hard to secure independence, whether they criticized Davis and his generals or claimed that the offensive-defensive was the best possible Confederate strategy, their accounts all concluded with the death of the Confederacy. Some argued that such an outcome was inevitable given superior northern resources, while more recently Gallagher and other historians have maintained that much depended on the outcome of battles. During the war itself, however, another factor loomed much larger than it has in the historiography: how would Europe respond to a Civil War in North America? Anyone reading the northern or southern newspapers of the period quickly notices extensive discussion about the possibility of foreign intervention, yet students of the Confederacy have curiously slighted the war's diplomatic history.

The standard account of Confederate foreign relations remains Frank Lawrence Owsley's *King Cotton Diplomacy* – a book that will soon be seventy years old. Traveling to Europe on a Guggenheim fellowship, Owsley conducted extensive research in both British and French archives. His book described efforts by Confederate diplomats to encourage European intervention in the Civil War whether through diplomatic recognition, mediation, or assistance against the Union blockade. The hope of Confederate political leaders – as expressed in Owsley's title – was that dependence on southern cotton would force the European powers to come to the southern nation's assistance. The early cotton embargo clearly rested on this nearly unshakeable assumption. Owsley noted how antebellum politicians had created the notion of King Cotton and how both politicians and newspaper editors had trumpeted it during the war. This theory was eventually modified, and the European powers weathered the "cotton famine," but the Confederate government continued to discourage cotton growing.

Although Napoleon III was favorably disposed toward mediation, the French government refused to act without British cooperation. Confederate diplomats also hoped that British hostility toward a powerful United States and French ambitions in Mexico might win support for their cause, but Owsley's book documented at length the reasons why such hopes were soon dashed. Owsley denied that idealism or fear of wheat shortages discouraged British intervention. Instead he maintained – with a flood of statistics but little direct evidence – that war profits drove British reluctance to help mediate the American conflict. His analysis of how the British substituted Indian cotton for southern cotton was much more persuasive. As did a number of later historians, Owsley noted how successfully ships ran the northern blockade and presumably became part of a lucrative wartime traffic; but he did not compare prewar and wartime trade levels – a truer measure of the blockade's effectiveness.

In treating Confederate diplomacy, Owsley was much more descriptive than analytical. He wrote traditional diplomatic history, crafting his narrative from notes and dispatches, and did not offer a critical assessment of Davis, Secretary of State Judah P. Benjamin, or the Confederate ministers in Europe. His research was deep and revealing, but his conclusions modest and in some cases hard to pin down. Owsley's book remains a readable and fairly comprehensive treatment that likely discouraged other scholars from tackling the subject, and so Confederate diplomacy remains a topic much in need of more creative approaches.

Instead scholars have looked for fresh subjects and new angles in studying the wartime South – many of them far removed from traditional concerns with Confederate nationalism and the war's outcome. To be sure, some recent works obviously addressed aspects of older questions, but virtually all of them reflected the explosion of interest in social history and the belated discovery of the war years by social historians.

As part of a rich and expanding scholarship on slavery that appeared during the 1960s and 1970s, James L. Roark's *Masters Without Slaves* (1977) essayed a comprehensive account of the slaveholding class in crisis. The result was an indispensable book based on thorough research that addressed a host of intriguing questions. For some planters, secession became a crusade to protect slave property, but war inevitably threatened the stability of the entire system. The central issue became whether slavery would be safer inside or outside the Union. Yet planters also worried about the future of a slaveholding society increasingly isolated in the world and feared the growth of class conflict at home. Early euphoria often overcame doubts, and for some planters a faith in King Cotton made them confident of victory.

Once the war began patriotic planters shifted from staple crops to food production, though some pointedly insisted on raising cotton. Planters struggled to get along without overseers, and with the exodus of men to the armies, many women had to manage plantations. Production and incomes plummeted as resentment against planter privilege grew. But for Roark, the real crisis came with the erosion and eventual destruction of slavery. Efforts to tighten control on slaves largely failed as the institution crumbled; planters lost slaves to impressment, runaways, and Union armies. Power shifted from the big house to the slave cabins as planters struggled with emotions ranging from pity to outrage. Saddened and disappointed – in many ways captives of their own ideology – they especially lamented the desertion of what they paternalistically called "their" black families.

Yet according to Roark, despite war weariness and the general demoralization of slave labor, proslavery ideology survived. Even in defeat, planters still assumed that black labor would be worthless without coercion, and adjustment to free labor occurred haltingly at best. The plantations had survived, but a way of life had vanished.

Roark's tight focus on the white elite left much of the story untold. In studying slavery in Civil War Georgia, Clarence Mohr (1986) examined the response of masters and slaves alike to a series of wrenching changes. By dealing with a single state, Mohr could assess the influence of geography on white and black behavior. In the coastal regions, for instance, slaves began entering Union lines as soon as the sea islands were captured by federal forces, and some enlisted in the army to rescue their families. In the interior, blacks proved more cautious. For their part planters also abandoned their coastal lands but found it difficult to resume farming operations elsewhere.

Mohr nicely recaptured the complexity of decisions made by both planters and slaves as their world fell apart. Like the planters, many slaves disliked being uprooted from familiar surroundings, but the war also revealed that their vaunted masters were no longer invincible. The transfer of slaves from agriculture to industry (in addition to work on fortifications) increased contacts with free blacks, separated families, and worried slaveholders. The growth of cities also undermined agrarian values and broke down slave discipline.

Mohr argued that the uncertainties of war not only changed the institution of slavery but fostered a significant movement to reform the institution. Methodist and Baptist ministers proposed legal recognition of slave marriages, prohibitions against breaking up families by sale, and the removal of restrictions on slave education. During the debate on enlisting slave soldiers at the end of the war, white Georgians were perhaps moving toward some form of gradual emancipation. Mohr undoubtedly exaggerated the strength of such reform impulses, but his book nicely described the breakdown of slavery in both the countryside and urban areas. A well-researched work attuned to subtleties of place and psychology, *On the Threshold of Freedom* established a model for similar studies of other states.

The disintegration of slavery indirectly raised other questions about wartime changes in the southern social order. Traditional Confederate narratives had presented heroic accounts of women's sacrifices and struggles, but the explosion of scholarly interest in gender history inevitably produced more challenging and ambivalent interpretations. In *Mothers of Invention*, Drew Faust (1996) did for white women of the slaveholding class what James Roark had done for male planters – carefully explore the war's impact on their lives and sense of identity.

Although recognizing the power of class and especially race, Faust argued that the war greatly affected gender relations. Elite women closely followed the secession debates and then searched for ways they could help the war effort. Some felt useless and frustrated, but many joined sewing circles and other organizations that offered a larger public role. In the meantime women had to assume greater responsibilities in their households as men trooped off to war. Difficult decisions about moving, the trials of refugee life, and the demands of household manufacturing all tested their mettle. Many women also had to assume "mastery" over slaves but sometimes found themselves fearfully "dependent" on their own "servants." Struggles with overseers and recalcitrant slaves added to their frustrations.

Economic hardship forced some middle- and upper-class women to work for wages for the first time. As teachers, government clerks, and nurses, women had decidedly mixed reactions to labor outside the household and often tried to preserve their class privileges at all costs. Yet many women also realized that they could no longer count on men. They missed husbands who were off fighting, struggled to manage unruly children, and tried to either express or stifle their own discontent. Single women worried about their marital prospects and became emotionally dependent on female friends. Faust tried to recapture the interior lives of these elite women by exploring their reading and writing habits. In diaries, letters, and petitions, and more indirectly in Augusta Evans's novel *Macaria*, women raised hard questions about gender, family, and war without abandoning traditional mores. Faust argued that many elite women used religious language to deal with public issues, though Confederate military defeats often caused despondency. She described a spiritual crisis for elite women but did not exaggerate their despair or fail to note the resiliency of their faith (see also Faust 1990).

The book focused on but did not become obsessed with gender and wore its theoretical garb gracefully. Faust dealt with the women who practiced shooting, dressed as men to enter the armies, or served as spies, but did not turn them into nineteenth-century feminists. Her attention to the material culture of clothing – a much neglected subject among historians – allowed for a perceptive exploration of changing boundaries of gender during the war. Suffering and sacrifice forever shaped women's lives even as they worked to restore families and some semblance of normal life after the war. The book closed with many ambiguities and contradictions for these women unresolved because Faust carefully avoided facile generalizations.

In Faust's book and an earlier study of white women from all classes (Rable 1989), the disillusionment, class resentments, and social tensions were sometimes overemphasized, but this is hardly surprising because quotations and anecdotes naturally focused on discontent. In a brilliantly original study of a single Virginia county, Daniel Sutherland (1995) nicely balanced traditional notions about Confederate persistence with the more recent emphasis on internal conflicts. His *Seasons of War* sought to recapture the life of what he called a "Confederate community" in Culpeper County, Virginia. In an area occupied by both armies at various times, citizens saw more than enough "hard war," and they witnessed battles fought in their own back yard at Cedar Mountain and Brandy Station.

Sutherland paid close attention to the mundane and sometimes sickening details of Union and Confederate camp life, his vivid descriptions and stories offering little comfort for romantics. He hauled readers into the midst of battle, and his daring choice to write much of this history in the present tense gave readers a wonderful sense of immediacy and contingency. He evoked an era filled with tales of fascinating people in a way that more professional historians should emulate. Sutherland's success rested on prodigious research in family papers, church records, court documents, deeds, marriage registers, tax reports, and of course soldier diaries and letters. But a strong sense of place and a talent for vivid descriptions of landscape, objects, and people transported readers back into the world of Culpeper County. He recounted moments from the lives of ordinary and extraordinary people and made the reader feel almost at home. Here were soldiers, local politicians, women, slaves, Yankee invaders, and generals, unforgettable characters each in their own right. Sutherland's book did not directly address any of the so-called big questions that normally occupy his professional colleagues, but his ability to bring to life a county and people at war nevertheless made his book a historiographical landmark.

Yet if historians have been narrowing their field of vision – Reid Mitchell (1996: 614) even predicted that the future of Civil War history lay in community studies – they have also tried to look at the war's larger picture from new angles. Stephen Ash's *When the Yankees Came* (1995) tackled the neglected topic of the southern states under military occupation. Even before the federal armies arrived, politicians and planters had stepped up slave patrols, imposed martial law, and generally sought to preserve their own authority. Recognizing the diversity of civilian experience and federal policies, Ash explored the "garrisoned towns," the Confederate frontier (areas vulnerable to Union raids), and a "no man's land" (not under direct Yankee control but not subject to Confederate authority either). Southern Unionists faced the greatest persecution on the Confederate frontier, held their own in areas near garrisoned towns, and gained the upper hand in places firmly held by federal armies. In all three areas, restless and increasingly assertive slaves eventually seized greater freedom.

Wartime deprivations fueled class resentments among whites, but sectional and racial loyalties kept such antagonisms from boiling over into a social revolution. Yet spying, thievery, illicit trade with slaves, and free-labor ideology all produced fissures that set neighbor against neighbor. Refugees and especially women felt the social strains and endured the economic hardships.

Ash maintained that Confederate resistance inevitably spurred the federals to move from a conciliatory approach to a policy of confiscation and emancipation. Therefore the experience of occupation had a lasting influence on the psyches of white southerners, though the greatest irony of all was that Appomattox left many Confederates with both the will and wherewithal to resist what at first seemed to be the growing power of native Unionists and the advent of a free-labor system that promised to revolutionize race relations. Although most white southerners found little cause for joy in the spring and summer of 1865, many others clung to a traditional faith that in God's good time all might be well with them again.

Indeed scriptural references pervaded both public and private discourse during war, yet the whole topic of religion's role in the war has been scandalously neglected. The monographs dealing with the subject have generally been narrowly conceived, and even though several scholars (see especially Faust 1987) have treated the war's spiritual aspects at least in passing, no large synthetic work has yet appeared. *Religion and the American Civil War* (Miller, Stout, and Wilson 1998) presented a collection of essays originally delivered as papers at a 1994 conference on religion and the war held at the Louisville Presbyterian Theological Seminary. These creative and well-crafted pieces were pathbreaking in their own right and should inspire much future work. The editors concluded that "religion stood at the center of the American Civil War experience" (ibid: 4), but most of the essays focused on the southern side of the story. Mark Noll (1998) dealt with the evolution of more general American attitudes toward the Bible – especially a belief in biblical literalism – though his treatment of southern defenses of slavery was in many ways the most interesting and most import-ant aspect. Taking the argument one step further, Eugene Genovese (1998) main-tained that Christian orthodoxy buttressed southern slavery and vice versa, allowing southerners to stand firm in defense of biblical teachings and resist northern "Higher Law" arguments. Unlike Genovese, Bertram Wyatt-Brown (1998) described the southern clergy as ambivalent about both slavery and secession, in part because they feared the effects of revolutionary upheaval. This sometimes sharp disagreement hearkened back to questions about the nature and strength of Confederate will.

Debate about such fundamental ideas, however, ignored important distinctions between ideologues and audiences, between timeless and time-bound rationaliza-tions. What Kurt Berends (1998) termed the "religious military press" in the Con-federacy made piety more masculine, emphasized the workings of divine providence, helped soldiers cope with death, developed a Confederate civil religion, and even tried to explain battlefield defeats. Yet all these issues presented dilemmas not only for individual believers but for their denominations. An essay by Paul Harvey (1998) highlighted the divisions among antebellum southern Baptists, the sometimes uncer-tain support for the Confederate cause, and the struggles to explain the southern nation's demise. On a more microscopic level, Daniel Stowell (1998) showed how Stonewall Jackson's death raised hard questions about sin, punishment, and divine purpose.

One great virtue of Miller, Stout, and Wilson's volume was that the authors paid suitable attention to the efforts of the laity at home and in the armies to fathom the war's religious significance and thus went beyond the usual kind of organizational study. Elizabeth Fox-Genovese (1998) emphasized the commitment of women (North and South) to traditional biblical teachings on female roles in home and church. Yet with the men off fighting, as Drew Faust (1998) observed in an essay that nicely dovetailed with her book *Mothers of Invention*, religious practice during the war became more private and more dominated by women. As the casualties mounted, a crisis of faith forced women into even greater struggles against hardship and foisted on them larger religious responsibilities. But if women's religious convictions were sorely tested, what of the men in uniform? Reid Mitchell (1998) argued that the southern Christian soldier was much more a postwar invention than a wartime reality, and in any case, the average enlisted man was more interested in finding ways to cope with suffering and death than in Confederate civil religion. Richmond, Virginia, of course, became the center of efforts to weld religion to the cause of southern independence, and an innovative essay by Harry S. Stout and Christopher Grasso

(1998) demonstrated how religious arguments buttressed citizen morale. Despite ambiguities and complexities, and the shifting emphases of official propaganda, Confederate religious themes survived long after the war.

Miller, Stout, and Wilson organized and linked these disparate essays, but the very incompleteness of the volume suggested a future research agenda. We know very little about African-American religious expression during the war, and we know virtually nothing about the operation of local congregations in either the North or the South. We may need more focused studies on particular places, and social historians may need to understand military matters much better, and surely writers mainly interested in generals and battles have much to learn from events, ideas, and people far removed from the camps and killing fields. To study more carefully overlooked areas and topics, while at the same time imagining broader and more creative answers to both old and new questions, will remain the challenge. And the more traditional biographies and campaign studies will still appear. All this will mean that the outpouring of new work about this most written-about period of southern history will not slow down any time soon.

BIBLIOGRAPHY

Ash, Stephen V. 1995: *When the Yankees Came: Conflict and Chaos in the Occupied South, 1861–1865.* Chapel Hill: University of North Carolina Press.

Bensel, Richard Franklin 1990: *Yankee Leviathan: The Origins of Central State Authority in America, 1859–1877.* Cambridge: Cambridge University Press.

Berends, Kurt O. 1998: Wholesome Reading Purifies and Elevates the Man: The Religious Military Press in the Confederacy. In Randall M. Miller, Harry S. Stout, and Charles Reagan Wilson (eds.), *Religion and the American Civil War.* New York: Oxford University Press, 131–66.

Beringer, Richard E., Hattaway, Herman, Jones, Archer, and Still, William N., Jr. 1986: *Why the South Lost the Civil War.* Athens: University of Georgia Press.

Blair, William Alan 1998: *Virginia's Private War: Feeding Body and Soul in the Confederacy, 1861–1865.* New York: Oxford University Press.

Connelly, Thomas Lawrence 1967: *Army of the Heartland: The Army of Tennessee, 1861–1862.* Baton Rouge: Louisiana State University Press.

Connelly, Thomas Lawrence 1971: *Autumn of Glory: The Army of Tennessee, 1862–1865.* Baton Rouge: Louisiana State University Press.

Connelly, Thomas Lawrence 1977: *The Marble Man: Robert E. Lee and His Image in American Society.* New York: Alfred A. Knopf.

Connelly, Thomas Lawrence and Jones, Archer 1973: *The Politics of Command: Factions and Ideas in Confederate Strategy.* Baton Rouge: Louisiana State University Press.

Cooper, William J. 2000: *Jefferson Davis, American.* New York: Alfred A. Knopf.

Daniel, Larry J. 1991: *Soldiering in the Army of Tennessee: A Portrait of Life in a Confederate Army.* Chapel Hill: University of North Carolina Press.

Davis, William C. 1991: *Jefferson Davis: The Man and His Hour.* New York: HarperCollins.

Escott, Paul D. 1978: *After Secession: Jefferson Davis and the Failure of Confederate Nationalism.* Baton Rouge: Louisiana State University Press.

Faust, Drew Gilpin 1987: Christian Soldiers: The Meaning of Revivalism in the Confederate Army. *Journal of Southern History,* 53 (February): 63–90.

Faust, Drew Gilpin 1988: *The Creation of Confederate Nationalism: Ideology and Identity in the Civil War South.* Baton Rouge: Louisiana State University Press.

Faust, Drew Gilpin 1990: Altars of Sacrifice: Confederate Women and the Narratives of War. *Journal of American History*, 76 (March): 1,200–28.

Faust, Drew Gilpin 1996: *Mothers of Invention: Women of the Slaveholding South in the American Civil War*. Chapel Hill: University of North Carolina Press.

Faust, Drew Gilpin 1998: Without Pilot or Compass: Elite Women and Religion in the Civil War South. In Randall M. Miller, Harry S. Stout, and Charles Reagan Wilson (eds.), *Religion and the American Civil War*. New York: Oxford University Press, 250–60.

Foote, Shelby 1958–74: *The Civil War: A Narrative*, 3 vols. New York: Random House.

Fox-Genovese, Elizabeth 1998: Days of Judgment, Days of Wrath: The Civil War and the Religious Imagination of Women Writers. In Randall M. Miller, Harry S. Stout, and Charles Reagan Wilson (eds.), *Religion and the American Civil War*. New York: Oxford University Press, 229–49.

Freeman, Douglas Southall 1934–5: *R. E. Lee: A Biography*, 4 vols. New York: Charles Scribner's Sons.

Freeman, Douglas Southall 1942–4: *Lee's Lieutenants: A Study in Command*, 3 vols. New York: Charles Scribner's Sons.

Gallagher, Gary W. 1997: *The Confederate War*. Cambridge, MA: Harvard University Press.

Genovese, Eugene D. 1998: Religion in the Collapse of the American Union. In Randall M. Miller, Harry S. Stout, and Charles Reagan Wilson (eds.), *Religion and the American Civil War*. New York: Oxford University Press, 74–88.

Harsh, Joseph L. 1998: *Confederate Tide Rising: Robert E. Lee and the Making of Southern Strategy, 1861–1862*. Kent, OH: Kent State University Press.

Harvey, Paul 1998: Yankee Faith and Southern Redemption: White Southern Baptist Ministers, 1850–1890. In Randall M. Miller, Harry S. Stout, and Charles Reagan Wilson (eds.), *Religion and the American Civil War*. New York: Oxford University Press, 167–86.

Hattaway, Herman and Jones, Archer 1983: *How the North Won: A Military History of the Civil War*. Urbana: University of Illinois Press.

Linderman, Gerald F. 1987: *Embattled Courage: The Experience of Combat in the American Civil War*. New York: Free Press.

McMurry, Richard M. 1989: *Two Great Rebel Armies: An Essay in Confederate Military History*. Chapel Hill: University of North Carolina Press.

Mcpherson, James M. 1988: *Battle Cry of Freedom: The Civil War Era*. New York: Oxford University Press.

McPherson, James M. 1997: *For Cause and Comrades: Why Men Fought in the Civil War*. New York: Oxford University Press.

McPherson, James M. and Cooper, William J., Jr. (eds.) 1998: *Writing the Civil War: The Quest to Understand*. Columbia: University of South Carolina Press.

McWhiney, Grady and Jamieson, Perry D. 1982: *Attack and Die: Civil War Military Tactics and the Southern Heritage*. Tuscaloosa: University of Alabama Press.

Miller, Randall M., Stout, Harry S., and Wilson, Charles Reagan (eds.) 1998: *Religion and the American Civil War*. New York: Oxford University Press.

Mitchell, Reid 1988: *Civil War Soldiers: Their Expectations and Experiences*. New York: Viking.

Mitchell, Reid 1996: Sitting on the Front Porch Watching the War. *Reviews in American History*, 4 (December): 613–17.

Mitchell, Reid 1998: Christian Soldiers? Perfecting the Confederacy. In Randall M. Miller, Harry S. Stout, and Charles Reagan Wilson (eds.), *Religion and the American Civil War*. New York: Oxford University Press, 297–309.

Mohr, Clarence L. 1986: *On the Threshold of Freedom: Masters and Slaves in Civil War Georgia*. Athens: University of Georgia Press.

Noll, Mark 1998: The Bible and Slavery. In Randall M. Miller, Harry S. Stout, and Charles Reagan Wilson (eds.), *Religion and the American Civil War*. New York: Oxford University Press, 43–73.

Owsley, Frank Lawrence 1959: *King Cotton Diplomacy: Foreign Relations of the Confederate States of America*, 2nd revd edn. Chicago: University of Chicago Press.

Power, J. Tracy 1998: *Lee's Miserables: Life in the Army of Northern Virginia from the Wilderness to Appomattox*. Chapel Hill: University of North Carolina Press.

Rable, George C. 1989: *Civil Wars: Women and the Crisis of Southern Nationalism*. Urbana: University of Illinois Press.

Rable, George C. 1994: *The Confederate Republic: A Revolution Against Politics*. Chapel Hill: University of North Carolina Press.

Roark, James L. 1977: *Masters Without Slaves: Southern Planters in the Civil War and Reconstruction*. New York: W. W. Norton.

Robertson, James I., Jr. 1988: *Soldiers Blue and Gray*. Columbia: University of South Carolina Press.

Robertson, James I., Jr. 1997: *Stonewall Jackson: The Man, The Soldier, The Legend*. New York: Simon and Schuster Macmillan.

Stampp, Kenneth M. 1980: The Southern Road to Appomattox. In *The Imperiled Union: Essays on the Background of the Civil War*. New York: Oxford University Press.

Stout, Harry S. and Grasso, Christopher 1998: Civil War, Religion, and Communications: The Case of Richmond. In Randall M. Miller, Harry S. Stout, and Charles Reagan Wilson (eds.), *Religion and the American Civil War*. New York: Oxford University Press, 313–59.

Stowell, Daniel 1998: Stonewall Jackson and the Providence of God. In Randall M. Miller, Harry S. Stout, and Charles Reagan Wilson (eds.), *Religion and the American Civil War*. New York: Oxford University Press, 187–207.

Sutherland, Daniel E. 1995: *Seasons of War: The Ordeal of a Confederate Community, 1861–1865*. New York: Free Press.

Thomas, Emory M. 1971: *The Confederacy as a Revolutionary Experience*. Englewood Cliffs, NJ: Prentice-Hall.

Thomas, Emory M. 1979: *The Confederate Nation, 1861–1865*. New York: Harper and Row.

Thomas, Emory M. 1995: *Robert E. Lee: Biography*. New York: W. W. Norton.

Wiley, Bell Irvin 1943: *The Life of Johnny Reb: The Common Soldier of the Confederacy*. Indianapolis, IN: Bobbs-Merrill.

Wiley, Bell Irvin 1956: *The Road to Appomattox*. Memphis: Memphis State College Press.

Williams, T. Harry 1952: *Lincoln and His Generals*. New York: Alfred A. Knopf.

Woodworth, Steven E. 1990: *Jefferson Davis and His Generals: The Failure of Confederate Command in the West*. Lawrence: University Press of Kansas.

Woodworth, Steven E. 1995: *Davis and Lee at War*. Lawrence: University Press of Kansas.

Wyatt-Brown, Bertram 1998: Church, Honor, and Secession. In Randall M. Miller, Harry S. Stout, and Charles Reagan Wilson (eds.), *Religion and the American Civil War*. New York: Oxford University Press, 89–109.

CHAPTER SIXTEEN

Emancipation and Its Consequences

LAURA F. EDWARDS

THE issue of emancipation has always been politically charged. In the nineteenth century the tension between slavery and the nation's founding ideals tore the country apart and threw it into the bloodiest war in its history. The Civil War ended the "problem of slavery," as David Brion Davis (1966) has called it. But it did not resolve what Thomas Holt (1992) has termed the "problem of freedom." In the post-emancipation United States, freedom was a problem of major proportions, extending beyond the status of former slaves to the nature of social, economic, and political relations in the nation as a whole. There was no consensus on any of these issues at the time. African-Americans tried to establish economic autonomy and claim full civil and political rights. Most white southerners resisted the concept of full citizenship for African-Americans, although they divided among themselves over other issues such as economic development and political leadership. Many white northerners hoped to remake the South in the image of the industrializing North, a vision at odds with those of many northerners and southerners, black and white.

When the federal government abandoned Reconstruction and pulled out of the South in 1876, these issues remained unresolved. By the turn of the century, southern "redeemers" appeared to be the clear winners in this battle: they had disfranchised most African-Americans and many poor whites; they had passed Jim Crow laws that would keep the South segregated well into the twentieth century; and they had created a low-wage economy that enriched the few and left the majority of southerners impoverished. But the process had been slow and uncertain. Redeemers' victories, moreover, did not erase the past. Neither southerners nor northerners let go of the hopes or the fears of the post-emancipation period.

These wounds still festered when the first generation of academic historians began writing the history of emancipation in the late nineteenth century. Many historians of the so-called Dunning school, named for William A. Dunning, a professor at Columbia University who trained a small army of southern historians, were open apologists for disfranchisement, Jim Crow, and the violent suppression of political dissent in the South. Historians today generally dismiss their scholarship as politically biased and historically unsound. Still, the Dunning school helped set the intellectual agenda that has since defined the field by framing their scholarship in terms of the relative merits of emancipation: was it good for African-Americans, the South, and the nation, or not? The question was not merely academic. Although addressed to the past, it spoke to current visions of social and political relations as well. Scholarship in the field has swung back and forth in its evaluation of emancipation's

results. But the question itself remains the same, revealing how politically charged –
and politically relevant – the topic of emancipation remains today.

The Dunning school characterized emancipation as an unmitigated disaster. Following William Dunning's pioneering analysis, first articulated in his *Essays on the
Civil War and Reconstruction* (1898), these historians argued that northern radicals
gave African-Americans, who were not yet ready for freedom, too much power.
African-Americans' abuse of freedom's privileges then threw the entire region into
political chaos, corruption, and economic despair. For Dunning school historians,
Reconstruction's end represented not just a political victory but a moral "redemption" – a term they coined. Such evocative language and imagery, so characteristic of
Dunning school histories, betrayed the substance and intensity of the politics that
fueled their academic arguments. In fact, these historians often spent as much time on
the collapse of Reconstruction as they did on emancipation itself.

The Dunning school actually discounted the agency of African-Americans in
defining the terms of freedom. Influenced by the pseudo-scientific racial theories
of the late nineteenth and early twentieth centuries, these historians were certain
that African-Americans' biological makeup made them inferior to the white race.
To them, African-Americans were incapable of ever exercising full civil and political
rights. The idea that emancipated African-Americans played a substantive role in
Reconstruction never entered into their calculations. Yet Dunning school racism also
had a distinctly paternalistic cast. These historians accepted African-Americans as a
necessary part of southern society, portraying them as easily manipulable children
who needed the right kind of supervision so as not to get out of hand. As they saw it,
emancipation was problematic because it destroyed the system – slavery – that had
contained African-Americans. The challenge, then, was to establish a new system of
control to replace the old one. In the work of the Dunning school, it was northern
radicals who prevented white southerners from doing so. These radicals, a lunatic
fringe who managed to seize power by deceit and manipulation, did not act out of
concern for the South, the nation, or even the welfare of African-Americans. They
wanted to enrich themselves, enhance their power, and punish white southerners for
the war. By irresponsibly and selfishly turning African-Americans against white southerners, these northern radicals wrecked the whole region. The results then tainted the
nation, leaving a legacy of problematic race relations and perpetuating ill will between
North and South.

The Dunning school was incredibly influential both inside and outside academia in
the first four decades of the twentieth century. Among the few dissenting voices was
W. E. B. Du Bois, a Harvard-trained sociologist and one of the most prominent
African-American political activists of his generation. Du Bois's *Black Reconstruction:
An Essay Toward a History of the Part which Black Folk Played in the Attempt to
Reconstruct Democracy in America, 1860–1880* (1935) completely reversed the conclusions of the Dunning school. For Du Bois, emancipation was a democratic
revolution that restored property in labor to its rightful owners and promised to
fulfill the nation's founding ideals. By redistributing power, emancipation opened all
sorts of social, economic, and political possibilities for African-Americans, ordinary
white southerners, and the South as a whole. African-Americans are central in Du
Bois's analysis, as suggested in the subtitle. His opening section shows how slaves
emancipated themselves and undermined the Confederacy by running to federal

lines. Subsequent chapters trace African-Americans' efforts to achieve economic independence and full civil and political rights. Du Bois, moreover, links the South's future to the status of black people. The great tragedy in *Black Reconstruction* is that ordinary white southerners did not make this same connection. Instead of identifying with blacks, they chose race over class and supported the policies of reactionary white leaders. Not only did ordinary white southerners wipe out the gains African-Americans had made, but they destroyed their own position as well. They were left only with a psychological sense of racial superiority. But this psychic benefit was a poor replacement for the tangible rewards they could have had.

Du Bois's *Reconstruction*, although largely ignored at the time, anticipated the research agenda and conceptual frameworks of subsequent scholarship on the subject. Still, it was World War II that had the most immediate impact on the next group of emancipation historians, known as the "revisionists." Fascism and the specific brand of racism that resulted in the Holocaust horrified revisionists. So, too, did the continued presence of both "isms" in the United States. Looking to the past for answers, they found them in the post-Civil War South. Like Du Bois, revisionists saw emancipation as period of great democratic possibilities for black and white southerners. Reactionary Democrats, the virtuous "redeemers" of the Dunning school, then smashed these possibilities, leaving a legacy of racism and political exclusion that still plagued the region and the nation.

Early revisionists focused on the Dunning school's characterization of Republican leaders as corrupt and Republican rule as destructive of the South's interests. One strand of the scholarship rehabilitated the so-called Radical Republicans in Congress. In revisionist hands, they became idealistic, self-sacrificing leaders who wanted to fulfill America's democratic ideals by extending full civil and political rights to African-Americans. Revisionists also interpreted congressional Republicans' policies in a favorable light. They characterized the previously reviled Freedmen's Bureau as a necessary and important presence in overseeing the transition from slavery to free labor in the South. Its officers, however, faced an uphill battle because of the recalcitrance of white planters who tried to exploit black workers at every turn. Revisionists underscored the devastating implications of Congress's failure to give former slaves land and the means to cultivate it. Property redistribution, revisionists argued, would have resolved African-Americans' problems by freeing them from dependence on whites and giving them a base of power from which to successfully defend their civil and political rights. Revisionists also criticized the Republican Party for abandoning the ideal of racial equality in 1876 when it agreed to the principle of "home rule" in the South.

As Radical Republicans' stock rose, that of moderate Republicans plummeted. According to revisionist historians, moderates' racism and their willingness to work with former Confederates undermined Radical Republican plans for racial equality. Not even Abraham Lincoln escaped censure. In *The Era of Reconstruction, 1865–1877*, Kenneth Stampp (1965) punctured the myth of the "Great Emancipator," arguing that Abraham Lincoln only freed the slaves as a last resort to save the Union and that he never believed African-Americans capable of exercising full citizenship rights. Had he lived, Lincoln's Reconstruction plan would have given power back to former Confederates and left African-Americans free in name only. Andrew Johnson did not come off much better. As Stampp argued, Johnson shared Lincoln's racism.

His deep resentment towards southern slaveholders and his belief in Jefferson's yeoman ideal did lead him to disfranchise Confederate elites, something that Lincoln did not plan to do and that would have leveled the political playing field somewhat. But Johnson's vanity and his desire to be accepted into elite southern society undercut the democratic implications of his policies. Instead of sticking by his plans, he gave personal pardons to virtually every prominent Confederate who asked for one.

Revisionists saved their most intense criticism for Democrats in the South. They scrutinized state budgets and expenditures to prove the fiscal integrity of Republican state governments and the corruption of subsequent Democratic regimes. They tracked voting records and debates in the state legislatures to show that other Republican policies – including public education, debt relief, democratization of local governments, and the elimination of voting restrictions – represented the interests of ordinary southerners generally. They unearthed biographical background on Republican politicians to disprove the Dunning school's claims that the white elected officials were self-interested "scalawags" and "carpetbaggers" and that black elected officials were illiterate buffoons controlled by whites. In *A Carpetbagger's Crusade: The Life of Albion Winegar Tourgée*, for instance, Otto Olsen (1965) argued that Albion Tourgée, an Ohio abolitionist who became active in Republican politics in North Carolina, was an idealistic leader. Not only was Tourgée committed to racial equality and political democracy, but he endured considerable personal danger to build a biracial coalition that could achieve these goals. Revisionists also documented how destructive the recalcitrance of southern Democrats was. State studies such as Joel Williamson's *After Slavery: The Negro in South Carolina During Reconstruction, 1861–1877* (1965) and William McKee Evans's *Ballots and Fence Rails: Reconstruction on the Lower Cape Fear* (1967) chronicled the barriers Democrats threw in the way of African-Americans. Other work highlighted the political role of the Klan in bringing down democratic governments and returning Democrats to power.

Although early revisionists elaborated on some of Du Bois's insights, they tended to emphasize race rather than class in the downfall of Recostruction and to highlight the role of political leaders rather than Du Bois's "Black Folk." There were notable exceptions. Evans's *Ballots and Fence Rails* and Williamson's *After Slavery* gave considerable attention to African-Americans' efforts to obtain full civil and political rights. Evans also noted efforts to achieve economic independence and to build a biracial political movement in eastern North Carolina based around the interests of the poor. Still, both analyses ultimately returned to institutional politics at the state level, detailing the coordinated efforts of the Democratic Party to squelch all opposition and to deny civil and political rights to African-Americans.

The revisionists' emphasis reflected the dominance of political history in the profession as a whole. But it was also based on these historians' views of race and politics. Working from liberal assumptions about human nature current in post-World War II America, most revisionists believed that all people were fundamentally the same. Social circumstances, not human nature, produced significant differences among groups of people. By shifting the blame for racial inequality to society, postwar liberalism provided a powerful counter to discriminatory practices based on the notion that African-Americans were inherently different from and inferior to whites. Even as it supported racial equality, however, postwar liberalism also downplayed conflict and diversity. Liberals assumed that human nature consisted of a specific constellation of values, namely those of market-oriented capitalism and liberal political democracy. They did not question the universality of these values. Given their experiences with World War II and the Cold War, they were convinced that the corresponding political and economic systems best served the common good. Once social aberrations such as racism or dictatorial political regimes were eliminated, people would naturally become self-interested, profit-maximizing individuals who would embrace wage labor and define freedom in terms of the ability to pursue their own economic interests and to participate in electoral politics. Any resistance would come from those few who remained invested in the old regimes.

This particular brand of liberalism profoundly shaped revisionist histories of emancipation. Revisionists assumed that the only thing separating African-American slaves from whites was the institution of slavery. Once released from unnatural bondage, African-Americans would behave as everyone else did. The South, by extension, would be like the rest of America. Southern slaveholders did not follow this pattern because slavery better served their immediate economic and political interests at the expense of everyone else. The problem of the post-emancipation period, as revisionists saw it, was in sustaining the South's newly created political institutions so that the region would not lapse into tyranny. Thus, the revisionist's conceptual framework did not depend on the study of ordinary people. Nor did it allow for the possibility that African-Americans and ordinary white southerners might not embrace the values that revisionists presumed to be universal.

Even as the revisionists were rewriting the political history of emancipation, a new wave of scholarship began shifting the focus to economic issues. These historians took their cues from the "new" social history, which maintained that the outcomes of people's daily struggles over economic resources and social relations were as pivotal to understanding the period as the decisions of political leaders. In this sense, they returned to a theme first introduced by W. E. B. Du Bois, although they used new methods and new sources to examine both the impact of emancipation on the lives of ordinary southerners and these people's efforts to shape the post-Civil War South.

History from the "bottom up" presented new research challenges because ordinary people did not leave the kind of written sources – diaries, letters, and reports – that literate leaders did. To ferret out information, some social historians applied statistical methods to data from such records as the manuscript census and tax lists. One of the most influential cliometric studies of the post-emancipation South was Roger Ransom's and Richard Sutch's *One Kind of Freedom: The Economic Consequences of Emancipation* (1977). Their basic question – why the South had remained so poor in comparison to the rest of the nation for so long after the Civil War – was deceivingly straightforward. With it, Ransom and Sutch were actually approaching the revisionists' indictment of Democratic rule from a different perspective, using empirical data to evaluate the failure of the post-emancipation period in economic rather than political terms. As they argued, the root of the South's problems was sharecropping. Sharecropping emerged in the 1870s as a compromise between freed African-Americans, who wanted to work their own land on their own terms, and white landowners, who needed labor but had no resources to pay wage workers. This compromise soon degenerated into an extremely exploitative, inefficient system that kept African-Americans and many whites locked in poverty and prevented the South from developing economically.

What explained the development of such an irrational system? The answer, according to Ransom and Sutch, lay in the perverse racism of white landowners and their Democratic allies. Together, they propped up the system in a shortsighted, self-destructive effort to keep African-Americans down. As Ransom and Sutch argued, racism robbed freedpeople of economic opportunities and market incentives, leaving them with only "one kind of freedom" – one far less meaningful than the kind of freedom they could have had. Although Ransom and Sutch were critical of the postwar southern economy, their data also indicated that African-Americans made impressive economic gains by the turn of the twentieth century. But such evidence, they argued, proved their point by suggesting what African-Americans could have achieved in the absence of racial barriers.

Other cliometricians arrived at the opposite conclusion. They argued that the economic devastation of the Civil War, not sharecropping or even race, explained the South's persistent poverty. In fact, these cliometricians characterized sharecropping as an efficient response to market incentives. Given the setbacks of the war years, both the South and black southerners made significant economic progress. Robert Higgs's *Competition and Coercion: Blacks in the American Economy, 1865–1914* (1977) is representative of this school of thought. Higgs argued that increases in African-Americans' income and landownership indicated a smoothly functioning economy that distributed its rewards equitably. To be sure, there were still large economic disparities between whites and blacks in the South. But, according to Higgs, race could not explain the difference: "It seems quite clear that a half century was not long enough for the blacks to close the economic gap separating them from the whites, even under the most favorable circumstances, including a complete absence of racial discrimination" (Higgs 1977: 127). Freed slaves, in other words, had done as well as could be expected, given that they started so far behind whites after emancipation. Race, moreover, did not have a significant effect on either African-Americans' economic fortunes or the southern economy generally.

Despite the radically different conclusions about the economic results of emancipation, this body of cliometric work rested on similar assumptions about freedpeople's goals. All these scholars saw emancipated African-Americans as profit-maximizing individuals governed by economic self-interest who responded to market forces and who defined freedom primarily in terms of material acquisitions. These historians also believed that a properly functioning market would produce optimal results for everyone in society. Indeed, critics dubbed this body of cliometric work "neoclassical" because of its reliance on classical, economic liberalism. Yet, conceptually, the cliometricians were not all that different from revisionist political historians. Both groups worked from a similar cluster of liberal ideas, although they were not always as obvious in revisionist political history as they were in neoclassical economic history.

Another group of historians, who were also connected to the "new" social history, challenged these liberal presumptions and the historical conclusions based on them. Like other social historians influenced by Marxism and the politics of the New Left, they rejected the notion of a liberal consensus that marked so much of the scholarship in the post-World War II era and were highly critical of capitalism and liberalism. For neo-Marxist historians of the post-emancipation South, the key event was the economic transition to market-oriented capitalism. This shift, they argued, foreclosed the possibility of black and white southerners controlling their own labor and exercising power within southern society. Instead, they became a powerless, landless laboring class dependent on exploitative, low-wage jobs as sharecroppers and factory hands. A properly functioning capitalist market would not have resolved anything. That was the root of the problem.

Neo-Marxists, however, did agree with Ransom and Sutch in one key respect. They, too, saw capitalist economic change in the South as distinctly exploitative. For them, the reason was not race *per se*, but the continued persistence of the class relations of slavery. In *Social Origins of the New South: Alabama, 1860–1885*, for instance, Jonathan Wiener (1978) argued that former slaveholders retained their economic and political power in post-Civil War Alabama, a conclusion at odds with C. Vann Woodward's classic argument that the Old South elite gave way to a new, commercial class that embraced capitalist change in the decades following the Civil War. According to Wiener, planters were not adverse to capitalism. But they did favor a particular form of capitalism that kept power in the hands of the elite and bypassed the adoption of bourgeois civil liberties and political rights. Wiener then elaborated on the implications of his findings in later writings. Drawing on the work of Barrington Moore Jr. and likening southern planters to German Junkers, Wiener argued that the South's leaders directed the region on a forced march down the "Prussian Road," which he defined as a decidedly undemocratic, demonstrably different capitalist path than that followed by the rest of the nation.

The debate between neo-Marxists and neoclassicists peaked in the late 1970s. The best critiques of it came from Harold Woodman, who straddled both camps as an economic historian with cliometric training and neo-Marxist sympathies. In his much-cited article, "Sequel to Slavery: The New History Views the Postbellum South," Woodman (1977) took both sides to task. Neoclassicists, he maintained, had produced valuable data on the postwar southern economy and the position of ordinary southerners within it. Yet, in interpreting the meaning of these statistics, they isolated economic variables that could not really be separated from the larger society. The market, in particular, was not an abstract entity that existed in ideal form outside society, as neoclassicists assumed. It was always a product of the larger society, shaped by the political decisions and social relations of the time. Woodman thus found unconvincing the neoclassicist assumption that a properly functioning market would have produced optimal results. After all, the social conditions for such a market never actually existed anywhere but in theory. Woodman found neo-Marxists' sustained analysis of the South's class structure and its effects on all southerners to be more historically useful. Yet he also thought the theoretical structure of neo-Marxist work to be too overdetermined and ahistorical. Not only did it lump all southerners into two overly broad classes, but it also ignored regional variations and change over time. In the last pages of the article, Woodman sketched out a new approach to avoid the pitfalls of both sides. The central problem for historians of emancipation, he argued, was understanding the process by which African-Americans became free laborers and planters became employers over time in different parts of the South. His approach, however, ultimately owed more to neo-Marxists than to neoclassicists. "The New South," he concluded, "might best be seen as an evolving bourgeois society in which a capitalistic social structure was arising on the ruins of a premodern slave society" (ibid: 554).

Although the rancor of the debate between neo-Marxists and neoclassicists has long since dissipated, the underlying issues still shape work on emancipation. This scholarship ultimately shifted the field to studies of political economy instead of partisan politics. It also opened up a new debate about the relative importance of race and class. For neoclassicists who saw capitalism as socially beneficial, class was not a particularly powerful explanatory tool. The issue for them was one of exclusion from the existing society. Race was what prevented African-Americans from participating. Although historians no longer align themselves with neoclassicists or label themselves as such, many still emphasize racial exclusion as the primary problem in the post-emancipation South.

For neo-Marxists, by contrast, the problem was African-Americans' inclusion in a particularly exploitative capitalist order shaped by class relations from the slave era. Race was a dependent variable. It could wreak all kinds of havoc, but it could never explain the development of the social structure that entrapped all southerners, white and black. Historians have since abandoned both the neo-Marxist label and the reductive two-class model of the late 1970s. But they still rely heavily on basic elements of the neo-Marxist critique of the South's social and economic structure.

The difference in work since the 1980s is the focus on the lives of ordinary white and black southerners. Neither neoclassicists nor neo-Marxists actually dealt with the experiences of these people in any sustained way. Black and white workers appear primarily as composite groups who either plodded along diligently or were victimized shamelessly by those in power. Either way, they were largely silent and inert. Harold Woodman obliquely raised this issue in the conclusion to "Sequel to Slavery," suggesting that the field needed a more nuanced approach that would engage the historical complexities of economic change in the post-emancipation South. He urged scholars to abandon the rigid two-class model and to explore instead the multiplicity of experiences among freedpeople, upcountry whites, and planters within the different parts of the South. He also advocated a closer examination of the motivations and goals of these different groups as they grappled with postwar change.

A number of historians were already working in this direction, taking inspiration from the "new" social history and building on W. E. B. Du Bois's pathbreaking analysis of former slaves' struggles to emancipate themselves and define the terms of their freedom. Willie Lee Rose's *Rehearsal for Reconstruction: The Port Royal Experiment* (1964) and Louis S. Gerteis's *From Contraband to Freedman: Federal Policy Toward Southern Blacks, 1861–65* (1973) focused primarily on federal policy toward southern African-Americans. But both also explored the motivations and actions of freedpeople and showed how northern policies actually thwarted African-Americans' goals and limited their freedom. In *A Right to the Land: Essays on the Freedmen's Community*, Edward Magdol (1977) examined African-Americans' efforts to build families and communities after the war. Central to Magdol's analysis was his discussion of freedpeople's sense of ownership in the land they worked as slaves and their attempts to acquire that land. This literature is often overlooked today because it did not fit within the historiographical debate between neo-Marxists and neoclassicists. But it provided the base on which the next body of scholarship was built.

Subsequent work focused specifically on the experiences of former slaves during and immediately after the war. One of the first, most notable works was Leon Litwack's *Been in the Storm So Long: The Aftermath of Slavery* (1979), which focused explicitly on emancipation through the lived experiences of former slaves. But the intellectual center of the historiography was the Freedmen and Southern Society Project, a collaborative project directed by Ira Berlin that included a number of key scholars working in the field. The resulting series, *Freedom: A Documentary History of Emancipation, 1861–1867*, worked on two levels. They were documentary volumes that told the history of the period through selections from the vast collections of federal records that had been largely unused by historians. At the same time, however, the editors' thematic organization of the material and their pathbreaking introductory essays made these volumes key historiographical works as well. The first, *The Black Military Experience* (1982), explored black soldiers' contributions to the war, with particular attention to the ways that they used military service as a means to achieve their own goals. What distinguished this and subsequent volumes was the way the authors treated southern African-Americans as independent historical actors who could not be understood as extensions of Republican policies or politics.

Much of the material in the *Freedom* volumes addressed the tensions between former slaves and northern officials. The editors combined the revisionist critiques of moderate Republicans with neo-Marxist critiques of capitalism and then took the analysis in new directions by highlighting former slaves' own views of the society and the economy. In so doing, they drew heavily on concurrent work in slavery and labor history influenced by the pioneering scholarship of English historian E. P. Thompson and his American popularizer, Herbert Gutman. The scholarship in both fields emphasized slaves' and workers' success in constructing cultural systems apart from those in power. In this view, workers entered the capitalist economy reluctantly. Once there, they tried to keep their traditional precapitalist values: a moral economy that placed limits on property accumulation and distributed goods on the basis of need; a work ethic that valued subsistence and freedom from labor over working regularly and continually to satisfy ever-expanding material desires; and family structures that turned outward and blended with the larger community instead of turning inward as privatized bourgeois families did. According to the editors of the *Freedom* series, these basic elements informed slaves' vision of freedom and clashed with that of most northern officials. The editors deemphasized race in this conflict, although they did not ignore it. As they showed, the racial views of northern officials ran the gamut from a firm conviction in African-Americans' inherent inferiority to an idealistic belief in racial equality. What united this diverse group of military officers, charity workers, and political appointees was an unquestioned faith in bourgeois social and economic relations. Some tried to woo former slaves to these values. Others tried to impose them by force. But all intended to replace freedpeople's communally oriented social structures and subsistence-centered work ethic with the social and economic relations of liberal capitalism. By these standards the only true radicals of the post-emancipation South were former slaves. Even most Radical Republicans fell short.

The first volumes of *Freedom*, because they were focused on the war years, dealt primarily with African-Americans' relations with federal officials. But other historians applied elements of this approach to the post-emancipation period, extending the analysis to include white southern planters. Eric Foner's essays in *Nothing But Freedom: Emancipation and Its Legacy* (1983) used just such a tripartite analysis, exploring northern efforts to construct capitalist labor relations in the South, white southern planters' attempts to reestablish the labor and racial controls of slavery, and African-Americans' resistance to proletarianization and anything that smacked of the slave system. Barbara Fields's *Slavery and Freedom on the Middle Ground: Maryland during the Nineteenth Century* (1985) was also influential. Fields, who was connected with the Freedmen and Southern Society project, traced the experiences of northern officials, former slaveholders, slaves, and common whites during the collapse of slavery and the transition to capitalism in Maryland. Central to her analysis are African-Americans' efforts to carve out some measure of independence on this new terrain and their ultimate failure to do so, given the combined forces of federal officials and white planters. As Fields shows, the federal agents who oversaw the transition from slavery to free labor believed that former slaves gained only the contractual right to sell their labor. They forced African-Americans into long-term, low-paying, restrictive labor contracts; they listened half-heartedly to African-Americans' complaints about lost wages and abuse; and they completely rejected African-Americans' hopes to own productive property and avoid wage labor altogether. Northern officials' visions of capitalist labor relations ultimately meshed with the goals of former planters, who wanted a cheap, captive, compliant workforce. Indeed, federal representatives did nothing to stop the restrictions placed on African-Americans' civil and political rights. Julie Saville (1994) revisited these themes in *The Work of Reconstruction: From Slave to Wage Laborer in South Carolina, 1860–1870*. In Saville's analysis, which focuses more on the organized efforts of African-Americans to establish economic independence and political power, African-Americans emerge even more clearly as active agents in the process of defining freedom.

Other scholars examined the impact of the evolving capitalist economy on ordinary white southerners. In *The Roots of Southern Populism: Yeoman Farmers and the Transformation of the Georgia Upcountry, 1850–1890*, Steven Hahn (1983) traced the collapse of the subsistence, household economy that had undergirded social relations in the southern countryside. Economic change began in the antebellum years, Hahn argued. But white yeoman families were able to use market-oriented agriculture to supplement their subsistence, safety-first economic strategies without becoming enmeshed in market capitalism. The destruction of the war and the economic changes thereafter forever altered their relations to capitalist economic change. The need for cash forced them to focus exclusively on cash crops such as cotton. Unable to negotiate the market's fickle swings and unable to get out of market agriculture, many farmers lost their land and entered the post-emancipation agricultural workforce as tenants and sharecroppers.

Other scholars questioned the distinctiveness of the southern yeomanry from the planter class and their distance from market capitalism in the antebellum period. Less contested, however, was the notion that post-emancipation economic change transformed the lives of ordinary white southerners. In contrast, earlier scholarship had viewed white southerners primarily through the lens of race; although some did ally with the Republican Party immediately after the war, they ultimately moved to the Democratic side out of a sense of white solidarity and a desire to preserve their racial privilege. As new work emphasized, however, the economic component of white southerners' politics made their commitment to racial unity and their Democratic proclivities less certain. Hahn, for instance, argued that white yeomen's traumatic economic experiences in the postwar years explained why they abandoned the Democrats for the Populists. Historians also uncovered other examples of "white flight" from the Democratic Party at key moments throughout the post-emancipation period. These scholars did not argue that the resulting biracial alliances transcended racial animosity, although they did imply that political cooperation across the color bar held out this possibility. Rather, these alliances were built despite entrenched racism, a testament to the depth of whites' and blacks' opposition to the Democratic leadership and the political power of their common economic interests.

The scholarship from the 1980s complicated, but did not reframe, the terms of the historiograpical debate set back in the 1890s by the Dunning school. Previously, historians told the story of Reconstruction in terms of two opposing sides: the Democrats versus the Republicans or the forces of racism versus those of liberal capitalism. Debate then centered on which side best represented the interests of the South and the nation. By separating former slaves and ordinary white southerners from political leaders, the work of the 1980s populated the social and political terrain of the post-emancipation South with new historical actors and uncovered new historical issues. Not only were there more than two sides, but the two sides of previous scholarship were both problematic. Representatives of both the Republican and Democratic parties betrayed the best interests of the region by purposefully squashing the democratic solutions offered by ordinary southerners, white and black. Yet the underlying question – whether or not emancipation was good for African-Americans, the South, and the nation – remained the same. In the scholarship of the 1980s, the post-emancipation period was a tragic one of lost opportunities, although for different reasons than for the Dunning school or earlier revisionist historians.

In 1988 Eric Foner pulled together the work on political economy and revisionist political history in a single, sweeping synthesis, *Reconstruction, 1863–1877: America's Unfinished Revolution* (Foner 1988). In Foner's analysis the process of Reconstruction reshaped both the North and the South. The narrative included the entire range of characters covered in the scholarship thus far: southern yeomen and northern workers, planters and industrialists, Republicans and Democrats, free blacks and former slaves. At this crucial juncture, all these people participated in a debate over the social, economic, and political direction of the entire country. In one sense, the results were clear. As Foner argued, the nation abandoned the economic and political ideals of the early republic to build a nation centered around industrial capitalism. The first casualty was the republican ideal of workers' control over their labor. Federal officials imposed a narrow definition of free labor on former slaves that would later become the model for the rest of the nation. At the same time, government policy at the state and national levels promoted capitalist economic change and undermined southern yeomen's and white workers' economic independence. Then the federal government rejected the republican ideals of civil equality and political participation, turning its back on African-Americans' claims to rights in ways that prefigured the fate of all Americans. Gutting the Fourteenth Amendment, the federal courts used it to expand corporate power instead of protecting the liberties of individual citizens.

Yet, in Foner's analysis, Reconstruction was still an "unfinished revolution" because the period also generated some of the most powerful defenses of individual freedom, racial equality, and economic justice. Although largely unsuccessful, the struggles over civil rights, political power, and economic change in that period still defined the political terrain – and the political possibilities – of the late twentieth century. Foner thus saw the implications of emancipation as both good and bad. The outcome was tragic. But the nation still had the opportunity to change all that, if it could build on the idealism that was also part of Reconstruction's legacy.

The historical and historiographical comprehensiveness of Foner's *Reconstruction* made it seem as if no stone had been left unturned. Indeed, many in the field still see the book as the definitive statement on the period. But *Reconstruction*, like the work on which it drew, left out one large, important group: women. Throughout the 1970s and 1980s a small but growing body of scholarship on women in the era of Reconstruction had emerged. Disaggregating women's experiences from those of men just as other historians separated white southerners from the Democratic Party and African-Americans from the Republican leadership, these historians cast women as independent political actors with their own, distinct interests. In *The Southern Lady: From Pedestal to Politics, 1830–1930*, Anne Scott (1970) argued that the Civil War and emancipation marked the beginning of southern women's independent political activism. Other women's historians examined suffragists' failed attempts to extend political rights to women. More recently, women's historians have explored conflicts between freedwomen and freedmen over domestic obligations and the different problems of slaveholding men and women in negotiating labor relations with former slaves.

In the late 1980s and 1990s women's historians increasingly emphasized racial and class differences among women. Black women, according to Jacqueline Jones in *Labor of Love, Labor of Sorrow: Black Women, Work, and the Family from Slavery to the Present* (1985), did not withdraw from the labor force to pursue a white middle-class ideal of domesticity within their homes, as many historians had assumed. Rather, they distanced themselves from wage work for whites to avoid abuse, particularly sexual abuse. Still, they considered it part of their role as women to contribute economically to their households, and they took up other forms of productive labor to fulfill those obligations.

This work suggested that emancipation had very different implications for women. By implication, historical evaluations of emancipation would be different if women's experiences were given as much weight as those of men. But even as women's history began to find its way into the historiography by the 1980s, it remained on the margins. In *Reconstruction*, for instance, Foner discussed black women's labor and the exclusion of women from political rights. These additions, however, did not alter the terms of the analysis, which took the experiences of men as representative of the period as a whole. Historians of Reconstruction also continued to discuss the period's brief affirmation of universal suffrage and full citizenship without any sense of contradiction or any curiosity as to why it was so easy to exclude women from those rights then and from the historiography now.

In the 1990s a new generation of historians directly challenged the historiographical marginalization of women. Their tool was the analytical concept of gender – the idea that masculine and feminine ideals are culturally constructed and key components in power relations of all kinds. Gender allowed these historians to illuminate the links between the "private" sphere of the household and the "public" world of politics in ways that also made women central to their analyses. Central to this work, for instance, was the idea that free white men in the mid-nineteenth century acquired public rights to protect and represent their property and their dependents as heads of household. Because only men could be household heads, only men could claim the rights of citizenship. As Leslie Schwalm argued in *A Hard Fight for We: Women's Transition from Slavery to Freedom in South Carolina* (1997), these presumptions undercut black women's economic position after emancipation. Northern officials presumed that all women were economically dependent on their husbands' wages, while simultaneously excluding black women from the category of womanhood because of their race. Their policies thus forced black women to work but did not recognize them as independent workers with the same rights over their labor and its product as men. These gendered assumptions affected men as well as women. In *White Women, Black Men: Illicit Sex in the Nineteenth Century South*, for instance, Martha Hodes (1997) used the connections between men's private authority and public power to explain why southern Democrats thought granting suffrage to black men would result in their sexual domination of white women. Laura Edwards argued in *Gendered Strife and Confusion: The Political Culture of Reconstruction* (1997) that gender inequality ultimately undercut men's claims to equality as well. African-American and common white men used their position as household heads to claim full citizenship, arguing that they needed civil and political rights to fulfill their obligations to their families. Similarly, African-American and common white women claimed the legal privileges previously granted only to elite white women on the basis of their position as legally dependent wives. Yet, by emphasizing gender differences rooted within a patriarchal family structure, these men and women left key components of the antebellum power structure in place. That patriarchal structure had been used to justify racial and class hierarchies in the past, and conservative Democrats mobilized it to those ends again in the post-emancipation period.

Once again the democratic solutions held up by a previous generation of scholars became part of the problem. From the perspective of new work on gender, the republican ideal of economic independence would never have resulted in equality because it presumed the subordination of women within households headed by men. "Manhood rights," as civil and political rights were then called, were not the solution either. Not only did the gender inequality embedded within the most radical political claims of the time foreclose equality for women, but it also undermined the possibility of democracy among men.

Emancipation continues to be a vibrant topic because this particular piece of our past speaks directly to current political concerns. It was a crucial period in the history of race relations and economic change. More importantly, it was one of the few times in the nation's history when Americans experimented boldly and openly with the concept of freedom. Generations of historians have hoped to find the reasons for inequality and unrest in their own times by looking to the post-emancipation past. Although they did not always admit it, they also hoped to find solutions there. Indeed, of all the chronological subfields in American history, the work on Reconstruction has been among the most didactic, moralistic, and passionate. Yet the work has never been purely presentist. As evaluations of the period have swung back and forth, analyses of the period have grown increasingly complex and sophisticated. The number of historical actors and issues has multiplied. We now know much more about the interaction between economic interests, racial ideology, and the identities of individual men and women, the contingencies of time and region in shaping the outcome of economic relations and political contests, and the range of differences among southerners and northerners on economic, social, and political relations. But that historical knowledge inevitably folds back into the present. The answers to our own questions may not lie in the post-emancipation period. But how we imagine that period still says a great deal about our own political problems and our own dreams of freedom today.

BIBLIOGRAPHY

Berlin, Ira, Reidy, Joseph P., and Rowland, Leslie S. (eds.) 1982: *Freedom: A Documentary History of Emancipation, 1861–1867*. Series 2: *The Black Military Experience*. New York: Cambridge University Press.

Davis, David Brion 1966: *The Problem of Slavery in Western Culture*. Ithaca, NY: Cornell University Press.

Du Bois, W. E. B. 1935: *Black Reconstruction: An Essay Toward a History of the Part which Black Folk Played in the Attempt to Reconstruct Democracy in America, 1860–1880*. New York: Russell and Russell.

Dunning, William Archibald 1898: *Essays on the Civil War and Reconstruction and Related Topics*. New York: MacMillan.

Edwards, Laura F. 1997: *Gendered Strife and Confusion: The Political Culture of Reconstruction*. Urbana: University of Illinois Press.

Evans, W. McKee 1967: *Ballots and Fence Rails: Reconstruction on the Lower Cape Fear*. Chapel Hill: University of North Carolina Press.

Fields, Barbara Jeanne 1985: *Slavery and Freedom on the Middle Ground: Maryland during the Nineteenth Century*. New Haven, CT: Yale University Press.

Foner, Eric 1983: *Nothing But Freedom: Emancipation and Its Legacy*. Baton Rouge: Louisiana State University Press.

Foner, Eric 1988: *Reconstruction, 1863–1877: America's Unfinished Revolution*. New York: Harper and Row.

Gerteis, Louis S. 1973: *From Contraband to Freedman: Federal Policy Toward Southern Blacks, 1861–65*. Westport, CT: Greenwood Press.

Hahn, Steven 1983: *The Roots of Southern Populism: Yeoman Farmers and the Transformation of the Georgia Upcountry, 1850–1890*. New York: Oxford University Press.

Higgs, Robert 1977: *Competition and Coercion: Blacks in the American Economy, 1865–1914*. Cambridge: Cambridge University Press.

Hodes, Martha 1997: *White Women, Black Men: Illicit Sex in the Nineteenth Century South*. New Haven, CT: Yale University Press.

Holt, Thomas C. 1992: *The Problem of Freedom: Race, Labor, and Politics in Jamaica and Britain, 1832–1938*. Baltimore: Johns Hopkins University Press.

Jones, Jacqueline 1985: *Labor of Love, Labor of Sorrow: Black Women, Work, and the Family from Slavery to the Present*. New York: Basic Books.

Kolchin, Peter 1982: *First Freedom: The Responses of Alabama's Blacks to Emancipation and Reconstruction*. Westport, CT: Greenwood Press.

Litwack, Leon 1979: *Been in the Storm So Long: The Aftermath of Slavery*. New York: Alfred A. Knopf.

Magdol, Edward 1977: *A Right to the Land: Essays on the Freedmen's Community*. Westport, CT: Greenwood Press.

Olsen, Otto 1965: *A Carpetbagger's Crusade: The Life of Albion Winegar Tourgée*. Baltimore: Johns Hopkins University Press.

Ransom, Roger L. and Sutch, Richard 1977: *One Kind of Freedom: The Economic Consequences of Emancipation*. Cambridge: Cambridge University Press.

Ripley, C. Peter 1976: *Slaves and Freedmen in Civil War Louisiana*. Baton Rouge: Louisiana State University Press.

Rose, Willie Lee 1964: *Rehearsal for Reconstruction: The Port Royal Experiment*. Indianapolis, IN: Bobbs Merrill.

Saville, Julie 1994: *The Work of Reconstruction: From Slave to Wage Laborer in South Carolina, 1860–1870*. New York: Cambridge University Press.

Schwalm, Leslie A. 1997: *A Hard Fight for We: Women's Transition from Slavery to Freedom in South Carolina*. Urbana: University of Illinois Press.

Scott, Anne Firor 1970: *The Southern Lady: From Pedestal to Politics, 1830–1930*. Chicago: University of Chicago Press.

Stampp, Kenneth M. 1965: *The Era of Reconstruction, 1865–1877*. New York: Alfred A. Knopf.

Wayne, Michael 1983: *The Reshaping of Plantation Society: The Natchez District, 1860–1880*. Baton Rouge: Louisiana State University Press.

Wiener, Jonathan M. 1978: *Social Origins of the New South: Alabama, 1860–1885*. Baton Rouge: Louisiana State University Press.

Williamson, Joel 1965: *After Slavery: The Negro in South Carolina During Reconstruction, 1861–1877*. Chapel Hill: University of North Carolina Press.

Woodman, Harold D. 1977: Sequel to Slavery: The New History Views the Postbellum South. *Journal of Southern History*, 43, 523–54.

CHAPTER SEVENTEEN

Political Reconstruction, 1865–1877

MICHAEL W. FITZGERALD

WORKING in the area of Reconstruction politics has been a modestly dispiriting endeavor in recent years, and not only because political history is regarded within the profession as somewhat *passé*. For most of the century, critiques of southern society animated American public discourse. Scholarship on the tumultuous era after the Civil War touched a larger audience, revolving as it did around race relations and the meaning of equality. This wider interest inspired those writing on Reconstruction politics. The great civil convulsions of the 1960s heightened scholarly engagement, and it seemed only fitting for the dean of southern historians, C. Vann Woodward, to march at Selma. As regional distinctiveness diminished in subsequent decades, southern political issues moved to the periphery of national consciousness, and the field lost some of its animating energy. For the moment, the politics of Reconstruction lacks the popular interest it held in some previous times, but whether this represents an eclipse, or an opportunity for scholarly reevaluation, remains to be seen.

In Reconstruction scholarship, methodological innovation has always been less significant than changes in the wider climate of opinion. From its inception as a distinct field early in the twentieth century, the writing about Reconstruction has had a pronounced political agenda, or at least contemporary overtones. Southern race relations remained under outside scrutiny as segregation solidified, and a body of historical literature emerged that ratified the region's racial practices. The "Dunning school" of William A. Dunning and his students long dominated the scholarship, aided by the emerging professionalization of history and the rise of graduate training as the credential for practice. Dunning's work clearly bore the impress of the racial settlement after the turn of the century, as the South adopted legal Jim Crow and the nation embraced imperialism. His *Reconstruction, Political and Economic* (1907) serves as the representative example of this literature. That work justified "Home Rule," and it implicitly buttressed the social order from internal and external criticism.

Dunning's *Reconstruction* provided a scholarly rationale of the earlier Democratic partisan critique of Republican policies, the outlines of which it followed closely. Dunning argued that after the Civil War, President Andrew Johnson pursued President Abraham Lincoln's benign policies for a magnanimous peace. Southern efforts under Presidential Reconstruction, while not perfect, basically ratified emancipation and were likely all that could be expected under the circumstances of defeat. Outside interlopers, like the Union army, the Freedmen's Bureau, and the various missionary societies, undermined black social discipline while providing a drumbeat of public criticism. Seizing on the imperfections, fanatics like Thaddeus Stevens and Charles Sumner enflamed northern prejudices and induced a compliant Republican Congress to intervene. The result was Radical Reconstruction, which bestowed suffrage on an ill-prepared African-American population under the protection of federal bayonets. With the ruling southern white elite largely disfranchised, northern migrants ("carpetbaggers") and embittered southern renegades ("scalawags") provided the white leadership for a mass of ignorant black voters. A wave of corrupt and oppressive government followed as extravagant subsidies for railroads generated immense legislative corruption along with escalating taxes. Goaded by Radical misrule and egalitarian extremism, white southerners eventually turned to extralegal violence to overturn Reconstruction. Though excesses occurred under the Ku Klux Klan and the later White Leagues, there was no alternative to intimidation, given the massive provocation. In the end even the northern public tired of the corruption and disorder, and in 1877 Redemption restored power to the native elite, thus rescuing white southerners from "permanent subjection to another race" (Dunning 1907: vii).

The underlying contention was that the federal mandate of black suffrage had been a mistake, motivated by malice and partisanship. Scholars' depiction of events had more nuance than its cinematic reflection, the wildly successful *Birth of a Nation*, but the 1915 movie popularized this interpretation before a national audience. The Dunning viewpoint still enjoys an unsettling popular credence outside the university, its stock images persisting as a folk memory. Dunning's influence was enhanced by his Columbia University graduate students, often from outside the South, who dominated the scholarship for decades. They produced a raft of state studies, some of them of more enduring interest for probing the racial orthodoxy. James W. Garner's *Reconstruction in Mississippi* (1901) demonstrated relative open mindedness, interviewing the African-American ex-Congressman John Roy Lynch. Garner also solicited the recollections of the reviled carpetbag Governor Adelbert Ames and concluded that the tales of corruption under his rule were wildly exaggerated. Similarly, Mildred Thompson's study of Georgia appeared in 1915, late enough for her to witness the rebirth of the Ku Klux Klan, and her enthusiasm for the Reconstruction terrorists is notably muted.

Some of the state studies, on the other hand, were less judicious than Dunning, with Walter Lynwood Fleming's *Civil War and Reconstruction in Alabama* (1905) being perhaps the most troublesome for modern sensibilities. Fleming derided egalitarian aspirations as folly: Republicans supposedly told blacks that "if they did not vote they would be re-enslaved and their wives made to work the roads and quit wearing hoopskirts" (Fleming 1905: 514). Almost as striking as his racial animus were his strictures against poorer whites, depicting their resentments as being the basis of Unionism during the war and scalawag sentiment afterwards. Fleming invidiously anticipated a class interpretation: his Alabama Tories, from the "lowest class of the population," were a century behind the times and "shut off from the world." Beyond animosity toward their betters, they knew "scarcely anything of the Union or of the questions at issue" (ibid: 114). His treatment of the Ku Klux Klan demonstrates similar tendencies. He depicts it as initially a restrained, defensive organization dominated by planters, mostly social rather than political in intent. The movement's increasing violence he blames squarely on the increasing control of the Klan bands by poorer whites, bent on havoc.

By the 1920s, as racial egalitarian ideas became increasingly influential among intellectuals, one might have expected such biases to have generated dissent, but criticism developed slowly. The Progressive historiography that dominated the era's scholarship downplayed racial matters in favor of the struggle between the democratic masses and corporate elites. The Beardsian view of the Civil War as the "Second American Revolution," the triumph of capital over the agrarian populace, depicted Republican humanitarian sentiments toward the black people as a front for less savory motivations. The anti-capitalist surge of the 1930s only augmented this tendency to subsume the racial justice issue. Andrew Johnson, for example, emerged as the champion of the older America, while the protectionist ironmaker Thaddeus Stevens became the ironic symbol of a new corporate order.

Early criticism of the Dunning school's findings came from the margins of academic life. African-American scholars and leftists, inside and outside the university, were among those who challenged the prevailing discourse first. Though professionally marginalized, they anticipated the themes so evident later on. The most prominent of these early critics was the noted scholar and activist W. E. B. Du Bois, whose *Black Reconstruction* (1935) was a landmark. By his own admission, Du Bois lacked extensive archival basis for his work; instead, he critiqued the intellectual grounding of the existing literature, especially the assumption that blacks were "sub-human and congenitally unfitted for citizenship and the suffrage" (ibid: 724, 731). As a civil rights leader, Du Bois's enthusiasm for federal activism disposed him to see the positive accomplishments of Reconstruction, like the humanitarian work of the Freedmen's Bureau and the expansion of public education under the Republicans. He combined an interest in African-American agency with the Marxist emphasis on class struggle to yield results far different from those of the Beardsians. Du Bois anticipated the later turn of the field toward racial egalitarianism, and several of his conceptions remain influential. His notion of a wartime "general strike" by plantation hands crippling the Confederate war effort and forcing the hands of Union policy makers remains compelling, as does his insistence that agricultural laborers took a direct political role through their workplace behavior (ibid: 55). Du Bois forcefully articulated the conception of Reconstruction as a biracial social movement, with poor blacks and poor whites uniting for democratic change against planter rule. Du Bois neatly inverted the previous ethical valuation of what previous scholars invidiously depicted as a lower-class phenomenon, white support for Reconstruction.

At the time he wrote, Du Bois conceded he was almost alone in his conclusions, but other historians gradually began to critique the prevailing view, if more gently. Though not focused directly on Reconstruction, the late C. Vann Woodward's reworking of the Progressive tradition offered an important corrective. His *Origins of the New South* (Woodward 1951a) assailed the Dunning school's heroes, the Redeemers who overthrew Reconstruction, as moneyed reactionaries who were often corrupt in their own right. His study of the 1876 election, *Reunion and Reaction* (Woodward 1951b), highlighted the role of corporate influence on the end of Reconstruction, while his *Strange Career of Jim Crow* (Woodward 1955) challenged the inevitability of the southern way of life, contending that wholesale apartheid had not characterized southern society until legislated into place. Woodward's emphases were broadly consonant with some of the themes of the revisionists later on, but these aspects of his work sparked scattered emulation at the moment.

With the Cold War, scholarly tastes turned at mid-century toward a more celebratory approach to the American past. Those highlighting the "consensus" undergirding American life somehow found little to say about the Civil War era, slowing the process of reevaluation.

It took the civil rights struggles of the 1960s for the trickle of revisionist scholarship to become a flood. The "Second Reconstruction" made the racial issues of a century earlier suddenly bear on pressing concerns. Historical analogies proliferated: John Kennedy once mused that "maybe Thaddeus Stevens was right," while a prominent study of civil rights activists termed them "the New Abolitionists." Learned monographs suddenly found mass distribution in paperback editions. Publishing scholars were almost universally sympathetic to contemporary civil rights struggles, in southern universities as elsewhere. All aspects of the older Dunning literature came under attack, repudiated by the literate public almost overnight; the older school found few articulate defenders, its leading lights being long since dead and buried. Republican Reconstruction was rehabilitated, the regimes' goals if not their actual accomplishments lauded. The astonishing if incomplete triumph of the southern civil rights movement, culminating in the abrupt federal dismantling of Jim Crow, only reemphasized the importance of this earlier moment of breathtaking change.

John Hope Franklin's *Reconstruction after the Civil War* (1961) commenced the decade's revisionist outpouring, and Kenneth M. Stampp's *The Era of Reconstruction* (1965) is the obvious exemplar of the new school of interpretation. Stampp's work demonstrates both the strengths and the liabilities of the wider shift in attitude, as he simultaneously mounted an attack on nearly all aspects of the "Tragic Legend of Reconstruction." One might almost compile a checklist as Stampp challenged the older depictions one after another: congressional Radicals were neo-abolitionists, struggling to secure the fruits of the war against a pig-headed and violently racist President Johnson, who was not at all following in his martyred predecessor's footsteps. Far from being victimized, white southerners experienced a postwar settlement unusual in its mildness. The Ku Klux Klan was a terrorist gang, pure and simple, while the carpetbaggers by contrast came in for rehabilitation; they were not freebooters but were often idealistic critics of the South's racial practices. Republican corruption was exaggerated, for the bulk of government revenues went to railroad subsidies and schools and other necessary social spending. Besides, he avers, "why was the tar brush applied to those who accepted the bribes and not to those who offered them?" (ibid: 180). Even taxation under Reconstruction was not excessive, since levies would inevitably have had to increase after the war, regardless of who was in power. While Stampp carefully conceded that the Reconstruction regimes had their drawbacks, his caveats tended to be overlooked in the polemical needs of the mid-1960s. Stampp's primary aim was a thoroughgoing rebuttal of the Dunning school version of Reconstruction.

Given the urgency of the surrounding events, a presentist orientation was inevitable. There was a certain uncritical quality to the reaction, the refutation of the previous racist literature being more urgent than formulating a coherent new version of what actually occurred. For example, the gigantic social changes accompanying emancipation are not prominent in his analysis, nor is African-American political agency all that evident. *The Era of Reconstruction* concentrates narrowly on formal politics, with racial justice overshadowing other concerns. This was most obvious in Stampp's approach to class issues among those whites most sympathetic to Reconstruction, a topic which he barely touches upon. Stampp demurs from the Dunning school depiction of white Republicans, pointing out that "all scalawags were not degraded poor whites," adding that individual native white leaders often had elite backgrounds (ibid: 160). He similarly calls W. E. B. Du Bois's account "disappointing," with its characterization of Reconstruction as a proletarian movement dismissed as "naïve" (ibid: 218). One problem with this approach is that it leaves the nature and composition of white Republican support rather unexplored.

Many other works pursued Stampp's general approach, the unifying feature of which was a forthright and sometimes indiscriminate rejection of the emphases of the previous writing. In 1968 Stampp and Leon Litwack coedited a revisionist anthology, noting that the literature was already so large that one book could only provide a small sample (Stampp and Litwack 1968: viii). Some of the very titles suggest the moral urgency of the moment, like Hans Trefousse's *The Radical Republicans: Lincoln's Vanguard for Racial Justice* (1969). The drastic changes in the wider political climate in the late 1960s only gradually influenced the direction of the work. Even after the emergence of "Black Power" and the disorienting events of the late 1960s, the outpouring of sympathetic scholarship continued. This made a certain sense: the white liberals who dominated the profession could easily identify with the demands of African-Americans for legal equality, so pronounced in the Reconstruction era's politics. One might almost discern a certain nostalgia for a time when African-Americans unambiguously sought incorporation into American life.

Still, the novelty of revisionism eventually passed, and gradually scholars began to reconsider the state of the field in light of contemporary events. By the 1970s straightforward celebration of federal activism and liberal reform seemed less compelling. No one mourned the Dunning literature, but new scholarship left some obvious loose ends. After all, the Reconstruction regimes were overthrown and the egalitarian upsurge of the era crushed. Simply decrying that outcome paled quickly. Whatever virtues of aspiration Reconstruction possessed, one could hardly maintain it was a wholesale success – though I recall trying to make this argument myself as a graduate student. Such aberrations aside, some effort to come to terms with the result was inescapable.

Over time, historians became less upbeat in dealing with the successes of Reconstruction, less inclined to see formal legal equality as a transcendent accomplishment while more skeptical of the northern social agenda. Louis Gerteis (1973) saw the origins of the repressive Black Codes in federal army policy toward the refugee population. A more general disillusionment with the federal government's role was common. In a startling reversal of the Dunning school, many scholars contended that Reconstruction hadn't gone far enough. Michael Les Benedict, for example, contended that congressional Reconstruction was fatally flawed by its accommodation of states' rights precedents: Republicans preferred to alter the government's traditional federal structure as little as possible. William McFeely's *Yankee Stepfather: General O. O. Howard and the Freedmen's Bureau* (1968) provides an early and influential example of this trend. His bureau is a study in co-optation. Commissioner O. O. Howard, knowing full well that land reform was the freedmen's most pressing need, found himself evicting thousands off confiscated farms in order to maintain his position under President Johnson. Howard replaced egalitarian officers with bureaucrats of a more conservative bent who pressed annual contracts as agricultural laborers on restive freedpeople. In sum, much of Howard's work "served to preclude rather than promote Negro freedom" (McFeely 1968: 5). McFeely reflects a common conviction of the insignificance of legal equality, that nothing short of revolutionary economic change – land redistribution – would have made much difference.

The emphasis on the half-hearted character of Reconstruction reform became the most coherent of several prospective "postrevisionist" formulations. One might see it as a historiographic analogue of the New Left mood of disillusionment with liberal reform, which usefully highlighted the distinction between the goals of the freedpeople and those of their Yankee benefactors. Though plausible in specific cases, this postrevisionist position was difficult to sustain as an overarching interpretation. Confiscation, however vital for the freedpeople, had limited support with the northern public, and presidential control of the pardoning process made constitutional obstacles daunting. Land redistribution was probably beyond the bounds of political possibility once the war ended and Andrew Johnson assumed office. More fundamentally, Radical Reconstruction, whatever its limitations, represented a serious attempt to enforce basic legal equality. This represented so drastic a departure in nineteenth-century practice that it seems almost utopian for scholars to underestimate its radicalism. After all, it took the nation nearly a century to regain the ground lost with Redemption. On the other hand, this postrevisionist approach had the major virtue of bringing the accomplishments of Reconstruction into question, opening the era's ultimate meaning to serious debate.

The theme of insufficient radicalism inspired the first critical examination of African-American political leadership, Thomas Holt's groundbreaking *Black Over White* (1977). This was an original effort to rethink the 1960s developments and their implications for the study of Reconstruction. In South Carolina, where African-American direct influence was strongest, Holt finds that a light-skinned and freeborn elite dominated black political life. These leaders pursued a civil rights agenda suited to their social circumstances, open accommodations laws and the like, as opposed to the land-reform measures that might have helped their poorer rural constituents. Thus the black leadership "failed," and the Republican majority, rather than being overthrown by outside force, was undermined from within. Black disunity, Holt contends, doomed Reconstruction because whites "would have chosen to make their peace with a strong government, responsive or not" (Holt 1977: 4). Clearly informed by contemporary debates in the black community over Black Power, Holt's work combines a fresh reading of the sources with a sophisticated analysis of legislative voting. However, several of his specific conclusions remain subject to dispute. One wonders about the author's belief that the state's notorious corruption did not undermine Republican rule, given the national political context and necessity for outside support. There is also little evidence that rural blacks were any less enthusiastic about civil rights laws than their freeborn social betters, which complicates depicting such measures as elitist. Furthermore, South Carolina was the only state that implemented a substantial program of land redistribution; rather than being indifferent to their poorer colleagues, the political leadership was thus unusually attentive to them. Francis Cardozo, the college-educated foil of much of Holt's book, was apparently the one honest man on the land commission, as opposed to his four white colleagues taking bribes. Privileged or not, it is hard to see him as unfaithful to his rural constituents. These issues aside, Holt's work was a unique contribution to Reconstruction political history, bringing a cogency to the analysis of social and class forces within the black community seldom seen to that point, or since, for that matter.

Perhaps the overriding influence on the historiography during this period was less specific works than the broader professional context, as the increasing vogue of "history from the bottom up" emphasized black popular agency. Encouraged by the outpouring of cutting-edge scholarship in the study of slavery, books like Herbert Gutman's *The Black Family in Slavery and Freedom* (1976) and Leon Litwack's *Been in the Storm So Long* (1979) heralded a similar approach to the postwar world. With the rise of social history to prominence in the discipline, the story of Reconstruction politics became less in demand. Some suggest the very "Era of Reconstruction" had been largely eclipsed by the "Era of Emancipation," with the former slaves' aspirations at the center of the narrative. Whatever challenges this posed, the new scholarship also opened up fresh avenues for understanding the social bases of politics. Increased emphasis on the era's intense grassroots movements suggested the necessity of breaking down the walls between social and traditional political history. For example, the influential volumes of *Freedom: A Documentary History of Emancipation* (Berlin, Reidy, and Rowland 1982–) document the wartime plantation crisis and its aftermath, demonstrating the interconnection between labor transformation and high politics. Michael W. Fitzgerald's *Union League Movement in the Deep South* (1989) interpreted Radical agitation as an outgrowth of the labor unrest sweeping the plantation system, much as did Julie Saville's *The Work of Reconstruction* (1994). In contemporary writing on Reconstruction politics, some of the most influential works are not strictly speaking political history at all, or rather, they manifest a broader definition of what is political. The newer work also extends the era far beyond the accepted chronological demarcations, based as they are on traditional political landmarks.

With respect to the white population, Steven Hahn's *The Roots of Southern Populism* (1983) illustrates these tendencies well. This study examines political and social developments among the yeomanry in the Georgia hill country, from the Jacksonian period through the 1880s. He uses the notion of the "dual economy" and the upcountry farmer's continuing dependence on the free ranging of livestock to illuminate traditional attitudes of the yeomanry relative to the planters of the rich cotton belt. Using census data, Hahn demonstrates the penetration of commercial credit and cash-crop agriculture into the upcountry, a decades-long process transforming traditional attitudes toward private property and community rights. Hahn devotes modest attention to the specific issues of Reconstruction, and he is in general little inclined to emphasize the racial limitations of his protagonists. For example, his brief discussion of the Ku Klux Klan describes it as elite led, without examining what impact fears of livestock theft might have had among his small farmers, in terms of encouraging support for extralegal violence (Hahn 1983: 212–14). Such questions aside, and despite subsequent challenges to his whole framework, Hahn's broad interpretation has been enormously influential in understanding Unionist and scalawag sentiments and their limitations. His book socially contextualized the tradition of upcountry dissent so evident in the politics of the Civil War and Reconstruction.

Beyond deepening scholars' understanding of the era, the emergence of social and labor history in emancipation studies had another effect on those writing on the politics. The stress on positive black agency in other spheres seemingly broke the taboo on criticizing Reconstruction – that is, for something besides being insufficiently drastic. A more pragmatic bent emerged, as political historians became increasingly willing to confront the electoral weaknesses of the Reconstruction regimes. The underlying issue is how Republicans might have breached the wall of conservative white hostility that eventually prevailed. Several studies appeared that sympathetically examined the "moderate" or scalawag faction within the southern Republican parties, as opposed to the black-dominated "Radical" or carpetbag faction. Sarah Wiggins (1977) argued the prominence of propertied scalawags in the Republican leadership in Alabama, while Elizabeth Nathans (1969) envisioned a Whig–black alliance behind a New South-style program of economic development in Georgia. William Harris's *Day of the Carpetbagger* (1979) was probably the most influential of these works, spelling out the viewpoint most explicitly. Harris's exhaustive study of Mississippi focuses on the administration of Governor James Lusk Alcorn. This rich planter and former Whig, an established political leader, was able to solidify some degree of acquiescence from the white population. His Radical opponent, Adelbert Ames, could never achieve this, and so despite his personal probity and egalitarian intent, Governor Ames presided over the overthrow of Reconstruction in a spasm of violence. For Harris, the moderate Republicans like Alcorn might have stabilized power had more Radical voices not undermined their black support.

This formulation is not to be readily dismissed. For Reconstruction to have succeeded, it probably required a substantial minority of the white vote, even in the few black-majority states, given the national context. Established scalawag moderates, attentive to white racial sensitivities, likely had the best opportunity to cobble together a majority coalition. Such leaders also arguably had a better chance to govern effectively, and whatever their liabilities, they should have been less racist than the Redeemers. Despite the obvious logic of this position, historians generally have been skeptical, much as were the freedpeople themselves. For moderate politicians, the search for legitimacy meant distancing themselves from civil rights demands. Moderate Republicans thus disappointed black expectations again and again, in Alcorn's case by appointing conservatives to local office. In some cases this was a matter of life and death, for moderate Republicans generally opposed federal anti-Klan legislation as an intrusion on state authority. Alabama's Governor William Hugh Smith actually denied the Klan's existence in his state, in the face of widespread political violence. Furthermore, the extravagant opportunism of men like Joseph Brown in Georgia is difficult to overlook, and as Armstead Robinson argued, Whiggish leadership had little to offer poorer Unionists in the upcountry – the backbone of scalawag support. In sum, the limitations of the moderate Republican leadership were so pronounced, especially on racial matters, as to render them implausible protagonists. Given the circumstances, African-Americans could hardly defer to their leadership and expect a positive outcome.

Other scholars challenged the favorable revisionist depiction of Reconstruction more directly by reexamining some of the older positions long since discredited. Several frankly dissected the defects of Republican rule. For example, J. Mills

Thornton examined Reconstruction tax policy, concluding that Republicans presided over a gigantic rise in property levies. The bulk of the white population, small farm owners, saw dramatic increases which drove them into the arms of the Redeemers (Thornton 1982: 350). Thornton concludes that tax policy rather than unvarnished racism offers an alternative "persuasive explanation" for the decline of scalawag sentiment (ibid: 391). In another influential article, Lawrence N. Powell builds on his work on northern planters in the South to reexamine the stereotype of carpetbaggers as opportunistic office seekers. Powell concludes that most Republican activists were financially marginal men, so ostracized from the white community as to be nearly unemployable. The resulting dependency on political jobs "greatly aggravated the factional weaknesses to which Southern Republicans were already prone" (Powell 1982: 316). Thus patronage disputes and office seeking became matters of personal necessity, which encouraged the infighting that facilitated Democratic victory. For all the criticism of Reconstruction, though, these scholars rather shied away from examining black agency on tax or patronage issues, or how these choices advanced a racial agenda. Given the earlier racist Dunning school depiction, it is as though to be skeptical of the Republicans in power, one has to write African-Americans out of the story.

This pattern is evident in the work of Mark W. Summers, the most prolific of these "post-postrevisionists," if such a cumbersome term might be employed. Summers has made something of a cottage industry of corruption studies in the Civil War era, and for southern history purposes his *Railroads, Reconstruction, and the Gospel of Prosperity* (Summers 1984) is his crucial work. It was the first substantial study of the railroad program in over half a century, itself a striking statement given the obvious significance of the topic. Though modern scholars recognized the problem of corruption, few seemed inclined to write on it at length. Summers concedes the plausibility, and even necessity, of subsidy policies, for without public aid railroads would not soon have been built in the devastated region. He also emphasizes that the program worked, that there was an enormous increase in mileage during the period, with tremendous long-term economic benefit. He stresses the substantial Democratic support for subsidy measures, which tended to be broadly popular among the white public. Still, the Republicans were in power and provided most of the votes for enactment, and Summers's depiction of their conduct is harsh: "Republicans had ruled badly, and they admitted it. They had elected incompetents and mountebanks, corruptionists and self-serving mediocrities." Bribery secured enactment of laws that were executed wretchedly, culminating in bankruptcy for several states. His "inescapable" conclusion was that, judged by the gap between their promises and actual performance, "the Republicans deserved to lose power" (ibid: 295). Few other scholars would agree, so overriding is continuing concern with civil rights. Still, no one has challenged Summers's findings, and certainly the more favorable revisionist depiction of Reconstruction's accomplishments has come full circle, when so distasteful a conclusion could be seriously entertained.

Where, then, stands the current study of the political history of the era? Writing after the revisionist and postrevisionist waves, two major 1980s works stand out as broad syntheses of the field, the differences between them providing some notion of areas most in contention. The first is *The Road to Redemption* by Michael Perman (1984), whose own work illustrates several of the major changes in the historiography of recent decades. Perman's previous venture, *Reunion without Compromise* (1973), depicted Reconstruction in postrevisionist terms, as hamstrung by the Republican Congress's desire for the acquiescence of the ex-Confederate elite. The crisis of Presidential Reconstruction "demanded a radical solution," like wholesale disfranchisement. Anything else was "dangerous and delusive," and would fail in the long run (ibid: 547). In *The Road to Redemption*, by contrast, Perman focuses on how the long-neglected Democratic opposition struggled during the Grant years, with particular attention to the Whiggish moderates whose allegiance was in flux.

For all the complexity of Reconstruction factionalism, Perman discerns a strikingly simple pattern. Among the Republicans, as Whiggish scalawags like Alcorn in Mississippi assumed leadership, they reached out to the white electorate, a majority in most places. Much the same thing happened in reverse on the Democratic side. After U. S. Grant's victory in the 1868 presidential election, many conservative whites reconsidered their public association with social extremism and Klan violence. They thus moved toward a "competitive" mode of centrist political behavior, as opposed to an "expressive" strategy of reflecting the intransigent views of their strongest supporters. The result for the next several years was a "politics of convergence" as both sides collaborated on several issues, most obviously on railroad aid. For Democrats, this "New Departure" politics took the form of public acceptance of the Fourteenth and Fifteenth Amendments, with at least implicit criticism of Klan terrorists.

The high point of the New Departure came in 1872 when Democrats reluctantly backed the presidential bid of the Liberal Republican insurgent, Horace Greeley. Greeley's catastrophic defeat forced reappraisal, while the depression of 1873 weakened President Grant and changed calculations of what the northern electorate would tolerate. In the South economic depression also bankrupted many railroad projects. Whiggish economic policies were abandoned, with "a resurgence of the party's agrarian constituency and of the ideas and men formerly associated with the Democracy" (Perman 1984: 265). The initiative thus passed to the proponents of the "White Line," who favored an aggressive assertion of race resentment laced with intimidation of black voters. On the Republican side, roughly analogous developments took place in reverse. After Grant's reelection the African-American electorate tired of conciliatory gestures. They insisted on more representation in leadership and more attention to their distinctive concerns, a process that culminated in the passage of the Civil Rights Act of 1875, integrating most public facilities by federal law. The difference, for Perman, is that the surge toward Radicalism was less a political strategy than a gut-level response to the failures of the moderate Republicans in power, exacerbated by the economic troubles.

According to Perman there was considerable debate within the Democratic ranks over the expediency of the White Line approach, especially among ex-Whigs who feared the social and political ramifications of violence. A groundswell of militancy among upcountry white voters overwhelmed them, and Democrats won smashing victories in 1874 on explicitly White Line campaigns. Republicans remained in power in only the few southern states where blacks were at or near a majority of the electorate. Only fraud and intimidation could prevail here, and the "Mississippi plan" of 1875 demonstrated that the federal government would not intervene, even when Democratic rifle clubs deterred blacks from voting. Thus the brokered outcome of the Hayes–Tilden election the following year only ratified a foregone conclusion. Perman concludes that agrarian racial extremists successfully "Redeemed" the South in the worst possible way.

As a top-down account of the region's political history Perman's account works admirably. He took the first serious look in decades at the Democrats, and he also took a body of bewildering political detail and imposed a coherent pattern upon it, one that is reasonably consistent with the evidence. Still, his account raises unresolved issues, most critically regarding the social constituency of the political forces he examines. For example, upcountry anti-Confederate sentiment had been substantial in the early postwar years, and the process by which Republicans alienated Unionist voters probably deserves more exploration, for they were arguably the whites most crucial to the outcome. More centrally, Perman's book implicitly relieves planters from blame for most of the violence. In Perman's words, the focus of racial moderation was in "the black counties" of areas like South Carolina's tidewater or the plantation belt of Mississippi (Perman 1984: 164). While this identification seems plausible, one wonders how far it resonated beyond the ranks of the political elite. After all, the White Line campaigns of mid-decade spread violence throughout the plantation regions, into areas where intimidation had seldom been seen on this scale before. Who was directing the operation, if not the planter elite? As with his earlier discussion of the Ku Klux Klan, the political sources Perman examines may be insufficient to document the actual attitudes of the planter class towards political violence and the range of social objectives such violence served.

If Perman's book devotes limited attention to social context, the other major overview certainly avoids this problem. Eric Foner's *Reconstruction: America's Unfinished Revolution* (1988) updates the basic revisionist interpretation in light of the literature on emancipation. Foner aims "to view the period as a whole, integrating the social, political, and economic aspects of Reconstruction into a coherent, analytical narrative" (Foner 1988: xxvii). This massively researched study is the preeminent synthesis of the field, with its excellent abridged version, *A Short History of Reconstruction* (1989), widely used as a college text. *Reconstruction*'s appearance was greeted by an outpouring of laudatory reviews, albeit with a smattering of criticism for neglect of gender issues. Even now, over a decade later, it seems unlikely that it will lose this premiere status soon.

Foner's work follows several of Du Bois's interpretive leads and is broadly consistent with the revisionists' main points as well. African-American agency is the central theme, as the ex-slave population moved to make freedom real in a variety of ways: through rebuilding and restructuring family life, securing education for their children, and establishing churches and mutual-aid societies under their own control. The plantations are the main focus of struggle, as traditional practices like gang labor, women and children in the workforce, tight supervision, and physical coercion came under intense black pressure. The slogan "Forty acres and a mule" encapsulated black demands for greater autonomy, even as the plantation elite utilized state power to buttress discipline. Thus the struggle over the future of the plantation fueled the mass insurgency after suffrage. One sometimes hears criticism of the Marxist overtones of Foner's work, but his stress on the centrality of the plantation conflict is difficult to dispute.

Foner reaffirms the Radicalism of the Reconstruction enterprise, which after all extended federal protection and a measure of state power to landless black laborers.

His previous book, *Nothing But Freedom* (1983), catalogues how unique the American grant of suffrage was in hemispheric context, with ferocious labor statutes being prevalent elsewhere. In *Reconstruction* he calls black suffrage "a massive experiment in interracial democracy" (Foner 1988: xxv). Foner acknowledges that northern egalitarian commitments coming out of the war were limited, and that the army and the Freedmen's Bureau often directed black behavior in ways thought appropriate. Even so, the postrevisionist emphasis on Reconstruction's essential conservatism did not seem "altogether persuasive" in the wider context of American history, and especially in view of the era's lively African-American political participation (ibid: xxiii). The book provides a detailed catalogue of black initiative: positive proposals for schools and expanded social services, blacks as jurors and in law enforcement. The argument is that African-Americans had a reasonable notion of what they needed, and they chose officials, black and white, who acted on their demands. In some areas, especially where black majorities were large enough to deter terrorist activities, Reconstruction came close to living up to its egalitarian promise.

Foner observes that in contemporary historical writing "changes in the relative power of social classes" had again become a "central concern," and class is certainly one of his major emphases (ibid: xxiv). He is sensitive to the issue within the black community, arguing that the more privileged segments gradually lost political leadership to more representative spokesmen, though these divisions were always secondary to the wider racial divide. Class differences were more pressing among those whites disposed toward Reconstruction. For Foner, wartime Unionists in the upcountry, often poor, were the crucial scalawag constituency. Their interests, however, contradicted those of other wealthier scalawags and northern newcomers interested in economic modernization or railroads. These differences over economic policy combined with distaste for civil rights placed the Republican coalition under strain from the beginning. Foner nonetheless emphasizes that "despite racism, a significant number of Southern whites were willing to link their political fortunes with those of blacks" (ibid: xxv).

This emphasis on class, combined with the centrality of the plantation labor struggle, raises interesting interpretive issues in terms of white behavior. For Foner, the Ku Klux Klan developed out of labor conflict as much as black enfranchisement – the two being thoroughly interconnected. While the Klan's membership crossed class lines and was composed mostly of smaller farmers, its leadership was politician and planter-dominated, and the organization pursued a labor-control agenda as well as a partisan one. This interpretation, it will be recalled, is at drastic variance from Perman's stress on the relative moderation of the Whiggish black Belt planters. These two views might be reconciled: by all accounts, the planter presence in the Klan was most pronounced before Grant's election, when labor unrest and white fears of insurrection were most intense. One might explain diminishing support for terror by wealthy planters with reference to greater awareness of the national political climate, especially as federal Klan prosecutions loomed. One suspects, though, that Foner's lack of sympathy for the planters' viewpoint makes him minimize the differences in racial attitudes and calculation of expediency within the conservative ranks.

Foner's account also raises the issue of the ultimate meaning of the era. He concludes that for blacks, Reconstruction's failure was "a disaster whose magnitude cannot be obscured by the genuine accomplishments" (ibid: 604). Still, the book as a whole emphasizes the positive legacy: Redemption destroyed "much, but by no means all, of what had been accomplished" (ibid: xxvii). Foner also persuasively argues that federal enforcement legislation temporarily crushed the Ku Klux Klan, which suggests that sufficient northern resolve might have yielded a different outcome. As an historian, I would like to believe Reconstruction accomplished something, and there certainly were benign results, direct and indirect. One might talk about the irreversible gains in public education, the disintegration of the centralized plantation system, and the Fifteenth Amendment, whose implementation in the North became crucial with the Great Migration. In terms of the African-American community, the memory of Reconstruction political struggle certainly informed later drives for civil rights.

All that said, Foner's discussion raises the issue of whether Reconstruction achieved anything overall, for one can point to negative results as readily as positive ones. The Reconstruction intervention, and its successful overthrow by force, strengthened the forces of reaction among southern whites. The memory encouraged xenophobia and fears of big government, especially an activist federal government. State bankruptcies after Reconstruction limited government spending for decades, while demonstrating that black suffrage meant fiscal ruin. Reconstruction's horrors would be the rallying cry for extremists for the next century, legitimizing racial excess as self-preservation. The turn of the century lynching craze is difficult to envision without Reconstruction, extralegal force having been proven the essential buttress of white supremacy. Foner notes all this but does not comment upon a crucial implication. If Reconstruction's legacy strengthened the most intransigent forces in southern life, it encouraged the traits that eventually forced federal intervention in the showdown of the 1960s. The memory of Nat Turner and John Brown once goaded the ruling class toward self-destruction, and a century later the egalitarian vision of Thaddeus Stevens encouraged a similar reaction, as the threat of the civil rights movement became real. Perhaps one might claim ultimate victory for Radical Reconstruction through disaster. Be this as it may, Foner's emphasis on the positive legacy of Reconstruction is one of the boldest and most thought-provoking of his conclusions.

Since the appearance of Foner's work, the most dramatic recent trend in the literature has been to incorporate gender, not surprisingly in view of wider changes in the profession. This tendency has been most apparent in the 1990s, but to an extent it has been happening for some time. For example, Jacqueline Jones's *Labor of Love, Labor of Sorrow* (1985) contextualizes the struggle to rebuild the slave family and the withdrawal of freedwomen from the workforce amid emancipation. In terms of Reconstruction and the role of women in public life, Ellen DuBois's *Feminism and Suffrage* (1978) raised political issues more directly. The book explores how white abolitionists like Susan B. Anthony and Elizabeth Cady Stanton dealt with the abandonment of women's suffrage in favor of suffrage for black men. Both works fit well with the conventional narrative themes of the era, and synthetic works readily incorporated their insights. More recent historians of gender, however, have challenged the conceptualization of the Civil War era more fundamentally. In southern history as a whole, Stephanie McCurry's *Masters of Small Worlds* (1995) encouraged a rethinking of politics. In her study of the antebellum era, McCurry contends that historians have overlooked the assumptions that encouraged proslavery unity. All white landowners shared privilege through control over their households of legally subordinate wives, children, and slaves. Anti-abolitionist and anti-feminist ideas thus went together logically, forming a sort of higher synthesis of reaction. Following this general line of analysis, Peter Bardaglio's *Reconstructing the Household* (1995) examines the legal sphere to find dramatic changes resulting from the Civil War.

More crucially for our purposes, Laura F. Edwards's *Gendered Strife and Confusion* (1997) extends this concept into Reconstruction politics. In examining one North Carolina locality, Edwards finds that the postwar redefinition of the household shaped "traditionally defined political demands" (Edwards 1997: 18). Rights like legal marriage, control over women's labor and that of one's children, became political issues. After emancipation, conservatives saw African-American men as subordinate beings but granted them significant authority over their families in order to bolster social order. Enfranchisement changed things much more drastically. To institutionalize racial equality, Republicans vested black men with the legal rights over their households enjoyed by other free males, despite the fact that their social circumstances were quite different as wage laborers. With the gradual restoration of conservative rule, the language of independent manhood was used to disparage not only black men but those poorer whites who cooperated with them during and after Reconstruction. Thus the household was redefined by conservatives from a racial to a class basis over the course of the era.

Gendered Strife and Confusion provides one of the bolder reconceptualizations of the era since Foner. As a description of how Republican Reconstruction redefined the household, Edwards effectively demonstrates how intertwined the family was with wider political issues. However, she wants also to critique the underlying bias of the whole language of the household, stressing the conservative implications. It was, in her estimate, very "problematic" for Republicans to rely on "gender hierarchy" to erase existing racial and class barriers. Republicans thus "built their politics around a patriarchal structure that would later prove to be their undoing" (ibid: 21). In the abstract, of course, this is persuasive; the language of the male-directed household clearly influenced the parameters of debate. Still, one wonders how far to pursue this logic, or how historians can utilize this insight in practice. For southern Republicans, mirroring established images of the family was less tragic flaw than imperative necessity. Those seeking egalitarian change seldom prosper by spelling out the ultimate radical implications. Rather the contrary: it was a measure of Republicans' pragmatism that they put a racially egalitarian spin on the prevailing discourse. Emphasis on the anti-egalitarian implications may thus appear as an extension of the postrevisionist viewpoint, arguably accurate but of limited practical import.

Save for the introduction of gender issues, the literature on Reconstruction has not changed basic direction in recent years. Beyond the continuing influence of social history throughout the discipline, the most obvious tendency has been toward a certain pragmatism in political writing, perhaps in reaction to the previous ideologically charged scholarship. One reflection of this touches on the era of Reconstruction violence. In contrast to Perman's depiction of a quasi-normal partisan competition, a "politics of convergence" during Grant's first term, other scholars have emphasized the Ku Klux Klan upsurge at this very time. George C. Rable (1984) provided an overview of political violence, making the significant point that Klan terror was politically double-edged. It provoked a northern outcry and federal intervention, and it was thus less effective than the open White Leagues and rifle clubs of the mid-1870s. Richard Zuczek's *State of Rebellion* (1996) depicts terrorism in South Carolina as a "people's war," with conservatives switching back and forth between electoral politics and terror as circumstances allowed. Zuczek concludes that the emphasis on the internal failures of Reconstruction is exaggerated, that southern white hostility eventually won out, exhausting the northern will to enforce civil rights. By contrast, Christopher Waldrep's *Roots of Disorder* (1998) analyzes the resort to violence in social terms as an outgrowth of the legal changes following emancipation. His detailed study of local justice in Vicksburg concludes that the much-maligned postwar Black Codes permitted blacks significant legal access. Military Reconstruction allowed them much more, even if the mass of landless African-Americans were dramatically underrepresented on juries. The result was a perceived loss of control over the African-American population, despite high conviction rates under the Republicans. Small-scale theft infuriated property holders. Most whites doubted that the judicial process would sufficiently protect their interests, even when under conservative control. An enormous surge toward extralegal violence ensued because "law could never be made oppressive enough to effectively control African-Americans" (ibid: 174). While Waldrep stresses the moderate character of the legal reforms achieved during Reconstruction, all these works highlight the practical obstacles white resistance placed in the way of change.

In a sense, historians' heightened awareness of the practical constraints posed by white hostility underscores the ambitiousness of what Reconstruction attempted. Following Foner's lead, much of the recent work critiques aspects of the postrevision-ist writing. Several works, for example, have defended the Freedmen's Bureau against the charge of buttressing social control. Paul Cimbala's *Under the Guardianship of the Nation: The Freedmen's Bureau and the Reconstruction of Georgia* (1997) is probably the most significant and thoroughgoing of these. Cimbala argues it "a mistake" to stress the continuity between repressive wartime labor codes and bureau contract policy because the bureau men "had a different purpose" from earlier army officers (Cimbala 1997: xv–xvi). Most strikingly, Cimbala rehabilitates Davis Tillson, one of the bureau officials most commonly decried as conservative. Tillson stopped bureau land redistribution in coastal Georgia, and his enthusiasm for annual labor contracts was pronounced. Still, according to Cimbala, given the limited resources at his disposal, and the temporary status of his agency, Tillson "might have" formulated the most logical plan to help freedpeople, while his efforts to "co-opt white Georgians were reasonable" (ibid: 223). Cimbala's study argues that more Radical officers often fared worse in practice, being unable to protect anybody effectively. Practical constraints, rather than individual preferences, were the crucial factor limiting bureau effectiveness.

The rehabilitation of the Freedmen's Bureau's most conservative officers has not gone uncontested, but a renewed awareness of political constraints has been evident in other venues. With respect to federal policy toward the South, for decades scholars decried the Republican betrayal of civil rights. William McFeely's *Grant* (1981) presented a devastating critique of his abandonment of southern allies to their fate. William Gillette's overview, *Retreat from Reconstruction* (1979), offers much the same view: Reconstruction had been "neglected, discredited and deserted by many of its friends" (Gillette 1979: 380). This reproachful tone is difficult to escape, given subsequent events, but recently a more fatalistic reading of the available choices is more evident. Brooks Simpson, for example, has written extensively on U. S. Grant, arguing that by the time he assumed the presidency, he had some real if limited commitment to civil rights. *The Reconstruction Presidents* (Simpson 1998) argues that President Grant faced severe practical limitations in aiding the southern Republican regimes. Most Republican governments lost power to white electoral majorities, and once Grant implemented anti-Klan legislation there was not much more he could do. When open terrorist campaigns overturned black majorities, Grant often did intervene, but his political situation was weakened by the time of the crucial confrontations. Simpson observes that Grant's modern critics could not suggest a policy that would have achieved both sectional reconciliation and racial justice. Perhaps, Simpson concludes, failure "simply wasn't his fault" (ibid: 196). Simpson comes to much the same conclusion about the termination of Reconstruction. By 1877 Redemption was inevitable, a conviction that is shared by Ari Hoogenboom's biography *Rutherford B. Hayes: Warrior and President* (1995).

Living in a time of historic retreat from egalitarian aspirations, perhaps the current pragmatic bent of much of the writing is inevitable. Beyond this overriding appreciation of the limitations of practical politics in the recent literature, one might touch on several secondary tendencies in the current writing as well. A number of works extend the geographic focus away from the Deep South. There are several recent studies on Texas alone, often focusing on the local level, along with Carl Moneyhon's examination of Reconstruction's impact on the distribution of wealth in Arkansas. As with the new emphasis on gender issues, much of the recent writing moves beyond the narrowly racial issues that dominated writing since the second Reconstruction. The current resurgence of religious history has inspired several major works exploring the interconnection of church and politics. Litwack and other social historians rightly conceptualized the newly black-controlled churches in the context of the drive for autonomy, but there was much else going on besides. In a scene of bewildering complexity, southern Methodists confronted northern Methodist missionaries as well as two northern African Methodist denominations, not to mention a conservative native "Colored" one. Clarence Walker's (1982) pathbreaking examination of internal rivalries among black Methodists moved the discussion beyond denominational celebration. Reginald F. Hildebrand examined the interplay of contending forces in ideological terms. In particular, Hildebrand explored the currents of black nationalist sentiment often overlooked in the era's universalistic Radical rhetoric. More recently, Daniel W. Stowell's *Rebuilding Zion: The Religious Reconstruction of the South, 1863–1877* (1998) offers a full-scale history of southern evangelical Protestantism. It usefully clarifies the bewildering array of churches and conflict so evident in the era. Stowell correctly observes that "many scholars have neglected the role of religion" (Stowell 1998: 11) in Reconstruction; however, it is unclear how his account, useful as it is, changes the fundamental direction of the writing on politics.

Overall, in evaluating the state of the Reconstruction scholarship at the turn of a new century, several broader points stand out. As Jim Crow recedes in memory, the immediate civil rights concerns and analogies that animated previous writing should become less evident. In the future, one hopes that southern distinctiveness will not inspire continuing interregional strife over race relations. Reconstruction politics is thus unlikely to reacquire the sort of contemporary relevance it once possessed, and the popular audience should remain relatively modest for the foreseeable future.

While this has its drawbacks, there are compensations. The study of gender, religion, and other new fields should become more compelling; so should a renewed interest in nuances within the black community, rather than exclusive stress on the stark racial divide. The previous tendency toward agenda-driven history should be less intense, with less temptation to insist on an immediately usable past. Reconstruction always defied easy solutions, and even now its meaning for American history remains problematic. Perhaps a more modest, realistic vision of its political possibilities will be this generation's contribution to future scholarship.

BIBLIOGRAPHY

Anderson, Eric and Moss, Alfred A., Jr. (eds.) 1991: *The Facts of Reconstruction: Essays in Honor of John Hope Franklin.* Baton Rouge: Louisiana State University Press.

Bardaglio, Peter W. 1995: *Reconstructing the Household: Families, Sex and the Law in the Nineteenth-Century South.* Chapel Hill: University of North Carolina Press.

Benedict, Michael Les 1974: Preserving the Constitution: The Conservative Basis of Radical Reconstruction. *Journal of American History,* 61, 65–90.

Berlin, Ira, Reidy, Joseph P., and Rowland, Leslie S. (eds.) 1982–: *Freedom: A Documentary History of Emancipation.* New York: Cambridge University Press.

Cimbala, Paul A. 1997: *Under the Guardianship of the Nation: The Freedmen's Bureau and the Reconstruction of Georgia, 1865–1870.* Athens: University of Georgia Press.

DuBois, Ellen 1978: *Feminism and Suffrage: The Emergence of an Independent Women's Movement in America, 1848–1869.* Ithaca, NY: Cornell University Press.

Du Bois, W. E. B. 1935: *Black Reconstruction: An Essay Toward a History of the Part which Black Folk Played in the Attempt to Reconstruct America, 1860–1880.* New York: Russell and Russell.

Dunning, William Archibald 1907: *Reconstruction, Political and Economic, 1865–1877.* New York: Harper.

Edwards, Laura F. 1997: *Gendered Strife and Confusion: The Political Culture of Reconstruction.* Urbana: University of Illinois Press.

Fitzgerald, Michael W. 1989: *The Union League Movement in the Deep South: Politics and Agricultural Change During Reconstruction.* Baton Rouge: Louisiana State University Press.

Fleming, Walter Lynwood 1905: *Civil War and Reconstruction in Alabama.* New York: P. Smith.

Foner, Eric 1983: *Nothing But Freedom: Emancipation and Its Legacy.* Baton Rouge: Louisiana State University Press.

Foner, Eric 1988: *Reconstruction: America's Unfinished Revolution, 1863–1877.* New York: Harper and Row.

Foner, Eric 1990: *A Short History of Reconstruction, 1863–1877.* New York: Harper and Row.

Franklin, John Hope 1961: *Reconstruction: After the Civil War.* Chicago: University of Chicago Press.

Garner, James W. 1901: *Reconstruction in Mississippi.* New York: Macmillan.

Gerteis, Louis S. 1973: *From Contraband to Freedman: Federal Policy Toward Southern Blacks, 1861–1865.* Westport, CT: Greenwood Press.

Gillette, William 1979: *Retreat from Reconstruction, 1869–1879.* Baton Rouge: Louisiana State University Press.

Hahn, Steven 1983: *The Roots of Southern Populism: Yeoman Farmers and the Transformation of the Georgia Upcountry, 1850–1890.* New York: Oxford University Press.

Harris, William C. 1979: *The Day of the Carpetbagger: Republican Reconstruction in Mississippi.* Baton Rouge: Louisiana State University Press.

Hildebrand, Reginald F. 1995: *The Times Were Strange and Stirring: Methodist Preachers and the Crisis of Emancipation*. Durham, NC: Duke University Press.

Holt, Thomas 1977: *Black Over White: Negro Political Leadership in South Carolina during Reconstruction*. Urbana: University of Illinois Press.

Hoogenboom, Ari 1995: *Rutherford B. Hayes: Warrior and President*. Lawrence: University Press of Kansas.

Jones, Jacqueline 1985: *Labor of Love, Labor of Sorrow: Black Women, Work, and the Family from Slavery to the Present*. New York: Basic Books.

Litwack, Leon 1979: *Been in the Storm So Long: The Aftermath of Slavery*. New York: Alfred A. Knopf.

McCurry, Stephanie 1995: *Masters of Small Worlds: Yeoman Households, Gender Relations, and the Political Culture of the Antebellum South Carolina Low Country*. New York: Oxford University Press.

McFeely, William S. 1968: *Yankee Stepfather: General O. O. Howard and the Freedmen*. New Haven, CT: Yale University Press.

Moneyhon, Carl H. 1994: *The Impact of the Civil War and Reconstruction on Arkansas: Persistence in the Midst of Ruin*. Baton Rouge: Louisiana State University Press.

Nathans, Elizabeth Studley 1969: *Losing the Peace: Georgia Republicans and Reconstruction, 1865–1871*. Baton Rouge: Louisiana State University Press.

Nieman, Donald G. 1979: *To Set the Law in Motion: The Freedmen's Bureau and the Legal Rights of Blacks, 1865–1868*. Millwood, NY: KTO.

Perman, Michael 1973: *Reunion Without Compromise: The South and Reconstruction, 1861–1868*. Cambridge: Cambridge University Press.

Perman, Michael 1984: *The Road to Redemption: Southern Politics, 1869–1879*. Chapel Hill: University of North Carolina Press.

Powell, Lawrence N. 1982: The Politics of Livelihood: Carpetbaggers in the Deep South. In J. Morgan Kousser and James M. McPherson (eds.), *Region, Race and Reconstruction: Essays in Honor of C. Vann Woodward*. New York: Oxford University Press, 315–47.

Rable, George C. 1984: *But There Was No Peace: The Role of Violence in the Politics of Reconstruction*. Athens: University of Georgia Press.

Saville, Julie 1994: *The Work of Reconstruction: From Slave to Wage Laborer in South Carolina, 1860–1870*. New York: Cambridge University Press.

Simpson, Brooks D. 1991: *Let Us Have Peace: Ulysses S. Grant and the Politics of War and Reconstruction, 1861–1868*. Chapel Hill: University of North Carolina Press.

Simpson, Brooks D. 1998: *The Reconstruction Presidents*. Lawrence: University Press of Kansas.

Stampp, Kenneth M. 1965: *The Era of Reconstruction, 1865–1877*. New York: Vintage Books.

Stampp, Kenneth M. and Litwack, Leon F. (eds.) 1968: *Reconstruction: An Anthology of Revisionist Writings*. Baton Rouge: Louisiana State University Press.

Stowell, Daniel W. 1998: *Rebuilding Zion: The Religious Reconstruction of the South, 1863–1877*. New York: Oxford University Press.

Summers, Mark W. 1984: *Railroads, Reconstruction, and the Gospel of Prosperity: Aid under the Radical Republicans, 1865–1877*. Princeton, NJ: Princeton University Press.

Summers, Mark W. 1993: *The Era of Good Stealings*. New York: Oxford University Press.

Thompson, C. Mildred 1915: *Reconstruction in Georgia: Economic, Social, Political, 1865–1872*. New York: Columbia University Press.

Thornton, J. Mills 1982: Fiscal Policy and the Failure of Radical Reconstruction in the Lower South. In J. Morgan Kousser and James M. McPherson (eds.), *Region, Race and Reconstruction: Essays in Honor of C. Vann Woodward*. New York: Oxford University Press, 349–94.

Trefousse, Hans L. 1969: *The Radical Republicans: Lincoln's Vanguard for Racial Justice*. New York: Alfred A. Knopf.

Waldrep, Christopher 1998: *Roots of Disorder: Race and Criminal Justice in the American South, 1817–1880*. Urbana: University of Illinois Press.

Walker, Clarence E. 1982: *A Rock in a Weary Land: The African Methodist Episcopal Zion Church during the Civil War and Reconstruction*. Baton Rouge: Louisiana State University Press.

Wiggins, Sarah Woolfolk 1977: *The Scalawag in Alabama Politics, 1865–1881*. Tuscaloosa: University of Alabama Press.

Woodward, C. Vann 1951a: *Origins of the New South, 1877–1913*. Baton Rouge: Louisiana State University Press.

Woodward, C. Vann 1951b: *Reunion and Reaction: The Compromise of 1877 and the End of Reconstruction*. New York: Little, Brown.

Woodward, C. Vann 1955: *Strange Career of Jim Crow*. New York: Oxford University Press.

Zuczek, Richard 1996: *State of Rebellion: Reconstruction in South Carolina*. Columbia: University of South Carolina Press.

CHAPTER EIGHTEEN

Economic Consequences of the Civil War and Reconstruction

JOSEPH P. REIDY

AT first glance, the economic consequences of the Civil War are so obvious that the merest mention suffices to convey their importance. From a weak antebellum base, industry began to flourish; railroad mileage grew to an extent matched by few independent nations; and trade networks proliferated and the volume of goods carried increased apace. Agriculture, the mainstay of the antebellum economy, rebounded from the destruction and neglect of the war years despite dramatic changes in the labor system and in the markets for agricultural staples.

Historians have uncovered a tangle of explanations for these apparently straightforward developments. In fact, every major historical interpretation of the economic consequences of the Civil War has appeared to reopen one or more of the political battles that raged during Reconstruction. Students of the postbellum South have begun with the suppositions that enjoyed nearly universal currency in the days after Appomattox. First, wartime destruction required rebuilding the region's economic infrastructure. Second, military defeat required enduring even if not necessarily imbibing Yankee notions of economic development whose first commandment was thou shalt not hold thy fellow man in bondage.

The changing political contexts in which the historians interpreting the postbellum South lived and worked profoundly influenced their interpretations. During the Depression of the 1930s, for instance, when images of southern poverty filled picture magazines and presidential reports, scarcely a historian of the region could escape the burden of poverty that southerners stoically but nonetheless tragically bore. The obligation to explain this poverty has lived on in the historiography. By the same token, since World War II, when the first stirrings of the Civil Rights movement began to emerge, historians have questioned the racial heritage of the South. The habits of segregation and disfranchisement that had grown so customary over the prior half-century appeared in flagrant contradiction to American ideals of freedom and equality.

The modern historiography of the economic consequences of the Civil War begins with C. Vann Woodward's *Origins of the New South* (1951), an elegantly crafted framework for understanding the region's postwar economic history. Tapping the political sensibilities of the post-World War II world, Woodward cast the economic relationship between the two sections in provocative terms: the southern economy was nothing more or less than a colonial dependency of the North. A coalition of industrialists, financiers, and New South propagandists helped develop and then popularize a program of economic improvement wherein the South produced raw materials for northern (and European) factories. While for a few this system proved profitable, for the many it exacted staggering social costs that were simply "charged to 'progress'" (Woodward 1951: 310). Moreover, colonial dependency left the South at a marked disadvantage to the North by "almost any regional comparison of the distribution of wealth, income, wages, and goods" (ibid: 318).

If Woodward's colonial analogy held a mirror up to the nation, he focused a separate lens on the South. With restrained but nonetheless biting sarcasm, he cut through contemporary rationales of racial segregation and disfranchisement, exposing the racial discrimination that accompanied allegedly "progressive" social legislation. But by far his most lasting contribution to later historical debates grew out of his characterization of the Civil War's effect on the region's class structure.

Even apart from subjecting the South to northern political and economic interests, the North's victory coupled with the destruction of slavery forced an internal reconfiguration of southern social classes. Not only did slaves become free laborers, but as a result planters also became dispossessed of their chief form of wealth and power. A new class of businessmen, merchants, and attorneys found openings to amass wealth and political influence both locally and regionally. The transformation was "revolutionary." "In the main," Woodward argued, the new men "were of middle-class, industrial, capitalist outlook, with little but nominal connection with the old planter regime." Big fish in the southern pond, they were little more than minnows in the national political economy (ibid: 22, 20).

As Woodward was penning his masterpiece, the Civil Rights movement began nudging southern history in a new direction, one that brought critical sensibilities to bear on white supremacist ideology and the institutions that had birthed and nurtured it. First evident in the pioneering reexaminations of slavery that were published in the 1940s and 1950s, the revisionist wave soon swept across the Civil War and Reconstruction. Scholars assumed a sympathetic posture toward black southerners, even if they still looked at white southerners as the makers of history. Although much of this work reprised themes that a host of black authors from Carter G. Woodson and Charles H. Wesley to W. E. B. Du Bois and Rayford W. Logan had earlier explored, the revisionist message began to register in the mainstream of the historical profession and to achieve a measure of broader popularity. And if this work often displayed a liberal, integrationist bias that by today's standards appears naive, there can be no denying the radical shift that it represented at the time.

By the light of the old plantation school of slavery and the newer sociological studies, historians remained focused on the plantation as the normative social institution of slavery and the cotton plantation as the normative plantation. Certain technological and methodological advances as well as broader theoretical debates in the social sciences reinforced this judgment. In the subdiscipline of economic history, for instance, the methodological revolution hit high gear. A spate of studies focusing on the economic consequences of the Civil War and the profitability of slavery demonstrated the interpretive fruits that the new technology made possible (Andreano 1962; Conrad and Meyer 1964). And Eugene D. Genovese's *The Political Economy of Slavery* (1965) made a provocative case for maintaining interpretive focus on the plantations as critical to understanding the mainspring of southern history.

In such a climate of theoretical and methodological vitality, it is not coincidental that just as the econometricians Robert William Fogel and Stanley Engerman released their controversial *Time on the Cross* (1974), another pair of econometricians, Roger L. Ransom and Richard Sutch, applied similar quantitative tools to much different results. Carefully researched and masterfully argued, *One Kind of Freedom* (1977) provides a panoramic survey of the postbellum cotton plantation system. Though not unmindful of the influence that wealthy planters continued to exert, Ransom and Sutch also largely ignored the interpretive issues of political economy that had been Woodward's chief preoccupation. Instead, the two kept their feet in the furrow, analyzing a sample of southern farms and plantations for insight into postbellum agricultural developments and – much like late-nineteenth-century southern farmers – venturing from the field only to visit the crossroads store. They concentrated primarily on two features. The first was the transformation of the plantation labor system from one based on large, centrally directed gangs to one based on small, decentralized farms operated by tenants and sharecroppers. In one of their most poignant, if controversial, observations, they contended "that by 1880 the old plantation system had ceased to exist" (Ransom and Sutch 1977: 56). Synthesizing recent prior work and anticipating the direction of even more specialized studies, the authors made a strong case for the important role that freedpeople played in determining the contours of the new labor relations. In particular, they cited the withdrawal of workers – specifically women and children – from field labor as a powerful weapon in the struggle for "alternative arrangements" to gang labor under overseers (ibid: 67).

In their second and ultimately more contentious argument, they posited that local merchants exerted a virtual "territorial monopoly" over the areas they serviced (ibid: 126–7). As a result, merchants could charge artificially high prices for a narrow range of food, clothing, shoes, and other necessities. Over time, such arrangements had disastrous consequences for the agricultural South, among which were poverty, a lack of capital investment from the North, and a debilitating reduction in the farmer's "pride, his ambition, and his efficiency as a tiller of the soil" (ibid: 170).

Like all seminal works of scholarship, *One Kind of Freedom* generated considerable debate and quickly became a benchmark for studies of postbellum southern agriculture. It focused lasting attention on the importance of the struggle between former masters and former slaves over the terms of compensated labor. It also reemphasized the importance of credit in agricultural operations large and small. The work has also produced some unintended consequences of similarly lasting significance. First, it reinforced the notion that cotton plantations were virtually synonymous with southern agriculture. Second, it suggested a linear progression in the evolution of cotton sharecropping: from wage labor during the war through share wages shortly thereafter to sharecropping by the end of Reconstruction. Third, the notion of merchants' territorial monopolies introduced an image of rigidity that belied the rich variety of postbellum credit arrangements.

As its title reveals, Jonathan Wiener's *Social Origins of the New South* (1978) took direct aim at Woodward's theory of origins. Whereas Woodward had stressed an abrupt discontinuity between the postwar and prewar ruling elites, Wiener argued that the leading prewar planters "persisted" (Wiener 1978: 16). Despite having forfeited their slaves, they retained considerable landholdings as well as the social status and political power they had enjoyed before the Civil War. Adopting an analogy first popularized by the political theorist Barrington Moore Jr., Wiener argued that southern planters charted a "Prussian Road" to modernization (ibid: 72). In this model, a powerful landed class exerts dominance over commercial and industrial classes to ensure that neither its political power nor its conservative social values become compromised as a result of industrialization.

In addition to describing the struggles between landholders and agricultural laborers, Wiener also examined the changed relationship between planters and merchants. Unlike Ransom and Sutch, Wiener claimed that Black Belt planters retained supremacy through legislative means, specifically by crafting lien laws that gave them primacy over the merchants. Denied such a lever over the freedpeople, the merchants had little chance to muscle their way into political control of the Black Belt. They soon abandoned the region entirely in favor of the yeoman-farming areas of the piedmont, where they had unrivalled access to the growing numbers of smallholders who were abandoning subsistence agriculture for cotton. The merchants pursued "wealth and power in the hills" but in distinct subordination to the planters (ibid: 107).

The economic historian Jay R. Mandle elaborated on the framework of a plantation mode of production that Wiener had suggested. His reasoning was straightforward: plantations dominated southern agricultural production and cotton dominated the plantations. Planters took advantage of a "nonmarket mechanism" to control labor (Mandle 1978: 14). The weight of the planters' extra-market influence, coupled with the landowners' insistence on controlling the labor of all who worked their land, combined to reduce the distinctions between sharecroppers and other tenants to "a matter of degree, not kind" (ibid: 44). Accordingly, Mandle argued that any attempt to draw similarities between postbellum southern agriculture and the northern capitalist economy could not withstand close scrutiny. The South possessed a distinct mode of production, predicated on sharecropping, that he depicted as a plantation mode of production or "a plantation economy." In such an economy, "profit-maximizing, large-scale farmers" produce staples "for an external market." The accompanying labor-intensive technology requires "more workers than would be made available if they were freely permitted to choose their employment in a competitive labor market." Preserving access to "a sufficient supply of workers" requires "some nonmarket mechanism," which, in turn, helps "to define the class relations of the society." "The culture which emerges," he concluded, "reinforces these class relations" (ibid: 10). In a slightly modified restatement of this argument, Mandle insists that the postbellum South does not fit the model of a capitalist mode of production. The "plantation mode of production," alone among the interpretive models, "emphasizes the sources of that region's unique racial etiquette and economic underdevelopment" (Mandle 1992: 67).

During the 1980s scholarly debates over the proper framework for understanding the evolution of the postbellum southern economy remained largely embedded in the mode of production controversy. The collection of essays edited by Thavolia Glymph and John J. Kushma, *Essays on the Postbellum Southern Economy* (1985), eloquently stated the case for conceptualizing the postbellum South as a region in evolution from a slave economy to a capitalist one. In characteristically sparkling prose, Barbara Jeanne Fields noted that "after the epochmaking upheaval of the Civil War and Reconstruction, a prolonged period of transition set in" that eventually culminated in "the consolidation of capitalist agriculture in the South . . . a process that had been underway for centuries on a world scale" (Fields 1985a: 74). Harold D. Woodman complemented Fields's analysis, arguing that the imperatives of emancipation – with regard to both the liquidation of capital and the transformation of labor relations – left no alternative to a revolutionary transformation for which "a bourgeois, free labor society" constituted the only available template (Woodman 1985: 99–100). And as employers and laborers thrashed out the terms of the new productive system, the "resulting conflict concerned the familiar problems of labor-management relations in a free labor, capitalist economy: rates of pay, hours of work, degree of supervision" (ibid: 112). "Put succinctly," Woodman concluded, "what finally emerged in the southern countryside was capitalist agriculture" (ibid: 113).

Armstead L. Robinson's contribution to the volume emphasized the importance of understanding how the Civil War initiated "a sweeping redefinition of the structural relationships among and between the South's constituent social classes and racial groups." Furthermore, he drew attention to the important precept of regional variation that so frequently fades to the background in sweeping generalizations about the wartime and postwar South. "Freedom came to mean sharply different things to different groups of freedpeople – depending on their personal situations, their location, and the timing of formal emancipation – and this spectrum," he cautions, "suggests that none of the groups involved in the southern transition to free labor held a unitary view" (Robinson 1985: 12–13). Thavolia Glymph examined the struggle whereby freedpeople sought independence amid efforts by both former masters and the Yankee newcomers to transform them into a laboring class. She also noted the difficulties many former masters experienced in trying to make "the transition from mastery to management" (Glymph 1985: 57). For their part, Yankee sponsors of the transition did not fully appreciate the inherent biases they brought to the project or the tenacity of "a racially determined slave economy" (ibid: 66).

Three important studies of the era sidestepped the mode of production debate. The first, Eric Foner's *Nothing But Freedom* (1983), constructed an interpretive framework that was international in scope and both sympathetic to the evolution of capitalism in the modern world and insistent that post-Civil War economic developments in the South had counterparts in the post-emancipation histories of other slave societies. Tapping the rich (and then rapidly growing) literature on emancipation in the plantation colonies of the European powers, Foner observed striking parallels to the southern experience. In addition to the persistent and all-encompassing struggles between former masters and former slaves, he identified "the effort to create a dependent labor force, the ideological conflict over changing definitions of labor and property, the impact of metropolitan policies, the place of the society in the larger world economy, and the uses of the state in bolstering the plantation regime" (Foner 1983: 38). In an especially fascinating chapter on postbellum rice plantations in South Carolina, he demonstrated the rich haul of insights to be derived from historical settings other than upcountry cotton plantations.

Ira Berlin and his colleagues at the Freedmen and Southern Society Project at the University of Maryland entered the debate with a series of documentary histories that sketched both the broad significance of emancipation and the detailed working of the process in the different subregions of the South. In both *The Destruction of Slavery* (1985) and the two volumes entitled *The Wartime Genesis of Free Labor* (1990 and

1993), Berlin et al. specifically addressed the revolution in southern labor relations that flowed from emancipation. A full appreciation of the complexity and contingency of the process requires accounting not only for time and place, but also for the myriad actions of the participants: slaves, former slaves, and free blacks and Yankee and Confederate politicians, generals, soldiers, and civilians.

In the third instance, Gerald David Jaynes's *Branches Without Roots* (1986) reex-amined many of the interpretations advanced by Roger Ransom and Richard Sutch while at the same time offering a broad interpretation of the freedpeople's stifled aspirations for economic independence. In some respects the chief virtue of the book lies in the richness of detail he drew from contemporary evidence. He resisted, for instance, the temptation to reduce postwar labor relations to schematic models in which cash wages led to share wages, which in turn led to sharecropping. His appreciation for the factors that might add variability to such terms, not the least of which was the freedpeople's varying ability to exert leverage on the contract process, marks the work as a model of interpretive subtlety despite its occasional lapses into neoclassical economic jargon.

The economic historian Gavin Wright has bent neoclassical economic theory to the political conditions of the postwar world even as he steered a path through the rocky theoretical shoals. Taking for granted that radical economic change had to follow Confederate defeat, he looked toward human relationships as the secret to unlocking the mystery. In his popular survey of economic change in the post-Civil War South, Wright offered a stunningly simple way to conceptualize how the war and emancipa-tion affected southern planters. In their relationships to the land and the labor force before and after the war, Wright argues in *Old South, New South* (1986), planters underwent a profound change. Economic relationships in the antebellum South de-rived from "property rights in human beings," and emancipation shattered that world. Unable to command laborers in the postbellum world, landowners none-theless still held dominion over their land. In a word, antebellum "laborlords" became postbellum "landlords" (Wright 1986: 11, 49).

The key to the transformation lay in many respects with the evolution of share-cropping. Wright argued that the system emerged "from a kind of market mechan-ism" that tended to decentralize the organization of labor from gangs to squads to individual households (ibid: 85). He noted the strong correlation "between wage labor and young, unmarried males" but also suggested that the key to a black family's prosperity lay in establishing a good reputation for credit in a local setting (ibid: 96). "It was this need to be known that kept black families in a local area; the great majority of family moves were to places in the same vicinity" (ibid: 98).

In surveying the transformation of the planter class, Wright made a number of useful observations about the relationship of the southern economy to the national and international economies. The "defining feature" of the postbellum southern economy, he argued, "was that the South constituted a separate regional labor market, outside the scope of national and international labor markets that were active and effective during the same era" (ibid: 7). By the 1870s, "the South was a low-wage region in a high-wage country" (ibid: 12). Strikingly, wage rates for "raw homogenized common labor" became very nearly equal across regions, even though discrimination continued to exclude black workers from entire industries and to keep them from advancing beyond common labor (ibid: 13).

Proponents of the theory that the postbellum South was a capitalist economy have made the case that by the 1880s, if not earlier, sharecroppers stood in the condition of wage laborers before the law, without any claims to the crops their labor enriched other than the laborer's liens that survived in the statutes of several states. In *New South, New Law* (1995) Harold Woodman reprised his earlier analysis of the origins of capitalist agriculture in the postbellum South. The earliest crop lien laws, he discovered, dated from the period immediately after the Civil War, when southern legislators hoped to feed the people and promote agricultural recovery by authorizing loans against growing crops. In the view of the lawmakers, laborers would stand outside of the credit relationship between landowner and lender. But in a cash- and credit-poor environment, wherein landowners offered to pay wages in a share of the harvest, laborers were more than interested observers. Judges conceded that laborers working according to such contracts possessed a valid claim to what was their due. What is more, "with the support of local merchants," freedmen "quickly discovered ways to take advantage of the lien laws in order to decrease their dependence upon their employers, a result completely unforeseen by those who wrote the initial laws" (Woodman 1995: 23).

Not surprisingly, given the politically motivated origins of the earliest lien laws, politics cast a long shadow over all future revisions of the laws. The Republican governments that came into power during congressional Reconstruction often authorized specific liens for laborers and in a few instances granted primacy to the laborer's lien over competing liens of landlords and merchants. By the same token, when Democrats returned to power, they modified the lien laws to suit the interests of large planters. By subordinating the merchants' claims to those of the landlords, the new laws weakened competition for the tenants' business, thereby giving landlords considerably more authority over their tenants (ibid: 63–4). Whereas Wiener concluded that planters wielded this renewed political leverage to banish merchants from the plantation districts to the hill country, Woodman reasoned that merchants and planters coexisted, with the former often "providing (as the prewar factors had done) supplies to the landlords, who then passed these supplies on to their tenants" (ibid: 64).

Woodman contended that within a few years after the end of the Civil War both legislators and courts in all the former slaveholding states began defining the status of sharecropper as legally equivalent to that of wage worker. The intent was simply to invalidate any claim that croppers stood as "partners" to the landlords with discretionary rights over their labor and the other productive resources and valid claims to the crops they produced. Disputing the contention that "the new system was ... little more than a continuation of slavery under a new guise," Woodman insisted that, however repressive, the legal changes gave rise to a free labor system that "in important respects was similar to that in the North.... Croppers, like northern workers, had a legal right to their wages but no legal right to the goods they produced and from which their wages would come; in both sections, employers owned the means of production, and they, not the employees, made the management decisions" (ibid: 104–5).

Several prize-winning works advanced the framework for understanding the economic consequences of emancipation both conceptually and geographically. Steven Hahn's *The Roots of Southern Populism* (1983) examined the circumstances that led to the dramatic spread of cotton agriculture into the upper piedmont of Georgia following the Civil War. Hahn rejected the notion that the piedmont farmers eagerly embraced the chance to enter commercial production. Instead, they found themselves on a slippery slope, where though they often found it useful to have cash at their disposal, their prime motivation had little to do with accumulation of cash or material goods.

From the early days of white settlement in the upper piedmont, the pioneers had taken great pride in subsisting themselves. The essence of survival lay in concentrating most productive activity on subsistence goods while forsaking neither cotton (which made comfortable clothing) nor cash (which though not essential was useful for market transactions). Piedmont farmers planted food crops, grazed their animals on the open range, and partook freely of the fish and game and other resources of woods and waterways, content that such a mixture promised them independence as well as subsistence.

The Civil War began to erode that world. With the able-bodied men absent under arms, and Confederate tax collectors obliged to collect wagons and work stock as well as grain and other foodstuffs, soldiers' families stretched traditional subsistence routines to the breaking point. With the return of peace and the subsistence crisis largely unresolved, they lent sympathetic ears to producing for the market. The construction of new rail lines into the region coupled with "the greater availability of commercial fertilizers . . . played a key role in propelling the expansion of Upcountry cotton production" (Hahn 1983: 145).

While aiming ultimately to explain the roots of the Populist revolt of the last two decades of the nineteenth century, Hahn also identified sources of class tension between the commercially oriented and the subsistence-oriented inhabitants of the upper piedmont. The revised fence laws that obligated animal owners to pen their livestock relieved planters from the cost of fencing their crops but exacted a heavy toll on "the smallholders, tenants, and laborers" for whom the traditional practice of granting animals free range had offered "special advantage" (ibid: 243). Because large landowners tended to champion the new fence laws at the expense of their poorer neighbors' access to the open range, the controversy soon inflamed both local and state-level politics. Indeed, related political struggles preoccupied all the former Confederate states (and not a few northwestern and western ones as well) from Reconstruction into the twentieth century.

By focusing attention on a mixed farming region of the Upper South, Barbara Jeanne Fields likewise helped refine the model posited by studies of the cotton plantation South. In particular, she found that in Maryland wage relations supplanted the master–slave relationship relatively quickly. One of the byproducts of wage labor in an agricultural setting was seasonal unemployment, which she theorized became more widespread as rural laborers scrambled to subsist themselves in circumstances where they, like the formerly independent farmers of the piedmont South, had diminished access to land and other necessary resources. On top of that, the recurrent depressions of the late nineteenth century created a pervasive "insecurity of employment" that multiplied the challenge of subsistence (Fields 1985b: 189).

Wage labor also derived from the relatively widespread influence of the commercial links that the city of Baltimore enjoyed with the surrounding countryside. Even before the Civil War, slave labor had been playing a smaller and smaller part in economic life of the city. The influx of European immigrants in the two decades prior to the war helps account for the declining importance of slavery, and slaveholders found themselves increasingly caught between the growing preference among businessmen for employing free laborers and the growing opposition among free white workers toward competition from slave laborers. As a result, Baltimore had taken on the aspect of a city where slavery was "a legal status attaching to individuals, not a system for the organization of social life" (ibid: 49).

Mark V. Wetherington's *The New South Comes to Wiregrass Georgia* (1994) is an elegantly written examination of the economic and social changes in a representative region of the South Atlantic coast that offers a nice corrective for theories deriving from the plantation zone. Wetherington's tale unfolds in a sequence of transformations. Before the war, a sturdy if often struggling yeomanry had planted homesteads and settlements among the longleaf pines and wiregrass barrens. During the Civil War, the Confederacy's growing need for resources disrupted the earlier quality of "timelessness" (Wetherington 1994: 25). With the return of peace, commercial interests from the North as well as the South began exploiting the pine forests. Lumbermen initiated this radical transformation, first clearing away the trees and then devising new commercial ventures. They quickly understood that railroads held the key to economic development: the rails that carried lumber out could also carry persons and goods back in. As the population of the region grew and the open range shrank, commercial agriculture took root with the railroads alternately hauling guano and cotton.

The boosters of economic development were a mixed group. Although local entrepreneurs played a small role, important players came from outside the state and the most important from outside the region. Whether they hailed from plantation or commercial backgrounds mattered little in the sense that, after the war, slaveholding planters did not oppose plans for the commercial development of viable ecological zones. In the sense that advocates of development represented "both the northern-inspired, bourgeois route to modernization and a modified version of the landed elite's 'Prussian Road' out of the preindustrial world," they ran roughshod over the analytical distinctions around which so much of the earlier historiography had turned (ibid: xxi–xxii).

Historians have not neglected the study of southern industrialization and urbanization, both of which were central to Woodward's thesis about the New South. There can be little denying that the Civil War removed the barriers that the antebellum planter class had erected in the path of industrial development. From the 1960s onward, historians of the South have recognized the extent to which the Confederate experience had weakened if not destroyed these obstacles, even before the Yankees achieved victory. Frank E. Vandiver's *Ploughshares into Swords* (1952) traced the remarkable efforts of Josiah Gorgas to produce the weapons of war, and Emory Thomas's brief but powerful meditation on *The Confederacy as a Revolutionary Experience* (1971) expanded upon these points. Under the demands of waging war against a foe that enjoyed advantages in almost every measurable category, Confederate planners "blazed economic trails" unimaginable before the contest. "The Confederate nation moved so far so fast toward industrialization and urbanization," Thomas concluded, that "economic revolution" is the only apt description (Thomas 1971: 98–9).

A recent modification of this thesis by Richard Franklin Bensel holds that such state interventionism was doubly revolutionary: it not only ran counter to the Confederacy's self-declared ideal of individual liberties and state rights, but it also provided one of the earliest examples of how a bureaucratic state could mobilize scarce resources for war. If in the North the war effort was "a more-or-less capitalist, market-oriented response to the mobilization," in the Confederacy the "war effort far outstripped the productive capabilities of the prewar economy and compelled a much more innovative, almost futuristic mobilization of resources" (Bensel 1990: 97–8). Mary A. DeCredico likewise modified the view to suggest how private entrepreneurs and not just establishments operated under Confederate auspices benefited from the military mobilization. Georgia's businessmen found that, however destructive, in the end the "war created nothing but opportunity" (DeCredico 1990: 152).

While acknowledging the significance of this effort at wartime industrialization, Emory Thomas also shrewdly observed that if the Confederacy "was born with little," it "died with less" (Thomas 1971: 87). The postwar period began with a memory of what had been but with few of the material resources intact. Would-be manufacturers had to start essentially from scratch. A small but influential group of studies appearing in the 1970s and 1980s recast the analytical framework for assessing industrial development in the postwar period. Addressing not so much the what as the wherefore, these studies followed Woodward's interest in exploring the social origins of the manufacturing class. Jonathan Wiener's treatment of the rise of Birmingham led the charge.

Consistent with his provocative thesis on planter persistence in shaping the contours of postbellum agricultural policy, Wiener's *Social Origins of the New South* also made a case for a strong degree of planter influence on industrial development. Wiener insisted that the return of peace "did not unleash southern industry," nor did it "release southern industrialists from their subservience to planter interests" (Wiener 1978: 148). The political history of efforts to create a favorable legal climate for industrial development, he insists, demonstrated time and again that "conservative lawmakers . . . were opposed to industrial development of the state" (ibid: 155). Apart from their fears that an upstart class might challenge their political hegemony, planters also "wanted to keep black labor tied to the plantations, to preserve the state's fundamentally agrarian society" (ibid: 184). To be sure, a group of local promoters eventually succeeded in fostering Birmingham's industrial development, but they walked a tightrope between Black Belt planter opposition and the demands of northern industrial, financial, and commercial overlords. If Birmingham's boosters found "important allies" among Kentucky and Tennessee investors, the alliance provided no long-term independence from the northern juggernaut. Just as important, Alabama's "combination of textiles plus iron plus railroads did not add up to a case of general and sustained industrialization" (ibid).

In *Planters and the Making of a "New South"* (1979), Dwight B. Billings Jr. argued that North Carolina's planters aimed not so much to stifle industrial development as to nurture it under their own domination. While clearly influenced by an eclectic group of social theorists, Billings concluded that an agrarian elite sponsored industrial development, citing a number of influential families whose pedigrees lay deep in the state's past and whose members had over the years combined interests in industry as well as agriculture. "The economic and social basis for this upper class," he argued, "was land ownership. Agriculture produced wealth that was used in diverse ways, including industry." The elite's hegemony "survived the Civil War and emancipation," and, though they continued to demonstrate their "agrarian moorings," they demonstrated "leadership in banking, insurance, railroad building, cotton mills, and other enterprises" (Billings 1979: 91–2). Tobacco manufacturers differed somewhat from this general profile in that they hailed from more modest landed wealth and therefore took less interest in preserving traditional social relations. Thanks to the elite's influence, labor relations in every industrial sector displayed a heavy dose of paternalism that to some extent persists to the present day.

David Carlton offered a contrary view from the experience of post-Civil War South Carolina. Struck by the remarkable growth of upcountry towns and the "striking commercial expansion" that accompanied it, Carlton followed Woodward's steps to conclude that the process gave rise to "a fundamental shift in economic and social power to a new class of merchants" (Carlton 1982: 21, 26). Steeped from youth in business culture rather than that of the plantation or the farm, these men were "modern industrial capitalists" who combined available resources shrewdly and identified markets carefully (ibid: 41).

Once established, the mill complexes took on something of a life of their own, with results that were often at variance with the vision of the founders. While achieving the objective of defusing the political rebelliousness of white yeomen by providing them employment off the farm, the mills quickly became associated with poverty, transience, and disease, not to mention the crass exploitation of children. Contemporaries dubbed this constellation of social maladies the "mill problem," the resolution of which became a political preoccupation throughout much of the twentieth century.

Don H. Doyle's survey of urban development, *New Men, New Cities, New South* (1990), provides a fresh perspective on the importance of cities in the making of the New South. The legacy of antebellum class structures and business habits strongly influenced postwar urban development, as of course did location. In the older seaport cities of Charleston and Mobile, the "old families" retained a kind of "moral capital" that outweighed the "material fortunes" of the entrepreneurs. In Charleston, for instance, the traditional elite's "inertia, if not opposition" to new varieties of enterprise relegated the city to "the backwater" (Doyle 1990: 129). In contrast, few of the urban leaders of the New South's cities "were sons of the slaveholding planter elite who commanded so much of the wealth and power in the Old South" (ibid: 92). Absent such an inheritance, the upstarts in cities like Nashville and Atlanta built new foundations of economic and social power in commerce, "with finance and manufacturing playing important supporting roles" (ibid: 39). "It was largely by the process of city building," he concludes, "that local business leaders became a class" (ibid: 19).

In addition to tracking the antebellum backgrounds of the new elites, Doyle explored the process by which they parlayed entrepreneurial skill into political and social power and influence. Business associations such as chambers of commerce proved especially critical to this process. In Atlanta, where businessmen scuttled the old-fashioned board of trade shortly after the Civil War, the chamber of commerce "moved beyond providing market quotes to address a range of issues affecting the local business environment" (ibid: 139). In short order it also began "to promote Atlanta's general economic development" (ibid: 140). But business groups alone did not account for the success of New South cities: entrepreneurs had to develop a broader framework, a new class, knit together as much by "neighborhoods, clubs, charity organizations, and marriages" as by business organizations as such (ibid: 190).

Just as emancipation studies have emerged as a thriving subfield within the framework of postbellum southern agriculture, both transcending as well as enriching the field, a new social history of the southern working classes has emerged from the topic of postbellum southern industrialization. In both cases, the new departure has both enriched and in some respects transcended its field of origin. Eric Arnesen's prodigiously researched study of the waterfront workers of New Orleans demonstrated the promise of exploring the economic history of southern industry from the viewpoint of the working class. Such an approach requires a careful delineation of industrial developments – particularly as they are reflected in changing patterns of trade in the region, the nation, and the world – and a subtlety that views sweeping historical interpretations with skepticism. Understanding the behavior of southern workers requires rejecting simple dichotomies, particularly "the race/class dichotomy" (Arnesen 1991: x). In a recent study of Alabama coal miners, Daniel Letwin demonstrated the attractiveness of Arnesen's approach by scarcely pausing to note the past interpretive battles over the planters' role in industrial development (Letwin 1998: 13, 198 n. 10). Only with additional studies "alive to the peculiar constraints and possibilities of each setting," Letwin argued, will the "sterile generalities about race and class" give way "to a more nuanced, historically credible picture" (ibid: 193).

Like all fields in US history, the study of the postbellum South has been transformed by recent scholarship on gender. Several works serve to illustrate how the earlier preoccupations with race relations or with relations among varying social classes have given way to an interest in domestic relations. Laura Edwards's *Gendered Strife and Confusion* (1997) has made the important case that much of the struggle over the meaning of emancipation derives from the struggles to define new domestic relations in the aftermath of slavery. Men with property viewed relations between employees and employers, like those between wives and husbands, within the framework of domestic relations. At the same time, northern white workers also appropriated the language of domestic relations to advance their own case for independence, citing "their responsibility for wives and children to emphasize their commonalities with self-employed artisans and farmers as household heads who provided for dependents" (Edwards 1997: 72). Moreover, by insisting that women and black men were inherently dependent, white workingmen aimed to exclude those groups from public recognition as workers, lest they parlay that status into a claim for independence. Poor black and white men and women refused to accept their appointed role as dependents. In countless confrontations, many of which eventually reached the public eye, they exposed the injustices of enforced subjugation, demanding and often getting redress.

By rejecting contemporary stereotypes, poor white and black southerners "provided a basis for a political vision that softened the sharp racial and class hierarchies of southern society" even while leaving themselves vulnerable to charges of violating the norms of proper manly and womanly behavior (ibid: 182). From a methodological standpoint, Edwards insisted that "the stuff of private life was inherently political." When black and white common folk brought domestic affairs into the public arena, they claimed both "political personas for themselves" and "the right to define the substance of public debate" (ibid: 18). In a similar study of domestic relations, Peter Bardaglio concluded that the Civil War and slave emancipation shook the patriarchal antebellum household to its foundation. Persons previously defined as dependents – women and children no less than slaves – began claiming rights that were threatening to the old order but compatible with the new. As government officials began recognizing former slaves' rights to marriage, mothers' rights to custody over their children, and women's and children's rights to protection against domestic violence and sexual abuse, the consequences of the failed bid for national independence became clear. If, at first, reluctance characterized these interventions, by the end of the century "an emergent state-centered paternalism" bore witness to how far the New South's political leaders had traveled toward "shaping the old hierarchy of power into a new social order" (Bardaglio 1995: 227, 136).

The greatest challenge facing historians of the postbellum southern economy is to develop a vocabulary that will be sufficiently general to describe the whole while at the same time not obliterating variations across time, space, and other particular circumstances. In that sense, the recent work exploring the intersections among class, race, and gender structures and the corresponding aspects of individual and group identity among historical actors has produced intriguing even if not always convincing results. As historians seek finer levels of meaning, it is evident that the vogue for sweeping interpretations has fallen from favor. With diversity all the rage in political life, small wonder that scholarship reflects a similar emphasis.

Despite the absence at the present time of a satisfying general synthesis concerning the economic development of the postbellum South, two observations are in order. First, the sheer number of practicing historians engaged in ever-more-specialized studies has cluttered as much as smoothed the path to such a synthesis. And second, by its very nature, the pursuit of historical understanding entails a dynamic and never-ending tension between the known and the unknown, between the general and the specific. An optimist need not have swallowed chaos theory whole simply to believe that a broader synthesis will emerge out of the present fixation with divergence from the norm and exceptions to the rule. Nor need the present day's pessimism about the limitation of the human mind to understand – and of human action to effect change – reign indefinitely into the future.

A possible path from the wilderness may lie in assuming the capitalist world system as given, as a major background context of human behavior over the past several hundred years, while at the same time recognizing that the development of such a system was neither preordained nor self-evident to historical actors. With fresh appreciation for the fact that even when the agents of capitalist transformation have worked so assiduously their efforts have rarely gone uncontested, the historical process will reveal itself as a mutual give-and-take rather than a one-way exchange of habits and ideas. At a time when historians of the American West and assorted other geographically specific regions are currently wrestling with interpretive challenges similar to those facing southern historians, it may be fruitful to seek synthetic frameworks that fit both equally well. Woodward's colonial analogy might serve again as a starting point, provided that his emphasis on the structural relationships of political and economic domination gives way to one rooted in the human interactions that alternately advanced, retarded, or simply accommodated to the encounter with metropolitan industrial capitalism. The growing body of scholarship on the dispossessed world's response to European colonialism illustrates ways of exploring these interactions that appreciate the developed world's might, while at the same time accounting for the political and cultural struggles that "modernization" has generated and that ultimately link the past to the present.

BIBLIOGRAPHY

Andreano, Ralph (ed.) 1962: *The Economic Impact of the American Civil War*. Cambridge, MA: Schenkman.

Arnesen, Eric 1991: *Waterfront Workers of New Orleans: Race, Class and Politics, 1863–1923*. New York: Oxford University Press.

Bardaglio, Peter W. 1995: *Reconstructing the Household: Families, Sex, and the Law in the Nineteenth-Century South*. Chapel Hill: University of North Carolina Press.

Bensel, Richard Franklin 1990: *Yankee Leviathan: The Origins of Central State Authority in America, 1859–1877*. Cambridge: Cambridge University Press.

Berlin, Ira, Fields, Barbara J., Glymph, Thavolia, Reidy, Joseph P., and Rowland, Leslie S. 1985: *Freedom: A Documentary History of Emancipation, 1861–1867. Series I, Volume I: The Destruction of Slavery*. Cambridge: Cambridge University Press.

Berlin, Ira, Glymph, Thavolia, Miller, Steven F., Reidy, Joseph P., Rowland, Leslie S., and Saville, Julie 1990: *Freedom: A Documentary History of Emancipation, 1861–1867. Series I, Volume III: The Wartime Genesis of Free Labor: The Lower South*. Cambridge: Cambridge University Press.

Berlin, Ira, Miller, Steven F., Reidy, Joseph P., and Rowland, Leslie S. 1993: *Freedom: A Documentary History of Emancipation, 1861–1867. Series I, Volume II: The Wartime Genesis of Free Labor: The Upper South*. Cambridge: Cambridge University Press.

Billings, Dwight B., Jr. 1979: *Planters and the Making of a "New South": Class, Politics, and Development in North Carolina, 1865–1900*. Chapel Hill: University of North Carolina Press.

Carlton, David L. 1982: *Mill and Town in South Carolina, 1880–1920*. Baton Rouge: Louisiana State University Press.

Conrad, Alfred H. and Meyer, John R. 1964: *The Economics of Slavery and Other Studies in Econometric History*. Chicago: Aldine Publishing.

DeCredico, Mary A. 1990: *Patriotism for Profit: Georgia's Urban Entrepreneurs and the Confederate War Effort*. Chapel Hill: University of North Carolina Press.

Doyle, Don H. 1990: *New Men, New Cities, New South: Atlanta, Nashville, Charleston, Mobile, 1860–1910*. Chapel Hill: University of North Carolina Press.

Du Bois, W. E. Burghardt 1935: *Black Reconstruction: An Essay toward a History of the Part Which Black Folk Played in the Attempt to Reconstruct Democracy in America, 1860–1880*. New York: Russell and Russell.

Edwards, Laura F. 1997: *Gendered Strife and Confusion: The Political Culture of Reconstruction*. Urbana: University of Illinois Press.

Fields, Barbara Jeanne 1985a: The Advent of Capitalist Agriculture: The New South in a Bourgeois World. In Thavolia Glymph and John J. Kushma (eds.), *Essays on the Postbellum Southern Economy*. College Station: Texas A & M University Press, 73–94.

Fields, Barbara Jeanne 1985b: *Slavery and Freedom on the Middle Ground: Maryland during the Nineteenth Century*. New Haven, CT: Yale University Press.

Fogel, Robert William and Engerman, Stanley L. 1974: *Time on the Cross: The Economics of American Negro Slavery*. Boston: Little, Brown.

Foner, Eric 1983: *Nothing But Freedom: Emancipation and Its Legacy.* Baton Rouge: Louisiana State University Press.

Genovese, Eugene D. 1965: *The Political Economy of Slavery: Studies in the Economy and Society of the Slave South.* New York: Pantheon Books.

Glymph, Thavolia 1985: Freedpeople and Ex-Masters: Shaping a New Order in the Postbellum South, 1865–1868. In Thavolia Glymph and John J. Kushma (eds.), *Essays on the Postbellum Southern Economy.* College Station: Texas A & M University Press, 48–72.

Glymph, Thavolia and Kushma, John J. (eds.) 1985: *Essays on the Postbellum Southern Economy.* College Station: Texas A & M University Press.

Hahn, Steven 1983: *The Roots of Southern Populism: Yeoman Farmers and the Transformation of the Georgia Upcountry, 1850–1890.* New York: Oxford University Press.

Jaynes, Gerald David 1986: *Branches Without Roots: Genesis of the Black Working Class in the American South, 1862–1882.* New York: Oxford University Press.

Letwin, Daniel 1998: *The Challenge of Interracial Unionism: Alabama Coal Miners, 1878–1921.* Chapel Hill: University of North Carolina Press.

Logan, Rayford W. 1954: *The Negro in American Life and Thought: The Nadir, 1877–1901.* New York: Dial Press.

Mandle, Jay R. 1978: *The Roots of Black Poverty: The Southern Plantation Economy After the Civil War.* Durham, NC: Duke University Press.

Mandle, Jay R. 1992: *Not Slave, Not Free: The African American Economic Experience since the Civil War.* Durham, NC: Duke University Press.

Ransom, Roger L. and Sutch, Richard 1977: *One Kind of Freedom: The Economic Consequences of Emancipation.* Cambridge: Cambridge University Press.

Robinson, Armstead L. 1985: "Worser dan Jeff Davis": The Coming of Free Labor during the Civil War, 1861–1865. In Thavolia Glymph and John J. Kushma (eds.), *Essays on the Postbellum Southern Economy.* College Station: Texas A & M University Press, 11–47.

Thomas, Emory M. 1971: *The Confederacy as a Revolutionary Experience.* Englewood Cliffs, NJ: Prentice-Hall.

Vandiver, Frank E. 1952: *Ploughshares into Swords: Josiah Gorgas and Confederate Ordnance.* Austin: University of Texas Press.

Wesley, Charles H. 1937: *The Collapse of the Confederacy.* Washington, DC: Associated Publishers.

Wetherington, Mark V. 1994: *The New South Comes to Wiregrass Georgia 1860–1910.* Knoxville: University of Tennessee Press.

Wiener, Jonathan M. 1978: *Social Origins of the New South: Alabama, 1860–1885.* Baton Rouge: Louisiana State University Press.

Woodman, Harold D. 1985: The Reconstruction of the Cotton Plantation in the New South. In Thavolia Glymph and John J. Kushma (eds.), *Essays on the Postbellum Southern Economy.* College Station: Texas A & M University Press, 95–119.

Woodman, Harold D. 1995: *New South, New Law: The Legal Foundations of Credit and Labor Relations in the Postbellum Agricultural South.* Baton Rouge: Louisiana State University Press.

Woodson, C. G. 1919: *The Education of the Negro Prior to 1861: A History of the Education of the Colored People of the United States from the Beginning of Slavery to the Civil War,* 2nd edn. Washington, DC: Association for the Study of Negro Life and History.

Woodward, C. Vann 1951: *Origins of the New South, 1877–1913.* Baton Rouge: Louisiana State University Press.

Wright, Gavin 1986: *Old South, New South: Revolutions in the Southern Economy since the Civil War.* New York: Harper-Collins.

PART IV

The New South

CHAPTER NINETEEN

Southern Politics in the Age of Populism and Progressivism: A Historiographical Essay

SAMUEL L. WEBB

Historians writing about Populism and Progressivism confront stubborn myths about southern politics, and W. J. Cash's popular but unreliable *The Mind of the South* (1941) spread many of them. Cash believed that the post-Reconstruction South was unified in opposition to Negro rights and Yankee meddling, leading it to remain unshakeably loyal to the Democratic Party. Populism was but a brief and uninfluential challenge to Democratic power. Regional politics was "devoid" of "economic and social focus," and was dominated by either "old captains" who guarded the interests of the upper class or slick demagogues who mesmerized the masses with Negrophobic rhetoric (Cash 1941: 252). Reformers failed to address pressing southern problems because "common whites" lacked the class consciousness needed to ignite effective change. Other writers reveal a more complex story.

A 1946 essay by Arthur Link puts southerners "in the vanguard" of the nation's reform movements before and after 1900 (Link 1946: 195). The impact of Populists was "profound," writes Link, "despite the paucity" of their victories (ibid: 176–7). They bequeathed a program to progressive Democrats and forced them to break with conservatives in their party. There was a "well-organized" southern Progressivism aimed at "remedying" regional ills and a more complex set of politicians than Cash detected (ibid: 194).

Two classic biographies support Link's claims, but both also raise troubling questions about southern reformers. C. Vann Woodward's *Tom Watson: Agrarian Rebel* (1938) and Francis Butler Simkins's *Pitchfork Ben Tillman: South Carolinian* (1944) reject Cash's simplism, stress that race was only one element in a multidimensional regional politics, and place their subjects in reform movements that threatened or overthrew elite power groups. Spanning Populist and Progressive periods, Watson's and Tillman's careers amplified the racism, rhetorical excess, and pathological public behavior perceived as typical of southern politicians. They became prototypes of the "Southern Demagogue," but Woodward discards this label, describing it as a "political epithet" that adds nothing "to our understanding of the men to whom it is applied" (Woodward 1938: preface, n.p.).

Influenced by the New Deal, and by Charles Beard and the "Progressive" historians, Woodward exudes sympathy for the struggling poor and suspicion of the moneyed interests in *Tom Watson*. He includes daring arguments about the "New South" capitalist impulses of Georgia's Democratic Party leaders, the power of dissent in a region believed to be solid, the courage of the Populists, and the hopeful signs of racial accord they raised. His main thesis is that Watson began as an idealistic reformer determined to restore the independence of American farmers but went through a transformation after Populism's demise that stifled his benevolence and made him a raving bigot.

Watson joined the most radical Populists in pushing for government help for farmers. Contending that economic or class interests were more important than race, he was, writes Woodward, "perhaps the first native white southern leader of importance to treat the Negro's aspirations with the seriousness that human strivings deserve" (ibid: 221). The nation's most renowned Populist orator, Watson's star fell when the Democratic Party's free silver movement co-opted Populism in 1896. After the party of white supremacy triumphed, a bitter Watson began to move from a politics of class to one of racial and religious hatred. In the decade before World War I he descended into a world where Jewish bankers, the Catholic church, and the Negroes he once asked for support became his demons. His widely read newspaper, *The Jeffersonian*, circulated his paranoia to the nation. Between 1906 and 1916 he tried to control Georgia politics by spitefully switching his influence from one gubernatorial aspirant to another, depending on how they danced to his discordant tune.

The sensational 1915 lynching of Leo Frank, a Jewish textile mill manager unjustly charged with raping and killing a female employee, might not have occurred, says Woodward, if Watson had not insisted on Frank's death. As "hysteria" over the case peaked, Georgia's Klan was reborn; and while Watson had no direct role in this, "if any mortal man may be credited . . . with releasing the forces of human malice and ignorance and prejudice, which the Klan merely mobilized," writes Woodward, "that man was Thomas E. Watson" (Woodward 1938: 450). This surmise conflicts with earlier conclusions by Woodward. The book's preface says that Watson was unjustly accused of producing Georgia's intolerance, which was "produced" by "forces" of "economics and race and historical heritage," that "thwarted" his "courageous struggles" for Populism and "led him into the futility and degeneration of his later career."

Woodward is more certain about the goals of Georgia's Democratic Party elite and those of the Populists. Contrary to prior historians, he asserts that Democratic leaders were not tools of the planter class but agents of northern industrial corporations complicit in making Georgia an economic colony of Yankee capital. Populists fighting this oligarchy were sincere reformers committed to rational and creative solutions to farm problems. Firmly behind the most radical planks in the People's Party platform, Watson and other southern Populists fought a losing battle against efforts by their northern and western brethren to hand their party over to free silverites in 1896.

Woodward's weakest argument makes Populists agents of racial tolerance and equal rights. They courted the black man's vote, invited him to meetings, appointed him to committees, and engaged in rhetoric that portended racial change. But the Populists' need to bind black and white farmers in class solidarity was purely pragmatic. Watson never wanted racial equality, and neither did the farmers whose sons were later as transfixed by Gene Talmadge's race-baiting oratory as their fathers had been by Watson's.

The reputation of *Tom Watson* grows more luminous along with that of its author, and scholars have been reluctant to challenge its assumptions, but in 1984 Barton Shaw assailed Woodward's thesis on Watson and Georgia's Populists. He argues that Watson had always been the fractious, violent, paranoid man Woodward found only after 1900, and that Populists were a cranky, racist, illiberal crowd driven more by a lust for power than by ideology or program. They accomplished so little because they were unclear about what they wanted to do. The Populism Shaw describes is similar to that described by Cash and resembles the pseudo-variety offered to South Carolina by Benjamin Ryan Tillman.

Pitchfork Ben Tillman and its author are not accorded the veneration given Woodward and *Tom Watson*, but critics recognized Simkins's exhaustive research and evenhanded approach, and it is a tribute to both authors that no biographies of Watson or Tillman have been published since theirs. Simkins's vivid portrayal of South Carolina's rough and tumble politics captures the tense drama and potential for violence that always trailed the crude, profane, overbearing Tillman. The central theme is Tillman's effort to subvert his state's ruling class, an elite similar to the one Woodward found in Georgia. Linked to railroads and urban merchants as well as lowcountry planters, these Bourbons were so entrenched that only a wild man could dislodge them.

Never an idealist with a radical program like Watson, the colorful Tillman did give "ordinary white men," writes Simkins, "the will to vote," creating a new "tradition of popular rule" (Simkins 1944: 554). Using "the state's race, sectional and class divisions," Tillman awakened the masses with stinging attacks on "aristocrats," on the failure of the upper crust to help average citizens, and on the lowcountry "niggerdom" (ibid: 153–7). He created a personal following based on the adulation of upcountry farmers angry about their decline, but the Tillmanites were never Populists. Tillman joined the Farmers' Alliance and paid lip service to its program in order to control it, yet he remained a free silver Democrat who ran his own farmers' organization and craved power more than the subtreasury.

Governor Tillman supported railroad rate regulation, higher taxes on railroads, and mild restrictions on child labor. These modest reforms fit within a "provincial framework" suitable to the state's lowcountry conservatives (ibid: 553). Doing little to ease the plight of his adoring farmers, Tillman is remembered for imposing state control over liquor sales, restricting Negro voting, and creating a statewide white Democratic primary. His racist tactics and justification of violence used in his behalf "imposed a dreadful tyranny" on South Carolina, says Simkins, stifling "free and progressive thought" (ibid: 551).

Tillman's US Senate career was filled with more rhetorical bombast than substance. A Progressive during Theodore Roosevelt's presidency, he led efforts to strengthen railroad regulations, but the reformer made coarse speeches attacking Negroes and engaged in needless feuds with Roosevelt. Turning conservative in his last term, says Simkins, Tillman sought support from the lowcountry elite he once damned. Opposing the ambitions of his state's newest champion of the masses, Cole Blease, cost Tillman the support of old allies and left him in the embrace of his former enemies, but he died before anyone could defeat him.

Simkins and Woodward confirm Link's view of strong regional reform impulses, but their evidence also casts suspicion on the reformers' motives, unwittingly reinforcing aspects of Cash's depiction of southern politics. Demagogues whipping up the coarsest emotions of "common whites," an obsession with race, feckless reformers, wealthy elites directing government policy, and voters incapable of recognizing their economic interests were all too apparent in South Carolina and Georgia. Woodward modifies this impression in *Origins of the New South 1877–1913* (1951), a comprehensive book about southern life in the reform era that presents a more contingent and complex regional politics. The most influential study of the period, *Origins* suggests that wrenching change left little continuity between the antebellum and post-Reconstruction South, and that southern life was marked by serious economic, class, and political conflict. Politics was raucous and unsolid, and Democrats faced a very real threat to the region's political and economic order from the Populists.

A Democratic Party bulging with ex-Whigs, Jacksonians, big planters, and small upcountry farmers, says Woodward, began to fracture immediately after it redeemed the South from Republican Reconstruction. Readjuster, Independent, and Greenbacker movements sprouted to oppose Redeemer Democrats but rarely defeated them. Some rebels were economic radicals, but they were mostly upset by Democratic Party election shenanigans such as the manipulation of black voters. The diffuse revolts had no unifying element except anger at the venal Democrats and ran their course by the mid-eighties, but they planted "seeds" that helped produce a great farmers' rebellion (Woodward 1951: 106).

Discontinuity between Old and New South is most obvious in Woodward's account of the falling cotton prices, sharecropping, crop liens, increasingly smaller farms, usurious merchants, and the desperate search for credit that obsessed postwar southern farmers. Currency contraction and control of the nation's money by eastern banks were blamed, but Redeemer Democrats in Congress were no help. They rejected a coalition with agrarians from the West in favor of one with easterners tied to banks and corporate interests. Farm discontent ignited only scattered political revolts in the 1880s but led to the decade's most important development, the rise of the Southern Farmers' Alliance.

Origins gives the organizational efforts and programs of the Southern Alliance credit for the rise of American Populism, breaking with John D. Hicks's *The Populist Revolt* (1931), the most comprehensive account of Populism when Woodward wrote. Hicks does not ignore the South or its Alliance but emphasizes the movement among western plains farmers. Woodward leans heavily on Hicks's findings, agreeing with his favorable view of Populism and his stress on economic rather than ethnocultural issues as the movement's progenitor, yet differing with his assessment of the demands, motives, and impact of southern Populists.

Hicks contends that the broad-based popularity of free silver led to its domination of the movement in all regions, and that by 1893 it had eclipsed support among Populists for more radical Alliance demands like the subtreasury. For Woodward, authentic Populism lay in adherence to Alliance goals and programs, and southerners were more committed to them than northwesterners. Many bimetallists wanted to destroy the third party, says Woodward, by luring Populists into a pro-silver Democratic Party. Since silver was only the minimum Alliance demand, the National People's Party abandoned the major goals of the organization that mothered

Populism and decimated agrarian reform when it supported William Jennings Bryan in 1896.

Black southerners were invited to Populist meetings and given responsible positions in the third party, and Populists showed more solicitude for their problems than Democrats or Republicans, but, adds Woodward, the "significance" of such gains "is easily exaggerated" (Woodward 1951: 258). Retreating from his glowing view of Populist tolerance in *Tom Watson*, the author admits that third-party leaders were more interested in votes than equality and, like the Democrats, tried to buy black voters.

In the 1950s a group of scholars rejected the emphasis that "progressive historians" such as Hicks and Woodward place on discord and unrest. Admitting serious disagreements in our past, these "consensus historians" argue that class conflict and economic radicalism were rare and that most reformers accepted fundamental aspects of the American system. Angry Populists remained capitalists and democrats, and like Progressives, were driven by ideas only tangentially related to their economic or class interests. Racial, ethnic, and religious prejudices, a decline in their societal status, or their fear of the ways that a complex urban–industrial society challenged their traditional ways were the real catalysts of their discontent. Richard Hofstadter's influential *The Age of Reform: From Bryan to F. D. R.* (1955) synthesized these views.

Hofstadter's Populists were not rational or programmatic rebels. Unrealistic about the vicissitudes of the economic marketplace, they held a mythical view of the nation's history that featured independent yeomen farmers living in a society less greedy than the one that ensnared them. This myth led Populists to believe that they were "innocent pastoral victims" of the nation's money managers (Hofstadter 1955: 35). As the new urban–industrial society devalued rural life and lowered the farmers' status, resentful Populists touted conspiracy theories that made Jewish bankers into scapegoats, helping to activate modern American antisemitism. Other historians and social scientists who, like Hofstadter, were educated in the 1930s and shaken by that decade's events, found Fascist elements in the rhetoric of midwestern Populists. They contend that Populist conspiracy-mindedness was symptomatic of the paranoid thinking evident in many mass movements. The roots of anti-communist hysteria and support for Joe McCarthy's demagogic crusade against subversives lay in Populism (Ferkiss 1957; Lipset 1964)

Answering the critics in a forceful essay, C. Vann Woodward counters that if Populism was not "class" politics, it was "agricultural interest" politics because it focused on remedies to economic problems (Woodward 1960: 112). He concedes some retrograde elements and antisemitic bigots in Populist ranks, but says there were just as many in the two major parties and other reform movements of the time. Southern Populists were more often victims of than purveyors of bigotry, and critics of their movement failed to point out its racial inclusiveness. Scholars finding continuity between conspiracy-minded midwestern Populism and McCarthyism got their history wrong, says Woodward, because Populists were weak in the Midwest and nearly nonexistent in Joe McCarthy's home state of Wisconsin. In the South, where they had been strongest, McCarthy never had much support.

For two decades after publication of *The Age of Reform* the dispute about Populism's character intensified. Studies of individual southern states produced conflicting views. Two authors whose books were published within a year of one another differ on what Populists were like in one state. Sheldon Hackney contends that Alabama's Populists were geographically and socially isolated farmers frustrated by their outsider status and unrealistic about their place in the emerging market-oriented world. They had no coherent ideology or program and substituted conspiracy theories for substantive ideas (Hackney 1969). William Warren Rogers demurs, contending that the state's Populists responded to real economic distress, were prepared for action by radical farm organizations, and proposed rational solutions to festering financial and political questions (Rogers 1970).

Seeking to clarify Populism's motivations and ideology, Lawrence Goodwyn wrote *Democratic Promise: The Populist Moment in America* (1976), an exhaustive study of the national movement that supplants Hicks's *Populist Revolt* as the leading work in the field. Passionate and reverential about the democratic aims of the agrarian rebels, Goodwyn rebukes critics who believe that Populists were obsessed with ethnocultural rather than economic issues, or that white southern farmers were too race conscious to seek substantive economic reforms. Populists were defeated because the nation's "hierarchical culture" was too entrenched to allow a truly authentic democratic mass movement to succeed (Goodwyn 1976: 540–3). The dominating financial and political edifice pulled every trick to keep farmers dependent, but Populists created a "moment" of hope that people could, if properly organized, challenge the power structure and defeat it.

The reformers' problem was how to create an economy in which farmers would be independent of those who controlled the nation's money supply. The Southern Farmers' Alliance had answers that helped it create "a movement culture" (ibid: 87–8). The People's Party and the ideology that undergirded it, argues Goodwyn, were Alliance products. Organized in Texas, it won western as well as southern converts, but the cooperative spirit that made Populism possible began in the South. Alliance leaders taught southern farmers the causes of their plight and the value of cooperation; formulated the influential subtreasury program as a method of gaining credit for farmers, and set up producing, manufacturing, and marketing cooperatives that led farmers to believe they could be independent. Alliance meetings provided rural southerners a place to talk to one another about mutual problems, eat and play together, and plan for their common good. This new cultural habitat led farmers to believe that they could oppose institutions that once awed them, says Goodwyn, and brought the possibility of real democracy to the countryside.

Goodwyn admits that some cooperatives ultimately failed from a lack of capital or mismanagement, but many were also felled by the clout of eastern banks, supply merchants, gin owners, and others whose prosperity depended on the farmers' subordinate position. The decline of cooperation came more quickly as the People's Party supplanted the Alliance as the central institution of agrarian reform. Like all other parties, it was hierarchical in structure and did not offer farmers the communal ties that had given them strength in the Alliance. The movement dissipated as it was captured by practical politics, and its effort to accommodate the free silver movement led directly to its demise.

Goodwyn's assessment of the 1896 election contradicts Robert F. Durden's *The Climax of Populism: The Election of 1896* (1965). Populists were indeed driven by economic issues, says Durden, and silver was one of them, but it was wrong to argue that they were beguiled into supporting Bryan by free silver conspirators or that fusion with Democrats destroyed the movement. Fusion was a sensible, even inevitable, political decision. Goodwyn argues that silverites were a "shadow movement" and a distraction from real Populism (Goodwyn 1976: 388–401). When northwestern Populists and a few southerners arranged fusion with silver Democrats, they sold out the great mass of southern Populists and destroyed the separate identity of the People's Party. Populism's death ended the possibility that Americans could continue to resist the power of giant corporations over their lives.

Democratic Promise makes convincing arguments that the problems of credit, currency, production, and marketing were the prime motivators of Populism, but some scholars argue that the economic analysis is too strict and leaves no room for other factors (Turner 1980). Others argue that the cooperatives were not as extensive or influential as Goodwyn contends (Parsons et al. 1983). Historians of midwestern Populism claim that *Promise* overemphasizes the Southern Alliance, puts too much blame on northerners for the fusion debacle, and unfairly puts Great Plains farmers on the Populist right wing (Cherny 1981; Clanton 1991). David Montgomery complains that Goodwyn fails to connect Populism to a class struggle against industrial capitalism that included urban workers (Montgomery 1978: 166–73). In his *American Populism: A Social History 1877–1898* (1993), Robert McMath finds that a rebellious, Democratic, rural political culture in which farmers were not awed by the power of powerful institutions existed long before the Farmers' Alliance.

Bruce Palmer's *"Man Over Money": The Southern Populist Critique of American Capitalism* (1980), while emphasizing that the Alliance shaped Populist thought, points out the influence of an older political culture that Goodwyn ignored. Newspapers, pamphlets, letters, and speeches of southern Populists prove that their Jeffersonian–Jacksonian heritage led them to dislike state-sponsored economic privileges, be suspicious of eastern banks, and believe that "producers" must stand against corporate-banker power. Neither Marxists nor socialists, says Palmer, Populists criticized capitalism from a moral viewpoint that grew from their religion. Far from wanting to overthrow the system, they only wanted it to be fair and hoped to retain the benefits industrial growth gave consumers. Large corporations producing goods for national and international markets, however, were incompatible with the "simple market society" Populists knew. Their experiences had not prepared them to live in the impersonal economic world created by the industrial revolution.

Past experiences of family and neighbors did shape farmers' responses to economic events, and in *The Roots of Southern Populism: Yeoman Farmers and the Transformation of the Georgia Upcountry, 1850–1890* (1983), Steven Hahn describes how social change in a Georgia region led farmers to revolt. Like Palmer, he believes historians too often limit their studies of Populism to postbellum or post-Reconstruction years. Offering a compelling account of how antebellum experiences affected postwar attitudes, Hahn argues that the postbellum economy alienated upcountry yeomen trained in a precapitalist world and that the encroaching market ethos eroded their independence.

According to Hahn, antebellum yeomen raised food crops and livestock for their families, only rarely sold produce for cash at the market, and bartered for items they needed. Upcountry culture molded social relations that led yeomen to expect an almost communal use of the area's land, livestock, and wild game. The "open range," a system of legal rights essential to yeomen whose grass lands were not extensive enough to sustain their livestock, permitted smaller farmers' hogs and cattle to forage on the unfenced lands of neighbors. People also hunted on the unfenced lands of neighboring farmers for game to feed their families. These practices led yeomen to believe that they had certain "common rights" on property owned by others.

This older way of living was threatened by the post-Civil War "cash nexus" economy. The war devastated northern Georgia's farms, says Hahn, and led to the replacement of food crops by cotton. A desperate need for money, penetration of the once isolated upcountry by railroads, and a demand by creditors that debtors grow a cash crop led farmers into the marketplace. Furnishing merchants entered the upcountry to loan farmers the necessities to begin production, and the proud yeomen eventually accumulated debts they could not pay. As cotton prices fell the need for credit increased, and thousands went from landownership to tenancy, or from self-sufficiency to dependency.

Elite groups found that the old antebellum ways restricted commercial development, contends Hahn, and they supported laws requiring farmers to fence in their livestock. Efforts to pass stock laws were led by large landowners wanting to increase the amount of produce they could sell to new markets made available by the railroads. Foraging animals threatened their crops. Stock laws made small landowners more dependent on larger landowners for essential foodstuffs they would have been able to produce on their own under the old system. Game laws supported by the commercial classes also restricted the hunting liberties of yeomen. These changes, says Hahn, along with debt, a lack of money or credit, growing tenancy rates, and the arrival of the Alliance, helped spur the third-party movement.

This story of class conflict and farmers justly concerned about their eroding "common rights" differs with Hofstadter, Cash, and Barton Shaw. Some historians criticize Hahn's "Marxist" analysis, but more relevant criticism comes from those who point out that he ignored Georgia's old plantation belt where Populism was strongest and where commercial farming was entrenched before the Civil War (Rothenberg 1987; Holmes 1990: 40–1). Critics also believe the stock law issue was less pivotal than Hahn claims (Kantor and Kousser 1993). Robert McMath's short synthesis of the national movement supports Hahn's view that Populism's roots lay in a "culture" much older than the Alliance (McMath 1993: 19–82).

Hahn's description of the upcountry's independent political culture includes sections on pre-Populist revolts against the Democratic Party in the area in the 1870s and 1880s, and Woodward also recognizes the impact of these dissenters, but three recent books dealing with southern Independents, Republicans, and Greenbackers prove that the strength of these groups was greater than previously recognized (Hyman 1990; Cresswell 1995; Webb 1997). They call into question Goodwyn's intense focus on the Alliance as the sole parent of Populism.

Studies of the Populists' roots are not matched by efforts to understand what happened to them after 1896. "Clearly the Populists were reformers," writes William F. Holmes, "but to understand them better we need to know more precisely how their movement related" to post-1900 reform (Holmes 1990: 57). The issue of whether or not there were strong Populist links to Progressivism has not been resolved, and a clear answer to that question is difficult because so many Populists lost their political rights. Populism's demise, the rise of the progressive movement, and the creation of a one-party political system were all, to some extent, produced by disfranchisement.

In *Race, Class, and Party: A History of Negro Suffrage and White Politics in the South* (1932), Paul Lewinson stressed that disfranchisement was designed not only to eliminate black voters, but also to protect the franchise of whites. The subsequent decline in white voting was not intentional. In *Southern Politics in State and Nation* (1949), V. O. Key asserts that legal provisions on voting adopted in the South between 1890 and 1910 merely formalized control of voting processes established earlier by whites. Thus, disfranchisement was a "fait accompli" before it was backed up by law (Key 1949: 535–54).

In *Origins of the New South* and in his acclaimed effort to explain the imposition of segregation in the South, *The Strange Career of Jim Crow* (1955), C. Vann Woodward differs with Lewinson and Key. He contends that racial motives alone do not explain disfranchisement and that Democrats could not have achieved their ends without laws. Motivation for voting restrictions came from ex-Populists frustrated by plantation belt manipulation of black voters and from elite Democrats threatened by a potential biracial coalition of poor farmers. The elite knew that the legal elimination of lower-class voters of both races was their only adequate security against another Populist-style uprising, and that without laws they would have to continue to stuff ballot boxes and engage in fraudulent practices to win. Woodward seems unable to decide who was more responsible for disfranchisement, but in *Strange Career* he asserts that a large portion of the region's Democratic elite were "conservatives" opposed to the elimination of Negro civil rights, and he places the greatest blame on frustrated ex-Populists.

The only book devoted entirely to disfranchisement, and the most thorough account of the subject, is J. Morgan Kousser's *The Shaping of Southern Politics: Suffrage Restriction and the Establishment of the One-Party South, 1880–1910* (1974). Kousser adopts many of Woodward's views but offers new evidence to support them and original interpretations of his own. He asserts that supporters of voting restrictions needed the force of law to achieve permanent results, and that Key was wrong to believe that dissident voters were controlled prior to legal disfranchisement. White dissidents allied with Republicans remained a threat to Democrats through the 1880s primarily because blacks were still voting in large numbers for GOP candidates. The rise of Populism, and fusion between the GOP and Populists, convinced Democrats that the only safe route to ending this incessant opposition lay in legal restrictions. Thus, the motive behind voter limitations was not race, but the Democrats' partisan desire for power.

Kousser finds little support for Woodward's theory of racial moderation among upper-class conservative Democrats. Party leaders from the region's Black Belt areas wanted to eliminate blacks and white hill-country dissidents. These white Democrats from elite backgrounds pushed for disfranchisement over the strong opposition of ex-Populists, who understood that the new laws might take the franchise from them as well. Statistical tables assembled by Kousser demonstrate that, while black voters were essentially wiped out by disfranchisement, a severe decline in white voting also resulted. Party competition ceased to exist in the Deep South, and, except for Tennessee, Republicans had little chance to win statewide offices in the Upper South states.

The Progressive movement that followed disfranchisement, writes Kousser, was for "middle class whites only," because the political system no longer included the poor of either race (Kousser 1974: 229–31). Progressivism did more for "large merchants and industrialists" who favored railroad regulation and social efficiency than for those who truly needed help (ibid: 229). The reformers' "rational" approach to governing led to a more stable and orderly society, but "usually at the expense of the lower strata of society" (ibid: 230). Disfranchisement typified most Progressive reforms because it "disarmed radical critics while strengthening the status quo" (ibid: 261).

C. Vann Woodward admits that southern Progressivism was for "white men only," but is not as cynical about its aims or as narrow in assessing its achievements as Kousser (Woodward 1951: 373). In *Origins of the New South* Woodward describes a vital Progressivism that was not a northern derivative but indigenous to the South. Differing with Link about connections between Populists and post-1900 reformers, he says that Progressivism owed little to its predecessor, lacked the "agrarian cast" and "radical edge" of the prior movement, was "urban and middle class" in origin, and its leaders were business and professional men (Woodward 1951: 371). All "progressive doctrines and experiments" were tried in the region (ibid: 373). Southern reform politicians created the first direct nominating primaries, regulated railroads and insurance companies, fought monopolies, and backed prohibition, but did far less for labor than citizen reformers operating outside of public office. Even rabid white supremacists like James K. Vardaman of Mississippi and Charles B. Aycock of North Carolina achieved important reforms for whites.

Jack Temple Kirby's *Darkness at the Dawning: Race and Reform in the Progressive South* (1972), the first comprehensive synthesis of southern Progressivism, argues that the South's desire for reform was "deeper and broader" than that of other regions because southerners had so much more to do (Kirby 1972: 2). Differing with Woodward, Kirby writes that the "most potent force for southern reform lay in the frustrations and yearnings of the rural and small town masses" (ibid: 26). Their pervasive resentment of corporate power and eastern banks buttressed an important antimonopoly aspect of reform. Kirby's brief volume, built around biographical sketches of reformers, contends that post-1900 reform was "variegated and convoluted," driven by multiple forces, "broad in scope," and led to "rich and multidirectional" change (ibid: 1). Impetus for reform also came from women's groups or ministers who did not hold office but who fought for prohibition, child labor laws, and more humane penal systems. A much-needed chapter by Kirby also deals with efforts by black reformers to uplift their people in the face of great obstacles.

Disfranchisement and segregation were the "seminal" reforms of southern Progressives, according to Kirby, because whites had to stabilize the region's fluid racial system before they would agree to tackle other issues (Kirby 1972: 1). Thus, barriers to black freedom made "whites-only" reform possible. A typical white southern reformer was Bryanite newspaper editor Josephus Daniels of North Carolina, who supported Progressive governor Charles Brantley Aycock and a variety of salutary reforms while leading the fight for white supremacy. Racist demagogues condemned by W. J. Cash often compiled enviable Progressive records. As Mississippi's governor, writes Kirby, Theodore G. Bilbo "was the most effective southern mass leader before Huey Long" (Kirby 1972: 28–9).

Both Kirby and George Brown Tindall see Progressivism as a paradox that brought great change while reinforcing the South's traditional social system. This led Tindall to express divergent attitudes toward reform in *The Emergence of the New South 1913–1945* (1967) and *The Persistent Tradition in New South Politics* (1975). The earlier volume emphasizes that southern reformers abandoned the region's traditional support for states' rights and limited government. The backing southern congressmen gave to Woodrow Wilson's reform programs and the progressive achievements of governors as diverse as Bilbo and the patrician Richard Manning of South Carolina proved that the South accepted the "public service" state (Tindall 1967: 31–2). A regional fondness for using government resources to improve the economy continued into the 1920s when "business progressives" provided public support for projects that accommodated a rising new urban–industrial order (ibid: 224–33).

This hopeful conception of change is absent from *Persistent Tradition*, where Tindall accepts Morgan Kousser's view that the superficial adjustments made by reformers buttressed the power of elite groups. While noting that Kousser "overstated the case," Tindall believes southern Progressivism inherited little from Populism, and was instead "the legatee, almost the inevitable corollary" of "Bourbonism" and its "New South" economic goals (Tindall 1975: 61–2). Reforms adopted in the South usually served the interests of business and the "better class."

Tindall's suggestion that reformers produced conservative results may be accurate, but scholars studying national politics argue that southern congressmen pushed their northern brethren leftward, leading the charge for the nation's most far-reaching reforms. In an influential essay Anne Firor Scott (1963) contends that a "progressive wind" from the South was behind most reform legislation in the Congress between 1906 and 1916, proving that southerners were not bound by outmoded ideas about states' rights. David Sarasohn also assails the myth that the South was a "reactionary weight" on the Progressive Era's national Democratic Party and provides ample evidence that "the reality was almost the exact opposite" (Sarasohn 1989: 17–18).

The major questions about post-1900 reform are addressed in Dewey Grantham's *Southern Progressivism: The Reconciliation of Progress and Tradition* (1983), the most complete survey of the subject. It is, writes one critic, a "calm account" marked by a "balanced and fair" narrative, an "even-handed" assessment of historical figures, and professional "detachment and restraint" (Gould 1984: 1,403). Drawing on all the secondary literature and most primary sources, the author analyzes every aspect of reform. Grantham is a political historian, and though he points out the humanitarian efforts of those who never ran for office and the work of private groups such as the Southern Sociological Conference, his main subject is candidates, elections, political ideology, party factions, and the actions of governors and legislators. He seeks to explain the paradox of widespread reform efforts in a region where sharecropping, poverty, segregation, disfranchisement, a one-party system, white primaries, and racial demagoguery remained fixed and unchanging.

With such varied people in mind as Hoke Smith and James K. Vardaman, Grantham says there was "no typical progressive in the South," but the "most characteristic and significant" reformers were the middle-class professionals in the South's urban areas (Grantham 1983: xv–xvi). These Progressives wanted "a clearly defined community" that "would accommodate a society differentiated by race and class but one that also possessed unity, cohesion, and stability" (ibid: xvii). A "strong conservative cast" was clear among reformers, who believed in "a democratic society for whites only," and "revealed a deep distrust of the masses, whether white or black" (ibid). They wanted government to make their society more orderly, moral, humanitarian, and efficient, and they believed southern problems could best be solved through the engine of capitalist economic development. Although there were radical elements among the Progressives, most reforms were made palatable to planters and business interests.

Southern reform was spurred, says Grantham, by the social change that led to the rise of cities, industry, and a larger factory class near the end of the nineteenth century. The new structure of southern politics, which eliminated blacks and institutionalized the white primary, led to the rise of avowed reformers. A strong humanitarian impulse also came from southern Protestantism, which had as its chief aim the abolition of alcoholic beverages. The writings of several social critics of the 1890s and the early years of the twentieth century also piqued the region's social conscience.

Grantham describes a variety of southern reform efforts to regulate railroads, abolish the convict leasing system, impose prohibition, limit child labor, gain the suffrage for women, create social welfare agencies, improve education, modernize southern cities, improve working conditions in the mills, and bring help to struggling southern farmers. Like Kirby, Grantham believes that these reform efforts would not have been seriously attempted by whites in the absence of the racial controls they imposed between 1890 and 1910. Disfranchisement was part of a broader movement to improve the quality and honesty of southern politics that included the passage of such measures as corrupt practices acts governing the conduct of elections. No southern reform had greater support than the campaign to end the sale of alcoholic beverages, and though prohibition was supported by reformers in all regions, the power of religious fundamentalism made it an even greater imperative in the South.

Realizing that southern politics has always been more diverse than W. J. Cash described, Grantham divides the states into subregions called the "Lower South," "Upper South," and "Southwest." The ensuing effort to generalize about these subregions and distinguish between them is arbitrary, forced, and unsupported by the evidence. The author's discussions of politics in individual states are more convincing. After Populism and disfranchisement, a one-party system developed in most southern states; and in the few Upper South states where Republicans remained competitive, they rarely won statewide races. Democratic primary fights were characterized by distinctive bifactional splits that developed around intrastate sectional divisions, colorful personalities, conflicting economic interests, and urban against rural counties. Race, particularly in the Lower South, continued to play a major role despite efforts by disfranchisers to eliminate it as an issue.

Every southern state produced reform factions led by either an urban businessman like Braxton Bragg Comer of Alabama or a rural demagogue like Vardaman. Strong conservative forces, usually led by lowland planters or business interests, opposed the reformers. In most instances the conservatives, usually through their control of legislatures, were able to soften the efforts of reformers. The South produced no reformers who were willing to overturn the conservative political and economic institutions that had been put into place by the Bourbon–Redeemer leaders of the late nineteenth century. As a result, Grantham believes that southern traditions remained firmly in place and reform produced more stability than change.

Despite his view of politics in the state capitals as essentially conservative, Grantham joins other historians who describe the key role that southern politicians played in the reform efforts of the Wilson administration. They strongly supported federal programs to aid farmers and small businessmen, and laws restricting monopolies. By concentrating on the arguments of the minority who opposed the prolabor measures of the Wilson years, Grantham obscures the support most southerners gave to these bills.

No one could accuse Grantham of agreeing with W. J. Cash, though he might have traded his "detachment" for some of the colorful prose in *The Mind of the South*. Yet, he does end his story by arguing that southern reformers "were in no sense involved in the promotion of fundamental social change" (Grantham 1983: 418). That conclusion puts him closer to the camp of Morgan Kousser than that of Arthur Link. Grantham admits the strong desire for reform in the South; but like all historians of southern politics he ultimately admits that reformers were held back by certain institutional constraints that kept them from supporting more radical measures. Racial institutions were the most constraining. Too much support by Progressives for small farmers might have led to biracial coalitions, and too much support for labor might have created working-class solidarity across racial lines. Support for women's suffrage might have reopened the disfranchisement issue. Because of such fears, southern reformers always left out too many people, and that is why so few have noticed the diversity and complexity of southern politics reported by Link and Woodward. It is also why so many still agree with Cash, despite his oversimplifications.

BIBLIOGRAPHY

Boles, John B. and Johnson, Bethany L., (eds.) 2003: *"Origins of the New South" Fifty Years Later: The Continuing Influence of a Historical Classic*. Baton Rouge: Louisiana State University Press.

Cash, W. J. 1941: *The Mind of the South*. New York: Alfred A. Knopf.

Cherny, Robert W. 1981: Lawrence Goodwyn and Nebraska Populism: A Review Essay. *Great Plains Quarterly*, 1 (2), 181–94.

Clanton, Gene 1991: *Populism: The Humane Preference in America, 1890–1900*. Boston: Twayne Publishers.

Cresswell, Stephen Edward 1995: *Multiparty Politics in Mississippi, 1897–1902*. Jackson: University Press of Mississippi.

Durden, Robert F. 1965: *The Climax of Populism: The Election of 1896*. Lexington: University Press of Kentucky.

Ferkiss, Victor C. 1957: Populist Influences on American Fascism. *Western Political Quarterly*, 10 (2), 350–73.

Goodwyn, Lawrence 1976: *Democratic Promise: The Populist Moment in America*. New York: Oxford University Press.

Gould, Lewis L. 1984: Review of Dewey W. Grantham, *Southern Progressivism: The Reconciliation of Progress and Tradition. American Historical Review* 89 (5), 1,403–4.

Grantham, Dewey W. 1983: *Southern Progressivism: The Reconciliation of Progress and Tradition*. Knoxville: University of Tennessee Press.

Hackney, Sheldon 1969: *Populism to Progressivism in Alabama*. Princeton, NJ: Princeton University Press.

Hahn, Steven 1983: *The Roots of Southern Populism: Yeoman Farmers and the Transformation of the Georgia Upcountry, 1850–1890*. New York: Oxford University Press.

Hicks, John D. 1931: *The Populist Revolt: A History of the Farmers' Alliance and the People's Party*. Minneapolis: University of Minnesota Press.

Hofstadter, Richard 1955: *The Age of Reform: From Bryan to F. D. R.* New York: Vintage Books.

Holmes, William F. 1990: Populism: In Search of A Context. *Agricultural History*, 64 (4), 26–58.

Hyman, Michael R. 1990: *The Anti-Redeemers: Hill Country Political Dissenters in the Lower South from Redemption to Populism*. Baton Rouge: Louisiana State University Press.

Kantor, Shawn Everett and Kousser, J. Morgan 1993: Common Sense or Commonwealth? The Fence Law and Institutional Change in the Postbellum South. *Journal of Southern History*, 61 (2), 201–42.

Key, V. O. 1949: *Southern Politics in State and Nation*. New York: Alfred A. Knopf.

Kirby, Jack Temple 1972: *Darkness at the Dawning: Race and Reform in the Progressive South*. Philadelphia: Lippincott.

Kousser, J. Morgan 1974: *The Shaping of Southern Politics: Suffrage Restriction and the Establishment of the One-Party South, 1880–1910*. New Haven, CT: Yale University Press.

Lewinson, Paul 1932: *Race, Class, and Party: A History of Negro Suffrage and White Politics in the South*. New York: Oxford University Press (1959 and 1965 editions).

Link, Arthur S. 1946: The Progressive Movement in the South, 1870–1914. *North Carolina Historical Review*, 23 (1), 172–95.

Lipset, Seymour Martin 1964: The Sources of the Radical Right. In Daniel Bell (ed.), *The Radical Right: The New American Right Expanded and Updated*. Garden City, NY: Anchor Books.

McMath, Robert C., Jr. 1993: *American Populism: A Social History, 1877–1898*. New York: Hill and Wang.

Montgomery, David 1978: On Goodwyn's Populists. *Marxist Perspectives*, 1, 166–73.

Palmer, Bruce 1980: *"Man Over Money": The Southern Populist Critique of American Capitalism*. Chapel Hill: University of North Carolina Press.

Parsons, Stanley, et al. 1983: The Role of Cooperatives in the Development of the Movement Culture of Populism. *Journal of American History*, 69 (4), 866–85.

Rogers, William Warren 1970: *The One-Gallused Rebellion: Agrarianism in Alabama 1865–1896*. Baton Rouge: Louisiana State University Press.

Rothenberg, Winifred B. 1987: The Bound Prometheus. *Reviews in American History*, 15 (4), 628–37.

Sarasohn, David 1989: *The Party of Reform: Democrats in the Progressive Era*. Jackson: University Press of Mississippi.

Scott, Anne Firor 1963: A Progressive Wind From the South, 1906–1913. *Journal of Southern History*, 29 (1), 53–70.

Shaw, Barton 1984: *The Wool-Hat Boys: Georgia's Populist Party*. Baton Rouge: Louisiana State University Press.

Simkins, Francis Butler 1944: *Pitchfork Ben Tillman, South Carolinian*. Baton Rouge: Louisiana State University Press.

Tindall, George Brown 1967: *The Emergence of the New South 1913–1945*. Baton Rouge: Louisiana State University Press.

Tindall, George Brown 1975: *The Persistent Tradition in New South Politics*. Baton Rouge: Louisiana State University Press.

Turner, James 1980: Understanding the Populists. *Journal of American History*, 67 (2), 354–73.

Webb, Samuel L. 1997: *Two-Party Politics in the One-Party South: Alabama's Hill Country, 1874–1920*. Tuscaloosa: University of Alabama Press.

Woodward, C. Vann 1938: *Tom Watson: Agrarian Rebel*. New York: Oxford University Press.

Woodward, C. Vann 1951: *Origins of the New South 1877–1913*. Baton Rouge: Louisiana State University Press.

Woodward, C. Vann 1955: *The Strange Career of Jim Crow*. New York: Oxford University Press.

Woodward, C. Vann 1960: *The Burden of Southern History*. Baton Rouge: Louisiana State University Press.

CHAPTER TWENTY

The Rise of Jim Crow, 1880–1920

JAMES BEEBY AND DONALD G. NIEMAN

D URING the first half of the twentieth century, Jim Crow – a system of law and custom that took its name from an antebellum minstrel song-and-dance – rigidly separated blacks and whites and dominated virtually all aspects of southern life. For the past fifty years, as the nation has grappled with the bitter legacy of Jim Crow, historians have devoted considerable attention to the origins and development of segregation. Studies have examined the origins of segregation in the antebellum era, the development of northern ghettos in the twentieth century, and the long struggle against segregation. Most of the scholarship, however, has focused on the post-Civil War South, where the harshest form of American apartheid took shape. The result has been a sharp debate and a rich body of scholarship that has powerfully influenced our understanding of the southern experience.

In explaining the development of segregation, historians have emphasized a variety of factors: the emergence of white demagogues and their exploitation of race; the growth of pseudo-scientific racism and rapidly diminishing support for equality among northern whites; the rise of Populism and the bitter conflict among whites it produced; economic frustration produced by declining cotton prices, a colonial economy, and the sharp depression of the 1890s; a new generation of African-Americans who refused to accept their prescribed position in southern society; and psychosocial fears of the imagined threat black men posed to white women. The key historiographical differences revolve around the relative weight each element played in causing the rise of segregation and the degree of continuity or discontinuity between the 1890s and the preceding decades.

One book stands at the center of this debate: C. Vann Woodward's *The Strange Career of Jim Crow*, a classic of American historiography. First given as a series of lectures at the University of Virginia in October 1954, only months after the United States Supreme Court declared segregation in public schools unconstitutional, it offered a provocative interpretation of the origins of segregation.

Woodward argued that the Jim Crow system was of relatively recent origin and did not have deep roots in southern history and culture. Central to his argument was that a universal, legally prescribed system of segregation did not emerge during slavery or in the immediate aftermath of emancipation. Indeed, he insisted that the 1870s and 1880s were a period of "forgotten alternatives" (Woodward 1955: ch. 1), a time when there was flexibility in southern race relations and it was not unusual for whites and blacks to share the same public spaces. Not until the 1890s, according to Woodward, did Jim Crow crystallize, as states competed with each other to mandate racial separation by law and segregation became a universal feature of southern life.

To opponents of the Supreme Court's ruling in *Brown v. Board of Education* (1954) who contended that segregation was part of the natural order of things and was so deeply rooted that it could never be changed by law, Woodward suggested that Jim Crow was of relatively recent origin and, therefore, not immutable.

In addition to his concern with timing, Woodward sought to explain the forces that produced segregation. While crediting the growth of pseudo-scientific racism and declining northern support for equality, he placed special emphasis on politics. Utilizing a Beardian notion of historical causation, Woodward identified the rise of Populism as the key factor in hardening racial attitudes in the South and the emergence of Jim Crow. By appealing to African-American voters and raising the possibility of a powerful biracial coalition of poor farmers and tenants, the Populists challenged the hegemony of the Democratic elites who had dominated southern politics since the end of Reconstruction and pursued a neo-Whig policy of promoting economic development at the expense of the black and white masses. Frightened by this insurgency, Woodward explained, Democrats played the race card, reminding whites of the alleged horrors of black rule during Reconstruction and appealing to their sense of racial solidarity and fear of African-Americans. Combined with electoral fraud and outright violence, this strategy enabled Democrats to beat back the Populist challenge and force through disfranchisement policies that eliminated blacks and many poor whites from the political process. This climate – white-hot with racist vituperation – proved fertile soil for those who advocated rigid separation of the races. Indeed, Woodward emphasized that many Populists, feeling betrayed by their erstwhile black political allies, lent their support to extreme racist policies.

At the time Woodward's book appeared, historians had written little on the subject of post-Civil War race relations. *Strange Career* changed that, quickly generating a substantial body of scholarship on the origins of southern segregation. While some of this work supported Woodward (Blassingame 1973; Dethloff and Jones 1968; Logan 1964; Wynes 1961), many scholars took issue with Woodward's claims. Critics demonstrated that segregation had antedated the Civil War, finding that it had existed in antebellum southern cities with respect to slaves (Wade 1964) and restrictions on free blacks (Berlin 1974). More to the point, they charged that southern society became intensely segregated in the years immediately following the Civil War. Chiding Woodward for placing too much emphasis on law and too little on custom, these scholars found that white racism and aversion to contact with African-Americans led to a pervasive separation of the races in churches, schools, prisons, asylums, public transportation, and other forms of public accommodation very quickly after emancipation. The Jim Crow statutes that were enacted in the 1890s did not create segregation, these critics insisted, but rather formalized a system that had been created by custom (Cartwright 1976; Fischer 1974; Williamson 1965).

Although the critics made telling points, Woodward refused to concede defeat. He responded that he had never contended that segregation did not exist prior to the 1890s or that law was an accurate gauge of behavior. He admitted that custom played an important part in establishing segregation and that segregation had become widespread prior to the 1890s. Nevertheless, he maintained that there was a certain flexibility in postbellum race relations and that widespread adoption of Jim Crow laws in the 1890s was significant, signalling the emergence of a much more rigid and all-encompassing form of segregation (Woodward 1971, 1988).

While the debate between Woodward and his critics often seemed to narrow to a question of the degree of interracial contact that existed prior to the establishment of legally mandated segregation, new and more fruitful lines of inquiry soon emerged in the 1970s. Howard Rabinowitz's pathbreaking 1978 book, *Race Relations in the Urban South, 1865–1890*, significantly altered the course of the discussion by focusing on what the system of *de jure* segregation that emerged in the 1890s replaced. Rabinowitz argued that before legalized segregation, African-Americans had witnessed a period of exclusion, rather than integration, as Woodward suggested.

Unlike Woodward, Rabinowitz moved away from viewing African-Americans as victims, instead treating them as historical actors. He insisted that one must tie the rise of segregation to the actions of African-Americans themselves and not merely to the erosion of northern support for black political participation and the new wave of virulent white racism that emerged in the 1890s. In the 1880s, he argued, a new generation of African-Americans emerged, especially in the cities, who had been born in freedom and refused to accept their prescribed second-class position in southern society. As Rabinowitz eloquently stated, "Like youth in general, they tended to be impatient; born in freedom they had no fond memories of slavery or attachments to the past" (Rabinowitz 1978: 334). Consequently, they acted in an assertive manner and demanded their full rights as citizens. As African-Americans began to resist white rule and northern support for equal rights dwindled, Rabinowitz persuasively argued, white southerners took the opportunity to impose a rigid system of *de jure* segregation, formalizing custom that had been in place.

Because Woodward had treated African-Americans as victims and failed to acknowledge their agency, Rabinowitz's analysis represented an important contribution to the literature and reinvigorated what had become a rather stale discussion. Following Rabinowitz's work, a growing number of scholars wrote at length on the proactive nature of the African-American community in a number of southern states, and these studies lent support to Rabinowitz's basic thesis of increased black assertiveness and the resultant virulent reaction by southern whites (Cartwright 1976; Flynn 1983). Neil McMillen's work on Mississippi is perhaps the best example of an African-American-centered work on a Deep South state. McMillen argues that, in Mississippi at least, with a very few exceptions, segregation in all walks of life occurred well before the 1890s; but that by the last decade of the nineteenth century, *de jure* segregation was firmly in place. Although McMillen sketches the familiar outlines of the Jim Crow system, he takes his analysis to new heights with the subtle use of first-hand accounts of black life in Mississippi and his focus on local details and historical contingency. He argues that "black Mississippians resisted the erosion of their citizenship by every practical means" (McMillen 1989: 288). They did not see white supremacy as just, and therefore, even after the rise of Jim Crow, blacks continued to resist segregation. Although he carefully analyzed the virulent white racism against blacks, what makes McMillen's work so important is its attention to the agency of African-Americans as they resisted white hegemony and fought for their rights in the 1890s.

In addition to its welcome exploration of segregation from the African-American perspective, the scholarship of the 1980s and 1990s saw growing interest in sexuality and gender as concepts crucial to explain the rise of Jim Crow. In *The Crucible of Race* (1984), a sprawling analysis of changing white racial attitudes in the decades after emancipation, Joel Williamson argued that white men's determination to preserve their masculinity drove them to support lynching, disfranchisement, and Jim Crow. Poverty and economic depression undermined white men's ability to fulfill their prescribed roles as providers, thereby undermining their masculinity. Even their ability to protect their wives and daughters – a key element of their masculine identity – was called into question by fears that black men, freed from the constraints of slavery, would indulge their supposed lasciviousness and victimize white women. According to Williamson, these feelings of inadequacy, frustration, and fear led white men to participate in ritualistic lynchings of black men alleged to have transgressed racial mores and to support a rigid system of segregation that would protect white women from blacks. Even southern conservatives, who viewed Africans as inferior but benign, supported segregation as a way of shielding blacks from contacts with whites that often generated violence.

Many critics charged that Williamson focused too heavily on white fantasies and failed to treat African-Americans as actors. Nevertheless, appearing at a time of growing interest in gender as a powerful explanatory tool, *The Crucible of Race* pointed a new direction in scholarship on segregation. In the mid-1990s two deeply researched, highly imaginative works placed gender at the core of their analyses of the rise of Jim Crow: Glenda Gilmore's *Gender and Jim Crow: Women and the Politics of White Supremacy in North Carolina, 1896–1920* and Grace E. Hale's *Making Whiteness: The Culture of Segregation in the South, 1890–1940*. Although each work has a different emphasis and scope (Gilmore focuses on North Carolina while Hale examines the South as a whole), both address the complex dynamics of gender, masculinity, and the culture of Jim Crow, as well as the African-American response to the worsening state of race relations. Each offers compelling insights into the fluidity of race and gender relations in the 1890s that seem to shift the historiographical debate into new and exciting directions.

Glenda Gilmore agrees with Woodward that Jim Crow profoundly reordered southern society. However, she notes, in North Carolina at least, the emergence of Jim Crow was closely tied to the manipulation of gender by white supremacists. In other words – and here she is in disagreement with Rabinowitz – by focusing on the gendered nature of Jim Crow, Gilmore postulates that segregation was not the culmination of prevailing trends, but rather a reordering of society. By illustrating the agency of women – white and black – and black men, Gilmore provides the most nuanced view we have of the rise of the Jim Crow South. Essentially, Gilmore argues, white Democrats responded to a growing assertiveness among black men, to urban and social pressures (such as those in Wilmington), and to "spectacular African-American successes" (Gilmore 1996: xx), seeking to stave-off threats to white dominance. Gilmore, like Woodward forty years before her, focuses on politics, albeit more broadly defined. In her account, Democrats engineered a racialized and gendered campaign to defeat an alliance of Populists and Republicans and then to usher in a period of virulent Jim Crowism.

While Gilmore's work focuses on the political culture of gender and race in the New South state of North Carolina, Grace Hale's book explores the culture of segregation as it took shape across the South. Although the majority of Hale's analysis illuminates the subtlety of racial mores in the segregated South, she also explores the emergence of Jim Crow. Hale argues that southern whites "constructed their racial identities on two interlocking planes: within a regional dynamic of ex-Confederates versus ex-slaves and within a national dynamic of the South, understood as white, versus the nation" (Hale 1998: 9). In a fluid world, Hale argues, white southerners, seeking social order, evoked narratives through spectacles, such as lynchings, to ground their identity as white. African-Americans, she suggests, quickly discerned that whites were looking to unite the nation behind a construction of whiteness that left out blacks, especially at a time when some African-Americans had begun to prosper economically during the late nineteenth-century. According to Hale, whites created the culture of segregation in large part to counter black success, to make a myth of racial difference, and to stop the progress of African-Americans. In other words, historiographically, Hale is in general agreement with Rabinowitz, McMillen, and Gilmore on the agency of African-Americans, but also she agrees with the discontinuity thesis in race relations, first offered by Woodward and supported by Gilmore. Unlike these historians, however, Hale places the South within the broader context of changes in American culture and society as a whole during the Gilded Age and Progressive Era. In this regard, Hale's work may launch a new departure in historical scholarship on the South: the social construction of race – including white-ness – and the functioning of culture in society.

The vast majority of new writings on the rise of Jim Crow focus, correctly, on the agency of African-Americans and their refusal to remain quiet in the face of white racism. On the whole, however, these works, probably because of the nature of the sources, tend to privilege the African-American middle class at the expense of the vast majority of African-Americans who earned their livelihoods as sharecroppers and common laborers. Recently, Pulitzer Prize-winning historian Leon Litwack has shifted the focus of the study of Jim Crow to the black masses in his magisterial study, *Trouble in Mind: Black Southerners in the Age of Jim Crow.* Litwack (1998) agrees with Rabinowitz that the rise of Jim Crow coincided with the coming of age of a new generation of blacks who refused to accept a second-class status prescribed by whites. By chronicling the everyday lives of working-class African-Americans, in both rural and urban areas, as they confronted racism on a daily basis, tried to educate themselves to improve their lives, worked as sharecroppers or as poorly paid laborers in the cities, and struggled to advance economically, politically, and socially, Litwack details African-Americans' resistance to their prescribed position in society. He also explicates the violence and intimidation whites routinely employed against blacks and a legal system that afforded little protection to the most vulnerable in society. By illuminating the lives of poor blacks, Litwack adds credence and nuance to the work of Rabinowitz and others. At last, one clearly hears the voices of the disaffected and disfranchised.

Discussion of and debate over the causes of the rise of Jim Crow will not end any time soon. In many ways the central tenets of Woodward's thesis remain, like the Tower of London, the bedrock of historiography in southern studies. There is little doubt that successive generations of historians have modified his work, particularly with respect to the role of African-Americans, the reaction of whites to increased black assertiveness, and the importance of gender, but there is no sign that the ravens have left the Tower yet.

As Woodward suggested in *Strange Career,* the discussion of Jim Crow cannot be separated from disfranchisement. Although the importance of politics in the lives of African-Americans is perhaps exaggerated, politics meant far more to

African-Americans than merely voting and holding office. While many historians argue that blacks faced roadblocks – legal and extralegal – to voting, they nevertheless strategically used the ballot in many southern states, particularly in the Upper South, to elect sympathetic officials and to offset the most egregious forms of white violence and racial discrimination in the post-Reconstruction period (Anderson 1981; Beeby 1999; Goodwyn 1971; Nieman 1989). In the 1890s, however, southern states began to disfranchise black men and some poor whites. Most historians agree on the impact of disfranchisement, namely that African-Americans and many poor whites lost the right to vote, that a small cadre of whites would dominate politics for a generation, that overall voter turnout declined, and that once blacks lost the vote they had little, if any, protection from the most humiliating and violent aspects of segregation and Jim Crowism. However, there is strong disagreement among historians over what led to disfranchisement in the 1880s and 1890s, and much of the debate revolves around the same issues discussed with the rise of segregation.

By far the most significant work on the forces behind and the impact of disfranchisement is J. Morgan Kousser's *The Shaping of Southern Politics* (1974). Through sophisticated use of statistical analysis, case studies of all the southern states, and a thorough survey of the secondary literature, Kousser constructed a powerful analysis of disfranchisement that is nunaced, sensitive to locality and time, mindful of the interconnections of social customs and political actions in the electoral process, and attentive to race and class. Kousser argues that Black Belt Democratic elites, who had long been politically dominant and had always held a privileged position in southern society, demanded absolute control of their heavily black counties, an end to organized competition between politicians, and an end to lower-class interest in political decision making. Kousser carefully showed how Democrats, over a thirty-year period, expunged African-Americans from the electoral process and simultaneously stymied lower-class white opposition to Democratic hegemony. These white Democrats were determined to control the political process, and one way to cement their control was to divide the lower classes along race lines and push through disfranchisement.

In this respect Kousser is in agreement with the central tenets of Woodward's analysis. Woodward argues that disfranchisement came to the South after the economic depression of the 1890s swept away the Redeemer Democrats and ushered in the Populist revolt. As a result, Woodward argues, conservative Democrats (New Democrats) "raised the cry of 'Negro domination' and white supremacy, and enlisted Negrophobe elements" to defeat this political insurgency (Woodward 1955: 79). Once the Democrats defeated the Populists and their African-American allies, they used the race issue to bring together white men, rich and poor, by disfranchising African-Americans. The disfranchisement of blacks, Woodward argues, was a way for Democrats to advocate racial solidarity and consolidate their grip on power. In a remarkably short time – between 1890 and 1908 – all southern states effected disfranchisement of African-Americans and many poor whites.

If Woodward emphasized disfranchisement as a way for the Democrats to defeat Populism and end the specter of black rule, other historians chose to view disfranchisement as a response to increased demands by African-Americans for public office and political positions consistent with their numbers. Historians such as Glenda Gilmore, Edward Ayers, Neil McMillen, Leon Litwack, and Howard Rabinowitz illustrate, with good effect, the Democrats' abhorrence of black officeholding, particularly (but not solely) in the Black Belt (where African-Americans constituted a majority of the electorate in many counties), and the threat this posed, according to the Democrats, to southern white women.

Each of these historians argues that the Democrats believed that political equality between the races would inevitably lead to social equality. As a result, the Democrats, in light of continued black political participation, doubled their efforts to curtail black voting in the 1890s. Glenda Gilmore makes this point clear in her work on North Carolina, where white Democrats used the perceived threat to white womanhood by black officials such as Congressman George White or state legislator James H. Young to defeat a Fusionist coalition of Populists and Republicans in 1898 and the opponents of disfranchisement in 1900.

Neil McMillen focuses on similar events in Mississippi, and Leon Litwack makes the case for the South as a whole. Litwack is just one of many historians who tie the emergence of Jim Crow to disfranchisement. He notes that the issue of black political participation remained linked in the white man's mind with black assertiveness and argues that white men believed in their own superiority. To underscore this, whites "disfranchised black men, imposed rigid patterns of racial segregation, manipulated the judicial system, and sustained extraordinary levels of violence and brutality" (Litwack 1998: 218–19). Litwack believes that disfranchisement did not result from concerns about political power but rather from fear among many whites that African-American political equality would lead to social equality. In order to prevent this, white leaders created a system in which disfranchisement buttressed segregation to constantly remind African-Americans of their powerlessness and subordinate status.

These studies stand in sharp contrast to Rabinowitz, who argued that in many southern cities, at least, *de facto* disfranchisement of African-Americans existed before the 1890s. For Rabinowitz the exclusion of African-Americans from voting was already in effect a decade before states began adopting formal disfranchising devices. Although this may have been the case in the cities Rabinowitz studied, the work of Gilmore, Kousser, McMillen, and Litwack proves that black political participation was a reality well into the 1890s and that widespread disfranchisement came only in the 1890s and after.

Although historians have a clear sense of what caused disfranchisement, more analysis is needed of the attempts at political alliances between poor whites and blacks in the post-Reconstruction decades. Although both groups distrusted one another, at times race was put aside, however fleetingly, for cooperation based on mutual class interests. In recent years scholars have reapproached this subject and the contested nature of southern politics in the 1890s, and these new studies seem to suggest that the Populist threat *and* the increased political assertiveness of a new generation of African-Americans may have caused the virulent racist campaigns of the white Democrats in the 1890s and the eventual disfranchisement of blacks and many poor whites.

Like politics, the realm of work during the age of segregation has also attracted a great deal of scholarly attention. Historians have grappled with the effects of the changing southern economy and African-American responses to an economic system in which the opportunities open to them were sharply constrained by racism and segregation and the racially segmented labor markets they created. The central historiographical questions revolve around the degree to which the South underwent an economic transformation during the period from 1880 to 1920 and the impact of segregation on the working lives of African-Americans. Leon Litwack's *Trouble in Mind*, for example, argues that for most poor blacks poverty was due "not to the willingness of blacks to work the land they knew so intimately but in the betrayal of their expectations, in the failure to reap rewards that were in any way commensurate with their labor" (Litwack 1998: 115). Despite the poverty, hardships, violence, and discrimination that all blacks faced, Litwack elucidates the success stories of some rural blacks and their resistance to the most egregious forms of economic exploitation, as whites continued to own the land and demand a tractable black labor force. Black men and women, Litwack notes, were determined to advance themselves, their families, and their race, to gain dignity and independence in the face of white violence and legal machinations.

African-Americans' resistance to Jim Crow in both the workplace and in the larger society of the South, as well as their determination to gain personal autonomy, is best exemplified in the work of Tera Hunter. Her book, *To 'Joy My Freedom* (1997), specifically addresses African-American workers' lives in Atlanta and uses a wealth of new sources as well as a reinterpretation of existing ones to explore the lives of poor blacks. Hunter adds a new twist to the study of black labor by focusing on African-American women and their work. Her scholarship is truly groundbreaking, illuminating the subtle ways women struggled as laundresses and other service workers to construct their own world of work, play, resistance, and community organization in the face of virulent white racism. Hunter reinterprets the famous Atlanta laundry strike of 1881 as a pivotal moment in the agency of women and the African-American community when they demanded social and economic justice. She takes issue with those historians, such as Rabinowitz, who minimize the importance of the strike and the inefficacy of the women. Rather, Hunter persuasively argues, the strike was one of the largest and most effective by African-Americans in a southern city. It was led by black women, who were willing to jeopardize the sole source of family income in order to improve their lives and their community. In striking, these women faced class, gender, and racial hostility, and although the whites managed to defeat the strike, black women, Hunter argues, did not give up fighting for racial and economic justice, resorting to a variety of other tactics to improve their lives. As Jim Crow laws hardened and violence escalated, with sickening lynchings and anti-black pogroms, many black men and women took their resistance to the next level and migrated out of the South.

The efforts of African-Americans to maintain their dignity and pursue economic advancement in the face of segregation is a constant theme of the recent historical literature. One of the most illuminating studies of African-American workers in the South is Jacqueline Jones's prize-winning and groundbreaking work, *Labor of Love, Labor of Sorrow: Black Women, Work and the Family from Slavery to the Present* (1985). The strength of Jones's work is that she subtly weaves a powerful narrative around the lives of black women in the South and their responses to the increasing virulence of Jim Crow. No mere chronicler of events, she makes connections between the home and the workplace and the complex ways in which black women dealt with the stresses of family life and the demands of labor outside the home, particularly in the face of white suppression and segregation. Unlike Tera Hunter, Jones focuses on the rural South, contending that women worked in the hope that their sons and daughters would one day escape from the oppressive Cotton South and its grinding poverty. She persuasively argues that although the lives of black sharecroppers remained outside the mainstream of American society, these workers struggled to maintain their independence and the independence of their families and their communities as centers of racial pride and uplift.

Leon Litwack's rich, yet relentless, portrayal of work in the rural South makes for depressing reading. He notes the increasingly difficult position African-American sharecroppers faced as cotton prices plummeted and racial antagonisms hardened. He also notes that white landowners were not prepared to deal with free blacks on equal terms and, therefore, they demanded workers who would obey their commands and know their place. Litwack agrees with historians who argue that blacks were "cheated of their earnings, turned off their lands, or refused lands they could afford to purchase" and remained mired in poverty as white property owners retained control over most of the black population through debt peonage and crop liens (Litwack 1998: 115). The power of Litwack's analysis of the life of black rural workers comes through his use of interviews and first-hand accounts that give a more nuanced account of working conditions and the life of the poorest members of southern society. He notes that some blacks did manage to make money and own land, but that these successes occurred predominantly in the Upper South. Litwack carefully notes how blacks refused to passively respond to perceived limitations placed on their working lives and opportunities.

Although Jones, Hunter, and Litwack detail different arenas of work in the South, each illuminates the degree to which African-Americans refused to live the lives ascribed to them by whites, even when, as in the case of the rural South, whites owned most of the land, consciously stifled black economic development, and brutally suppressed black civil and political rights. At every opportunity, African-Americans sought to advance themselves, maintain their families, and uplift their race. Their perseverance in the face of increased violence by whites, through lynching and riots, as well as the legal hurdles placed in the way of the newly emancipated slaves, is a testament to the continued effort by blacks to move beyond their ascribed position. This opposition took its most organized form during the era of Jim Crow as a growing number of African-Americans chose to migrate from the poverty and violence of the South to the burgeoning industrial cities of the North, where they found problems both familiar and new.

The literature on the rise of Jim Crow still owes much to the work of C. Vann Woodward and the key themes he outlined fifty years ago. Nevertheless, as the work of Rabinowitz, Gilmore, Hale, Litwack, and Hunter suggests, scholarship has moved in exciting and productive new directions during the past two decades. The field, however, must pay even greater attention to the role of gender in the emergence of Jim Crow. More research is needed on the role of white and black women in the emergence of Jim Crow and how black women and white women related to one another in the social, economic, and political realms. In addition, we need studies of the differences within the ranks of those who supported Jim Crow, namely white Democrats. Although we have a good understanding of the motives that drove the leadership (e.g. James Vardaman, Charles B. Aycock, Furnifold Simmons, and Ben Tillman, among others), the attitudes of middle-class whites, who supported and were the vanguard in segregation and disfranchisement, remain more muted. In addition, more comparative work on the sites of contestation over Jim Crow (such as the railroads, sexual politics, politics, post offices, entertainment, and stores), where the races came into direct conflict, might elucidate subtleties of the emergence of Jim Crow. In addition, we need more work on the nature of the Populist insurgency and the political alliances it generated between white Populists and African-Americans to determine how much of a threat these groups presented to the upper- and middle-class Democrats in the Black Belt. Likewise, a full analysis of the nature of African-American political activism in all southern states is desperately needed. On the effects of disfranchisement the literature is never-ending. However, historians need to analyze, particularly in rural areas, how black men and women opposed disfranchisement. On the relationship between black labor and segregation, more historians need to follow in the footsteps of Tera Hunter's work on Atlanta. Historians need to flesh out the nature of African-American work in southern cities and in the countryside and the lives of the working-class blacks and whites.

BIBLIOGRAPHY

Anderson, Eric 1981: *Race and Politics in North Carolina, 1872–1901: The Black Second.* Baton Rouge: Louisiana State University Press.

Anderson, John D. 1988: *The Education of Blacks in the South, 1860–1935.* Chapel Hill: University of North Carolina Press.

Ayers, Edward L. 1984: *Vengeance and Justice: Crime and Punishment in the Nineteenth-Century South.* New York: Oxford University Press.

Ayers, Edward L. 1992: *The Promise of the New South: Life After Reconstruction.* New York: Oxford University Press.

Beeby, James 1999: Revolt of the Tar Heelers: A Socio-Political History of the North Carolina Populist Party, 1892–1901. Ph.D. dissertation, Bowling Green State University.

Berlin, Ira 1974: *Slaves Without Masters: The Free Negro in the Antebellum South.* New York: Pantheon Books.

Blassingame, John 1973: *Black New Orleans, 1860–1880.* Chicago: University of Chicago Press.

Brundage, W. Fitzhugh 1993: *Lynching in the New South: Georgia and Virginia, 1880–1930.* Urbana: University of Illinois Press.

Cantrel, Gregg and Barton, D. Scott 1989: Texas Populists and the Failure of Biracial Politics. *Journal of Southern History,* 55 (4), 659–92.

Cartwright, Joseph H. 1976: *The Triumph of Jim Crow: Race Relations in the 1880s.* Knoxville: University of Tennessee Press.

Cash, Wilbur J. 1941: *The Mind of the South.* New York: Alfred A. Knopf.

Cell, John W. 1982: *The Highest Stage of White Supremacy: The Origins of Segregation in South Africa and the American South.* New York: Oxford University Press.

Cohen, William 1991: *At Freedom's Edge: Black Mobility and the Southern White Quest for Racial Control, 1861–1915.* Baton Rouge: Louisiana State University Press.

Degler, Carl N. 1974: *The Other South: Southern Dissenters in the Nineteenth Century.* New York: Harper and Row.

Dethloff, Henry C. and Jones, Robert R. 1968: Race Relations in Louisiana, 1877–1898. *Louisiana History,* 9 (4), 301–23.

De Santis, Vincent P. 1959: *Republicans Face the Southern Question – The New Departure Years, 1877–1897.* Baltimore: John Hopkins University Press.

Dittmer, John 1977: *Black Georgia in the Progressive Era, 1900–1920.* Urbana: University of Illinois Press.

Dollard, John 1937: *Caste and Class in a Southern Town*. New Haven, CT: Yale University Press.

Edmonds, Helen G. 1951: *The Negro and Fusion Politics in North Carolina, 1894–1901*. Chapel Hill: University of North Carolina Press.

Fink, Leon 1983: *Workingmen's Democracy: The Knights of Labor and American Politics*. Urbana: University of Illinois Press.

Fischer, Roger A. 1974: *The Segregation Struggle in Louisiana, 1862–1877*. Urbana: University of Illinois Press.

Flynn, Charles L. 1983: *White Land, Black Labor: Caste and Class in Nineteenth-Century Georgia*. Baton Rouge: Louisiana State University Press.

Foster, Gaines M. 1987: *Ghosts of the Confederacy: Defeat, the Lost Cause and the Emergence of the New South, 1865–1913*. New York: Oxford University Press.

Gaston, Paul M. 1970: *The New South Creed: A Study in Modern Mythmaking*. New York: Alfred A. Knopf.

Gilmore, Glenda Elizabeth 1996: *Gender and Jim Crow: Women and the Politics of White Supremacy in North Carolina, 1896–1920*. Chapel Hill: University of North Carolina Press.

Goodwyn, Lawrence C. 1971: Populist Dreams and Negro Rights: East Texas as a Case Study, *American Historical Review* 76 (4), 1,435–56.

Goodwyn, Lawrence C. 1976: *Democratic Promise: The Populist Moment in America*. New York: Oxford University Press.

Grantham, Dewey W. 1983: *Southern Progressivism: The Reconciliation of Progress and Tradition*. Knoxville: University of Tennessee Press.

Graves, John William 1990: *Town and Country: Race Relations in an Urban–Rural Context, Arkansas, 1865–1905*. Fayetteville: University of Arkansas Press.

Grossman, James R. 1989: *Land of Hope: Chicago, Black Southerners and the Great Migration*. Chicago: University of Chicago Press.

Hale, Grace Elizabeth 1998: *Making Whiteness: The Culture of Segregation in the South, 1890–1940*. New York: Pantheon Books.

Hall, Jacquelyn Dowd, et al. 1987: *Like a Family: The Making of a Southern Cotton Mill World*. Chapel Hill: University of North Carolina Press.

Harlan, Louis R. 1972: *Booker T. Washington: The Making of a Black Leader, 1856–1901*. New York: Oxford University Press.

Harlan, Louis R. 1983: *Booker T. Washington: The Wizard of Tuskegee, 1901–1915*. New York: Oxford University Press.

Haws, Robert (ed.) 1978: *The Age of Segregation: Race Relations in the South, 1890–1945*. Jackson: University Press of Mississippi.

Hirshson, Stanley P. 1962: *Farewell to the Bloody Shirt: Northern Republicans and the Negro, 1877–1893*. Bloomington: Indiana University Press.

Hunter, Tera W. 1997: *To 'Joy My Freedom: Southern Black Women's Lives and Labors After the Civil War*. Cambridge, MA: Harvard University Press.

Janiewski, Delores E. 1985: *Sisterhood Denied: Race, Gender, and Class in a New South Community*. Philadelphia: Temple University Press.

Jones, Jacqueline 1985: *Labor of Love, Labor of Sorrow: Black Women, Work and the Family from Slavery to the Present*. New York: Basic Books.

Key, V. O. 1949: *Southern Politics in State and Nation*. New York: Vintage.

Kousser, J. Morgan 1974: *The Shaping of Southern Politics: Suffrage Restriction and the Establishment of the One-Party South, 1880–1910*. New Haven, CT: Yale University Press.

Leloudis, James L. 1996: *Schooling the New South: Pedagogy, Self, and Society in North Carolina, 1880–1920*. Chapel Hill: University of North Carolina Press.

Litwack, Leon F. 1998: *Trouble in Mind: Black Southerners in the Age of Jim Crow*. New York: Alfred A. Knopf.

Logan, Frenise A. 1964: *The Negro in North Carolina, 1876–1894*. Chapel Hill: University of North Carolina Press.

McLaurin, Melton A. 1971: *Paternalism and Protest: Southern Cotton Mill Workers and Organized Labor, 1875–1905*. Westport, CT: Greenwood Press.

McLaurin, Melton A. 1978: *The Knights of Labor in the South*. Westport, CT: Greenwood Press.

McMillen, Neil R. 1989: *Dark Journey: Black Mississippians in the Age of Jim Crow*. Urbana: University of Illinois Press.

Marks, Carole 1989: *Farewell – We're Good and Gone: The Great Black Migration*. Bloomington: Indiana University Press.

Meier, August 1963: *Negro Thought in America, 1880–1915: Racial Ideologies in the Age of Booker T. Washington, 1880–1915*. Ann Arbor: University of Michigan Press.

Myrdal, Gunnar 1944: *An American Dilemma: The Negro Problem and Modern Democracy*. New York: Harper and Row.

Nieman, Donald G. 1989: Black Political Power and Criminal Justice: Washington County, Texas, 1868–1884. *Journal of Southern History*, 55 (3), 391–420.

Nieman, Donald G. 1991: *Promises to Keep: African-Americans and the Constitutional Order, 1776 to the Present*. New York: Oxford University Press.

Rabinowitz, Howard N. 1978: *Race Relations in the Urban South, 1865–1890*. New York: Oxford University Press.

Sims, Anastatia 1997: *The Power of Femininity in the New South: Women's Organizations and Politics in North Carolina, 1880–1930*. Columbia: University of South Carolina Press.

Wade, Richard C. 1964: *Slavery in the Cities: The South, 1820–1860*. New York: Oxford University Press.

Webb, Samuel L. 1997: *Two-Party Politics in the One Party South: Alabama's Hill Country, 1874–1920*. Tuscaloosa: University of Alabama Press.

Whites, LeeAnn 1992: Rebecca Latimer Felton and the Wife's Farm: The Class and Racial Politics of Gender Reform. *Georgia Historical Quarterly*, 76, 354–72.

Williamson, Edward C. 1976: *Florida Politics in the Gilded Age, 1877–1893*. Gainesville: University of Florida Press.

Williamson, Joel 1965: *After Slavery: The Negro in South Carolina during Reconstruction 1861–1877*. Chapel Hill: University of North Carolina Press.

Williamson, Joel 1984: *The Crucible of Race: Black–White Relations in the American South since Reconstruction*. New York: Oxford University Press.

Woodman, Harold D. 1995. *New South, New Law: The Legal Foundations of Credit and Labor Relations in the Postbellum Agricultural South*. Baton Rouge: Louisiana State University Press.

Woodward, C. Vann 1951: *Origins of the New South, 1877–1913*. Baton Rouge: Louisiana State University Press.

Woodward, C. Vann 1955: *The Strange Career of Jim Crow*. New York: Oxford University Press.

Woodward, C. Vann 1971: *American Counterpoint: Slavery and Racism in the North–South Dialog*. Boston: Little, Brown.

Woodward, C. Vann 1988: *Strange Career* Critics: Long May They Persevere. *Journal of American History*, 75 (3), 857–68.

Wright, Gavin 1986: *Old South, New South: Revolutions in the Southern Economy since the Civil War*. New York: Basic Books.

Wynes, Charles E. 1961: *Race Relations in Virginia, 1870–1902*. Charlottesville: University of Virginia Press.

CHAPTER TWENTY-ONE

Women in the Post-Civil War South

ELIZABETH HAYES TURNER

THE study of women in the post-Civil War South has evolved in the last thirty years to become one of the most dynamic new fields in the history of the region. Since 1970, when Anne Firor Scott published her pathbreaking *The Southern Lady: From Pedestal to Politics, 1830–1930*, a host of articles and books have emerged to complement her analysis and explore new questions about the experience of women in the New South. Because the study of southern women is a relatively young discipline within an older established field – the history of the South – scholars have been surprised to discover that information, often extracted from familiar sources, has yielded new answers when seen through a gendered perspective.

Southern women's history is also a subfield of the larger discipline of women's history and gender studies, which emerged in the 1960s with the revitalization of feminism following the civil rights movement (Hall and Scott 1987). As the study of women and gender systems has matured in the national context, so has the field of southern women's history, but with a difference. The South was a multiracial, multicultural (and some would add multireligious) region with a predominantly agricultural economic base that supported both rural and urban livelihoods. The region's preoccupation with race relations and white male dominance and control, particularly in agriculture and industry, created political systems that challenged current notions of democracy. Conservative ideas on politics, race, and gender tended to mark the region as "backward" in comparison to the North and West despite a "New South" rhetoric from such spokespersons as Henry Grady and Booker T. Washington. National studies of women in the 1960s and 1970s looked idealistically to progressive women who broke gender barriers or who championed movements for women's rights. Except for the civil rights movement, the South, it seemed, had little to offer feminists searching for heroic history.

Because women in the New South were comparatively understudied, it may have appeared there were few subjects worth researching. But an exceptional book, published in 1979, proved this assumption false. Jacquelyn Dowd Hall's biography of Jessie Daniel Ames, a white woman from Texas who directed the Association of Southern Women for the Prevention of Lynching, challenged readers to see southern women, black and white, in the context of powerful hierarchical gender and race relationships. These stemmed from the South's "peculiar institution" – slavery – and its sexual taboos. That some white women were willing to confront lynchers, sheriffs, and their political cronies with their misdeeds of miscegenation, violence, and repression of women generally revealed women's oppositional stance toward the dominant culture, provided glimpses of interracial cooperation, and aided in discovering the roots of the freedom struggles of the 1960s. No longer could the study of women in the New South be dismissed by national scholars as a barren field.

By the 1980s women's historians had shifted from searching for notable women to explaining historical events with a broader understanding of what these meant to women or how women's attitudes and actions affected the outcome. At the same time, the subject of southern women began to attract both history graduate students and established scholars. The complexities of race, class, and gender beckoned scholars to revisit familiar time periods and episodes in southern history with an eye to understanding the role and experience of women. University offerings in women's history and gender studies promoted the investigation of the relatively uncharted domain of postbellum southern women.

In the last decade gender analysis – the examination of socially constructed behavior systems categorized as feminine and masculine that affected family, home, work, leisure, religious, cultural, and political life – has engaged scholars of the South. In addition, the post-Civil War South is rich with regional symbols and rituals to which southerners attach great cultural weight and from which racial identities have been solidified. Historians have begun to decode these images and events, often created and employed by women, to understand the construction of white supremacy and black pride. Finally, in the last five years, scholars have turned their attention toward careful analyses of women who helped to create and maintain the status quo, from white supremacists of the 1880s to opponents of the Equal Rights Amendment in the 1980s. No longer are historians interested only in the lives of dissenters or reformers – those whom feminists admire. We must know more about all of those who made the South what it is today, including the attitudes and actions of women who worked against change. Cultural studies, gender analysis, and women's history have added methodological depth to the historical narrative of the South. The result is a far more complex and rich version of the past.

The "New South" formally began with the transition from slavery to freedom for ex-slaves and from separate nationhood to conquered region for all southerners, black and white. Older studies of this period have focused on the nation's major postwar problems: how to reorganize southern state governments and readmit them to the union as well as how to administer the civil and economic transition to self-sufficiency for ex-slaves. LeeAnn Whites (1995) brings a gendered analysis to the subject of the Civil War and the years that followed. White elite men, she argues, had constituted the keystone to power and authority in public life and in private affairs of the home. White women and all other dependents, including children and slaves, well understood this hierarchy and ordered their lives within it. In the course of the war, however, white male power came into question. Confounding the issue was the fact that black men "stood to win their 'manhood'" too, causing uncertainty for white males (Whites 1995: 3). Womanhood, on the other hand, had traditionally been defined in contrast to masculinity – and war was not a woman's business. Always mindful that these claims to true manhood and womanhood were social constructs, Whites nonetheless shows that they held enormous import for white southerners. The crisis in gender, then, was intimately tied to the course of the war.

By April 1861 war's reality began to threaten the circumscribed roles accorded by social convention. Almost immediately, life changed for white women as they faced the difficult task of home management. Roles that formerly had belonged to men blurred as women assumed control over children and slaves. Confederate soldiers found their lives and their futures brutally battered at the front; at the same time they realized that white southern manhood could not be maintained without the help of women at home. Their ultimate humiliation came with surrender and return to a devastated southern economy. How could manhood be redeemed in defeat?

Here Whites suggests that the Reconstruction of white manhood was achieved in part by white women who continued their wartime "empowerment" by applauding the efforts of Confederate soldiers. Publicly, they formed voluntary associations such as the Ladies' Memorial Association designed to rehabilitate the failed sense of manhood. By helping to create Lost Cause celebrations, symbolisms, memorials to the Confederate dead, and homes for aged veterans, white women developed a "public cultural power" that threatened to upend gender structures (ibid: 14). Lest women take their public power too far, Whites claims that veterans reinstituted their own manhood via the development of the Confederate Survivors' Association and the creation of textile mills, which reestablished white men in powerful positions over women and children.

Whites's study brings gender to a central position in understanding the meaning of war and its aftermath for white southerners. This book should be read in tandem with Grace Elizabeth Hale's *Making Whiteness: The Culture of Segregation in the South, 1890–1940* (1998), a *tour de force* in exploring the origins and development of white racial identity. Hale's book incorporates gender in unraveling the history of "making whiteness," but because its focus is not strictly on women, it will not receive full review here. Still, historians exploring the meaning of the Civil War, the Lost Cause, or the culture of segregation will find in nearly every chapter evidence of women's participation, compliance, and sometime opposition.

In *Gendered Strife and Confusion: The Political Culture of Reconstruction*, Laura F. Edwards (1997) also uses gender analysis to argue that the household and its social and economic realities held the key to reshaping political and legal relations. In this legal and social history of elite white, African-American, and white working-class families in transition at war's end in Granville County, North Carolina, Edwards eschews the fixed boundaries of "private" and "public" described by historians as domestic and female versus political and male. She contends that these were not "fixed categories, but ideological ones" that changed over time and were influenced by race and class as well as by women and men (Edwards 1997: 5).

Edwards demonstrates that every political decision made "from above" resulted in unexpected results from the "periphery." The case of legalizing marriages for ex-slaves, previously seen as simply formalizing unions and obligating men and women to assume conjugal responsibilities, actually expanded civil rights for the head of the household and dependents therein. "The marriage covenant is at the foundation of all our rights," a statement made by a black corporal in Virginia, epitomized the results of the marriage ruling (ibid: 47). Black heads of households, though recently freed and untrained, used the legal system to defy the newly instituted Black Codes and establish their rights. One threat came from apprenticeship laws that allowed the courts to remove children from kinfolk and return them to their former masters or other white households. This infuriated freedpeople, who, after establishing their ability to support their children, used the courts or the Freedmen's Bureau to attempt to win them back. Marriage protected children by establishing households, and households, assured of male leadership, remained the economic unit responsible for raising families. Married women and men who petitioned the courts for the return of their children were much more likely to get them back than unmarried women.

If blacks had difficulty wresting their rights from the courts, they had an equally difficult time securing independent status as laborers. Southern white employers, unaccustomed to wage labor and laborers' independence, relied on the model provided by slavery and insisted that hired workers act as dependents. Freedmen and women would have none of it, understanding far more clearly than their employers the principles of wage labor. The only dependencies freedpeople accepted were within their own households where they had the right to order their domestic lives. Edwards takes the reader through a familiar landscape of Reconstruction history in North Carolina, but along the way shows that private, domestic arrangements blurred into public political and legal space, producing a gendered perspective of a period of national turmoil.

Willie Lee Rose, in her pathbreaking book *Rehearsal for Reconstruction: The Port Royal Experiment* (1964), adumbrated future patterns for race relations in the Reconstruction era by chronicling the Union Army occupation of the Sea Islands of South Carolina. Lively in detail and lavish in quotable aphorisms, the book opened a window onto a world in transition from slavery to freedom, but the perspective was mainly from officiating whites with limited but tantalizing views of freedwomen. Then in 1985 Jacqueline Jones's *Labor of Love, Labor of Sorrow: Black Women, Work, and the Family from Slavery to the Present* took stock of African-American women and their work from slavery to the present, presenting a generalized version of post-emancipation history. Since then, Julie Saville (1994) and Leslie A. Schwalm (1997) have presented landmark studies of the transition from slavery to freedom in South Carolina.

In the first years after the war, ex-slave women learned that their definition of freedom – to be as free of white intervention as possible and to define their lives and labor on their own terms – was not universally shared by army and Freedmen's Bureau personnel, let alone white planters. Freedwomen refused to work at certain aspects of plantation upkeep – repairing and maintaining the irrigation systems, weaving, spinning, butchering – and insisted that their labor end with the harvest. Schwalm deftly interprets their balkiness as evidence of the need to care for their own families and gardens and to maintain their homes while their male kin sought day work. Clashes between white planters and freedwomen were sometimes brutal, and yet freedwomen were defining with their acts of defiance the conditions of freedom as they understood them. They refused to enter into contracts that resembled reinslavement. In this Schwalm agrees with Laura Edwards that freedwomen were learning the lessons of a wage economy more quickly than their former owners.

When contracts were finally negotiated between freedwomen and planters in the lowcountry rice fields between 1866 and 1868, women signed on for fewer hours than men, rejected full-time field labor, and sometimes refused to work for former overseers. Schwalm argues that women were not retreating from field labor, as previous historians have maintained, but were establishing the right to control their lives and their labor and to remove themselves from slavery's memory. Freedwomen who sought domestic work also reshaped their jobs by insisting that the work be broken down into specific tasks.

Schwalm found that when freedwomen tried to establish freedom on their own terms, they provoked opposition not only from planters and overseers but also from northern military and Freedmen's Bureau officials who held bourgeois gendered ideals regarding masculinity, femininity, sexuality, and free labor. These officials set out to instill their ideals in black families, she argues, "to rebuild lowcountry culture and society in their own image of free-labor society" (Schwalm 1997: 266). She regards these efforts as bungling and intrusive, since freedwomen insisted on reconstructing their lives in freedom according to their needs and that of their families and community.

In a similar vein, black urban women exulted in the hope that freedom would bring opportunities for education and full employment independent of white control. White employers, according to Tera W. Hunter's *To 'Joy My Freedom: Southern Black Women's Lives and Labors after the Civil War* (1997), expected black women to remain servile, dependent, and exploitable. Hunter's study focuses mainly on Atlanta, where the tensions between black female workers and their white employers were never fully resolved. Hunter argues that black women workers countered a climate of oppression with myriad acts of resistance in an attempt to maintain their independence and humanity. While 98 percent of African-American women were categorized as domestics in 1880, few lived with the white families they served. Black workers preferred to live in their own neighborhoods to escape the constant surveillance and exploitation by white employers. Laundresses, though performing physically demanding work six days a week, chose this occupation for the independence it gave them. Although washerwomen remained underpaid, they demonstrated resilience and strategic timing when in 1881 they organized a trade union, the Washing Society. They held white households in thrall as they fomented a strike that spread to other domestics on the eve of the opening of the International Cotton Exposition in Atlanta. Just at the moment when the South had hoped to attract northern visitors and investors with images of southern industry and benign race relations, the Washing Amazons, as the press called them, countered with a striking image of their own.

In the years between 1900 and 1910 the percentage of black women in domestic service declined from 92 percent to 84 percent as commercial opportunities increased. But employment in cotton mills remained closed to them even during the labor shortages that accompanied World War I. In those same years, white fears of black independence resulted in stricter segregation laws, disfranchisement, police brutality, and finally violence acted out in the 1906 Atlanta race riot. Black resistance took many forms, however. Middle-class African-American women formed the Neighborhood Union under the leadership of Lugenia Burns Hope, and by their own labor brought substantial improvements to black communities. Others found the night life of Atlanta a compelling outlet for their individuality and desires for independence. Dance halls, despised by whites but cherished by working-class blacks for the release it gave them from working drudgery, provided public space for the development of musical talent and style. Blues singer Bessie Smith, the Whitman Sisters, and Thomas A. Dorsey all began their musical journeys in Atlanta's Decatur Avenue clubs. In the end, however, repression took its toll. This tale of struggle for dignity and autonomy ended in bitterness as many black families escaped to the North. In the Great Migration, Atlanta's working women sought release from the multiple bonds placed upon them by employers and city and state governments.

Hunter's work fills an important gap in our understanding of urban working women, but her book should be complemented by and contrasted with studies by Dolores Janiewski (1985) and Jacquelyn Dowd Hall et al. (1987), which discuss white and black labor in North Carolina tobacco factories and cotton mills.

At one time the study of the Progressive movement was confined to the northern and western states. But Arthur Link and C. Vann Woodward demonstrated a half-century ago that southern Progressivism was a subject quite distinct from that of other parts of the nation. Perhaps the most significant book to reinterpret our understanding of women in the Progressive Era South is Glenda E. Gilmore's *Gender and Jim Crow: Women and the Politics of White Supremacy in North Carolina, 1896–1920* (1996). Written largely from the perspective of African-American women, Gilmore subtly shifts the reader's focus from the actions of white men and women in public places at the turn of the century to the important, but previously undiscovered, roles played by middle-class black women. Understanding the Progressive movement from this angle necessitates incorporating the history of politics in North Carolina and of race relations at its most violent point since emancipation. Gilmore is among a growing number of historians who have found that the study of women cannot be complete without examining political history and women's part in it.

Gilmore begins by introducing the reader to black middle-class women and their families living in North Carolina before 1900. A sense of service to their community and a clear understanding of gender equality within their churches, colleges, and families led them to become outspoken advocates for their race. As middle-class matrons, they found themselves seeking leadership roles just as the state launched a prohibition referendum and Frances Willard brought the Woman's Christian Temperance Union (WCTU) to North Carolina. Black and white women for a time cooperated in separate unions under a single state organization, but white women thought themselves superior to their black coreligionists. Chafing under the humiliation, black women formed chapters outside the state structure and won affiliation with the national WCTU. An uneasy cooperation existed between the two unions, but this ended in 1898 when disfranchisement began to eliminate black voters, proving, Gilmore argues, that politics had a far more powerful impact on women's lives than had been formerly understood.

Any achievements of blacks toward middle-class professionalism threatened white assumptions of racial supremacy. Darkening clouds of violence gathered as Populist/Republican coalitions campaigned to victory at the statehouse. Laws intended to democratize elections in townships across the state resulted in an increase in black officeholding. The familiar history of the threat to Democratic Party hegemony is retold here, but differently, through a gendered approach that includes notions of manhood mingled with national imperialism. During the Spanish–American War the army invited recruits from across the nation to join, and black men saw a chance to "prove their manhood and patriotism" (Gilmore 1996: 65). In direct conflict with this impulse came *Plessy v. Ferguson* (1896), proclaiming the constitutionality of separate but equal facilities, and a new generation of younger white Democrats who were determined to dominate state politics. Thomas Dixon, Furnifold Simmons, and Walter Hines Page represented the "Best Men" of this new generation intent on developing a superior government based on a "superior" race. It was a brew that could only poison whatever positive race relations existed at the turn of the century.

Whites invented the myth of the black rapist, the pure white woman, and the fiction that all black men wanted to marry white women. Democrats launched a campaign to retake the reins of government by appealing to poor white farmers, whose womenfolk, they said, would be thereby protected from black outrages. This served two purposes – to discredit black achievements by painting all black men as base and to limit the advance of white women into public and political space. Hysteria followed as sexual innuendo flamed the fires of race prejudice. The result was the kind of racial violence in Wilmington and across the state that altered North Carolina's population. Thousands of middle-class blacks fled North to safety. No amount of protest from black writers and leaders could change the new order. Black men would have to leave the state or submit to humiliating and unmanly rules of disfranchisement and segregation. Black women, on the other hand, discovered a new role in the midst of their people's darkest hours.

Following thirty years of community building through separate voluntary organizations, black middle-class women began the task of fighting white supremacy. With black men removed from politics, African-American women became diplomats between the races. Through their own civic leagues, the YWCA, and community improvement associations, black women sought and won contacts with white club women, ushering in the tentative first steps toward interracial dialogue. Seeking to capitalize on the Progressive movement, black women went before local and state governing bodies to request better state services for their communities; and they fought for the right to vote.

Gilmore's achievement has been to build a historical bridge between two eras, that of the hopeful 1880s, when blacks voted and whites accepted their political coexistence, and the more oppressive but calm years after World War I. The years in between marked the nadir of race relations in the South, a troubled time when the only solution to wholesale violence seemed to be separation of blacks and whites and nearly complete domination by whites. Using gender analysis to interpret the often chaotic action of white supremacists and the rise of black women as advocates for reform, Gilmore enriches our understanding of politics, defined broadly, by filling in the gaps left by older historians who failed to see the multiple instances of resistance and resilience by black women.

Anastatia Sims documents the history of white and black club women in a parallel study, *The Power of Femininity in the New South: Women's Organizations and Politics in North Carolina, 1880–1930* (1997). She addresses women's participation in or resistance to white supremacy as well as the successes and limitations in ameliorating the effects of industrialization. As women sought broader applications for their education and interests through such voluntary associations as the WCTU, patriotic–hereditary organizations, religious and charitable groups, women's clubs, suffrage associations, and the League of Women Voters, they brought with them an image of ladyhood that Sims labels "the power of femininity." The concept of the southern lady held white women to an exacting ideal but one that Sims found to be malleable as well as useful to women even as it was limiting.

For white and black women after 1900, the ladyhood ideal translated into more opportunities for their expanded public roles. Sims agrees with Gilmore that

African-American women, empowered by the southern lady image, served as emissaries for the black community; they employed the image to win respect, gain racial equality, and push against the bonds of segregation. African-Americans aimed their messages most successfully at white women, who they said held the power to end lynchings and the sexual abuse of black women by white men.

By examining one of the South's strongest and most enduring cultural icons in the context of the Progressive Era, Sims points out its contradictory but powerful effects. Black and white women used the concept of ladyhood to promote Progressive reforms in their communities and in the state; conservative women used notions of ladyhood to maintain elitism, to support the Lost Cause, and to oppose woman suffrage. The power of femininity worked both ways, but there were limits to its effectiveness. As Sims states, men still controlled the worlds of politics and industry and would go to great lengths to oppose women who challenged them.

Middle-class African-American Progressive reformers whose activism was tempered by the double burdens of race and sex profoundly understood the power of opposition. Additional portrayals of their frustrations and triumphs are offered by Elsa Barkley Brown (1989), Jacqueline A. Rouse (1989), Cynthia Neverdon-Morton (1989), and Stephanie J. Shaw (1996).

Shaw (1996) examines three generations of black women who achieved remarkable successes in their professions (librarians, teachers, nurses, and social workers) and as volunteer community leaders. As the title suggests, *being* and *doing* were at the heart of women's lives: these verbs also determine the structure of Shaw's book. The institutions that nurtured the eighty subjects of her study were family and community members; they provided "highways" for young black women to incorporate dreams of achievement, obtain higher education, and escape lives of menial labor and exploitation. Their lives of "doing" reflected personal struggles to succeed as well as sacrifices in labor-intensive occupations and volunteer work beyond their long workdays. These women bore their "womanly responsibilities" by working tirelessly for causes that would help build race pride and combat discrimination: in literacy programs; cooking, canning, and sewing classes; and youth programs for urban teenagers. They worked in antilynching campaigns and joined the NAACP when it was dangerous to do so; they campaigned for equal salaries in school systems that had underfunded black education and thus "stunted the development of whole black communities" (Shaw 1996: 201).

For women like Septima Clark, who allowed her NAACP affiliation to be made public in 1954 and thus lost her teaching position with the South Carolina school system, transferring to the civil rights movement was the logical extension of her "race work." One of the remarkable findings in Shaw's study is the absence of sex discrimination from the parents who sought education and promotion for these young women headed toward professional life. Those who remained in the South were confined to sex- and race-segregated positions, but their professional roles gained for them positions of leadership that profoundly affected black communities. Shaw's analysis contributes to our understanding of the development of a black professional class, yet she is quick to point out that these women did not follow the traditional patterns of professionalization that often resulted in co-optation. Her subjects compromised their individual privileges for community service.

As the study of southern women in the Progressive Era has matured in the last fifteen years, more research has moved beyond the eastern seaboard to states and cities further west. Marsha Wedell (1991) focused on Memphis; Mary Martha Thomas (1992) on Alabama; and Margaret Ripley Wolfe (1995) on the entire South. Although some trans-Appalachian states still await a full-scale women's history, Texas has been the subject of three women's histories – one statewide and two urban. Each concentrates on the late nineteenth and early twentieth centuries but approaches the era with a different emphasis, proving that women's history can be richly multifaceted when combined with economics, religion, and politics.

Elizabeth York Enstam's *Women and the Creation of Urban Life: Dallas, Texas, 1843–1920* (1998) demonstrates the extremely broad range of activities of women in a single city. Applying an economic perspective to the emergence of women from private to public roles, Enstam provides a rich tapestry of city life woven by women and men. Her fundamental point is that cities were not male preserves created solely by them for the benefit of dependents. Both women and men shaped the contours of life in Dallas; but, she asks, "When, and at what level of development did women's work become important and noticeable in Dallas?" (Enstam 1998: xiv). This began, she answers, in the 1880s, when Dallas reached a point in its physical and economic development where commerce no longer depended solely on the produce of the surrounding farms but also on commercial trade and banking. Then the city's inhabitants, in all their ethnic diversity, found resources to sponsor regular cultural events, church services, and popular entertainments. In this milieu women established permanent institutions and organizations that recontoured urban services and civic space. In the decades following, some women continued to enter professions and the wage-earning workforce, while others in voluntary organizations and elected offices moved beyond charitable and cultural pursuits to urban policy making and political authority. Although women often used gendered themes such as motherhood to achieve their goals, Enstam refuses to allow Dallas women to be typed as simply creators of the social and cultural side of life. She insists that women in cooperation with each other formed institutions and agencies that changed governmental policies, altered the built environment, and transformed the way citizens thought about public life.

Almost 300 miles south of Dallas lies Galveston, an island city that has always been dependent upon shipping, merchandising, and banking for its livelihood. Although the city's business climate set the stage for this women's history, the questions that Elizabeth Hayes Turner asks in *Women, Culture, and Community: Religion and Reform in Galveston, 1880–1920* (1997) differ from those posed by Elizabeth Enstam. Turner wanted to know the details of women's church involvement and the effects of religion on women's activism in a southern city. Historians of women's Progressive reform movements in the South have tended to link evangelical churches and activism in the WCTU to later reforms such as woman suffrage. In this case study, after creating a database of 370 white activist women, Turner found that women from evangelical churches or those few who joined the WCTU were less involved with urban reform and suffrage than Jewish women or women from Protestant churches considered highly liturgical and elitist. Turner concluded that class status had as much to do with women's civic reform as did religious motivation.

Other factors contributed to the entry of both white and black women into public activism: education, the creation of charitable societies to care for the poor, benevolent institutions, and the women's club movement. All bore fruit by transforming the city's social and welfare structure at a time when Galveston experienced exceptional economic growth. Then disaster struck.

The hurricane of September 8, 1900 altered the city forever and changed the dynamic for women's public presence. Two other events marked a change for women: the creation of city commission government and black disfranchisement. White women found that by creating progressive organizations they could successfully introduce their agenda to city commissioners and thereby shape public policy and share in the city's rebuilding. This was in part facilitated by disfranchisement measures adopted by the state and the city. Black males were not included in city commission government, nor were African-American concerns given the same attention as those of white women. As segregation increased after 1900, black women formed their own organizations to improve their community and to combat segregation. Separately, black and white women formed their own activist communities. Each one, however, reshaped Galveston.

In *Creating the New Woman: The Rise of Southern Women's Progressive Culture in Texas, 1893–1918*, Judith N. McArthur (1998) portrays women as political activists long before they had the power to vote. How women became sufficiently politically minded to form what McArthur terms their "progressive culture" is the subject of this concise, well-written book. McArthur teaches us that events and movements, which to our modern eyes might seem stifling, actually opened avenues for women toward progressive reform.

The debate over the importance of the WCTU in women's political development continues in McArthur's book. Elsewhere in the South the WCTU had an enlightening effect on southern women – especially black women – as shown most recently by Glenda Gilmore and Anastatia Sims. However, the contention supported by Dewey Grantham (1983), Jean Friedman (1985), and Anne Firor Scott (1970) that much of the political activism by white women came from the WCTU, an outgrowth of evangelical churches, does not hold in Texas. If evangelicalism, the South's dominant religious preference, and the WCTU, the nineteenth century's largest women's organization, did not pull white Texas "women out of their cultural isolation and into progressivism," then what did (McArthur 1998: 3)? On this subject McArthur leads us in new – and some rediscovered – directions.

A network of women's voluntary organizations set the stage for their emergence. This is not a new insight, except that McArthur looks beyond the General Federation of Women's Clubs and the National Association of Colored Women to discover the National Congress of Mothers. Mothers' clubs, organized in nearly every school, focused on improvements for children and led women to run for school board elections. Links between the private home and society were also forged through the National Home Economics Association, which "led middle-class women directly into municipal housekeeping," hence passage of a state pure-food and drug law, the fight for a water filtration plant in Dallas, pure milk and clean food markets in Galveston, and a state college for women, now Texas Woman's University (McArthur 1998: 33). Domestic science courses at the other Texas universities introduced black and white women to advanced concepts of hygiene for home and community, and, bolstered by the support of women's clubs, led to enforcement of the pure-food law by volunteer women inspectors.

In visualizing these "New Women" of Texas it is not difficult to see how they moved almost seamlessly into the national woman suffrage movement after 1910. Engaging fully in party and state politics and eschewing the rhetoric of white supremacy, the Texas Equal Rights Association, especially under the leadership of Minnie Fisher Cunningham, became a sophisticated political "machine" that knew how to take advantage of opportunities for public approval during World War I. Here McArthur cleverly links the women's anti-vice campaign to suffrage, but she cautions that for all the sacrifices women made during the Great War, probably nothing would have turned Texas into a suffrage-granting state had there not been a rift in the Democratic Party. Fortunately, Cunningham and her supporters manipulated this to their advantage. Texas granted women the right to vote in primaries in 1918 and became the first state in the South to ratify the Nineteenth Amendment.

The woman suffrage movement in the South has had a number of historians. A. Elizabeth Taylor, the first to tackle this immense subject, is renowned for her state studies and for her book *The Woman Suffrage Movement in Tennessee* (1957), the fulcrum state in the ratification process. Anne Firor Scott took up the cause in *The Southern Lady* (1970), as did Aileen S. Kraditor, who first suggested in *The Ideas of the Woman Suffrage Movement: 1890–1920* (1965) that white women sought the vote in order to maintain white supremacy. It was not until 1993, however, when Marjorie Spruill Wheeler published *New Women of the New South: The Leaders of the Woman Suffrage Movement in the Southern States*, that a comprehensive single-volume regional history emerged. She examines in detail the professional careers of eleven suffrage leaders from seven southern states – Virginia, Kentucky, Tennessee, Georgia, Alabama, Mississippi, and Louisiana – and divides them not by ideology so much as by age, illuminating the efforts of the "first generation" in the 1890s and the "second generation" in the decades between 1910 and 1920. An epilogue describing the continuing careers of each woman shows even more clearly the divergent views of these leaders, who at one time campaigned together for a single purpose. Complementing Sims's study, Wheeler states that these "New Women" leaders were also "Southern Ladies" who upheld white supremacy and the disfranchisement of blacks even while they campaigned to end discrimination against white women. Indeed, she argues that the strategies of southern suffragists in the 1890s were based on the assumption that white supremacy would be strengthened by extending the franchise to carefully qualified white women. In that case, they reasoned, black disfranchisement, which might bring down the wrath of the US Supreme Court, would be unnecessary. The National American Woman Suffrage Association (NAWSA) leaders acquiesced to this discriminatory view in part because they felt it held promise for victory and because they too were frustrated by voting rights extended to "inferior" immigrant men. Hoping to find victory in the "southern strategy," NAWSA conventions were held in Atlanta in 1895 and in New Orleans in 1903.

It became clear that the southern strategy had failed when state after state found ways to eliminate black male voters. Suffrage leagues across the South died, and NAWSA turned its attention toward the West. Some southern leaders, without support from the NAWSA, tried to launch a campaign to enfranchise white women only, but this too failed. The movement in the South came to a halt because, as

McArthur and Turner have pointed out in Texas studies, there was no mass following at the grassroots yet; women's clubs were just beginning to become involved in politics. The Progressive movement later gave new life to southern suffragists, and thereafter the racial rhetoric changed to an assured tone that disfranchisement would take care of the "problem" of black women voting.

By 1915 the whole nation had become more enthusiastic over suffrage, and the NAWSA focused its attention on a federal amendment, awakening the chords of disunity in southern ranks with the rise of the Southern States Woman Suffrage Conference (SSWSC) on the right and the National Woman's Party (NWP) on the left. Southern suffragists were disappointed when Carrie Chapman Catt, president of the NAWSA, declared most southern states unwinnable and counseled the state leaders to work towards primary or partial suffrage. Arkansas, Texas, and Tennessee granted women partial suffrage victories before 1919. And loyalists to states' rights, particularly the Gordon sisters of Louisiana, actually campaigned against the federal amendment. Victory, when it came in 1920 with ratification of the Susan B. Anthony Amendment, was bitter-sweet for the eleven southern suffrage leaders profiled here. Only four southern states – Texas, Arkansas, Kentucky, and Tennessee – ratified the federal amendment. The majority of southern states did not, disappointing those who had worked for state endorsement and angering others who opposed a federal amendment.

Although Texas and Arkansas leaders are not represented, Wheeler's work should be the starting point for any student of the southern woman suffrage movement. For years historians criticized the movement in the United States for abandoning democratic ideals and succumbing to the expediency of racial strategies and class-exclusive tactics. Any study of the South, however, must take race and class into consideration, as political control derived from their manipulation. Yet Wheeler leaves the impression that the second generation of suffragists were amenable to interracial cooperation once the amendment had passed. This is more than can be said of the antisuffragists.

Elna C. Green's *Southern Strategies: Southern Women and the Woman Suffrage Question* (1997) is among the first studies to include the southern antisuffrage movement. She describes its leaders and analyzes their motives and strategies for halting the march toward full suffrage. Conservative leanings were, of course, at the heart of it, but Green also discovered political connections and familial links between antisuffragist women and conservative male power brokers within the Democratic Party. Women antis received financial backing and some administrative direction from the men who opposed the vote.

Antisuffrage ties reached back to the planter aristocracy and extended forward to the new industrial elites. Green also found that those who spearheaded the black disfranchisement measures backed the antisuffrage movement. Their entire plan was to uphold white supremacy at any cost, even if it meant withholding the vote from white women of their own class. This same group of New South entrepreneurs worried that voting women would impose protective legislation for women and children working in the mills, close down the breweries and liquor distributors with prohibition, and challenge the political hegemony enjoyed by "big agriculture and big business" (Green 1997: 55). Women antisuffragists, who conveniently and openly opposed the amendment, cited as their reasons biblical proscriptions, female biological inferiorities, the potential breakdown of the home, states' rights, and white supremacy. Both Wheeler and Green agree that antisuffragists used race-baiting and fear tactics to oppose woman suffrage, while suffragists employed statistical arguments to show that white votes could outnumber black.

Green's work is valuable because it demonstrates that female antisuffragists were the accomplices of and the facilitators for Democratic Party conservatives, that they revered white supremacy, and that they accepted women's subordinate role within a patriarchal system. Green's study allows readers to comprehend the roots of a whole range of conservative and antifeminist leanings in the South – women in the Ku Klux Klan (see also Blee 1991; MacLean 1994), women red baiters of the 1950s, women "cheerleaders" who screamed epithets at black children attempting to integrate schools, women opposed to the Equal Rights Amendment, and supporters of the prolife movement. Fortunately, the reluctance of feminist historians to analyze women on the extreme right is fading, and scholarship is the richer for it.

After 1920 "suffs and antis" alike were confronted with the reality of woman suffrage. What did that mean in the South, where voter registration was foreign to most white women and nearly impossible for black women? How did women use voting power and how did they master a male-controlled political system? This is answered in Pam Tyler's *Silk Stockings and Ballot Boxes: Women and Politics in New Orleans, 1920–1963* (1996), which ably demonstrates the degree to which white Louisiana women and New Orleans women in particular came to be thoroughly immersed in politics after 1920.

The vote for women came to Louisiana just as it did for all states in 1920; the question was how would Louisiana women use it? At first, women voters were few; 28.3 percent of Orleans Parish registered voters were women in 1924; and for black women it was far worse; only 152 black women's names were on the rolls, representing 0.1 percent of registered voters. As for white women, they stayed away because of tradition, lack of information, and true fear of the polling places, which were often in bars, juke joints, and other unsavory locations dominated by machine precinct workers.

Perhaps women would have stayed away from the polls much longer had it not been for the dazzling pyrotechnics of the state's governor and then US senator, Huey Long. He was detested among the "silk stocking" coterie of women for his vulgarity, venality, and power-grabbing arrogance; he served as a catalyst for a series of women's political reform movements. Hilda Phelps Hammond and the Women's Committee of Louisiana hounded Long and his protégé Senator John Overton through the Senate subcommittee on campaign expenditures until his death in 1935. Here Tyler takes issue with the leading biographers of Huey Long for ignoring or belittling the important role of women in creating a viable anti-Long faction.

The logical organization to introduce women to political issues was the League of Women Voters in New Orleans, but the league had been taken over by a group devoted to the Old Regulars, who controlled the city. When the national headquarters rescinded the New Orleans chapter's affiliation due to partisanship (later reinstated in 1942), this opened the door for another group, an offshoot of the Honest Election League, to teach women the mechanics of political behavior. Martha Robinson headed the women's division, later the Woman Citizens' Union (WCU), and began to learn how the well-oiled New Orleans political machine kept running.

Members of the WCU began by monitoring elections, starting with the registration rolls and continuing through the long voting day at each of the 262 polling places in the city. Their aim was to fight voter fraud, and they noted every irregularity. The women wanted to reform the structure of government, including election proceedings, with voting machines, decent polling places, and civil service laws to end patronage. Women had to fight for jury service, for the right to be included in party decision making, and for the power to run for office.

By 1940 many of the same women entered partisan politics as anti-Long advocates. They formed the Independent Women's Organization (IWO) and worked successfully in 1940 to oust the Long regime from the governor's mansion. In 1946 they succeeded in electing a progressive New Orleans mayor, Chep Morrison. They improved the turnout of women voters until, by 1962, more white women than white men and more black women than black men registered to vote. Their organizations continued to monitor city politics, managed to get women elected to the school board, and sponsored Martha Robinson's campaign for city council. (She lost mostly due to her own divisive nature.) These were not radical women; rather, they enjoyed privilege and security and most often maintained the same racial prejudices as their male peers. But in areas other than race, they were not conservatives; they chose to become active and to form women's political organizations because they found their efforts effective. Tyler calls this era "their golden age of unity in politics" as middle- and upper-class white women discovered the excitement of political participation (Tyler 1996: 245). Historians familiar with volunteer studies also know the limits of such organizations. The purpose was to mold good government out of entrenched bossism, but the IWO envisioned politics through the lens of privilege, with little understanding of the effects of disfranchisement.

The decades of the 1950s and 1960s turned toward race relations and rising expectations for desegregation. Here we see a sharp turn, for before 1961 the IWO was not interested in advancing desegregation, although the group endorsed improved but separate facilities for blacks. One white woman stood out in marked contrast: Rosa Keller, who in 1953 headed the New Orleans Urban League and worked assiduously for improved health facilities for African-Americans, for equal access to city libraries, for decent housing for blacks, for desegregation of Tulane University, for voter registration, and of course for public school desegregation. The book ends in 1963, just as enormous changes were sweeping the South. But it is a satisfying end, knowing that women in New Orleans struggled for sensible government.

This era from 1920 to 1963 – between winning the vote and the birth of the "new" women's revolution of the late 1960s – is dubbed "the doldrums" by feminist historians chronicling the advance of the women's movement. A decided women's voting bloc did not emerge as expected, the dedication of former suffragists could not be resurrected with the same intensity after the vote was won, and economic opportunities for women waxed and waned according to national emergencies and measures. A series of historians have pondered this "decline" in the feminist movement. Tyler challenges the doldrums – not by claiming gains in the women's movement but by proving that economically independent Louisiana women became pupils in the hard-knock school of politics. Winning the vote was only the beginning; once achieved, there were years of intensive training in how to vote, run for office, combat voter fraud, find women to back reform candidates, and win victories for progressive reform. Without actually claiming feminist goals for themselves, New Orleans reformers secured the right (sometimes against ruffian opponents) to use politics and prepared the way for a day when civil rights and women's rights could be seriously entertained. Tyler argues that in gaining the vote, women changed the political process – in parties, politics, and elections.

In 1984 Julia Kirk Blackwelder completed *Women of the Depression: Caste and Culture in San Antonio, 1929–1939*, a book important for its social and economic discussion of Mexican American, black, and white women during the years of the Great Depression in a city on the western edge of the New South. Since then other scholars (Hewitt 1993; Ruiz 1991) have included Hispanic women in New South studies of Florida and Texas, and this will undoubtedly become a growing field. Blackwelder found that in San Antonio race, class, and ethnicity conspired to form a caste culture that severely affected women of color as they competed for the limited resources available during the years of the Great Depression. She analyzed the sources available to women – family, community, church, labor unions, relief organizations, and crime – and women's methods of coping within a socially stratified society.

San Antonio was one of the hardest hit of all southern cities during the Great Depression, compounded by the fact that the federal government's military bases in close proximity provided no direct tax revenue, although they did offer some employment to residents. The city divided into ethnic enclaves; politics was dominated by an entrenched machine; and relief organizations, not large to begin with, soon were overwhelmed by hunger and need. Federal programs designed to aid families were administered by local residents, usually white, who protected white men and women more than minorities. Labor was segregated by sex and by ethnicity: white women landed clerical jobs, black women provided domestic services, and Mexican American women worked in food processing, garment, and tobacco factories. The latter group suffered more than whites or blacks, were more fearful of deportation and therefore more hesitant to ask for relief. Moreover, passage of the Fair Labor Standards Act, which legislated a minimum wage for hourly workers, pushed some companies out of San Antonio, where labor had been cheap, resulting in no jobs for the most vulnerable population.

Blackwelder's study points out the damaging results of continued discrimination toward women and minorities. By maintaining a segregated system, cities such as San Antonio lost opportunities for economic expansion. Prejudices were upheld at the expense of fair market competition. The Great Depression reinforced occupational segregation, and federal programs were more advantageous to white men than to any other sector of the workforce. While Blackwelder in this and other urban studies found that women experienced fewer benefits from New Deal programs, Martha Swain (1995), in a study of New Deal administrator and Mississippian Ellen S. Woodward, examines New Deal advantages for women. To be sure, Hispanic, Native American, and black women suffered greater discrimination from state officials administering federal programs. Still, Swain argues, that against a public often hostile to changing work roles for women and minorities, lasting gains came from New Deal agencies.

Sara Evans (1979) wrote one of the first books to elucidate the invaluable role of women in the civil rights movement. *Personal Politics: The Roots of Women's Liberation in the Civil Rights Movement and the New Left* was a triumph of scholarship and established the fact that black women served as role models in organizing and training young white women workers from the South and the North. Eventually internal politics and sexual discrimination within the movement led to the rise of the modern women's rights movement. Since then scholarship on the South's freedom struggles has enjoyed a parallel rapid growth with southern women's history. The two fields have found common ground in *Women in the Civil Rights Movement: Trailblazers and Torchbearers, 1941–1965* (Crawford, Rouse, and Woods 1990). The seventeen separate articles are organized according to distinct themes that include women and the religious roots of nonviolent direct action; empowerment, citizenship, and community building; civil rights activism and gender, class, and race; and the future of civil rights.

In the early stages of writing the history of the civil rights movement, scholars tended to focus on its male leaders, their lives, and the significant events that advanced or retarded the movement's progress in the 1950s and 1960s. The historiography of the field changed dramatically when feminist historians insisted on equal representation of women in the movement, social historians concentrated on activists in southern rural settings, and scholars of the twentieth century searched for the roots of civil rights in the years before its full emergence. All of these areas of new scholarship can be found in this volume. Civil rights activists Septima Clark, Ella Baker, and Fannie Lou Hamer, represented here, are just a few of the notable women who have now become as well known as Robert Moses and Fred Shuttlesworth. Septima Clark found her calling in developing workshops first at the Highlander Folk School and later with the Southern Christian Leadership Conference (SCLC). Clark's work at age sixty-three in establishing Citizenship Schools, which delivered training in constitutional rights and voting, provided "the base upon which the whole civil rights movement was built" (ibid: 91). Baker's ideology of participatory democracy, her experience with NAACP work, and her grassroots organizing talents shaped the contours of one of the movement's most vibrant organizations, the Student Nonviolent Coordinating Committee (SNCC). Hamer's sharecropping background, her religiosity, and her determination to bring voting rights and liberation to Mississippians led to the co-founding of the Mississippi Freedom Democratic Party in 1964. Alongside the histories of these leaders are explorations of Eleanor Roosevelt's early civil rights activism, of connections between organized labor struggles of the 1930s and the Highlander Folk School, and of Methodist churchwomen in the integration of public schools. Each chapter provides a glimpse of the larger picture of women in the movement. This book should be followed by reading Belinda Robnett's *How Long? How Long? African-American Women in the Struggle for Civil Rights* (1997), which offers an interpretive overlay and highlights the roles of local leaders, mainly women, who constituted a bridge between state and national leaders and movement followers. As with the women's club movement and woman suffrage, Robnett finds that local leaders were essential to the development of a successful movement for change.

There is an old saw, however, that changing public opinion toward gender is far more difficult (and radical) than changing public opinion toward race. This proved to be true in the case of ratification of the Equal Rights Amendment and the South. Donald G. Mathews and Jane Sherron De Hart take an in-depth look at the failure of

North Carolina to ratify the amendment in *Sex, Gender, and the Politics of ERA: A State and the Nation* (1990). In the wake of passage of the twenty-fourth amendment outlawing poll taxes in 1965, the nation seemed poised to make constitutional adjustments for its women citizens who "wanted to forbid the government to deny citizens their rights 'on account of sex' " (ibid: vii). It was not to be, and the South had a share in its defeat. White backlash studies, like civil rights scholarship twenty years ago, have gained sufficient distance in time to be pursued by historians. This study should be considered part of a growing number of books and articles on the powerful reemergence of conservative politics in the South and the nation with the election of Richard Nixon in 1968. But as with each work mentioned in this essay, Mathews and De Hart find gender at the core.

The authors compare the modern movement for equal rights with the woman suffrage campaign in the 1910s – the parallels are striking, for the North Carolina legislature refused to ratify the Equal Rights Amendment just as it had defeated the Anthony Amendment in 1920. There is a certain sense of *déjà vu* in reading the rationale for ERA's failure, and connections to the historical antisuffragist campaign are by no means out of place. The same sentiments expressed by antisuffragists were finding new life in anti-ERA rhetoric. "Essentially the conflict was about gender," and the threat of change riding on the ERA was too great for many in the South to accept (ibid: xii).

The word "sex" held meaning well beyond biological differences to opponents. In short, opponents believed that the "physiological and functional differences" attributed to women allowed them protection in the law (ibid: 28). Equality, they feared, would threaten this protection. Issues such as compulsory military service, women in combat, protective legislation for women workers and widows, integration of public restrooms, and loss of child support payments all became potent arguments for opponents. Senator Sam Ervin of North Carolina and Phyllis Schlafly worked together; he dispatched his anti-ERA Senate speeches to constituents from lists provided by her. Schlafly founded the national STOP ERA organization, which allied itself with the New Right, and quietly they sent coded images that linked feminists with civil rights workers and the intrusion of the federal government in state affairs. "Forced busing" came to North Carolina just as the amendment was making its ratification rounds, suggesting that the ERA would also bring "forced equality" (ibid: 172). The Religious Right mounted opposition based on traditional biblical views of women's subordination, while a more liberal US Supreme Court in *Roe v. Wade* countenanced abortion rights for women. The mix was volatile and lethal to the proponents, who were not prepared for the battle that ensued. It all seemed familiar; African-Americans had made their bid for social justice and now women sought to undermine white male control. Echoes of the Old South, replicated in the New South of the late nineteenth century, again resurfaced in the 1970s and 1980s. Nonetheless, southern women were once again engaged in politics, blurring the lines between public and private realms, and challenging the status quo. This book is one of a growing number of studies that seek a new direction – the study of conservative women and their influence on the South's political power. Following the lead of Sims and Green, Mathews and DeHart show the connection between antisuffragists and the current-day political Right. Historians are acknowledging that women's history must include all points of view from Mildred Rutherford (Historian of the United

Daughters of the Confederacy) to Mary McCleod Bethune (African-American founder of Bethune-Cookman College). To do otherwise is to diminish the truth.

In pursuing further study of the New South women, students should also consult the three edited volumes published under the auspices of the Southern Association for Women Historians (Bernhard et al. 1992, 1994; Coryell et al. 1998). Every three years since 1988 the SAWH has sponsored a southern conference on women's history, which has resulted in the publication of the best papers. Also a growing number of anthologies contain useful original articles: Hewitt and Lebsock (1993) and Farnham (1997). The *Georgia Historical Quarterly* has devoted two issues (1992, 1998) to women's history. Added to this are several biographies of postbellum southern women and an extensive collection of first-hand accounts written by southern women. There is, in fact, an abundance of riches, which continues to expand as graduate students complete their studies and established historians seek new topics.

Yet there is always room for more work to be done. One of the most needed areas of research is continued exploration of the impact of women on southern politics and reform, especially in the years between 1945 and 1955 and during the civil rights movement. We need to know more about Hispanic women, women of Asian ancestry, and especially about working women in general. And while there are studies of women in the 1930s and during World War II, there is room for more. We need to continue studying conservative southern women from the Daughters of the Confederacy to members of the Religious Right and their influence on southern culture and politics. There is a history waiting to be written about women and the rise of the Republican Party in the South between the 1950s and the present. One thing is certain, the history of the post-Civil War South, whether it relates to economics, politics, race, social, or cultural affairs, can no longer exclude gender and pretend to represent the whole of society. Women's history, gender analysis, and the most recent political and cultural studies have found rich soil in the New South.

BIBLIOGRAPHY

Alexander, Adele Logan 1991: *Ambiguous Lives: Free Women of Color in Rural Georgia, 1789–1879*. Fayetteville: University of Arkansas Press.

Bailey, Fred Arthur 1994: Mildred Lewis Rutherford and the Patrician Cult of the Old South. *Georgia Historical Quarterly*, 78, 509–35.

Bernhard, Virginia, Brandon, Betty, Fox-Genovese, Elizabeth, and Perdue, Theda (eds.) 1992: *Southern Women: Histories and Identities*. Columbia: University of Missouri Press.

Bernhard, Virginia, Brandon, Betty, Fox-Genovese, Elizabeth, Perdue, Theda, and Turner, Elizabeth H. (eds.) 1994: *Hidden Histories of Women in the New South*. Columbia: University of Missouri Press.

Blackwelder, Julia Kirk 1977: Quiet Suffering: Atlanta Women in the 1930s. *Georgia Historical Quarterly*, 61, 112–24.

Blackwelder, Julia Kirk 1984: *Women of the Depression: Caste and Culture in San Antonio, 1929–1939*. College Station: Texas A & M University Press.

Blee, Kathleen M. 1991: *Women of the Klan: Racism and Gender in the 1920s*. Berkeley: University of California Press.

Brown, Elsa Barkley 1989: Womanist Consciousness: Maggie Lena Walker and the Independent Order of Saint Luke. *Signs*, 14, 610–33.

Coryell, Janet, Swain, Martha H., Treadway, Sandra Gioia, and Turner, Elizabeth Hayes (eds.) 1998: *Beyond Image and Convention: Explorations in Southern Women's History.* Columbia: University of Missouri Press.

Cottrell, Debbie Mauldin 1993: *Pioneer Educator: The Progressive Spirit of Annie Webb Blanton.* College Station: Texas A & M University Press.

Crawford, Vicki L., Rouse, Jacqueline Anne, and Woods, Barbara (eds.) 1990: *Women in the Civil Rights Movement: Trailblazers and Torchbearers, 1941–1965.* Brooklyn, NY: Carlson Publishing.

Edwards, Laura F. 1997: *Gendered Strife and Confusion: The Political Culture of Reconstruction.* Urbana: University of Illinois Press.

Enstam, Elizabeth York 1998: *Women and the Creation of Urban Life: Dallas, Texas, 1843–1920.* College Station: Texas A & M University Press.

Evans, Sara 1979: *Personal Politics: The Roots of Women's Liberation in the Civil Rights Movement and the New Left.* New York: Alfred A. Knopf.

Farnham, Christie Anne (ed.) 1997: *Women of the American South: A Multicultural Reader.* New York: New York University Press.

Friedman, Jean E. 1985: *The Enclosed Garden: Women and Community in the Evangelical South, 1830–1900.* Chapel Hill: University of North Carolina Press.

Gilmore, Glenda Elizabeth 1996: *Gender and Jim Crow: Women and the Politics of White Supremacy in North Carolina, 1896–1920.* Chapel Hill: University of North Carolina Press.

Grantham, Dewey W. 1983: *Southern Progressivism: The Reconciliation of Progress and Tradition.* Knoxville: University of Tennessee Press.

Green, Elna C. 1997: *Southern Strategies: Southern Women and the Woman Suffrage Question.* Chapel Hill: University of North Carolina Press.

Guy-Sheftall, Beverly 1990: *"Daughters of Sorrow": Attitudes toward Black Women, 1880–1920.* Brooklyn, NY: Carlson Publishing.

Hale, Grace Elizabeth 1998: *Making Whiteness: The Culture of Segregation in the South, 1890–1940.* New York: Pantheon.

Hall, Jacquelyn Dowd 1979: *Revolt Against Chivalry: Jessie Daniel Ames and the Women's Campaign Against Lynching.* New York: Columbia University Press.

Hall, Jacquelyn Dowd 1986: Disorderly Women: Gender and Labor Militancy in the Appalachian South. *Journal of American History,* 73, 354–82.

Hall, Jacquelyn Dowd 1998: "You Must Remember This": Autobiography as Social Critique. *Journal of American History,* 85, 439–65.

Hall, Jacquelyn Dowd and Scott, Anne Firor 1987: Women in the South. In John B. Boles and Evelyn Thomas Nolen (eds.), *Interpreting Southern History: Historiographical Essays in Honor of Sanford W. Higginbotham.* Baton Rouge: Louisiana State University Press, 454–509.

Hall, Jacquelyn Dowd, Leloudis, James, Korstad, Robert, Murphy, Mary, Jones, Lu Ann, and Daly, Christopher B. 1987: *Like a Family: The Making of a Southern Cotton Mill World.* Chapel Hill: University of North Carolina Press.

Hawks, Joanne V. and Skemp, Sheila L. (eds.) 1983: *Sex, Race, and the Role of Women in the South.* Jackson: University Press of Mississippi.

Hewitt, Nancy A. 1993: In Pursuit of Power: The Political Economy of Women's Activism in Twentieth-Century Tampa. In Nancy A. Hewitt and Suzanne Lebsock (eds.), *Visible Women: New Essays on American Activism.* Urbana: University of Illinois Press, 199–222.

Hewitt, Nancy A. and Lebsock, Suzanne (eds.) 1993: *Visible Women: New Essays on American Activism.* Urbana: University of Illinois Press.

Hine, Darlene Clark 1992: Black Women's History, White Women's History: The Juncture of Race and Class. *Journal of Women's History,* 4, 125–33.

Hunter, Tera W. 1997: *To 'Joy My Freedom: Southern Black Women's Lives and Labors after the Civil War*. Cambridge, MA: Harvard University Press.

Janiewski, Dolores E. 1985: *Sisterhood Denied: Race, Gender, and Class in a New South Community*. Philadelphia: Temple University Press.

Jones, Jacqueline 1985: *Labor of Love, Labor of Sorrow: Black Women, Work, and the Family from Slavery to the Present*. New York: Basic Books.

Kraditor, Aileen S. 1965: *The Ideas of the Woman Suffrage Movement, 1890–1920*. New York: Columbia University Press.

Lasch-Quinn, Elisabeth 1993: *Black Neighbors: Race and the Limits of Reform in the American Settlement House Movement, 1890–1945*. Chapel Hill: University of North Carolina Press.

Lebsock, Suzanne 1993: Woman Suffrage and White Supremacy: A Virginia Case Study. In Nancy A. Hewitt and Suzanne Lebsock (eds.), *Visible Women: New Essays on American Activism*. Urbana: University of Illinois Press, 62–100.

Leloudis, James L., II 1983: School Reform in the New South: The Woman's Association for the Betterment of Public School Houses in North Carolina, 1902–1919. *Journal of American History*, 69, 886–909.

Leslie, Kent Anderson 1995: *Woman of Color, Daughter of Privilege: Amanda America Dickson, 1849–1893*. Athens: University of Georgia Press.

Lumpkin, Katharine Du Pre 1946: *The Making of a Southerner*. New York: Alfred A. Knopf.

McArthur, Judith N. 1998: *Creating the New Woman: The Rise of Southern Women's Progressive Culture in Texas, 1893–1918*. Urbana: University of Illinois Press.

McCandless, Amy Thompson 1999: *The Past in the Present: Women's Higher Education in the Twentieth-Century American South*. Tuscaloosa: University of Alabama Press.

McElhaney, Jacquelyn Masure 1998: *Pauline Periwinkle and Progressive Reform in Dallas*. College Station: Texas A & M University Press.

MacLean, Nancy 1994: *Behind the Mask of Chivalry: The Making of the Second Ku Klux Klan*. New York: Oxford University Press.

Mathews, Donald G. and De Hart, Jane Sherron 1990: *Sex, Gender, and the Politics of ERA: A State and the Nation*. New York: Oxford University Press.

Neverdon-Morton, Cynthia 1989: *Afro-American Women of the South and the Advancement of the Race, 1895–1925*. Knoxville: University of Tennessee Press.

Robnett, Belinda 1997: *How Long? How Long? African-American Women in the Struggle for Civil Rights*. New York: Oxford University Press.

Rose, Willie Lee 1964: *Rehearsal for Reconstruction: The Port Royal Experiment*. New York: Oxford University Press.

Rouse, Jacqueline A. 1989: *Lugenia Burns Hope: Black Southern Reformer*. Athens: University of Georgia Press.

Ruiz, Vicki 1991: Dead Ends or Gold Mines?: Using Missionary Records in Mexican-American Women's History. *Frontiers: A Journal of Women's Studies*, 12, 33–56.

Salem, Dorothy 1990: *To Better Our World: Black Women in Organized Reform, 1890–1920*. Brooklyn, NY: Carlson Publishing.

Saville, Julie 1994: *The Work of Reconstruction: From Slave to Wage Laborer in South Carolina, 1860–1870*. New York: Cambridge University Press.

Schwalm, Leslie A. 1997: *A Hard Fight for We: Women's Transition from Slavery to Freedom in South Carolina*. Urbana: University of Illinois Press.

Scott, Anne Firor 1970: *The Southern Lady: From Pedestal to Politics, 1830–1930*. Chicago: University of Chicago Press.

Scott, Anne Firor 1994: *Natural Allies: Women's Associations in American History*. Urbana: University of Illinois Press.

Shaw, Stephanie J. 1996: *What a Woman Ought to Be and to Do: Black Professional Women Workers During the Jim Crow Era*. Chicago: University of Chicago Press.

Sims, Anastatia 1997: *The Power of Femininity in the New South: Women's Organizations and Politics in North Carolina, 1880–1930*. Columbia: University of South Carolina Press.

Swain, Martha 1995: *Ellen S. Woodward: New Deal Advocate for Women*. Jackson: University Press of Mississippi.

Taylor, A. Elizabeth 1957: *The Woman Suffrage Movement in Tennessee*. New York: Bookman Associates.

Terborg-Penn, Roslyn 1998: *African American Women in the Struggle for the Vote, 1850–1920*. Bloomington: Indiana University Press.

Thomas, Mary Martha 1987: *Riveting and Rationing in Dixie: Alabama Women and the Second World War*. Tuscaloosa: University of Alabama Press.

Thomas, Mary Martha 1992: *The New Woman in Alabama: Social Reforms and Suffrage, 1890–1920*. Tuscaloosa: University of Alabama Press.

Thomas, Mary Martha (ed.) 1995: *Stepping Out of the Shadows: Alabama Women, 1819–1990*. Tuscaloosa: University of Alabama Press.

Thompson, Mildred I. 1990: *Ida B. Wells-Barnett: An Exploratory Study of an American Black Woman, 1893–1930*. Brooklyn, NY: Carlson Publishing.

Tucker, Susan 1988: *Telling Memories Among Southern Women: Domestic Workers and Their Employers in the Segregated South*. Baton Rouge: Louisiana State University Press.

Turner, Elizabeth Hayes 1997: *Women, Culture, and Community: Religion and Reform in Galveston, 1880–1920*. New York: Oxford University Press.

Tyler, Pamela 1996: *Silk Stockings and Ballot Boxes: Women and Politics in New Orleans, 1920–1963*. Athens: University of Georgia Press.

Wedell, Marsha 1991: *Elite Women and the Reform Impulse in Memphis, 1875–1915*. Knoxville: University of Tennessee Press.

Wheeler, Marjorie Spruill 1993: *New Women of the New South: The Leaders of the Woman Suffrage Movement in the Southern States*. New York: Oxford University Press.

Wheeler, Marjorie Spruill (ed.) 1995: *Votes for Women! The Woman Suffrage Movement in Tennessee, the South, and the Nation*. Knoxville: University of Tennessee Press.

Whites, LeeAnn 1995: *The Civil War as a Crisis in Gender: Augusta, Georgia, 1860–1890*. Athens: University of Georgia Press.

Wolfe, Margaret Ripley 1995: *Daughters of Canaan: A Saga of Southern Women*. Lexington: University Press of Kentucky.

CHAPTER TWENTY-TWO

The Discovery of Appalachia: Regional Revisionism as Scholarly Renaissance

JOHN C. INSCOE

JOHN Shelton Reed once noted that Appalachia has always served as "the South's South" (Reed 1986: 42). By that he meant that for all the mythmaking, distortion, and negative stereotyping to which the South has been subjected by other Americans, Southern Appalachia has faced much more of such abuse. In many ways, the burdens borne by the South, whether experienced historically, economically, socially, or interpreted literarily, are burdens shared, often in more acute form, by its highlanders. And if the "Sunbelt" phenomenon has somehow eased much of that burden – in both economic reality and national perception – for the larger region in recent years, Appalachia seems to remain as benighted as ever. As Ronald D. Eller, one of the region's foremost historians, recently noted: "Appalachia continues to languish backstage in the American drama, still dressed, in the popular mind at least, in the garments of backwardness, violence, poverty, and hopelessness once associated with the South as a whole. No other region of the United States today plays the role of 'other America' quite so persistently as Appalachia" (Billings, Norman, and Leford 1999: ix).

For that reason, southern Appalachians have also shared with other southerners a degree of regional self-consciousness more intense and deeply rooted than that of almost any other part of the country. Given the pejorative and patronizing nature of so much of the vast literature on the region and how deeply ingrained such assumptions are in the American consciousness, it is no wonder that, as Knoxville novelist and historian Wilma Dykeman noted as recently as the mid-1980s, Appalachians found it hard "to be neither defensive nor offensive about the region where we live" (Dykeman 1984: 14).

In a 1977 essay, Eller condemned historians for their failure to confront these distortions and simplifications more forthrightly. He bemoaned both the static nature of the historiography, still all too willing to buy into the perpetual myths of the region "as a vanishing frontier, and its people as frontiersmen, suspended and isolated," and the marginalization or even the absence of the region's history in broader treatments of southern or American history, "guided by the tacit assumption that nothing significant ever happened in the mountains" (Eller 1977: 75). He went on to note that "our efforts to explain and deal with the social problems of the region have focused not on economic and political realities in the area as they have evolved over time, but on the supposed inadequacies of a pathological culture that is seen to have equipped mountain people poorly for life in the modern industrial world" (Eller 1982: xvii).

Eller's call for a "new history" of Appalachia was timely; for it was at just that point – the late 1970s and early 1980s – that influential new work appeared (including his own) that would mark the beginning of a two-decade-long era of resurgence and revisionism in our understanding of the Appalachian experience and an appreciation for its relevance to the rest of southern and American history. One would be hard-pressed to find any other geographic region of the country whose history had been neglected for so long by serious scholars. Yet given the rapidity with which that void has been filled, it would also be difficult to find another part of the country that has been subjected to so vast a range of innovative scholarship spanning as many topical, chronological, and geographic fronts as has Appalachia over the course of the 1980s and 1990s. Historians of the region, many of them natives, have indeed been driven by both the defensive and offensive impulses that Wilma Dykeman acknowledged. But in the process, they have produced an extraordinary body of work that, taken together, provides a very different portrait of the region and its past, revealing it to have been far more dynamic, more complex, and more diverse than once assumed. With this belated maturation of serious study of the mountain South, historians have challenged the image of "a strange land and peculiar people" (a phrase coined in 1873; see Harney 1873), so deeply ingrained in the American consciousness with their portrayal of a much more multifaceted historical experience of considerable depth and complexity. The editors of a recent collection of essays on the region, *Appalachia in the Making*, characterized this recent scholarship as an "effort to deconstruct the concept of an essential and universalistic Appalachian past." Of the essays in their volume, they noted that "unlike a long tradition of Appalachian regional studies, none claims that the patterns described were necessarily unique to the highland South or general to the whole mountain region," a statement that is equally applicable to the recent historiography of Appalachia as a whole (Pudup, Billings, and Waller 1995: 3).

The current generation of historians of the region have recognized just how much the historical forces apparent in the mountain South were forces at work elsewhere in America as well – frontier settlement, slavery, the sectional crisis and Civil War, industrialization and modernization, violence, rural poverty, labor unrest, the exploitation of the land and its resources – though topography and other geographic factors often dictated significant variations in how such forces played out. And if Southern Appalachia did become increasingly marginalized and its development increasingly out of kilter with that of the rest of the country as the nineteenth century moved into the twentieth, recent historians have been far more likely to look to national events and trends in explaining why this was so. Connectedness has become a key term in Appalachian studies of late and an integral part of the explanatory force of regional identity and development.

Yet, at the same time, an equally important trend in the recent scholarship has been the particularization – even fragmentation – of the Appalachian experience. As will be demonstrated in the works discussed below, much of the most valuable work on the region have been studies focused on either a single community or a multicounty area. When juxtaposed with each other (as has often been the case in several influential collections of essays on the region), it becomes readily apparent that the mountain South cannot be considered a single geographic or social entity, and that the broad generalizations that were once so pervasive in characterizing mountain life and culture are now inapplicable and unconvincing. We are now more aware than ever that Appalachian society developed in different ways and at different rates, and was driven by different forces. As John C. Campbell once noted, the southern highlands make up "the backyards of several different states" (Campbell 1921: 42). As subsections of different political entities that were, in all instances but one (West Virginia), more nonmountainous than mountainous in character, the states of which they were a part defined, or at least influenced, much of the political and economic course of their highland regions. Thus, not only was the North Georgia experience quite different from that of eastern Kentucky or western Virginia, but that even adjacent regions, such as West Virginia and southwest Virginia or western North Carolina and East Tennessee, evolved differently, often with important political consequences, as the sectional crisis and Civil War revealed.

To explore these trends through specific books, it seems more logical to move chronologically through the two and a half centuries of Appalachian history rather than through the two decades or so over which that history has been produced. Because these works deal, for the most part, with a particular historical era, it is easy to proceed from eighteenth-century settlement through twentieth-century modernization, with one significant exception. Although the history of Appalachia – social, economic, and cultural – is grounded in the reality of the region or its various parts, there is also a strong scholarly impulse to analyze the intellectual concept of the southern highlands, the very idea of Appalachia – how it emerged and to what uses it has been put.

Those scholars certainly share in the goals of this new generation of chroniclers of the mountain South in eradicating the firmly entrenched misconceptions and stereotypical images about the region and its residents. As one scholar has noted, "In the Appalachian studies industry, an entire shop floor is devoted to the labor-intensive task of debunking these stereotypes" (Batteau 1990: 7). And yet, for these particular works, "debunking" has been almost a byproduct of more probing analyses of the processes by which these perceptions were created in the first place. Because this has long been so pervasive a theme, so broad in its chronological range, and so basic to our understanding of the region and the revisionist scholarship it has inspired, several of these books will be discussed up front, before moving backward to the mid-eighteenth century and then proceeding forward through time.

The first such effort appeared in 1978 and served as both a clarion call and a foundation for the revisionist scholarship that followed so quickly on its heels. Henry D. Shapiro's *Appalachia on Our Mind* established a theme that others would revisit and refine: that for the mountain South, perception trumped reality, or the medium was the message. Focusing on the crucial era from 1870 to 1920, when Appalachia "otherness" was discovered and defined so indelibly by outsiders – local color writers and journalists, missionaries and educators, public and private agencies – Shapiro emphasizes the external agendas that drove the distorted and simplistic ideas of the southern highlands as a primitive land inhabited by backward people. These ideas and the related impulses to reshape, reform, and revitalize the mountaineers and their antiquated ways, Shapiro asserted, tell us much about "new notions about the nature of America and American civilization" in the post-Civil War era and the discomfort many Americans felt in finding so anomalous a region that flew in the face of their concepts of progress, enlightenment, modernization and national homogeneity (Shapiro 1978: 3).

In *The Invention of Appalachia* cultural anthropologist Allen Batteau took Shapiro's thesis a step farther. He argued that Appalachia was not so much a social or geographic reality as it was a construct "invented" by political, journalistic, and literary forces to serve interests and agendas that had little or nothing to do with the highlands or highlanders. The region was, Batteau claimed, "a creature of the urban imagination" that has "provided American society with colorful characters for its fiction, perfect innocents for its philanthropy, and an undeveloped wilderness in which to prove its pioneering blood" (Batteau 1990: 1). The case studies with which he makes his argument cover a vast and varied range, far more eclectic than Shapiro's tighter chronological and thematic focus. The revolutionary battle of King's Mountain, John Brown's raid on Harpers Ferry, the Tennessee Valley Authority, Lyndon Johnson's "War on Poverty," and Harry Caudill's classic treatise on the devastation coal wrought to the Kentucky mountains, *Night Comes to the Cumberland*, all brought considerable visibility to Southern Appalachia. These and other episodes demonstrate how writers, journalists, and government policy makers used the region for agendas far broader than its own betterment – often applying more positive connotations to its frontier-like society, when viewed in contrast to the increasingly industrial, urban, pluralistic, and often morally uncertain nation from which it seemed more and more removed. In that respect, Batteau argues, the region was a mere accident of history, and any other semiremote populace could have served much the same purpose.

If Batteau pushed these issues forward in time, other rather inventive studies have pushed them backward. In *Two Worlds in the Tennessee Mountains* David Hsiung (1997) took a unique approach to explaining the earliest manifestations of Appalachian identity and distinctiveness. From early settlement on, upper East Tennesseeans found themselves situated in varying degrees of removal from or accessibility to the world and markets beyond. The isolation or connectedness of these residents dictated their views of themselves and their fellow highlanders. Local elites with a vested interest in promoting economic outreach, Hsiung argued, imposed the first pejorative images of backwardness and ignorance on those more remotely situated who resisted such change and refused to buy into the opportunities and investments pushed so by their "betters." Those politically motivated characterizations proved pervasive, and over the course of the nineteenth century, as two worlds did indeed emerge between the area's broad valleys with their thriving towns and the remote highlands and hollows nearby, became more imbedded in literary and popular perceptions of the mountains.

Rodger Cunningham, on the other hand, worked from an even more original interpretive model. His *Apples on the Flood* is an exploration of the ancestry of Appalachia's people and the geographical and ethnic baggage they brought with them. Evoking what he called "peripheralization theory," Cunningham saw the mountain South as part of a historic pattern of regional juxtapositions in which a metropolitan core that saw itself as "civilized" imposed labels of "savage" or "barbaric" on an outside, underdeveloped periphery. Just as ancient Romans perceived the Germanic peoples to their north, and the English saw those Celtic "edges" of the British Isles, so the intellectual and political elite of America's eastern seaboard have always viewed Appalachia (Cunningham 1987: xxi–xxii). Drawing on mythology, comparative literature, and both Freudian and existential psychology as much as cultural history to make his case, Cunningham celebrated the tenacity and the traditionalism of Appalachian folk and culture and argued that a mountain periphery is often the ultimate testing ground for the survival and workability of a civilization's values.

Two very different books have recently tackled the image issue by examining the popular media as a prime instigator of some of the most debasing and durable of Appalachian stereotypes. J. W. Williamson's *Hillbillyland* is among the liveliest and most provocative books on regional stereotyping. Williamson, like Batteau, began from the premise that Americans need hillbillies, and that as they've been portrayed by Hollywood in particular, they serve as a mirror to the best and the worst in all of us – they can flatter, frighten, or humiliate. Exploring the vast range of ways in which Hollywood created and Americans responded to mountain characters, both fictional and real – Sergeant York, Ma and Pa Kettle, Andy Griffith, Norma Rae, L'il Abner, Davy Crockett, and Dolly Parton, just to name a few – Williamson demonstrates the variety of comic and dramatic guises that have served throughout most of the twentieth century to make "the normative middle-class urban spectator feel better about the system of money and power that has him or her in its grasp" (Williamson 1995: 20).

The title of an even more recent essay collection – *Confronting Appalachian Stereotypes: Back Talk from an American Region* – suggests just how feisty regional scholars can be in this ongoing battle against myth and misconception. The book was inspired by Robert Schenkkan's 1992 Pulitzer Prize-winning play, *The Kentucky Cycle*, and the unwarranted acclaim many Kentuckians felt had been bestowed on a work that gave in to the negative stereotypes and patronizing portrayals they had fought against for so long. A nine-act, multi-generational saga, the play perpetuated the most egregious imagery of the region's poverty, degeneracy, and environmental abuse, all of which was brought on by stock hillbilly characters whose inherent weaknesses allowed them to be victimized by outside forces. It didn't help that Schenkkan stated that he got the idea of using the Appalachian experience as a metaphor for what is wrong with America after he spent a "day" traveling in eastern Kentucky in 1981. To scholars of the region, particularly Kentuckians, the play was yet another example of how outsiders had always portrayed the region; George Ella Lyon expressed the assessment shared by many, that it was "the same weary plod through outrage, pity, preconceived notions, self-righteous reductionism and psycho-social projection that has been the mark of literary tourism for so long" (Billings, Norman, and Leford 1999: 10).

While the play and the response to it proved to be the initial impetus for this volume, editors Dwight Billings and Gurney Norman (a sociologist and a short-story writer, in the long-standing Appalachian studies tradition of interdisciplinary collaboration) turned it into a much more extensive and multifaceted study of the roots of the literary, journalistic, and historical stereotyping to which the region has been subjected. It went even farther than most of the other books discussed above to explore the realities of the region as conveyed by residents and grassroot activists, testimony that even more effectively than the scholarly analyses conveyed the inadequacies and the distortions of the popular myths that still prevail about the mountain South.

If these works put the mythmaking front and center in their treatments of the region, most others in this great wave of regional revisionism expose the myths more by virtue of full-fledged historical research and analysis, using facts and often figures to refute the misconceptions. The remainder of this essay will focus on some of the most significant of those works, moving roughly chronologically across the two and a half centuries or so of Appalachia's past, rather than in sequence of their publication, as significant as that is.

Robert Mitchell's *Commercialism and Frontier* was one of the earliest and most influential of the revisionist studies. In this 1977 study of Virginia's Shenandoah Valley, Mitchell challenged the Turner thesis and other frontier myths by demonstrating the strong entrepreneurial impulses that were inherent in the earliest stages of settlement. These manifested themselves in a variety of ways: rampant land speculation, thriving trade linkages between frontier mercantile establishments and eastern seaboard cities linked by intra-and interregional road networks, a rapid increase in marketable agricultural surpluses and home manufactures, and a culturally diverse populace. Like the best of the work that would follow Mitchell's, the model of frontier development in the Shenandoah Valley has had significant implications not just for other parts of Appalachia but for much of North America's colonial and frontier experiences as well.

Mitchell did not have to wait long to see the proliferation of work his own had inspired. From a conference he and others organized in 1985 that reflected much of the scholarship then in progress, he edited a collection of essays entitled *Appalachian Frontiers*, which would prove to be merely the first of several conferences and subsequent essay collections that expanded upon the issues he had raised in *Commercialism and Frontier*. The sheer range of work examining this formative phase of southern highland settlement has been among the most effective in challenging the romanticized notions of preindustrial Appalachia as "isolated, rural, homogeneous populations relatively untouched or even bypassed by the mainstream of American life." Indeed, that range of experience, and the fluidity that characterized it, is just the point, Mitchell maintained. Appalachia, like other frontier regions, should be viewed as "becoming, as a place in process," or as "a series of frontiers" in which the mode, timing, and rate of local and regional development differed considerably and must be appreciated on their own terms and in juxtaposition with each other (Mitchell 1991: 3).

Wilma Dunaway and Paul Salstrom vastly expanded Mitchell's concept of the complex nature of Southern Appalachia's development by the bold, if somewhat controversial, application of theoretical models that they used to link the region in somewhat different ways to much larger forces beyond it. Dunaway, a historical sociologist, applied the "world systems" paradigm of Immanuel Wallerstein to the first century and a half of Appalachian development in *The First American Frontier* (Dunaway 1996). She argued that from first settlement on, the region was part of a remote periphery of a world economic system and remained a dependent element of that system through the mid-nineteenth century. Capitalist exploitation characterized even the first European activity in the southern highlands, as English deerskin traders undermined and ultimately displaced Cherokee presence in the highlands. By the late-eighteenth century it was the absentee speculators who bought up and controlled vast amounts of land, thus diminishing opportunities for small family farms and forcing many of the postrevolutionary generation of settlers into tenantry or even "coerced labor." The prevalence of this "landless agrarian semiproletariat" stifled agricultural or other forms of economic development and thus kept Appalachia fully marginalized and even in decline by the mid-nineteenth century. Dunaway supported her thesis with a massive, stratified sample of over 22,000 households in the 1860 census, but critics have questioned various elements of her methodology, her definition of terms, and the sweeping generalizations she applied to the region as a whole. Nevertheless, her book has commanded much attention and discussion among scholars of the region and raised new questions about both the conceptualization and the methodologies through which we can explain the complex economic forces that shaped Appalachian development.

In *Appalachia's Path to Dependency* Salstrom (1994) posited an equally bold thesis. He, like Dunaway and others, attempted to get at the root of Appalachian poverty and found the downward trend underway well before the industrialization of the region and before the Civil War, the two traditional culprits of Appalachian decline and dependency. Looking at agricultural productivity, market access, and farm size over the course of the nineteenth century, Salstrom argued that economic decline took place in stages, the first of which was evident in some parts of the mountain South in the 1840s and 1850s, when population growth and soil exhaustion were already taking their toll on farm size and output. Equally important to Salstrom's analysis was his differentiation of Appalachian subregions defined by the rates and degrees of settlement, thus reiterating one of the central components of Appalachian revisionism – its defiance of generalization. Both Dunaway and Salstrom have contributed significantly to the revisionist history of Appalachia by demonstrating the chronological connectedness in how the region developed – that in order to fully understand the emergence of Appalachian "otherness" in the late nineteenth and early twentieth centuries, we must pay close attention to patterns and trends already at play in the eighteenth and early nineteenth centuries.

The antebellum era has been the focus of an equally significant share of the new scholarship underway on Southern Appalachia. Following the themes established by Mitchell for the eighteenth century, most work on the first half of the nineteenth century has portrayed a society far more complex and varied than once assumed. In 1988 a community study by Durwood Dunn quickly emerged as not only one of the most popular scholarly works published on the region but one of the most influential as well. *Cade's Cove* (Dunn 1988) is a meticulously documented history of a small, rural community in the heart of Tennessee's Great Smoky Mountains. Dunn challenged the idea that this relatively remote settlement (and, by very qualified extension, others throughout the mountain South) was merely a "neo-frontier" that stagnated or even retrogressed to levels of subsistence, poverty, and isolation after its first generation or so. Instead he portrayed a much more dynamic and fluid set of social and economic conditions that characterized Cades Cove over the course of the nineteenth and early twentieth centuries, demonstrating that broader regional and even national trends – in politics, market forces, religion, and war – shaped the fortunes of its residents, who were themselves more varied in their socioeconomic circumstances and outlook than had been generally acknowledged.

A year later John Inscoe published the first of what would be several books examining the impact of slavery and slaveholders on the economics and politics of the mountain South. *Mountain Masters* (Inscoe 1989) focused on a small but influential elite in western North Carolina and the variety of ways in which they profited from slave ownership in this decidedly nonplantation environment. These men wielded considerable political and economic power locally and regionally, and under their leadership, Carolina highlanders were ultimately far more supportive of secession and the Confederate war effort than was true of other parts of the mountain South. Key to these sentiments were the vital economic ties that bound western Carolinians to the plantation markets of South Carolina and Georgia, which gave the region a vested interest in casting its fate with that of its southern neighbors when the secession crisis forced those choices upon them.

Slavery's impact on the region was often tied to mining and other industrial pursuits, as several book-length case studies of such industries have demonstrated. Charles Dew's *Bond of Iron* is a remarkable reconstruction of the intricacies in the relationships between masters and their slaves (often as individuals) at the iron works of Buffalo Forge in the Valley of Virginia (Dew 1994), while John Stealey (1993) has explored similar dynamics in his study of the salt furnaces of the Kanawha Valley in what would later be south-central West Virginia. Both operations became increasingly dependent on a slave workforce and thus became more inextricably bound to southern slave markets as they expanded their own trade in iron and salt. Ronald Lewis has documented a similar dependence on slavery in the nascent coalmining operations in Virginia and western Maryland before the Civil War (Lewis 1987: ch. 1), and David Williams has chronicled slaves' participation in the gold rush that swept several Georgia mountain counties in the 1830s and 1840s (Williams 1993). All of these works demonstrated the extent to which industrialization and market forces were very much antebellum developments that infused the highland economy and social structure in ways long obscured by the more simplistic and romanticized imagery to which preindustrial Appalachia has so long been subjected.

Kenneth Noe's *Southwest Virginia's Railroad* is one of the most thorough explorations of the forces of modernization in mid-nineteenth-century Appalachia. The Virginia and Tennessee Railroad transected the southwestern corner of Virginia in the mid-1850s, and Noe examined the multiple impacts it had on the region. By commerically linking this remote highland region to the eastern part of the state and by recasting the role of slavery and southwest Virginians' commitment to it, the railroad transformed the economic prospects and political alignments of those counties it served. In short, Noe argued, "the leading factor convincing most Southwest Virginians to don gray and most Northwest Virginians blue in 1861 was the divergence among western Virginians caused by their railroads: where they ran and what they carried, and how economic change caused by railroad building shaped ideology" (Noe 1994: 8). Like Inscoe's *Mountain Masters*, Noe's study confirmed the "southerness" of Appalachia, in itself a corrective to the long-standing northern perception of the region's isolation from and alienation toward the proslavery, prosecession, and pro-Confederate South.

The "whiteness" of the mountain South was a central component of this myth. Thus a major part of the revisionist scholarship on the region, particularly that covering the nineteenth century, has been the documentation of the black presence, both slave and free, throughout the region. All of the works just discussed and others have effectively refuted what historian Edward Cabbell has termed black invisibility in the region, or "a neglected minority within a neglected minority" (Cabbell and Turner 1985: 3). Two collections of essays perhaps best exemplify the range of work that has focused on race relations in the mountain South. *Blacks in Appalachia* (Cabbell and Turner 1985) included a rich sampling of work by African-American scholars native to the region, such as Booker T. Washington and Carter G. Woodson, along with newer studies by sociologists, anthropologists, folklorists, and historians. Much of the volume's focus was on the impact of African-Americans on the coalmining industry of Central Appalachia, but other essays and interviews dealt with issues of urban Appalachia, racial demographic shifts, and the political and educational impact of a biracial presence in certain parts of the region. A new volume, *Appalachians and Race* (Inscoe 2000), serves as a sequel of sorts to *Blacks in Appalachia*. While more tightly focused on nineteenth-century race relations, it includes eighteen essays or excerpts from larger works that reflect the vast expansion of scholarship on the black presence in the mountain South both before and after the Civil War. At the same time, this newer work is even more sensitized to the localized contexts in which blacks and whites interacted in mountain settings and thus adds to our appreciation of the social, economic, and geographical diversity that has always characterized Southern Appalachia and its past.

Curiously, the Civil War era has been among the last to attract the full-fledged attention of Appalachian scholars. Until the last five years one of the only book-length studies of the war and its impact on the region was Phillip Paludan's *Victims*, published in 1981. Paludan focused on what became an infamous mass execution of thirteen Unionist civilians by Confederate troops, mostly local, in a remote Blue Ridge community in North Carolina in 1863. He used the "Shelton Laurel massacre," as it came to be known, to explore the larger issues of the loyalty and disloyalty at the community level and the extent to which local conditions as well as tensions, when conventional troops were subjected to guerrilla warfare, contributed to this particular atrocity. In effect, Paludan both challenged and confirmed two of the most long-standing generalizations about the war in the mountains, what Kenneth Noe has termed the "myth of Unionist Appalachia": first, that southern highlanders were united in their alienation and isolation from the slaveholding lowlands; and second, that according to the "myth of savage Appalachia," violence and primitivism were inherent to its inhabitants (Noe and Wilson 1997: xiv). In so doing Paludan provided a new appreciation for the complex social and political conditions that allowed the war to degenerate so quickly into such localized terrorism and destruction.

It has only been in the latter half of the 1990s that Appalachian scholars have mounted a massive assault on the war, with yet another extraordinary essay collection leading the charge. Under the title of simply *The Civil War in Appalachia*, Kenneth Noe and Shannon Wilson (1997) collected and edited essays by eleven historians, almost all of whom drew on parts of their own larger projects dealing with the war in some part of Appalachia. Spanning the highland South from North Georgia to Kentucky and West Virginia, these essays reflected a wide variety of regional and local approaches to the war as experienced by highlanders who found themselves part of the Confederate South – the political and class divisions wrought by the secession crisis and the war's onset, the differing dynamics of the brutal guerrilla warfare that beset many sections of the region, the emancipation of slaves, the economic hardship and opportunities the war posed in different parts of the region, and its postwar legacy and the regional mythmaking that grew out of it. The very range of topics and the different conclusions drawn as to either the long- or short-term effects of the war on Appalachia reflected in these essays suggests the same complexity, diversity, and lack of consensus that has characterized most of the other revisionist scholarship on the region. There are no easy answers to the questions of what determined whether or not one became a Unionist or a secessionist, or what factors drove the internal guerrilla violence that characterized the war in many parts of the highland South, or the extent to which the war impeded or encouraged the industrialization and other forms of modernization that transformed so much of the region in the postbellum decades. When the findings suggested in these essays are expanded into monographs, as many of them will surely be, we will likely see an even greater range of treatments and interpretations of the conflict's multiple effects on individuals, on communities, and on the region as a whole.

Reconstruction remains one of the least examined eras and politics one of the least explored topics in the new Appalachian history. There is one major exception on both fronts – Gordon McKinney's *Southern Mountain Republicans, 1865–1900*, published in 1978. McKinney offered what remains the only full-scale analysis we have of what is indeed one of the most conspicuous manifestations of Appalachian exceptionalism – the fact that at the Civil War's end, it became the only sustained geographic base of the Republican Party south of the Mason-Dixon line (as it continued to be through the 1950s). In analyzing the reasons for this anomaly over its first third of a century, McKinney found that while initially rooted in the region's anti-Confederate biases and the traumatic upheavals of the war years, mountain Republicanism actually slowed during Reconstruction as the party's commitment to racial equality dominated its rationale in the South. Local issues and skillful leadership sustained the party through those years until the 1880s and 1890s, when the impact of regional industrialization created a new commercial elite who took control of the region politically as well as economically and brought highland Republicans more fully in synch with the party's national agenda. The strength of McKinney's work is that he acknowledged the complexities of social and economic forces at a variety of levels and how they impacted political behavior. At the same time, he demonstrated, as no one has since, just how much electoral politics can tell us about Appalachia and its transformation during this crucial era in its history.

That social and economic transformation has inspired some of the most significant and most varied scholarship on Appalachia in recent years. The appearance of Ronald D. Eller's *Miners, Millhands, and Mountaineers* in 1982 was a quantum leap forward in our understanding of the tremendous impact of late-nineteenth-century industrialization on the region and of how highlanders responded to it. Eller provided not only the first but the most comprehensive account of this traditionally recognized era of modernization and economic upheaval throughout the entire region, demonstrating the rapid and devastating effects of the intrusion first of lumber barons and then of coalmine companies, both of which stripped the land of its natural resources and harshly exploited a large local labor force to do so. He documented the social transformation that accompanied the economic exploitation and dislocation, during and after both industries peaked early and national markets for both timber and coal collapsed in the 1920s. It was a bleak picture, vividly described and effectively documented. Only Eller's rather idyllic and oversimplified portrayal of preindustrial family and community life generated skepticism from critics and was subsequently undermined by the later work on the complexities of antebellum life and labor discussed above.

Two books have examined the impact of modernization by demythologizing two of the more enduring components of Appalachian imagery – its feuds and its moonshiners. Altina Waller's *Feud*, published in 1988, quickly became as influential as Eller's book in altering our understanding of the internal dynamics of Appalachia's late-nineteenth-century transformation. In analyzing the multigenerational feud between the Hatfields and McCoys, Waller constructed a complex community study of the Tug Valley that straddled Kentucky and West Virginia. Drawing on a vast array of land, business, and legal records (for it was through law suits and in courtrooms that much of the feud played itself out), she demonstrated that the personal animosities that fueled the feud emerged as much from class differences as from familial rivalries. It was, in effect, a struggle between those highlanders who bought into the industrial–capitalist opportunities that presented themselves after the Civil War and their kinsmen and neighbors who sought to preserve the traditions of community autonomy and family loyalty that were so threatened by such entrepreneurial forces, both internal and external.

In 1991 Wilbur Miller chronicled yet another means by which southern highlanders resorted to violent resistance of outside intrusions on their traditional values and livelihoods. In *Revenuers and Moonshiners* he portrayed this struggle as far more complex and far more bound up in the same transforming effects of modernization than popular imagery of mountain moonshine wars have ever acknowledged. Miller admitted that his focus was more on the federal agents and their efforts to enforce newly imposed taxation on homemade whiskey than on the mountaineers who made those efforts so challenging. Yet he effectively deromanticized the latter, portraying these highland men – and women – not as "backward, quaint, squirrel-rifle-and-whiskey-jug-toting hillbillies," but as individuals and communities caught up in the same transformative forces of modernization that drove Hatfields and McCoys to part ways during approximately the same period (Miller 1991: x–xi).

Not all parts of the mountain South experienced this transformation because of industrialization. A very different type of community study explores facets of change and persistence during the postbellum era in a purely rural, agricultural environment. In *The Road to Poverty* historical sociologists Kathleen Blee and Dwight Billings (1999) explore the life course of residents of Beech Creek, Kentucky, from 1850 to 1910. Like Paul Salstrom, Wilma Dunaway, and others, they see the roots of regional impoverishment in factors other than the incursion of industrialization in the late nineteenth century. In a community that remained untouched by coalmining far longer than most in eastern Kentucky, Blee and Billings trace the agricultural decline of Beech Creek in comparative terms. They note that in 1860 its output was comparable to that of many northern and midwestern farm regions, but that over the course of the next two decades local farms decreased in size and productivity as the strains of significant population growth imposed severe limitations on the capacity of subsistence farming to support it. The issues Blee and Billings raise and the innovative statistical strategies with which they address them have important implications not only for our understanding of Appalachian agriculture and community, but for all of rural America in those crucial decades of the late nineteenth century.

Much of the most important work on the late-nineteenth and early-twentieth-century Appalachia has centered on West Virginia. Among the earliest was John Alexander Williams's (1976) *West Virginia and the Captains of Industry.* Williams noted that there were many factors that contributed to the abysmal failure of the state to turn its rich natural resources into statewide prosperity and a more mature and balanced economy, not all of which were intangible or unintentional. His insightful analysis of the state's business and industrial elite who masterminded much of that economic transformation from the 1880s through the 1910s focused on four of the wealthiest and most powerful of their number, each of whom wore the multiple hats of coalmining magnates, railroad tycoons, bankers, and/or timber barons.

Most of the subsequent scholarship on the region has taken a more bottom-up approach, with a particularly rich output of work on coalminers. Ronald Lewis's study of black miners (including his coverage of slaves, discussed above) remains the most comprehensive work on that topic, both geographically and chronologically. By spanning the entire region and beyond over nearly two centuries, he put the racial aspects of central Appalachian mining enterprises in comparative perspective. Compared with slavery, convict labor, or the sheer exclusion of African-Americans from the labor forces of coalmines elsewhere, their full employment alongside whites in turn-of-the-century Kentucky and West Virginia, to which they were so heavily recruited, led to what Lewis called "a judicious mixture" in terms of the working and living conditions they experienced there (Lewis 1987: esp. chs 7 and 8).

A number of books have dealt with other aspects of Central Appalachia's coalmines, as business history, labor history, social history, environmental history, and often as innovative combinations of all of the above. Three of the most influential studies are those by David Corbin, Joe William Trotter, and Crandall Shiftlett. Corbin's *Life, Work, and Rebellion in the Coal Fields* (1981) traced the evolution of tensions between southern West Virginia miners and management from the 1880s through the violent uprisings that characterized strikes in 1912 and 1921. His perspective was primarily that of the miners and their perceptions of an increasingly repressive regime under which they worked and lived. Corbin traced their valiant efforts to exert some autonomy in the company towns in which they lived through the development of their own social, political, and religious institutions, and eventually through labor organizations, particularly the United Mine Workers.

Trotter told a similar story for much the same area during a slightly later era, but he kept his focus on the African-American workers. In *Coal, Class, and Color* Trotter (1990) traced the proletarianization process experienced by blacks migrating to West Virginia mines in the 1910s and 1920s. It involved adjustments on a number of fronts, with most migrants moving from the rural, agricultural South into semirural, industrialized settings. As communities at the height of the Jim Crow era, they managed simultaneously to carve out their own social and political space within a large, multi-ethnic workforce and to join with those fellow workers in union organizing.

In *Coal Towns* Crandall Shifflett (1991) described a very different scenario from the class-conflict model laid out by Eller and Corbin. Even more than Trotter, he focused on the dynamics of social life in the mining towns of West Virginia and southwest Virginia. By comparing living conditions in those communities, bleak as they seemed, with the rural poverty from which its residents had come, Shifflett argued that the mining towns often represented a step up socially and materially. He used oral histories by former miners and their families to demonstrate that their own initiatives and community spirit, along with certain paternalistic impulses by owners, created a variety of institutional and cultural amenities that enhanced their lives far more than any other viable option would have.

Ronald Lewis (1998) reminds us that West Virginia's economic transformation was never limited to coal. The timber industry was equally as devastating in its impact on the state, and in *Transforming the Appalachian Countryside* Lewis provides the fullest account to date of the social and agricultural disruption and the environmental damage wrought by the timber companies from the 1880s through the 1910s. They thoroughly and systematically destroyed West Virginia's forests and did so with the full compliance of the state's railroads, and its increasingly capitalistic political and legal system. As environmental history, Lewis's book breaks important new ground and serves as a model of the complexities created by the multiple forces that so readily transformed the forests and countryside of much of the rest of the southern highlands as well.

Two works set West Virginia firmly within the context of defining eras of twentieth-century America – that during and after World War I and that of the Great Depression. In his very title, *The Americanization of West Virginia*, John Hennen (1996) suggested a rather new approach to Appalachian studies by keeping his focus on both national and state developments throughout the war years and the early 1920s. Moving well beyond but never neglecting the industrial forces so central to the state's progress during the decade of World War I and its aftermath, Hennen produced a multifaceted portrait of West Virginians as educators, as social reformers and religious leaders, as businessmen and politicians, who like Americans elsewhere responded in various ways to the war and the social and labor crises it set in motion. This era and these issues – wartime mobilization, patriotism, postwar subversion and labor unrest – have never been explored in an Appalachian setting, and Hennen's insightful treatment of them serves as a model that could well be applied not only to other parts of the mountain South but to other southern states as well.

Equally impressive and worthy of emulation for other parts of the region is Jerry Bruce Thomas's comprehensive treatment of the Great Depression in West Virginia in *An Appalachian New Deal* (1998). Problems of economic and social dislocation had become acute well before the stock market crash of 1929, and yet the national crisis intensified those problems within the region and led to a variety of relief and reform efforts, not only through FDR's federal programs but through local and regional programs as well. In analyzing one Appalachian region's response to national forces of war, depression, and government policy, both Hennen and Thomas provide powerful examples of the relativity of Appalachia's "otherness," reminding us that the region was never so isolated from the broader cross-currents of the American experience that it was not seriously impacted by them. West Virginians, from grass-roots levels to governmental and business policy makers, responded in ways not unlike their counterparts across the country, thus demonstrating both southern highlanders' commonalities and their distinctiveness.

Other than the extensive work on the Central Appalachian coalfields during and just after the turn of the century, the historical analysis of Appalachia in the twentieth century has not yet been quite as extensive or as probing as that of the eighteenth and nineteenth centuries. Certain themes have merited more attention than others. One of the most fruitful concerns is the exploitation and manipulation of mountain culture. By the early twentieth century, as Appalachia came to be seen as the last great resevoir of American folk, or pioneer, traditions, forces outside the region sought to disseminate and commodify the manifestations of those traditions. David Whisnant, in *All That is Native and Fine* (1983), used three very different enterprises to demonstrate the processes by which educated, urban elites from the North commandeered particular aspects of the indigenous culture they discovered in the southern highlands in order to make them marketable for mass consumption elsewhere. Through a phenomenon he calls "systematic cultural intervention," Whisnant examined the Hindeman Settlement School in eastern Kentucky from its founding in 1902 until World War II, the various activities of Olive Dame Campbell over the first half of the twentieth century in the Carolina highlands, and the White Top Folk Festival in southwestern Virginia in the 1930s, as examples of this redefinition and commodification at work throughout the region.

Jane Becker's more recent *Selling Tradition* (1998) cast a much more tightly focused view on the same phenomenon. She documented the establishment of the Southern Highland Handicraft Guild in the 1930s and placed its activities firmly within a broader Depression-era folk-culture movement. Becker used the Guild's efforts in fostering the production of such handicrafts (often under exploitative working conditions), in marketing them, and in shaping perceptions of the mountain people who made them to explore the changing meanings of tradition and of folk culture, as those terms were applied to Southern Appalachia.

David Whisnant has contributed significantly in other ways to our understanding of twentieth century Appalachia. His *Modernizing the Mountaineer* (1980) remains the broadest coverage yet of the institutional development of the region from mid-century on. Whisnant argued that the various state and federal programs directed at the mountain South derived from the same impulses that "a hundred years of exploitative private development in the mountains, and the condescending middle-class missionary activities and attitudes that accompanied it" (Whisnant 1980: xv). Again, he used multiple case studies to explore the dynamics of these impulses by several agencies and organizations, public and private, from the New Deal through the "Great Society" of Lyndon Johnson, from the Council of the Southern Mountains and TVA to the Appalachian Regional Commission and the Office of Economic Opportunity. Like so much of the work that would follow this 1980 publication, Whisnant's analysis was as concerned with the national agendas and circumstances outside the region that inspired these efforts as he was with how they impinged upon the lives of the many highlanders they touched.

In some respects this essay only scratches the surface in terms of the full range of historical literature on the region. Not covered here are substantive pieces of work, much of it by historians, on Appalachian music, literature, and particularly on its richly diverse religious heritage. (Deborah McCauley's massive *Appalachian Mountain*

Religion [1995], is merely the tip of a large iceberg of work on a variety of mainstream denominations and more regionally based sects.) At the same time, there are several aspects of the Appalachian past that remain curiously neglected, topics that have not yet inspired more than a few isolated works at best. These include politics, women and gender issues, the social and economic impact of tourism, and the urban experience within the region. While there are several excellent institutional histories of individual schools and colleges in the region (Glen 1996; Puckett 1989), there is no comprehensive or systematic analysis of the impact of education and educational institutions on the region, as Deborah McCauley has produced on religion. And curiously, there has not yet been much biographical work on the numerous men and women whose activities and/or writings proved so influential in shaping either Appalachia's development or perceptions of it.

Two of the distinguishing aspects of Appalachian scholarship are the extent to which it derives from a strong sense of mission to the region and its people, and the interdisciplinary nature of so much of that scholarship. Historians listen to, learn from, and collaborate with sociologists, economists, anthropologists, folklorists, fiction writers, and poets in ways that historians in other fields would find quite extraordinary. (We also argue with them as much as we argue with each other.) More often than not, those studying the region have a strong attachment to place and commitment to those living there, both of which drive the passion with which scholars seek to overturn the stereotypes and promote a real understanding of the region and its past in all its complexity and richness. The gaps between activists and academics certainly exist, but the latter seem far more aware of and interact with the former in more meaningful ways than is true in many other areas of history.

Allen Batteau once noted that "the falseness of most of the images of Appalachia lies not in their substance, in the various elements or themes they contain, but in the social context of their propagation, in the manner in which their facts and themes are presented to the audience" (Batteau 1990: 13). This is perhaps the greatest change that has characterized the scholarship on the region in the last two decades. The depth, complexity, and diversity of the topics explored has meant that there is far more substance now to be dealt with; but perhaps equally important, the respect with which historians and other scholars have approached the region and conveyed its history to their readerships have been vital to the new realities they are creating. There is a contagious spirit of discovery and commitment that infuses much of this scholarship. For all of its disciplinary diversity and often disagreement in terms of models used and conclusions drawn, all scholars of the region share a conviction that the Appalachian experience is well worth writing about because the region itself is well worth understanding, not only for the people who live there, but also for what it can teach us about the development of other rural regions and communities throughout the South and the nation.

BIBLIOGRAPHY

Batteau, Allen W. 1990: *The Invention of Appalachia*. Tucson: University of Arizona Press.
Becker, Jane S. 1998: *Selling Tradition: Appalachia and the Construction of an American Folk, 1930–1940*. Chapel Hill: University of North Carolina Press.

Billings, Dwight B., Norman, Gurney, and Ledford, Katherine (eds.) 1999: *Confronting Appalachian Stereotypes: Back Talk from an American Region*. Lexington: University Press of Kentucky.

Blee, Kathleen B. and Billings, Dwight B. 1999: *The Road to Poverty: The Making of Wealth and Hardship in Appalachia*. New York: Cambridge University Press.

Bradshaw, Michael 1992: *The Appalachian Regional Commission: Twenty-five Years of Government Policy*. Lexington: University Press of Kentucky.

Cabbell, Edward J. and Turner, William H. (eds.) 1985: *Blacks in Appalachia*. Lexington: University Press of Kentucky.

Campbell, John C. 1921: *The Southern Highlander and His Homeland*. New York: Russell Sage Foundation.

Corbin, David Alan 1981: *Life, Work, and Rebellion in the Coal Fields: The Southern West Virginia Miners, 1880–1922*. Urbana: University of Illinois Press.

Crass, David Colin et al. (eds.) 1998: *The Southern Colonial Backcountry: Interdisciplinary Perspectives on Frontier Communities*. Knoxville: University of Tennessee Press.

Cunningham, Rodger 1987: *Apples on the Flood: The Southern Mountain Experience*. Knoxville: University of Tennessee Press.

Davis, Donald E. 2000: *Where There Are Mountains: An Environmental History of the Southern Appalachians*. Athens: University of Georgia Press.

Dew, Charles B. 1994: *Bond of Iron: Master and Slave at Buffalo Forge*. New York: W. W. Norton.

Dunaway, Wilma A. 1996: *The First American Frontier: Transition to Capitalism in Southern Appalachia, 1700–1860*. Chapel Hill: University of North Carolina Press.

Dunn, Durwood 1988: *Cade's Cove: The Life and Death of a Southern Appalachian Community, 1818–1937*. Knoxville: University of Tennessee Press.

Dunn, Durwood 1997: *An Abolitionist in the Appalachian South: Ezekiel Birdseye on Slavery, Capitalism, and Separate Statehood for Tennessee, 1841–1846*. Knoxville: University of Tennessee Press.

Dykeman, Wilma 1984: *Explorations*. Newport, TN: Wakestone Books.

Eller, Ronald D. 1977: Toward a New History of the Appalachian South. In Stephen L. Fisher, J. W. Williamson, and Juanita Lewis (eds.), *A Guide to Appalachian Studies*. Special issue of *Appalachian Journal* 5 (Autumn): 74–81.

Eller, Ronald D. 1982: *Miners, Millhands, and Mountaineers: Industrialization of the Appalachian South, 1880–1930*. Knoxville: University of Tennessee Press.

Fisher, Noel C. 1997: *War at Every Door: Partisan Politics and Guerrilla Violence in East Tennessee, 1860–1869*. Chapel Hill: University of North Carolina Press.

Fisher, Stephen L., Williamson, J. W., and Lewis, Juanita, (eds.) 1977: *A Guide to Appalachian Studies*. Special issue of *Appalachian Studies* 5 (Autumn).

Glen, John M. 1996: *Highlander: No Ordinary School*, 2nd edn. Knoxville: University of Tennessee Press.

Groce, W. Todd 1999: *Mountain Rebels: East Tennessee Confederates and the Civil War, 1860–1870*. Knoxville: University of Tennessee Press.

Harney, Will Wallace 1873: A Strange Land and Peculiar People. *Lippincott's Magazine*, 12 (October), 429–38.

Hennen, Jonn C. 1996: *The Americanization of West Virginia: Creating a Modern Industrial State, 1916–1925*. Lexington: University Press of Kentucky.

Higgs, Robert J., Manning, Ambrose N., and Miller, Jim Wayne (eds.) 1995: *Appalachia Inside Out, Vol. 1: Conflict and Change; Vol. 2: Culture and Custom*. Knoxville: University of Tennessee Press.

Hsiung, David C. 1997: *Two Worlds in the Tennessee Mountains: Exploring the Origins of Appalachian Stereotypes*. Lexington: University Press of Kentucky.

Inscoe, John C. 1989: *Mountain Masters: Slavery and the Sectional Crisis in Western North Carolina*. Knoxville: University of Tennessee Press.

Inscoe, John C. (ed.) 2000: *Appalachians and Race: The Mountain South from Slavery to Segregation*. Lexington: University Press of Kentucky.

Inscoe, John C. and McKinney, Gordon B. 2000: *The Heart of Confederate Appalachia: Western North Carolina and the Civil War*. Chapel Hill: University of North Carolina Press.

Lewis, Ronald L. 1987: *Black Coal Miners in America: Race, Class, and Community Conflict, 1780–1980*. Lexington: University Press of Kentucky.

Lewis, Ronald L. 1998: *Transforming the Appalachian Countryside: Railroads, Deforestation, and Social Change in West Virginia, 1880–1920*. Chapel Hill: University of North Carolina Press.

McCauley, Deborah Vansau 1995: *Appalachian Mountain Religion: A History*. Urbana: University of Illinois Press.

McKenzie, Robert Tracy 1994: *One South or Many? Plantation Belt and Upcountry in Civil War-Era Tennessee*. New York: Cambridge University Press.

McKinney, Gordon B. 1978: *Southern Mountain Republicans, 1865–1900: Politics and the Appalachian Community*. Chapel Hill: University of North Carolina Press. New edn, 1998: Knoxville: University of Tennessee Press.

McNeil, W. K. (ed.) 1994: *Appalachian Images in Folk and Popular Culture*, 2nd edn. Knoxville: University of Tennessee Press.

Miller, Wilbur R. 1991: *Revenuers and Moonshiners: Enforcing Federal Liquor Law in the Mountain South, 1865–1900*. Chapel Hill: University of North Carolina Press.

Mitchell, Robert D. 1977: *Commercialism and Frontier: Perspectives on the Early Shenandoah Valley*. Charlottesville: University Press of Virginia.

Mitchell, Robert D. (ed.) 1991: *Appalachian Frontiers: Settlement, Society, and Development in the Preindustrial Era*. Lexington: University Press of Kentucky.

Noe, Kenneth W. 1994: *Southwest Virginia's Railroad: Modernization and the Sectional Crisis*. Urbana: University of Illinois Press.

Noe, Kenneth W. and Wilson, Shannon H. (eds.) 1997: *The Civil War in Appalachia: Collected Essays*. Knoxville: University of Tennessee Press.

Paludan, Phillip S. 1981: *Victims: A True Story of the Civil War*. Knoxville: University of Tennessee Press.

Puckett, John L. 1989: *Foxfire Reconsidered: A Twenty-Year Experiment in Progressive Education*. Urbana: University of Illinois Press.

Pudup, Mary Beth, Billings, Dwight B., and Waller, Altina L. (eds.) 1995: *Appalachia in the Making: The Mountain South in the Nineteenth Century*. Chapel Hill: University of North Carolina Press.

Puglisi, Michael (ed.) 1997: *Diversity and Accommodation: Essays on the Cultural Composition of the Virginia Frontier*. Knoxville: University of Tennessee Press.

Rasmussen, Barbara 1994: *Absentee Landowning and Exploitation in West Virginia, 1760–1920*. Lexington: University Press of Kentucky.

Reed, John Shelton 1986: *Southern Folk, Plain and Fancy: Native White Social Types*. Athens: University of Georgia Press.

Salstrom, Paul 1994: *Appalachia's Path to Dependency: Rethinking a Region's Economic History, 1730–1940*. Lexington: University Press of Kentucky.

Shapiro, Henry D. 1978: *Appalachia on Our Mind: The Southern Mountains and Mountaineers in the American Consciousness, 1870–1920*. Chapel Hill: University of North Carolina Press.

Shifflett, Crandall A. 1991: *Coal Towns: Life, Work, and Culture in Company Towns of Southern Appalachia, 1880–1960*. Knoxville: University of Tennessee Press.

Stealey, John E., III 1993: *The Antebellum Kanawha Salt Business and Western Markets*. Lexington: University Press of Kentucky.

Thomas, Jerry Bruce 1998: *An Appalachian New Deal: West Virginia in the Great Depression*. Lexington: University Press of Kentucky.

Trotter, Joe William, Jr. 1990: *Coal, Class, and Color: Blacks in Southern West Virginia, 1915–1932*. Urbana: University of Illinois Press.

Waller, Altina L. 1988: *Feud: Hatfields, McCoys, and Social Change in Appalachia, 1860–1900*. Chapel Hill: University of North Carolina Press.

Whisnant, David E. 1980: *Modernizing the Mountaineer: People, Power, and Planning in Appalachia*. Boone, NC: Appalachian Consortium Press. Revd edn 1994: Knoxville: University of Tennessee Press.

Whisnant, David E. 1983: *All That is Native and Fine: The Politics of Culture in an American Region*. Chapel Hill: University of North Carolina Press.

Williams, Cratis D. 1961: The Southern Mountaineer in Fact and Fiction. Ph.D. dissertation, New York University.

Williams, David 1993: *The Georgia Gold Rush: Twenty-niners, Cherokees, and Gold Fever*. Columbia: University of South Carolina Press.

Williams, John Alexander 1976: *West Virginia and the Captains of Industry*. Morgantown: West Virginia University Library.

Williams, John Alexander 1984: *West Virginia, A History*. New York: W. W. Norton.

Williamson, J. W. 1995: *Hillbillyland: What the Movies Did to the Mountains and What the Mountains Did to the Movies*. Chapel Hill: University of North Carolina Press.

CHAPTER TWENTY-THREE

Religion in the American South Since the Civil War

PAUL HARVEY

IN the 1920s H. L. Mencken slammed the South as "a cesspool of Baptists, a miasma of Methodism, snake-charmers, phony real-estate operators, and syphilitic evangelists" (quoted in Wilson 1995: 2). In the 1930s John Dollard's *Caste and Class in a Southern Town* (1937) underscored how southern churches reinforced the caste system of the region. In his 1941 classic *Mind of the South*, Wilbur J. Cash said that there was no mind of the South but only a temperament torn between a "hell-of-a-fellow" sociability and a primitive religious fundamentalism.

In recent years, however, the South has undergone a renaissance. With it has come a revitalized scholarship, largely freed of older defensiveness and denominational hagiography on the one hand and academic iconoclasm on the other. In the 1960s and 1970s an initial burst of interest in southern religious history, spurred on by both the civil rights movement and the resistance to it, established the field. Works by scholars such as Samuel S. Hill Jr. (1967), John B. Boles (1972), and Donald G. Mathews (1977) ushered in an era of serious historical inquiry that continues today. Meanwhile, the burgeoning field of slavery studies produced classics in the study of antebellum southern religion, most notably Eugene D. Genovese's provocative *Roll, Jordan, Roll* (1974) and Albert J. Raboteau's synthetic *Slave Religion: The "Invisible Institution" in the Antebellum South* (1978). Most recently, Christine Leigh Heyrman's *Southern Cross: The Beginnings of the Bible Belt* (1997), focusing on the early days of southern evangelicals and their accommodation to the moral reality of a patriarchal slave society, shows how much can still be gleaned from rereading the sources with a fresh set of questions.

If religion in the Old South has become a mature field, scholarship on the era since the Civil War is still, relatively speaking, in its adolescence. As a result, many of the works discussed here date from the last decade. Questions remain as to whether studies in post-Civil War southern religion will add detail to, or fundamentally change, dominant paradigms for understanding southern history. For example, women's historians seeking to understand social reform in the South repeatedly have discovered religion at the center of it. In the process they have added significantly to the body of literature on southern religion, even though many of the studies are about other topics. Some important areas, such as the history of southern Pentecostalism, cry out for more research. There is hardly any substantial scholarship on some key figures, such as Charles Harrison Mason, founder of the Memphis-based black Pentecostal Church of God in Christ. Some topics (such as Appalachian mountain religious expression) have drawn the attention of anthropologists but not often of historians. The area also lacks a general study that serves as the equivalent of Donald Mathews's *Religion in the Old South* (1977). However, the impact of a new generation of scholarship and the recent establishment of the *Journal of Southern Religion* (one of the first of a growing number of wholly online journals, with the permanent web address of http://purl.org/jsr) will provide an agenda for the scholarly future.

Any discussion of southern religion must begin with the landmark works of Samuel S. Hill Jr., whose 1967 *Southern Churches in Crisis* and subsequent books, including *Religion in the Solid South* (1972) and *The South and the North in American Religion* (1980), defined the field. If historians, as the cliché goes, are divided into lumpers and splitters, Hill is a classic "lumper." That is, Hill's original work concerned itself not with variety and diversity within a tradition so much as with what unites the tradition, what made southern religion *southern*. Focusing almost exclusively on whites, *Southern Churches in Crisis* defined the archetypal "culture-religion" of the South. Southern Christianity was more experiential and emotional, less doctrinal and intellectual than religion outside the region. Southern orthodoxy, according to Hill, has been characterized by an inward-looking conservatism that sees individual conversion (rather than social reform or any larger purpose) as the central role of religious institutions – an argument later dubbed the "conversionist paradigm." Southern believers historically have seen their own region as a Zion, set apart from the secularizing currents of the rest of the country, and more pure, more godly. Thus, southern believers have been "otherworldly" even while theologically defending the southern status quo. *Southern Churches in Crisis* evinced considerable skepticism about whether there were any forces that could break the stranglehold of the insular nature of southern belief patterns. One of Hill's contemporaries, John Lee Eighmy, provided a useful catch phrase to summarize this argument in his work *Churches in Cultural Captivity*, published originally in 1972. Eighmy's work was actually mildly revisionist, as he traced the impact of a limited social gospel in early twentieth-century southern religious life (especially in the Prohibition movement). Yet his book is remembered now primarily for the phrase "cultural captivity," as it encapsulated (if also oversimplified) the arguments made by this first generation of scholars.

As Hill and Eighmy wrote, a new generation of scholars recovered the history of African-Americans as agents, over and above being victims or foils to white histories. Scholars have also investigated more thoroughly the religious history of southern whites, providing greater empirical data and new conceptual understanding to that topic. The fruits of this research on the white and black religious histories of the South appear in a number of recent studies, including Daniel W. Stowell's *Rebuilding Zion: The Religious Reconstruction of the South, 1863–1877* (1998). Stowell studies Baptists, Methodists, and Presbyterians in Georgia and Tennessee, states with Civil War and Reconstruction-era histories indicative of the experience of the Upper South and the Deep South. He traces the development and interaction of three religious "visions" for the religious life of the postwar South. The first vision, variously labeled "southern" (meaning *white* southern) or (more accurately) "Confederate," suggested that God's purpose in the Civil War and Reconstruction was to purify "His people" (white southerners) for greater glory. The second part of Stowell's story follows the Yankee missionaries and their few southern religious allies who pursued a policy of political and ecclesiastical reunion together with an effort towards "the evangelization and Christianization of the benighted South and its black and white inhabitants" (Stowell 1998: 7). Finally, the third vision expressed itself in Christian freedpeople together with black northern missionaries creating separate and independent religious denominations, institutionalizing the African-American dream of political citizenship and ecclesiastical freedom. In the end, Stowell argues, none of the three visions triumphed completely or failed totally; as Lincoln expressed it in his Second Inaugural Address, "the prayers of both could not be answered; that of neither has been answered fully." Yet the evidence Stowell presents certainly suggests that some prayers were more equal than others. By the 1890s, Stowell recounts, northern denominations had very nearly left the South completely. African-Americans escaped the bondage of white religious dictates, yet the Promised Land was nowhere in sight. It was a somewhat altered yet still recognizably Confederate vision, ultimately, that was the victor: "the [white] southern vision prevailed through its unyielding commitment to the Confederate interpretation of the Civil War" (Stowell 1998: 178).

Stowell's work, focusing on religious institutions after the war, is nicely complemented by William E. Montgomery's synoptic and more culturally analytical account, *Under Their Own Vine and Fig Tree: The African-American Church in the South, 1865–1900* (1993). Montgomery's work brings together numerous studies on post-Civil War black evangelicalism, including notable works by James Melvin Washington on the formation of the black National Baptist Convention (1986) and studies of the rise of the AME church in the South by Clarence Walker (1982) and Stephen Angell (1992). Montgomery's argument emphasizes the "merging" of the folk religiosity of the slaves with the institutional churches of American denominationalism brought to the South by northern missionaries. The resulting black denominations were "complex and factious" (Montgomery 1993: xii) precisely because of their mixed heritage. Overnight, a northern denomination such as the African Methodist Episcopal (AME) Church became a predominantly southern institution as black Methodist leaders welcomed legions of ex-slaves into their ranks and attempted to teach them the ways of "dignified" and "rational" worship. Montgomery offers a compelling look at the controversies over "the spirit of worship," arising out of the continued vitality of folk traditions in countryside churches: "The differences between the folk churches of the antebellum slaves and the denominational churches of northern blacks . . . produced tension within the merging black communities of the postwar period" (ibid: 305). Mongtomery carefully assesses the church and black nationalism, finding the church divided within itself between integrationism and separatism and thus voicing a multiplicity of views from conservative accommodationism to radical separatism. While carefully noting the divisions that sometimes paralyzed churches and recognizing the expediently calibrated ecclesiastical response to the rise of Jim Crow, Montgomery nevertheless stresses how the church was "an important instrument for the steady advancement of African-Americans" (ibid: 5). If not outstandingly innovative, Montgomery's work provides an indispensable resource for future studies of post-Civil War black churches. Readers of Montgomery's work will also want to consult James Campbell's magnificent *Songs of Zion: The African Methodist Episcopal Church in the United States and South Africa* (1995), although the majority of the work concerns the antebellum North and AME mission churches in South Africa.

Evelyn Brooks Higginbotham's theoretically informed and influential *Righteous Discontent: The Women's Movement in the Black Baptist Church, 1880–1920* (1993) is the first serious and extended study that places black women at the center of African-American religious life. As Higginbotham shows, since women made up over 60 percent of black Baptist church congregants and Baptists claimed over 60 percent of the black churchgoing population, black Baptist women must be at the center of post-Civil War southern and African-American religious history. Though not advertised as specifically "southern," the preponderance of women in the church were southerners. Higginbotham narrates the remarkable careers of black Baptist women who organized missionary societies, notably Virginia Broughton, Lucy Cook, and (especially) Nannie Helen Burroughs. She argues that women in the black Baptist Convention forged a space, a "public sphere," for themselves, outside the dictates of the male-dominated convention structures. Organized into the Woman's Auxiliary of the National Baptist Convention, black Baptist women such as Burroughs pursued racial justice politics, progressive reform, and racial uplift. If their distinctly bourgeois agenda sometimes misunderstood or repressed the expressive choices of black working-class women, they nonetheless seized the limited means available to resist the imposition of Jim Crow. They also articulated a nascent but powerful "feminist theology" that challenged the masculinist tone and style of the male church leader-ship. Higginbotham's work has been widely cited among historians in several fields, not least because of the sophisticated situating of her analysis in postmodernist discourse (opened up by Jürgen Habermas and Mikhail Bakhtin) about the multiple "weapons of the weak" open to subjugated groups.

Montgomery, Higginbotham, and others have provided excellent accounts of black southern religion from the Civil War through the Progressive Era. White southern religion receives equally sophisticated study in Beth Barton Schweiger's *The Gospel Working Up: Progress and the Pulpit in Nineteenth-Century Virginia* (2000), a work based on a database of 800 white Baptist and Methodist ministers in Virginia from 1830 to 1900. Schweiger insists that southern religious leaders expressed the strivings of an aspiring and progressive people and were not the reactionary toadies of a landed elite. These Virginia ministers used religious institutions as a springboard from which to launch their own bourgeois aspirations. They served as advocates, Schweiger explains, for good religion, good roads, and good education. Many of the ministers served as superintendents of education and in other important bodies, consistently taking positions that put them at the forefront of what would later become the southern Progressive movement. Schweiger's briskly written work provides the most vigorous challenge to date of the Hill–Eighmy cultural captivity thesis. It should serve to awaken studies of white churches, which have not matched the innovative scholarship that has graced black religious history.

The lumper tradition in this field has been well represented by the older works of Samuel Hill and Donald Mathews, who understood southern evangelicalism as a solid and singular formation. More recently "splitter" historians have emerged; they look into the crevices of the formation and find contrasting layers and individually interesting pebbles. Christopher H. Owen's *The Sacred Flame of Love: Methodism and Society in Nineteenth-Century Georgia* (1998) and Paul Harvey's *Redeeming the South: Religious Cultures and Racial Identities Among Southern Baptists, 1865–1925* (1997) have provided two recent studies of this sort. Each monograph also shows the possibilities of, and the difficulties involved in, writing biracial histories of southern religion that comprehend whites and blacks in relationship to one another. Owen draws on the Troeltschian "despised sect to established church" paradigm as the framework for his analysis, as he traces the rise of the Methodist church in Georgia from the late eighteenth century to the Civil War. Owen then details the postwar alliance of convenience between the AME church (black) and the Methodist Episcopal Church, South (white). Both possessed an interest in resisting encroachments from the northern Methodist church, which confidently moved into the region but gained only a few adherents. In the late nineteenth century, as southern Methodism modernized, the appeal of old-time Methodism remained strong among the people who were southern evangelicalism's original base of support, farmers and plain folks in the upcountry. They increasingly turned to Holiness associations to provide the emotional warmth and "old-time religion" that established town churches had forsaken in favor of civic religion and social benevolence – a story covered in considerably more detail in Briane Turley's work on the Holiness movement in late-nineteenth-century Georgia (Turley 1999). By the 1890s the split between the two was particularly bitter precisely because Methodism was so well represented in both places, unlike the overwhelmingly rural Baptists and the predominantly urban Presbyterians and Episcopalians.

Paul Harvey's *Redeeming the South*, although covering a somewhat different time period, follows a similar track to Owen's. Harvey traces the rebuilding of the white Southern Baptist Convention from its lowpoint after the Civil War to its becoming a denominational behemoth in the twentieth century. He parallels this story with the creation of a black Baptist denominational world, solidified in the creation of the National Baptist Convention in 1895, which itself grew to be the largest black religious formation in the country. Harvey's work, like Owen's, emphasizes tensions, contradictions, and ambiguities, finding that the struggle between traditionalists and progressives characterized the history of both white and black Baptists (seen especially in the struggle over what constituted "intelligent" worship practices). Like Owen as well, Harvey's narrative does not fully integrate the "white" story and the "black" story but places them along two parallel tracks. The difficulty of writing a truly integrative biracial history of southern religion sets a compelling challenge for the next generation of scholarship.

Harvey and Owen's works represent recent trends of emphasizing diversity and variety even in mainstream and established southern denominations. Middle-class denominational leaders of both races, for example, certainly realized that the folk in the pews were hardly poster children for respectability but were instead given to ecstatic expressions as well as bitter infighting and theological disputation. Southern evangelical culture also varied greatly by subregion – between city and country, Southeast and Southwest, Virginia and Texas, Florida and Kentucky, the Appalachian mountains and the lowcountry, the piney woods and the Black Belt, the Dust Bowl and the Florida swamplands. Where historians have (until recently) generalized about the regional religion, scholars from other disciplines, especially folklore, musicology, and religious studies, have brought their expertise into the study of practices that exist on the margins of dominant evangelicalism. Pioneered by Lawrence Levine's *Black Culture and Black Consciousness: Afro-American Folk Thought from Slavery to Freedom* (1997), scholars have addressed subjects such as ring shouts, conjure rituals, chanted sermonizing, and blues hollers. In such activities, students of religious culture have discovered a rich tradition of black expressive culture underneath the smothering rhetoric of "uplift" pervading black church organizations. Notable works to be discussed here are Jon Spencer's provocative extended essay *Blues and Evil* (1993) and Yvonne Chireau's sweeping study *Black Magic: Dimensions of the Supernatural in African-American Religion* (2000). For white churches, Deborah McCauley's *Appalachian Mountain Religion* (1995) covers many of the same issues of folk sacred expression in the context of an urbanizing and secularizing region. Meanwhile, recent (if still considerably underdeveloped) work on southern Pentecostalism has investigated these avenues for southern folk religious tradition (see Woods 1997).

In *Blues and Evil*, Jon Spencer (1993), a prolific author in the field of black theomusicology (the study of the theology of black musical forms and lyrics), depicts rural southern bluesmen as folk theologians who asked serious questions about the nature of evil and lampooned the hypocrisies of supposedly respectable community leaders. The blues, he argues, was one medium for older African-derived spiritualities driven underground by the assimilationist tendencies of late-nineteenth-century black religious leaders. Bluesmen spun tales of their selling their souls to the devil – most famously, Robert Johnson's story of selling his soul to the devil at the crossroads – but they may have done so, Spencer speculates, precisely because they were not that frightened of the evil presence. Closer to the trickster gods of Africa than to the darkly powerful Satan of Western Christianity, the devil in African-American folklore was a force at once attractive, amusing, and frightening, just as were the bluesmen themselves. As Spencer summarizes, the country blues "tended to be more ritualistic than performance oriented, . . . tended to be more priestly than artistic, . . . tended to be more committed than merely appreciative" (Spencer 1993: 95). The preachers and the bluesmen pitted themselves as ferocious competitors in a zero-sum game. They offered two seemingly contradictory but ultimately complementary versions of black folk spirituality. Providing neither the collective solace of spirituals nor the optimistic swing of gospel, the blues instead commented on the inability of humans to sustain relationships, improve their condition, or encounter the Sacred as something other than a trickster. The country blues sketched a collective folk theodicy that spoke truth to power but also reinforced social enmities.

The power of folk traditions as both internally cohesive and destructive forces receives sweeping historical analysis in Yvonne Chireau's (2000) study of four centuries of *Black Magic*. Chireau's work provides a most fascinating contribution to the long ongoing discussion of "magic" and "religion," of how informally envisioned and formally/theologically wrought worlds of the supernatural interact, collide, complement, and supplement one another. Chireau shows how, for African-Americans both slave and free, religion and magic provided complementary strategies to deal with the most philosophical and long-range (religion) as well as the most immediate and practical (magic) needs of their spiritual and quotidian lives. She offers wonderfully textured narratives and analyses of how conjure and magic provided psychological sustenance against the overwhelming power blacks faced in white America, and at the same time she shows how destructive and internally divisive conjuration could be within the African-American world. Additionally, Chireau pulls together research on how the belief patterns and practices of conjure found their way into African-American Pentecostalism, the Spiritualist churches in New Orleans and elsewhere, and the blues. Chireau also analyzes the commodification of this folk culture in new urban settings, in "High John the Conqueror" potions and the like. The Reverend Charles Harrison Mason, to cite another example, invoked conjure magic and Christianity alike in his spiritual performances at the mother congregation of the Church of God in Christ, merging chanted sermonizing with supernatural healing and the manipulation of root bags. Spiritualist churches scattered through the Crescent City also brought legacies from the conjure world (roots, candles, ointments, chants, and notions of bodily possession) into urban religious settings, attracting a clientele of recent urban migrants.

In the Appalachian mountains, another distinctive subregional religious tradition with considerable folk supernaturalistic roots of its own lived on in the face of the rise to respectability of the southern denominations. Deborah Vansau McCauley's (1995) work *Appalachian Mountain Religion* should be required reading for all who would too quickly adopt a unitary label of "southern evangelicalism." As McCauley demonstrates in a wonderful series of historical chapters, mountain religious worship and theology derive from a mixture of Scots–Irish "sacramental revivalism," German Pietism, colonial Baptist revival culture, and the anti-missions impulse in the southern backcountry. All of these came together after the camp meetings of the early nineteenth century (centered in the Upland South, particularly in Cane Ridge in Kentucky) to form what later became "mountain religion." In the antebellum era, as the benevolent empire began its march through America's religious heartland, religious folk in the Upland South took a determined stand against the increasingly Arminian theology of standard American evangelicalism. They remained true to their doctrines of waiting with a "sweet hope" for the action of the Spirit. Later in the nineteenth century, Protestant denominations began extensive home missions work in the mountains, disparaging the vital religiosity of the people while ignoring the tradition of native preaching. This continued in the twentieth century with the retranslation of "Social Gospel" ideas into current-day "liberation theology" in the mountains, again assuming the paternalist's prerogative of shining the light of true religion to deprived folk. McCauley's penchant for lambasting denominationalism, the flip side of her loving description of mountain worship ways, is overdone. At the level of actual practice, thousands of southern churches across the region remained much more closely tied to traditionalist practices than McCauley would allow. Interspersed with the historical and sociological chapters are accounts of religious services and tales drawn from the lives of contemporary mountain preachers. To McCauley's synthetic and highly academic survey may be added a corpus of literature, mostly by anthropologists and sociologists, who have studied specific mountain traditions, preachers, and musicians, including Elaine Lawless's (1988) study of Pentecostal women's preaching and religious expression in the Upper South, David Kimborough's (1995) analysis of Kentucky snake handlers, and Howard Dorgan's numerous works on Primitive Baptist traditions (see, for example, Dorgan 1989).

Holiness-Pentecostalism in the South awaits its own scholarly breakthrough literature. Mickey Crews's *The Church of God: A Social History* (1990) provides one pioneering denominational history of the Church of God, Cleveland, Tennessee. But the most illuminating study to date remains David Edwin Harrell's (1985) biographical treatment of Oral Roberts. Born in 1918 to Pentecostal parents, the future faith-healing evangelist's mother marked him for special service, an anointing confirmed when, at age seventeen, Roberts felt the Lord heal him of the tuberculosis that had long bedeviled him. Roberts became an itinerant minister in the Pentecostal Holiness Church (a denomination based in Franklin Springs, Georgia, and concentrated in the southeastern states). Early in his ministry Roberts itinerated through the cities and small towns of the South, setting up gigantic tents and attracting tens of thousands of excited spectators to his special divine healing services. His name and personal ministry outgrew the provincial hold of the Pentecostal Holiness Church, creating one of America's first interdenominational megachurch establishments. As he joined the more established church world, he yearned to be recognized by establishment figures themselves. Billy Graham and others took him under their wing and helped him shed his bumpkin image. When Roberts opened his own university in Tulsa, he did not make professors sign denominational pledges. He looked favorably on any charismatic ministry, whether in the Pentecostal church or in older established denominations. Harrell's biography joins a very short shelf of critical and biographical studies of Pentecostalism. Given Pentecostalism's origins as an outgrowth (in part) of the preaching of a black minister (William L. Seymour) native to Louisiana, and its subsequent history as currently the fastest growing brand of Protestantism worldwide, the history of southern Holiness/Pentecostalism remains a most fertile field for exploration.

Approaches drawn from cultural studies have influenced many recent religious history scholars. One who has incorporated those methods with particular success has been Charles Reagan Wilson, director of the Center for the Study of Southern Culture at the University of Mississippi and author of the widely read *Baptized in Blood* (1980). Wilson argues that white southerners after the war created a new civil religion, one with its own theology, myths, rituals, and saints. Lost Cause evangelists placed white southerners squarely in God's hands and propounded a mythical interpretation of the past that exalted the deeds of the fallen heroes. Wilson focuses especially on John William Jones, an elite Virginia minister and historian and author of *Christ in the Camp* (1887), an early work detailing the impact of revivals in the Confederate army. Jones was a Lost Cause itinerant who campaigned for South-wide memorial days to sanctify the memory of the Confederacy. The Lost Cause religion also served to instill a deep conservatism in the white southern churches, to exalt the past rather than look to the future. God's people (white southerners), according to the tenets of Lost Cause theology, were baptized in blood and thus had been purified. "Redemption" served as the perfect slogan to describe the end of Reconstruction, for it married the political events of the 1860s and 1870s to the religious imagery increasingly favored by white southern conservative elites.

Wilson's work should be read in conjunction with Gaines Foster's *Ghosts of the Confederacy* (1987). Foster demonstrates how, in the early twentieth century, the Lost Cause evolved into a predominantly middle-class movement that served New South leaders who wanted to pay homage to a moonlight-and-magnolias past before rushing off to a future of industry. Wilson's work also contrasts with much of the newer "splitter" scholarship, which emphasizes the diversity and variety to be found even in white southern evangelical churches and depicts ministers who served as agents of bourgeois progress and change. All that being said, Wilson's anthropologically informed work will remain required reading for southern historians.

Wilson extends his approach in *Judgment and Grace in Dixie* (1995), a compilation of essays that collectively provide a picture of "folk" and "popular" religion in the South (terms Wilson carefully defines, drawing on the work of folklorist Donald Yoder). Wilson discusses topics ranging from religion in Faulkner and the deification of Elvis to church fans, religious symbolism in the funeral of Paul "Bear" Bryant, death themes in country music, beauty pageants, and services at the First Baptist Church of Dallas. The overall thesis emerges in " 'God's Project': Southern Civil Religion, 1920–1980," the most effective essay in the collection. Wilson believes that the common evangelical heritage of southerners, white and black, may lead to a new civil religion in which the difficult and painful truths of the southern past may teach humility and a sense of history to a nation noticeably lacking in both. Wilson spends some time on black cultural symbology, but his major theme is the white working-class South. He is aware of the faults of the regional religion, its anti-intellectualism, its long refusal to countenance African-Americans as equal partners in "God's project." But he sees the potential for the traditional southern virtues of humility and gentle politeness in everyday life reigning in the equally historically rooted traditions of violence and oppression. Whether this optimism is applicable to an increasingly urbanized and multicultural South remains to be seen.

Ted Ownby's *Subduing Satan: Religion, Recreation, and Manhood in the Rural South, 1865–1920* (1990) also employs a cultural studies approach. Ownby describes and explains the "tension between the extremes of masculine aggressiveness and home-centered evangelicalism" that "gave white Southern culture its emotionally charged nature" (Ownby 1990: 14). Part one of *Subduing Satan* portrays "male culture," focusing especially on hunting, drinking, carousing in town, attending professional entertainments, mocking preachers, and generally raising hell. The second, more somber third of the work describes evangelical culture at home, in the church, and in the revival meeting. The male honor and self-assertion required by notions of southern honor was the antithesis of the self-denial and humbling implicit in the evangelical code. This explains, Ownby argues, why evangelical conversions required great struggle and were often emotional – the "self" really did have to be defeated. Even if evangelicalism was never as all-pervasive as the believers hoped, "people who rarely attended church and who lived far outside the evangelicals' moral code nevertheless found ways to express their belief in the virtues of the dominant religion" (ibid: 162). Because so much of male culture took place in isolated locales – on the hunting fields, in the backwoods tippling house, in the shady part of town – the church did not have to discipline society as a whole but could be content to police members. Later in the nineteenth century, discipline within churches declined dramatically. Meanwhile, the male honor culture seemed increasingly repellent to postwar middle-class southern boosters. The personal excesses required by the honor code were inimical to the construction of a bourgeois order in the South, which required the inculcation of methodical accumulation. Evangelicals then, Ownby contends, moved from church discipline to disciplining society as a whole, most particularly in the Prohibition movement.

While offering a fresh understanding of post-Civil War southern culture, Ownby's work sometimes conflates gender "ideal types" with the actual behavior of men and women. The current wave of scholarship in women's history has emphasized how the "cult of true womanhood," while powerful as an image, was itself riddled with contradictions and often ignored in personal behavior. Indeed, gender remains one of the great areas for further research in southern religious history. The pioneering scholars have been Anne Firor Scott and Jacquelyn Hall, historians not identified specifically as doing "religious history" but who have laid the groundwork for studies in this field.

Anne Firor Scott's *The Southern Lady: From Pedestal to Politics* (1970) has influenced now more than one generation of scholars. Scott was one of the first to take southern women's history into the modern feminist-influenced era of scholarship. Scott's work, sometimes explicitly and sometimes by implication, also showed the central importance of the church to southern women's lives. More to the point here, Scott's important 1972 article "Women, Religion, and Social Change in the South" was one of the first to link the large-scale organizing of women's missionary societies in the nineteenth century and the movement of women into Progressive Era reform in the twentieth century.

Jacquelyn D. Hall's *Revolt Against Chivalry* (1979) also remains essential reading. Hall traces the story of Jesse Daniel Ames, a Texas native, businesswoman, and Methodist who in the early 1920s became involved with the Commission on Interracial Cooperation, a group organized by Nashville Methodist minister Will Alexander in response to the shocking violence of the Red Summer of 1919. An independent woman, strong-minded and entrepreneurial, Ames in the 1920s formed the Association of Southern Women for the Prevention of Lynching. In the 1930s the Association collected tens of thousands of signatures imploring southern sheriffs to restrain mob violence against black suspects. At the same time, as Hall makes poignantly clear, Ames resisted the very political measures (such as federal anti-lynching legislation) that most clearly might have punished perpetrators of the violence. Still, Ames successfully organized thousands of southern church women (mostly Methodists) who made some of the first tentative steps outside the enclosed garden of a pseudo-chivalry. Hall's deeply insightful biography probes Ames's psychological motivations as well as her numerous connections in the church world, showing both the great possibilities as well as the self-imposed limitations of southern white liberalism during these years.

The pioneering works of Hall and Scott now have several worthy successors (and several more on the way in dissertation form), that look at the context of religion, social reform, and women's lives in the South. Elizabeth Hayes Turner's *Women, Culture, and Community: Religion and Reform in Galveston, 1880–1920* (1997) is a well-documented study that refines Scott's thesis about the progression from missionary society to progressive reform. Turner focuses on Galveston, where an entirely new city, and consequently social order, had to be reconstructed after the 1900 hurricane (and the old city government's inability to respond adequately) leveled everything in its path. In the late nineteenth century, argues Turner, women developed public leadership roles in church, first through memorials, cemeteries, and music programs, expressing a different, more aesthetic vision of church than men did. Presbyterian, Jewish, and Episcopalian women especially took the lead. Women transformed churches into multifaceted institutions that focused on family needs. In the early twentieth century, women in churches that deemphasized a traditional sense of "missions" and placed believers instead in social reform work provided the female foot soldiers for progressive battles. Episcopal, Presbyterian, and Jewish women staffed progressive health and community groups (most importantly, the local Women's Health Protective Association). Women's missionary societies and the WCTU, dominated by Baptist and Methodist women, played virtually no role in the creation of a coterie of progressive female reformers in Galveston. The YWCA was the only group where upper-class and more middle-class and working women served together; the YWCA's explicitly Christian emphasis attracted evangelical women, while the goal of reaching young working women appealed to the socially conscious Episcopalian and Presbyterian parishioners. Likewise, suffragist leaders came from the same groups, "because in these churches status and wealth interfaced with a strong tradition of community service" (Turner 1997: 270). Turner concludes that the active participation of Presbyterian, Episcopalian, and Jewish women in socially progressive secular organizations and their "relative inactivity in church prayer groups and women's societies suggests that civic-mindedness, a sense of status, and notions of the unfairness of woman's political inequality were at heart more important motivators than faith" (ibid). Turner's local study compels a rethinking of Scott's original (and tentative) hypothesis about the connection between women's religious societies and social change in the Progressive Era South.

Glenda E. Gilmore's passionately written study, *Gender and Jim Crow: Women and the Politics of White Supremacy in North Carolina 1896–1920* (1996), provides a striking counterpoint to Turner's findings, for in the black world, evangelical women were at the forefront of politics. Gilmore argues that women entered the political sphere by demanding resources from the Progressive Era state after whites closed ranks around segregation and disfranchisement laws and ejected black men from the electoral political realm. As Gilmore explains, "contact between black and white women came about not because the two groups felt gender solidarity but because white women controlled the resources that black women needed to improve their communities" (ibid: 172). Gilmore traces the tentative steps of black and white women in North Carolina WCTU chapters. Black women, she argues, tried to use the temperance society to "build a Christian community that could serve as a model of interracial cooperation on other fronts" (ibid: 49). White women, however, envisioned such cooperation as helping the less fortunate. The small but emerging black middle class adopted what Gilmore terms the "Best Man" and "Best Woman" ideology of the age, as class distinctions grew in the African-American community. Sarah Dudley Pettey, wife of an African Methodist Episcopal Zion bishop and heroine of the first half of Gilmore's work, believed that the Black Best Woman would have to speak for uneducated women of her race. After the Wilmington riot of 1898, which Gilmore depicts in chilling and fresh detail, disfranchisement closed off the electoral realm. In the second half of the work Gilmore argues that political activity among black women increased after disfranchisement. Women in churches, WCTU chapters, and clubs provided both an ideological basis and an organizational structure from which black women challenged the notion that Progressivism was "for whites only." Gilmore's stirring study ends with the meeting of white and black church women in Memphis in 1921, organized by the Commission on Interracial Cooperation. At the convention, Charlotte Hawkins Brown (black North Carolina educator) evoked the pain of racial injustice for the white assemblage, some of whom (such as Jesse Daniel Ames) subsequently devoted careers to racial reformism. The Memphis convention set an agenda for women interested in working for racial reform but as yet unable to directly attack the Jim Crow system. They served as a bridge from Jim Crow's darkest days to the beginnings of the civil rights movement. Methodist women who fought first for laity rights in their own denomination soon found themselves at the cutting edge of white racial liberalism, as detailed in John Patrick McDowell's (1982) study of southern Methodist women's missionary societies.

Gilmore ends her work optimistically, reminding her readers that what appears to us a defeat (the failure of blacks to forestall the imposition of Jim Crow) established important precedents for organizing work. Thus, Gilmore's study serves as a sort of prologue to understanding the later civil rights movement. And to understand the movement, one must grapple with its deep grounding in southern religious understandings of sin, grace, redemption, and conversion. In looking at the civil rights movement, scholars have come to a new understanding of, and appreciation for, southern religion itself.

As he took over the pulpit of Ebenezer Baptist in Montgomery, intent on preaching and finishing his studies at Boston University, Martin Luther King had no idea of the history that was about to overtake him, but long-time community activists such as JoAnne Gibson Robinson and E. D. Nixon quickly recognized the usefulness of the young doctoral student. David Garrow's *Bearing the Cross: Martin Luther King, Jr., and the Southern Christian Leadership Conference* (1988) provides a landmark scholarly biography that places King firmly in the context both of his southern religious roots as well as his northern theological training and his connections with political organizers outside the church world such as Bayard Rustin. Garrow places much emphasis on King's second conversion experience, sitting alone in his kitchen one night in the mid-1950s, agonizing over the pressures of being a young minister suddenly lifted to national prominence by the movement. King's spiritual vision that night steeled him for the battles to come, including the numerous attempts on his life and the constant internecine struggles within movement organizations. Garrow details King's battles within his home denomination, the National Baptist Convention, the denomination to which his father had devoted his life. Garrow also follows the rise and internal workings of the Southern Christian Leadership Conference (SCLC), and its ability (through sagacity and luck) both to stumble into as well as to intentionally provoke salutary confrontations with Jim Crow's enforcers.

Another seminal work in religion and civil rights is Aldon D. Morris's *The Origins of the Civil Rights Movement: Black Communities Organizing for Change* (1984). He begins his story not with Montgomery but with an earlier boycott led by black Baptist pastor T. D. Jemison in Baton Rouge, Louisiana, in 1953, an action that set the stage for mass mobilizations to come. Morris follows events in well-known arenas such as the Montgomery bus boycott as well as lesser-known venues, concluding with the "planned exercise in mass disruption" (Morris 1984: 229) in Birmingham, Alabama, in 1963. Morris refers to the SCLC as the "decentralized arm of the black church" (ibid: 77). Throughout the work he argues strongly for the central role of churches in organizing and carrying out the black freedom struggle, noting that only an indigenous organization such as the church could have served so effectively as an agent of mass mobilization. Organizers for the Student Non-Violent Coordinating Committee (SNCC) and other groups built on this model of leadership, one that depended on great internal organization as well as charismatic leadership to endure repression and emerge triumphant in the national arena. The argument advanced by Morris is furthered by Andrew Manis's (1999) memorable biography of Fred Shuttlesworth, which shows the longtime Baptist pastor in Birmingham at the forefront of civil rights crusades in this most brutally racist of southern cities long before the more well-known names from SCLC showed up in 1963. Shuttlesworth's relentless drive for equal rights, captured in Manis's title *A Fire You Can't Put Out*, persisted despite numerous attempts on his life and despite the heavy price Shuttlesworth paid in his personal life because of the requirements of his public role as civil rights leader.

What Morris refers to as "Movement Halfway Houses" – including the Southern Conference Educational Fund, the Fellowship of Reconciliation, the Fellowship of Southern Churchmen, and (most notably) the Highlander Folk School in Tennessee – have also drawn increasing attention in more recent literature. Historians have searched out southerners who challenged Jim Crow in the years before the civil rights movement, including New Deal liberals such as Virginia Foster Durr, benevolent paternalists such as Willis Duke Weatherford, and reformists affiliated with the Southern Conference on Human Welfare. John Egerton's *Speak Now Against the Day: The Generation Before the Civil Rights Movement in the South* (1974) provides an interpretive synthesis of this literature. Egerton deals only in small bits with religion *per se*, as he argues that churches as institutions (not unlike universities) were conservative and cautious in dealing with racial matters, but that individuals imbued with religious ideals often strode out ahead of their complacent church homes.

Among this group, but going far beyond liberalism in his radical commitment to Christian community, was a Southern Baptist-trained minister named Clarence Jordan, founder of Koinonia farm in Southwest Georgia, between Americus and Albany. Jordan's legendary work has now finally received extended scholarly study in Tracy Elaine K'Meyer's *Interracialism and Christian Community in the Postwar South: The Story of Koinonia Farm* (1997). Begun in 1942 as a kind of home mission rural settlement, the farm attracted a small group of evangelicals equally interested in progressive farming, biracial evangelical outreach, and interracial Christian communalism. Always a Southern Baptist in theology, and nationally known in the 1960s for his "cotton patch" translation of the gospels, Jordan placed his faith in Christian individuals living together in community as his answer to the race problem. Jordan's vision of complete economic sharing, however, inevitably contradicted his equally fervent vision of whites and blacks living together in community. Local blacks needed economic opportunity and stability and could ill-afford to dump their meager resources into a community pot, a reality that Jordan understood very well. Attempts by local authorities and vigilantes to drive out the farm from Sumter County further frayed the small and fragile community. Koinonia attracted numerous visitors from national church groups who assumed that the farm was there primarily to establish a base for civil rights activities, despite Jordan's repeated explanations that Koinonia was foremost an experiment in Christian communalism. Though it harbored black activists such as Charles Sherrod and other SNCC members involved in movement activities in Albany, Clarence Jordan resisted SNCC's philosophy of active non-violence, clinging instead to a Quaker-like faith in nonresistance and a progressive farmer's belief in economic independence.

Clarence Jordan is an example of an "inside agitator," a white southerner who employed the deepest assumptions (including religious beliefs) of the white South to undermine the very segregationist system cherished by white southerners. David L. Chappell's *Inside Agitators: White Southerners in the Civil Rights Movement* (1994) follows the stories of the white men and women who became movement supporters, whether quiet and behind the scenes or out in public. Chappell draws heavily from well-known inside agitators such as Virginia Durr, but to his credit he also highlights the lesser-known folk who provided necessary behind-the-scenes support to the larger public movement's activities. They were in no way responsible for the movement, of course, but many of them felt compelled by Christian belief to reject Jim Crow. Most of them seem to have understood their attraction to the cause in the language of conviction and conversion drawn from their church backgrounds. Chappell also points out that the inability of southern trad-itionalists to come up with compelling prosegregationist biblical arguments (in con-trast to their antebellum forebears, who devised powerful proslavery biblical arguments) hampered defenders of the *ancien régime* in the South, particularly when Jim Crow's opponents drew from such a deep well of biblical mythology for their cause.

Egerton and Chappell's works both illuminate how churches, themselves conser-vative and even reactionary, often inspired feats of organizing and leadership. This argument also finds support in the black world in Charles M. Payne's compelling study *I've Got the Light of Freedom: The Organizing Tradition and the Mississippi Freedom Struggle* (1995). Payne suggests that religion provided for women the same kind of organizing and sustaining gumption that landownership provided for men in Mississippi. Because there was more religion than there was landownership, women were largely responsible for keeping the movement alive at the grassroots in Mis-sissippi. Men led, he argues, while women organized. The churches themselves were often resistant to movement personnel, fearing retaliation by white landlords. And whites in Mississippi, of course, were experts at coercion both subtle and brutal. After one visit from the White Citizen's Council of Mississippi, a group of leading Mis-sissippi blacks, including the president of the General Baptist Convention in the state, publicly endorsed separate-but-equal education. During the Greenwood campaign, the few liberal whites in the state (including the Reverend Archie Meadows of First Methodist) and civil rights activists came under the surveillance of the notorious Mississippi Sovereignty Commission.

Despite the fearful conservatism of many ministers and the determined resistance of the white Mississippi establishment, black churchgoers (and a few white religious radicals) made up the front lines of the movement. Even Ella Baker, godmother to SNCC and skeptic of organized religion, noted how her mother's religious faith energized her own activism. Although a higher-up in SCLC for two years, she remained suspicious of SCLC's dependence on charismatic leadership (which she considered susceptible to media manipulation) and top-down leadership styles. At the grassroots level, people like Cleveland Jordan of Greenwood made up the rank-and-file of the movement. A Baptist deacon, he boasted a "for-midable knowledge of the Bible" (Payne 1995: 140) that belied his fourth-grade education. Amzie Moore, another legend of the movement, accosted one Holiness minister in this way:

I used to say, "Reverend Robb, you preaching holiness, you say God can do everything. Now don't come back off your profession. If God can do everything and we done dedicated and give this church to God and if God can't take care of his own house, it's got to go, 'cause we gonna have the meetings.''...All these preachers, Baptists, Methodists, claim like they had so much God, but they didn't believe the God they served could keep this white man off him. I used to tell them that white man was their God. If you gon' trust God, trust him for everything. (Payne 1995: 196)

Some ministers felt sufficiently pressured from below to pretend at least to align themselves with the movement. More to the point, the women who filled the majority of church pews had to "have that something on the inside" to inspire them to feats of defiance, and Payne finds that the deep-rooted legacy of black evangelical culture provided that "something." As one poor Mississippi woman explained her conversion to movement activism, "Something hit me like a new religion" (ibid: 231).

Recent studies have emphasized the connection – indirect at times, more evident at others – between black religion and civil rights organizing. Scholars have drawn similar connections between white southern religion and the rise of the contemporary "Religious Right" in politics. Fundamentalism, of course, was once thought to have perished in the embarrassment of the Scopes "monkey trial" of 1925, only to resurrect itself as part of the backlash to the 1960s. In fact, it never died, but went underground through the middle decades of the century. Fundamentalists set about developing networks and schools that prepared them for their reemergence in the 1970s and 1980s as a powerful political force (seen today in the southern-dominated Christian Coalition and in religio-political figures such as Jerry Falwell and Pat Robertson).

The Scopes trial was the turning point, the moment when fundamentalism discovered the necessity of political organizing. Long misunderstood, in large part because of the play and movie *Inherit the Wind*, the closely watched battle is given full-length treatment in Edward J. Larson's *Summer for the Gods: The Scopes Trial and America's Continuing Debate Over Science and Religion* (1997). Like a number of other recent observers, Larson finds that the trial is remembered more for its legacy of interpretation and reinterpretation than for the actual story of what happened there, which is more complicated and nuanced than legend (on either side) would have it. Far from being a simple two-sided battle between the forces of reason and the agents of darkness, the trial had many facets, and it was not even clear at the time which side had "won." The ACLU sought to make the case one of individual conscience over majoritarian tyranny, but Darrow insisted on publicizing the science versus religion aspect of the case (which many in the ACLU considered a publicity stunt on Darrow's part). William Jennings Bryan (with famous incoherence) defended the biblical story of creation, but the prosecution's case was based on the right of local communities to control what was taught in schools. Scholars (such as William L. Poteat of Wake Forest University, who has received perceptive biographical treatment in Randal Hall's recent work) taught evolution at many southern evangelical schools prior to the 1920s with little controversy, and some fundamentalists conceded that evolution might have been biology's rule for animals of a lower order than man. Bryan, a professional speechmaker by that time, had planned to carry on his anti-evolution crusade on the stump until his death, which occurred only a few days after the trial. He died neither of a broken heart (as some said) nor of a busted belly (as Darrow quipped), but rather of natural causes. The legal proceedings ended, as everyone knew they would, with Scopes being charged and fined for breaking the law. An expected major showdown in the state supreme court came to naught, as the court threw out the conviction on a technicality and refused to have anything more to do with the case. Debate over issues related to the trial, however, remains strong, namely the contest between liberty of individual conscience and the rights of the majority in a democracy, seen most recently in debates over the teaching of evolution and creationism.

Despite popular perception, the Scopes trial hardly killed fundamentalism, but it did represent a moment when fundamentalists began to change their tactics. To understand the underground nitty-gritty organizing efforts of southern fundamentalists in the first half of the twentieth century, readers should turn to William Glass's as-yet-unpublished "The Development of Northern Patterns of Fundamentalism in the South, 1900–1950" (1991). Glass traces how southerners learned fundamentalism just as northern conservative evangelicals had earlier, from itinerant Bible teachers in Bible conferences. Conservative southern preachers replicated those meetings in their own region, building allies in the struggle against what they perceived as creeping liberalism in their denominations. Some early fundamentalists stayed in their own denominations to fight liberalism. Others separated and formed denominations and fellowships along the lines of the theological traditions they left. Still others formed interdenominational groups, some explicitly separatist and others trying to be cooperative with all theologically conservative factions regardless of denominational affiliation. Gradually fundamentalists developed a network of schools and colleges (many of which were essentially institutes with informal courses in English Bible for full-time pastors).

Glass ends his study in 1950, just as evangelicals allied with each other in the new National Association of Evangelicals. Southern fundamentalists found new media-savvy spokespersons, took advantage of the Cold War to press the cause of Christianity versus communism, and seized on race as another issue to circle southern conservative wagons. Southern evangelical preachers such as Billy Graham, whose life is perceptively explored in William Martin's *Prophet With Honor: The Billy Graham Story* (1991), capitalized on America's spiritual hunger and Cold War fears – though he insisted on preaching to integrated audiences. Graham created a well-oiled machine of evangelical proselytizing that drew hundreds of thousands of Americans to his crusades, and compelled millions more to watch them on television. Southern evangelicalism had emerged from the shadows and entered the major media limelight.

After the civil rights movement, liberalism in the 1960s, and the Supreme Court's *Roe v. Wade* (1973) decision on abortion, fundamentalists allied with other conservatives in grassroots organizing campaigns, doing precisely what the New Left often preached but rarely practiced. They took over local school boards, filled state legislative seats, and pushed the national Republican Party to the right. While still preaching a pessimistic premillennialism, fundamentalists adopted positions identified with the political Right (including American triumphalism), forming what soon came to be called the "New Religious Political Right." In the 1990s, the Christian Coalition, the brainchild of southern televangelist Pat Robertson and Emory

University-trained southern evangelical historian Ralph Reed, emerged as a major force in national politics.

Led by conservative Texas lawyer Paul Pressler and his theological educator ally Paige Patterson, Southern Baptist fundamentalists took over the largest Protestant denomination in the United States, the Southern Baptist Convention. Theirs was a political masterstroke described in full detail in David T. Morgan's *The New Crusades, the New Holy Land* (1996). The fundamentalists argued that theological modernism and political liberalism were weaning Southern Baptists away from their historically conservative stance. Learning from previous fundamentalist failures, Pressler and Patterson formulated a strategy for ultimate victory: place the right men in the presidency of the SBC, and then use the power of the presidency to appoint only men and women affiliated with the fundamentalist faction to the boards of trustees of the SBC seminaries and to the various agencies of the denomination. An ugly battle for control of the SBC soon ensued, complete with mass rallies at the annual SBC meetings, secret tape-recordings of meetings, locks mysteriously changed on doors, and spies planted in agencies to report evidence of liberalism. By 1991 the fundamentalists (who termed themselves "conservatives") achieved a complete victory. The "moderates" (whom the most polite fundamentalists referred to as "liberals" but other conservatives called "rats" and "skunks") charged that the fundamentalists were leaders of an Inquisition, but they were routed. Nancy T. Ammerman's *Baptist Battles* (1990) and David Stricklin's *A Genealogy of Dissent* (1999) should also be consulted for readers who seek broader historical and sociological explanations for the controversy. But Morgan's book will be essential reading for those who want a clear, blow-by-blow (literally) account.

Studies of southern religion now make up a vital part of American religious history. The imbalance between work on the antebellum and postbellum eras is being redressed. The distorting influence of racial segregation is being dissolved as scholars attempt culturally complex histories of southern religious cultures. The overemphasis on the homogeneity of evangelical Protestantism in the region is giving way to an appreciation of diversity and complexity within the regional religious traditions. Simplistic interpretations of sectarian movements, especially Holiness-Pentecostalism, while still prevalent in American religious history generally, will not survive the coming generation of scholarship on this topic, much of it now unpublished but soon to have a major impact on the field.

Important questions and avenues of scholarship remain. The discovery of southern Jewish history goes on apace. Eli Evans's classic *The Provincials: A Personal History of Jews in the South* (1973) has now been supplemented by other published diaries and studies of Jewish communities in the urban South (Malone 1997; Lewis 1998). Meanwhile, the diversification of the contemporary South brings religious pluralism to the region. Thomas Tweed's study of a Cuban Catholic shrine in Miami (Tweed 1997) is one of the first of what will be many more works on non-Protestant religious expressions in the recent South. Since much of this concerns contemporary groups, anthropologists and sociologists have been the pioneers of this work.

Important questions remain in understanding religion in the present-day South. The new South, symbolized by rising mega-regions such as Atlanta, Dallas, and Houston, stems in part from the successes of local leaders in attracting corporate enterprises to their region. Can southern religion remain "distinctive" in such settings? Is "Sunbelt Religion" a different species than "southern religion," given that the religion of the Sunbelt is attracting business enterprise while the religion of the South historically has provided spiritual comfort to those in relative poverty?

Most importantly, the field awaits a successful integration of scholarship on white and black religious traditions. A number of scholars have attempted studies that present southern religion as the product of mutual interactions, hostilities, and influence between whites and blacks. No one, really, has succeeded fully in that venture yet. Southern religious history since the Civil War awaits the synthetic work that captures southern religious expressive cultures in all their complexity, tragic pain, and reconciling possibilities.

BIBLIOGRAPHY

Ammerman, Nancy Tatom 1990: *Baptist Battles: Social Change and Religious Conflict in the Southern Baptist Convention*. New Brunswick, NJ: Rutgers University Press.

Angell, Stephen Ward 1992: *Bishop Henry McNeal Turner and African-American Religion in the South*. Knoxville: University of Tennessee Press.

Boles, John B. 1972: *The Great Revival, 1787–1905: The Origins of the Southern Evangelical Mind*. Lexington: University Press of Kentucky.

Campbell, James T. 1995: *Songs of Zion: The African Methodist Episcopal Church in the United States and South Africa*. New York: Oxford University Press.

Cash, W. J. 1941: *The Mind of the South*. New York: Alfred A. Knopf.

Chappell, David L. 1994: *Inside Agitators: White Southerners in the Civil Rights Movement*. Baltimore: Johns Hopkins University Press.

Chireau, Yvonne 2000: *Black Magic: Dimensions of the Supernatural in African-American Religion*. Berkeley: University of California Press.

Crews, Mickey 1990: *The Church of God: A Social History*. Knoxville: University of Tennessee Press.

Dollard, John 1937: *Caste and Class in a Southern Town*. New Haven, CT: Yale University Press.

Dorgan, Howard 1989: *The Old Regular Baptists of Central Appalachia: Brothers and Sisters in Hope*. Knoxville: University of Tennessee Press.

Egerton, John 1994: *Speak Now Against the Day: The Generation Before the Civil Rights Movement in the South*. New York: Alfred A. Knopf.

Eighmy, John Lee 1972: *Churches in Cultural Captivity: A History of the Social Attitudes of Southern Baptists*, ed. Samuel S. Hill Jr. Knoxville: University of Tennessee Press.

Evans, Eli N. 1973: *The Provincials: A Personal History of Jews in the South*. New York: Atheneum.

Foster, Gaines M. 1987: *Ghosts of the Confederacy: Defeat, the Lost Cause, and the Emergence of the New South, 1865 to 1913*. New York: Oxford University Press.

Garrow, David J. 1988: *Bearing the Cross: Martin Luther King, Jr., and the Southern Christian Leadership Conference*. New York: Vintage.

Genovese, Eugene D. 1974: *Roll, Jordan, Roll: The World the Slaves Made*. New York: Pantheon Books.

Gilmore, Glenda Elizabeth 1996: *Gender and Jim Crow: Women and the Politics of White Supremacy in North Carolina, 1896–1920*. Chapel Hill and London: University of North Carolina Press.

Glass, William Robert 1991: The Development of Northern Patterns of Fundamentalism in the South, 1900–1950. Ph.D. dissertation, Emory University.

Hall, Jacquelyn Dowd 1979: *Revolt Against Chivalry: Jesse Daniel Ames and the Women's Campaign Against Lynching*. New York: Columbia University Press.

Hall, Randal Lee 2000: *William Louis Poteat: A Leader of the Progressive-Era South*. Lexington: University Press of Kentucky.

Harrell, David Edwin 1985: *Oral Roberts: An American Life*. Bloomington: University Press of Indiana.

Harvey, Paul 1997: *Redeeming the South: Religious Cultures and Racial Identities Among Southern Baptists, 1865–1925*. Chapel Hill: University of North Carolina Press.

Heyrman, Christine Leigh 1997: *Southern Cross: The Beginnings of the Bible Belt*. New York: Alfred A. Knopf.

Higginbotham, Evelyn Brooks 1993: *Righteous Discontent: The Women's Movement in the Black Baptist Church, 1880–1920*. Cambridge, MA: Harvard University Press.

Hill, Samuel S., Jr. 1967: *Southern Churches in Crisis*. New York: Holt, Rinehart, and Winston.

Hill, Samuel S., Jr. (ed.) 1972: *Religion and the Solid South*. Nashville: Abingdon Press.

Hill, Samuel S., Jr. 1980: *The South and the North in American Religion*. Athens: University of Georgia Press.

Jones, J. William 1887: *Christ in the Camp: or, Religion in Lee's Army*. Richmond, VA: B. F. Johnson.

Journal of Southern Religion: http://purl.org/jsr

K'Meyer, Tracy Elaine 1997: *Interracialism and Christian Community in the Postwar South: The Story of Koinonia Farm*. Charlottesville: University Press of Virginia.

Kimbrough, David L. 1995: *Taking Up Serpents: Snake Handlers of Eastern Kentucky*. Chapel Hill: University of North Carolina Press.

Larson, Edward J. 1997: *Summer for the Gods: The Scopes Trial and America's Continuing Debate Over Science and Religion*. New York: Basic Books.

Lawless, Elaine J. 1988: *God's Peculiar People: Women's Voices and Folk Tradition in a Pentecostal Church*. Lexington: University Press of Kentucky.

Levine, Lawrence H. 1977: *Black Culture and Black Consciousness: Afro-American Folk Thought from Slavery to Freedom*. New York: Oxford University Press.

Lewis, Selma S. 1998: *A Biblical People in the Bible Belt: The Jewish Community of Memphis, Tennessee, 1840s–1960s*. Macon, GA: Mercer University Press.

McCauley, Deborah Vansau 1995: *Appalachian Mountain Religion: A History*. Urbana: University of Illinois Press.

McDowell, John Patrick 1982: *The Social Gospel in the South: The Woman's Home Mission Movement in the Methodist Episcopal Church, South, 1886–1939*. Baton Rouge: Louisiana State University Press.

Malone, Bobbie 1997: *Rabbi Max Heller: Reformer, Zionist, Southerner, 1860–1929*. Tuscaloosa: University of Alabama Press.

Manis, Andrew 1999: *A Fire You Can't Put Out: The Civil Rights Life of Birmingham's Reverend Fred Shuttlesworth*. Tuscaloosa: University of Alabama Press.

Martin, William J. 1991: *Prophet With Honor: The Billy Graham Story*. New York: William Morrow.

Mathews, Donald G. 1977: *Religion in the Old South*. Chicago: University of Chicago Press.

Montgomery, William E. 1993: *Under Their Own Vine and Fig Tree: The African-American Church in the South, 1865–1900*. Baton Rouge: Louisiana State University Press.

Morgan, David T. 1996: *The New Crusades, the New Holy Land: Conflict in the Southern Baptist Convention, 1969–1991*. Tuscaloosa: University of Alabama Press.

Morris, Aldon D. 1984: *The Origins of the Civil Rights Movement: Black Communities Organizing for Change*. New York: Free Press.

Owen, Christopher H. 1998: *The Sacred Flame of Love: Methodism and Society in Nineteenth-Century Georgia*. Athens: University of Georgia Press.

Ownby, Ted 1990: *Subduing Satan: Religion, Recreation, and Manhood in the Rural South, 1865–1920*. Chapel Hill: University of North Carolina Press.

Payne, Charles M. 1995: *I've Got the Light of Freedom: The Organizing Tradition and the Mississippi Freedom Struggle*. Berkeley: University of California Press.

Raboteau, Albert J. 1978: *Slave Religion: The "Invisible Institution" in the Antebellum South*. New York: Oxford University Press.

Schweiger, Beth Barton 2000: *The Gospel Working Up: Progress and the Pulpit in Nineteenth-Century Virginia*. New York: Oxford University Press.

Scott, Anne Firor 1970: *The Southern Lady: From Pedestal to Politics, 1830–1930*. Chicago: University of Chicago Press.

Scott, Anne Firor 1972: Women, Religion, and Social Change in the South, 1830–1930. In Samuel S. Hill (ed.), *Religion and the Solid South*. Nashville: Abingdon Press.

Spencer, Jon Michael 1993: *Blues and Evil*. Knoxville: University of Tennessee Press.

Stowell, Daniel W. 1998: *Rebuilding Zion: The Religious Reconstruction of the South, 1863–1877*. New York: Oxford University Press.

Stricklin, David 1999: *A Genealogy of Dissent: The Culture of Progressive Protest in Southern Baptist Life, 1920–1995*. Lexington: University Press of Kentucky.

Turley, Briane K. 1999: "A Wheel Within a Wheel": Southern Methodism and the Georgia Holiness Association. Ph.D. dissertation, University of Virginia. Forthcoming from Mercer University Press.

Turner, Elizabeth Hayes 1997: *Women, Culture, and Community: Religion and Reform in Galveston, 1880–1920*. New York: Oxford University Press.

Tweed, Thomas A. 1997: *Our Lady of the Exile: Diasporic Religion at a Cuban Catholic Shrine in Miami*. New York: Oxford University Press.

Walker, Clarence Earl 1982: *A Rock in a Weary Land: The African Methodist Episcopal Church during the Civil War and Reconstruction*. Baton Rouge: Louisiana State University Press.

Washington, James Melvin 1986: *Frustrated Fellowship: The Black Baptist Quest for Social Power*. Macon, GA: Mercer University Press.

Wilson, Charles Reagan 1980: *Baptized in Blood: The Religion of the Lost Cause, 1865–1920*. Athens: University of Georgia Press.

Wilson, Charles Reagan 1995: *Judgment and Grace in Dixie: Southern Faiths from Faulkner to Elvis*. Athens: University of Georgia Press.

Woods, Daniel Glenn 1997: Living in the Presence of God: Enthusiasm, Authority, and Negotiation in the Practice of Pentecostal Holiness. Ph.D. dissertation, University of Mississippi.

PART V

The Modern South

CHAPTER TWENTY-FOUR

Southern Environmental History

MART A. STEWART

ENVIRONMENTAL history is both old and new in the South. The efforts of scholars to unearth the complex history of the South have always required some consideration of the history of the land southerners have lived on and the climate they lived in. Until well into the twentieth century, the South was an agricultural region, and every attempt by historians to understand, as Lewis Gray explained his mission at the outset of his now-classic *History of Agriculture in the Southern United States to 1860*, "the way of life of a great section of a country which was almost entirely agricultural," has required a close look at the interaction of cultivators and the cultivated (Gray 1933, I: xi). And one of Gray's contemporaries, Ulrich B. Phillips, urged students of the South's history "to begin with the weather, for that has been the chief agency in making the South distinctive" (Phillips 1929: 3). Historians of medicine, of African-American culture, and of the peculiar regimens of specific staple crops have also often promoted the importance of the environment of the region that has come to be known as the South.

But for these historians nature has been a given and mainly the scene in which historical action has taken place. The intricacy of human interactions with nature, and the agency of nature itself as a powerful historical force, can seldom be found in traditional agricultural history or other studies of southerners and the land. Though environmental history is a relatively new field that is only now developing interpretative perspectives and key issues and debates, in southern history it has had scant development at all. Many works of southern history have been sensitive to the environment, but few are *environmental*. Nonetheless, environmental history has historiographical ancestors in southern history, and several key works have been published in the field in the more recent past.

Environmental historians of the South need not begin, as have historians of the West, with Frederick Jackson Turner. Turner's frontier thesis implicitly recognized the importance of geography and the interaction between humans and the environment. But no consideration of the South's long agricultural history can ignore the avid student of Turner's, Avery Craven. Craven took his master's degree at Harvard with Turner in 1914, and in his early books Craven followed his mentor's lead in identifying and spatializing stages of economic and political development.

Craven's most important work was decidedly – and perhaps, deliberately – an antifrontier history. In *Soil Exhaustion as a Factor in the Agricultural History of Virginia and Maryland, 1606–1860*, first published in 1926, Craven studied "old" America, the part that had been left behind and that had been "exhausted" by the skimming practices of frontier farmers. Though the concept of "soil exhaustion," which was central to Craven's argument, is essentially – and narrowly – agricultural, it is also about an interaction between humans and nature. The first farmers in Virginia merely *mined* the soil, he argued, and thereby created an environmental problem that undermined the social and economic order of early Virginia. He joined with his antebellum Virginia heroes, John Taylor and Edmund Ruffin, in roundly condemning the farming practices of frontier farmers and in celebrating the problem-solving skills and practices of progressive agriculturists. By the 1850s, he argued, Ruffin's soil improvement system had been adopted by a significant number of Chesapeake planters, who laid the groundwork for a revivified Chesapeake agriculture.

Geographer Rupert Vance, a contemporary of Craven's who worked with the group of social scientists who called themselves the Chapel Hill Regionalists, also celebrated the efficacy of human actions against or in harmony with nature. The Regionalists sought to identify a factual foundation for New Deal-style regional housekeeping, a goal that assumed that comprehensive planning – rational human agency and applications of the new discipline of regionalism – could identify funda-mental regional patterns of all kinds and facilitate a better adaptation to nature. Their portrayal of the region solidified around an affirmation of the importance of geography as part of the organic whole that was the culture of each region, but in the end the Regionalists emphasized the power of human action. Vance was especially interested in considering the relationship between the physiographic features of the South and the cultural evolution of the region, and he shaped an argument that deliberately focused on the relationship between humans and nature. In his important study *Human Geography of the South*, Vance argued that humans "[have] not evolved in a vacuum, and... when nature prevents she also determines," but "history, not geography, made the solid South" (Vance 1932: 482). Environment and humans interacted in an organic relationship that developed a distinctive shape in each region, Vance and the Regionalists assumed, and the physiography of the South provided both conditions and constraints for the cultural evolution of the area.

In spite of the focus on the interaction of humans and the environment by these scholars, historians of the South gave scant attention to the environment even while the field of environmental history bloomed elsewhere. The first study of the South that was deliberately environmental was Albert Cowdrey's *This Land, This South: An Environmental History*, published in 1983. Cowdrey attempted a task he himself admits was "daunting:" to survey the environmental history of the South from the beginning of human habitation to the present. He accomplished this task by present-ing his study in a series of essays and by focusing on some subjects and excluding others. The book is strong, for example, on the engineering of the Mississippi River and on the problems southerners have had with a hostile "disease environment," but scarcely mentions the Pee Dee and Savannah Rivers or the Great Dismal Swamp. And it gives more attention to the snail darter than to the development of the sprawling automobile landscapes of the metropolitan Sunbelt. As a grand summary that looks mainly at the rural and wild environments of the South and that does not so much advance an argument as yield a persuasive point of view, Cowdrey's book was a real benchmark in the development of environmental history of the South. For many years, *This Land, This South* was virtually the only book-length environmental history of the South available.

Several article-length studies were important in the development of the field in the 1980s, however. In the long term, the most important of these has been Steven Hahn's "Hunting, Fishing, and Foraging: Common Rights and Class Relations in the Postbellum South," published in *Radical History Review* in 1982. This fine-grained and deeply researched article about the closure of the "commons" in the South, but especially in South Carolina and Georgia, linked the "grid of use rights," especially on lands that were uncultivated, with "basic social relationships" (Hahn 1982: 37). In the aftermath of the emancipation of the slaves, he argues, modification of many of these use rights by trespass, enclosure, game and stock laws resulted in "skirmishes... [that] helped define the longer meaning of sectional reconciliation" (ibid). The effective enclosure of lands that were once open for hunting, fishing, foraging, and, most importantly, the free ranging of livestock, severely handicapped white and black semi-subsistence farmers who depended on access to uncultivated lands, whoever they belonged to, for part of their sustenance.

Use rights and the labor issue after emancipation were deeply linked, Hahn argues. When white property owners were able to restrict poorer whites and blacks from access to important resources, they also amplified their dependence on wage or share labor. Everywhere commercial farming advanced in the 1870s and 1880s, enclosure laws followed. Those whose economic independence were restricted by such laws resisted haphazardly but with a common sensibility about rights to the land that eventually "formed the heart of an emergent popular radicalism that would be harnessed by Populism" (ibid: 57).

Hahn might be surprised to have this essay tagged as environmental history, yet it made an important analytical advance in linking the practice of land use with social relationships. The land itself scarcely appears, except as marked out by the "grid of use rights." Historians have to go elsewhere to find out what cattle ate, where the cornfields were, whether this region was hilly or flat, what the relationship of water-ways to farmsteads was, and what kinds of birds and animals filled the pots of yeoman farmers. But Hahn's essay explains how even the "wild" parts of the southern environment were cross-hatched with social and racial relationships. The environment, then, was not simply something "out there" that was used, abused, or left alone but the terrain of important class and social contests.

Environmental history in the 1980s was transformed by several pioneering studies that brought together social history and historical ecology. Instead of merely identifying environmental problems and "damage," and analyzing how human behavior had caused them, a new environmental history took seriously William Cronon's argument, in *Changes in the Land: Indians, Colonists, and the Ecology of New England* (1983), that when historians studied the different livelihoods created by different groups of people, they needed to understand how these livelihoods were composed of ecological as well as social and economic relationships. Cronon also pioneered a regional approach to environmental history that encouraged historians to take into account the findings of ecologists when reconstructing past environments and marking the changes caused in them by their human occupants. Timothy Silver's *A New Face on the Countryside: Indians, Colonists, and Slaves in South Atlantic Forests, 1500–1800*, published in 1990 as part of the prestigious Cambridge University Press Studies in Environment and History series, took advantage of these analytical advances and pushed them in a direction that revealed the complex social and environmental history of the colonial South. *A New Face* also linked social conflict and land use but was much more explicit than Hahn and other social and agricultural historians in identifying the complexity of these links.

Silver's region of focus stretches from the South Atlantic to the Appalachians, an area that was originally largely forested and that was carved up by the British into the colonies of Virginia, South and North Carolina, and Georgia. Between the first contacts of Indians and Europeans and the cotton boom in the 1790s, he explains, the development of these areas, population growth, and the introduction of varieties of resource exploitation that were new to the Americas drastically changed the face of the countryside. Euro-American attempts to "improve" on nature and to manipulate it for commercial purposes transformed forests into farmland, replaced wild animals with domestic ones, and wrenched South Atlantic ecosystems into new alignments. At the same time, Europeans and Africans supplanted Native Americans as the primary population groups in the region.

Silver in this study does not claim a paradise lost. He does not revive an older declensionist paradigm for understanding ecological change, and he does not explain the changes he outlines by testing them against a static model of ecosystem health or by measuring them against an imagined pristine state of nature. And Indians, in this study, are not the first ecologists. Silver makes it abundantly clear that all humans, Native Americans included, are agents of change in nature.

Europeans intensified and accelerated change, however. Though Native Americans used fire to hunt game and clear land, Europeans bumped that use up to the conflagration level. In the process, he explains, they disturbed natural ecosystems beyond their ability to recover some measure of diversity and health. Though Silver strongly implies this change was sometimes damage, his analysis of countryside faces, new and old, is noticeably unsentimental. He makes it clear that the story of the interaction between humans and nature is always a story about change, and he recognizes that humans are always in a process, good or bad, of remaking their relationships with nature.

A New Face made an important advance among historians of the South and connected the environmental history of the South with important and influential work that had been done in the 1980s by environmental historians elsewhere. It looked carefully at a specific region, identified the complex changes in the physical environment wrought by human hands in the region, and considered both the social and ecological consequences of those changes.

How environments are racialized or riven by class, ethnicity, and other social relationships has become an important area of study for environmental historians in general in the 1990s. Several scholars have published benchmark works in southern environmental studies that take as fundamental the social construction of the environment. Essential to this area of study has been the work of sociologist Robert D. Bullard. His *Dumping in Dixie: Race, Class and Environmental Equality* (1990) has been important to historians who are studying the uneven control of environments along class and race lines in the modern South. Bullard argued that because of their "political and economic vulnerability," black communities in the South have suffered more than others from "environmental stressors" produced by toxin-producing industries, hazardous waste landfills, toxic waste dumps, and other environmental hazards. In the 1980s, one-third of the hazardous waste landfills in the United States were located in five southern states (Alabama, Louisiana, Oklahoma, South Carolina, and Texas), and all of them were sited in places where neighboring residents were largely black and always poor. This environmental racism has been especially intense in the South because of the plantation-economy legacy, the history of racism, and an approach to economic development by southern leaders that has emphasized economic growth over environmental protection.

Communities threatened by "environmental stressors" have often organized to protest environmental inequalities. And in the five case studies Bullard includes (Northwood Manor in Houston; West Dallas; Institute, West Virginia; Alsen, Louisiana; and Emelle-Sumter County, Alabama), they have met with varying degrees of success. Several studies since *Dumping in Dixie* was published have questioned and added complexity to Bullard's larger conclusions about environmental racism. But this study of environmental inequalities, grassroots protest, and the politics they have engendered has successfully challenged historians who would write any history of environmental damage and not take into account the relationship between race, class, and the environment.

Though environmental history continues to be weakly developed in the South, the number of studies published that were explicitly environmental began to multiply in the 1990s. Two recent studies successfully integrate the various models for doing environmental history that are represented by earlier studies. Jack Temple Kirby's *Poquosin: A Study of Rural Landscape and Society* (1995) and Mart Stewart's *"What Nature Suffers to Groe": Life, Labor, and Landscape on the Georgia Coast, 1680–1920* (1996) look at specific regions in the South – Kirby, the Abermarle Sound–James River region in Virginia; Stewart, the Coastal Plain and lowcountry of Georgia – and identify the most salient ecological characteristics of these regions. Both studies place at center stage the relationships between humans – but humans of different sorts – and the environment, as these humans engaged in the process of creating and sustaining livelihoods. Both recognize the importance of race, class, and gender in identifying different perspectives on and uses of the land. They also understand that some terrain is contested terrain because of contrasting notions about how the land should be (and was) used. And both books look at environmental change not simply in terms of problems, but of the different landscapes created by different groups of people over the long duration.

Though both *Poquosin* and *"What Nature Suffers to Groe"* take the interdisciplinary approach to the study of humans and nature that is common among environmental historians, they acknowledge the instability of ecology as a guide to reconstructing past environments (Stewart's more deliberately and usefully than Kirby's). By the late 1980s environmental historians had begun to lose the confidence that they could go to scientists, and especially ecologists, to find a usable model of nature to integrate into their scholarly work. The question, "what is nature?" that they needed to answer before they could measure change in nature was no longer clearly answered by ecologists. Ecology also has not escaped history (and increasing complexity) and no longer gives the sure answers that environmental historians could depend upon in the 1970s and early 1980s.

In the 1970s a new generation of ecologists discovered much more disorder, disequilibrium, and disturbance in nature than ecologists had previously imagined. They began to argue that nature is not the relatively stable complex of either organisms or processes that ecologists had earlier in the century said it was. Nature, some have argued, is little more than a fluctuating array of populations of individuals with no inherent ties that bind. The central certainty, these ecologists say, is that things change, and change erratically and unpredictably. The consequence of this shift in the science of the study of nature, according to Donald Worster, who among environmental historians has written most perceptively about this development, has been that environmental historians no longer have a yardstick against which they can measure change. If nature is nothing but a shimmer of populations in space and time, then any effort to explain "nature" and compare human impact against it – other than the most obvious environmental disasters, the dust bowls, toxic waste deserts, and strip mines – becomes only a guessing game. The splendid consensus of the late 1950s and 1960s and on into the 1970s, when ecologists were secure as gurus for the environmental movement and as guides for environmental historians, is gone. Ecologists can no longer provide the sure model of nature against which historians can measure human impact.

Both *Poquosin* and *"What Nature Suffers to Groe"* acknowledge, at least implicitly, that the line demarcating nature from culture can no longer be clearly drawn or borrowed from the studies of scientists without privileging these studies. Instead of focusing just on changes in the land, both books analyze changes in the relationships between humans and the land. *"What Nature Suffers to Groe"* is the more self-conscious of the two books in foregrounding purpose and method and in integrating the insights of previous models in environmental history with a postmodern perspective.

Both books connect insights wrested from interdisciplinary analysis and the methods of modern environmental history with issues that have had long currency in southern history. Kirby builds on and questions the discussion of "soil exhaustion" begun by Avery Craven in *Soil Exhaustion* and introduced again to discussions among historians of southern agriculture in the 1960s by Eugene D. Genovese in a brief chapter in *The Political Economy of Slavery* (Genovese 1965: 85–105). *Poquosin* country is Edmund Ruffin country, and one of the arguments ribboning through Kirby's book is that progressive agriculturists like Ruffin were more important as representatives of the advance of cosmopolitan knowledge and associated market forces than for any resolution they brought to the problem of soil fertility. Kirby also develops a discussion proposed by Carville Earle (1988) in an important article that also questions the uncritical acceptance of Craven's condemnation of frontier farmers. "Hinterland" swidden (slash and burn) farming was better adapted to the soils of Virginia, if "sustainability" was the measure, than the improving methods of reformers.

Among other traditional chestnuts of southern history, *"What Nature Suffers to Groe"* engages the large literature on the political economy of plantations. The book resolves problems that emerge in the discussions of the relationships between ecological and social change by introducing the notion of "landscapes" as a nexus of ecological and social relations. Many cultural geographers, historical archeologists, social anthropologists, historians, and other scholars who have studied the interaction of nature and culture share an understanding of "landscape" as land shaped by human hands and agree that humans create landscapes in accordance with both aesthetic and social values or in order to organize or facilitate certain kinds of production. Landscapes also reflect social and productive relationships and can themselves become modes of production. When planters and slaves constructed tidewater rice and sea island cotton plantations, they not only reinforced a complex of economic and social relationships but created meaningful landscapes as well. Cultivation engraved culture in the land. Landscapes in the lowcountry were both agro-ecosystems and an embodiment of social relations. And within the plantations, planters, plantation mistresses, overseers, and slaves created different, though often overlapping or overlaid, landscapes.

When nature challenged, through a gale or pest invasion or fertility decline, the people who made plantation landscapes were forced to make responses that both shaped and reinforced social relations. Prominent historians of the South have long acknowledged and have more recently demanded that *labor* was the cornerstone of plantation society and should be studied more carefully; *"What Nature Suffers to Groe"* argues that a study of labor *only* gives short shrift to the experience of those who did it, and *labor on the land* must be studied if scholars are to understand the fundamentals of plantation culture – or indeed, of any relationship between a working culture and its environment.

Much of the literature in the larger field of American environmental history has been, up until the mid-1990s, focused on the American West – and much of it, on landscapes that are more arid than any part of the South. Both Stewart and Kirby's books analyze swampy regions, and the environmental and cultural conditions created and reinforced by drainage and hydraulic systems. Several books about the twentieth-century engineering of watery places in the South recapitulate Marc Reisner's observation in *Cadillac Desert*, that outside California, more waterways in the South have been engineered than anywhere else. The successive massive efforts of the Corps along the Mississippi River or the enormous Tennessee Valley Authority project in the New Deal South were important manipulations of nature that have begun to find their historians. The most important of recent studies of attempts to engineer waterways in the South has been Jeffrey Stine's masterful *Mixing the Waters: Environment, Politics, and the Building of the Tennessee–Tombigbee Waterway.* In terms of "earth moved and dollars spent" (Stine 1993: 254), the Tenn–Tom project was the nation's largest water project. The project also had a political and economic complexity that distinguished it from other efforts to engineer American waterways. But the real significance of the Tenn–Tom, Stine argues, is that it was a project that revealed a sea change in attitudes toward large-scale public works in the United States and especially in the South. The Tenn–Tom was built, but only after a long struggle between environmental groups and supporters of the water project. This struggle revealed much about the evolution of environmentalism in this region and in America in the 1970s and 1980s.

Most of *Mixing the Waters* focuses on the architecture of support and defense of the Tenn–Tom and the sources of the opposition to it, and is a political history of environmentalism. But the book also presents a fine-grained account of the massive reconstruction of the environment in the region by the Corps. One can learn here about the Corps' design of river, canal, and divide portions of the waterway, the new disposal concept of dredged material developed by the builders of the waterway, the "chain-of-lakes" design, how "cut slopes" were stabilized, what the "Rock Monster" did, and how construction sites were "dewatered." Stine's careful tracking of

the technology of waterway construction constitutes a model study of the relationship of technology and the environment in the modern South.

But environmental politics shaped this relationship at every stage and determined
the final contours of the Tenn–Tom. The waterway was strongly supported by
regional commercial and political interests who were represented by congressmen
who had acquired seniority. It was at first opposed by national environmental groups,
then also by a regional group, CLEAN (the Committee for Leaving the Environment
of America Natural). CLEAN found its most powerful ally in a strange quarter, the
railroads, who were concerned about the waterway's potential for competition in the
hauling of freight. The Tenn–Tom was at first opposed by leaders and organizations
representing the residents who lived in the area along its route – one of the poorest
areas in the South and with a population that was predominantly African-American.
These interests were fairly easily bought out by the builders and supporters of the
Tenn–Tom with promises of jobs for minorities and of improved economic health for
the region.

The waterway was eventually completed but became exactly what its critics said it
was, a boondoggle. Moving freight on the Mississippi was usually faster and cheaper,
even if a longer haul. Shippers there could move freight in thirty-to-forty-barge tows.
The Tenn–Tom could accommodate only eight-barge tows, and the locks slowed
traffic significantly. Most traffic on the waterway was through traffic, and it brought
few economic benefits to the residents along the Tenn–Tom corridor. Bass fishing
boats have been more common than barge traffic on the Tenn–Tom, and pleasure
boats use the waterway to move throughout the South. The Tenn–Tom, like the
numerous lakes built in the South by the US Army Corps of Engineers and by the
TVA, has been more valuable to recreational users than commercial ones. Stine
suggests that this reflects a tendency in the development of water resources in the
South, emphasizing recreational more than other commercial purposes.

Impoverished African-Americans who live in the region have remained poor.
Ironically, the waterway stimulated the waste-dump industry in the region, which
brought something quite different than economic benefits to the area's residents.
One of these, the largest commercial hazardous waste dump in America, was sited in
Emelle, Alabama, where, as Robert Bullard has explained, it reinforced the usual race
and class patterns of dumping in Dixie. The Tenn–Tom not only did not bring
economic opportunity to impoverished African-Americans in rural Alabama, but it
has facilitated yet another kind of exploitation.

"The history of the Tennessee–Tombigbee Waterway reflects many of the crucial
changes in the development of large-scale public works in the United States," Stine
concludes (Stine 1993: 251). The project was conceived, designed, and justified
according to political and cultural values that came from an earlier time, when the
large-scale wrenchings of water resources by public agencies were seen as a positive
good. But the project was caught up in a major change in the "social consensus" on
the appropriate relationship between technology and the environment in the region
and in the nation. Regional and national environmental groups, by way of their
opposition to the waterway, illuminated this deep change. At the same time, they
failed to do what most environmental groups failed to do in the 1970s and 1980s:
link environmental issues with civil rights ones. Environmental politics during the
period was more concerned with environmental quality in terms of the amenities of

the white middle class and usually ignored environmental issues that affected the quality of life of poor people and racial and ethnic minorities. The history of this waterway is not only intrinsically interesting because of magnitude and complexity but because it illuminates the "course of engineering and environmental politics in late twentieth-century America" (ibid: 255), and especially in the South.

The mountain South has also begun to receive attention by environmental historians, most notably in Ronald L. Lewis's *Transforming the Appalachian Countryside: Railroads, Deforestation, and Social Change in West Virginia, 1880–1920* (1998). Lewis explains the arrival of industrial capitalism in the West Virginia countryside – particularly in the state's Allegheny Highland counties – in the late nineteenth century and the institutional, economic, social, and cultural transformation it wrought. In less than fifty years, industrial logging companies stripped West Virginia of most of its hardwood forests, turned them into forest "products," and hauled them on new railroads to larger markets. The subsistence economy that had developed in the woods and that depended on timber for a variety of uses and for cash was also permanently changed. Forest inhabitants became laborers in sawmills and logging camps. When these disappeared, West Virginians who had been backcountry farmers became unemployed laborers, forced to move with the jobs or remain rooted in a derelict landscape and mired in poverty. Those who were able to continue farming were wedded to the market not because they were forced to grow new or inedible commodities, but because they had to expand operations in order to turn a profit.

Lewis draws upon the world-system theory of Immanuel Wallerstein to place the transformation of West Virginia's countryside within the context of the global evolution of industrial capitalism. Lewis's book is not so much about the dynamic compulsions of the "core," however, as about the transformation of social and political institutions and lifeways on the "periphery." Some chapters say very little about the ecological change that accompanied and shaped other changes, but focus instead on cultural and political changes that organized and ratified the commodification of West Virginia forests, on the construction of railroads into the area, on the influx of capital, and on the transformation of law to favor investing capital. Part of the study looks closely at labor practices and logging camp life and on the consequences of the influx of laborers of different ethnic backgrounds. One chapter analyzes the "county seat wars" and the change of local political institutions – a change, Lewis argues, that was powered by economic change (Lewis 1998: 211–34).

The stripping of the hardwood forests of the region was the predominant development in the larger transformation of the Appalachian countryside, however. Lewis's account is overall a tale about a virgin forest despoiled, with very little in the story that adds saving grace (even attempts at conservation were defeated by some of the same forces that were originally opposed to deforestation). Lewis's tale might reveal an appropriate trajectory for any environmental history of Appalachia, though declensionist narratives have attracted considerable criticism recently by historians who question the reductionist views of nature such accounts assume. Forest history in the South is still a vastly underdeveloped field and is likely much richer than lamentations about a forest that has been lost will reveal. Nonetheless, this book constitutes a valuable model for studies both of mountain landscapes and forested ones in the South.

Several essays have begun to reframe a discussion of the South's distinctive climate. Instead of accepting climate as merely an objective force that has shaped culture, historians more recently have identified the conceptual biases that shaped the perceptions of those who have settled and lived in the region. The most influential of recent works is Karen Kupperman's "Fear of Hot Climates in the Anglo-American Colonial Experience" (1984). Kupperman looks at the encounter between Europeans and, simply, hot weather, in the colonial era and explains how they conceptualized this encounter and how they explained away discomfort and anxiety about a climate that appeared so different from northern European ones. Two essays have discussed the relationship between perceptions of the climate and the evolution among elite southerners of an argument or a "problem" that used these perceptions to naturalize a political ideology: Joyce Chaplin's "Climate and Southern Pessimism: The Natural History of an Idea, 1500–1800," in Griffin and Doyle (1995) and Mart Stewart's "'Let Us Begin with the Weather?': Climate, Race, and Cultural Distinctiveness in the American South," in Teich, Porter, and Gustafsson (1997). Stewart's begins a discussion of the relationship between constructions of climate and the evolution of a colonizing science (medicine, especially) in nineteenth-century America that destabilizes traditional southern conceits about climate. And an essay by Ray Arsenault about artificial climates in the South has become a classic. "The End of the Long Hot Summer: The Air Conditioner and Southern Culture" (1984) examines the impact of controlled climates on the culture of the South and the transformation of the hot and humid South to the Sunbelt.

Finally, the South's unique disease environments have received much attention from medical historians, and this literature is a cumulative resource that is of importance to students of the environmental history of the South. A good entry into a discussion of the South's struggle with various maladies is a collection of essays edited by Todd Savitt and James Harvey Young, *Disease and Distinctiveness in the American South* (1988). In an introductory essay, "Disease as a Factor in Southern Distinctiveness," James Breeden surveys the distinctive history of disease and disease environments in the region. Both culture and environment contributed to the South's unique health problems, Breeden explains. The insect vectors for malaria, yellow fever, and typhoid fever thrived in southern environments. Malaria and yellow fever were especially important in gaining for the South a reputation for sickliness – and as "diseases of laziness" in the common image of the "lazy Southerner" (Breeden 1988: 11). The hot summers made the preservation of food difficult, intensified sanitary and public health problems, and encouraged inhabitants to go barefoot (which made them vulnerable to hookworm). In the late nineteenth century, tuberculosis was more common in the South than elsewhere in the United States. Poverty and poor public health services reinforced the distinctive patterns of disease in the South. "After the war (Civil War) as before it," Breeden explains, "the South's health woes set the region apart from the rest of the nation and promoted regional ethnicity" (ibid: 13).

The conquest of yellow fever and malaria and the progressive decline in hookworm in the twentieth century made the region less dangerous, especially to newcomers who had no immunities. The virtual eradication, after World War II, of the vector for malaria, the *Anopheles* mosquito, through the use of DDT in government-sponsored programs, was especially dramatic. Malaria had made the South a land of fever since the disease first became endemic in the early colonial era. The relationship between southerners and disease in the twentieth century was a story of the gradual control of disease environments and of the success of public health programs.

Disease and Distinctiveness includes essays on the most serious of diseases that plagued the South – on malaria, yellow fever, and hookworm – which are, in part, discussions of the environments of these diseases. Several studies have gone much further in explaining the etiology of these diseases and the particular combination of cultural and environmental factors that fostered their success. Darrett and Anita Rutman's essay, "Of Agues and Fevers: Malaria in the Early Chesapeake" (1976), continues to be the place to begin in any study of malaria. More recently, Margaret Humphreys has synthesized the many case studies of yellow fever and discussed the public health campaign that ended yellow fever's reign as "the scourge of the South," in *Yellow Fever and the South*. "Perhaps the most significant characteristic of yellow fever…was the disease's well-marked geographic selectivity" Humphreys explains (Humphreys 1992: 32). Though yellow fever could be a serious threat outside the South, it could be so only in "extraordinary conditions of filth and heat" (ibid). Yellow fever, then, was mainly a disease of southern environments. Culture reinforced geography as the identity of the South came to be connected to this and to other diseases. Finally, the public health measures to control these diseases, especially drainage schemes to destroy mosquito habitats and spraying to kill the mosquito itself, were environmental ones.

Landscapes of forests and fields were often racialized and contested in the South, but diseases made bodies themselves contested terrain. In a chapter on tuberculosis in her study of black working women in Atlanta, *To 'Joy My Freedom: Southern Black Women's Lives and Labors after the Civil War*, Tera Hunter (1997) discusses how southern urban dwellers shaped an understanding of the disease that was both racialized and gendered and at the same time connected to how blacks and whites worked. Tuberculosis became a medium for southern assumptions about racial inequalities and for framing tensions in labor and race relations in southern cities, when whites began to associate the disease with the black domestics who worked in their homes or to whom they sent their laundry. Residential segregation in southern cities kept private black and white spaces entirely separate, but most middle-class whites hired black domestics, who moved across the color line into the homes of white people. Whites used perceptions that these African-Americans were carriers of the disease – a disease, they claimed, that was more common among African-Americans in the urbanizing South than among slaves in the healthier planta-tion South – to encourage live-in domestics and to suggest a return to Old South social relations and a higher level of supervision of African-American servants. Per-ceptions of disease – and especially tuberculosis – became justification for further control of workers who were also black, and especially when they moved into white environments. Demarcations of social space, social and racial expectations, and per-ceptions of disease all converged in the struggles of Atlanta's blacks and whites to master tuberculosis.

Though environmental history in the South has lagged in development to the field elsewhere, it has become a much richer field in the last twenty-five years. At the same time, regional history of any kind has been destabilized by new examinations of the cultural meanings of *region*. A new emphasis on internationalizing American history and on global history has taken historians away from the study of regional and local history. It has also, paradoxically, reinforced the need for the careful study of regional and local history. Interactions between humans and the environment in the past has often been an intensely local affair. And the study of global history also needs the balancing counterpoint of the analyses of terrains of differences, of regions, and of cultural differences because of them and within them. Environmental history of the South, then, will continue to develop and grow, as questions of global versus regional forces acquire significance.

BIBLIOGRAPHY

Aiken, Charles S. 1998: *The Cotton Plantation South Since the Civil War.* Baltimore: Johns Hopkins University Press.

Arsenault, Raymond 1984: The End of the Long Hot Summer: The Air Conditioner and Southern Culture. *Journal of Southern History,* 50 (4): 597–628.

Barry, John M. 1997: *Rising Tide: The Great Mississippi Flood of 1927 and How it Changed America.* New York: Simon and Schuster.

Bartlett, Richard A. 1995: *Troubled Waters: Champion International and the Pigeon River Controversy.* Knoxville: University of Tennessee Press.

Berlin, Ira and Morgan, Philip D. (eds.) 1993: *Cultivation and Culture: Labor and the Shaping of Slave Life in the Americas.* Charlottesville: University of Virginia Press.

Blake, Nelson 1980: *Land into Water – Water into Land: A History of Water Management in Florida.* Tallahassee: University Presses of Florida.

Bonner, James 1964: *A History of Georgia Agriculture, 1732–1860.* Athens: University of Georgia Press.

Breeden, James 1988: Disease as a Factor in Southern Distinctiveness. In Todd L. Savitt and James Harvey Young (eds.), *Disease and Distinctiveness in the American South.* Knoxville: University of Tennessee Press, 1–28.

Breen, T. H. 1985: *Tobacco Culture: The Mentality of the Great Tidewater Planters on the Eve of Revolution.* Princeton, NJ: Princeton University Press.

Brown, Margaret Lynn 2000: *The Wild East: A Biography of the Great Smoky Mountains.* Gainesville: University Press of Florida.

Bullard, Robert D. 1990: *Dumping in Dixie: Race, Class, and Environmental Equality.* Boulder: Westview Press.

Cashin, Joan E. 1994: Landscape and Memory in Antebellum Virginia. *Virginia Magazine of History and Biography,* 102 (4): 477–500.

Chaplin, Joyce E. 1995: Climate and Southern Pessimism: The Natural History of an Idea, 1500–1800. In Larry J. Griffin and Don H. Doyle (eds.), *The South as an American Problem.* Athens: University of Georgia Press.

Clark, Thomas D. 1984: *The Greening of the South: The Recovery of Land and Forest.* Lexington: University of Kentucky Press.

Cobb, James C. 1984: *Industrialization and Southern Society 1877–1984.* Lexington: University Press of Kentucky.

Cotterill, R. S. 1936: *The Old South: The Geographic, Economic, Social, Political, and Cultural Expansion, Institutions, and Nationalism of the Ante-bellum South.* Glendale, CA: Arthur H. Clark.

Cowdrey, Albert E. 1983: *This Land, This South: An Environmental History.* Lexington: University of Kentucky Press.

Craven, Avery 1926: *Soil Exhaustion as a Factor in the Agricultural History of Virginia and Maryland, 1606–1860.* Urbana: University of Illinois Press.

Cronon, William 1983: *Changes in the Land: Indians, Colonists, and the Ecology of New England*. New York: Hill and Wang.

Daniel, Pete 1985: *Breaking the Land: The Transformation of Cotton, Tobacco, and Rice Cultures since 1880*. Urbana: University of Illinois Press.

Davis, Donald Edward 2000: *Where There Are Mountains: An Environmental History of the Southern Appalachians*. Athens: University of Georgia Press.

Dewey, Scott H. 1999: The Fickle Finger of Phosphate: Central Florida Air Pollution and the Failure of Environmental Policy, 1957–1970. *Journal of Southern History*, 65 (3): 565–603.

Dorman, Robert L. 1993: *Revolt of the Provinces: The Regionalist Movement in America, 1920–1945*. Chapel Hill: University of North Carolina Press.

Drobney, Jeffrey A. 1997: *Lumbermen and Log Sawyers: Life, Labor, and Culture in the North Florida Timber Industry, 1830–1930*. Macon, GA: Mercer University Press.

Earle, Carville 1979: Environment, Disease, and Mortality in Early Virginia. In Thad W. Tate and David L. Ammerman (eds.), *The Chesapeake in the Seventeenth Century: Essays on Anglo-American Society*. Chapel Hill: University of North Carolina Press, 96–125.

Earle, Carville 1987: Regional Economic Development West of the Appalachians, 1815–1860. In Robert Mitchell and Paul Groves (eds.), *North America: The Historical Geography of a Changing Continent*. London: Hutchinson, 172–99.

Earle, Carville 1988: The Myth of the Southern Soil Miner: Macrohistory, Agricultural Innovation, and Environmental Change. In Donald Worster (ed.), *The Ends of the Earth: Perspectives on Modern Environmental History*. Cambridge: Cambridge University Press, 175–210.

Earle, Carville and Hoffman, Ronald 1976: Staple Crops and Urban Development in the Eighteenth-century South. In Donald Fleming and Bernard Bailyn (eds.), *Perspectives in American History*. Cambridge: Charles Warren Center, 7 80.

Fisher, Stephen L. (ed.) 1993: *Fighting Back in Appalachia: Traditions of Resistance and Change*. Philadelphia: Temple University Press.

Genovese, Eugene D. 1965: *The Political Economy of Slavery*. New York: Pantheon Books.

Gray, Lewis Cecil 1933: *History of Agriculture in the Southern United States to 1860*, 2 vols. Washington: Carnegie Institution of Washington.

Hahn, Steven 1982: Hunting, Fishing, and Foraging: Common Rights and Class Relations in the Postbellum South. *Radical History Review*, 26: 37–64.

Haygood, Tamara Miner 1986: Cows, Ticks, and Disease: A Medical Interpretation of the Southern Cattle Industry. *Journal of Southern History*, 52 (4): 551–64.

Healy, Robert G. 1985: *Competition for Land in the American South: Agriculture, Human Settlement, and the Environment*. Washington, DC: Conservation Foundation.

Hilliard, Sam Bowers 1972: *Hog Meat and Hoecake: Food Supply in the Old South, 1840–1860*. Carbondale: Southern Illinois University Press.

Hilliard, Sam Bowers 1975: The Tidewater Rice Plantation: An Ingenious Adaptation to Nature. *Geoscience and Man: Coastal Resources*, 12: 57–66.

Hilliard, Sam Bowers 1979: Site Characteristics and Spatial Stability of the Louisiana Sugarcane Industry. *Agricultural History*, 53 (1): 254–69.

Humphreys, Margaret 1992: *Yellow Fever and the South*. New Brunswick, NJ: Rutgers University Press.

Hunter, Tera 1997: *To 'Joy My Freedom: Southern Black Women's Lives and Labors After the Civil War*. Cambridge, MA: Harvard University Press.

Hurley, Andrew (ed.) 1997: *Common Fields: An Environmental History of St. Louis*. St Louis, MO: Historical Society Press.

Jackson, Harvey H. 1995: *Rivers of History: Life on the Coosa, Tallapoosa, Cahaba, and Alabama*. Tuscaloosa: University of Alabama Press.

Jordan-Bychkov, Terry G. 1993: *North American Cattle-Ranching Frontiers: Origins, Diffusion, and Differentiation.* Albuquerque: University of New Mexico Press.

Kiple, Kenneth F. and King, Virginia 1981: *Another Dimension to the Black Diaspora: Diet, Disease, and Racism.* Cambridge: Cambridge University Press.

Kirby, Jack Temple 1987: *Rural Worlds Lost: The American South, 1920–1960.* Baton Rouge: Louisiana State University Press.

Kirby, Jack Temple 1995: *Poquosin: A Study of Rural Landscape and Society.* Chapel Hill: University of North Carolina Press.

Kupperman, Karen Ordahl 1984: Fear of Hot Climates in the Anglo-American Colonial Experience. *William and Mary Quarterly,* 3rd ser. 41: 213–40.

Lewis, Ronald 1998: *Transforming the Appalachian Countryside: Railroads, Deforestation, and Social Change in West Virginia, 1880–1920.* Chapel Hill: University of North Carolina Press.

McCally, David 1999: *The Everglades: An Environmental History.* Gainesville: University Press of Florida.

McDonald, Michael J. and Muldowny, John 1982: *TVA and the Dispossessed: The Resettlement of Population in the Norris Dam Area.* Knoxville: University of Tennessee Press.

MacKethan, Lucinda Hardwick 1980: *The Dream of Arcady: Place and Time in Southern Literature.* Baton Rouge: Louisiana State University Press.

Merrens, H. Roy and Terry, George D. 1984: Dying in Paradise: Malaria, Mortality, and the Perceptual Environment in Colonial South Carolina. *Journal of Southern History,* 50: 533–50.

Miller, David C. 1989: *Dark Eden: The Swamp in Nineteenth-Century American Culture.* Cambridge: Cambridge University Press.

Miller, James J. 1998: *An Environmental History of Northeast Florida.* Gainesville: University Press of Florida.

Mohai, Paul 1990: Black Environmentalism. *Social Science Quarterly,* 71: 744–65.

Numbers, Ronald L. and Savitt, Todd L. (eds.) 1989: *Science and Medicine in the Old South.* Baton Rouge: Louisiana State University Press.

Odum, Howard W. 1936: *Southern Regions of the United States.* Chapel Hill: University of North Carolina Press.

Outland, Robert B., III 1996: Slavery, Work, and the Geography of North Carolina Naval Stores Industry, 1835–1860. *Journal of Southern History,* 62 (1): 27–56.

Percy, William Alexander 1941: *Lanterns on the Levee: Recollections of a Planter's Son.* New York: Alfred A. Knopf.

Phillips, Ulrich Bonner 1929: *Life and Labor in the Old South.* Boston: Little, Brown.

Rasmussen, Barbara 1994: *Absentee Landowning and Exploitation in West Virginia, 1760–1920.* Lexington: University Press of Kentucky.

Reuss, Martin 1998: *Designing the Bayous: The Control of Water in the Atchafalaya Basin, 1800–1995.* Alexandria, VA: Office of History, US Army Corps of Engineers.

Rutman, Darrett B. and Rutman, Anita H. 1976: Of Agues and Fevers: Malaria in the Early Chesapeake. *William and Mary Quarterly,* 33: 31–60.

Savitt, Todd L. and Young, James Harvey (eds.) 1988: *Disease and Distinctiveness in the American South.* Knoxville: University of Tennessee Press.

Silver, Timothy 1990: *A New Face on the Countryside: Indians, Colonists, and Slaves in South Atlantic Forests, 1500–1800.* Cambridge: Cambridge University Press.

Steinberg, Theodore 1997: Do-It-Yourself Deathscape: The Unnatural History of Natural Disaster in South Florida. *Environmental History,* 2 (4): 414–38.

Stewart, Mart A. 1991a: Rice, Water, and Power: Landscapes of Domination and Resistance in the Lowcountry, 1790–1880. *Environmental History Review,* 15 (3): 47–64.

Stewart, Mart A. 1991b: "Whether Wast, Deodand, or Stray": Cattle, Culture, and the Environment in Early Georgia. *Agricultural History,* 65: 1–28.

Stewart, Mart A. 1996: *"What Nature Suffers to Groe": Life, Labor, and Landscape on the Georgia Coast, 1680–1920*. Athens: University of Georgia Press.

Stewart, Mart A. 1997: "Let us Begin with the Weather?": Climate, Race, and Cultural Distinctiveness in the American South. In Mikulá Teich, Roy Porter, and Bo Gustafsson (eds.), *Nature and Society in Historical Context*. Cambridge: Cambridge University Press, 240–56.

Stewart, Mart A. 1998: The Natural Environment: The South. In Mary Kupiec Cayton, Elliott J. Gorn, and Peter W. Williams (eds.), *Encyclopedia of American Social History*. New York: Charles Scribner's Sons.

Stine, Jeffrey K. 1993: *Mixing the Waters: Environment, Politics, and the Building of the Tennessee–Tombigbee Waterway*. Akron: University of Akron Press.

Strom, Claire 2000: Texas Fever and the Dispossession of the Southern Yeoman Farmer. *Journal of Southern History*, 66 (1): 49–74.

Valenĉius, Conevery Bolton 2002: *The Health of the Country: How American Settlers Understood Themselves and Their Land*. New York: Basic Books

Vance, Rupert 1932: *Human Geography of the South: A Study in Regional Resources and Human Adequacy*. Chapel Hill: University of North Carolina Press, 3–23, 357–79, 482–4.

Warner, John Harley 1985: The Idea of Southern Medical Distinctiveness: Medical Knowledge and Practice in the Old South. In Ronald L. Numbers and Todd L. Savitt (eds.), *Science and Medicine in the Old South*. Baton Rouge: Louisiana State University Press, 179–205.

Warren, Christopher 1997: Northern Chills, Southern Fevers: Race-specific Mortality in American Cities, 1730–1900. *Journal of Southern History*, 63 (1): 23–6.

Wetherington, Mark V. 1994: *The New South Comes to Wiregrass Georgia: 1860–1910*. Knoxville: University of Tennessee Press.

Worster, Donald 1990: Transformation of the Earth: Toward an Agroecological Perspective in History. *Journal of American History*, 76 (4): 1,087–106.

Worster, Donald 1994: *Nature's Economy: A History of Ecological Ideas*. Cambridge: Cambridge University Press.

Young, Jeffrey 1991: Ideology and Death on a Savannah River Rice Plantation, 1833–1867: Paternalism Amidst "A Good Supply of Disease and Pain." *Journal of Southern History*, 59 (4): 673–706.

CHAPTER TWENTY-FIVE

Labor Relations in the Industrializing South

Daniel Letwin

FROM the Gilded Age to the Nuclear Age, most southerners were working folk. Regardless of station, those who lived by their hands were bound by common threads of experience. Like workers everywhere, they aspired to fulfilling labor, dignified treatment, material comfort, civic esteem, and a stable future. Like workers across industrializing America, they strained to reconcile the promise of democracy with the dislocations of emergent capitalism. But they also faced circumstances distinctive to their region; not least, slow economic development, raw exploitation of labor, sharp repression of unionism, and steadfast neglect of popular concerns.

Yet for all they shared in common, New South workers were a study in diversity. Male and female, black and white, native-born and foreign, settled and mobile, paid and unpaid, skilled and unskilled, aged and juvenile, they toiled across a mosaic of farmlands, railroads, forests, factories, coalmines, docks, laundries, homes, craftshops, and offices. How and on what terms southerners worked were matters inseparable from their standing in society, from their self-identity, from their sense of where the line lay between "us" and "them." No strand of southern life can be fully grasped without regard to issues of labor; no serious chronicle of working-class America can slight the South.

Still, the vitality of Dixie's labor past has not always emerged in either field. Consider how the topic looked as recently as 1965. The South, it was widely thought, had precious little labor history to speak of. Few monographs on the subject were in the works; few overviews of the modern South gave it much prominence; few histories of American labor cast more than a sidelong glance below the Mason-Dixon Line. This is not to suggest that the field was barren. A visit to a good library could turn up sketches of Black Belt sharecroppers, Appalachian coalminers, Gulf Coast longshoremen, and, most abundantly, Piedmont textile workers. Yet most of these treatments were dated, the product of journalists, activists, or social scientists. Much of what historians had to offer was compressed into general surveys on southern or labor history.

Why was the field so thin just a few decades back? In part, this merely reflected the pallor of working-class history at large. Most who examined that marginal slice of the national past focused on unions and institutional politics. Through this lens, southern labor itself seemed marginal. But entrenched assumptions about the region played their part as well. According to received wisdom, the common people of Dixie were steeped in a culture of docility, individualism, and racial division, opening them up to paternal control and closing them off to collective action. Essentially a variant on the theme of regional exceptionalism, images like these gave the story of southern labor a two-dimensional quality. The picture was not, of course, unvaried. Depictions of employers ran from benevolent reformer to rapacious capitalist; of workers, from hopeful object of New South uplift to hapless object of New South avarice. (The benign outlook found its classic expression in Broadus Mitchell's *The Rise of Cotton Mills in the South*, 1921; the dismal portrayal, in Frank Tannenbaum's *Darker Phases of the South*, 1924: 39–73, or W. J. Cash's *The Mind of the South*, 1941.) Either way, a dominant strain of passivity and subordination was taken to be pervasive, if not congenital. For much of the past century, the perpetual weakness of southern labor was raised more as an explanation for other outcomes – for example, the limited achievements of American unionism, the persistence of southern poverty, or the protracted reign of Bourbon Democracy – than as an outcome itself to be explored. It was a perspective that did little to prompt fresh inquiry into the region's working-class past.

Yet by the 1960s other trends were beginning to do just that. The civil rights movement threw into question the proverbial acquiescence of black southerners, spurring interest in earlier waves of resistance. The rise of the New Left awakened younger scholars to forgotten traditions of social protest. At once whetting and reflecting that impulse was a radically new approach to the study of working-class history. Eschewing doctrinaire models of all stripes, practitioners of the "new labor history" traced currents of dissent in every area of workers' lives. Challenging the institutional confines of the older school, they expanded the meanings of "work," and thus the parameters of working class experience. How workers perceived their options and identities in industrializing America was found to be considerably more fluid than previously recognized. By the late 1960s, pioneering "new labor historians" such as Herbert Gutman and David Montgomery were publishing their seminal works, and an army of graduate students were following their lead. (For an introduction to the new labor history, see Arnesen, Greene, and Laurie 1998: 1–15.)

The New South offered a natural frontier for the new labor history. Years earlier, C. Vann Woodward's *Origins of the New South* had skewered the placid assumptions of both Bourbon and "consensus" historiography, presenting instead a region wracked by class and racial conflict. Yet in its initial focus on urban manufacturing centers, the new labor history was slow to look southward. Taking stock of southern labor historiography as it appeared in the mid-1970s, one is struck by how little had changed. To be sure, one dimension of southern labor, slavery, had burst onto the cutting edge of American historical research. But this only accentuated the dearth of attention to New South labor. Perhaps the most widely noted volume to appear in the previous decade was F. Ray Marshall's (1967) historical survey of organized labor in the South, a valuable work, but very much a product of the old school.

The imbalance was not absolute. Important new work, for example, had appeared on labor in the New South farmlands. Pete Daniel's *The Shadow of Slavery: Peonage in the South, 1901–1969* (1972) traced the myriad forms of coercion that ensnared rural laborers of the twentieth-century South. Donald Grubbs's *Cry from the Cotton* (1971) recounted the interracial campaigns of the Southern Tenant Farmers' Union during the Great Depression. Illuminating the experience of black farmers was *All God's Dangers*, the vivid reminiscences of the aged sharecropper and veteran labor activist Ned Cobb (Rosengarten 1974).

There were intriguing glimpses too of industrial life below the Mason-Dixon Line. Some concerned the interplay of racial and class experience, particularly where blacks and whites toiled together. Herbert Gutman pointed the way with an evocative 1968 essay about Richard Davis, a black organizer for the United Mine Workers (UMW), who toured the coal fields from Illinois to Alabama during the 1890s (Gutman 1968). Intermingled with his frustration over the barriers of racism was an abiding faith in labor solidarity. How, Gutman asked, could the odyssey of this obscure unionist be squared with models that depicted "blacks" and "workers" as mutually alienated (and, by implication, mutually exclusive)? Gutman answered in the empathetic spirit of the new labor history: only fine-grained inquiry could reveal "the quality of life and the complexity of thought and feeling of ordinary white and Negro workers" (ibid: 125–6). Endorsing Gutman's intuition were essays by Paul Worthman and James Green on interracial unionism in the mineral district of Alabama and timberlands of the Old Southwest, respectively. The dynamics of race and labor in industrializing America were, it would seem, less fixed and more varied than generally assumed.

Reassessment of the Piedmont textile region was germinating as well. Kicking off the trend was Melton McLaurin's *Paternalism and Protest: Southern Cotton Mill Workers and Organized Labor, 1875–1905* (1971). Resurrecting little-known campaigns of the Knights of Labor and the National Union of Textile Workers, McLaurin challenged the culture-of-docility thesis that had long dominated studies of southern millhands. He attributed the defeats of these early efforts less to the pliability of labor than to the ferocity of management. Yet brute force was only part of the story; vital as well, McLaurin acknowledged, were residual, backcountry strains of individualism and racial xenophobia. That millworkers left their own stamp on the outcome would become a premise of historical writing in the years to come. In what measures their actions bore the stamp of ingrained culture and immediate circumstances would, however, fuel ongoing debate.

By 1975, then, a new ripple of interest in sharecroppers, coalminers, timber workers, and millhands signaled that swelling attention to labor in the slave South and industrial North might soon spill over to the New South. And so it did. A glance at the field just ten years later would disclose an acceleration of research on the farmlands, coalfields, the industrial Piedmont, and urban centers. A biennial Southern Labor History Conference had been inaugurated in 1976, and the proceedings of the first two gatherings had each appeared as edited volumes (Fink and Reed 1977; Reed, Hough, and Fink 1981). Courses on the topic were multiplying, their syllabi filled with current books and articles.

Much of this attention flowed to the industrial Piedmont, where scholars pursued questions long associated with that area (but relevant to the New South as a whole): To what extent have the actions (or inaction) of millworkers flowed from rational calculation, and to what extent inbred character? Where has company power left off, and labor autonomy begun? How have operatives weighed the respective appeals of employer paternalism and organized labor, and why especially has the latter fared so poorly? Of this generation of Piedmont studies, perhaps the fullest contribution was David L. Carlton's *Mill and Town in South Carolina, 1880–1920* (1982).

Like McLaurin, Carlton rejected the stereotypes of passive mill folk and gauzy paternalism. In their place he depicted a nascent textile world ridden with tension and conflict. At once incensed and daunted by the hard-edged power of management – and either way, ambivalent about the moral claims and tactical promise of unionism – the millworkers asserted their autonomy in the political realm. Rallying to the backwoods appeal of Governor (and later Senator) Cole Blease, textile operatives challenged what they saw as the intrusive "uplift" measures of the New South's middle-class Progressives: child-labor reform, compulsory education, and the like. If company paternalism was far from benevolent, the same, Carlton stressed, could be said of millworker solidarity; integral to the class awareness crystallizing among the predominantly white operatives was an acute sensitivity (artfully inflamed by Blease) to the "black peril."

Interest in the contours of solidarity informed research on Appalachian coalfields as well – another stretch of New South industry marked by arduous labor, low pay, and expansive company power. Yet here the racial diversity of labor injected its own set of dynamics. How black and white workers resolved the tensions between labor unity and racial antipathy was a fascinating question, amenable only to the kind of in-depth research envisioned by Gutman. In the decade following his pathbreaking essay, the interplay of race and labor – especially the breadth and character of interracial unionism – remained a focus of research on southern coalminers. An essay by Stephen Brier (1977) uncovered a rich vein of black–white cooperation in the southern West Virginia coalfields, involving the Knights of Labor and the early UMW. Interracial solidarity figured prominently as well in David A. Corbin's full-length study, *Life, Work, and Rebellion in the Coal Fields: The Southern West Virginia Coal Miners, 1880–1922* (1981).

New findings on black unionism extended beyond the coalfields. The place of African-American workers in the labor movement – and of the labor movement in the black community – was an emerging theme in the study of urban labor. The port city of Richmond provided the setting for the first full length treatment of black working-class activism in the New South, Peter Rachleff's *Black Labor in the South* (1984). Rachleff's contribution was to locate this dynamic tradition equally in Richmond's civil rights and union movements – in both the associational matrix of its black community and an expansive network of labor organizations. For Rachleff, the rise of a Knights of Labor "movement culture" was the high-water mark of labor inter-racialism in postbellum Richmond, while its demise showed the formidable obstacles it ran up against.

The social history of New South agriculture was undergoing its own revision. Spotlighting popular reaction to the acquisitiveness and inequalities of the Gilded Age, scholars revealed a republican current galvanizing city and countryside alike. Lawrence Goodwyn's *Democratic Promise: The Populist Moment in America* (1976) restored to that crusade a transformative vision overlooked in more skeptical accounts. While historians would debate how fully he captured tensions of class or race within Populism's "movement culture," *Democratic Promise* clearly owed as much to E. P. Thompson as to C. Vann Woodward. The same could be said of Steven Hahn's *The Roots of Southern Populism: Yeoman Farmers and the Transformation of the Georgia Upcountry, 1850–1890* (1983). In presenting the struggles of small-scale cultivators to retain their independence amid the relentless commodification of agriculture, Hahn found a strain of Gilded Age dissent no less vital than that found by Rachleff in working-class Richmond. If scholars like Goodwyn and Hahn exposed a variant of labor republicanism in the rural South, James R. Green did the same for Debsian radicalism in *Grass-Roots Socialism: Radical Movements in the Southwest, 1895–1943* (1978). At once extending and departing from the Populist tradition, the American Socialist Party of the early twentieth century found its largest per capita following in the Old Southwest states of Arkansas, Louisiana, Oklahoma, and Texas.

Continued inattention to working-class women, and to gender as a tool of analysis, drew increasing notice by the early 1980s. David Katzman's book on women and domestic service in late nineteenth- and early twentieth-century America conveyed the unique dynamics of a labor–management relation conducted at each end by women (Katzman 1978; on the South in particular, pp. 184–222). Essays on the distinctive experience of women in the textile mills had begun to appear (Newman 1978; Fredrickson 1982, 1985; Frankel 1984; Beatty 1984). Especially pathbreaking was Delores Janiewski's *Sisterhood Denied: Race, Gender, and Class in a New South Community* (1985), which examined the passage of black and white women from the hardscrabble farmlands of the Carolina Piedmont to the textile and tobacco mills of Durham. Janiewski examined their comparative experiences in the spheres of labor, home-life, community association, and grassroots politics. Like Rachleff's *Black Labor in the South, Sisterhood Denied* explored the capacity (or inclination) of hetero-geneous workers to join around shared class concerns. In showing how extensively their horizons were affected by gender, as well as by class and race, Janiewski deepened the complexity of southern working-class identity even as she broadened the cast of characters.

On the rise by 1985, the historiography of southern labor would explode in the years to follow. An observer revisiting the field today cannot help but notice how lively and nuanced the picture has become. While textile workers and coalminers retain leading roles, they have been joined by an enlarged roster: longshoremen, migrant farmworkers, steelworkers, shipyard workers, and southerners from a variety of other trades. (Samplings of this growing diversity can be found in essay collections edited by Fink and Reed 1994, and Zieger 1991, 1997.) Familiar questions – the "character" of southern workers, the aims and impact of paternalism, the ingredients of solidarity, the failings of unionism, the dialectics of race and class – have taken on new twists, and the debates surrounding them, new subtlety. Other questions marginal to the field in 1985, such as the multifaceted meanings of gender or the ambiguous role of the state, have risen in prominence. While labor research on the early New South shows little sign of abating, attention has extended to the eras of the New Deal, World War II, and the Cold War.

Fueled by a rush of oral history projects, the study of textile workers has flourished as never before. How an ancestral upcountry culture flavored their response to life and labor in the milltowns remains a live issue. If wellsprings of mutuality figure in all writing on millworker society, historians differ over where and against whom the boundaries of community were drawn, how closely those boundaries corresponded to class, and how readily class sensibilities translated into unionism. How and on whose terms company paternalism functioned; how millhands received the labor movement and New Deal liberalism; how, finally, all these questions look when refracted through prisms of gender and race – here again, opinion continues to divide.

Several works capture this interpretive diversity. Warmly if not uncritically received was *Like a Family: The Making of a Southern Cotton Mill World* (Hall et al. 1987). Blending broad archival research with a wealth of new oral accounts, *Like a Family* offered the liveliest portrayal yet of millworker life from the outset of Piedmont textile production through the Great Depression. Here was a world interwoven with social ties extending from mill to household to public life. Hall et al. throw particular light on the divergent experiences of women and men. But collective resilience is the unifying theme of *Like a Family*. Behind the operatives' manifest wariness of "outsiders" – including labor organizers and New Dealers – lay a vibrant community, rooted in the interdependency of upcountry life and reinforced by the class realities of their industrial environment. It was from this soil that the labor unrest of the late 1920s and early 1930s emerged. Stressing irrepressible solidarity over oppression and division, *Like a Family* marked the new labor history's heartiest venture below the Mason-Dixon Line.

If *Like a Family* won acclaim for restoring flesh-and-blood agency to the millworkers, not everyone endorsed so affirmative a portrayal. In I. A. Newby's *Plain Folk in the New South: Social Change and Cultural Persistence, 1880–1915* (1989), employer hegemony overshadows labor autonomy. Like most current writing, Newby recognizes a tight-knit millworker culture; however (also like most), he finds less within it to celebrate. Curtailing its powers of mutuality, he contends, were streaks of racism, lethargy, and social deference. Despite flashes of labor protest, textile operatives were more apt to target African-Americans, social reformers, or union organizers than they were their employers. Likewise, the millhands portrayed in James Hodges's *New Deal Labor Policy and the Southern Cotton Textile Industry, 1930–1941* (1986) were more fractious and fatalistic than those in *Like a Family*. But he attributes their circumspection about the New Dealers and the CIO less to a primordial conservatism than to a rational reading of management's power and the shortcomings of the national union and federal labor policy – instincts dolefully confirmed by the strike defeat of 1934. Barbara Griffith brings a comparable analysis to the postwar period in *The Crisis of American Labor: Operation Dixie and the Defeat of the CIO* (1988). Focusing largely on textiles, Griffith invokes a myriad of obstacles to mass unionism, including the structures of key southern industries, the interlocking power of civic and economic elites, the relentless use of race-baiting and red-baiting, the foibles and flaws of union organizers, the weakness of federal labor law, and a pervasive heritage of labor deference.

These variations in tone have much to do with the questions scholars bring to the mill towns. By their very nature, inquiries into the perpetual weakness of southern unionism tend toward a brooding pessimism. A more sanguine spirit flows from the mission of *Like a Family*, which is not so much to explain a failed outcome as to discover how millworkers retained dignity and community amid harsh circumstances. Douglass Flamming's *Creating a Modern South: Millhands and Managers in Dalton, Georgia, 1884–1984* (1992) represents a third approach. Focused evenly upon the interaction of workers and employers, *Creating a Modern South* brings new light to the origins and impact of company paternalism. Detailing a century of labor relations in a Georgia textile center, Flamming challenges the image of paternalism as a legacy of the Old South (plantation or upcountry); to the contrary, he notes, cotton mill paternalism emerged only in response to New South, industrial imperatives (above all, mounting demand for labor). Nor was paternalism a unilateral enterprise. Recalling Eugene Genovese's *Roll, Jordan, Roll: The World the Slaves Made* (1974), Flamming's paternalism is elaborate, malleable, and the collective handiwork of managers and workers, each responding to a constellation of factors. Further echoing Genovese, Flamming tests the notion that company welfare preempted militancy, arguing rather that they fostered millhand communities and sowed within them expectations that converted readily to unionism in the 1930s, when employers failed to fulfill them. Alternately resisting and accommodating company power, Flamming's millhands were neither abject nor autonomous. Like Hall et al. (1987), he stresses that unionism was not the only measure of mutuality; like critics of Hall et al., he stresses that class solidarity was not the only face of mutuality, nor inclusion the only thrust of community.

The Piedmont shows no sign of receding from the forefront of historical research on southern labor. Bryant Simon's *A Fabric of Defeat: The Politics of South Carolina Millhands, 1910–1948* (1998) employs the new labor history's broad idea of politics, spanning from voting place to workplace, front porch to company store. Picking up where Carlton's *Mill and Town in South Carolina* left off, *A Fabric of Defeat* digs deeper into the appeal of the young Cole Blease, conveying his feel for the anxieties of gender, race, and class haunting white men at the mills. Simon tracks their gradual disenchantment with the blustery demagogue during the interwar years. Blease's indifference to labor activism and hostility to state activism (except in the service of white supremacy) proved ill-suited for a time of wrenching hardship, surging militancy, and incipient New Dealism. The eventual demise of textile unionism and pro-labor politics in South Carolina owed not, Simon insists, to the operatives' racism or insularity; they were simply out-muscled on the field of class warfare. It was only after that bruising defeat, and the incremental decline of Jim Crow in the years to come, that the politics of race regained its traction among white millworkers. Thus, Simon's closing section speaks not only to the ebbs and flows of millworker consciousness but also to the fragmenting of the New Deal coalition in America.

If the works of Flamming and Simon conclude with the postwar era, two other recent narratives unfold wholly within it: Daniel Clark's *Like Night and Day: Unionization in a Southern Mill Town* (1997) and Timothy Minchin's *What Do We Need a Union For? The TWUA in the South, 1945–1955* (1997). In a vivid study of Henderson, North Carolina, where the TWUA enjoyed recognition from 1943 to 1958, Clark probes the meanings of the union shop in workers' lives. Scouring grievance and arbitration records, the author shows how representation enhanced the capacity of millhands to resist stretch-outs, cost-cutting technologies, and other mainstays of operator domination. In this regard, *Like Night and Day* challenges depictions of the postwar CIO as a calcified bureaucracy whose "business union" proceduralism sapped workers' shop-floor power. Of course, the TWUA's 15-year run in Henderson was exceptional. In his wide-angle survey, Minchin explores a more familiar outcome: the ineffectiveness of textile unionism in the postwar South (reconfirmed in the ill-fated regionwide strike of 1951). To the standard medley of obstacles – repression, red-baiting, racial division, industrial competition, fractious leadership, anemic federal policy – Minchin adds a novel explanation: as mid-century operatives acquired increased earning power, and hence the trappings of credit-financed goods such as cars and homes, the risks of union affiliation grew ever-more apparent than the promise. Under the circumstances, he argues, organized labor's failure to present itself first-and-foremost as an instrument of *social* power sealed its defeat.

African-Americans have been marginal to the study of Piedmont labor, reflecting their sparse presence (until recently) at the mills. Where race intrudes at all, it is usually as an element of white workers' consciousness. (A pioneering essay on black textile workers was Fredrickson, 1982. A more recent effort to fill this gap is Minchin, 1999.) But for the wider South, research has burgeoned on black labor – and, more generally, on the ways issues of race and class have affected workers on each side of the color line. A number of historians have unearthed the extensive mobility of blacks and whites across the southern countryside. The regularity with which rural people shifted (perennially or even seasonally) from one landowner to another, or between tenant farming and a host of other callings, suggests that the region's labor-repressive apparatus was never total. Particularly evocative is Jacqueline Jones's survey of the many modes of labor coexisting along Dixie's hinterlands (Jones 1992: 127–66). Here was a world of phosphate mining and oyster shucking, lumbering and turpentine production, sugar refining and sawmilling, peopled by "foreign immigrants and native white and black men, women, and children, organized as wage earners, contract laborers, unpaid family members, peons, and convicts" (ibid: 132). Growing recognition of the fluidity of rural life has altered portrayals of the black exodus North as well. Discarding the traditional picture of the Great Migration, which showed peasant folk dispatched by a swirl of "pushes" and "pulls" to the industrial city, historians like Peter Gottlieb and James Grossman show black migrants proceeding deliberately, often by degrees, from the southern farmlands to the urban North (Gottlieb 1987; Grossman 1989).

If the winding path from farm to factory provides one way into the history of black workers, their relation to black elites offers another. Tensions between the unifying power of race and the diversifying thrust of class were a constant feature of African-American life across the New South, and scholars continue to present them in differing ways. Some recent works – such as Joe William Trotter, Jr.'s *Coal, Class, and Color: Blacks in Southern West Virginia, 1915–32* (1990) and Earl Lewis's *In Their Own Interests: Race, Class, and Power in Twentieth-Century Norfolk, Virginia* (1991) – accentuate the shared perspectives of black workers and the black middle class. Rural African-Americans arriving at the coalfields of central Appalachia, Trotter observes, found only limited avenues of response to the dual barriers of race and class. Discouraged from interracialism by the weakness of the UMW and persisting racism of white miners, Trotter argues, black miners were more inclined to ally with the local black elite, notwithstanding class tensions between them. It is this latter relation that makes up the core of *Coal, Class, and Color*. Lewis reaches similar conclusions in his study, which recreates the network of race-based institutions that anchored Norfolk's black working class. In contrast to Rachleff, and more emphatically than Trotter, Lewis finds the bonds of race between black workers and the black middle class to have been far stronger than whatever bonds of class arose between black and white workers.

Class cleavages in black life, by contrast, loom large in Robin D. G. Kelley's *Hammer and Hoe: Alabama Communists during the Great Depression* (1990). Central to the study are the thousands of poor blacks, rural and urban, who disregarded injunctions from the black elite that they should spurn the Communist

Party. According to Kelley, black workers played a leading part in Alabama communism, bringing distinctive forms of resistance to its drives against unemployment and evictions, segregation and disfranchisement, labor exploitation and lynching. Thus, *Hammer and Hoe* shows reservoirs of independence among black workers usually obscured in studies of the black community and American communism alike. Kelley (1993) broadens this perspective in a widely noted article. Decrying the "romantic" presumption of a "tight-knit, harmonious black community" (ibid: 80–1), Kelley stresses informal displays of resistance from black workers falling outside organized struggle. Transmitted through "daily conversations, folklore, jokes, songs, and other cultural practices," this "dissident political culture" emerged through shop-floor sabotage, theft, and transiency, and boisterous comportment and raucous recreation in the public sphere. Historians might question whether the meaning of "political resistance" can be viably stretched to include such activities as dancing, drinking, and making love, without finally vanishing into the overall phenomenon of human behavior. Either way, Kelley's attention to subtle, often discordant layers of mass culture adapts an approach long applied to American slaves and wage-earners to the black poor of urban Dixie.

Divergent experiences of gender as well as class in the urban black community are brought to life in *To 'Joy My Freedom* (1997), Tera Hunter's pioneering study of black working women in the half-century following emancipation. Concentrating on Atlanta, Hunter details the quest of domestic servants and washerwomen for fulfillment and independence. In this they faced social constraints at every turn: white employers, in whose homes many lived and worked; white civic leaders, who regarded them as dissolute objects to monitor; white workers, who saw them as a social and material threat; and black elites, who approached them with didactic condescension. Hunter shows the many ways black working women sought to maintain their autonomy, including work-based resistance (informal and organized), pooling of job and familial obligations, and involvement in community campaigns for black rights and advancement. They also found release and self-identity in a world of saloons, juke joints, and dance halls; a scene inaccessible (and generally scandalous) to their social "betters," white and black. Few studies have more effectively captured the overlaps among African-American, women's, and labor history.

The past decade-and-a-half has seen an outpouring of work on race and southern unionism. While some focus on single-race endeavors (either lily-white or all-black), most examine unions that brought black and white workers into some manner of association. At issue have been the scope, character, and outcome of interracial unionism. In what measures did organized labor serve as a bulwark of segregation, a rallying point for racial equality, or the setting for a raft of agendas ranging between those two poles? To whom, ultimately, did the labor movement belong? Opened by Gutman a generation before, these questions had a number of researchers (mostly doctoral students) combing the archives by the mid-1980s.

Theirs would prove an absorbing exploration, filled with untold stories, unpredictable outcomes, and at times animated debate. The latter heated up in the late 1980s, when Herbert Hill (1988–9) issued a withering critique of Gutman and his so-called disciples. Upon scrutiny, Hill claimed, Gutman's 1968 essay on race and the UMW stood exposed as an exercise in "mythmaking" – a Marxian bid to sanitize working-class racism, to obscure it beneath a fantasy of interracial fellowship. For Hill, organization across the color line was too infrequent, too transient, too suspect in purpose and mired in racism to warrant serious consideration. Race, not class, he insisted, was the paramount theme of America's labor past. As the field polarized between supporters of Hill and defenders of Gutman (who had himself died in 1985), word spread of a "race–class debate" among labor historians.

Thus framed, the "debate" was itself a myth. Sure enough, an ardent "race-over-class"(or "Hill") school had surfaced, chiefly in the form of critical essays. But the "class-over-race" school flayed by Hill and company existed only as a caricature of their own making. The late scholar's impatience with fixed equations of social identity mocked the very notion of a "Gutman school." If Gutman acquired a following in the study of race and southern unionism, it might better be termed a "persuasion" – a diverse assemblage sharing the freewheeling spirit of the new labor history. It is in the contrast between a Hill *school* and a Gutman *persuasion* that the so-called Hill–Gutman debate finds its authentic shape. The former was prosecutorial in tone; the latter, inquisitive. The former highlighted the actions of white workers; the latter focused more widely, restoring agency to African-Americans as framers of interracial unionism, and to employers (among others) as architects of discrimination. For the Hill school, the pervasive racism of white workers and their unions was the salient (if not only) theme. For those of the Gutman persuasion, Jim Crow's presence in the House of Labor was not in itself a finding, or conclusion, so much as a well-established starting point. Their guiding purpose was rather to survey how black and white workers in particular settings resolved the dual claims of class and color, and to identify the circumstances that either prompted or discouraged their collaboration. (There is much here that mirrors the age-old debate over "American Exceptionalism," with proponents of the question seeking to explain labor's deviation from an expected path, and critics preferring to examine workers' options and actions on their own terms.) For all its initial splash, the Hill critique was ultimately too coarse and polemical to leave a lasting mark. As research mounts in volume and subtlety, allusions to a dichotomous "race-versus-class" debate grow evermore out-of-touch. This is not, however, to suggest that the historiography of interracial unionism proceeds in lockstep; to the contrary, its momentum has fed upon compelling differences of narrative and analysis.

For the late nineteenth and early twentieth centuries, historians of race and organized labor have remained especially interested in port towns and mineral districts, where relations between black and white workers were most indeterminate. Particularly influential is Eric Arnesen's *Waterfront Workers of New Orleans: Race, Class, and Politics, 1863–1923* (1991). Recounting two waves of organization along the New Orleans riverfront (the first spearheaded by the Cotton Men's Executive Council of the late nineteenth century, and the second by the Dock and Cotton Council of the early twentieth), Arnesen resurrects one of the New South's most arresting, if complicated, traditions of interracial unionism. Designed to preserve racial comity – an imperative affirmed by chronic eruptions of violence over the postbellum decades – black and white waterfront unions forged biracial mechanisms of work-sharing on the docks and power-sharing in the union hall. That their alliance stemmed from pragmatic concerns should not, Arnesen insists, trivialize the results. At its height, black and white dockworkers attained appreciable improvements in wages and conditions, and control over the work process.

In *The Challenge of Interracial Unionism* (1998), Daniel Letwin explores a comparable heritage in the Birmingham mineral district, where black and white miners joined forces under the banners of the Greenback-Labor Party (late-1870s), the Knights of Labor (1880s), and, most enduringly, the United Mine Workers (1890–). The docks of New Orleans and the mines of Alabama have long stood out as exceptions to the juggernaut of Jim Crow – C. Vann Woodward noted as much in the *Origins of the New South* (1951: 360–4) – and their common features magnify upon close review. Each trade was structured more along industrial than craft lines, accentuating the logic of cooperation for black and white workers alike. In each case, interracial unions passed through alternating stretches of dormancy and revival; the latter marked by periods of contractual recognition, punctuated by major strikes. While neither was conceived by participants of either race as a civil rights crusade, "separate" came closer to "equal" in their unions than in any other enterprise around. And if neither movement overcame racial tension, within or beyond its ranks, neither succumbed to it either. Ultimately, the defeat of labor interracialism in each venue owed not to internal discord but rather to an open-shop drive that decimated unions across postwar America. Like Arnesen, Letwin presents labor interracialism as a decidedly complex phenomenon, anchored in but never reducible to the calculus of self-interest for workers of each race. In assessing what allowed this phenomenon to persist so long into the era of segregation, Letwin calls attention to the gender composition of the labor force. Voluntary association of the races, he notes, was less provocative in the all-male setting of the union hall than in other parts of the miners' world, where "race-mixing" raised the specter of "social equality" between black men and white women.

A very different perspective on race and early New South unionism is found in Henry M. McKiven, Jr.'s *Iron and Steel: Class, Race, and Community in Birmingham, Alabama, 1875–1920* (1995). Where others track unpredictable tensions in the identities of black and white workers, McKiven finds a more-or-less unqualified racism among the whites who monopolized skilled positions at Birmingham's furnaces and foundries. More than succumbing to the dictates of white supremacy, he argues, white iron and steel workers and their unions ranked among its framers, within and beyond the mills. Even their willingness to join forces with black mill labor and iron miners in the World War I era reflected more an impulse to control than to unite with workers of color.

No doubt, these contrasting pictures have much to do with the cases examined. When it came to race and labor in the postbellum South, the waterfronts and coalmines were a far cry from the iron and steel mills. (It is indicative that, in his subsequent work on the racial practices of railroad brotherhoods and longshore unionism beyond New Orleans, Arnesen [1994, 1995] presents white unionists in a less flattering light.) And yet differing portrayals like these turn upon more than the stories themselves; they also illustrate how varied the historiography has become. If the passions still roused by the interracial possibility promote debate, so does its intrinsic complexity. In casting the narrative, the historian must determine in what measure this is the story of white workers, black workers, their families, union leaders, or allied associations (not to mention an array of external forces). One scholar might focus on the gains reaped by workers of each race through joint organization (whether these be reckoned in wages, benefits, conditions, dignity, or shop-floor power); for another, the essence of the story lies in a union's position on Jim Crow (whether at the workplace, the union hall, or in the social and political realms beyond). Not least, scholars are prone to differ in the historical (or even moral) yardsticks they bring to a union of white and black workers – some appraising its racial performance against current standards of absolute equality, others against the constraints of time and place, or the expressed aims of participants themselves. In sum, race relations in the New South's rickety House of Labor could take many forms, each of which can be assessed in dramatically different ways.

These complexities of narrative and analysis are amply reconfirmed with the recent surge of attention to race and southern unionism in the CIO years. Here was an era of exceptional possibility for the interracial project, as extreme hardship engulfed workers of each race, industrial unionism regained its vitality, union rights and labor standards attained federal sanction, and the return of war boosted the stature of African-Americans and organized labor. Never had black and white workers coalesced in such numbers, or the promise of racial equality found broader endorsement (at least rhetorical), either within or beyond the labor movement. And yet the incipient alliance of black and white workers encountered, and quickened, a fierce backlash – a frothy brew of segregationism, anticommunism, and antiliberalism, it too swelling both within and beyond the union hall. All told, these years brought the tension between labor solidarity and racial division onto explosive new ground.

And never, before or since, have the outcomes been so manifold. Snapshots from current research suggest how kaleidoscopic relations between black and white workers – and between unions and the wider racial order – had grown by the 1930s, 1940s, and 1950s. In Winston-Salem, tobacco workers of each race congregate at picket lines, union meetings, and social affairs, interbraiding the causes of labor and racial equality (K. Korstad 1992); in Tennessee, a regional CIO director rebukes white labor activists for addressing their black confederates as "Mr" and "Mrs" (Honey 1993: 210). In Fort Worth, white and black packinghouse workers walk out over the firing of black butchers (Halpern 1991: 168); in Mobile, white CIO shipyard workers violently expel black workers from their midst (Nelson 1993). In Memphis, white workers climb aboard left-led, black-majority unions (Honey 1993); in the Birmingham district, white ore miners spurn the equal rights agenda of another largely black union in favor of a company union (Draper 1996). Countless variations on these contrasts fill the landscape of mid-century southern labor.

Of course, historians approach the topic of interracial unionism with different notions of its breadth and import. Not surprisingly, the more skeptical assessments tend to come from those exploring bastions of white labor privilege. Robert Norrell's (1986) essay on the Birmingham steel mills stresses how white workers used CIO representation (through the Steel Workers' Organizing Committee and its successor, the United Steel Workers) to tighten their hold on skilled positions. In an article on wartime Mobile, Bruce Nelson (1993) details the fierce resistance of white shipyard workers (especially those fresh off the countryside) to the rights, or even presence, of African-Americans. Conversely, the more generous verdicts on labor interracialism have tended to accompany studies of the radical, civil rights wing of organized labor; thus, a 1988 piece by Robert Korstad and Nelson Lichtenstein on the tenacious egalitarianism of black and white unionists in Winston-Salem (and, up North, in Detroit), or Rick Halpern's (1991) comparable findings on the United Packinghouse

Workers in Ft Worth. Yet contrasting depictions reflect more than the stories themselves; at times they flow to the same case. Take essays by Norrell (1986) and Judith Stein (1991) on steelworker unionism in Alabama: if Norrell presents the union as a tool of white privilege, Stein emphasizes how industry-wide contracts, governed by federal code, afforded workers of each race leverage and benefits once unimaginable.

Comprised chiefly of article-length essays by a host of authors, this new scholarship defies easy encapsulation. The first (and thus far only) local study to appear as a monograph is Michael Honey's *Southern Labor and Black Civil Rights: Organizing Memphis Workers* (1993). Much of the book's drama lies in its locale; not even the daunting fiefdom of Boss Crump could escape the transformative effects of the Great Depression and World War II. By the late 1930s, thousands of black and white workers from a range of trades had rallied to industrial unionism. Black labor activists, along with a cadre of white radical organizers, challenged racial discrimination at work, in the union hall, and in the public arena. An impressive minority of white workers turned to labor interracialism, if only for practical reasons, and World War II accelerated its momentum. The industrial alliance of black and white labor would soon succumb, in Memphis as elsewhere, to the postwar reaction. But if repression hastened the demise of civil rights unionism, so too, Honey argues, did the failure of most white workers and CIO leaders to resist race-baiting and red-baiting – to overcome their racism and embrace the cause of civil rights. If Honey's judgment of white unionists evokes the moral impatience of Herbert Hill, his attention to a complex range of players, and the roadblocks facing any coalition of black and white workers in mid-century Memphis, lend his work a texture foreign to the Hill critique. Like so much of the current output, *Southern Labor and Black Civil Rights* affirms how far the study of interracial unionism has moved beyond "race-versus-class" or "were-they-or-weren't-they-racist?" dichotomies. (For important historiographical surveys of – and contributions to – the field, see Arnesen 1993, 1998; Halpern 1994; Goldfield 1993, 1994; Trotter 1994; Nelson 1996.)

For all its diversity, the emerging record of southern labor's encounter with the "race question" has reinforced several broad themes, concerning, in turn, agency, purpose, motivation, and causation. First, organized labor was never the exclusive domain of white workers; as a whole, it is better seen as an assortment of visions and initiatives, arising each side of the color line. Second, only at its very boldest did interracial unionism expand into a full-fledged civil rights crusade or flaunt the taboo against "social equality." Third, seldom did white and black workers test the hegemony of Jim Crow without compelling material incentives all around; not often did white workers forsake tangible fruits of racial privilege for a venture in inter-racialism. Finally, the factors shaping the extent and character of interracial solidarity were legion: in any given situation, these could turn upon the structure and circumstances of the industry; the racial demography of the workforce; the state of the labor market; the political climate of the community, region, and nation; or the stance of government (local, state, or federal).

Recent years have also brought attention to neglected corners of New South labor, to workers and labor systems little touched by unionism. The laundresses and domestics examined by Hunter represent one such area. In *The Fruits of Their Labor: Atlantic Coast Farmworkers and the Making of Migrant Poverty, 1870–1945*

(1997), Cindy Hahamovitch illuminates another. The driving problem of *The Fruits of Their Labor* is not why unionism has failed to do better, but, one level deeper, why migrant farmworkers have always been so poor and powerless. This means unraveling how and on what terms migrants were recruited and put to work. With an eye for the constant presence (if evolving forms) of labor coercion, Hahamovitch reviews the eras of Italian labor contractors ("Padroni"), Progressive reformers, wartime "work-or-fight" sanctions, and finally, the New Deal and World War II. It is the multifaceted approaches of the labor movement and the federal government in this latter period to the employment of migrant farm labor – now predominantly black – that make up the heart of her study. Challenging models that reduce government to either an "autonomous actor" or an agent of labor co-optation, Hahamovitch shows the capacity of an ascendant national state alternately to empower and constrain migrant workers. All told, a series of forces conspired to deny them the fruits of their labor.

Another topic finally receiving serious attention is the system of convict labor that thrived in the decades following emancipation. Of particular note are Alex Lichtenstein's *Twice the Work of Free Labor: The Political Economy of Convict Labor in the South* (1996) and Karin Shapiro's *A New South Rebellion: The Battle Against Convict Labor in the Tennessee Coalfields, 1871–1896* (1998). Reflecting current approaches to the world of workers, slave and free, both regard the overwhelmingly black corps of convict labor as historical actors in their own right, doing what they could to check a welter of dehumanizing circumstances as they toiled across the plantations, railroads, mines, roads, and assorted light industries of the New South. But it is the problem of convict labor in the broader sweep of southern society that lies at the core of each study. In *Twice the Work of Free Labor*, Lichtenstein argues for the vital place of convict labor in the South's political economy. Focusing chiefly on Georgia, he charts this form of neo-slavery from its postbellum rise through its transformation (and ultimate abolition) at the hands of Progressive reformers. In casting convict labor more as a New South than an Old South phenomenon, Lichtenstein echoes Woodward's analysis of emergent Jim Crow, or Flamming's of Piedmont paternalism.

In *A New South Rebellion* Shapiro lifts from obscurity one of the more dramatic instances of labor protest of late nineteenth-century America and situates it within the deep social tensions attending New South industrialization. In a protracted series of forays over 1891–2, miners of eastern and central Tennessee seized the convicts leased to the mines and dispatched them from the district (often torching their stockades for good measure). The miners were no foes of market capitalism; it was indeed in the budding coal towns that they sought to recover an independence that the land no longer ensured them. At issue, Shapiro stresses, were the rightful terms of industrialization. Where the coal operators saw in the convict lease a source of cheap, pliable labor, the miners (and sympathetic merchants and farmers) saw an assault on their dignity and livelihood. Only after labor bargaining, lobbying, legal challenge, and finally the election of a Farmers Alliance ticket failed to bring about its abolition, did these avowed adherents of law and property resort to extralegal measures. The anti-convict rebellion convulsed the state, as public aversion to the miners' "lawlessness" (interracial at that) vied with repugnance over the use of convicts. Shapiro's narrative illuminates roiling discord over the meanings of labor, independence, and citizenship in the industrializing South.

No historiographical revolution is ever complete. In the case of southern labor, some outstanding verities of the traditional school – the breadth of poverty and depth of exploitation, the fragility of unionism and virulence of racism, the power of capital and the business slant of Bourbon rule – remain staples of historical writing. Still, at the heart of the new southern labor history are discontinuities worthy of the New South itself. To contest the image of an essentially passive people, fragmented and ill-equipped for collective action, has been a defining mission of the scholarship surveyed above. And on this front, the revolution can claim victory. Themes that seemed revelatory not so long ago are now axiomatic. That New South workers were not naturally quiescent; that the region and the labor movement were not intrinsically incompatible; that unionism is not the only index of militancy or mutuality; that race and class interact subtly in the lives of workers; that the experience of southern labor is distinctive, but not fundamentally exceptional – if these constituted pathbreaking arguments a generation back, they are widely recognized premises today. But the clearing away of stale assumptions has hardly concluded the work of the new southern labor history. To the contrary, it has prompted inquiry unprecedented in scope or energy.

In part, this testifies to the expansive areas still ripe for investigation. Even those sectors traditionally emblematic of New South labor, such as mining or textiles, are filled with stories and angles yet to be explored. And beyond these lies a multiplicity of groups and settings only beginning to enter the annals of southern labor. For a number of years, Piedmont milltowns and Black Belt farmlands were the chief frontiers of research on working women. More recently, interest has extended to domestic servants and laundry workers, although one suspects that the attention of Hunter and others to unexplored spheres of female labor will inspire many to follow their lead in the years ahead. Public employment, municipal to federal, presents another broad horizon of research on the working-class South. The dearth of attention here is remarkable, given the diversity of the work, and workers, involved. Here was a distinctive cluster of occupations – from teachers to secretaries, postal workers to firefighters, paper-pushers to sanitation workers – all shaped by political as much as market forces, and yet each having its own stature, its own relation to the public, its own correlation to the race and gender hierarchies of the day. Many further sectors await investigation: among them, the shadowy assortment of casual rural occupations glimpsed in Jones's *Dispossessed*, the rush of defense-related industrial work during World War II, and the surge of advanced manufacturing employment across the postwar South (particularly the Sunbelt region) spawned by the vaunted "military–industrial complex."

The ongoing arrival of fresh sources, methods, and sensibilities replenish interest in the old haunts of southern labor history even as they hasten the turn to less familiar vistas. Further fueling current research are a raft of questions scarcely raised in earlier times, ranging from the multiple impacts of gender upon the lives and perspectives of working men and women to the ways in which ethnicity shaped the identities of working-class southerners, to the effects of an expanded federal presence upon labor relations in the modern South, to the interconnections between southern unionism and a series of other causes, above all the civil rights movement.

The story of southern labor is interwoven with many other strands of history, regional and beyond. And in recent decades its historians have drawn upon, and refined, an ever-widening range of perspectives and agendas. Consider a selection of leading works. Delores Janiewski's *Sisterhood Denied* is a contribution to the studies of southern women, rural-to-urban migration, community organization, and the connections between hierarchies of work and social background. Two works on race and organized labor – Peter Rachleff's *Black Labor in the South* and Eric Arnesen's *Waterfront Workers of New Orleans* – enter as well into the histories of Reconstruction, New South urban politics, early civil rights campaigns, Gilded Age labor movements, and issues of workplace control. *Like a Family*, Jacquelyn Hall et al.'s examination of cotton mill workers, engages the literatures on working-class culture and community, labor and gender, class resistance, and worker response to the New Deal and the CIO. Robin Kelley's *Hammer and Hoe* is of relevance to historians of depression-era unionism, race and labor, American communism, and the informal politics of the African-American poor. Tera Hunter's *To 'Joy My Freedom* intertwines the historiographies of laboring women, working-class leisure and resistance, class dynamics in black life, Progressive reform, and the relations of white and black women of the New South. Michael Honey's *Southern Labor and Black Civil Rights* straddles the fields of machine politics, American radicalism, race and the CIO, the civil rights movement, and the regional impacts of the Great Depression, New Deal, World War II, and postwar reaction. No one interested in the varieties of labor coercion, federal labor policy, the social repercussions of war mobilization, or the mechanics of poverty and powerlessness in rural America can ignore Cindy Hahamovitch's *The Fruits of their Labor*. Karin Shapiro's *A New South Rebellion* illuminates the complexities of convict labor in the industrializing South, Populism, race and New South unionism, the political ideologies of working-class southerners, and the dynamics of popular dissent. Other volumes mentioned in this essay (and many more not) bring together their own respective blends of historical inquiry.

Clearly, the time is past when southern labor can be compartmentalized from broader themes of southern or American history. It is because of this – above and beyond the wealth of untapped sources and untold stories – that the field remains so fertile. The coming decade or two will no doubt see the panorama of New South labor enriched, transformed, and still, as ever, the subject of vigorous debate. And much of the trend-setting scholarship will be the work of historians only now entering the profession.

NOTE

I am grateful to Eva Maczuga and Eric Arnesen for their commentary on drafts of this essay.

BIBLIOGRAPHY

Arnesen, Eric 1991: *Waterfront Workers of New Orleans: Race, Class, and Politics, 1863–1923.* New York: Oxford University Press.

Arnesen, Eric 1993: Following the Color Line of Labor: Black Workers and the Labor Movement Before 1930. *Radical History Review*, 55, 53–87.

Arnesen, Eric 1994: "Like Banquo's Ghost, It Will Not Down": The Race Question and the American Railroad Brotherhoods, 1880–1920. *American Historical Review*, 99, 1,601–33.

Arnesen, Eric 1995: "It Aint Like They Do in New Orleans": Race Relations, Labor Markets, and Waterfront Labor Movements in the American South, 1880–1923. In Marcel Van Der Linden and Jan Lucassen (eds.), *Racism and the Labour Market: Historical Studies*. Bern: Peter Land AG, 57–100.

Arnesen, Eric 1998: Up From Exclusion: Black and White Workers, Race, and the State of Labor History. *Reviews in American History*, 26, 146–74.

Arnesen, Eric, Greene, Julie, and Laurie, Bruce (eds.) 1998: *Labor Histories: Class, Politics, and the Working-Class Experience*. Urbana: University of Illinois Press.

Beatty, Bess 1984: Textile Labor in the North Carolina Piedmont: Mill Owner Images and Mill Worker Response, 1830–1900. *Labor History*, 25, 485–503.

Brier, Stephen 1977: Interracial Organizing in the West Virginia Coal Industry: The Participation of Black Mine Workers in the Knights of Labor and the United Mine Workers, 1880–1894. In Gary M. Fink and Merl E. Reed (eds.), *Essays in Southern Labor History*. Westport, CT: Greenwood Press, 18–41.

Carlton, David L. 1982: *Mill and Town in South Carolina, 1880–1920*. Baton Rouge: Louisiana University Press.

Cash, W. J. 1941: *The Mind of the South*. New York: Alfred A. Knopf.

Clark, Daniel J. 1997: *Like Night and Day: Unionization in a Southern Mill Town*. Chapel Hill: University of North Carolina Press.

Corbin, David Alan 1981: *Life, Work, and Rebellion in the Coal Fields: The Southern West Virginia Miners, 1880–1922*. Urbana: University of Illinois Press.

Daniel, Pete 1972: *The Shadow of Slavery: Peonage in the South, 1901–1969*. New York: Oxford University Press.

Draper 1996: The New Southern Labor History Revisited: The Success of the Mine Mill and Smelter Workers Union in Birmingham, 1934–1938. *Journal of Southern History*, 62, 87–108.

Fink, Gary M and Reed, Merl E. (eds.) 1977: *Essays in Southern Labor History: Selected Papers, Southern Labor History Conference, 1976*. Westport, CT: Greenwood Press.

Fink, Gary M and Reed, Merl E. (eds.) 1994: *Race, Class, and Community in Southern Labor History*. Tuscaloosa: University of Alabama Press.

Flamming, Douglass 1992: *Creating the Modern South: Millhands and Managers in Dalton, Georgia, 1884–1984*. Chapel Hill: University of North Carolina Press.

Frankel, Linda 1984: Southern Textile Women. In Karen Brodkin Sacks and Dorothy Remy (eds.), *My Troubles Are Going to Have Trouble with Me: Everyday Trials and Triumphs of Women Workers*. New Brunswick, NJ: Rutgers University Press, 39–60.

Fredrickson, Mary 1982: Four Decades of Change: Black Workers in Southern Textiles, 1941–1981. *Radical America*, 16, 27–44.

Fredrickson, Mary 1985: "I Know Which Side I'm On": Southern Women in the Labor Movement in the Twentieth Century. In Ruth Milkman (ed.), *Women, Work, and Protest: A Century of U.S. Women's Labor History*. Boston: Routledge and Kegan Paul, 156–80.

Goldfield, Michael 1993: Race and the CIO: The Possibilities for Racial Egalitarianism During the 1930s and 1940s. *International Labor and Working-Class History*, 44, 1–32. (Followed by responses by Gary Gerstle, Robert Korstad, Marshall F. Stevenson, Jr., and Judith Stein, 33–63.)

Goldfield, Michael 1994: Race and the CIO: Reply to Critics. *International Labor and Working-Class History*, 46, 142–60.

Goodwyn, Lawrence 1976: *Democratic Promise: The Populist Moment in America*. New York: Oxford University Press.

Gottlieb, Peter 1987: *Making Their Own Way: Southern Blacks' Migration to Pittsburgh, 1916–30*. Urbana: University of Illinois Press.

Green, James R. 1973: The Brotherhood of Timber Workers, 1910–1913: A Radical Response to Industrial Capitalism in the Southern USA. *Past and Present*, 60, 161–200.

Green, James R. 1978: *Grass-Roots Socialism: Radical Movements in the Southwest, 1895–1943*. Baton Rouge: Louisiana University Press.

Griffith, Barbara S. 1988: *The Crisis of American Labor: Operation Dixie and the Defeat of the CIO*. Philadelphia: Temple University Press.

Grossman, James R. 1989: *Land of Hope: Chicago, Black Southerners, and the Great Migration*. Chicago: University of Chicago Press.

Grubbs, Donald H. 1971: *Cry from the Cotton: The Southern Tenant Farmers' Union and the New Deal*. Chapel Hill: University of North Carolina Press.

Gutman, Herbert G. 1968: The Negro and the United Mine Workers of America: The Career and Letters of Richard L. Davis and Something of Their Meaning: 1890–1900. In Julius Jacobson (ed.), *The Negro and the Labor Movement*. Garden City, NY: Anchor Books, 49–127.

Hahamovitch, Cindy 1997: *The Fruits of Their Labor: Atlantic Coast Farmworkers and the Making of Migrant Poverty, 1870–1945*. Chapel Hill: University of North Carolina Press.

Hahn, Steven 1983: *The Roots of Southern Populism: Yeoman Farmers and the Transformation of the Georgia Uncountry, 1850–1890*. New York: Oxford University Press.

Hall, Jacquelyn Dowd, Leloudis, James, Korstad, Robert, Murphy, Mary, Jones, Lu Ann, and Daly, Christopher B. 1987: *Like a Family: The Making of a Southern Cotton Mill World*. Chapel Hill: University of North Carolina Press.

Halpern, Rick 1991: Interracial Unionism in the Southwest: Fort Worth's Packinghouse Workers, 1937–1954. In Robert H. Zieger (ed.), *Organized Labor in the Twentieth-Century South*. Knoxville: University of Tennessee Press, 158–82.

Halpern, Rick 1994: Organized Labour, Black Workers, in the Twentieth-Century South: The Emerging Revision. *Social History*, 19, 359–83.

Hill, Herbert 1988–9: Myth-Making as Labor History: Herbert Gutman and the United Mine Workers of America. *International Journal of Politics, Culture, and Society*, 2, 132–200. (With responses by Steven Shulman, Nell Irvin Painter, David Roediger, Francille Rusan Wilson, Stephen Brier, Irving Bernstein, and Albert Fried, 361–403.)

Hill, Herbert 1989: Rejoinder to Symposium on "Myth-Making as Labor History: Herbert Gutman and the United Mine Workers of America." *International Journal of Politics, Culture, and Society*, 2, 587–96.

Hodges, James A. 1986: *New Deal Labor Policy and the Southern Cotton Textile Industry, 1933–1941*. Knoxville: University of Tennessee Press.

Honey, Michael 1993: *Southern Labor and Black Civil Rights: Organizing Memphis Workers*. Urbana: University of Illinois Press.

Hunter, Tera 1997: *To 'Joy My Freedom: Southern Black Women's Lives and Labors After the Civil War*. Cambridge, MA: Harvard University Press.

Janiewski, Delores E. 1985: *Sisterhood Denied: Race, Gender, and Class in a New South Community*. Philadelphia: Temple University Press.

Jones, Jacqueline 1992: *The Dispossessed: America's Underclasses from the Civil War to the Present*. New York: Basic Books.

Katzman, David M. 1978: *Seven Days a Week: Women and Domestic Service in Industrializing America*. New York: Oxford University Press.

Kelley, Robin D. G. 1990: *Hammer and Hoe: Alabama Communists During the Great Depression*. Chapel Hill: University of North Carolina Press.

Kelley, Robin D. G. 1993: "We Are Not What We Seem": Re-thinking Black Working-Class Opposition in the Jim Crow South. *Journal of American History*, 80, 75–112.

Korstad, Karl 1992: Black and White Together: Organizing in the South with the Food, Tobacco, Agricultural & Allied Workers Union (FTA-CIO), 1942–1952. In Steve

Rosswurm (ed.), *The CIO's Left-Led Unions*. New Brunswick, NJ: Rutgers University Press, 64–94.

Korstad, Robert and Lichtenstein, Nelson 1988: Opportunities Found and Lost: Labor, Radicals, and the Early Civil Rights Movement. *Journal of American History*, 75, 786–811.

Letwin, Daniel 1998: *The Challenge of Interracial Unionism: Alabama Coal Miners, 1878–1921*. Chapel Hill: University of North Carolina Press.

Lewis, Earl 1991: *In Their Own Interests: Race, Class, and Power in Twentieth-Century Norfolk, Virginia*. Berkeley: University of California Press.

Lichtenstein, Alex 1996: *Twice the Work of Free Labor: The Political Economy of Convict Labor in the South*. London: Verso Press.

McKiven, Henry M., Jr. 1995: *Iron and Steel: Class, Race, and Community in Birmingham, Alabama, 1875–1920*. Chapel Hill: University of North Carolina Press.

McLaurin, Melton A. 1971: *Paternalism and Protest: Southern Cotton Mill Workers and Organized Labor, 1875–1905*. Westport, CT: Greenwood Press.

Marshall, F. Ray 1967: *Labor in the South*. Cambridge, MA: Harvard University Press.

Minchin, Timothy J. 1997: *What Do We Need a Union For?: The TWUA in the South, 1945–1955*. Chapel Hill: University of North Carolina Press.

Minchin, Timothy J. 1999: *Hiring the Black Worker: The Racial Integration of the Southern Textile Industry, 1960–1980*. Chapel Hill: University of North Carolina Press.

Mitchell, Broadus 1921: *The Rise of Cotton Mills in the South*. Baltimore: Johns Hopkins University Press.

Nelson, Bruce 1993: Organized Labor and the Struggle for Black Equality in Mobile during World War II. *Journal of American History*, 80, 952–88.

Nelson, Bruce 1996: Class, Race, and Democracy in the CIO: The "New" Labor History Meets the "Wages of Whiteness" (with responses by Elizabeth Faue and Thomas J. Sugrue, and rejoinder by Nelson). *International Review of Social History*, 41, 351–420.

Newby, I. A. 1989: *Plain Folk in the New South: Social Change and Cultural Persistence, 1880–1915*. Baton Rouge: Louisiana State University Press.

Newman, Dale 1978: Work and Community in a Southern Textile Town. *Labor History*, 19, 204–25.

Norrell, Robert J. 1986: Caste in Steel: Jim Crow Careers in Birmingham, Alabama. *Journal of American History*, 73, 669–94.

Rachleff, Peter J. 1984: *Black Labor in the South: Richmond, Virginia, 1865–1890*. Philadelphia: Temple University Press.

Reed, Merl E., Hough, Leslie S., and Fink, Gary M (eds.) 1981: *Southern Workers and their Unions, 1880–1975: Selected Papers, The Second Southern Labor History Conference, 1978*. Westport, CT: Greenwood Press.

Rosengarten, Theodore 1974: *All God's Dangers: The Life of Nate Shaw*. New York: Alfred A. Knopf.

Shapiro, Karin A. 1998: *A New South Rebellion: The Battle Against Convict Labor in the Tennessee Coalfields, 1871–1896*. Chapel Hill: University of North Carolina Press.

Simon, Bryant 1998: *A Fabric of Defeat: The Politics of South Carolina Millhands, 1910–1948*. Chapel Hill: University of North Carolina Press.

Stein, Judith 1991: Southern Workers in National Unions: Birmingham Steelworkers, 1936–1951. In Robert H. Zieger (ed.), *Organized Labor in the Twentieth-Century South*. Knoxville: University of Tennessee Press, 183–222.

Tannenbaum, Frank 1924: *Darker Phases of the South*. New York: G. P. Putman's Sons.

Trotter, Joe William, Jr. 1990: *Coal, Class, and Color: Blacks in Southern West Virginia, 1915–32*. Urbana: University of Illinois Press.

Trotter, Joe William, Jr. 1994: African-American Workers: New Directions in US Labor Historiography. *Labor History*, 35, 495–523.

Woodward, C. Vann 1951: *Origins of the New South, 1877–1913*. Baton Rouge: Louisiana State University Press.

Worthman, Paul B. 1969: Black Workers and Labor Unions in Birmingham, Alabama, 1897–1904. *Labor History*, 10, 375–407.

Zieger, Robert H. (ed.) 1991: *Organized Labor in the Twentieth-Century South*. Knoxville: University of Tennessee Press.

Zieger, Robert H. (ed.) 1997: *Southern Labor in Transition, 1940–1995*. Knoxville: University of Tennessee Press.

CHAPTER TWENTY-SIX

The Impact of the New Deal and World War II on the South

PAMELA TYLER

IN combination, Margaret Mitchell and Hollywood had a sure touch for melodrama. Recall the scene during the dramatic flight from Atlanta in flames when Rhett Butler gibed at the distraught Scarlett, "Take a good look, my dear – it's a historic moment." As the tattered remnants of the city's last Confederate defenders staggered past in ragged retreat, he mocked, "You can tell your grandchildren how you watched the old South disappear one night." The never-resolved question of change versus continuity in the so-called New South makes Rhett's assertion debatable, but if Mitchell had survived to pen a sequel to her page-turner, she might well have used that line again. Scarlett O'Hara's grandchildren, elderly Georgians at mid-twentieth century, would indeed have lived to see the disappearance of the Old South. Unlike Rhett, they probably would not have been able to pinpoint and agree on the exact date and event that drove old Dixie down. One grandson might have cited the Triple A, another the federal minimum wage act, another the remaking of the Party of the Fathers, still another the urbanization of the southern region or the growing assertiveness of African-Americans or the day he sold his mules at auction and put a red Farmall in the barn. But if, at some fictional family reunion of O'Hara descendants, the talk turned to drastic changes in the Southland, the consensus that emerged would most likely have been that all was traceable to the impact of the New Deal and World War II.

The more one reads in sources on the period 1933–45, the less possible it becomes to assess the impact on the South of the New Deal and World War II *separately*. What appears certain is that *trends* begun during the 1930s *accelerated* during the war years. The 1930s and 1940s saw the growing disappearance of tenant houses, mules, sharecroppers, and mill villages, all real and tangible entities, and the decline or endangerment of long-standing southern institutions such as paternalism, white supremacy, the one-party South, and the white primary. These changes and others were not completed between 1933 and 1945, but they are *rooted* there. Indeed, George B. Tindall (whose *The Emergence of the New South 1913–1945* is the essential starting point for anyone wishing to understand the impact of the 1930s and 1940s on the American South) felt that "recurrent themes of emergence" (Tindall 1967: ix) characterized the period. Other historians echo his judgment: "The soil had been tilled. The seeds that would later bear fruit had been planted. ... Harvest time would come in the next generation" (Sitkoff 1978: 335). "The New Deal set in motion forces ..." (Cobb 1992: 184). "The Great Depression, the New Deal farm programs and the demographic chaos occasioned by World War II all conspired to end or alter the main elements of the old system" (Kirby 1987: xiv). The language in these quotes is revealing. Historians in general do not allege that the New Deal, or later World War II, *finished*, *ended*, *completed*, or *accomplished* concrete actions; rather, these upheavals in American life were *catalysts for change* in the American South. "Metamorphoses of social structure, economy, beliefs, or mental attitude cannot conform to an overly precise chronology without distortion," warned Marc Bloch nearly half a century ago, and historians of the South in the 1930s and 1940s agree (quoted in Sosna 1987: 161).

In the 1930s and 1940s the federal presence in the South grew enormously, with momentous implications, but historians find room for disagreement about the exact meaning of that presence for southerners. For example, there is no unanimity of understanding about the intents or the effects of the Agricultural Adjustment Act (Triple A) in the South. Because agriculture so obviously occupied an economic and cultural status of great importance in the South, historians have written extensively about the effects of the New Deal on southern farmers, who were, by any assessment, suffering from Depression-like conditions years before the rest of the country felt them. Things only got worse during the national economic crisis. Roving journalist and federal employee Lorena Hickok wrote from the Delta to her boss Harry Hopkins of "an illiterate, wretched people, undernourished, with standards of living so low that, once on relief, they are quite willing to stay there the rest of their lives," and a federal report branded the agricultural South as "a belt of sickness, misery, and unnecessary death" (both quoted in Mertz 1978: 4, 13).

Paul Mertz in *New Deal Policy and Southern Rural Poverty* (1978) contends that the New Deal never found an effective way dealing with the South's rural poor or of reforming the pernicious conditions that governed their lives. In early 1933 the collapse of cotton prices had resulted in the near collapse of the fragile world of those who grew the white fiber. Congress passed the Triple A in the belief that scarcity, coupled with parity pricing, would bring recovery, an old idea that had been the heart of McNary-Haugenism in the 1920s. But AAA administrators never saw their agency as intended to deal with deep-seated social problems of the rural South and operated instead on the principle that a rising tide lifts all boats. However, the tide of benefit checks flowed to landowners, who were then on their honor to share the benefits with tenants and croppers working for them. When planters pocketed most or all of the benefits they were paid for growing fewer acres, the already impoverished tenants and croppers with fewer acres of crop to sell absorbed the pain of a well-meaning system that, in Mertz's view, was full of abuses. Mertz traces the inadequate early efforts of the federal government to get relief to destitute rural families, examining the workings of the Federal Emergency Relief Administration (FERA) and the Resettlement Administration (RA).

A faction of liberal administrators within AAA advocated extensive help for the neediest farmers and thorough reform of the southern agricultural system via a program of rural rehabilitation. The majority of AAA officials, however, operated conservatively and worked to advance the interests of the landowning class of farmers, maintaining, Mertz charges, that "prosperity was largely a matter of twelve cent cotton" (Mertz 1978: 257). He presents the story of the Farm Security Administration, which, in its eleven years of life, spent $1.9 billion to aid the South's poorest farm families, largely through loans for farm purchase or purchase of implements and household goods, coupled with a program of intensive supervision and instruction on progressive methods of farming and housekeeping. After 1941 attacks against the FSA mounted. Southern bankers and merchants resented its competition; others bitterly protested its services to blacks. "No New Deal agency worked more con-scientiously than the FSA to eliminate racial discrimination," Mertz noted (ibid: 193). Congress slashed the FSA budget repeatedly during the war and ultimately killed it in 1946. Mertz concludes that New Dealers were slow to see the limitations inherent in their "recovery through scarcity" agricultural policy, failing to realize that southern rural poverty was a chronic condition, predating 1929 and demanding extraordinary efforts from the federal government. Interestingly, FDR himself always leaned toward fostering the ideal of the yeoman farmer, using federal powers to turn landless tenants into self-supporting small farmers. It was one of his "oldest and most enduring dreams," notes his biographer Frank Freidel (1965: 64). It also ran counter to the trend toward rationalized commercial farming that his AAA aided and abetted.

Other historians agree with Mertz that the AAA, intent on raising crop prices and uninterested in reforming southern agricultural practices, was a boon for planters and a burden for tenants. Gavin Wright in *Old South, New South* branded the AAA "planter's heaven" (Wright 1986: 236), while Jack Temple Kirby, in *Rural Worlds Lost*, agreed that AAA rescued and enriched planters while inflicting "frustration and suffering on the already poor and landless" (Kirby 1987: 56). Bruce Schulman, in *From Cotton Belt to Sunbelt*, called AAA "a precision tool for raising farm prices and not . . . a multi-purpose vehicle for effecting social reform in rural areas" (Schulman 1991: 16). Tindall agreed, noting that "it had neither the organization nor the mandate to reform the landlord–tenant relationship" (Tindall 1967: 413).

A highly controversial aspect of the AAA concerned its alleged acceleration of the decline in numbers of tenants and croppers, whom planters increasingly evicted. As Rupert Vance put it in the 1930s, "With one hand the cotton landlord takes agricultural subsidies and rental benefits from his government; with the other he pushes his tenant on relief" (quoted in Tindall 1967: 409). The displacement of tenants was a demographic fact of the 1930s, but the causes remain in dispute. Acreage reductions mandated by the federal government led to evictions even though AAA contracts included clauses designed to protect tenants and croppers. However, imprecise wording ("insofar as possible" planters were to keep "the normal number of tenants" on their land) and a generous loophole that allowed planters to evict those who became "a nuisance or a menace" only reinforced the prolandlord outlook of the AAA cotton section. At the same time many planters began mechanizing their operations. A dispute has centered around this question: what explains the displace-ment of tenant farmers in the South? Did tenants leave because tractors came, or did planters buy machines because their labor left them?

Mechanization of cotton cultivation proceeded in stages, with tractors first used to break and till land and pull planting equipment. Though the labor-intensive tasks of chopping out weeds and picking the mature bolls still defied mechanization, many commercial farmers bought tractors in the 1930s, sold their mules, and displaced tenant families. They then relied on cheap surplus day labor for picking in the fall. Pete Daniel, in *Breaking the Land: The Transformation of Cotton, Tobacco, and Rice Cultures since 1880*, argues that such mechanization displaced perhaps from one-fifth to two-fifths of all uprooted tenants, with AAA acreage reduction accounting for much of the remainder (Daniel 1985: 175). Bruce Schulman stresses that it was never lack of capital that had kept cotton growers from mechanizing but concern about labor supply if they displaced their tenants. Planters were unwilling to risk complete dependence on day labor, making tenancy "the price," as Gavin Wright explains it, paid for "certainty of harvest labor" (Wright 1986: 235). Once the New Deal began providing relief for unemployed rural ex-tenants, in effect acting as surrogate "furnishing merchant" for part of the year, planters evicted more tenants and used their AAA checks to buy tractors. To ensure a ready supply of cheap labor when needed, they learned to manipulate local relief officials, pressuring them to strip the relief rolls of beneficiaries when cotton was ready for harvest. Thus deprived of any means of support other than the meager wages paid to day laborers, reluctant men and women picked cotton for fifty cents a hundredweight. After the harvest, planters coolly encouraged resumption of relief efforts to remove their obligation to furnish croppers at their commissaries. Daniel noted, "So long as federal relief policy did not displace the seasonal work force or drive wages too high, planters accepted it" (Daniel 1985: 72).

Tindall argues that displacement of tenants was not entirely the fault of AAA, which became "a scapegoat for sins not altogether its own" (Tindall 1967: 414). Rural poverty had existed long before 1933, agrees Harvard Sitkoff, causing migration of thousands of landless farmers out of the South in the teens and twenties as well. Civil rights activists were voluble in their charge that AAA was perpetrating a mass eviction of black croppers, but Sitkoff notes that more African-Americans left the South in the years 1931–3 than in the first two years of the New Deal. The problem of high rates of reproduction among tenants and croppers, both black and white, combined with the onslaught of the boll weevil and the South's falling share of the world cotton market to mean that fewer and fewer southerners could make a living growing cotton. Many chose to try their luck elsewhere, swelling the populations and the relief rolls of cities and towns. The coming of mechanized farming surely fed this trend but cannot be said to have started it (Sitkoff 1978: 53).

Overall, Tindall gives the most favorable assessment of the AAA's effects on the South, noting that rural poverty might have been worse without AAA-brought stabilization and that many, many southerners were helped to better lives by the AAA. Its soil conservation programs succeeded in fostering contour plowing, cover crops, crop rotation, and terracing, and its credit agencies helped many middle-class borrowers. A 1936 Gallup poll showed that while 59 percent of national voters regarded AAA as more harmful than helpful, 57 percent of southerners supported it. Pete Daniel (1985) takes a dimmer view, noting the chaos caused by competing factions of officials within the AAA. The dominant group pushed to sweep away the old system of tenancy while a minority of officials fought to reform that system. The one fueled the drive toward bigger commercial farms and more machinery – a capitalist agricultural structure more like that of the business world – while the other struggled to provide small farms for self-supporting farmers. AAA policies pushed people off the land, but FSA policies resettled them on it. AAA reduced acreage under cultvation, but county agents taught farmers to grow more on fewer acres. Sounding a bit like a Vanderbilt agrarian, Daniel laments the passing of the self-sustaining family farmer and his folk culture, deplores commercial farming, and is frankly nostalgic for the agrarian way of life. He maintains, if not persuasively, that there were options that could have kept people farming on the small scale and preserved their rural culture and communities. Like Gunnar Myrdal, who coined the phrase, Daniel sees the AAA as a "southern enclosure movement." Kirby says, laconically but realistically, "mechanization would ultimately doom most ordinary farmers" (Kirby 1987: 335).

Of course there was more to southern agriculture than cotton. Daniel observes that AAA stabilized tobacco and rice cultures with little disruption of tenant arrangements. Because tobacco was a labor-intensive crop requiring steady work over the months, tobacco growers evicted fewer tenants and were more likely to share AAA subsidy payments with them. Kirby notes that in nonplantation areas, AAA's effects were inadequate but primarily beneficial.

Kirby's thesis in *Rural Worlds Lost*, namely that a transformation of the South occurred between 1920 and 1960, with the most intense changes coming in the 1930s and 1940s, is persuasive. The South that was swept away was marked by deep rural poverty, croppers and mules, more farmers than industrial workers, and urbanites in the minority. Key elements of change were the mechanization of agriculture, expensive but labor-saving agricultural science, government subsidies, and government regulation.

The South of the 1930s was not exclusively rural and agrarian; while it had not measured up to boosters' ballyhoo, it was not without industry. Indeed, the authors of *Like A Family* (1987), an award-winning study of southern laborers, open their book with the line, "Textile mills built the New South" (Hall et al. 1987: xi). For an understanding of how New Deal policies affected southern industries, the essential works are Hall et al., Gavin Wright's *Old South, New South* (1986), Bruce Schulman's *From Cotton Belt to Sunbelt* (1991), and Tindall's *Emergence of the New South* (1967). Wright, a historical economist, addresses himself to the question of how the South accomplished its transformation from a poor, rural region to the dazzling Sunbelt South of Houston, Atlanta, and North Carolina's Research Triangle Park. In a nutshell, he answers that until the grip of the southern *regional* economy was broken, the South remained isolated and poor, with the southern wage below national norms. In the 1930s and 1940s came a set of federal policies that undermined the separate southern labor market and produced a revolution. Southern mill owners had long used the lure of low wages to entice textile operations south from New England. In the 1930s the collapse of tenancy reinforced an industrial labor surplus as destitute men and women sought work in the rural and small-town mills. The New Deal's National Industrial Recovery Act of 1933 arrived as an assault on the low-wage economy of the South, with codes prohibiting "cutthroat competition," stabilizing industries, and ensuring purchasing power for labor by setting a minimum wage. Its effects were greatest on low-wage industries, which meant the NIRA had a greater impact on the South than any other region. Key southern enterprises like textiles, tobacco, lumber, and furniture-making all saw overnight wage increases, and although NIRA permitted a southern wage differential (based on the argument that the cost of living in the South was lower), the codes still significantly reduced the North–South wage differential and began the process of bringing the South into the national labor market. (Of this fact, Tindall commented drily, "The conclusion is unavoidable that the differential, like so many other things, reflected differences not in the cost but in the *standard* of living": Tindall 1967: 481.)

Jacquelyn Dowd Hall and her co-authors reveal in *Like A Family* (1987) that the NIRA minimum-wage requirements led to a frenzy of rationalization in southern mills as owners, determined to get the most from workers in return for the increased wages they were forced to pay, fired slower, weaker workers and upped production quotas for the able-bodied who remained. Small, inefficient mills had often kept slower workers on because they were the cheapest of cheap labor, but NIRA took away this advantage; consequently, mills shifted their policies. Though owners generally observed wage guidelines, they slashed the work week in order to regulate swollen inventories that had resulted when they drove workers to peak efficiency. Moreover, mill owners began charging workers for water and electricity in mill villages to offset the wage hikes mandated by NIRA. Having heard on their radios invitations to write to the Roosevelts, southern workers took up their pens and poured out candid accounts about the most intimate details of their working lives. One of the greatest strengths of this well-written book is its use of long-forgotten letters in NIRA files to reveal vivid glimpses of the realities of workers' lives. In particular, this book includes gender as a category of analysis, examining how changes in mill operations affected women and reporting how women viewed themselves as workers and as mothers.

Believing that in FDR they had a friend who had extended rights and privileges to them, southern textile workers began to voice long-repressed grievances. A revolution of rising expectations appeared to be underway. Section 7(a) of the NIRA had injected the South with the virus of unionism, one casualty of which was paternalism. Citing the lame excuse of "inferior work," owners fired union leaders and railed against "outside agitators." Hall notes the delicious irony that the chief agitator was likely President Roosevelt himself, whose radio broadcasts had helped to convince people that "the President wants you to join the union" (Hall et al. 1987: 304).

Like A Family provides a memorable account of the disastrous general strike of 1934, which erupted when the Textile Code authority ignored southern workers' discontent and approved a 25 percent cut in hours. Strikes spread throughout the South, growing in two weeks' time to "the largest single labor conflict in American history" (ibid: 329). FDR disappointed workers when he ducked calls to intervene and instead punted to a special mediation board, which studied rather than mediated. When the strike ultimately failed, a mass purge of strikers followed, with evictions from mill villages and blacklistings common. The 1934 strike revealed the inadequacy of New Deal labor policy, which, having encouraged unionism, could neither compel arbitration nor protect workers from unfair labor practices or brutal retaliations. The legacy of the strike was "a deep distrust of government and trade unions alike" (ibid: 354) as the textile industry remained the major failure of southern unionism.

Wayne Flynt agrees with Hall about the strike's consequences. In an essay on southern labor, he notes that the change represented by southern workers turning to the federal government to redress their grievances in the 1930s was extraordinary (Flynt 1984: 94). He also suggests that the owners' strategy of locating southern mills in rural areas beyond cities kept unionism blunted. When mills were in or near cities with strong union movements already in existence (Birmingham, for example), the outlook for textile unions was better.

Bruce Schulman's *From Cotton Belt to Sunbelt* advances an interesting and unique thesis. He challenges the conventional view that the New Deal waned after 1938 as conservative advisers to FDR replaced more liberal voices, sapping the will to reform socioeconomic conditions, while gathering war clouds overshadowed everything else. Instead, Schulman holds that "it was not so much that the New Deal withered after 1938 as that it headed south" (Schulman 1991: viii). In his second term, Roosevelt, with strong support from southern liberal allies, abandoned his more cautious relief and recovery approach and worked to reform the southern economy and to transform the Democratic Party. In a speech at Gainesville, Georgia, in 1938, FDR branded the South a feudal economy and said that there was little difference in a feudal and a fascist system. As a way of focusing national attention and preparing the way for more extensive federal intervention in the South, the president that year commissioned the National Emergency Council to write its *Report on Economic Conditions of the South*, in which the southern liberals who compiled the report factually surveyed economic and social conditions in the region, examining housing, income, education, health, credit, purchasing power, and more. In the introduction to the report, FDR famously called the South "the Nation's No. 1 economic problem." To Schulman, this was a watershed, marking "the onset of a concerted effort to restructure the region's economy and the end to the national administration's conciliation of southern interests" (Schulman 1991: 51). Morton Sosna has labeled it a call for "a regional affirmative action program" (Sosna 1987: 149). Initiatives that followed included the FSA's program to assist landless black and white farmers to better themselves economically, the National Youth Administration's plan to aid poor young people of both races to stay in school, and efforts to achieve abolition of the poll tax in southern states. All provoked storms of furious negative reaction from local elites in the South.

Schulman also includes the Fair Labor Standards Act of 1938 (FLSA) as part of FDR's initiative to reform the South. Walter Lippmann had called the FLSA "really a sectional bill thinly disguised as a humanitarian reform" (quoted in Schulman 1991: 54), because the South remained the only region without minimum-wage laws. To Schulman, passage of the FLSA was evidence of the Roosevelt administration's intention to break the grip of low-wage, labor-intensive industries on the South despite incurring the wrath of mill owners. An unforeseen consequence of this new direction was the pain inflicted on many southern workers as owners rushed to adopt labor-saving machinery. Southern industry became more modern and competitive, but many unskilled workers lost their jobs to the higher wage scale. Schulman says the president and his southern liberal allies "never considered who would pay for the restructuring of southern industry" (ibid: 72). Furthermore, federal legislation on wages made mill housing a liability to owners, who had traditionally provided it as a sort of wage supplement. The new forty-hour week meant that mills ran two shifts to meet production, but owners had no desire to build more company housing for the new workers who were, after the New Deal, being paid at rates much higher than before 1933. Moreover, the collapse of tenancy provided a stream of southerners eager for mill jobs even without a guarantee of housing. Mill owners, who felt that the expense of mill villages was less and less justified, began selling off the houses. The passing of the mill village was one more consequence of the New Deal.

Overall, an eager Dixieland learned the Roosevelt alphabet: NIRA, AAA, CCC, TVA, FERA, CWA, PWA, WPA, REA, RA, FSA, NYA. Ironically, the region that had long retained an obsessive fear of federal intervention came to rely on that very intervention for anything approaching economic prosperity, and thus the New Deal brought a major shift in the relationship between the South and the federal government. Unwittingly, various New Deal agencies helped to erode the "vestigial paternalism of the landlord–tenant relationship" (Schulman 1991: 20) and of the mill worker–mill owner relationship as well (as Hall et al. and Flynt noted). Well before the Roosevelt administration, southerners had learned that the federal government could function as an ally rather than an adversary. In the wake of floods and droughts, the Corps of Engineers, the Red Cross, and various federal relief agencies addressed southern needs and simultaneously reinforced the existing economic and social order. James C. Cobb discusses this phenomenon insightfully in his study of the Mississippi Delta, *The Most Southern Place on Earth* (1992). After brief exposure to the workings of the New Deal, however, the landowning establishment realized that the extent of federal intrusion into life in the heretofore isolated South threatened to upset the status quo and alter cherished institutions. With previously subservient tenants and workers looking to Washington rather than to local planters, merchants, and mill owners for assistance came a shift in relationships. Landlords had quite willingly let the federal government take the role of providing for their dependents during winter off-seasons, as they let croppers draw relief checks rather than "furnish" them. For their part, poor blacks and whites saw that government checks carried no interest charges and found that at least some government officials treated them with more dignity than planters had. When the desperate times of 1933 temporarily altered a regional outlook that had long resisted federal intervention, conservative planters had clamored for federal action. Gaining the sought-after funds, they came to resent federal interference with regional ways, but the camel's nose was under the tent; relief interposed federal officials between the laboring people and the local bosses and abetted the undermining of the oppressive authority of local elites.

Obviously, no group of southerners felt the oppressive authority of local elites more heavily than African-Americans. The impact of the New Deal on blacks is a subject addressed by Harvard Sitkoff and Nancy Weiss, who reach different conclusions about it. In nearly all of its alphabetic manifestations, the New Deal discriminated against black recipients. In the South, local administrators of programs prevented blacks from sharing fully in benefits, but, preferring to keep intact his working relationship with powerful congressional southerners who wanted the southern racial status quo to remain undisturbed, FDR offered no challenge to their discriminatory ways. Alan Brinkley analyzes Roosevelt's failure to reform southern politics, his steadfast avoidance of antagonizing issues, and his preference for working with existing political elites. In all the southern region, no AAA county committee included blacks; of over 10,000 WPA supervisors in the South, a total of 11 were black; Mississippi, over half black, allotted but 1.7 percent of its CCC allotment to African-Americans (Sitkoff 1978: 53, 49, 51). However, Sitkoff ultimately sees a glass that is half-full. Negro expectations rose because of the Roosevelt administration's racial gestures; allies who wanted to challenge the reactionary South materialized in the president's circle and began to assist a nascent civil rights movement (ibid: 330–3).

Though Sitkoff credits the New Deal with making few substantive changes for African-American welfare, he articulates the view that the Roosevelt administration recognized and took responsibility for the plight of blacks and created "a reform atmosphere that made possible a major campaign for civil rights" (ibid: 59). He sees Eleanor Roosevelt as first among all for altering the relationship between the New

Deal and civil rights, noting how boldly she moved toward publicly embracing civil rights issues (challenging the segregation ordinance in 1938 in Birmingham, addressing conferences of the NAACP, accepting awards for crusading for racial justice, joining the campaign for abolition of poll taxes, speaking in favor of an anti-lynching bill, being photographed frequently with African-Americans). He attributes the shift of black votes from Republican to Democratic in 1936 (a trend that really began in the off-year elections of 1934) to the identification of key New Dealers with the cause of civil rights. Observing that black leaders and newspapers had stressed civil rights issues emphatically in the 1936 campaign, he concludes that "economic matters were secondary in their endorsement of Roosevelt" (ibid: 96).

In *Farewell to the Party of Lincoln* Nancy Weiss (1983) counters that blacks became wedded to the Democratic Party not because of the Roosevelt administration's record on civil rights, which she sees as anemic, but because of the economic gains they made under the New Deal. However, her thesis is less than persuasive and she sometimes seems to make the case for Sitkoff with more evidence than she brings to her own ideas. Her inclusion of an entire chapter on the role of Eleanor Roosevelt in changing the loyalty of black voters seems to undercut her argument that blacks turned Democrat because of economic benefits. Weiss insists that the racial gestures made by FDR or his administation "did not betoken any growing commitment by the administration to the cause of civil rights" (ibid: 157). She argues that black support for FDR did not mean support for the Democratic Party, since in 1936, when 71 percent of blacks polled backed FDR, only 44 percent identified themselves as Democrats. Blacks surely understood that Congress enacted economically beneficial legislation, but they also understood that Franklin Roosevelt, his wife, and his appointed officials (notably Harold Ickes, Clark Foreman, Will Alexander, Mary McLeod Bethune, Aubrey Williams) had granted blacks a measure of dignity and friendship by showing an interest never before shown by the White House. Like Weiss, Sitkoff reports frankly the racism with which New Deal programs operated and its failures at fairness. However, he concludes that, because of previous administrations' indifference, the New Deal exceeded blacks' expectations and kindled their enthusiastic loyalty, based on much more than economic rewards alone. Their shift in allegiance from "the party of Lincoln" to the Democrats is yet another legacy of the New Deal, and, although few southern blacks outside cities were registered voters in the 1930s, Roosevelt's pictures adorned their walls too. The Voting Rights Act of a later generation would be the final piece in the political puzzle; when enfranchised, southern blacks would become mainstays of the remade Democratic Party.

Bruce Schulman and Harvard Sitkoff have argued that in its second term, the Roosevelt administration turned to the left in its relations with the South. The New Deal created an atmosphere that encouraged nascent liberalism in the South. White southern liberals advocated many reforms: unionization, tenant resettlement, public power, generous relief measures, minimum wages, improved public health and public schools. Southern planters and mill owners, alarmed at the New Deal's reduction of dependency and paternalism and at the metamorphosis of the national Democratic Party into one in which their views were all but ignored, feared that outside interference would lead farm workers and factory workers to demand justice. To prevent any class-based movement of have-nots, they played the race card, railing at the New Deal's plans to pay equal wages to blacks, build integrated housing projects, and, allegedly, promote social equality and even intermarriage (Sitkoff 1978: ch. 5). They were further inflamed by FDR's ill-advised and ultimately unsuccessful efforts to purge ultraconservative southern members from Congress, depicting his intervention as another Yankee invasion.

While southern liberals had hoped reforms would ease racial tensions by improving life for southern blacks as well as whites, they did not call for an end to segregation. They viewed economic injustice as the primary problem in the South. In 1938, with President Roosevelt's approval and his wife's direct participation, they organized the Southern Conference for Human Welfare to focus on bringing the New Deal to all poor people in the South. The nucleus of liberals who established SCHW were middle-class, white, and urban, united in their belief that they must make common cause with the rural poor, organized labor, and blacks in order to rejuvenate the South and liberate it from the stifling grip of reaction. But SCHW was tarred at the outset with the brush of interracialism and suffered a loss of credibility in the eyes of many white southerners, even reputedly liberal ones, who feared being branded as a racial-equality organization. Harvard Sitkoff says it "made more headlines than progress" (Sitkoff 1978: 137).

The story of the SCHW in particular and of southern liberalism in general during the New Deal period is told in Thomas Krueger, *And Promises to Keep* (1967), Morton Sosna, *In Search of the Silent South* (1977), Linda Reed, *Simple Decency and Common Sense* (1991), and Patricia Sullivan, *Days of Hope* (1996). Sullivan's book is particularly well written and well researched, weaving together fascinating stories of remarkable men and women like Virginia Foster Durr, Lucy Randolph Mason, Ella Baker, Clark Foreman, Walter White, Charles H. Houston, and others into a narrative of efforts that "reached across racial boundaries to advance political and economic democracy in the region, with the support of the federal government and a strong national labor movement" (Sullivan 1996: 273). Tindall, however, judges the southern liberals as "generals without an army, leaders with little influence among the mass of workers, farmers and middle class, and with almost no foothold in politics" (Tindall 1967: 633). An especially good article that examines the failed attempt at interracial, class-based action in one southern city is Robert J. Norrell's "Labor at the Ballot Box: Alabama Politics from the New Deal to the Dixiecrat Movement." Norrell, too, sees that signs of interracial working-class cooperation "worked to reinforce the concerted effort of Birmingham's upper class to make all whites think in racial or sectional ways – indeed, in any terms *except* class" (Norrell 1991: 227).

Ultimately, race trumped class. The weakness of the southern labor movement and the fact that few blacks and working-class whites voted meant that a class view could not be heard in politics. The elite understood only too well that "to preserve their hegemony in the local community they had to destroy the possibility of working-class cohesion" (ibid: 233), and when they succeeded in rousing the masses into a defense of white supremacy, fledgling southern liberalism failed to take root. Thus, the New Deal did not debilitate the southern political structure but shook it, threatened it, and forced it to take the defensive. In resorting to race-based appeals to maintain itself in power, the southern elite marginalized themselves more than ever and positioned themselves far outside the national mainstream of thought. The coming war, with its emphasis on democracy versus fascism, would marginalize southern institutions even further.

The most obvious effect of World War II on the American South was the creation of thousands upon thousands of jobs. "For the first time since the War Between the States," noted *Fortune Magazine* in 1943, "almost any native of the Deep South who wants a job can get one." Schulman argues that, coming at the time when AAA policies and mechanization of farming had displaced armies of rural laborers, and mill owners had laid off multitudes of unskilled workers rather than pay them the federally mandated minimum wage, the massive war mobilization averted a southern economic catastrophe in the making by creating a huge demand for labor. Pete Daniel agrees, calling the armed forces and defense plants "the resettlement administration for rural southerners" (Schulman 1991: 72; Daniel 1985: 243).

So great was the demand for industrial labor in the South that there were labor shortages in agriculture, with German POWs pressed into service at harvest time on southern farms and plantations. These shortages meant higher wages for cotton pickers, which resulted in new leisure and independence among blacks, which infuriated many southern whites, as Jim Cobb noted in *The Most Southern Place on Earth*. Particularly galling was the difficulty in getting black women to do domestic service when they had other and more attractive ways of earning a living. This situation led to rumors of Eleanor Clubs, supposedly inspired by the First Lady: groups of African-American women pledged to put "a white woman in every kitchen" by Christmas (Cooper and Terrill 1991: 692). The wartime South was awash with rumors about uprisings among blacks, fueled by the stresses of war and the real changes in black confidence and assertiveness. An old but worthwhile book that treats the phenomenon of southern whites' wartime fears is Howard Odom's *Race and Rumors of Race* (1943). Cobb also addresses the war's contribution to escalating racial tensions (Cobb 1992: chs 8–9). Attributing these unwanted changes to the impact of the New Deal, which had inclined blacks to look to Washington for security and support, many southern whites turned against the Roosevelt administration's domestic efforts with energy and vitriol, while supporting FDR's foreign initiatives enthusiastically.

Morton Sosna charted new interpretative waters with his original essay, "More Important Than the Civil War?" and continued to probe the subject in "The GIs' South and the North–South Dialogue During World War II" (Sosna 1988: 311–26). In the latter essay, he notes that the stationing of at least half of the nation's servicemen and women in the South for military training during the war created and mobilized "an army of critics against the South" (ibid: 312). Personal contact with the region confirmed them in viewing the South as exotic, discomforting, and shocking.

In 1997 nine scholarly papers presented at a conference commemorating the fiftieth anniversary of the end of World War II were published in McMillen (1997b). These selections, plus Morton Sosna's introduction to the topic, constitute a good overview of the thinking and scholarship on the subject today. In his essay, James C. Cobb agrees with Sosna that by bringing millions of Yankee soldiers into the South, "the war had not only highlighted the South's abnormalities but helped to transform the nation into one where these abnormalities could no longer be tolerated." He also insists that a new periodization would be useful to historians. Since separating the impact of war from the impact of the New Deal is well nigh impossible, he prefers to view the war as "a sort of unarticulated Third New Deal, one freed from some of the most severe economic restraints that hampered the first two" (Cobb 1997: 14, 10).

Dewey Grantham's essay ("The South and Congressional Politics") also notes that during the war, non-southern Americans increasingly began to ask, "What can be done about the South?" Thus, Sosna, Cobb, and Grantham view the war years as a watershed during which the nation at large developed a heightened consciousness of the South's undesirable extremes of conservatism and a resolve to intervene to change things.

In another essay in the same volume ("African-American Militancy in the World War II South"), Harvard Sitkoff casts doubt on the conventional view that depicts the war years as a time when "blacks belligerently assaulted the racial status quo," noting rightly that the most important signs of African-American militancy (protest editorials, threats by protest organizations, lukewarm support for the Allied cause, violent interracial clashes on military bases) came most frequently in the *pre*-Pearl Harbor period. He also counters the familiar idea that military service provided a coterie of future southern civil rights leaders radicalized and energized by their war experiences, insisting that blacks "modernized" by their war service left the South in greatest numbers. "Those militantly fighting for change in the 1960s would not look to the agenda and actions of World War II blacks and racial organizations as models to emulate" (Sitkoff 1997: 92). Neil McMillen's entry in this volume, "Fighting For What We Didn't Have: How Mississippi's Black Veterans Remember World War II," suggests both that the war experience "touched the lives of Mississippi's black service men and women in ways their white oppressors both feared and underestimated" and that it did not cause them to press for changes in the racial status quo in any immediate way (McMillen 1997a: 95). On the whole, he agrees with Sitkoff that the war did *not* ignite a Negro Revolution, as is often asserted.

In the decade after World War II it became clear that the American South was in the midst of a transformation from a provincial, rural, impoverished, low-wage society to a more nearly modern society, with race relations, economic conditions, and urbanization patterns increasingly like those in the rest of the United States. Not all historians will agree that the alterations were an unmixed blessing. Pete Daniel and Numan Bartley sound decidedly doubtful about the salutary effects of some of the changes, the former writing wistfully of disappearing community and continuity in the years since the 1930s and 1940s, and the latter noting that "progress" meant, among other things, bringing the South into the national labor market, and that that meant commodity labor, which depersonalized the southern work place.

An examination of the literature on the impact of World War II on the South reveals that I. A. Newby's comment in 1978 is still valid: the "history of the South during World War II is still largely unwritten" (Newby 1978: 546). Historians have been more thorough and inquisitive in charting the impact of the New Deal on Dixie, but there remain many likely directions for further study on aspects of the years 1933–45. A longitudinal or follow-up study to determine the short-term and long-term effects of Farm Security Administration expenditures in the South would be useful, combining statistical data, departmental reports, and interviews with survivors, both aid recipients and FSA employees, somewhat in the manner of the follow-up to James Agee and Walker Evans's 1941 classic, *Let Us Now Praise Famous Men*. Such a study would provide analysis of the effectiveness of this early effort to attack southern poverty. *Like A Family* stands as a model for sensitive use of oral history supported by manuscript sources. Following its lead, others might contribute detailed local studies of southern industrial communities and their reactions to unions, strikes, the Roosevelt administration, and the strains on housing and transportation facilities caused by the war. There is no complete study of the southern exodus in the twentieth century, the massive out-migration of black and white southerners to regions beyond their places of birth. How did their residence in northern and western cities affect them, and how did they affect their new communities? Other areas are suggested by other questions: What exactly was the economic impact of World War II on the South? How did southern communities react to German prisoners-of-war interned in their vicinities, and what types of work, under what conditions, did these prisoners do? What was the relationship between southerners and the peripatetic Eleanor Roosevelt? With so many men away for military service, what new patterns of activities among southern women emerged? And with what, if any, lasting effects?

For anyone wishing to understand the impact of the New Deal and World War II on the American South, there are useful tools beyond the historians' arts. The novels of William Faulkner paint memorable pictures of the assumptions governing race and class relations in the rural and small town South of that era; particularly good are *The Hamlet* (1940) and *Intruder in the Dust* (1948). Harriette Arnow's *The Dollmaker* (1954) traces vividly the upheaval visited in the lives of an Appalachian family by the war, with particular emphasis on women's culture and ways of coping. Two videos deal with the agricultural and industrial experience of the South during the New Deal. *Mean Things Happening in This Land* (60 minutes; part of a series entitled *The Great Depression*, produced by Henry Hampton for Blackside, Inc., and the Corporation for Public Broadcasting in 1993) focuses memorably on the plight of landless southern farmers who attempted an interracial effort to improve wages and conditions when they formed the Southern Tenant Farmers Union in Arkansas. *The Uprising of '34* (87 minutes; produced and directed by Geroge Stoney and Judith Helfand, for First Run/Icarus Films in 1995) recounts the largest labor uprising ever in the United States, when southern textile workers struck against intolerable conditions. Both films intercut interviews with elderly survivors of the events with black-and-white archival footage to achieve gripping immediacy.

The years 1933–45 were not the beginning of the end, but were, as Winston Churchill said of a crucial battle in early World War II, "the end of the beginning." These years mark *starts* that were made, seeds planted, forces set in motion, trends begun. When 1945 arrived, it indeed marked the end of the beginning, the beginning of the South's transformation into a more national, less sectional piece of the United States. Many had hoped to see the South join the national mainstream. However, there was more than a little bittersweet reflection among southerners as they marked the alteration. Wrote Flannery O'Connor, more than a decade after war's end, "The anguish that most of us have observed for some time now has been caused not by the fact that the South is alienated from the rest of the country, but by the fact that it is not alienated enough, that every day we are getting more and more like the rest of the country, that we are being forced out, not only of our many sins but of our few virtues" (quoted in Bartley: 1984: 145). This is the paradox that John Egerton (1974) later captured in his book, *The Americanization of Dixie/The Southernization of America*. For good or ill, this is what came, finally, of the impact of the New Deal and World War II on the American South.

BIBLIOGRAPHY

Agee, James and Walker, Evans 1941: *Let Us Now Praise Famous Men*. Boston: Houghton-Mifflin.

Anderson, William 1975: *The Wild Man From Sugar Creek: The Political Career of Eugene Talmadge*. Athens: University of Georgia Press.

Angelou, Maya 1969: *I Know Why the Caged Bird Sings*. New York: Random House.

Arnow, Harriette Louisa Simpson 1954: *The Dollmaker*. New York: Macmillan.

Ashby, Warren 1980: *Frank Porter Graham: A Southern Liberal*. Winston-Salem, NC: Wake Forest University Press.

Badger, Anthony 1981: *Prosperity Road: The New Deal, Tobacco, and North Carolina*. Chapel Hill: University of North Carolina Press.

Baldwin, Sidney 1980: *Poverty and Politics: The Rise and Fall of the Farm Security Administration*. Chapel Hill: University of North Carolina Press.

Barnard, Hollinger (ed.) 1984: *Outside the Magic Circle: The Autobiography of Virginia Foster Durr*. Tuscaloosa: University of Alabama Press.

Bartley, Numan 1984: The Era of the New Deal as a Turning Point in Southern History. In James C. Cobb and Michael V. Namorato (eds.), *The New Deal and the South*. Jackson: University Press of Mississippi, 135–46.

Bartley, Numan 1995: *The New South 1945–1980*. Baton Rouge: Louisiana State University Press.

Biles, Roger 1994: *The South and the New Deal*. Lexington: University Press of Kentucky.

Brinkley, Alan 1984: The New Deal and Southern Politics. In James C. Cobb and Michael V. Namorato (eds.), *The New Deal and the South*. Jackson: University Press of Mississippi, 97–115.

Carter, Dan T. 1969: *Scottsboro: A Tragedy of the American South*. Baton Rouge: Louisiana State University Press.

Cobb, James C. 1982: *The Selling of the South: The Southern Crusade for Industrial Development, 1936–1980*. Baton Rouge: Louisiana State University Press.

Cobb, James C. 1992: *The Most Southern Place on Earth: The Mississippi Delta and the Roots of Regional Identity*. New York and Oxford: Oxford University Press.

Cobb, James C. 1997: World War II and the Mind of the Modern South. In Neil R. McMillen (ed.), *Remaking Dixie: The Impact of World War II on the American South*. Jackson: University Press of Mississippi, 3–20.

Cobb, James C. and Namorato, Michael V. (eds.) 1984: *The New Deal and the South*. Jackson: University Press of Mississippi.

Conkin, Paul 1959: *Tomorrow a New World: The New Deal Community Program*. Ithaca, NY: Cornell University Press.

Conrad, David 1965: *The Forgotten Farmers: The Story of Sharecroppers in the New Deal*. Urbana: University of Illinois Press.

Cooper, William J. and Terrill, Thomas E. 1991: *The American South: A History*. New York: Alfred A. Knopf.

Crews, Harry 1978: *A Childhood: Biography of a Place*. Athens: University of Georgia Press.

Cronenberg, Allen 1995: *Forth to the Mighty Conflict: Alabama and World War II*. Tuscaloosa: University of Alabama Press.

Daniel, Pete 1984: The New Deal, Southern Agriculture, and Economic Change. In J. C. Cobb and M. V. Namorato (eds.), *The New Deal and the South*. Jackson: University Press of Mississippi, 37–61.

Daniel, Pete 1985: *Breaking the Land: The Transformation of Cotton, Tobacco, and Rice Cultures since 1880*. Urbana: University of Illinois Press.

Daniel, Pete 1990: Going Among Strangers: Southern Reactions to World War II. *Journal of American History*, 77: 886–911.

Dykeman, Wilma and Stokely, James 1962: *Seeds of Southern Change: The Life of Will Alexander*. Chicago: University of Chicago Press.

Egerton, John 1974: *The Americanization of Dixie: The Southernization of America*. New York: Harper's Magazine Press.

Egerton, John 1994: *Speak Now Against the Day: The Generation Before the Civil Rights Movement in the South*. New York: Alfred A. Knopf.

Faulkner, William 1940: *The Hamlet*. New York: Random House.

Faulkner, William 1948: *Intruder in the Dust*. New York: Random House.

Fite, Gilbert 1984: *Cotton Fields No More: Southern Agriculture, 1865–1980*. Lexington: University Press of Kentucky.

Flynt, J. Wayne 1979: *Dixie's Forgotten People: The South's Poor Whites*. Bloomington: Indiana University Press.

Flynt, J. Wayne 1984: The New Deal and Southern Labor. In James C. Cobb and Michael V. Namorato (eds.), *The New Deal and the South*. Jackson: University Press of Mississippi, 63–95.

Freidel, Frank 1965: *FDR and the South*. Baton Rouge: Louisiana State University Press.

Freidel, Frank 1984: The South and the New Deal. In James C. Cobb and Michael V. Namorato (eds.), *The New Deal and the South*. Jackson: University Press of Mississippi, 17–36.

Grantham, Dewey W. 1997: The South and Congressional Politics. In Neil R. McMillen (ed.), *Remaking Dixie: The Impact of World War II on the American South*. Jackson: University Press of Mississippi, 21–32.

Grubbs, Donald 1971: *Cry From the Cotton: The Southern Tenant Farmers Union*. Chapel Hill: University of North Carolina Press.

Hagood, Margaret J. 1939: *Mothers of the South: Portraiture of White Tenant Farm Women*. Chapel Hill: University of North Carolina Press.

Hall, Jacquelyn Dowd, et al. 1987: *Like A Family: The Making of a Southern Cotton Mill World*. Chapel Hill: University of North Carolina Press.

Hargrove, Erwin and Conkin, Paul (eds.) 1983: *TVA: Fifty Years of Grass Roots Bureaucracy*. Urbana: University of Illinois Press.

Herring, Harriet 1949: *The Passing of the Mill Village*. Chapel Hill: University of North Carolina Press.

Hevener, John C. 1978: *Which Side Are You On? The Harlan County Coal Miners*. Urbana: University of Illinois Press.

Holley, Donald 1975: *Uncle Sam's Farmers: The New Deal Communities in the Lower Mississippi Valley*. Urbana: University of Illinois Press.

Holmes, Michael 1975: *The New Deal in Georgia: An Administrative History*. Westport, CT: Greenwood Publishing.

Kelley, Robin 1990: *Hammer and Hoe: Alabama Communists During the Greeat Depression*. Chapel Hill: University of North Carolina Press.

Kirby, Jack Temple 1983: The Southern Exodus, 1910–1960: A Primer for Historians. *Journal of Southern History*, 49, 585–600.

Kirby, Jack Temple 1987: *Rural Worlds Lost: The American South 1920–1960*. Baton Rouge: Louisiana State University Press.

Krueger, Thomas 1967: *And Promises to Keep: The Southern Conference for Human Welfare*. Nashville: Vanderbilt University Press.

Loveland, Anne C. 1986: *Lillian Smith: A Southerner Confronting the South*. Baton Rouge: Louisiana State University Press.

McMillen, Neil R. 1997a: Fighting For What We Didn't Have: How Mississippi's Black Veterans Remember World War II. In Neil McMillen (ed.), *Remaking Dixie: The Impact of World War II on the American South*. Jackson: University Press of Mississippi, 93–110.

McMillen, Neil R. (ed.) 1997b: *Remaking Dixie: The Impact of World War II on the American South*. Jackson: University Press of Mississippi.

Maharidge, Dale and Williamson, Michael 1989: *And Their Children After Them: The Legacy of Let Us Now Praise Famous Men, James Agee, Walker Evans and the Rise and Fall of Cotton in the South*. New York: Pantheon Books.

Mertz, Paul E. 1978: *New Deal Policy and Southern Rural Poverty*. Baton Rouge: Louisiana State University Press.

Morgan, Chester 1985: *Redneck Liberal: Theodore Bilbo and the New Deal*. Baton Rouge: Louisiana State University Press.

National Emergency Council 1938: *Report on Economic Conditions of the South*. Washington: US Government Printing Office.

Nelson, Lawrence 1984: Welfare Capitalism on a Mississippi Plantation During the Great Depression. *Journal of Southern History*, 50, 225–50.

Newby, I. A. 1978: *The South: A History*. New York: Holt, Rinehart, and Winston.

Norrell, Robert J. 1991: Labor at the Ballot Box: Alabama Politics from the New Deal to the Dixiecrat Movement. *Journal of Southern History*, 57, 201–34.

Odom, Howard Washington 1943: *Race and Rumors of Race: Challenge to American Crisis*. Chapel Hill: University of North Carolina Press.

Percy, William A. 1941: *Lanterns on the Levee: Memoirs of a Planter's Son*. Baton Rouge: Louisiana State University Press.

Reed, Linda 1991: *Simple Decency and Common Sense: The Southern Conference Movement, 1938–1963*. Bloomington: University of Indiana Press.

Reed, Merl 1991: *Seedtime for the Modern Civil Rights Movement: The President's Committee on Fair Employment Practices, 1941–1946*. Baton Rouge: Louisiana State University Press.

Salmond, John A. 1967: *The Civilian Conservation Corps, 1933–1942: A New Deal Case Study*. Durham, NC: Duke University Press.

Salmond, John A. 1983: *A Southern Rebel: The Life and Times of Aubrey Williams, 1890–1965*. Chapel Hill: University of North Carolina Press.

Salmond, John A. 1988: *Miss Lucy of the CIO: The Life and Times of Lucy Randolph Mason, 1882–1959*. Athens: University of Georgia Press.

Schulman, Bruce J. 1991: *From Cotton Belt to Sunbelt: Federal Policy, Economic Development, and the Transformation of the South, 1938–1980*. New York: Oxford University Press.

Simon, Bryant 1998: *A Fabric of Defeat: The Politics of South Carolina Millhands, 1910–1948*. Chapel Hill: University of North Carolina Press.

Sitkoff, Harvard 1978: *A New Deal for Blacks: The Emergence of Civil Rights as a National Issue*. New York: Oxford University Press.

Sitkoff, Harvard 1984: The Impact of the New Deal on Black Southerners. In James C. Cobb and Michael V. Namorato (eds.), *The New Deal and the South*. Jackson: University Press of Mississippi, 117–34.

Sitkoff, Harvard 1997: African-American Militancy in the World War II South: Another Perspective. In Neil R. McMillen (ed.), *Remaking Dixie: The Impact of World War II on the American South*. Jackson: University Press of Mississippi, 70–93.

Skates, John R. 1975: World War II as a Watershed in Mississippi History. *Journal of Mississippi History*, 37, 131–42.

Smith, C. Calvin 1986: *War and Wartime Change: The Transformation of Arkansas, 1940–1945*. Fayetteville: University of Arkansas Press.

Smith, Douglas 1988: *The New Deal in the Urban South*. Baton Rouge: Louisiana State University Press.

Sosna, Morton 1977: *In Search of the Silent South: Southern Liberals and the Race Issue*. New York: Columbia University Press.

Sosna, Morton 1987: More Important Than the Civil War? The Impact of World War II on the South. In James C. Cobb and Charles Reagan Wilson (eds.), *Perspectives on the American South: An Annual Review of Society, Politics, and Culture 4*. New York: Gordon and Breach Science Publishers.

Sosna, Morton 1988: The GI's South and the North–South Dialogue in World War II. In Winfred B. Moore Jr., Joseph F. Tripp, and Lyon G. Tyler Jr. (eds.), *Developing Dixie: Modernization in a Traditional Society*. Westport, CT: Greenwood Press, 311–26.

Strahan, Jerry 1994: *Andrew Jackson Higgins and the Boats That Won World War II*. Baton Rouge: Louisiana State University Press.

Sullivan, Patricia 1996: *Days of Hope: Race and Democracy in the New Deal Era*. Chapel Hill: University of North Carolina Press.

Swain, Martha 1995: *Ellen S. Woodward: New Deal Advocate for Women*. Jackson: University of Mississippi Press.

Thomas, Mary Martha 1987: *Riveting and Rationing in Dixie: Alabama Women and the Second World War*. Tuscaloosa: University of Alabama Press.

Tindall, George Brown 1967: *The Emergence of the New South 1913–1945*. Baton Rouge: Louisiana State University Press.

Weiss, Nancy J. 1983: *Farewell to the Party of Lincoln: Black Politics in the Age of FDR*. Princeton, NJ: Princeton University Press.

Woodruff, Nan Elizabeth 1994: Mississippi Delta Planters and Debates over Mechanization, Labor, and Civil Rights in the 1940s. *Journal of Southern History*, 60, 263–84.

Wright, Gavin 1986: *Old South, New South: Revolutions in the Southern Economy since the Civil War*. New York: Basic Books.

CHAPTER TWENTY-SEVEN

The Civil Rights Movement

CHARLES W. EAGLES

IN the middle third of the twentieth century a movement for equal rights for African-Americans worked a revolution in southern race relations. The period became known as the Second Reconstruction because it ushered in changes comparable in significance to the first Reconstruction after the Civil War. The earlier era had by constitutional amendment abolished slavery, guaranteed the former slaves the rights of citizenship, and given the freedmen the right to vote, but the changes proved transitory. By the early twentieth century a new pattern of racial segregation, discrimination, and oppression had emerged in the South. The Second Reconstruction, under the pressure of black protests and orders by the federal courts and Congress, replaced the system of white supremacy with greater social, political, and economic equality for blacks. Though the reforms brought about by the civil rights movement were not easy, smooth, or complete, the gains of the twentieth-century black freedom struggle included desegregation of public education, opening of public accommodations without regard to race, protection of the right to vote, equal employment opportunities, and equitable treatment in the legal system.

Journalists provided remarkably comprehensive contemporary coverage of the southern civil rights struggle, and participants and scholars, especially social scientists, also wrote extensively about it. Professional historians waited until about 1970 to begin setting down the complex history of the movement, and in the succeeding three decades scores of books have examined a multitude of topics from a variety of historical perspectives. Historians, along with sociologists, political scientists, and independent authors, have probed the origins of the freedom struggle, chronicled the movement's crucial events, examined its major organizations and leaders, explored particular themes within the movement, focused intensively on changes within individual communities, and produced helpful reference works dealing with civil rights. In general, the scholarship on the movement has proceeded from an initial emphasis on big events, organizations, and leaders to a greater appreciation of the role of ordinary people at the local community level; at the same time, affected by developments in social history, the growing literature has broadened to include previously neglected diverse topics such as women, labor, and religion (Fairclough 1990; Lawson 1991; Eagles 2000).

The relative newness of the scholarly literature on the black freedom struggle has resulted in an as yet undeveloped historiography. No clashing schools of interpretation have yet developed. Research that has covered topics for the first time has had no earlier interpretations to revise or refute. In addition, the closeness of the people and events has resulted in a lack of the detachment necessary to produce contentious works. Writing on the movement has, nonetheless, involved implicit disagreement on a number of issues. Scholars have variously suggested, for example, that the movement actually began in the 1930s with the New Deal, in 1954 with the case of *Brown v. Board of Education*, or even in 1960 with the sit-ins. By the focus of their works, historians have also placed different emphases on the roles of the federal government, major protest organizations, and prominent leaders, and they have stressed the efficacy of different strategies and tactics – violent or non-violent action, litigation or mass protest, national or grassroots efforts. Students of the movement have also viewed white segregationists in different ways, and they have reached conflicting conclusions about the results of the civil rights movement. Seldom have the disagreements among scholars become explicit in their publications; more commonly they are implied or have to be inferred by their experienced readers. As the volume of work continues to increase, differing perspectives will likely emerge and interpretive disagreements will probably also increase.

In spite of the outpouring of scholarly work on the movement, however, two very early books have become undisputed classics that still provide invaluable background for understanding the civil rights movement. Gunnar Myrdal's incomparable *An American Dilemma: The Negro Problem and Modern Democracy*, completed in 1944, offered the most extensive examination of United States race relations (Myrdal et al. 1944; Jackson 1990). Hired by the Carnegie Corporation in the late 1930s to direct the study, the Swedish economist in turn relied on a small army of American social scientists, black and white, to conduct research. Myrdal combined his colleagues' findings with his own observations to produce a massive analysis of more than one thousand pages of text and nearly three hundred pages of notes and bibliography. The comprehensive social science assessment ranged from demography to psychology, from biology to employment economics, but its main argument emphasized the moral dimension of racial relations.

The national racial problem, Myrdal concluded, actually existed as a problem within the minds of whites. Without denying the importance of economics, politics, and social structures in racial matters, Myrdal identified the central dilemma in American race relations as one involving the psychology and ideology of whites. They faced powerful conflicting demands: the American creed that stressed democratic and egalitarian values versus ingrained racial prejudice against blacks that in practice caused discrimination and oppression. Myrdal explained in detail how the racial dilemma pervaded American institutions of all kinds. In spite of his encyclopedic evidence of the results of racism, however, Myrdal the liberal social engineer remained optimistic that the democratic and Christian components of the American creed would triumph. *An American Dilemma*, according to Walter Jackson, its most careful student, had long-term effects for the civil rights movement that was just dawning because it "played a major role in articulating and shaping a new racial liberalism for postwar America" (Jackson 1990: 240).

A second classic work that illuminated the movement's background and thereby provided historical support for it came in 1955 from C. Vann Woodward, the dean of southern historians. A brief collection of lectures delivered originally in the immediate aftermath of the *Brown* decision, *The Strange Career of Jim Crow* (Woodward 1974) surveyed southern racial segregation from emancipation to the United States Supreme Court's decree that school segregation was unconstitutional. In his pathbreaking study, Woodward pointed out that the southern experience of racial segregation had been strange because it had not, as most people at the time would have assumed, always existed. In the southern past he found not an unbroken pattern of segregation but instead discontinuity in black–white relations. After the end of slavery, whites and blacks did not immediately segregate but instead lived for a generation in a fluid state in which considerable variety prevailed. According to Woodward, only after 1890 with the passage of laws mandating separation of the races in public transportation, in recreation, and in most public facilities did segregation become the inflexible norm. At the time of the *Brown* decision, therefore, living southerners had known nothing but strict segregation, but it had not always existed.

Like Myrdal's monumental work, Woodward's slim volume of essays had a profound effect on the study of race relations and also on the emerging civil rights movement. With his essential argument for discontinuity, an optimistic Woodward sought to encourage his fellow white southerners to understand that they could survive the court-ordered end of segregation because it was of only relatively recent origin. He was also sanguine because he thought successful reform more likely in what he termed the Second Reconstruction of the mid-twentieth century than it had been after the Civil War. Woodward's bold view of the southern past as well as his hopeful assessment of contemporary conditions provided added impetus to the civil rights movement; and in later, widely selling editions, *The Strange Career of Jim Crow* influenced many students.

Woodward's interpretation of segregation's history has, however, been criticized by many historians. Critics have especially questioned his emphasis on discontinuity regarding the post-Civil War years in the South. Most have agreed with Woodward that something profound happened in the 1890s, but his challengers have argued that he overstated the fluidity between the end of the war and the turn of the century. In 1974 in the third revised edition of *The Strange Career of Jim Crow*, after the heyday of the civil rights movement, Woodward also moved away from the optimism of his original lectures because he saw the movement floundering. The problematic fate of the struggle for equality prompted him to change his focus from white attitudes and segregation toward a more direct consideration of the actions and attitudes of African-Americans. In spite of the criticism of the book by other scholars and in spite of Woodward's own growing pessimism about racial reform, *The Strange Career of Jim Crow* remains, according to Howard Rabinowitz, "the best available brief account of American race relations" (Rabinowitz 1988: 856).

Where Woodward perceptively canvassed race relations since the Civil War, many others have provided capable appraisals of the modern civil rights movement itself. Two have been especially popular. Harvard Sitkoff's *The Struggle for Black Equality, 1954–1980* (1981), the first synthesis of the movement's history, offered in seven swift chapters a standard and reliable narrative of the major national events in the quarter century after *Brown*. A more contentious but also popular account came from Manning Marable in *Race, Reform, and Rebellion: The Second Reconstruction in Black America, 1945–1982* (1984). A sociologist, Marable emphasized the significance of the Cold War, anticommunism, black nationalism, and economic class in the movement. More negative than most analysts in his assessment of the Second Reconstruction, Marable argued the need for yet a Third Reconstruction to rectify the structural shortcomings still preventing the emergence of a pluralistic democracy in which blacks could receive fair treatment because they have obtained real power.

Perhaps the most insightful survey came in David R. Goldfield's *Black, White, and Southern: Race Relations and Southern Culture, 1940 to the Present* (1990). Though known primarily as a southern urban historian, Goldfield in several ways crafted an unusually comprehensive treatment of the civil rights era. First, by starting before World War II and concluding two decades after the death of Martin Luther King Jr., Goldfield both portrayed southern culture before the movement and assessed the impact of the movement. Second, Goldfield wisely considered all of southern culture, which included white segregationists as well as civil rights activists, and thereby told a much more complete story than others who dealt almost exclusively with the movement. Third, and perhaps least satisfying, Goldfield argued that it was a religious movement in which guilty whites had their sin of white supremacy expiated and "the sinner and the redeemer managed to be transformed without destroying their unique land, the South" (Goldfield 1990: xv). Though based largely on published sources, Goldfield's work presented the best comprehensive account of the southern movement.

Two volumes in a far more popular, award-winning narrative of the civil rights movement have so far been written by journalist Taylor Branch. *Parting the Waters* (1988) and *Pillar of Fire* (1998) did provide, as their subtitle "America in the King Years" suggested, a sweeping life-and-times story of the movement with King at its center but without any dominating interpretive framework. Based on prodigious research, Branch's compelling account moved deftly from King to the broader movement and back. In addition to the events that involved King directly, he discussed, for example, Vernon Johns (King's predecessor at Montgomery's Dexter Avenue Baptist Church), the Freedom Rides, the Kennedy administration's civil rights policies, and Freedom Summer. In the second volume, which in the beginning overlapped considerably with the first, Branch also expanded his focus to include the non-southern aspects of the movement such as Malcolm X and developments in Chicago and Los Angeles, but Branch always returned to his emphasis on King. Branch promises to continue his story through the death of King and the end of the Johnson administration.

More than Branch's bestsellers, however, the most influential survey of the civil rights movement appeared in a major television documentary series, the two parts of *Eyes on the Prize* (1986, 1990). Produced by Blackside, Inc., they consisted of two sets of hour-long shows, six up through 1965 and eight after. Dealing mainly with the southern movement, the first six episodes covered events from the *Brown* decision to the Selma-to-Montgomery march and passage of the Voting Rights Act in 1965. Henry Hampton and the Blackside staff effectively combined contemporary newsreel footage with more recent interviews with participants to create a vivid and dramatic portrait of the struggle for civil rights. The second set paid far less attention to the South as it shifted to northern urban areas and politics. The first *Eyes on the Prize*, especially when combined with books such as Sitkoff's survey, contributed to the establishment of a canonical view of the movement that grew linearly from *Brown* through Montgomery and Little Rock, followed by the freedom rides and the sit-ins, to King's Albany, Birmingham, and Selma campaigns, and including Mississippi's James Meredith and Freedom Summer. Early scholarly works tended to conform to the *Eyes on the Prize* model.

Scholars have, for instance, generally agreed on the centrality of the *Brown* decision for the civil rights movement, and many have written about the Supreme Court's handling of the school desegregation cases. The premier work was *Simple Justice* by Richard Kluger (1976), a journalist and publisher. Employing fascinating detail, captivating anecdotes, and irresistible writing, Kluger explained the vital role of the National Association for the Advancement of Colored People's (NAACP) twenty-year campaign against school segregation and delineated the course of the court cases that eventually made up *Brown*. In his magisterial work, Kluger crafted telling portraits of the major and minor figures involved and set the entire story within a fully developed legal and racial context. Except for a brief epilogue, Kluger ended his massive account with the *Brown* decision itself and did not explore the controversial effects of the decision, but many scholars have examined the implementation of *Brown*. One of the better studies of the effects of *Brown* looked at the desegregation of the public schools of Charlotte, North Carolina, where busing became an inflammatory issue in the 1960s (Douglas 1995). A significant dissent from the consensus on *Brown* came from Michael J. Klarman (1994), a University of Virginia law professor, who argued that the court decision's importance derived not from its ostensible igniting of the civil rights movement but instead from its inciting a backlash among southern white segregationists. The white reaction in turn, according to Klarman's provocative thesis, spurred the mobilization of pro-civil rights forces outside the South that later successfully pushed for the civil rights legislation of the 1960s.

Whatever the ultimate verdict on the importance of the *Brown* case, the role of the NAACP specifically in school desegregation and more generally in the movement for equal rights cannot be denied. No historian has, however, written a major work on the NAACP, the oldest and largest civil rights organization, or its influential offshoot, the Legal Defense and Education Fund. Some civil rights organizations have had their stories told in scholarly studies. Clayborne Carson (1981) provided the southern movement's best institutional history in his account of the Student Nonviolent Coordinating Committee. In a clearly organized argument, Carson identified three stages in SNCC's life. First, in the aftermath of the 1960 sit-ins, SNCC emphasized radical local action seeking political rights. After the defeat of the Mississippi Freedom Democratic Party at the 1964 Democratic convention, SNCC, with considerable internal dissension, reevaluated its strategy. According to Carson, SNCC in its final phase moved toward racial separatism and black power. In addition to Carson's cogent analysis of SNCC, the histories of the Congress of Racial Equality and the Southern Christian Leadership Conference have also been chronicled (Meier and Rudwick 1973; Garrow 1986; Fairclough 1987).

While some scholars have attended to the significant histories of protest organizations, others have focused on the role of politics and government in bringing racial change. Equal access to the ballot box was a long-held goal of civil rights activists, and Steven F. Lawson's *Black Ballots: Voting Rights in the South, 1944–1969* (1976) explored the campaign for black suffrage in the South. Starting his well-researched account in the 1930s and 1940s, he explained the importance of *Smith v. Allwright* in eliminating the white primary and described the less successful challenges to poll taxes. Lawson continued through the postwar battles over suffrage between southern blacks and intransigent whites in the years before the *Brown* decision. In an essentially national, political study, he clearly explained the political maneuverings and compromises behind the passage of the Civil Rights Acts of 1957 and 1960. Though critical of presidential caution and timidity and of the Justice Department's slowness to prosecute cases involving voting rights, Lawson appreciated the ultimate importance of the Voting Rights Act of 1965. Following up on Lawson's work, two key books have assessed the impact of the Voting Rights Act in the South. One charted the devious efforts of white Mississippians to thwart the law and prevent the empowerment of blacks and the litigation blacks pursued in response (Parker 1990). A second, more comprehensive collection of essays employed detailed quantitative analyses to measure the law's results in southern states and concluded that the Voting Rights Act was crucial to the success of the Second Reconstruction (Davidson and Grofman 1994).

The involvement of the federal government in voting rights and other civil rights issues has concerned many historians. Serious studies have appeared, for example, on the Eisenhower administration and the Kennedy administration and civil rights (Burk 1984; Brauer 1977). Numerous other works have examined the federal courts and judges, the Justice Department, and the Federal Bureau of Investigation. The most original probed the FBI's hounding of Martin Luther King (Garrow 1981). Using the Freedom of Information and Privacy Act to pry thousands of documents on King from the FBI's files, David J. Garrow revealed the bureau's systematic, pervasive pursuit and harassment of King in the 1960s. Garrow's study of the FBI and King was part of his larger biographical work on the civil rights leader.

With popular and charismatic figures such as Martin Luther King Jr., the civil rights era, like other historical periods, has provided many subjects for biographers. The best of the biographies has been Garrow's (1986) study of King, *Bearing the Cross.* *Bearing the Cross* was an enormous research accomplishment. Out of his research in hundreds of interviews, scores of manuscript collections, innumerable newspapers and magazines, and the federal documents he obtained under the Freedom of Information Act, as well as his command of the secondary literature, Garrow fashioned an encyclopedic story of King's civil rights career from his initial involvement with the Montgomery bus boycott to his death in Memphis. Garrow's six hundred pages of text lacked any major interpretation, but his authoritative chronicle contained a wealth of new information about the head of the Southern Christian Leadership Conference. His chapters on the movement in Albany, Georgia, and on King's last major effort in Chicago broke new ground.

Although actually only a small part of his massive book, Garrow's most sensational revelations involved the FBI's surveillance of King and the resulting information about his sexual life. He mentioned King's "various sexual involvements with a number of different women," his "incidental couplings that were a commonplace of King's travels," and "his compulsive sexual athleticism" (Garrow 1986: 374–5). In spite of his brief but explicit references to sex, Garrow did not create an intimate portrait of King or analyze his personality and character; he did not probe his family background or explain the complexities of King's personal life. Garrow nonetheless wrought a valuable account of King's public life. He fruitfully charted King's changing ideas on the Vietnam war, described his growing economic radicalism after 1965, and generally avoided idolizing the Nobel Prize winner. His work garnered the Pulitzer Prize for biography.

Where Garrow's book demonstrated the strengths and liabilities of a rigorously factual and relentlessly chronological study, Keith D. Miller demonstrated the virtues of an imaginative and creative analysis of one part of King's life. An English professor, Miller carefully studied King's use of language to discover the sources of his ideas and rhetorical style. In *Voice of Deliverance: The Language of Martin Luther King, Jr., and Its Sources* (1992), Miller argued that King did not absorb his ideas from the great theological treatises of the past that he encountered in seminary; instead, King drew both on the African-American folk religious culture that he learned in his father's church and on the widely available published sermons of liberal white preachers like Harry Emerson Fosdick. Moving between and merging the two homiletic traditions was, according to Miller, important not just to King's development but "it was absolutely crucial to the triumph of the civil rights movement." He points to "King's distinctive ability to synthesize two sermonic traditions and use them to propel and interpret a vast social upheaval" (ibid: 9, 12). King's unusual voice allowed him to appeal to both white and black Christians across the racial divide. One consequence of Miller's subtle and sophisticated analysis was to diminish the significance of the plagiarism charges that had earlier been lodged against King.

Even if few biographical studies have had the subtlety of Miller's work on King, a number of others have been written. They range from a solid biography of the rather unexciting Whitney Young to the sometimes enticing collection of brief biographical essays on women in the civil rights movement (Weiss 1989; Crawford, Rouse, and Woods 1990). Many important figures from the freedom struggle still await their biographers.

Just as significant individuals have attracted researchers, so exciting events have drawn their attention. Using the tools of social history, the better books have situated their dramatic subjects within a richly rendered local context. Since about 1980, the local community approach to studying the civil rights struggle has in fact nearly supplanted the earlier emphasis on great men and big organizations operating on the national stage. At the local level, historians have examined sit-ins, lynchings, and mass marches, as well as apparently more prosaic activities such as community organizing. Even local studies varied in approach, from one examining individual communities to others spanning an entire state.

One important book ranged across several communities to make its larger interpretive argument. Sociologist Aldon D. Morris found the "origins of the civil rights movement" in indigenous social institutions, especially the black churches and colleges, in dozens of local movement centers (Morris 1984: 84). Spanning the decade from 1953 to 1963, Morris sketchily considered civil rights activities in the predictable locales of Montgomery, Greensboro, and Birmingham, but he ingeniously started with the less well known bus boycott in Baton Rouge in 1953. Making his work more complex, he also included smaller organizations such as the Highlander Folk School and the Fellowship of Reconciliation. Morris stressed the connections and continuities among the early civil rights protests and the ties across generational lines.

Where Morris's *Origins of the Civil Rights Movement* gained importance from its theoretical approach, its inclusive coverage, and its wide applicability, the fine craftsmanship and deep research in Robert J. Norrell's *Reaping the Whirlwind: The Civil Rights Movement in Tuskegee* (1985) has made it the best of the community studies.

Even though Tuskegee, as home of Booker T. Washington's famous school, may be atypical, it provided Norrell a rich opportunity to trace in a single place the development of the struggle for civil rights, particularly the right to vote. *Reaping the Whirlwind* provides a convincing description of change spanning the century from Reconstruction through the civil rights movement of the 1960s. In an original interpretation, Norrell identified 1941 as the beginning of the movement in Tuskegee, but he wisely devoted several chapters to its crucial antecedents. Included in his thorough discussion were the beginning of Tuskegee Institute in the 1880s and the establishment of a veterans' hospital in the 1920s; whites, whom Norrell also portrays fully and sensitively, supported the start of each institution without realizing how each would fundamentally affect black–white relations. Norrell emphasized the role of Tuskegee sociologist Charles Gomillion and the creation in 1941 of the Tuskegee Civic Association (TCA) that pressed for equal voting rights. The TCA fought gerrymandering and, in the 1950s, school segregation. Arguing that Washington's experiment ultimately succeeded in Tuskegee, Norrell traced the growth of black political power that resulted, in spite of major fractures in the black community, in the election of a black mayor in 1972. In the end, however, Norrell boldly concluded that the civil rights movement had disappointed all sides: black political power alienated whites but at the same time it did not bring the economic equality blacks wanted.

Falling between the local community studies exemplified by Norrell and Morris and the examinations of the movement on a national level have been works that described and assessed the freedom struggle in individual states. John Dittmer won numerous prizes for his *Local People: The Struggle for Civil Rights in Mississippi* (1994). Instead of canvassing the entire state in the 1950s and 1960s, however, it dealt primarily with the efforts of the Student Nonviolent Coordinating Committee in just the early 1960s. Although less heralded, the best state study so far has been Adam Fairclough's comprehensive assessment of the movement in Louisiana.

In *Race and Democracy* (1995), Fairclough ranged across more than fifty years and virtually the entire state. Though events in Louisiana have lacked the notoriety of Mississippi or Alabama, Fairclough's prodigious research uncovered plenty for him to write about in his 600-page book. Breaking out of the consensus that gripped much of the historiography, Fairclough argued that the larger civil rights struggle came in two stages, divided about 1954. Although he saw continuities between the two, especially in individuals such as the activist lawyer Alexander Pierre Tureaud, even more Fairclough posited a major break between the two eras; and he sought to correct the imbalance caused by an overemphasis on the dramatic direct-action phase after the *Brown* decision. In the earlier period, he found considerable protest against discrimination in voting, parks and playgrounds, teacher salaries, and other facets of everyday life, as well as the omnipresent violence against blacks, but he also unromantically acknowledged that for most blacks most of the time accommodation to racism proved the best policy. Fairclough also described early efforts at interracial cooperation, the crucial activities of the NAACP, and the activities of labor organizations. Fairclough further deepened his story for the post-1954 period. For example, he dealt with bus desegregation, the NAACP's continued litigation, the desegregation of public schools, the role of the federal courts, the fight for voting rights, and myriad other subjects, all explained within the interesting context of Louisiana.

The rich and variegated detail provided by Fairclough cannot easily be summarized. Where more timid scholars would have been intimidated by the religious, cultural, economic, and political complexities of Louisiana, Fairclough seemed to thrive on them. Throughout his excellent study, Fairclough continually explored the differences and similarities among religious groups, the sections of the state, blacks, whites, politicians, civil rights activists, businessmen, and nearly every demographic category; but even the abundant evidence that he marshaled did not slow or confuse his story. The special merits of Fairclough's work included its serious consideration of the pre-1954 era, its attention to the unorganized grassroots of protest as well as the often dismissed work of the NAACP, and its informed treatment of segregationists as well as civil rights activists

A common failing of local studies, and of much of the literature on the civil rights era, has been a neglect of the opponents, the white segregationists of the South. In a study of the killing of a white northern civil rights worker, Charles W. Eagles (1993) provided a portrait of one southern white segregationist and analyzed the surrounding culture of the Black Belt, but such attempts to plumb the segregationist side of the struggle have been rare. Only a few researchers have written entire books concentrating on the ideas and actions of the white supremacists, and their books appeared a generation ago. Numan Bartley pioneered in the field with his *The Rise of Massive Resistance* (1969). Examining race and politics in the 1950s South, Bartley focused on the southern white conservative leaders who supported white supremacy, who opposed racial change, and who advocated states' rights. Starting with the Dixiecrat movement of 1948, Bartley traced the development of massive resistance to racial change through the reaction to the *Brown* decision, the advocacy of the doctrine of interposition, the Little Rock crisis, the closure of some public schools to avoid integration, and the eventual decline of white resistance in the late 1950s. In the program of massive resistance, Bartley found a dilemma: its advocates could not maintain their segregated racial past and achieve economic development for their region. After achieving its greatest popularity in 1957, according to Bartley, a growing white southern preference for economic progress combined with increasing black protests in the sit-ins to spell the end of massive resistance by 1960. Although Bartley concluded that massive resistance failed, he acknowledged that the movement had pulled southern politics to the right and prevented the development of any moderate or liberal alternative. As a result, Bartley found significant continuity in southern politics even at a time of great social and economic change.

Where Bartley included one chapter on the Citizens' Councils, Neil R. McMillen devoted a major book to an analysis of the leading southern organization opposed to racial change. *The Citizens' Council* (McMillen 1971) chronicled the white supremacist group's story from its formation in the immediate aftermath of the 1954 school desegregation decision through the 1964 presidential campaign of Barry Goldwater and the rise of George Wallace as a national political force. McMillen commenced with an account of the Citizens' Council's beginning in Mississippi in the summer of 1954, and he followed state by state its spread across the South, with special attention to its strongholds in Mississippi, Alabama, and Louisiana. Going beyond organizational history, McMillen allotted a major part of his book to the actions of the Council in response to the growing civil rights movement. Particularly in the Deep South, the Citizens' Council employed intimidation, economic retaliation, and even violence against blacks to combat racial change. Against wavering whites, the Council used coercion to ensure that its racial orthodoxy prevailed.

In a middle section of his work, McMillen paid careful attention to the ideology of the Council. Though varying across the South and among its membership, its fundamental belief was in white supremacy. To support its prosegregation position, councilors drew on various ideas from physiology, psychology, history, and religion. The Citizens' Council's bedrock argument for segregation, according to McMillen, was simply that integration was "the very quintessence of ignorance, evil, and unholiness – was so utterly wrong" (McMillen 1971: 188). A more detailed examination of scientific segregationist thought had preceded McMillen's work by several years. I. A. Newby's *Challenge to the Court: Social Scientists and the Defense of Segregation, 1954–1966* (1967) surveyed the major social scientists and their works that sought to prevent racial integration. Two years after its publication, Newby and his publisher issued a revised edition with replies by several of Newby's subjects. Newby's original work and his critics' responses revealed much about segregationist thought.

While historians have for nearly three decades paid insufficient attention to the white opponents of the civil rights movement, scholars in several disciplines have produced an increasingly rich array of topical and thematic studies of the movement that complement the large number of biographies, institutional studies, and newer community analyses. Two works from nonhistorians stand out in significance. In 1982 sociologist Doug McAdam employed social science theories to analyze the emergence, growth, and decline of the civil rights movement. After finding the classical and resource mobilization theories lacking in explanatory power, McAdam proposed a political-process model that stressed – in the period from 1930 to 1954 – greater political opportunities for blacks, their growing sense of the possibilities for change, and the strengthening of black colleges, churches, and the local NAACP. After 1954 vital external support led to the development of an insurgent movement that reached its heyday between 1961 and 1966. The movement's success in the early 1960s derived, according to McAdam, from organizational strength, a favorable national political context, the movement's internal unity, and the positive response of external groups; by 1970, however, internal divisions, an increasingly hostile environment, and a decline in liberal support caused decline in black insurgency. Marshaling an array of empirical evidence to buttress his theoretical concerns, McAdam's *Political Process and the Development of Black Insurgency, 1930–1970* (1982) asked original questions and suggested innovative approaches to studying the movement, but in the intervening years few scholars have followed his lead.

A second important, specialized study of the movement came from Charles Marsh, a theology professor. Shunning the theoretical approach of McAdam, Marsh instead told powerful personal stories about the impact of religion on individuals on both sides of the civil rights movement. *God's Long Summer* (Marsh 1997) profiled the religious lives and beliefs of five people involved in Mississippi's Freedom Summer in 1964. Marsh's carefully selected subjects included Sam Bowers of the Ku Klux Klan as well as famed civil rights activists Fannie Lou Hamer and Cleveland Sellers. According to Marsh's interviews with Sam Bowers, the Klansman's Bible study convinced him that God had called him to preserve the white race. As Imperial Wizard of the White Knights of the KKK in the 1960s, Bowers helped lead white Mississippi's opposition to what he saw as the heretical movement, and his group frequently resorted to violence against what they believed were the forces of the Antichrist, including civil rights workers Michael Schwerner, James Chaney, and Andrew Goodman. On the other hand, Marsh found that Fannie Lou Hamer "gave eloquent witness to a liberating, reconciling faith, shaped by a skillful blending of African-American hymnody and spirituality, prophetic religion, and an indefatigable belief in Jesus as friend and deliverer of the poor" (Marsh 1997: 4). The experience of Cleveland Sellers in the movement offered yet a different view of the role of religious faith. An Episcopalian in South Carolina, Sellers saw the movement as evidence of God's providence, but defeat and disappointment in the mid-1960s drove him into Black Power and away from his Christian witness.

As might have been expected in a book stressing religion, two white ministers of quite different persuasions also came in for consideration – white Methodist minister Ed King who served as chaplain at black Tougaloo College and segregationist William Douglas Hudgins of a prominent Jackson Baptist church. In each case, Marsh described how religious belief undergirded the person's racial stance, whether it be rabid segregationist or ardent integrationist. Though probably less surprising than the other three, their stories clearly disclosed how deeply held faiths came into conflict because each believed God was on his side in the racial battle. The beauty of Marsh's work derived from his capacity to treat each of his dissimilar subjects seriously and sympathetically, with neither condescension nor veneration.

As Marsh revealed the variety of expressions of Christian faith in the movement, three other books have demonstrated the diversity of scholarship about the civil rights movement. Elizabeth Jacoway and David R. Colburn (1982) brought together original essays on the role of businessmen in the desegregation of fourteen southern cities. The essays explored the complex accommodations made by important businessmen to the forces influencing them during the 1950s and 1960s. Alan Draper (1994) addressed the support of organized labor for the southern civil rights movement, even though the rank and file opposed racial change. He discussed labor's reaction to *Brown* and massive resistance, efforts to desegregate union conventions, and the work of the AFL-CIO in Alabama and Mississippi. In an unusual approach to the study of the desegregation of southern transportation, Catherine A. Barnes (1983) spanned the period from the case of *Plessy v. Ferguson* through the Montgomery bus boycott and the Freedom Rides. Although Barnes concluded that the federal government repeatedly played a crucial role, she argued that it only responded to black demands. Though black leaders paid little attention, the desegregation of transit was, according to Barnes, important because it proved structural change was possible and encouraged protests against other forms of discrimination. Although none of the books about businessmen, labor, or southern transit is a comprehensive, definitive account of its subject, each initiated study of a crucial topic.

Finally, two books have made a wealth of information readily available to scholars of the movement as well as interested laypeople. The 600-page *Encyclopedia of African-American Civil Rights: From Emancipation to the Present* (Lowery and Marszalek 1992) consisted of more than eight hundred brief essays on many events, people, organizations, concepts, court cases, and places important to the modern movement. Like other standard reference works, it contains bibliographical sources, a chronology, and a full index. A more pathbreaking work was Townsend Davis's *Weary Feet, Rested Souls: A Guided History of the Civil Rights Movement* (1998). With many maps of individual communities and complementary photographs, it offered a vivid geographical approach to the movement. Individual chapters narrate events in Alabama, Arkansas, Georgia, Mississippi, North Carolina, South Carolina, and Tennessee, with Alabama and Mississippi receiving more comprehensive coverage. David J. Garrow's comment on the dust jacket summed up the book's many virtues: "Even if – *especially* if – you've never read a single book on America's Black freedom struggle, read Townsend Davis's *Weary Feet, Rested Souls* ... a moving and accurate guide, and an invaluable contribution to civil rights history." It provides a good starting point for anyone studying the movement.

BIBLIOGRAPHY

Barnes, Catherine A. 1983: *Journey From Jim Crow: The Desegregation of Southern Transit.* New York: Columbia University Press.

Bartley, Numan V. 1969: *The Rise of Massive Resistance: Race and Politics in the South During the 1950s.* Baton Rouge: Louisiana State University Press.

Branch, Taylor 1988: *Parting the Waters: America in the King Years, 1954–63.* New York: Simon and Schuster.

Branch, Taylor 1998: *Pillar of Fire: America in the King Years, 1963–65.* New York: Simon and Schuster.

Brauer, Carl M. 1977: *John F. Kennedy and the Second Reconstruction.* New York: Columbia University Press.

Burk, Robert Fredrick 1984: *The Eisenhower Administration and Black Civil Rights.* Knoxville: University of Tennessee Press.

Carson, Clayborne 1981: *In Struggle: SNCC and the Black Awakening of the 1960s.* Cambridge, MA: Harvard University Press.

Crawford, Vicki L., Rouse, Jacqueline Anne, and Woods, Barbara (eds.) 1990: *Women in the Civil Rights Movement: Trailblazers and Torchbearers, 1941–1965.* New York: Carlson.

Davidson, Chandler and Grofman, Bernard (eds.) 1994: *Quiet Revolution in the South: The Impact of the Voting Rights Act, 1965–1990.* Princeton, NJ: Princeton University Press.

Davis, Townsend 1998: *Weary Feet, Rested Souls: A Guided History of the Civil Rights Movement.* New York: Norton.

Dittmer, John 1994: *Local People: The Struggle for Civil Rights in Mississippi.* Urbana: University of Illinois Press.

Douglas, Davison M. 1995: *Reading, Writing, and Race: The Desegregation of the Charlotte Schools.* Chapel Hill: University of North Carolina Press.

Draper, Alan 1994: *Conflict of Interests: Organized Labor and the Civil Rights Movement in the South, 1954–1968.* Ithaca, NY: ILR Press.

Eagles, Charles W. 1993: *Outside Agitator: Jon Daniels and the Civil Rights Movement in Alabama.* Chapel Hill: University of North Carolina Press.

Eagles, Charles W. 2000: Toward New Histories of the Civil Rights Era. *Journal of Southern History,* 66, 815–48.

Eyes on the Prize: America's Civil Rights Years 1986: Produced and directed by Judith Vecchione for WGBH Boston, Blackside, Inc., and the Corporation for Public Broadcasting. Alexandria, VA: PBS Video.

Eyes on the Prize: American at the Racial Crossroads 1990: Alexandria, VA: PBS Video.

Fairclough, Adam 1987: *To Redeem the Soul of America: The Southern Christian Leadership Conference and Martin Luther King, Jr.* Athens: University of Georgia Press.

Fairclough, Adam 1990: Historians and the Civil Rights Movement. *Journal of American Studies,* 24, 387–98.

Fairclough, Adam 1995: *Race and Democracy: The Civil Rights Struggle in Louisiana, 1915–1972*. Athens: University of Georgia Press.

Garrow, David J. 1981: *The FBI and Martin Luther King, Jr.: From "Solo" to Memphis*. New York: Norton.

Garrow, David J. 1986: *Bearing the Cross: Martin Luther King, Jr., and the Southern Christian Leadership Conference*. New York: Morrow.

Goldfield, David R. 1990: *Black, White, and Southern: Race Relations and Southern Culture, 1940 to the Present*. Baton Rouge: Louisiana State University Press.

Jackson, Walter A. 1990: *Gunnar Myrdal and America's Conscience: Social Engineering and Racial Liberalism, 1938–1987*. Chapel Hill: University of North Carolina Press.

Jacoway, Elizabeth, and Colburn, David R. (eds.) 1982: *Southern Businessmen and Desegregation*. Baton Rouge: Louisiana State University Press.

Klarman, Michael J. 1994: How *Brown* Changed Race Relations: The Backlash Thesis. *Journal of American History*, 81, 81–118.

Kluger, Richard 1976: *Simple Justice: The History of Brown v. Board of Education and Black America's Struggle for Equality*. New York: Alfred A. Knopf.

Lawson, Steven F. 1976: *Black Ballots: Voting Rights in the South, 1944–1969*. New York: Columbia University Press.

Lawson, Steven F. 1991: Freedom Then, Freedom Now: The Historiography of the Civil Rights Movement. *American Historical Review*, 96 (2): 456–71.

Lowery, Charles D. and Marszalek, John F. (eds.) 1992: *Encyclopedia of African-American Civil Rights: From Emancipation to the Present*. New York: Greenwood.

McAdam, Doug 1982: *Political Process and the Development of Black Insurgency, 1930–1970*. Chicago: University of Chicago Press.

McMillen, Neil R. 1971: *The Citizens' Council: Organized Resistance to the Second Reconstruction, 1954–1964*. Urbana: University of Illinois Press.

Marable, Manning 1984: *Race, Reform, and Rebellion: The Second Reconstruction in Black America, 1945–1982*. Jackson: University Press of Mississippi.

Marsh, Charles 1997: *God's Long Summer: Stories of Faith and Civil Rights*. Princeton, NJ: Princeton University Press.

Meier, August and Rudwick, Elliott 1973: *CORE: A Study in the Civil Rights Movement, 1942–1968*. New York: Oxford University Press.

Miller, Keith D. 1992: *Voice of Deliverance: The Language of Martin Luther King, Jr., and Its Sources*. New York: Free Press.

Morris, Aldon D. 1984: *The Origins of the Civil Rights Movement: Black Communities Organizing for Change*. New York: Free Press.

Myrdal, Gunnar with Sterner, Richard and Rose, Arnold 1944: *An American Dilemma: The Negro Problem and Modern Democracy*. New York: Harper and Row.

Newby, I. A. 1967: *Challenge to the Court: Social Scientists and the Defense of Segregation, 1954–1966*. Baton Rouge: Louisiana State University Press.

Norrell, Robert J. 1985: *Reaping the Whirlwind: The Civil Rights Movement in Tuskegee*. New York: Alfred A. Knopf.

Parker, Frank R. 1990: *Black Votes County: Political Empowerment in Mississippi after 1965*. Chapel Hill: University of North Carolina Press.

Rabinowitz, Howard N. 1988: More Than the Woodward Thesis: Assessing *The Strange Career of Jim Crow*. *Journal of American History*, 75, 842–56.

Sitkoff, Harvard 1981: *The Struggle for Black Equality, 1954–1980*. New York: Hill and Wang.

Weiss, Nancy J. 1989: *Whitney M. Young, Jr., and the Struggle for Civil Rights*. Princeton, NJ: Princeton University Press.

Woodward, C. Vann 1974: *The Strange Career of Jim Crow*, 3rd revd edn. New York: Oxford University Press.

CHAPTER TWENTY-EIGHT

The Rise of the Sunbelt:
Urbanization and Industrialization

DAVID R. GOLDFIELD

THE "Sunbelt" is more a journalistic shorthand for metropolitan prosperity below the 37th parallel than it is a viable analytical or historical concept. There is no consensus on the precise geographic boundaries of the Sunbelt, and the works discussed below variously identify areas as diverse as the South Atlantic and the Pacific Northwest as parts of this same region. Most writers include the South as only part of the Sunbelt and, even at that, only part of the South. But southern historians and other social scientists of the South have used the concept as a synonym for economic and urban development in the region in exploring how the nation's economic problem became an international success, and how a suddenly urban and prosperous region has affected regional culture politics since World War II.

This is a relatively new historiography. We are eyewitnesses to an ongoing event and, therefore, lack the salutary benefit of the perspective of time. But a mitigating factor is that these urban and economic changes have occurred in a context familiar to students of southern history. The interaction between change and tradition, between new influences and old culture, is nothing new in most writing about the South. For a region where past, present, and future often merge into the same time zone, current events are rarely only current. Though it is always more difficult to write about the recent past, there is the deep and rich background of southern history to provide the intellectual foundation for such analysis.

The earliest identification of the geographic area that came to be known as the Sunbelt appeared in an Army/Air Force report in the early 1940s. The report referred to a "sunshine belt" south of the 37th parallel suitable for new air training facilities. The concept languished for another generation until it reappeared in Kevin Phillips's book, *The Emerging Republican Majority* (1969). Phillips used the term "Sun Belt" to describe a region of conservative voters who would forge a new Republican majority. They resided in states such as California, Arizona, Florida, and Texas, where the allures of climate, leisure activities, and high-wage employment were most pronounced. Where Phillips found the emergence of this new population a positive event in the nation's political history, Kirkpatrick Sale, in *Power Shift: The Rise of the Southern Rim and its Challenge to the Northern Establishment* (1975), discovered a sinister movement to undermine the liberal consensus of the 1960s. Despite the sometimes intemperate tone, Sale's work at least placed the Sunbelt in a broader national context, an approach followed in a series of *New York Times* articles in 1976 and in a number of scholarly works later in the decade (*New York Times*, February 9–13, 1976, p. 1).

Two works appearing after the *New York Times* articles established the Sunbelt as a topic worthy of scholarly analysis, if somewhat imprecise in its geography. They responded quite consciously to the criticisms that the emergence of the region portended adverse economic and political consequences for the Northeast and Midwest. Two economists, Bernard L. Weinstein and Robert E. Firestine, in *Regional Growth and Decline in the U.S.: The Rise of the Sunbelt and the Decline of the Northeast* (1978), argued that the Sunbelt (which they defined rather awkwardly as East South Central and West South Central) did not emerge as a result of firms fleeing the high-wage, high-tax, unionized North for more business-friendly locations in the South. Rather, the emergence of new economic activities, the expansion of firms already in place, and the branching of companies headquartered elsewhere actually accounted for most of the economic upsurge. Weinstein and Firestine's work was important from a policy perspective in that northeasterners and midwesterners were already forming coalitions in Congress to head-off what they perceived as southern economic imperialism. From Weinstein and Firestine's perspective, the economic prosperity of the Sunbelt reflected more the emergence of the region as a key consumer base than a glandular hucksterism. Besides, they noted, the economic growth of the South and West need not imply a decline of the North. Indeed, in subsequent decades, this bit of wisdom has been borne out as northern states and cities, often borrowing strategies from their Sunbelt competitors, have enjoyed an economic renaissance of sorts.

Where Weinstein and Firestine emphasized the Sunbelt's economic basis, two political scientists, David C. Perry and Alfred J. Watkins, focused on urbanization in *The Rise of Sunbelt Cities* (1977). The writers urged their readers to move away from conceptualizing northeastern and midwestern cities as *the* models of urbanization. The Sunbelt offered a new type of urban development, a regional urbanization, where cities act "in environments that far exceed their metropolitan hinterlands" (Perry and Watkins 1977: 9). In fact, had they looked at the literature on nineteenth-century urbanization, they would have discovered that every major American city, regardless of location, had a significant impact far beyond their boundaries. Ironically, southern urbanization, at least until the past thirty years or so, did not attain the economic, political, or cultural dominance of cities in other sections of the nation.

Despite their misreading of American urban history, Perry and Watkins provided a sound economic historical context for the emerging Sunbelt phenomenon of the 1970s. They identified six new "pillars" of post-World War II economic growth – agriculture, defense, advanced technology, oil and natural gas, real estate and construction, and tourism and leisure – all of which flourished, for various reasons, more in the Sunbelt than in the older industrial cities of the northeast and midwest. Perry and Watkins also identified the crucial role of the federal government in serving as a catalyst (especially in terms of infrastructure) to facilitate the location of the new economy in the Sunbelt.

The contributors to the Perry and Watkins anthology, with remarkable prescience, outlined some of the research agenda for the next two decades. These included the distinctions in land use between northern cities and urban areas in the South, Southwest, and West (the broad Sunbelt defined by Perry and Watkins), the differences in cultural and political perspectives toward the responsibilities of urban governments (especially the strong proclivity toward "privatism" in the Sunbelt), and the signs of trouble with respect to poverty, race relations, and urban decline that portended a fate not unlike the urban North.

The emphasis of the Perry and Watkins collection on regionalism as a key to understanding the emergence of the Sunbelt suggests the importance, in turn, of understanding the relationship between southern history and southern economic development. Although that is a much broader topic than can be covered in this chapter, perhaps the best place to begin to discern the underlying bases of the Sunbelt South is Howard W. Odum's *Southern Regions of the United States* (1936). To be sure, Odum's magnificent opus does not explain the rise of a prosperous region; rather, it tells the tale of why the South is not as economically strong as it should be. First, there is the absence of certain economic prerequisites – technological skills in the workforce, artificial wealth (capital and credit), and institutional services. Second, there is the South's ruinous (both environmentally and economically) system of agriculture. And, finally, there is a stifling culture characterized by a restrictive religious and social orthodoxy. Accordingly, Odum was not sanguine that industrialization and urbanization, by themselves, would create a prosperous region. Odum's nostrums for change, however, such as regional planning, greater support for higher education, and a complete overhaul of agriculture ignore the tenacity of underlying racial and social constraints that remained relatively unaddressed in an otherwise valuable study.

Nearly a half-century later, inspired by Odum's regionalism and less constrained than he in including the racial dimension in a telling of southern economic development, I embarked on a comprehensive study of southern urbanization where I discovered a new type of urban formation primarily as a result of the cultural and economic factors cited by Odum. Unlike Perry and Watkins who had assumed the cultural preeminence of southern cities across a wide regional swath, I argued in *Cotton Fields and Skyscrapers: Southern City and Region, 1607–1980* (Goldfield 1982) the opposite: that southern urbanization, even into the 1980s, continued to reflect regional attributes, particularly those shaped in small towns and the countryside. Such factors as urban density, landscape, political culture, race relations, and religious practices and beliefs accompanied the migrants to the city from the more typical southern settlements of small towns and farms. Modifications occurred to be sure, but, by and large, the southern city was primarily a creature of regional culture. That accounted, I argued, for the fact that southern cities did not assume progressive positions on issues that threatened regional traditions, and that, even after the civil rights victories of the 1960s, regional patterns persisted in the urban South.

Looking back from the perspective of the turn of the twenty-first century, I must modify my relentless regional perspective. The rise of the South as a banking center (a phenomenon of the 1990s), the emergence of indigenous high-tech industries, and the ballooning of the mailbox economy (leisure residents and retirees) has lessened the region's colonial economic dependence considerably. And race relations are probably as good if not better in the urban South than many places elsewhere. Even the landscape has capitulated in many cities, surrendering to other southern phenomena, such as rigorous boosterism and the sanctity of private property. But amid the bagel shops and coffee boutiques, there are still elements of regional culture that persist in religion, food, music, political culture, and gender relations. The main difference, I think, is that the urban South has now become the regional arbiter of these cultural attributes in much the same way that our national metropolitan culture has pervaded every corner of the country. Part of this national imperialism reflects the significant migration that has occurred over the past two decades. But there are no serious studies of the impact of Yankees; from just an anecdotal observation, they have fit in quite well with the moderate-to-conservative suburban lifestyle of the urban South. And, finally, were I to offer a sequel to *Cotton Fields and Skyscrapers*, I would pay greater attention to the great diversity of the urban South and how the difference in annexation laws, racial mix, and state influence have affected the prosperity and image of various southern cities.

Gavin Wright in *Old South, New South: Revolutions in the Southern Economy Since the Civil War* (1986) offered the strongest and best-argued attack on my continuarian view of southern urbanization. Wright contended that until the 1930s the South's isolated labor market – a legacy of slavery and a depressed agricultural sector after the Civil War – restricted wages throughout the regional economy and, in turn, reinforced low educational levels and white supremacy. The consequent shortage of capital inhibited industrial development and the emergence of technology and technological expertise. The New Deal and World War II, however, destroyed the isolation of southern labor by destroying (unwittingly) southern tenancy and setting in motion migration, mechanization, and the South's entrance into the national labor market. Wright also noted the importance of the civil rights movement in the 1960s in nationalizing the southern labor market.

While New Deal agricultural policy and such measures as the minimum wage indeed divested the South of its distinctive labor market, it does not necessarily follow, however, that the region's colonial relationship to the rest of the nation disappeared, or that the elements that the isolated labor market complemented, diminished altogether either. Wright clearly demonstrated the importance of the labor market as a prerequisite for substantial positive economic change in the region – the rise of the Sunbelt, to put it another way – but he did not make the case that these economic changes altered traditional elements in southern society or the patterns of southern urbanization. This is not to say that history and culture are immutable, and, from a statistical standpoint at least, there is a convergence of northern and southern urbanization and economic development. Culture is a matter of process; it is always changing, however imperceptible at times. But it is possible, and I would argue, probable, that the South absorbed the great economic changes wrought by depression and war, while adjusting its traditional attitudes toward race, the white working class, and political structure in a manner that did not disturb the basic framework of southern society.

In writing *Cotton Fields and Skyscrapers* I had few models to build on, other than the anthologies discussed earlier and the work of Odum. Rupert B. Vance and Nicholas Demerath, both of whom were sociologists who worked with Odum at Chapel Hill, edited an anthology, *The Urban South* (1954), which probably was the first scholarly book devoted to just that subject. The collection appeared in the midst of two major events in the South: postwar prosperity and the advent of the civil rights revolution. Blending quantitative analysis, a staple of Chapel Hill researchers, with qualitative data, the anthology emphasized the great changes that had occurred during the 1940s, especially the move from farm to town. The writers also noted the differences between southern and northern urbanization, especially the tendency of southern industry to concentrate in rural areas and small towns; that industry did not necessarily function as a city-builder in the manner that it did in other parts of the United States. One of the contributors, sociologist T. Lynn Smith, predicted that southern cities would never be more than "auxiliaries" to the great urban centers of the nation and that the agrarian tradition of the South as well as the region's relatively late entrance into urban development militated against the rise of great cities (Vance and Demerath 1954: 37). But, as events and further research demonstrated, agrarian traditions do not necessarily imply modest urban development, and timing is not as important as seizing upon particular trends, such as global competition, and changes in corporate practices, leisure and tourism preferences, and infrastructure development that may favor a particular region.

While all of the writers in the anthology viewed urbanization as the next great southern phenomenon, several predicted that southern cities would continue to evolve differently from the urban North. Vance supported this perspective by noting that the South was still overwhelmingly a region of small cities with relatively low densities, a geography that the growth in automobility would only reinforce, and that the biracial, segregated nature of the urban South would continue to affect the urban landscape in distinctive ways. Steeped in the tradition of regionalism, Vance and fellow contributor and sociologist Sara Smith were also cognizant of the problems that smaller communities and rural areas faced as a result of migration and the growth of metropolitan areas. Vance and Smith believed that, given the South's history and the recent migrations, rural and urban ways would merge into a distinctive way of life that would relieve southern cities from many of the problems that plagued cities elsewhere in the country. In contrast to some writers in the 1930s and 1940s, the contributors did not see the southern city as an environment conducive to challenging white supremacy; in fact, Nicholas Demerath predicted that as migrations from rural areas continued, the southern city would become even more segregated over time. Nor did Demerath and his colleagues view the southern city as a place to promote the upward mobility of the white working class.

But not all of the contributors to *The Urban South* perceived southern cities as merely carrying forward rural traditions. Several noted that cities tended to provide more opportunities and fewer restrictions for blacks who sought to protest against Jim Crow, and their urban residents tended to be more politically active and less likely to support traditional rural-based elites. As the contributors looked around them, of course, there were numerous examples of progressive urban regimes, at least progressive to the extent that economic development rather than white supremacy came foremost as policy issues. So *The Urban South* concluded with the acknowledgment that southern urbanization is and will be different, but with the hope that it will follow some of the liberalizing tendencies common to urban areas in the rest of the nation. Although the collection is nearly half a century old, this basic tug between southern tradition and urban modernization still characterizes the urban South today.

Another model study appeared two decades later, probably the first major attempt by a historian to treat southern urbanization as a theme unto itself. Blaine A. Brownell's *The Urban Ethos in the South, 1920–1930* (1975) focused on seven southern cities and the attitudes of their "commercial–civic elite" (a phrase now indelibly part of the urban historiographical lexicon) toward urbanization and how they promoted their cities in the decade of Babbitry. Although some historians have misread Brownell's work as a statement of how southern cities closely resembled cities elsewhere in the country, the author demonstrated the agrarian perspective of the urban boosters, how they viewed the importance of preserving and promoting farm life and the countryside in general, and how they delicately balanced urban growth with changes in the social structure and patterns of civic leadership. The commercial–civic elite wanted the former without incurring the latter and, by and large, according to Brownell, they succeeded. The study is significant precisely because Brownell showed his leaders as virtually indistinguishable from their counterparts in other cities of the country but with an agenda and an approach that reflected distinctive regional values. Brownell's work provided an excellent perspective on how the booster ethic, or urban ethos, can be turned toward conservative ends. There remains the question, not resolved in Brownell's study, of the exaggerated promotionalism and defensiveness of southern boosters and how that may have reflected regional culture as well. The tension between tradition and modernization that the contributors to the Vance and Demerath volume noted existed only minimally for Brownell's commercial–civic elite. They blended a vigorous economic development program with strong fealty to the traditional elements of southern society and demonstrated that one did not necessarily contradict the other.

This last point was especially important in James C. Cobb's *The Selling of the South: The Southern Crusade for Industrial Development, 1936–1980* (1998). Cobb's searing portrait of southern economic development strategies from the New Deal to the Sunbelt era emphasized the disjunction between economic growth and regional change. Although the setting of industrial recruitment shifted from the cotton fields of Mississippi under Governor Hugh White's Balance Agriculture With Industry program of 1936 to the state and local government office buildings of the 1960s and after, the message remained remarkably similar: nonunion workers, lower costs, lower taxes, fewer regulations, and an array of government subsidies. But Cobb also noted that selling the South bought some amenities, particularly for metropolitan areas where newcomers came to expect more and better social services, transportation, and educational facilities.

Yet, in the rural and small-town South, what may be termed the heartland of southern industry, the pitch has remained remarkably consistent. In the metropolitan South, however, the presence of coffee shops, book stores, good restaurants, a top-notch university, and cultural amenities are likely to transcend the importance of traditional inducements in the coming years. When Charlotte lured the huge university pension plan, TIAA-CREF, from New York in 1999, recruiters stressed sophistication, the environment, culture, and education, and soft-pedaled cheap labor, cheap land, and cheap taxes, though the firm will certainly save a bundle on all three in its move to the Queen City. Cobb's work points out, like Vance and Demerath, Brownell, and Goldfield, that the South continues to live in two worlds simultaneously and, for the most part, comfortably.

In a thoughtful 1993 revision to *The Selling of the South*, Cobb placed the crusade for industrial development in a broader national and international context. By the beginning of the 1990s the South had gone "global," though the region had been involved in a global economy of sorts ever since the first tobacco shipment made it across the Atlantic. In the decade since the first edition appeared, national deindustrialization had accelerated, spurred by changes in the global economy and domestic trade legislation. These trends exposed the unevenness of the South's industrial development. Rural areas and small towns, not metropolitan regions, suffered the greatest relative loss in jobs and tax revenues. In addition, as Cobb indicated, the South continued to lag behind the rest of the nation in almost every category of worker welfare. The region persistently tops lists of good places to do business, but falls to the bottom in terms of protecting and paying its industrial workforce. And despite the overall prosperity of the Sunbelt South, African-Americans, Cobb asserted, continued to benefit less than whites from outside investment. The theme of continuity in the midst of change that has characterized much of Sunbelt historiography from the 1980s onward remained a strong presence in Cobb's revised work.

By the mid-1980s enough scholars were involved in Sunbelt-related research that a conference was held in Miami in 1985 to assess the state of the new field to date and suggest an agenda for future work. Many of the presenters had already established reputations as Sunbelt scholars, and the resulting volume from the conference, *Searching for the Sunbelt: Historical Perspectives on a Region*, edited by Raymond A. Mohl (1990), offered both synopses of past research as well as previews of future books. The collection emphasized the political and policy dimensions of the Sunbelt's emergence (and few of the participants agreed on where or what the Sunbelt was) with essays by Roger W. Lotchin, Richard M. Bernard, political scientist Amy Bridges, and Ronald Bayor. James C. Cobb wrote about the South's peculiar path to industrialization, Raymond A. Mohl focused on the ethnic dimensions of Miami, and Elliott Barkan took a broad view of Sunbelt immigration. Carl Abbott opened the volume with a delightful essay on the Sunbelt's discovery; perhaps "manufacture" might be a more appropriate description. The editor also had the good sense to reprint Raymond Arsenault's *Journal of Southern History* essay, "The End of the Long Hot Summer: The Air Conditioner and Southern Culture," a technology without which the Sunbelt could hardly be thinkable.

The two concluding essays, Bradley R. Rice's "Searching for the Sunbelt" and the Epilogue, entitled "The Vanishing Sunbelt," which Howard N. Rabinowitz and I co-authored, implied that while the "Sunbelt" was a helpful public relations ploy, its reality in terms of a prosperous South and a struggling North was becoming less accurate with each passing year. The sectional antagonisms that fueled 1970s Sunbelt research and produced the volumes by Weinstein and Firestine, and Perry and Watkins, were abating. As Rabinowitz and I concluded, "In the end it is the uneasy alliance of South and West in the Sunbelt and the equally oversimplified view of the Frostbelt that exposes the weakness of the [Sunbelt] concept. ...We can more profitably understand America in terms of North, South, and West, or urban, rural, and suburban. Either of these more traditional models works better than the Sunbelt stereotypes of more recent theorists" (Mohl 1990: 231). Indeed, the volume exposed so many differences between South and West and within the South that the Sunbelt concept proved to be a weak analytical tool.

These distinctions within the South were already apparent by 1990, especially in the research of scholars devoted to studying the rural South. The persistent struggle of the southern countryside to attain economic parity with the South's more prosperous metropolitan areas was a theme of Cobb's study and of Sunbelt historiography in general. Vance and Demerath also noted the close connection between city and countryside in migration patterns and cultural and economic influences. In contrast, the economists and political scientists writing in the 1970s explained how the Sunbelt evolved, but they left unexplained the key role played by southern agriculture in this transformation. No story of the Sunbelt's rise could be complete without an analysis of the rural South and the people who live and who have lived there.

Fortunately, there are several excellent studies of this agricultural transformation, foremost among them Pete Daniel's *Breaking the Land* (1985) and Jack Temple Kirby's *Rural Worlds Lost* (1987). Daniel focused on the impact of federal policy in particular on the South's major agricultural staples of rice, tobacco, and cotton. Perhaps he waxed a bit too nostalgic for the small family farm or the lost promise thereof. But Daniel's work is still the best in print on the impact of the Agricultural Adjustment Act and subsequent federal policies on staple agriculture in the South. Kirby's work is more comprehensive and more balanced in tone. His book centered on the post-1940 transformation of southern agriculture when, in a relatively few years, southern agriculture mechanized and people moved off the land and into cities. Kirby, like writers before him, cited the transforming impact of New Deal agricultural policies, but especially World War II and the accompanying technological innovations that freed southern farm labor to pursue more remunerative occupations elsewhere. Kirby also made the point that industrialization and urbanization did not occur in the South until after World War II. The apparent moves in that direction in the late nineteenth and early twentieth centuries represented growth but did not generate the types of economic activities, cultural changes, and political transformations that typically have accompanied urban and industrial development elsewhere.

What is most impressive about Kirby's findings is the scale of agricultural and rural transformation. The South, by 1970, became the quintessential home of the corporate farm, leading the nation in that category. And the people who once worked in and around agriculture have now become commuters to factories in small towns or, if they are fortunate in their proximity to larger metropolitan areas, to jobs in Sunbelt cities. To Kirby, the changes have been a mixed blessing, increasing the dependence of the rural population in one sense, but also enhancing their security in another.

The human costs and benefits of the agricultural transformation and its impact on urban and industrial development are best seen in an underappreciated book by Linda Flowers, an English professor at North Carolina Wesleyan University. *Throwed Away: Failures of Progress in Eastern North Carolina* (Flowers 1990) is part autobiography, part history, and part anthropology. In it, the major themes of Sunbelt historiography are played out. Flowers demonstrated the consequences of selling the South in rural, small-town eastern North Carolina from the 1950s through the 1980s, attracting foot-loose industries intent on exploiting land and labor and then thinking nothing of pulling up stakes and leaving. She wrote of the young people who no longer can parlay basic skills and inadequate education into entry-level industrial jobs because such work is disappearing. And their chances of competing for work in the state's prosperous metropolitan areas are reduced by the poor public school systems in eastern North Carolina, where local and county governments remain relatively unresponsive to social and educational needs but very supportive of economic development efforts and low taxes. This is the dark side of the Sunbelt, almost literally within the shadow of one of its monuments, the Research Triangle Park in the Raleigh–Durham–Chapel Hill area.

Flowers correctly located southern postwar industrialization in a rural, small-town context. Ironically, the portrait she drew of disconnected young workers, isolated from the prosperity of metropolitan areas to the west, is strikingly similar to the depiction of the rise of an industrial workforce in the Piedmont during the late nineteenth century. David L. Carlton's *Mill and Town in South Carolina, 1880–1920* (1982) revealed the antagonisms of the new proletariat toward middle-class urban reformers and paternalistic bosses and the isolation of the workers from the growing urban, commercial world out of their reach. Although manufacturing continues to occupy an important segment of the South's economy today, it is not a key element in the historiography of the Sunbelt. Perhaps it should be, as the petrochemical industry, various high-tech enterprises in the Silicon Hills in and around Austin, Texas, and the smaller steel and truck and auto-manufacturing concerns in the Piedmont remain a largely untold story in the South's postwar economic transformation. Texas now has the nation's second largest number of high-tech employees, and they outnumber workers in the state's petroleum industry. Works such as Carlton's and Henry M. McKiven, Jr.'s *Iron and Steel: Class, Race, and Community in Birmingham, Alabama, 1875–1920* (1995), have no late-twentieth-century counterparts. Part of the problem is that manufacturing firms, especially the oil and natural gas companies, are very reluctant to share their archives with historians not in their employ. Also, the racial and class issues that occupy many historians today are perhaps not very interesting when applied to urban industries that have more open employment practices and better wages and working conditions than the traditional rural-based industries. In fact, while the South continues to lag behind the rest of the nation in most indices of working safety, wages, and benefits, the differences are much more narrow in metropolitan areas.

But it would be a mistake to view the Sunbelt phenomenon as solely a metropolitan presence. Sunbelt economic prosperity appeared outside metropolitan areas and was selective within metropolitan areas. Unfortunately, there is no major work on the booming leisure and tourist industry in the South, and particularly how a region that experienced few tourists and retirees (except for New Orleans and Florida) prior to the 1960s, suddenly became a haven for both. Did state political and economic leaders implement the same strategies for attracting tourist activities as they did for other economic endeavors? Is the tourist industry merely a perpetuation of the rural and small-town labor and land exploitation that characterized industrial growth? And to what extent did the federal government subsidize the southern tourist and leisure industries in terms of transportation, home loans, and tax structure? Who has benefited from the tourist and leisure boom? And what national and international trends have abetted these activities in the South? And, in a region where "fitting in" has been essential to economic and personal well-being, especially in nonmetropolitan areas, how has the adjustment process occurred with newcomers, and how has it changed them and the South? Disney World, Busch Gardens, Six Flags, Williamsburg, battlefield sites, beaches, planned communities such as Seaside, and the beach cultures of South Padre Island, Myrtle Beach, and much of Florida, the attractions of New Orleans and San Antonio, and the mountain resorts in western North Carolina, east Tennessee, and parts of Arkansas remain unaddressed topics that can say as much about southern history and culture as about contemporary economic trends in the Sunbelt economy. Though some of these activities and places are located in and about major metropolitan areas, many are not. And in some respects the physical and economic changes occurring in these small towns and rural areas may be more wrenching than those occurring elsewhere.

While economic prosperity has now filtered into certain nonmetropolitan areas, it is clear that such prosperity is selective within metropolitan areas as well. Some cities resemble the hollowed-out shells of northeastern and midwestern metropolises, while even in some of the more prosperous urban areas, pockets of poverty and disillusionment persist. Much of this selectivity resulted from the peculiar historical circumstances of the urban South brought out in the works of the 1970s and early 1980s. Historians Richard M. Bernard and Bradley R. Rice collected profiles of Sunbelt cities from the South Atlantic to the Southwest and presented them in an anthology, *Sunbelt Cities: Politics and Growth since World War II* (1983). The writers, historians for the most part, employed politics and political leadership as the focal point for a broader discussion on race, economic development, and ethnicity. Since few of the cities covered had been the subject of a monograph, the anthology introduced these post-World War II Sunbelt cities to the professional historical community. The volume also highlighted the differences between southern cities such as New Orleans, Miami, and Dallas, with their distinctive economic prospects, political systems, and ethnic and racial mixes. The essays served as a warning to future scholars who might generalize about the urban South to the neglect of the variable nature of urbanization in the region.

Politics, though, remained the major focus of the anthology. Although the writers emphasized the interaction between politics and economic development, what is most interesting about a new breed of Sunbelt city leader emerging after World War II, at least in the southern portion, is how readily they adapted to new racial and political realities yet maintained a tight rein on public spending and taxes. Generally, fiscal conservatism combined with a modicum of social progressivism to make the Sunbelt city appealing to business and to refugees escaping high taxes and racial strife in the North.

Studies that appeared after the pioneering Bernard and Rice (1983) volume expanded the political focus to include other aspects of Sunbelt city development. Taking their cue from the regional obsession with race, a number of fine studies appeared in the 1980s and 1990s, some of them written by contributors to the Bernard and Rice anthology, that placed white supremacy at the center of urban analysis. These works most often related how racial perceptions literally shaped southern cities to the point that land-use patterns and residential development differed from those in cities elsewhere in the country. Where Vance and Demereth had viewed the spatial configuration of the urban South as primarily a reflection of the small scale and timing of southern urban development, historians of the 1980s and 1990s saw race as the major factor in the physical formation of southern cities.

Three works in particular stand out. The first major study of this genre was Christopher Silver's *Twentieth-Century Richmond: Planning, Politics, and Race* (1984). Silver demonstrated how racial concerns among white leaders literally shaped the city of Richmond, especially its residential and commercial land use. Silver also showed that the planning profession, generally viewed as a progressive force holding back rapacious developers and their political allies, acted as willing accomplices to the carving up of Richmond. The turning point occurred during the 1950s and 1960s just when the Sunbelt economy began to emerge. Richmond's elite focused on refurbishing the downtown core to attract more business and destroyed surrounding residential neighborhoods with urban renewal projects. It was a scenario repeated in cities throughout the country during this time. And it proved devastating to Richmond. Downtown office towers gleam in the sun, but the increasingly black and poor city, and a struggling public education system, could not compete with the attractions of suburbia for growing numbers of businesses and erstwhile city residents. More recently, neighborhood preservation advocates have had their voices heard, but the planning and development focus remains fixated on downtown.

A similar story emerged in one of the Sunbelt's showcase cities, Atlanta, a place perennially associated with the New South and the booster mentality. Even more forcefully than Silver, Ronald H. Bayor, in *Race and the Shaping of Twentieth-Century Atlanta* (1996), showed that white racism provided the policy engine for Atlanta's residential patterns, transportation systems (including the MARTA subway system), and the development of educational and social services. As black political power grew after World War II, the city's African-American community increasingly received benefits from the white power structure, while the elites attempted to annex as much suburban territory as possible to "whiten" the electorate. The inattention to the needs of black citizens, as in Richmond, did not serve Atlanta well. As neighborhoods and schools deteriorated, the middle class of both races fled to the suburbs, most of which successfully fought off annexation.

Bayor also indicated that even after blacks won city hall in 1973, white economic power continued to shape the city – though blacks had considerably more voice, as the construction of the Georgia Dome and the 1996 Olympics attested. In any case, the aesthetic results have been awful: empty concrete canyons of high-rise islands, interminable traffic jams, deteriorating air quality, and a suburb–city standoff reflecting racial polarization.

The most recent foray into land use and planning in the Sunbelt South is Thomas W. Hanchett's *Sorting Out the New South City: Race, Class, and Urban Development in Charlotte, 1875–1975* (1998). The story of Charlotte was similar to the Atlanta saga: a progressive business elite concerned with isolating black from white, building up the downtown, leveling older, minority districts, and preserving historically white neighborhoods. But Hanchett noted significant differences as well, including a more cordial relationship between black and white Charlotteans, especially those of the middle class, than existed in Atlanta prior to the 1950s. Such cordiality was reflected in the attention to parks for blacks and decent, if spartan, new neighborhoods for the city's African-American residents. Most important, perhaps, Charlotte's black population rarely exceeded a quarter of the total, and North Carolina's liberal annexation laws significantly dampened the adverse racial impact of white flight.

These studies, and the Bernard and Rice anthology before them, raised an important question, mostly unanswered by the authors, about the role of the respective states, especially the prevailing political and racial culture, in affecting urban policy. The differences in annexation law provided one example, but also the racial climate of each state – North Carolina, Georgia, and Virginia – may have had some impact on urban policy, especially as rural migrants, black and white, moved to nearby cities. And, finally, what of the political culture of each state? How did the distinctions between Talmadge-led Georgia, the Byrd machine in Virginia, and the relatively anonymous white, rural oligarchy that governed North Carolina well into the 1970s affect urban policies?

This broader context may be crucial to understanding the emergence of the Sunbelt and the development of southern cities during the post-World War II era. The urban-planning case studies have already indicated how and why southern cities developed differently from northern cities: the compelling interest of race since the late nineteenth century relentlessly shaped public policy and, in turn, shaped the city. This should not imply that racial concerns were absent in the planning of northern cities, but in many older metropolises racial issues were relative latecomers to the political equation as ethnicity served as a more likely influence on land use and other policies. Besides, many black residential areas in the North emerged in succession-fashion as African-Americans moved into older ethnic neighborhoods, replacing upwardly mobile white ethnic groups, while in the South, a combination of succession and new settlement characterized black residential patterns. And quite often these new settlements were planned to keep the races separate.

But the traditional view of the urban, ethnic North and the urban biracial South needs some correction. A new historiography on southern ethnicity has emerged in the past two decades. It is hardly surprising that immigrants are seeking out Sunbelt locations, for newcomers have always come to places of great economic promise. But the new research has also demonstrated that ethnicity is hardly a new phenomenon in the urban South. The more recent influx of immigrants and their interaction with southerners (and Yankee transplants) could adjust immigration historians' view of the assimilation process.

As with most studies of the urban South over the past two decades, the key factor here is the distinctive history and culture of the South itself. The book that set the research agenda for this topic was a collection of essays, *Shades of the Sunbelt: Essays on Ethnicity, Race, and the Urban South* (1988), edited by Randall M. Miller and George E. Pozzetta. Perhaps the most insightful piece in the collection was Deborah Dash Moore's "Jewish Migration in the Sunbelt," which showed why Jewish migrants prefer some southern cities over others. Occupational interests, the history of a place, the image of a particular city, and the extent and position of the Jewish community all have relevance for Jewish newcomers. But once Jews are settled, they apparently undergo a change, particularly with respect to the strengthening of their ethnic and religious awareness. This change reflects, in part, a defense against the overwhelming evangelical Protestantism of the region, which may be a major reason why Jewish migrants to, say, Los Angeles, behave differently from Jewish migrants to Charlotte. It is not yet clear, though, how Jewish migrants, in turn, have influenced southern cities apart from the ubiquitous bagel shops which, like pizzerias, have passed into the general American food vernacular anyway.

As to whether the political pluralism that characterized the experience of northern cities will occur in the South, the results are mixed. In Miami, as Raymond A. Mohl argued in Miller and Pozzetta (1988), dominance, rather than the pluralistic model, seems a more appropriate description of the Cubans' status, while Hispanic and recent migrants from Southeast Asia and Eastern Europe may or may not evince "northern" urban patterns of residence and political affiliation. Historically in the urban South, the dividing line has been racial, not ethnic, and it remains to be seen whether that boundary will remain the key feature of political life in southern cities.

What also remains unclear is how these recent immigrants are changing southern cities and how those changes distance the urban South from the rest of the region, a region where small towns still have some political and cultural influence. Finally, writers need to distinguish between the experiences of ethnic migrants who have lived in the metropolitan North for several generations before moving South – their "Americanness" may be at least if not as important as their ethnicity – and recent arrivals to this country whose foreign culture is more evident. The South has absorbed newcomers in the past, often making them dyed-in-the-wool southerners before a generation has passed; whether the allure of the region continues to hold for a new and larger and more diverse group of migrants will have crucial ramifications for the nature of the urban South in the coming decades.

A common theme of the essayists in Miller and Pozzetta (1988) was the role of the federal government in placing and assisting immigrant newcomers in the urban South. Mohl's essay on Cubans in Miami demonstrated the federal role in particular, but Hispanics, Southeast Asians, migrants from the former Yugoslavia, and from Somalia have received special assistance from the federal government as well. That influence contrasted with the federal government's ambiguous assistance over the years to African-Americans residing in the urban South, a fact of contemporary urban life that has led to some racial–ethnic friction.

While most Sunbelt writers have noted federal influences in spurring economic development and urbanization in the South, none offered a systematic analysis of how federal programs and policies specifically benefited southern states and localities. An anthology edited by Roger W. Lotchin, *The Martial Metropolis: US Cities in War and Peace* (1984), though national in scope, provided the first solid evidence of the depth of the federal commitment and support for the Sunbelt. Bruce J. Schulman's *From Cotton Belt to Sunbelt: Federal Policy, Economic Development, and the Transformation of the South, 1938–1980* (1991) more than responded to the need for a southern perspective on the issue. Though some critics have averred that Schulman's single-minded pursuit of federal influence omitted other local, regional, and national factors that generated Sunbelt prosperity, he in fact never claimed an exclusive priority for federal influence. Rather, Schulman demonstrated how federal policy and programs since the New Deal era served as a catalyst for postwar economic development, while steering clear of inducing social and political changes.

The story is a testimony to the federal system of government that left national programs in the hands of local leaders who manipulated guidelines or ignored them altogether to build roads, hospitals, government buildings, and other infrastructure that sustained their power and minimized social change. These "neo-Whigs," as Schulman called them, differed from the old plantation elite more in degree than in kind. They eschewed welfare programs, or at least steered funds away from the most needy, in favor of infrastructure and defense spending, activities that had many fewer social ramifications. Schulman noted that, by 1980, the Sunbelt economy had emerged full-blown, but the South remained the nation's poorest region. Moreover, federal programs such as agricultural subsidies and military spending invariably benefited whites more than blacks. And federal programs such as social security, the interstate highway system, and airport construction and expansion, which are national in intent, provided an inordinate boost to southern tourism and retirement businesses. The success of southern leaders in deflecting funds and programs away from social objectives reflected their power in Washington, initially in the Democratic Party and, more recently, in the Republican Party.

Schulman concluded by noting that southern strategies and responses to federal programs provided a national model, as other states and localities adopted the South's craving for defense industries, its antipathy toward welfare and trade unions, and a promotional bent to leverage federal funds with private investment. Selling the South has been a successful activity, not only in luring investment, but in attracting federal funds and programs as well.

The fact that social change has lagged considerably behind the South's economic transformation is not surprising to any student of southern or American history. Yet a significant revolution occurred in the 1960s, the civil rights movement, which altered southern race relations immensely, even if the objectives of that era remain only partially fulfilled. It is a "given" of Sunbelt historiography that the civil rights movement released the South from having to support an increasingly illogical social construction – segregation – and allowed all southerners to direct their energy instead to making money. The timing of the Sunbelt phenomenon – Kevin Phillips's book and the 1976 *New York Times* series, the reversal of historic migration patterns, and the election of a president from the Deep South that same year – supported the view that the civil rights movement was an important catalyst for economic development. But the evidence remains circumstantial. Elements of economic development and urbanization that eventually comprised the Sunbelt phenomenon appeared as early as the years immediately following World War II. The evidence that racial resistance hurt southern economic development is mixed. We have not yet had studies of individual cities and the relationship between civil rights and economic take-off. The issue is important because the conventional wisdom is that racial harmony precedes economic prosperity. Perhaps the opposite is the case: the end of segregation became possible because of the growing prosperity of the urban South and the promise of more to come.

One measure of what needs to be done in Sunbelt historiography is to see how recent major synthetic works on the South treat postwar economic and urban development. Dewey W. Grantham's *The South in Modern America: A Region at Odds* (1994) followed the traditional periodization, emphasizing the changes that occurred nationally during the 1930s and 1940s as key turning points for the South. The result, according to Grantham, has been a convergence with the rest of the nation: a two-party region, a consumer-oriented lifestyle, and a prosperous and politically active suburban middle class, all at the expense of the southerner's traditional sense of place and family. In other words, the postwar economic transformation has altered southern culture. But the South has, at various times in its history, converged with American trends such as Progressivism, technology, and internationalism. Yet southerners have either molded such elements to fit their culture or have followed them only to the point where relatively little has changed. It is far from certain whether the Sunbelt is another southern ruse on social scientists, or whether we have, at last, written the epitaph for Dixie.

More pertinent to the Sunbelt era is Numan V. Bartley's excellent synthesis, *The New South, 1945–1980* (1995). Bartley argued that the modernization of the South depended on the elimination of two elements: white supremacy, as reflected in segregation and disfranchisement, and the dominance of elite white rural political leaders. Both factors were eliminated by the 1960s, replaced by metropolitan business leaders and a black and white middle class – the shock troops for the emergence of the Sunbelt South. But Bartley was quick to point out that the economic transformation on which the Sunbelt prosperity rested occurred during the era of white supremacy. By 1980 a moderate consensus had emerged in the metropolitan South that promoted economic development and cordial race relations, especially among the middle class. Working-class blacks and whites, however, remained outside the consensus, much like in the rest of the country. Bartley, therefore, like Grantham, argued for southern convergence. Unlike Grantham, however, Bartley believed that similarities aside, the South remains the most distinctive American region, even though the postwar economic and racial transformations have brought the South in alignment with the rest of the country. Place and family still matter, contra Grantham, and a rural culture persists in attitudes such as religion, gun control, and private property.

Some of the differences and similarities are obviously in the eye of the beholder, and the perennial conflict between continuity and discontinuity in southern history may be a worn, if not irrelevant contest, as most scholars find patterns of both. The key is to find places of interaction and change between the traditional and the modern, not necessarily merely one or the other.

And it may be that southern postwar economic and racial changes have vaulted the region beyond the rest of the country, so that the distinctions remain, though the relationship of the South to the rest of the nation is very different from what it was fifty years ago. The South is becoming the nation's prime economic and demographic generator, while in race relations (as measured by migration patterns, officeholding, and desegregation in neighborhoods and schools) black and white southerners may have surpassed the rest of the country as well. That may be the more substantive distinction of the South, rather than the food, music, and sense of place that often turn the South into a caricature of itself.

Southern novelists have displayed insights that historians of the region have found helpful, especially when studying this tug between tradition and modernization and the interactions between them. Unfortunately, there are very few Sunbelt scribes to be found. Most southern novels today are set in the rural, small-town South which still exists, of course, but not as a lifestyle for most of us. The great southern suburban novel has yet to be written. There is no *Great Gatsby* in the works, or a *Sister Carrie* for that matter. Atlanta, perhaps because the tension between Old South and newest South is epitomized best there, has been the subject of several novels, such as Anne Rivers Siddons's two books, *Peachtree Road* (1988) and *Downtown* (1994). The latter work captures the excitement and possibility that pervaded the city and, I suspect, many urban places in the South during the mid-1960s. But somehow that possibility was squandered, not in an economic sense, but in a sense of losing something that was precious, something southern. As one of her characters in *Downtown* noted, returning to the city in 1991 after a decade absence, "I might as well have come and gone to Dayton" (Siddons 1994: 494).

Siddons's disappointment transforms into ribald caricature in Tom Wolfe's novel, *A Man in Full* (1998), blending what's new about the New South, including the clichés of racial harmony and vast urban wealth, with more traditional elements such as greed, white supremacy, and misogyny into a wild concoction that often reads more like a journalistic account than a work of fiction. This is more like it, but it lacks the subtlety and insight of great literature, though it certainly is fun to read, especially if you are not from Atlanta.

While we are waiting for the great southern Sunbelt novel, there are a number of topics that historians can profitably address to help compose a fuller picture of the metropolitan South. First, in addition to studies of southern industries since World War II, the bellwethers of the service economy that dominates the Sunbelt economic profile – banking, real estate, insurance, and retail – remain untreated for the most part. Sandra S. Vance and Roy V. Scott's *Wal-Mart: A History of Sam Walton's Retail Phenomenon* (1994) begins to address this gap, but the retail giant's initial success in smaller urban areas, with less sophisticated consumers, and the impact of such a retail giant on downtown shops remain elusive subjects. In some respects, the story of Wal-Mart (and the home improvement giant, Lowe's) is a throwback to the traditional economic development scenario of small-town exploitation moving to the fringes of larger cities. Yet there is something to be said for indigenous enterprise that lowers consumer costs in a region historically gouged by corporate conglomerates head-quartered elsewhere.

Second, a profitable merger could occur if historians studied the environmental impact of postwar economic development and how southern states and their residents responded to environmental concerns. Again, the mixture of Old South attitudes with New South activities provides an interesting framework for such studies. R. Bruce Stephenson, in *Vision of Eden: Environmentalism, Urban Planning, and City Building in St. Petersburg, Florida, 1900–1995* (1997) demonstrated that Florida's urban ecological disasters were rarely natural. St Petersburg's story reflects the rabid boosterism of the 1920s uncovered by Blaine Brownell and others, while recent measures reveal a sinner brought to the altar of conservation. Whether the conversion will take remains to be seen. Still, the point is that the story of the urban South is also a saga of how urban and rural environments have interacted, of how citizens perceive these environments, and of how civic leaders deal with a resource that attracts people while, at the same time, those very migrants place inordinate pressures on the landscape they have come to enjoy.

Third, the issue of higher education and its relationship to urban economic development remains understudied. The urban university has been a relatively new feature in the South. Flagship state schools were usually located in smaller communities away from the corrupting influences of the metropolis. But the urban university has and can play a crucial role as a mediator between public and private interests, especially with respect to planning, race relations, and health care. The role of the University of Alabama in Birmingham, for example, in moderating that city's racial reputation, in attracting a new educational and cultural elite into what had been essentially a blue-collar town, awaits a book-length study.

There is also room for comparative work. The early studies of the Sunbelt phenomenon explicitly compared the rise of the South and the West with the decline of the North. By the 1990s such sharp distinctions proved inaccurate. Comparative studies on land use, economic development, ethnic and racial residential and employment patterns, and political structure and process will add important perspectives on the nature of urbanization and industrialization in the late twentieth-century South. What can we learn about the urban South, present and future, from studies such as Thomas J. Sugrue's *The Origins of the Urban Crisis: Race and Inequality in Postwar*

Detroit (1996)? In a sense, the South exported its potential urban problems, but, apparently, as the cases of Atlanta and Richmond indicate, not all of them. In another comparative sense, urban historians should pay as much attention to Dallas, Houston, and New Orleans as to Charlotte, Richmond, and Atlanta, in part to better understand how diverse southern cities are – and the Sunbelt is.

Finally, Sunbelt historiography needs to connect with other major trends in southern historiography, particularly the literature on gender. To what extent has the new urban environment provided a breakthrough for traditional perceptions and roles of southern women? How has the migration of women from other parts of the country and the world affected the status of southern women? What are the racial divisions, and what do they mean? How do southern women feel about the changes in and expansion of their occupational and lifestyle options? Do these perceptions have class, racial, and generational distinctions? We know the statistics that southern women still earn less, are more segregated in pink-collar occupations, and enjoy fewer benefits than women elsewhere, and live in the most anti-Equal Rights Amendment region in the country, but that is merely saying that southern workers, regardless of gender, fall behind their counterparts in other parts of the country. If we are to argue that Sunbelt prosperity, urbanization, and demographic diversity have changed both the southern economy and its culture, then the gender dimension needs close scrutiny.

It may be argued that southern economic development and urbanization holds much less drama than, say, the stories of slavery, segregation, civil rights, labor, and agricultural work and tenure, and that the historiography will build more slowly as a result. But for decades, work on the rural South and on agriculture has revealed how closely rural locales and culture, and the activities derived from them, have shaped the South and the region's reaction to and position in the nation. It is not too much to say that the southern city and its economy since World War II are now deserving of scholarly focus, because the urban South and the people who live and work there now define the region more than anything or anyplace else.

BIBLIOGRAPHY

Abbott, Carl 1987: *The New Urban America: Growth and Politics in Sunbelt Cities.* Chapel Hill: University of North Carolina Press.

Applebome, Peter 1996: *Dixie Rising: How the South is Shaping American Values, Politics and Culture.* New York: Times Books.

Bartley, Numan V. 1995: *The New South, 1945–1980.* Baton Rouge: Louisiana State University Press.

Bayor, Ronald H. 1996: *Race and the Shaping of Twentieth-Century Atlanta.* Chapel Hill: University of North Carolina Press.

Bernard, Richard M. and Rice, Bradley R. (eds.) 1983: *Sunbelt Cities: Politics and Growth since World War II.* Austin: University of Texas Press.

Biles, Roger 1986: *Memphis in the Great Depression.* Knoxville: University of Tennessee Press.

Biles, Roger 1994: *The South and the New Deal.* Lexington: University Press of Kentucky.

Bilstein, Roger E. 1996: *The American Aerospace Industry: From Workshop to Global Enterprise.* New York: Twayne Publishers.

Brownell, Blaine A. 1975: *The Urban Ethos in the South, 1920–1930.* Baton Rouge: Louisiana State University Press.

Bullard, Robert D. (ed.) 1989: *In Search of the New South: The Black Urban Experience in the 1970s and 1980s*. Tuscaloosa: University of Alabama Press.

Bullard, Robert D. 1994: *Dumping in Dixie: Race, Class, and Environmental Quality*. Boulder, CO: Westview Press.

Carlton, David L. 1982: *Mill and Town in South Carolina, 1880–1920*. Baton Rouge: Louisiana State University Press.

Cobb, James C. 1977: Urbanization and the Changing South: A Review of Literature. *South Atlantic Urban Studies*, 1, 253–66.

Cobb, James C. 1984: *Industrialization and Southern Society, 1877–1984*. Lexington: University Press of Kentucky.

Cobb, James C. 1998: *The Selling of the South: The Southern Crusade for Industrial Development, 1936–1990*. Baton Rouge: Louisiana State University Press. Urbana: University of Illinois Press.

Daniel, Pete 1985: *Breaking the Land: The Transformation of Cotton, Tobacco, and Rice Cultures since 1880*. Urbana: University of Illinois Press.

Doyle, Don H. 1985: *Nashville since the 1920s*. Knoxville: University of Tennessee Press.

Dunbar, Leslie W. 1980: *The South of the Near Future*. Atlanta: Southern Center for Studies in Public Policy, Clark College.

Eller, Ronald D. 1982: *Miners, Millhands, and Mountaineers: Industrialization of the Appalachian South, 1880–1930*. Knoxville: University of Tennessee Press.

Estall, Robert 1980: The Changing Balance of the Northern and Southern Regions of the United States. *Journal of American Studies*, 14, 365–86.

Falk, William W. and Lyson, Thomas A. 1988: *High Tech, Low Tech, No Tech: Recent Industrial and Occupational Change in the South*. Albany: State University of New York Press.

Feagin, Joe R. 1985: The Global Context of Metropolitan Growth: Houston and the Oil Industry. *American Journal of Sociology*, 90, 1,204–30.

Fite, Gilbert C. 1984: *Cotton Fields No More: Southern Agriculture, 1865–1980*. Lexington: University Press of Kentucky.

Flowers, Linda 1990: *Throwed Away: Failures of Progress in Eastern North Carolina*. Knoxville: University of Tennessee Press.

Garreau, Joel 1981: *The Nine Nations of North America*. Boston: Houghton Mifflin.

Garren, Robert Earl 1957: Urbanism: A New Way of Life for the South. *Mississippi Quarterly*, 10, 65–72.

Goldfield, David R. 1982: *Cotton Fields and Skyscrapers: Southern City and Region, 1607–1980*. Baton Rouge: Louisiana State University Press.

Goldfield, David R. 1987: *Promised Land: The South Since 1945*. Arlington Heights, IL: Harland Davidson.

Goldfield, David R. 1997: *Region, Race, and Cities: Interpreting the Urban South*. Baton Rouge: Louisiana State University Press.

Grantham, Dewey W. 1994: *The South in Modern America: A Region at Odds*. New York: HarperCollins.

Grenier, Guillermo J. and Stepick, Alex, III (eds.) 1992: *Miami Now! Immigration, Ethnicity, and Social Change*. Gainesville: University Press of Florida.

Hall, Robert L. and Stack, Carol B. (eds.) 1982: *Holding on to the Land and the Lord: Kinship, Ritual, Land Tenure, and Social Policy in the Rural South*. Athens: University of Georgia Press.

Hanchett, Thomas W. 1998: *Sorting Out the New South City: Race, Class, and Urban Development in Charlotte, 1875–1975*. Chapel Hill: University of North Carolina Press.

Hartshorn, Truman A. 1997: The Changed South, 1947–1997. *Southeastern Geographer*, 37, 122–39.

Hudson, Mike and McCue, Cathryn 1996: Virginia for Sale. *Southern Exposure*, 24, 10–14.

Jacoway, Elizabeth and Colburn, David R. (eds.) 1982: *Southern Businessmen and Desegregation*. Baton Rouge: Louisiana State University Press.

Kirby, Jack Temple 1987: *Rural Worlds Lost: The American South, 1920–1960*. Baton Rouge: Louisiana State University Press.

Lewis, W. David 1994: *Sloss Furnaces and the Rise of the Birmingham District: An Industrial Epic*. Tuscaloosa: University of Alabama Press.

Liner, E. Blaine and Lynch, Lawrence K. (eds.) 1977: *The Economics of Southern Growth*. Research Triangle Park, NC: Southern Growth Policies Board.

Lotchin, Roger W. (ed.) 1984: *The Martial Metropolis: US Cities in War and Peace*. New York: Praeger.

McComb, David G. 1981: *Houston: A History*. Austin: University of Texas Press.

McComb, David G. 1986: *Galveston: A History*. Austin: University of Texas Press.

McDonald, Michael J. and Wheeler, William Bruce 1983: *Knoxville, Tennessee: Continuity and Change in an Appalachian City*. Knoxville: University of Tennessee Press.

McKiven, Henry M., Jr. 1995: *Iron and Steel: Class, Race, and Community in Birmingham, Alabama, 1875–1920*. Chapel Hill: University of North Carolina Press.

Maril, Robert Lee 1986: *Cannibals and Condos: Texans and Texas along the Gulf Coast*. College Station: Texas A & M University Press.

Matherly, Walter J. 1936: The Emergence of the Metropolitan Community in the South. *Social Forces*, 14, 311–25.

MDC 1996: *The State of the South: A Report to the Region and Its Leadership*. Chapel Hill, NC: MDC.

Miller, Randall M. and Pozzetta, George E. (eds.) 1988: *Shades of the Sunbelt: Essays on Ethnicity, Race, and the Urban South*. New York: Greenwood Press.

Moeser, John V. and Dennis, Rutledge M. 1982: *The Politics of Annexation: Oligarchic Power in a Southern City*. Cambridge, MA: Schenkman Publishing.

Mohl, Raymond A. (ed.) 1990: *Searching for the Sunbelt: Historical Perspectives on a Region*. Knoxville: University of Tennessee Press.

Moore, Deborah Dash 1988: Jewish Migration to the Sunbelt. In Randall M. Miller and George E. Pozzetta (eds.), *Shades of the Sunbelt: Essays on Ethnicity, Race, and the Urban South*. New York: Greenwood Press, 41–52.

Moore, Deborah Dash 1994: *To the Golden Cities: Pursuing the American Jewish Dream in Miami and L.A.* New York: Free Press.

Naylor, Thomas H. and Clotfelter, James 1975: *Strategies for Change in the South*. Chapel Hill: University of North Carolina Press.

Nicholls, William Hord 1960: *Southern Tradition and Regional Progress*. Chapel Hill: University of North Carolina Press.

Nixon, Ron 1998: Toxic Gumbo. *Southern Exposure*, 26 (2 & 3), 11–15.

Odum, Howard W. 1936: *Southern Regions of the United States*. Chapel Hill: University of North Carolina Press.

Perry, David C. and Watkins, Alfred J. (eds.) 1977: *The Rise of the Sunbelt Cities*. Beverly Hills, CA: Sage Publications.

Persky, Joseph 1973: The South: A Colony at Home. *Southern Exposure*, 1 (2), 14–22.

Phillips, Kevin P. 1969: *The Emerging Republican Majority*. New Rochelle, NY: Arlington House.

Preston, Howard L. 1979: *Automobile Age Atlanta: The Making of a Southern Metropolis, 1900–1935*. Athens: University of Georgia Press.

Rutheiser, Charles 1996: *Imagineering Atlanta: The Politics of Place in the City of Dreams*. New York: Verso.

Sale, Kirkpatrick 1975: *Power Shift: The Rise of the Southern Rim and its Challenge to the Eastern Establishment*. New York: Random House.

Schrag, Peter 1972: A Hesitant New South: Fragile Promise on the Last Frontier. *Saturday Review*, February 12, 51–7.

Schulman, Bruce J. 1991: *From Cotton Belt to Sunbelt: Federal Policy, Economic Development, and the Transformation of the South, 1938–1980*. New York: Oxford University Press.

Siddons, Anne Rivers 1988: *Peachtree Road: A Novel*. New York: Harper and Row.

Siddons, Anne Rivers 1994: *Downtown: A Novel*. New York: HarperCollins.

Sigafoos, Robert A. 1979: *Cotton Row to Beale Street: A Business History of Memphis*. Memphis, TN: Memphis State University Press.

Silver, Christopher 1984: *Twentieth-Century Richmond: Planning, Politics, and Race*. Knoxville: University of Tennessee Press.

Smith, Douglas L. 1988: *The New Deal in the Urban South*. Baton Rouge: Louisiana State University Press.

Smith, T. Lynn 1954: The Emergence of Cities. In Rupert B. Vance and Nicholas J. Demerath (eds.), *The Urban South*. Chapel Hill: University of North Carolina Press, 24–37.

South Coast Follies 1982: *Southern Exposure*, 10 (3), 90–120.

Stephenson, R. Bruce 1997: *Visions of Eden: Environmentalism, Urban Planning, and City Building in St. Petersburg, Florida, 1900–1995*. Columbus: Ohio State University Press.

Sugrue, Thomas J. 1996: *The Origins of the Urban Crisis: Race and Inequality in Postwar Detroit*. Princeton, NJ: Princeton University Press.

Suro, Roberto 1998: *Strangers Among Us: How Latino Immigration is Transforming America*. New York: Alfred A. Knopf.

Tindall, George B. 1979: The Sunbelt Snow Job. *Houston Review*, Spring, 3–13.

Tindall, George B. 1995: *Natives and Newcomers: Ethnic Southerners and Southern Ethnics*. Athens: University of Georgia Press.

Twelve Southerners 1930: *I'll Take My Stand*. New York: Harper and Brothers.

Vance, Rupert B. and Demerath, Nicholas J. (eds.) 1954: *The Urban South*. Chapel Hill: University of North Carolina Press.

Vance, Rupert B. and Smith, Sara 1954: Metropolitan Dominance and Integration. In Rupert B. Vance and Nicholas J. Demerath (eds.), *The Urban South*. Chapel Hill: University of North Carolina Press, 111–34.

Vance, Sandra S. and Scott, Roy V. 1994: *Wal-Mart: A History of Sam Walton's Retail Phenomenon*. New York: Twayne Publishers.

Weinstein, Bernard L. and Firestine, Robert E. 1978: *Regional Growth and Decline in the United States: The Rise of the Sunbelt and the Decline of the Northeast*. New York: Praeger.

Whisnant, David E. 1994: *Modernizing the Mountaineer: People, Power, and Planning in Appalachia*. Knoxville: University of Tennessee Press.

White, John 1994: Safe to Have on Your Coffee Table: *Southern Living* Reconsidered. *Alabama Review*, 47, 185–209.

Wolfe, Tom 1998: *A Man in Full: A Novel*. New York: Farrar, Straus, Giroux.

Wright, Gavin 1986: *Old South, New South: Revolutions in the Southern Economy Since the Civil War*. New York: Basic Books.

CHAPTER TWENTY-NINE

The Transformation of Southern Politics, 1954 to the Present

Wayne Flynt

O NE of the South's chief claims to exceptionalism has been its unique
political culture. In a vibrant two-party America, the South featured a stagnant
one-party system. In New England, town meetings thrived. In northern cities,
rough-and-tumble political machines flourished. Nationwide, interest-group politics
predominated. But the South's claim to political notoriety and power originated in
personality cults, demagogues, and congressional seniority that rewarded congressmen from the safest districts with the weakest opposition party.

On the eve of tumultuous upheaval in southern politics, V. O. Key Jr. with the
assistance of Alexander Heard described the old political order in a classic treatise,
Southern Politics in State and Nation, published in 1949. Focusing on courthouse
gangs, localism, the friends-and-neighbors vote, poll taxes, literacy tests, Mountain
Republicanism, and other political aberrations, Key and Heard carefully dissected
regional politics state by state. Politics was a personal, not a party enterprise.

"Every man for himself" was the unofficial Democratic credo. Key and Heard also
noted that southern Democrats boasted the highest level of party cohesion in
Congress. Although divided along ideological and class lines, they were pretty
much of one mind concerning race. Even former New Dealers toed the orthodox
segregationist line. And in state legislatures virtually all the faces were white and all
the bodies were male.

Half a century after the publication of *Southern Politics* the South no longer
manifested a political system exceptional to the American experience. Although
southern voters overall were somewhat more conservative than American voters
generally, these differences could be explained largely by the region's greater ruralism
and the predominance of evangelical religious values. The two parties competed on
relatively equal footing, with Democrats winning statewide offices when issues centered on education and economics and Republicans triumphing when social and
"culture wars" issues were uppermost in the minds of voters. After a century of
presidential exile, three times during the postwar era southern Democrats were
elected president. By the end of century some political pundits claimed no Democrat
could be elected president unless he came from Dixie, and southern Republicans also
dominated their party.

The extent of this half-century change was bewildering to many observers but
generated substantial scholarly interest from journalists, political scientists, and historians. Jack Bass and Walter De Vries in *The Transformation of Southern Politics*

(1976) described the transition of the Democratic Party into a more moderate biracial coalition. But this very transition gave rise to a drastically larger GOP whose power is well described by Earl and Merle Black in *Politics and Society in the South* (1987). In 1945 all southern governors, all 22 US Senators, 118 of 120 US Representatives, and the overwhelming majority of state legislators were white, male Democrats. By 1999, 7 of 11 southern governors were Republicans. After the Republican sweep of off-year elections in 1994, Republicans controlled 13 of 22 US Senate seats and 67 of 125 congressional slots, with some female and black faces among them. In the seventeen presidential elections from 1880 to 1944, the belt of six Deep South states stretching from South Carolina to Louisiana and Arkansas voted Democratic every time. Virginia, North Carolina, Florida, and Texas voted Republican only once. Tennessee cast its lot with the GOP twice. In the eight presidential elections from 1968 through 1996, despite the presence of candidates from the South heading the ticket half the time, Democrats were drubbed 20 to 78 in the 11 former Confederate states.

Obviously the central question concerning southern politics during the past half-century involves causation. What caused this massive transformation in the South's political culture? Numan V. Bartley, in a series of volumes including a masterful synthesis of the era – *The New South* (1995) – attributes the change primarily to the politics of race. As blacks entered the Democratic Party in huge numbers, they made it more liberal. In reaction, conservative whites deserted it for the Republican Party in even larger numbers. The combination of losing conservative whites and gaining liberal blacks has been a very significant moderation, even liberalization, of the southern Democratic Party.

But for a number of reasons the question is harder to answer than it seems. Many political scientists have explored the complex changes state by state. Baker et al. (1990), Havard (1972), Lamis (1999), and Steed, Baker, and Moreland (1998) all essentially revise V. O. Key's masterpiece with particular attention to the growth of Republicanism state by state. Republican dominance did not occur evenly across the region or for the same reasons. As northern blacks entered the Democratic Party and made it more liberal, many southern Democrats deserted the party of their fathers even before the Voting Rights Act of 1965. The South began voting solidly Republican in presidential elections long before it began electing GOP candidates to state or local offices. The border states and suburbs fell into the Republican column long before the Deep South and rural areas did so. Factors contributing to Republican ascendency included suburbanization, growing prosperity, changes in party perception, the Wallace factor, and new GOP leadership, as well as racial, class, and religious changes.

Even before race became central to the story, a mixture of factors was altering historic voting patterns. Southern constitutions drafted on each side of the dawning of the twentieth century put in place an elaborate scheme to deny not only blacks the right to vote, but poor whites as well. Poll taxes, literacy tests, residency and property ownership requirements, and other barriers slashed voting lists by nearly half in many states. These policies deepened both racial and class grievances. Partly, disfranchisement was aimed at Populists who had threatened Democratic hegemony. Partly, it was aimed at Republicans whose origins in the racially troubled years of Reconstruction made them pariahs in most southern communities. Southerners had long memories. To blacks, the GOP was the party of emancipation and opportunity. It stood for change, racial equality, higher taxes, and improved public services. As poor people who benefited from improved services and paid few taxes, African–Americans had much to gain and little to lose from such policies. But small subsistence white farmers and townspeople resented Republican taxes nearly as much as they did black officeholders.

Changing perceptions of the two parties owed much to the 1954 *Brown v. Board of Education* desegregation decision. The perception of the two parties in the South also changed because of their shifting constituencies. The conservative, white, low-tax, limited public services, traditional values-oriented Democratic Party began to desert all these positions while the Republican Party began to espouse them. In that sense, race was merely the catalyst for a massive reversal among both blacks and whites in how they perceived the two parties.

Another key to this role reversal was the New Deal and the enduring political bifactionalism produced by it. As Numan Bartley (1995) demonstrates in *The New South*, the rise of labor unions and white southern liberalism split the Democratic Party along class and ideological lines, with many poor farmers, laborers, returning veterans, and others voting out mossback conservatives and replacing them with New Deal liberals. The conservative failure to carry even a majority of southern states against Harry Truman in the 1948 Dixiecrat revolt embarrassed the old guard and revealed how deeply divided southern Democrats were.

But the 1954 *Brown* decision went a long way toward repairing this fissure. Issues such as TVA's competition with private energy companies to provide electric power or the open/closed shop for factory workers seemed less urgent than the question of what color child would sit next to one's own offspring in public schools. As the focus of Democratic politics switched from class to race, a steady erosion began in Democratic ranks.

That erosion compounded and accelerated underlying economic and demographic changes. During the Great Depression, the South's per capita income was only half the nation's. More than half its people lived in rural areas and earned their primary income from agriculture. World War II began a massive transition in both the South's economy and its population. As businesses flourished because of cheap electrical power, low taxes, inexpensive labor, weak environmental restrictions, and anti-union policies, fortunes were made, suburbs constructed, and political loyalties altered. By the end of the century the per capita income of many southern states was approaching the national average and Florida and Virginia equaled or exceeded it.

A new political cadre was also eager for action. This younger generation of state Republican leaders consisted of "true believers" who were more interested in winning elections and imposing conservative values than in controlling patronage. They invigorated like-minded young business people and professionals living in the suburbs.

The profile of southern white middle-class suburbanites did not exactly fit the national profile (they were less educated and more Protestant–evangelical). But their voting patterns were just as likely to reveal a shift from Democratic to Republican, especially in presidential elections. Dwight D. Eisenhower and Richard M. Nixon in 1952 were the first to exploit this shift, even before racial differences began to cause hemorrhaging of whites away from the Democratic Party. In his successful bid for the presidency in 1952, Eisenhower carried 48 percent of the South's popular vote and won four southern states despite the presence of an Alabamian on the Democratic ticket.

As Numan Bartley argues (Bartley 1975; Bartley and Graham 1969) the desegregation crisis initially benefited neither party much in the South. The fact that the so-called Warren Court, which contained several Republican justices including Chief Justice Earl Warren, decided the 1954 *Brown* case unanimously, and that the decision was followed by President Eisenhower's reluctant use of federal troops to enforce school integration in Little Rock, Arkansas, gave southern Democrats wiggle room. Almost solidly opposed to racial integration themselves, the South's congressional Democrats during the 1950s swore allegiance to Jim Crow while urging white farmers and industrial workers to worry less about race and more about bread-and-butter issues. And besides, Republican congressional delegations and presidential candidates were arguably as liberal on desegregation as Democrats.

For a time this strategy held white voters in line. But with the elections of John F. Kennedy and Lyndon B. Johnson in 1960 and 1964, the rise of the civil rights movement, pressure on the federal government to become more interventionist, greater legal activism by federal courts, and racial confrontations in southern communities, white voters began to waver in their loyalties. Lyndon Johnson, trying to position himself as a national candidate for a 1960 presidential race, had endorsed some civil rights reforms during the 1950s. Following John Kennedy's assassination, LBJ moved deftly to advocacy of public accommodations, voting rights, and other reforms.

Lyndon B. Johnson rates as one of the most enigmatic presidents of the twentieth century. Obsessed with politics and willing to drive himself and others to unprecedented lengths, Johnson emerged from Depression-era Texas as a New Dealer whose commitment to the poor and ordinary people was matched by a sometimes erratic moral compass when it came to election returns, business deals, or coalition building (see Caro 1982, 1990).

After finally reaching the nation's highest office following the assassination of President Kennedy in 1963, Johnson proved himself as much a genius when holding power as when seeking it. Skillfully courting some southern politicians while isolating others, he used patronage, flattery, and threats to obtain a stunning legislative agenda. Multiple civil rights laws, crafted in the aftermath of shocked national reaction to violence in Mississippi and Alabama, overturned barriers to black voting, desegregated southern schools, and opened public accommodations. Johnson's lifelong concern for the poor found expression in his War on Poverty. The Appalachian Regional Commission funneled money to one of America's poorest regions much as the Tennessee Valley Authority had in LBJ's young manhood. Thanks to a booming economy and low inflation, Johnson compiled an amazing record of legislative accomplishments. Unfortunately his escalating intervention in the Vietnam war offended liberal supporters, alienated many Americans, and ultimately cost him the presidency.

It was precisely at this critical moment that Governor George Wallace emerged from the shadows of Alabama politics onto the national stage. The best biographer of Wallace (Dan Carter 1996) demonstrates how Wallace's long career mirrored the politics of the white South. Initiated into politics through the populistic liberalism of Governor James E. (Big Jim) Folsom, Wallace ran his early campaigns with substantial yeoman farmer, working-class, and black support. But after his defeat in the 1958 governor's race, Wallace hitched his cause to a different star, the rising specter of working-class white racial resentment. After his election as governor in 1962, he declared verbal war on the Kennedys, federal judges, "briefcase-carrying bureaucrats," "pointy-headed intellectuals," "bleeding heart do-gooders," and a variety of other villains, both real and imagined. Though his fiscal policies in Alabama cast doubt on his Populist ancestry, his appeals to working-class white southerners against the elites that tried to run their lives resonated not just across Dixie, but throughout the nation. Slicing into Democratic support among "Archie Bunker" voters (so-called in honor or defamation of the working-class, native-born, bigoted, white but northern antihero of the popular 1960s television sitcom *All in the Family*), Wallace formed a movement that allowed angry white Democrats to leave their party without having to become Republicans. After gingerly testing the presidential waters in 1964, Wallace plunged in neck-deep four years later. Running under the banner of the American Independent Party, Wallace scared the wits out of Richard Nixon and the Republican Party, which stood poised to win easily except for a three-way race in which Wallace carried much of the South and nearly cost Nixon the election.

Wallace reached a peak in the polls at the end of October 1968 at 21 percent of the anticipated vote, arguing that there was not a "dime's worth of difference between the two major parties." Even that dime was devalued by an inflated economy, heated up by Vietnam war spending, which had markedly eroded the purchasing power of blue-collar Americans. A vigorous labor-union drive brought many wavering members back into Democratic ranks by election day, but even then Wallace won 13 percent of the presidential vote. Redoubling his efforts in 1972, Wallace swamped nine Democratic contenders in the Florida and North Carolina primaries before garnering nearly the same victory margins in Indiana, Michigan, and Maryland. In all of the Democratic primaries up until Arthur Bremer's assassination attempt in Maryland, Wallace had won 3.3 million Democratic primary votes, 700,000 more than former vice-president Hubert H. Humphrey, and a million more than the eventual Democratic nominee, George McGovern. Rumors (subsequently denied) even circulated that Humphrey operatives approached Wallace to discuss a possible vice-presidential nomination.

In his controversial book *From George Wallace to Newt Gingrich*, Dan Carter (1996) contends that the impact of Wallace's career literally reshaped both parties but had a particularly conservatizing influence on the GOP. Although Wallace's wounds removed him from presidential politics, the Alabamian had led millions of Democrats out of their historic home and into a new political environment. Richard Nixon and his southern-leaning lieutenants were the first to take advantage of this transitional stage. Having adopted a moderately successful "Southern Strategy" in 1968, Republicans moved cautiously further right in 1972, especially on racial matters, then capitulated entirely to the conservative wing of the party with Ronald Reagan's nomination in 1980. Although religious concerns about declining moral standards and fiscal conservatism account for some of this shift, much of rising southern Republicanism remained race-driven.

Long the darling of conservatives, Reagan galvanized the amorphous forces that had been slowly altering southern politics for more than three decades. With Wallace out of the way, only Georgia's favorite son, Jimmy Carter, stood between Reagan and a fundamental reshaping of American politics.

Jimmy Carter had emerged in the 1970 gubernatorial class of "New South" governors. Characterized by racial inclusiveness, constitutional and educational reforms, and pro-business policies, they prospered from the votes of newly enfranchised blacks and moderate whites. Profiting both from his southern birth and born-again Baptist faith, Carter won the presidency in 1976. Carter's triumphant campaign unified the South and served much the same prideful function for southern Baptists that John Kennedy's 1960 victory had for American Catholics.

Carter's 1980 reelection bid would have been rough in the South even without international calamities. But an Arab oil embargo, the Iranian hostage crisis, rampant inflation, and anti-Carter religious zeal, directed by independent Virginia Baptist preacher Jerry Falwell and his newly organized Moral Majority, doomed Carter's presidency. American evangelicals were disappointed that Carter did not adopt their agenda of moral reform on issues such as abortion and school prayer. Reagan beat the incumbent president in every southern state except his home state of Georgia. And Wallace completed this transition by endorsing a series of state and national Republican candidates in the 1990s.

The Reagan era forced the level of change well beneath the veneer of presidential politics. Actually, Republican governors had been occasionally elected in the southern border states of Virginia, Tennessee, Arkansas, Texas, and Florida. But the 1960s shifted this phenomenon into high gear. Republican candidates won the governorships of Louisiana, Mississippi, and Alabama in the 1970s and 1980s, finally conquering all the Deep South states except Georgia. But even Georgia, like other southern states, elected a series of Republicans to the US Senate, and a majority to the US House of Representatives.

Another central theme in the transformation of recent southern politics, the growing involvement of religious and social conservatives, is explored by political scientists Wayne Parent and Peter Petrakis (1998), Oran Smith (1997), and Matthew C. Moen (1989, 1992). Accelerating the rightward shift were the "culture wars" raging in American society. Beginning in the later 1960s and early 1970s, in reaction to the moral relativism of the era, traditional southerners demanded that what they perceived as assaults on their religious and family values cease. Issues such as school prayer, public financing of private and parochial schools, abortion and sex education, homosexuality, women's liberation and feminism, the Equal Rights Amendment, and the gratuitous violence and sex available on television and in movies swept large numbers of both black and white southerners into outrage. Some joined emerging so-called nonpartisan lobbying efforts such as the Moral Majority, although these organizations' outright or implied endorsement of Republican candidates kept most blacks at arms' length. To combat a negative public image, such groups reorganized by the 1990s into more generic and innocuous-sounding groups, such as the Christian Coalition, Family Research Council, American Freedom Federation, and Freedom Council.

Evangelical Christians – led by Southern Baptists, Pentecostals, and the Presbyterian Church in America – virtually turned their churches into Republican precinct headquarters, registering new voters, distributing voter guides, and warning delinquent members who neglected to vote that they were partly responsible for murdering fetuses and destroying the moral fiber of this country.

Political polls revealed that only 29 percent of Southern Baptist ministers considered themselves Republicans in 1980, but that 66 percent did so five years later. Whereas in the 1970s progressive white Baptist clergymen were more likely to be politically active than their conservative brethren, the opposite was true by the 1990s. Three in four Southern Baptist ministers expressed more than "mild interest" in politics by 1992. And after voting three to two for Jimmy Carter in 1976, Southern Baptists voted against him by almost the same margin four years later.

After Fundamentalist–Conservatives took control of the Southern Baptist Convention (SBC) in 1979, they turned it into a religious rally for Republican candidates and causes. During the 1970s, 1980s, and 1990s, SBC officials invited non-Baptist Republican presidents Gerald Ford, Ronald Reagan, and George Bush to speak to their annual June convention but refused to offer a podium to Southern Baptist Presidents Jimmy Carter or Bill Clinton. These practitioners of a revised politics of morality defined moral issues as matters of personal behavior rather than issues of racial or economic justice.

Few doubted the power of this newly mobilized Religious Right. Ironically, national observers had long accused southern evangelicals of being otherworldly and disengaged from politics. But by the 1980s evangelicals were about as non-active as an April tornado. Indeed, so politicized were they that, at one point in 1998, seven of the eight political officials of both parties in the line of presidential succession, including the president and vice-president, were members of churches affiliated with the Southern Baptist Convention.

Southern white Democrats were caught off-guard by the politics of morality. Uncomfortable discussing their private religious beliefs in a public forum, they oftentimes left the impression either that they had no religious convictions or were hiding some personal moral failure. Gradually, Democrats recovered, thanks partly to the arrogance and hypocrisy of the Religious Right. Sexual scandals embarrassed both evangelical religious leaders (Jimmy Swaggart, Jim Bakker, and Pat Robertson) and self-proclaimed pro-family Republican officeholders (Bob Barr, Newt Gingrich, and Robert Livingston).

Shrewd Democrats also learned to speak the language of Zion. In her victorious 1998 US Senate race, Arkansas Democrat Blanche Lambert Lincoln described her personal relationship with Jesus Christ: "When I talk to Him it's pretty informal. I just lay it all out there, say it like it is." Lincoln, the centrist Democrat, addressed members at white and black Arkansas churches as her "brothers and sisters in Christ" (*Birmingham News*, November 1, 1998). The strategy earned her a 55 to 42 percent victory over State Senator Fay Boseman, a conservative Christian Right advocate, who based much of her senate campaign on her opposition to abortion. In the 1998 elections the Christian Coalition seemed to have lost its edge in southern politics. Democrats picked up strength among self-described religious conservative voters (in 1994 about two-thirds of them voted Republican, compared to only 54 percent in 1998; the Democratic share of this vote rose from 25 to 31 percent). In defining gubernatorial races in South Carolina and Alabama, pro-education and pro-lottery Democrats defeated incumbent anti-gambling Republicans.

Contributing to this changing political landscape was the centrist drift of the so-called New Democrats who took control of the party apparatus during the Clinton–Gore era. As Wayne Parent and Peter Petrakis (1998) demonstrate in an essay entitled

"Populism Left and Right," the New Democrats began to distance themselves from traditional Democratic core constituencies. Alienating some blacks by welfare reform proposals, many unionists by GATT and NAFTA free trade agreements, and liberals by calls for lower taxes, fewer federal programs, and more efficient government, administration Democrats began to sound like moderate Republicans. The electoral successes of the Clinton–Gore ticket emboldened centrist Democrats even as it caused them problems within their diminished congressional caucus. As conservative white southern Democrats were defeated by Republicans, the Democratic delegation became smaller, blacker, more urban, and more liberal.

This transition cut both ways. It allowed local white Democrats to reassure voters that the party had repented of the wayward political candidacy of the Humphreys, McGoverns, and Mondales. But by shifting Democratic rhetoric away from bread-and-butter economic issues, which had once distinguished Democrats – as the party of ordinary Americans – from Republicans, whom they described as plutocrats who favored business and "the country club crowd," the party also left political differentiation to social issues. And on issues such as family values, school prayer, and welfare reform (for) – and gun control, gay and women's rights, crime, and affirmative action (against) – the Republican agenda was far more appealing, especially to traditionally Democratic white rural southerners. This shift away from economic issues allowed rural white southerners to center their attention on the new class of elite technocrats who frightened them and on traditional religious and family values, none of which augured well for Democrats.

James F. Lea in *Contemporary Southern Politics* (1988) has examined the result of these forces in presidential elections such as the 1984 race between Walter Mondale and Reagan, which turned out a four-to-one margin among white middle-class southerners for the Republican incumbent, compared to only a three-to-one margin among such voters nationally. Rural white districts in particular began to elect Republican congressmen, and the Farm Bureau and County Extension agents, once the bedrock of the conservative Democratic Party, now mobilized for Republicans. With so many trends favoring Republicans, the miracle may have been the survival of the Democratic Party. But Democrats were not without their own advantages.

Political scientists Ronald Hrebenar and Clive Thomas (1992) have traced the changes in interest-group politics state by state. As labor-union membership declined and rural whites defected to the GOP, the Democratic Party became more and more dependent on black voters. Rae (1994) and Moreland, Steed, and Baker (1987) have measured the political earthquakes that reshaped racial politics in the South. The civil rights movement, the 1965 Voting Rights Act, and the Twenty-Fourth Amendment to the Constitution (abolishing the poll tax) allowed millions of unregistered black adults to become politically active. In 1966 some 2.3 million blacks were registered to vote. By 1972, 3.5 million were eligible. In Alabama and Mississippi in 1964 less than 20 percent of eligible black adults were on voting rolls, and in some counties not a single African-American was registered. After passage of the Voting Rights Act, Alabama's black registration increased from 19.3 percent to 51.6 percent in 1967 (although, in a little-noticed reaction, white registration during the same period increased from 69.2 to 89.6 percent). By the 1970s these two Deep South states furnished the highest number of elected African-American officials in the nation.

Black voters also furnished the victory margin for Lyndon Johnson in most southern states in 1964 and contributed significantly to the election of a series of moderate "New South" governors of both parties during the 1960s, 1970s, and 1980s (Republicans Winthrop Rockefeller and Lamar Alexander, Democrats Jimmy Carter, Reuben Askew, and John West, among others).

Federal court rulings also strengthened black voters. Supreme Court cases such as *Baker v. Carr* (1962) established the principle that political districts should be of relatively equal size ("one man, one vote") and denied depopulated rural areas dominance in state legislatures. *Bolden v. Mobile* in the 1980s ruled in favor of single-unit districts over at-large or countywide districts that diluted black voting strength.

In many state legislatures, opportunistic black leaders joined with Republicans to create majority black electoral districts. Taking areas with African-American voters out of largely white districts and reassigning them to precincts with black majorities assured the election of many new African-Americans. At the same time, such maneuvers left white districts much "whiter" and more conservative, paving the way for Republican victories.

The result was evident in Alabama: Republican victories. During some years in the 1940s, all 140 members of the legislature were white Democratic males; but by 1994, white Democrats were reduced to only 44 percent. Republicans controlled forty-three legislative seats, blacks thirty-five (their exact share of Alabama's population), and six women served (although this was still the lowest percentage of women in the nation). Predictably, as the Democratic Party became "blacker" and more liberal, the South became more Republican as a result of white voter reaction.

There were signs by the end of the century that racially polarized politics might be passing slowly from center stage. Many factors accounted for this. Closer contact with blacks had sufficiently softened white hostility, and some black Democratic incumbents were reelected in majority white districts even after reapportionment or court-ordered redistricting. Conservative, middle-class, black voters began to flirt with Christian Coalition and Republican candidates. Some blacks disliked the welfare system as much as middle-class whites. Others were attracted to Republican messages on crime, family values, school prayer, and school vouchers. African-Americans began to compete in and occasionally to win Republican primaries.

In Memphis, Tennessee, Harold E. Ford Jr. remained in the Democratic Party and replaced his father in the US Congress. As Dana Milbank (1998) demonstrated in a perceptive essay in *The New York Times Magazine*, both black congressmen represented the same predominantly black district, but that is where similarities between father and son ended. Harold Ford Sr. had grown up poor in a house without running water and had obtained little education. His son grew up in a three-floor Washington, DC, townhouse in the trendy Chevy Chase neighborhood. Harold Jr. attended exclusive St Albans School, wore "Polo" cologne, and drove a silver BMW. After graduating from the University of Pennsylvania, he earned a law degree from the University of Michigan. The senior Ford, elected to Congress with the "Watergate babies" in 1974, participated in a liberal assault on conservative southern Democratic control of the congressional caucus. Galvanized by a black political agenda, he alienated Memphis's white Democrats as well as conservative southern Democratic colleagues in the House.

Harold Ford Jr. entered the House in 1996 as one of twenty-two freshman Democrats. His goal was to install new centrist Democratic leaders and policies. He became a key player in the so-called New Democrat coalition and an uneasy member of the congressional Black Caucus. He shunned racial politics and adopted an agenda that appealed more to middle-class than to impoverished voters. Not only did such an agenda better suit his own upbringing, it also appealed to his increasingly affluent black constituency. At Mount Moriah-East Baptist Church, where both Fords were members, the congregation had changed in three decades, since the elder Ford won his congressional seat. Then the church contained only four college graduates. By the beginning of the younger Ford's tenure, half the adult members had college degrees, and comfortable houses in the suburbs had replaced public housing.

By the late 1990s other changes also fostered equilibrium between the two parties in the South. Despite Clinton's moral lapses, voters approved his policies and basked in the national prosperity that paralleled his years in office. Revelation of moral lapses by Republicans who claimed to represent family values neutralized the morality issue. Some evangelical churches became concerned about the increasingly partisan political endorsements of the Christian Coalition and refused to distribute its literature on the Sunday before election days. Democrats began to focus more sharply on education and economic issues, and the party became more disciplined and willing to share power with blacks. Indeed, Democrats discovered that having a popular black candidate on a statewide ballot was often the key to black voter turnout, and hence to Democratic chances.

Republican reverses during the 1998 off-year elections convinced the party that it had to broaden its appeal beyond conservative, white, Sunbelt males. That led to a declining emphasis on abortion and other Religious Right issues. Even in the South, focus on the moral lapses of Democrats did not play well. Slashing attacks on Bill Clinton's moral deficiencies generated a backlash among African-American voters. In Georgia's 1998 off-year election, blacks cast 29 percent of the votes, although they constituted only 24 percent of registered voters, making the difference in many close elections. And by refocusing the Democratic message toward saving Social Security and Medicare, restricting handgun availability, and improving education, Democrats significantly cut into Republican strength among older women. In Georgia, ten days before the November 1998 election, only 31 percent of women older than fifty said they planned to vote Democratic in the governor's race. But 43 percent ended up doing so.

Moreover, Republican reversals in 1998 did not mean the reinstitution of a one-party Democratic South. The average 1996 victory margin in the region (33 percent, compared to 30 percent nationally) and the turnout (40 percent regionally, compared to 46 percent nationally) suggest that the South is still the least politically active and politically competitive region of America. Furthermore, many Republicans now vote as blindly partisan as Democrats once did. In Lee County, Alabama, 37 percent of the straight-ticket voters in 1998 were Republicans and 63 percent were Democrats. Apparently "Yellow Dog" (meaning a voter who would vote even for a yellow dog if it was on his party's ticket) was no longer a phrase that applied solely to Democrats.

Whatever the course of the South's new political culture on the eve of a new century, it bore little resemblance to the one that V. O. Key described fifty years earlier.

BIBLIOGRAPHY

Baker, Tod A., Hadley, Charles D., Steed, Robert P., and Moreland, Laurence W. (eds.) 1990: *Political Parties in the Southern States: Party Activists in Partisan Coalitions.* New York: Praeger.

Bartley, Numan V. 1969: *The Rise of Massive Resistance: Race and Politics in the South During the 1950s.* Baton Rouge: Louisiana State University Press.

Bartley, Numan V. 1995: *The New South, 1945–1980.* Baton Rouge: Louisiana State University Press.

Bartley, Numan V. and Graham, Hugh D. 1975: *Southern Politics and the Second Reconstruction.* Baltimore: Johns Hopkins University Press.

Bass, Jack and De Vries, Walter 1976: *The Transformation of Southern Politics: Social Change and Political Consequence Since 1945.* New York: Basic Books.

Black, Earl and Black, Merle 1987: *Politics and Society in the South.* Cambridge, MA: Harvard University Press.

Black, Earl and Black, Merle 1992: *The Vital South: How Presidents Are Elected.* Cambridge, MA: Harvard University Press.

Bourne, Peter 1997: *Jimmy Carter: A Comprehensive Biography from Plains, Georgia to Post-presidency.* New York: Scribners.

Brinkley, Douglas 1998: *Unfinished Presidency: Jimmy Carter's Journey Beyond the White House.* New York: Viking Press.

Caro, Robert T. 1982: *The Years of Lyndon Johnson: The Paths to Power.* New York: Alfred A. Knopf.

Caro, Robert T. 1990: *The Years of Lyndon Johnson: Means of Ascent.* New York: Alfred A. Knopf.

Carter, Dan T. 1995: *The Politics of Rage: George Wallace, the Origins of the New Conservatism, and the Transformation of American Politics.* New York: Simon and Schuster.

Carter, Dan T. 1996: *From George Wallace to Newt Gingrich: Race in the Conservative Counter-revolution, 1963–1994.* Baton Rouge: Louisiana State University Press.

Dallek, Robert 1991: *Lone Star Rising: Lyndon Johnson and his Times, 1908–1960.* New York: Oxford University Press.

Dallek, Robert 1998: *Flawed Giant: Lyndon Johnson and his Times, 1961–1973,* New York: Oxford University Press.

Havard, William C. (ed.) 1972: *The Changing Politics of the South.* Baton Rouge: Louisiana State University Press.

Hrebenar, Ronald J. and Thomas, Clive S. 1992: *Interest Group Politics in the Southern States.* Tuscaloosa: University of Alabama Press.

Hurt, R. Douglas (ed.) 1998: *The Rural South Since World War II.* Baton Rouge: Louisiana State University Press.

Key, V. O., Jr., with assistance of Heard, Alexander 1949: *Southern Politics in State and Nation.* New York: Alfred A. Knopf.

Lamis, Alexander P. 1990: *The Two-Party South.* New York: Oxford University Press.

Lamis, Alexander P. (ed.) 1999: *Southern Politics in the 1990s.* Baton Rouge: Louisiana State University Press.

Lea, James F. (ed.) 1988: *Contemporary Southern Politics.* Baton Rouge: Louisiana State University Press.

Milbank, Dana 1998: Harold Ford, Jr., Storms His Father's House. *The New York Times Magazine,* October 25.

Moen, Matthew C. 1989: *The Christian Right and Congress.* Tuscaloosa: University of Alabama Press.

Moen, Matthew C. 1992: *The Transformation of the Christian Right*. Tuscaloosa: University of Alabama Press.

Moreland, Laurence W., Steed, Robert D., and Baker, Tod A. (eds.) 1987: *Blacks in Southern Politics*. New York: Praeger.

Parent, Wayne and Petrakis, Peter 1998: Populism Left and Right. In Douglas Hurt (ed.), *The Rural South Since World War II*. Baton Rouge: Louisiana State University Press.

Rae, Nicol C. 1994: *Southern Democrats*. New York: Oxford University Press.

Smith, Oran P. 1997: *The Rise of Baptist Republicanism*. New York: New York University Press.

Steed, Robert P., Baker, Tod A., and Moreland, Laurence W. (eds.) 1998: *Party Organization and Activism in the American South*. Tuscaloosa: University of Alabama Press.

Index

11850500R00304

Made in the USA
San Bernardino, CA
30 May 2014